WORLD CHRISTIANITIES
c. 1815–c. 1914

This is the first scholarly treatment of nineteenth-century Christianity to discuss the subject in a global context. Part I analyses the responses of Catholic and Protestant Christianity to the intellectual and social challenges presented by European modernity. It gives attention to the explosion of new voluntary forms of Christianity and the expanding role of women in religious life. Part II surveys the diverse and complex relationships between the churches and nationalism, resulting in fundamental changes to the connections between church and state. Part III examines the varied fortunes of Christianity as it expanded its historic bases in Asia and Africa, established itself for the first time in Australasia, and responded to the challenges and opportunities of the European colonial era. Each chapter has a full bibliography providing guidance on further reading.

SHERIDAN GILLEY is an Emeritus Reader in Theology, Durham University. He is the author of *Newman and His Age* (republished, 2003) and of numerous articles on modern religious history. He is co-editor, with Roger Swift, of *The Irish in the Victorian City* (1985), *The Irish in Britain 1815–1939* (1989) and *The Irish in Victorian Britain* (1999), and with W. J. Sheils, of *A History of Religion in Britain* (1994).

BRIAN STANLEY is Director of the Henry Martyn Centre for the Study of Mission and World Christianity in the Cambridge Theological Federation and a Fellow of St Edmund's College, Cambridge. He has written and edited a number of books on the modern history of Christian missions, including *The Bible and the Flag* (1990), *The History of the Baptist Missionary Society 1792–1992* (1992), *Christian Missions and the Enlightenment* (2001) and *Missions, Nationalism, and the End of Empire* (2003).

THE CAMBRIDGE HISTORY OF
CHRISTIANITY

The Cambridge History of Christianity offers a comprehensive chronological account of the development of Christianity in all its aspects – theological, intellectual, social, political, regional, global – from its beginnings to the present day. Each volume makes a substantial contribution in its own right to the scholarship of its period and the complete *History* constitutes a major work of academic reference. Far from being merely a history of Western European Christianity and its offshoots, the *History* aims to provide a global perspective. Eastern and Coptic Christianity are given full consideration from the early period onwards, and later, African, Far Eastern, New World, South Asian and other non-European developments in Christianity receive proper coverage. The volumes cover popular piety and non-formal expressions of Christian faith, and treat the sociology of Christian formation, worship and devotion in a broad cultural context. The question of relations between Christianity and other major faiths is also kept in sight throughout. The *History* will provide an invaluable resource for scholars and students alike.

List of volumes:

Origins to Constantine
EDITED BY MARGARET M. MITCHELL AND FRANCES M. YOUNG

Constantine to c.600
EDITED BY WINRICH LÖHR, FRED NORRIS AND AUGUSTINE CASIDAY

Early Medieval Christianity c.600–c.1100
EDITED BY THOMAS NOBLE AND JULIA SMITH

Christianity in Western Europe c.1100–c.1500
EDITED BY MIRI RUBIN AND WALTER SIMON

Eastern Christianity
EDITED BY MICHAEL ANGOLD

Re-Formation and Expansion c.1500–c.1660
EDITED BY RONNIE PO-CHIA HSIA

Enlightenment, Reawakening and Revolution 1660–1815
EDITED BY STEWART J. BROWN AND TIMOTHY TACKETT

World Christianities c.1815–c.1914
EDITED BY BRIAN STANLEY AND SHERIDAN GILLEY

World Christianities c.1914–c.2000
EDITED BY HUGH MCLEOD

THE CAMBRIDGE
HISTORY OF CHRISTIANITY

WORLD CHRISTIANITIES
c.1815–c.1914

★

VOLUME 8

★

Edited by

SHERIDAN GILLEY
Durham University

and

BRIAN STANLEY
University of Cambridge

CAMBRIDGE
UNIVERSITY PRESS

CAMBRIDGE UNIVERSITY PRESS
Cambridge, New York, Melbourne, Madrid, Cape Town, Singapore, São Paulo

Cambridge University Press
The Edinburgh Building, Cambridge CB2 2RU, UK

Published in the United States of America by Cambridge University Press, New York

www.cambridge.org
Information on this title: www.cambridge.org/9780521814560

First published 2006

Printed in the United Kingdom at the University Press, Cambridge

A catalogue record for this book is available from the British Library

Library of Congress Cataloguing in Publication data
World Christianities, c.1815–c.1914 / edited by Sheridan Gilley and Brian Stanley.
p.   cm. – (The Cambridge history of Christianity; vol. 8)
Includes bibliographical references and index.
ISBN 0 521-81456-1 (hardback)
1. Church history – 19th century.   2. Church history – 20th century.
1. Gilley, Sheridan.   II. Stanley, Brian, 1953–   III. Title.   IV. Series.
BR477.W87   2005   270.8 – dc22   2005008392

ISBN-13 978-0-521-81456-0 hardback
ISBN-10 0-521-81456-1 hardback

Contents

v

112697

Contents

Contents

PART III
THE EXPANSION OF CHRISTIANITY

Contents

Contributors

GABRIEL ADRIÁNYI is Emeritus Professor of Church History (including East European Church History) in the Catholic Theological Faculty, University of Bonn, and is Professor of Church History at the Lorand-Eötvös-University at Budapest. He has written and edited a number of books on modern church history, including *Geschichte der katholischen Kirche in Ungarn* (Cologne: Böhlau, 2004), *Die Ostpolitik des Vatikans 1958–1978 gegenüber Ungarn: der Fall Kardinal Mindszenty* (Herne: Schäfer, 2003), *Kleine Kirchengeschichte Ungarns* (Herne: Schäfer, 2003), *Prohászka és a római index* (Budapest, 2002) and *Geschichte der Kirche Osteuropas im 20. Jahrhundert* (Paderborn: Schöningh, 1992).

URS ALTERMATT has been Professor of Contemporary History at the University of Fribourg, Switzerland, since 1980, and Rector since 2003. He has been Visiting Professor at various central and eastern European universities (Cracow, Budapest, Sarajevo and Sofia). His numerous publications on modern European and Swiss political, social and religious history include *Der Weg der Schweizer Katholiken ins Ghetto* (Zurich and Cologne: Benziger, 1972, 3rd edn 1995), *Katholizismus und Moderne* (Zurich: Benziger, 1989), *Rechtsextremismus in der Schweiz*, with Hanspeter Kriesi *et al.* (Zurich: Neue Züricher-Zeitung, 1995), *Das Fanal von Sarajevo: Ethnonationalismus in Europa* (Zurich: Neue Züricher-Zeitung, 1996), *Katholizismus und Antisemitismus* (Frauenfeld, Stuttgart and Vienna: Huber, 1999) and *Katholische Denk- und Lebenswelten*, ed. (Fribourg: Academic Press, 2003).

DANIEL H. BAYS is Professor of History and Director of the Asian Studies Program at Calvin College, Grand Rapids, Michigan. He has written or edited several articles, chapters and books on the history of Christianity in China in the nineteenth and twentieth centuries, among them *Christianity in China, from the eighteenth century to the present*, ed. (Stanford: Stanford University Press, 1996), *The foreign missionary enterprise at home*, co-ed. (Tuscaloosa: University of Alabama Press, 2003), 'Chinese Protestant Christianity today', in *The China Quarterly* 174 (June 2003), and 'A tradition of state dominance', in Jason Kindopp and Carol Lee Hamrin (eds.), *God and Caesar in China* (Washington, DC: Brookings Institution Press, 2004).

DAVID BEBBINGTON is Professor of History at the University of Stirling. He has written *Patterns in history* (Leicester: Inter-Varsity Press, 1979), *The nonconformist conscience: chapel and politics, 1870–1914* (London: Allen and Unwin, 1982), *Evangelicalism in modern Britain: a history from the 1730s to the 1980s* (London: Unwin Hyman, 1989), *William Ewart Gladstone:*

faith and politics in Victorian Britain (Grand Rapids, MI: Eerdmans, 1993), *Holiness in nineteenth-century England* (Carlisle: Paternoster, 2000), *The mind of Gladstone: religion, Homer and politics* (Oxford: Oxford University Press, 2004) and *The dominance of evangelicalism: the age of Spurgeon and Moody* (Leicester: Inter-Varsity Press, 2005). His edited works include *Protestant nonconformist texts: the nineteenth century* (Aldershot: Ashgate, 2005).

WILLIAM J. CALLAHAN is Emeritus Professor of History at the University of Toronto. His book *Church, politics and society in Spain, 1750–1874* (Cambridge, MA: Harvard University Press, 1984) was awarded the Wallace K. Ferguson Prize of the Canadian Historical Association. Other works by him include *Honor, commerce, and industry in eighteenth-century Spain* (Boston: Baker Library, Harvard Graduate School of Business Administration, 1972) and *The Catholic Church in Spain, 1875–1998* (Washington, DC: Catholic University of America Press, 2000). He has edited, with David Higgs, *Church and society in Catholic Europe of the eighteenth century* (Cambridge: Cambridge University Press, 1979).

FRANK COPPA is Professor of History and Director of Doctoral Studies in Modern World History at St John's University in New York. He has written and edited more than a dozen volumes on united Italy and the modern papacy. His work has explored the *Risorgimento* as well as the counter-*Risorgimento*, including biographies of Camillo di Cavour as well as Pius IX and Cardinal Giacomo Antonelli. His most recent volumes include *The modern papacy since 1789* (London and New York: Addison Wesley Longman, 1998) and *The papacy confronts the modern world* (Krieger, 2003), and he has edited and contributed to *Controversial concordats* (Washington, DC: Catholic University Press, 1999) and the two-volume *Great popes through history* (Westport, CT: Greenwood Press, 2002).

ALLAN DAVIDSON is Director of Postgraduate Studies and teaches church history in the School of Theology at the University of Auckland. He has written extensively on the history of Christianity in New Zealand and the South Pacific. The books he has written and edited include *Semisi Nau: the story of my life: a Tongan missionary at Ontong Java* (Suva, Fiji: Institute of Pacific Studies, 1996), *Tongan Anglicans 1902–2002* (College of the Diocese of Polynesia, 2002), and *Christianity in Aotearoa: a history of church and society in New Zealand*, 3rd edn (Wellington, New Zealand: Education for Ministry, 2004).

JEREMY DIBBLE is Professor of Music at the University of Durham. His specialist interests in the Victorian, Edwardian and Georgian eras are reflected in the two major studies *C. Hubert H. Parry: his life and music* (Oxford: Oxford University Press, 1992) and *Charles Villiers Stanford: man and musician* (Oxford: Oxford University Press, 2002) and in his recent volume of Parry's violin sonatas for the Musica Britannica Trust. He has written on a wide range of topics including historiography, opera and church music in Britain and is currently working on a study of the life and music of John Stainer and a volume of Parry's piano trios for Musica Britannica. His future plans are to write a study of the music of Frederick Delius.

JOSÉ MARIO C. FRANCISCO has been Director of the East Asian Pastoral Institute since 1996 and will hold the Gasson Chair at Boston College for 2005–6. After graduate studies in literature and theology, he began teaching at Loyola School of Theology and Ateneo de Manila University in Manila and lecturing at the Jesuit School of Theology at Berkeley. In addition to organising and lecturing at conferences around Asia, he has written essays on religion and culture for journals and anthologies and has published books on Philippine vernacular texts from the Spanish colonial period such as *Sermones [Francisco Bloncas de San José O.P.]* and *Bocabulario Tagalo [Miguel Ruiz, O.P.]*.

ROBERT ERIC FRYKENBERG is Professor Emeritus at the University of Wisconsin-Madison. His works include: *Guntur district, 1788–1848: a history of local influence and central authority* (Oxford: Clarendon Press, 1965), *Land control and social structure in Indian history* (Madison: University of Wisconsin Press, 1969, 1978), *Land tenure and peasant in South Asia* (New Delhi: Manohar, 1977, 1981), *Delhi through the ages* (New Delhi: Oxford University Press, 1986, 1993) and *History and belief: the foundations of historical understanding* (Grand Rapids, MI: Eerdmans, 1996). Co-general editor, with Brian Stanley, of the Studies in the History of Christian Missions series, including *Christians, cultural interactions, and India's religious traditions* (Grand Rapids, MI: Eerdmans, 2002) and *Christians and missionaries in India* (Grand Rapids, MI: Eerdmans, 2003), he is writing the *Oxford history of Christianity in India*.

SHERIDAN GILLEY is an Emeritus Reader in Theology of the University of Durham. He is the author of *Newman and his age* (republished London: Darton, Longman, and Todd, 2003) and of numerous articles on modern religious history. He is co-editor, with Roger Swift, of three volumes on the Irish in Britain: *The Irish in the Victorian city* (London: Croom Helm, 1985), *The Irish in Britain, 1815–1939* (London: Pinter, 1989) and *The Irish in Victorian Britain: the local dimension* (Dublin: Four Courts Press, 1999); and, with W. J. Sheils, of *A history of religion in Britain* (Oxford: Blackwell, 1994).

JAMES H. GRAYSON is Professor of Modern Korean Studies in the School of East Asian Studies at the University of Sheffield. An anthropologist, Methodist minister and former missionary to Korea, he has written extensively on the religious traditions of Korea, including Christianity. His books include *Early Buddhism and Christianity in Korea* (Leiden: E. J. Brill, 1985) and *Korea: a religious history* (Oxford: Clarendon Press, 1989, revised edition Routledge-Curzon 2002). Among his articles on the socio-cultural aspects of Korean Christianity are 'The Shintô shrine conflict and Protestant martyrs in Korea, 1938–1945', *Missiology* 29 (2001), and 'Cultural encounter: Korean Protestantism and other religious traditions', *International Bulletin of Missionary Research* 25 (2001).

DOUGLAS HEDLEY is Senior Lecturer in the Philosophy of Religion at the University of Cambridge and a Fellow of Clare College. In 2002 he was Directeur d'études invité at the Ecole pratique des hautes études, Sorbonne, Paris, and he was the Alan Richardson Lecturer in Christian Apologetics at the University of Durham in 2004. He is a past Secretary of the British Society for the Philosophy of Religion and a past President of the European Society for the Philosophy of Religion. He is the author of *Coleridge, philosophy and religion: aids to reflection and the mirror of the spirit* (Cambridge: Cambridge University Press, 2000).

MARY HEIMANN is Senior Lecturer in History at the University of Strathclyde, and associate editor, with responsibility for Catholic entries, for the *Oxford Dictionary of National Biography* (Oxford: Oxford University Press, 2004). She is the author of *Catholic devotion in Victorian England* (Oxford: Oxford University Press, 1995), and has contributed to a number of surveys of modern religious history. She is currently completing a political history of Czechoslovakia, to be published by Hambledon and London, as well as planning a history of modern British attitudes towards the supernatural.

JANICE HOLMES is Lecturer in Irish History at the University of Ulster, Coleraine. Her specialisms include religious revivals, female ministry and Irish Presbyterianism. She has edited, with Diane Urquhart, *Coming into the light: the work, politics and religion of women in Ulster, 1840–1940* (Belfast: Institute of Irish Studies, 1994) and published *Religious revivals in Britain and Ireland, 1859–1905* (Dublin: Irish Academic Press, 2000).

OGBU U. KALU is the Henry Winters Luce Professor of World Christianity and Missions, McCormick Theological Seminary, Chicago, and Associate Director of the Chicago Center for Global Ministries. He has written and edited a number of books, including *Divided people of God: church union movement in Nigeria, 1875–1966* (New York: NOK Publishers,1978), *The history of Christianity in West Africa* (London: Longman, 1980), *Power, poverty and prayer: the challenges of poverty and pluralism in African Christianity, 1960–1996* (Frankfurt: Peter Lang, 2000) and *Embattled gods: the Christianization of Igboland, 1841–1991* (Lagos: Africa World Press, 2003).

JERZY KŁOCZOWSKI is Professor of History at the Catholic University of Lublin, Director of the Institute of East-Central Europe in Lublin, Chair of the International Federation of Institutes of East-Central Europe, Chair of the Polish Commission of the Comparative History of Churches and Vice-Chair of the International Commission of the Comparative History of Churches, and Chair of the Polish Commission for UNESCO. His numerous publications include *A history of Polish Christianity* (Cambridge: Cambridge University Press, 2000), *Chrześcijaństwo i historia [Christianity and history]* (1990), *Młodsza Europa [The younger Europe]* (Cracow: Znak, 2004) and *Historia Europy Środkowo-Wschodniej [A history of East-Central Europe]* (Paris: PUF 2004).

JOHN LYNCH is Emeritus Professor of Latin American History in the University of London. He is the author of numerous works on Spain and Latin America, including *Bourbon Spain 1700–1808* (Oxford: Blackwell, 1989), *Argentine dictator: Juan Manuel de Rosas 1829–1852* (Oxford: Clarendon Press, 1981), *The Spanish American revolutions 1808–1826* (New York: Norton, 1986), *Caudillos in Spanish America 1800–1850* (Oxford: Clarendon Press, 1992), *Massacre in the Pampas, 1872: Britain and Argentina in the age of migration* (Norman: University of Oklahoma Press, 1998) and *Latin America between colony and nation* (Basingstoke: Palgrave, 2001).

JAMES F. MCMILLAN is Richard Pares Professor of History at the University of Edinburgh. He is the author of many articles and chapters on the religious history of modern France, with a focus particularly on the French culture wars, political Catholicism and the relationship between religion and gender. Other publications include *France and women 1789–1914: gender, society and politics* (London: Routledge, 2000) and (as editor and contributor) *Modern France 1880–2002 (The short Oxford history of France)* (Oxford: Oxford University Press, 2003). He has been awarded a Major Leverhulme Research Fellowship to work on his next project, *War and belief: the Great War and the western religious imagination.*

FRANZISKA METZGER is Assistant in Contemporary History, University of Fribourg. Her publications on religious history and history of historiography include: *Die 'Schildwache': Eine integralistisch-rechtskatholische Zeitung 1912–1945* (Fribourg: Universitätsverlag, 2000), *Nation und Nationalismus in Europa: Festschrift für Urs Altermatt*, ed. with C. Bosshart-Pfluger and J. Jung (Frauenfeld: Huber, 2002), 'Die Reformation in der Schweiz zwischen 1850 und 1950. Konkurrierende konfessionelle und nationale Geschichtskonstruktionen und Erinnerungsgemeinschaften', in H.-G. Haupt and D. Langewiesche (eds.), *Nation und Religion in Europa* (Frankfurt a.M.: Campus, 2004), and 'Milieu, Teilmilieus und Netzwerke', with Urs Altermatt, in Urs Altermatt (ed.), *Katholische Denk- und Lebenswelten* (Fribourg: Academic Press, 2003).

JOHN MOLONY is Emeritus Professor of History and Visiting Fellow in the Australian Dictionary of Biography at the Australian National University. He is also Adjunct Professor, Australian Catholic University. He is the author of *The Roman mould of the Australian Catholic Church* (Carlton, Victoria: Melbourne University Press, 1969), *The emergence of political Catholicism in Italy, Partito Popolare, 1919–1926* (London: Croom Helm, 1980), *The Penguin bicentennial history of Australia* (Ringwood, Victoria: Viking, 1987), *The worker question: a new historical perspective on Rerum Novarum* (Dublin: Gill and Macmillan, 1991) and *Luther's pine* (Pandanus Books, 2004).

HELEEN MURRE-VAN DEN BERG is Associate Professor for the History of World Christianity at Leiden (Netherlands). She specialises in Middle Eastern Christianities, with special attention to the history of the Assyrian Church of the East and of western missions in the Middle East. Recent publications include 'Migration of Middle Eastern Christians to western countries and Protestant missionary activities in the Middle East: a preliminary investigation', *The Journal of Eastern Christian Studies* 54, 1–2 (2002), 39–49, and 'Generous devotion: women in the colophons of the Church of the East (1550–1850)', *Hugoye: Journal of Syriac Studies* 7/1 (2004) (http://syrcom.cua.edu/Hugoye).

MARK A. NOLL is McManis Professor of Christian Thought at Wheaton College, Illinois. His books include *America's God, from Jonathan Edwards to Abraham Lincoln* (New York: Oxford University Press, 2002), *The rise of evangelicalism: the age of Whitefield, Edwards, and the Wesleys* (Leicester: Inter-Varsity Press, 2004), *The old religion in a new world: the history of North American Christianity* (Grand Rapids, MI: Eerdmans, 2002) and *Turning points: decisive moments in the history of Christianity* (2nd edn Grand Rapids, MI: Baker Book House, 2000).

SUSAN O'BRIEN is an independent scholar, a Senior Member of St Edmund's College, Cambridge, and the Chair of Directors of the Margaret Beaufort Institute of Theology, Cambridge Theological Federation. Until 2002 she was Deputy Vice-Chancellor of Staffordshire

University. She has written extensively, in journal articles and essays, both on eighteenth-century transatlantic revivalism and on the history of Roman Catholic nuns and sisters in modern Britain and Ireland.

PETER C. PHAN is currently the Ignacio Ellacuria Professor of Catholic Social Thought at Georgetown University. He has published over 250 essays and a dozen books, including *Mission and catechesis: Alexandre de Rhodes and inculturation in seventeenth-century Vietnam* (1998) and his trilogy on Asian theology: *Christianity with an Asian face, In our own tongues* and *Being religious interreligiously*, all published by Orbis Books (Maryknoll, NY).

STUART PIGGIN is Director of the Centre for the History of Christian Thought and Experience (incorporating the Centre for the Study of Australian Christianity) at Macquarie University in Sydney, Australia. He has written over a hundred articles on the history of evangelicalism, missions and disasters. His books include *Making evangelical missionaries: the social background, motivation, and training of British Protestant missionaries* (n.p.: Sutton Courtenay Press, 1984), *The Mount Kembla disaster* (South Melbourne: Oxford University Press, 1992), *Evangelical Christianity in Australia: Spirit, word and world* (Melbourne: Oxford University Press, 1996) and *Firestorm of the Lord: the history of and prospects for revival in the church and the world* (Carlisle: Paternoster, 2000).

ANDREW PORTER is Rhodes Professor of Imperial History at King's College in the University of London. He has written extensively on imperial issues from the mid-eighteenth to the mid-twentieth century. Books include *The origins of the South African War* (Manchester: Manchester University Press, 1980), *Victorian shipping, business and empire* (Woodbridge: Boydell Press, 1986) and *An atlas of British overseas expansion* (London: Routledge, 1991). Editor of the *Oxford history of the British Empire*, vol. IV: *The nineteenth century* (Oxford: Oxford University Press, 1999) and *The imperial horizons of British Protestant missions, 1880–1914* (Grand Rapids, MI: Eerdmans, 2003), his most recent book is *Religion versus empire? British Protestant missionaries and overseas expansion, 1700–1914* (Manchester: Manchester University Press, 2004).

JOHN ROGERSON is Professor Emeritus of Biblical Studies at the University of Sheffield. His main publications have centred on the history and assumptions of Old Testament interpretation, and the use of the Bible today. They include *Myth in Old Testament interpretation* (Berlin: De Gruyter, 1974), *Anthropology and the Old Testament* (Oxford: Blackwell, 1978), *Old Testament criticism in the nineteenth century: England and Germany* (London: SPCK, 1984) and *The Bible and criticism in Victorian Britain: profiles of F. D. Maurice and William Robertson Smith* (Sheffield: Sheffield Academic Press, 1995).

NICOLAAS A. RUPKE is Professor of the History of Science and Director of the Institut für Wissenschaftsgeschichte, University of Göttingen. The topic of religion and the sciences figures prominently in his books *The great chain of history* (Oxford: Clarendon Press, 1983) and *Richard Owen* (New Haven, CT: Yale University Press, 1994). Currently he is working on a project entitled 'Eminent lives in twentieth-century science and religion'.

ANDREW SANDERS is Professor of English in the University of Durham. He has written extensively on nineteenth-century literature and especially on the work of Charles Dickens. He has edited a number of Victorian novels and is the author of *The short Oxford history of English literature* (3rd edn, Oxford: Oxford University Press, 2004). He has maintained an active scholarly interest in art and architecture and served as a member of the committee of the Victorian Society for many years.

JON SENSBACH is Professor of History at the University of Florida. He is the author of *Rebecca's revival: creating black Christianity in the Atlantic world* (Cambridge, MA: Harvard University Press, 2005) and *A separate Canaan: the making of an Afro-Moravian world in North Carolina, 1763–1840* (Chapel Hill and London: University of North Carolina Press, 1998).

BRIAN STANLEY is Director of the Henry Martyn Centre for the Study of Mission and World Christianity in the Cambridge Theological Federation and a Fellow of St Edmund's College, Cambridge. He has written and edited a number of books on the modern history of Christian missions, including *The Bible and the flag* (Leicester: Apollos, 1990), *The history of the Baptist Missionary Society 1792–1992* (Edinburgh: T. &. T. Clark, 1992), *Christian missions and the Enlightenment* (Grand Rapids, MI and Richmond: Eerdmans and Curzon, 2001) and *Missions, nationalism, and the end of empire* (Grand Rapids, MI: Eerdmans, 2003).

ANTHONY J. STEINHOFF is an Assistant Professor of Modern European History at the University of Tennessee at Chattanooga. He has published articles on modern European religious and cultural history in *Central European History*, *Geschichte und Gesellschaft* and the *Journal of Urban History*, and contributed to: the *Blackwell companion to nineteenth-century Europe*; *Protestants, Catholics, and Jews in Germany, 1800–1914*, ed. Helmut Walser Smith (New York: Berg, 2001); and *Religiöse Vergemeinschaftung in der Moderne*, ed. Lucian Hölscher (Göttingen: Wallstein, 2005). He is currently completing a monograph on Protestantism and urban religious culture in late nineteenth-century Strasbourg.

ROBERT J. TAFT is Professor Emeritus of Oriental Liturgy at the Pontifical Oriental Institute, Rome, and Consultor for Liturgy of the Vatican Congregation for the Oriental Churches. He has authored over 690 publications, chiefly on Oriental liturgy, including fifteen books.

DAVID M. THOMPSON is Fellow and President of Fitzwilliam College, Reader in Modern Church History in the University of Cambridge and Director of the Centre for Advanced Religious and Theological Studies. He has published widely on Victorian nonconformity, nineteenth-century Christian social thought and the history of the ecumenical movement.

DAG THORKILDSEN is Professor in the Faculty of Theology at the University of Oslo. He has specialized in the study of Norwegian and Scandinavian church history and has written several publications dealing with nation-building and religion, and religious awakenings and the modernisation of society: *Nationality, identity and morality* (KULTs skriftserie, 1995), 'Church and nation in the 19th century – the case of Norway', in Ingmar Brohed (ed.), *Church and people in Britain and Scandinavia* (Lund: Lund University Press, 1996), *Grundtvigianism and nationalism in Norway during the 19th century* (KULTs skriftserie, 1996), and 'Religious identity and Nordic identity' in Øystein Sørensen and Bo Stråth (eds.), *The cultural construction of Norden* (Oslo: Scandinavian University Press, 1997).

MICHAEL WINTLE is Professor of European History at the Universiteit van Amsterdam, where he directs the degree programmes in European Studies. Prior to 2002, he held a chair of European History at the University of Hull, UK, where he had taught since 1980. He has published widely on the modern history of the Netherlands, including *Pillars of piety* (Hull: Hull University Press, 1985) and *An economic and social history of the Netherlands* (Cambridge: Cambridge University Press, 2000). He also has research interests in European identity and especially the visual representation of Europe.

JOHN WOLFFE is Professor of Religious History at the Open University. He is the author of *The Protestant crusade in Great Britain, 1829–1860* (Oxford: Oxford University Press, 1991), *God and Greater Britain: religion and national life in Britain and Ireland, 1843–1945* (London: Routledge, 1994) and *Great deaths: grieving, religion and nationhood in Victorian and Edwardian Britain* (Oxford: Oxford University Press, 2000).

Introduction

SHERIDAN GILLEY

Historians of modern Christianity in western Europe, writing amid the chill winds of secularism at the beginning of the twenty-first century, may be tempted to apologise for their subject. Why write about something of diminishing importance, which has been in decline since the French Revolution? No student of the medieval or early modern eras doubts the central role of religion, but modern historiography can get along without it. In fact, the historian of nineteenth-century Christianity need not be defensive about his or her theme, which still entered into the very fabric of the social and political conflicts of the era, and just as the creation of a united Italy was on one level a defeat of Catholicism, and the creation of the German Empire a victory for Protestantism, so the attack upon the churches, in what some have seen as the beginning of secularisation, makes a fascinating story which, at least in the immediate term, led not only to religious decline but also to renewal and revival.

Western Europe might, however, be considered something of an anomaly even in the present, in which Christianity continues to grow and expand elsewhere, in the Third World, in the United States and, with the collapse of atheistic communism, in eastern Europe. This must be one reason for the somewhat unconventional appearance of this volume by the standards of other histories of the nineteenth-century Christian faith, as here at least a third of the space is given to the new Christian churches outside Europe. Catholic Christianity became a global religion through the Spanish and Portuguese empires in the sixteenth century and French missionaries in the seventeenth and eighteenth. There are chapters here reflecting the legacy of this earlier era. These include Latin America, where the Roman Catholic Church in the nineteenth century displayed a whole range of splendours and miseries, from post-colonial anticlerical attack and with too few priests; the Philippines, where Catholicism set down deep roots in native culture and with a native clergy, sometimes resistant to Spanish rule; and India, where the Portuguese had both persecuted and tried to convert the ancient Christian communities of Mar-Thomas in founding their own. Other old Catholic mission fields were Indochina, acquired in the nineteenth century by France; Canada, where the Quebecois renewed an older model of an integrally Catholic society; China, where Catholicism remained despite savage attempts to suppress it; and most remarkably Japan, where in 1865 a small Catholic Church was found to have survived the closure of the country in the seventeenth century to foreigners and the execution or exile of its clergy. The cruel martyrdom of Catholics in China, Indochina, Japan and Korea, another heroic missionary country, was connected to local fears of European invasion and conquest, which in some cases were not unjustified.

The emergence of the American colonies, and the rise of the British Empire and of the new international evangelical Protestant missionary movement of the eighteenth century, created by the leader of the Moravians, Count Nikolaus von Zinzendorf, and the founder of Methodism, John Wesley, also made Protestantism a global religion, through a complicated combination of mission and settlement. Its enormous expansion came in the nineteenth century, especially through voluntary bodies outside the established churches in the Protestant countries, spectacularly enough in Great Britain, among several varieties of Methodist, Baptists, Congregationalists and Presbyterians, as well as many minor or purely local bodies, and within the new Britain in Canada, but most dramatically in the United States, with hundreds of denominations, most of them of British origin, but some from the continent or home-grown. Indeed in spite of failures over slavery and of missions to Native Americans, and interdenominational rivalries and divisions, the new nation was dominated during the first half of this period by evangelical revivalism, although this was disturbed after 1860 by the arrival of still greater numbers of Roman Catholics and, in lesser measure, of Jews and Eastern Orthodox.

A burgeoning missionary Protestantism from Britain, northern Europe and the United States itself, sometimes fed by the premillennial expectation of Christ's Second Coming which was also rooted in revivalism, created new churches in many places in which Christians remain numerous to this day, though as small minorities of the general population. Amid the extraordinary babel of cultures and languages in India, Protestant missionary effort appealed to some of the educated as well as to marginal castes and ethnic groups. In China, Protestant institutions provided an educated minority with a western education, where, as elsewhere, Catholics sought to create wholly Catholic communities in the countryside. In both countries there was alarm among local elites at an alien western threat to their authority and culture, as well as a

European reluctance to adapt Christianity to wholly different ancient civilisations. One area of general missionary failure was the Middle East, where the recovery of the Holy Land had an important place in Protestant ambitions. Neither Catholic nor Protestant missionaries managed to convert many Muslims or Jews. While Catholics strengthened their own eastern Uniate churches, in the hope of reconciling the Orthodox churches to them, Protestants did not succeed in 'reforming' the Eastern Orthodox along their own lines, and ended by setting up numerous small Christian congregations, with a superior educational provision which was often an important part of a more general modernising mission.

Missionary Christianity often had a difficult and ambiguous relationship to the spread of the colonial empires, which had quite separate agendas: sometimes, as in India and the Sudan, in opposition to missions. Despite its idealism of purpose, however, missionary enterprise could not but be influenced by the nineteenth-century assumptions of racial and cultural superiority arising in part from greater European wealth and power, especially towards Africans. That raised difficult issues about whether to make independent native churches or churches controlled by Europeans, in a retreat from the optimism common early in the century about the innate Christian capacities of native peoples. Imperial white attitudes also produced by reaction 'Ethiopianism' as the hope for an intrinsically African form of Christianity, which would restore the black Christian's sense of dignity and worth. This led to the emergence of indigenous black African churches sometimes inspired by the flourishing black Protestant churches in the United States, themselves the outcome of Protestant missionary activity, but in reaction against the prejudice of other churches, with a faith deeply founded in their historic experience of servitude and oppression.

This growth of Christianity abroad was not always paralleled in Europe. Some of the challenges to the faith were intellectual, leading to the attempt of German and English Protestant thinkers to answer the problems posed by the spirit of the age in terms sympathetic to it, as by Hegel and Coleridge. The Romantic movement was in revolt against eighteenth-century rationalism and brought with it a renewed sense of the value of awe and mystery and wonder. Romanticism was, therefore, strongly inclined to Christianity, in both its Protestant and Catholic forms, and had a major influence upon the Christian dimension of nineteenth-century literature, especially in English-speaking countries, the subject of a separate chapter here. The Romantic insistence upon social cohesion appears in Chateaubriand's apologetic for Catholic civilisation, in the opposing conservative and liberal Catholic Ultramontane theories of de Maistre and the young Lamennais, within the Catholic Tübingen School in Germany, and in the Oxford Movement in England. The debt of Romanticism to Plato, Spinoza and even Unitarianism, however, sometimes inclined it to a one-sided immanentism as well as to orthodoxy, as in identifying Christianity with the Prussian *Zeitgeist* in Hegel, while the counter-cultural view of Christianity in Schelling and Kierkegaard insisted upon its autonomy, anticipating Barth, and the atheist possibilities of the tradition were made explicit in the writings of Feuerbach and Nietzsche.

Meanwhile a new historicism brought about a revolution in biblical criticism among Protestants, though this took a number of different positions according to the degree of radicalism of the scholar. Here German theology and philosophy, especially Hegel's, had a major influence upon scholarship. Regardless of such assumptions, it became more intellectually difficult if by no means impossible, for the educated at least, to adopt the literal view of Scripture which emerged from the premillennial movement of the 1820s. At a more popular level, traditional attitudes to hell fire and predestination were weakened, and some Protestant bodies were deeply influenced by a post-Enlightenment optimism and progressivism which harmonised with political liberalism. The new evolutionary biological science of Darwinism, seeming to require a view of the creation and of man very different from the one set forth in the Book of Genesis, posed particular problems for a literal Bible-based religion, although here the Christian reaction was a great deal more nuanced and complicated than is sometimes understood. Among Catholics, there were smaller liberal Catholic and later modernist movements to meet the criticism of the age.

This in turn, with the wider attacks upon the churches, also produced a reaction. Both Roman Catholicism and evangelical Protestantism proved resistant to the new liberalism. Yet even in its rural heartland, Christianity was sometimes weakened by social and political change, and there were major regional variations in churchgoing which had little reference to the new intellectual scepticism, and far more to do with politics and economics. In Spain, Portugal and Italy, a thoroughly Christianised north of small peasant farmers stood in contrast to the latifundia of the partly dechristianised south. But urbanisation and industrialisation created the new problem of an irreligious working class, though here again there were common devout exceptions to the rule, as among British miners and fishermen. The shock of industrialism was first felt in Great Britain, and in both England and Scotland the delay in the provision of new places of worship, especially by the established Anglican and Presbyterian churches, left many people unchurched. The strains of adaptation to the population explosion, which the fast-expanding non-established Noncon-formist churches were at first better able to provide, led to the secession after 1800 of most of the population of Wales to various forms of voluntarist Non-conformist evangelicalism, and contributed to the disruption of the Church of Scotland in 1843, with the formation of a new Free Church which was vol-untarist in practice though not in principle. The great British church-building boom after 1830, partly sustained by denominational rivalry, did not in itself win back the slums for religion, as popular alienation from formal religious practice, if not from faith itself, had more complicated causes, which partly lay in the middle-class character of so much British Christianity. On the conti-nent, the urban working classes were influenced by anticlerical socialism and, at the extremes, communism, though again with powerful differences from one place to another. In both Europe and North America, Protestant pastoral outreach, social Christianity and Christian Socialism attempted to address this, as did the social teaching of the Catholic Church enunciated by Leo XIII in his encyclical *Rerum Novarum*, and the great growth of Catholic self-help organ-isations in the last quarter of the nineteenth century. There is much here for the secular humanitarian to commend, as in the evangelical crusade against the slave trade and the condemnation of slavery by the papacy, the great many voluntary associations which tried to assist the poor and provided a frame-work for vast numbers of ordered and sober lives, and the churches' massive contributions to family welfare, medicine and education.

Certain kinds of response to secularisation and liberalism cut across denom-inational boundaries. In the aftermath of the French Revolution and later in the nineteenth century, with the advent of secular socialism, religious prac-tice was weakened among men rather than women, and, especially in Roman Catholicism, there was a feminisation of religion in many places, contributing to the huge growth in the numbers of new female religious orders active in education and social work, especially in France. Women also played a vital part in the multi-form vitality of British Nonconformity, where leadership and congregations, as distinct from actual membership, were often predominantly male. Female preaching and full equality of ministry tended to be confined to unsacramental charismatic bodies like the Salvation Army or liberal ones like the Unitarians. Women made a major contribution to the new Protestant missions, going where men could not, although this had partly to do with perceptions of the inferiority of the heathen.

Growth meant competition, and one consequence of the competition between churches in some countries was the reinforcement of denomina-tional differences. These became parts of wider political conflicts as between

Catholics and Protestants in Ireland, in the war between the Catholic and Protestant cantons in Switzerland, and in the *Kulturkampf* in Protestant Prussia, which attempted and failed to place Catholicism under strict regulation by the state. The most extraordinary expression of such conflict was the 'pillarisation' of nineteenth-century Dutch society, in which Calvinists, both moderate and conservative, Catholics and secular socialists could live entirely separate lives in institutions which only met at the leadership level for negotiation with one another.

A tendency accompanying conflict and competition among the churches in old Europe, even in some Protestant countries, was the development of a higher doctrine of church, ministry and sacrament, partly in a strengthening of clerical elites against the tendency by governments to invade the traditional province of established churches in family matters and education. The reaction was strongest in the Catholic Church, where the expropriation of ecclesiastical property began in the suppression of the Society of Jesus in 1773 and the reforms of the Emperor Joseph II, and resulted in the nationalisation of all French religious property in 1790, the suppression of the ecclesiastical principalities of the Holy Roman Empire and, for a time, Napoleon's seizure of the Papal States themselves. The papal reaction to the whole revolutionary tradition and to the subsequent *Risorgimento* to create a united Italy which annexed the States of the Church inspired the new or neo-Ultramontane movement to elevate the claims of the pope to govern the whole church, leading to the definition of papal infallibility in matters of faith and morals at the First Vatican Council of 1869–70. Neo-Ultramontanism prevailed in the Catholic churches of the Mediterranean and Latin America, in opposition to liberal anticlericalism, as the hierarchies and clergy of Italy, Iberia, Latin America and even Gallican France increasingly looked to Rome for inspiration and salvation from an anti-Christian state. Again, part of the reaction lay in a powerful revival of traditional devotions partly sustained by new apparitions of the Blessed Virgin to children and female visionaries, as the church reaffirmed the power of the miraculous and the supernatural to men who did not believe. This devotional movement was far more than the response of authority to political challenge, as spirituality has its own energies and reflected more immediate and domestic concerns as well as feminisation, but Pope Pius IX himself saw an intimate connection between his definition of the dogma of the Immaculate Conception in 1854 and the Syllabus of Errors in which he condemned 'progress, liberalism and modern civilisation', again on the feast of the Immaculate Conception, exactly ten years later to the day. A striking example of this new stress upon clerical authority and the new ardour of devotion occurred in the Church of England in the Oxford Movement, which arose in the University of Oxford in 1833 among Anglican High Churchmen who resented the weakening of the established character of the Church of England and sought ways of resisting a Whig government's reform of the church, then united to the even more Protestant Church of Ireland. The Oxford Movement's appeal, not to the official and national character of the church as by law established, but to the God-given authority of the threefold Catholic ministerial order of bishop, priest and deacon, and to the tradition of the early church as well as to Scripture, led to the secession of some of the movement's leaders, like John Henry Newman, to Roman Catholicism, while others, inspired by Edward Bouverie Pusey and John Keble, continued to press the Church of England's claim to be a part of the wider Holy Catholic and Apostolic Church. The outcome was that one whole section of a traditionally Protestant church disowned its Protestant inheritance, adopting a more Catholic theology and pastoral practice, with daily services, auricular confession, the worship of the Blessed Sacrament and prayer to the Virgin and saints, while Anglican ritual moved in a more Catholic direction, and the clergy assumed a more ecclesiastical character and dress which, after an initial reaction, reinforced an existing trend to clericalism among the British Nonconformist clergy.

Given the pre-existing renaissance of the British Protestant traditions between 1790 and 1830, especially in the form of evangelicalism, the rise of a counter-catholicising movement created bitter tensions within the Church of England with Protestants and liberals, as well as exacerbating conflict with the Protestant Nonconformist churches. Chapter 7 on church architecture and art shows some of the consequences in stone and paint of this kind of catholicising church revival, especially in the increasing popularity in the Protestant world of medieval neo-Gothic for churches and educational institutions, in a widespread, though far from universal, rejection of classicism as reflecting a secular pagan spirit. The resort to Gothic in such modern buildings as town halls and railway stations was a more general aspect of the Romantic liking for a medieval Catholic style. There was also an impressive Christian musical achievement, in both formal Catholic and Lutheran liturgical music as well as in hymnody and sacred song, though this was beset by diminished resources among Catholics and attended by controversy, which the papacy tried to control, over traditional plainchant and polyphony and the influence of opera, in the quest for a properly ecclesiastical style.

The neo-medievalism so powerful in art and architecture often went hand in hand with a new romantic nationalism, and if Rome opposed such nationalism in Italy, it found itself strengthened by the new intensity of nationalist

Catholic resistance to the multi-national empires of Britain, Prussia, Russia and Austria in Ireland, Poland and Hungary, as well as among the diasporas of emigrants from those countries. Faith flourished among regional groups like the Bretons, resistant to the centre, and more could be said here about smaller nationalities which achieved a greater self-consciousness in the nineteenth century, like the Croats, Slovenes and Czechs. Religion, however, also acted as a spur to European imperialism, and Protestantism could be described as the ideology of the global British empire, and as part of the manifest destiny of the expanding United States. In the new French empire, anticlericalism was not for export, until the advent of the administration of Emile Combes, as in spite of tensions the church was seen as an instrument of France's civilising mission. In some new British colonies like New Zealand, the French missionaries found the Protestant churches and settlers already in possession, and British Protestant and French Catholic rivalry in evangelism spurred their competing wills to empire across the Pacific and through Africa. Religion was intimately bound up with national culture and character: British Australia was predominantly Protestant, and reproduced the denominational divisions of Victorian Britain with fervently Catholic and Nonconformist minorities, though after 1840 without an established church. Yet it wore its Protestantism with a difference – some might say with an indifference – combining generally Christian convictions with strong culture-based reservations in the national psyche about the institutional churches.

One purpose of this work is simply to supply the necessary information for understanding a subject and its latest literature. There is one wholly regrettable omission from this volume, in its aspiration to give the whole of Christianity a fair coverage, and that is of the Eastern Orthodox, which leaves the work with an unhappy appearance of incompletion. They are to be covered in a volume of their own; this was not by a decision of the editors. The Eastern rite Christians sometimes called Greek Catholics or Uniates in communion with the pope, who were awkwardly poised between the Orthodox and overregulation from Rome, have their own chapter, and references to them occur in others.

In a volume of this kind, there is bound to be some variety of method and approach, in the use of narrative and the balance between breadth and depth of analysis, though all contributors claim the kind of unity of subject indicated in their titles. As the chapters are intended to be read as self-sufficient entities, there is also an overlap of subject matter, as in the various discussions of social patterns of religious practice; in the two accounts of the Scottish Disruption, seen from different angles; in the chapters on the papacy and the *Risorgimento*; and in the matter of the Irish Catholic diaspora, which has its own chapter and is treated separately and more briefly in the various countries across the world in which it found a home. There has been no attempt by the editors to impose their own views upon contributors. Contrary opinions will be found in the two discussions of the separation of church and state in France. The editors have not interfered simply because they have considered a matter of interpretation to be mistaken. Clio, the muse of history, is seldom definitive, for historical judgement as to the wisdom or desirability of a course or movement will vary with the general convictions of the historian.

There is a great deal about religious belief which lies in the human heart beyond historical observation and generalisation, and a summary is not easy. There is sympathy here, but also criticism. Like most periods of Christian history, seen from different angles, it was the best of times and the worst of times. It is difficult to define a criterion for the success of religious faith; how many Christians got to heaven is known to God alone. But if sheer influence and level of commitment count for anything, this was possibly a more successful period for Christianity than most.

PART I

*

CHRISTIANITY AND MODERNITY

2

The papacy

SHERIDAN GILLEY

The nineteenth century was a period of paradox in the history of the Roman Catholic Church. It was an age of revival, especially through the growth of active religious orders of women, and the strengthening of Catholicism in areas in which it suffered from disadvantage or minority status – Germany, Holland, the British Isles and the English-speaking world – while coming under pressure or persecution in the traditionally Catholic Latin states of southern Europe and South America. Both renewal and decline had, however, a common strand, the new or neo-Ultramontane movement to exalt the authority of the pope as an inspiration for revival and a defence against decline among the 'integrally' religious. Neo-Ultramontanism was the trades unionism of priests resistant to bishops in France, the protection of bishops resistant to the state in Spain and Prussia, and the enthusiasm among converts from Protestantism to Catholicism resistant to various forms of unbelief in England, and among Catholics everywhere opposed to the seizure of the Papal States by the kingdom of Piedmont-Savoy between 1860 and 1870.

Neo-Ultramontanism upheld the traditionally Ultramontane doctrines of the infallibility of papal teaching in faith and morals and the universal jurisdiction of the Roman pontiff; it opposed the old Gallican theory, ascendant in the Catholic world before 1789, of an infallible authority restricted to general councils of the whole church, and of independent national churches effectively controlled by kings and states and acknowledging only a titular papal primacy. Gallicanism still prevailed in 1829, when, of the 646 diocesan bishops, the pope appointed only twenty-four outside the Papal States. Neo-Ultramontanism differed from the traditional view in its populism, which carried it sometimes into an excess beyond the theories of the Roman theologians, and entailed its transformation by the modern means of communication into a *cultus* of the pope himself. The Parisian lady who reacted to the pope's new status as the 'Prisoner of the Vatican' after the Italian occupation of Rome in 1870 by sending him underclothes, hearing of his lamentable deprivation in this regard, was as much a part of the Ultramontane movement as the great bishops, journalists and theologians who espoused it, as papal prestige and authority over the church flourished by ways and means which Rome itself had often done little to inspire.

Yet neo-Ultramontanism was also sustained by a succession of strong, attractive papal personalities who, in the Catholic view, were martyrs. Pius VII, who was held prisoner from 1809 to 1814, reverted to the role of the monk who mended his own soutane. In 1814, the defeat of the Emperor Napoleon allowed him to return to Rome, where he revived the Society of Jesus. Almost alone among the numerous ecclesiastical principalities of the *ancien régime*, the astute Cardinal Ercole Consalvi negotiated the restoration almost *in toto* of the Papal States at the Congress of Vienna, losing Avignon and the Venaissin in France, before taking up the reins of papal government. The papal archives and many of the artistic treasures looted by the French were returned to Rome. The recovery in papal prestige was marked by concordats with Bavaria and Sardinia (1817), Naples (1818) and Prussia (1821) and the Upper Rhine Provinces (1821). The portrait of Pius by Sir Thomas Lawrence commissioned by the Prince Regent conveys the weariness of the man in the beauty of his wasted face and the long hands never raised except in blessing. It was the first papal icon of the coming age.

The restoration of the Papal States belonged to the conservative reaction to the revolutionary turmoil of the French Revolution and the Napoleonic wars, as the Austrian foreign minister (later chancellor) Prince Metternich, the 'coachman of Europe', guided the continent back into its ancient political paths. Catholicism remained the most popular religion in Europe – there were about 100 million Catholics to 40 million Protestants and 40 million Orthodox – but the 'Congress system' left the continent dominated by the non-Catholic powers (Great Britain, Prussia and Russia) with millions of Irish, German and Polish Catholics under their rule. These Catholics might feel more affinity with radical politics, even revolution, than with the status quo. Yet the new arrangement also left the papacy to a degree the creature of the conservative order of Metternich's creation. One of its foremost new apologists, Count Joseph de Maistre, author of *Du Pape* (1819), was an arch-conservative who looked to Rome as the sanction for monarchic rule, although Rome refused to join the Holy Alliance of non-Catholic Russia and Prussia with Catholic Austria which sought to give Metternich's order a religious colouring.

Rome's main problems were nearer home. Consalvi's division of the Papal States into four legations and thirteen delegations involved an element of lay participation and a compromise between Napoleonic and canon law, but the Romagna had been lay since 1800, and its more affluent citizens would never be happy again with government by priests. The *politicani* cardinals who supported Consalvi's reforms were outvoted in the conclave of 1823 by the *zelanti* who elected Consalvi's enemy, the conservative Annibale della Genga as Leo XII (1760–1829; ruled 1823–9). He abolished lay participation in the higher levels of government, banned the waltz at carnival and reopened the Jewish ghetto. Such conservatism drove opposition underground among the secret revolutionary brotherhood of *carbonari* or 'charcoal-burners', and there was a reaction in the conclave of 1829, when Consalvi's disciple Cardinal Albani worked to secure the election of the moderate Francesco Xaverio Castiglione, bishop of Montalto, who took the name Pius VIII (1761–1830; ruled 1829–30). He attempted, unsuccessfully, to reach a compromise with the Prussian government which wanted him to authorise mixed marriages in the Catholic Rhineland provinces it had acquired in 1815, and after initial distress he recognised the July Monarchy established by the French revolution of 1830. Meanwhile a small but influential body of French Catholic Ultramontanes, led by Robert Félicité de Lamennais, demanded that the pope champion liberal reform. Indeed the third Catholic Relief Act in the United Kingdom in 1829, the union of Catholics and Liberals in Belgium in 1830 to overthrow the rule of Protestant Holland and the Polish rising against Russia in 1830–1, all indicated, despite the pope's reservations, that liberalism might sometimes be in the church's interests. Pius was, however, already ill with a neck abscess at his election, and after a pontificate of just over a year and a half, he died in November 1830.

As the conservative Leo succeeded the moderate Pius VII and was followed by the moderate Pius VIII, so Pius was succeeded by the most conservative pope of the nineteenth century, the Camaldolese monk Bartolomeo (in religion Mauro) Cappellari who took the name Gregory XVI (1765–1846; ruled 1831–46). An inveterate snuff-taker – it gave rise to a facial tumour – Cappellari was a hale and vigorous old man, whose theology had always been strongly Ultramontane: his best-known book was called *The triumph of the Holy See* (1799). On his election there was a rising in the Romagna which Austria crushed at the pope's request, leading the liberal government of Louis-Philippe in France, supported by England, to organise a Memorandum signed by the Roman ambassadors of the great powers demanding reforms in his administration. Gregory gave the rebels an amnesty which was followed by a further revolt and Austrian occupation. The three most famous liberal Catholics of their generation, Lamennais, Lacordaire and the comte de Montalembert, visited Rome to persuade him of the value of a liberal Catholicism. Lamennais was politely received, but his liberalism was anathematised in the encyclical *Mirari Vos* in 1832, and his apocalyptic tract *Paroles d'un croyant* (1834) bitterly satirised Gregory, who condemned the work in his encyclical *Singulari Nos* in 1834. Lamennais left the church, but his followers did not, and their contribution to the Catholic revival was largely responsible for the church's popularity in the French revolution of 1848. Gregory, however, remained intransigent: he urged his faithful Catholic Poles to obey the Tsar after their rising, while the secretary of state, Cardinal Bernetti, in 1832 created a civil guard, the Centurions, whose unruly behaviour contributed to the unpopularity of papal rule. The liberal conspiracy to kidnap three leading ecclesiastics (one of them the future Pius IX) in 1843 was repressed by another secretary of state, Luigi Lambruschini, with executions and condemnations to the galleys. Gregory's antiliberalism was confirmed by the destruction of Spanish monasticism by anticlerical administrations from 1835, and the imprisonment of the archbishop of Cologne in 1837 for his resistance to Prussian legislation on mixed marriages. The pope's opposition to building railways in his states was taken by European liberals to symbolise his hostility to change. This was not wholly fair, as Gregory reorganised the Vatican and Lateran museums and refounded the Catholic missions, creating more than seventy new dioceses and vicariates apostolic, doubling those in England from four to eight. In the freshly independent states of Latin America and in India, he ignored Spain's *patronato real* and Portugal's *padroado* in appointing to bishoprics, and in 1839, in *In Supremo*, he condemned the African slave trade. He pragmatically accepted the liberal Belgian constitution, but he made the papacy appear the main obstacle to Italian unity, an omen for the future.

The Italian Catholic revival included such major figures as the theologian Antonio Rosmini and the novelist Manzoni, and liberals like Count Cesare Balbo who sought an accommodation between the church and the spirit of the age. Thus the priest Vincenzo Gioberti, in his *Moral and civil primacy of the Italians* (1843), defended the ideal of a united Italy under a papal presidency. Gioberti influenced Giovanni Maria Mastai Ferretti, the cardinal bishop of Imola, and the conclave of 1846 elected him pope, under the name of Pius IX, Pio Nono (1792–1878; ruled 1846–78), the longest-reigning pope in history. Pius had pleaded with the rebels in 1831 and had given a safe conduct to the young *carbonaro* Louis Napoleon. He announced an amnesty for political prisoners and the appointment of a consultative lay council. When a dove alighted on his coach, it seemed to liberals that heaven had come to earth.

The papacy was the weak point in Metternich's Congress system, and the election of a liberal pope precipitated the 1848 revolutions. Charles Albert of Piedmont-Savoy went into battle to expel Austria from Italy in 1848, and the excitable Roman revolutionary clubs put pressure on Pius through great public demonstrations to join the Piedmontese crusade against Austrian rule. The papal minister Count Pellegrino Rossi was assassinated, and Rome came under a Committee of Public Safety which made the pope a prisoner. In November 1848, he fled by night in a closed carriage to Gaeta in the kingdom of Naples, carrying the Blessed Sacrament in a ciborium borne into exile by Pius VI. An elected constituent assembly in Rome in February 1849 declared a Roman Republic, which was fired by Giuseppe Garibaldi and the visionary journalist Giuseppe Mazzini, for whom the republican 'Third Rome' would supersede the former Romes of the universal empire and papacy as symbolic of a regenerate humanity.

The victory of Austria over Piedmont at Novara in 1849 restored Habsburg rule in northern Italy, while a French army reinstated papal power. Pius returned to Rome in April 1850. He was a patriotic Italian but was committed to the integrity of his states, and he was henceforth the most resolute of the public enemies of liberalism, a course confirmed by the attacks upon church property, the religious orders and ecclesiastical jurisdiction in Piedmont in the 1850s under Count Camillo di Cavour. Pius's astute and courageous if self-aggrandising secretary of state, Giacomo Antonelli, encouraged him to resist any surrender of his kingship. The victory of France over Austria in 1859 brought about the Piedmontese invasion of the Papal States and the union, in 1861, of most of Italy, including the Papal States outside the Patrimony of St Peter, under the anticlerical government of King Victor Emmanuel II.

The city of Rome was protected by Napoleon III until 1870, who was under pressure from French Catholics, but the pope's predicament had an enormous impact on Ultramontane Europeans, some of whom volunteered to fight for him. He was encouraged by the mystical and visionary elements in Romanticism which contributed to the Catholic revival, while new apparitions of the Virgin, to St Catherine Labouré in Paris in 1830 and to children at La Salette in 1846, were given official encouragement. Our Lady confirmed to a peasant girl, St Bernadette, at Lourdes, in 1858, the dogma of the Immaculate Conception defined by Pius in 1854, and the spread of Marian pietism went with what one Anglican convert, Frederick William Faber, called devotion to the pope: Pius declared Mary Immaculate, and the church declared him infallible.

Kindly, handsome and witty, unlike his dour and ugly predecessor Gregory, and given to mildly sacrilegious jokes from Scripture – he wrote for a nun on a hideous portrait of himself, 'Fear not, it is I' – Pius was the first pope to be known as a personality to ordinary Catholics. The greatest propagandist of this 'new' populist Ultramontanism was a French journalist, Louis Veuillot, its high priest was an ex-Anglican archdeacon, Henry Edward Manning, later second cardinal archbishop of Westminster, and it created a popular culture through the new means of industry and communication, in mass-produced newspapers, books, pictures and devotional objects, with the pope's portrait in every Catholic presbytery, school and home. This inspired Cardinal Wiseman's comparison, in his hymn 'Full in the panting heart of Rome', of neo-Ultramontane loyalty with the electric telegraph. In this triumphalist mood, the pope negotiated concordats with Spain (1851 and 1859) and Austria (1855), and restored the episcopal hierarchies of England and Wales (1850) and Holland (1853), and later in Scotland (1878), the last completed by Pope Leo. Pius also greatly extended the Catholic hierarchy in the mission fields in Africa and Asia pioneered by the French, and in the United States and the British empire, as the church grew and flourished through European and especially Irish emigration.

The pope built railways in the Papal States, was an admirer of English manufactures, and commissioned an English screw steamship called *The Immaculate Conception* from a Thameside dockyard. Ideological liberalism was something else, and the persecution of the church by anticlerical liberals called from him in 1864 the encyclical *Quanta Cura* and its accompanying Syllabus of Errors, a list of the eighty great intellectual, social and political errors of the age, published on the feast of the Immaculate Conception ten years after the promulgation of the dogma and culminating in the condemnation by the Syllabus of 'progress, liberalism and recent departures in civil society', the last sometimes translated as 'modern civilisation'.[1] These errors were quoted from previous papal responses to attacks upon the church in its Latin heartlands, and need to be read in context, but they did not properly distinguish between the northern European liberalism which gave a new freedom to the church to open churches, schools and monasteries, and the Latin liberalism which closed them down. The astute Bishop Dupanloup of Orléans argued that the Syllabus described an ideal world in which every one was Catholic, not the real world in which the church must compromise. The case for the pope was that he saw the self-interested character of much nineteenth-century liberalism, its selfish conception of individual autonomy and its greed to do well out of the properties of the church which were public patrimony and the patrimony of the poor. The criticism of Pius is that he bound the church to the values of

---

1 Ehler and Morrall (eds.), *Church and state through the centuries*, p. 285.

an older social order, and that he did not, in the manner of liberal Catholics, welcome that element in liberalism which was, as Pius VII had recognised, an outgrowth of Christianity itself.

Meanwhile, great international gatherings of priests and bishops in Rome, for the canonisation of the Japanese martyrs in 1862 and for the eighteenth centenary of the martyrdoms of St Peter and St Paul in 1867, were the preliminaries to the Ecumenical Council opened in 1869. About a third of the prelates attending were Italian, with large blocs from the Spanish-speaking states, the great majority of them Ultramontanes. The Council set the seal on the triumph of the Holy See over the church by declaring the pope infallible in matters of faith and morals, in a repudiation of all the forms of Gallicanism which had haunted Rome for centuries. The pope was a partisan for his own position – he remarked that 'I am tradition' – and some eighty prelates, mostly from northern Europe, declined to vote for the final form of the decree, in *Pastor Aeternus*, although only two voted against it. The concomitant definition on papal jurisdiction over the whole church was also far reaching, and the withdrawal of the European states from control of the church during the next half-century made it realisable. But the outbreak in 1870 of the Franco-Prussian war caused the departure of the French garrison from Rome and its occupation by Italy, and with the loss of French protection the Council dispersed with its business incomplete, while the pope retreated from his city as 'the prisoner of the Vatican', to rule a new empire of the spirit.

European liberal reaction to Vatican I was hostile. Italy remained partly estranged for a generation. The pope repudiated the Law of Guarantees in 1871, in which the Italian government unilaterally offered him an annual payment, a measure of freedom for the Italian church from the state and protection for the curia and for the exercise of its spiritual authority, in return for a settlement of the Roman Question. The Law operated in a quasi-official manner in spite of conflict over the state's confirmation of episcopal appointments and further seizures of church and monastic property, especially in Rome itself. One of Pio Nono's last anxieties was that his despoiler Victor Emmanuel II should die with the rites of the church. Austria repudiated its concordat, while in the new predominantly Protestant German *Reich* formed in 1871 after the Prussian defeat of France and the fall of Napoleon III in 1870, the Iron Chancellor, Otto von Bismarck, launched a persecution of Catholicism called the *Kulturkampf* or 'culture struggle' in Prussia from 1872 which was copied in a number of German states, though the persecution of the clergy only strengthened the pre-existing impressive solidarity of German Catholicism. A small number of educated middle-class Catholics in Germany and Switzerland, who rejected the Vatican decrees, went off to found or join the Old Catholic Churches in union with the schism of Utrecht. In France, the conservative reaction to the violence of the Commune of 1871 seemed likely to restore the French Catholic monarchy, but in 1875 the country drifted into its Third Republic, leaving the church exposed to an anticlericalism which would greatly weaken its influence. Yet despite these setbacks, Pio Nono was the maker of the modern papacy. The loss of the Papal States was a blessing in disguise, as it diminished the Vatican's immersion in Italian politics, and marked its transformation into a more exclusively global spiritual power.

Pio Nono's strategy of opposition to ultra-modernity had its losses and gains, and left a difficult legacy to his successor, Gioacchino Vincenzo Raffaele Luigi Pecci, Pope Leo XIII (1810–1903; ruled 1878–1903). By living to 93, Leo was, until the reign of John Paul II, the second-longest ruling pope in history, only after Pius himself.

Born the sixth son of a minor Italian nobleman, and educated for the priesthood at the Roman College and the Academy of Noble Ecclesiastics, Leo was the last pope to exercise civil authority, as governor of the papal enclave of Benevento in 1838 and of Perugia in 1841. After a brief period as nuncio in Belgium, he remained for over three decades bishop of Perugia, being distrusted by Antonelli. Skilled as a diplomat and administrator, he sought a new *modus vivendi* with the European states, and was thought too liberal to succeed Pius, though his aims were still more extensive, the re-creation of Catholic Christendom. Leo's vision, like his name, was an imperial one, his favourite pope being the all-powerful Innocent III, whose remains he had reburied in his cathedral of the Lateran, opposite his own tomb.

Leo also looked to the thirteenth century for the renewal of Catholic intellectual life. In the encyclical *Aeterni Patris* (1879) he declared that all Catholic philosophy should be based on the study of St Thomas Aquinas, thereby producing a revival of Thomist thought that lasted into the twentieth century. Leo's philosophy of society is derived from Aquinas's doctrine of natural law, the eternal law as imprinted on the human mind, which was accessible in principle to the reason of all, but had the church for its guardian and protector. Rome therefore claimed a new universal importance for everyone as the custodian of the one right political and social philosophy.

This philosophy, though medieval in inspiration, was designed for the needs of a living Catholic world. In the 1870s, the extension of the franchise and of education beyond liberal middle-class elites to the Catholic masses resulted in the emergence of new populist political parties and social institutions. Catholic newspapers, peasant co-operatives, banks, youth organisations, schools and parishes marshalled the faithful, in Italy under the aegis of the Opera dei Congressi, while religious orders and foreign missions boomed. From the 1880s, populist cardinals in the English-speaking world – Manning in Westminster, Gibbons in Baltimore, Moran in Sydney – gave guidance to the infant labour movement, and tried to keep it from running to a secularist, socialist or Marxist extreme.

Leo provided this popular political movement, the largest in the western world, with its philosophy. As a fine Latinist and diplomat, he was the quintessence of the universal Latin mind, of its urbane familiarity with literatures, cultures and languages, and its consciousness of standing not in some merely Italian tradition but in the great name of Rome. His social teaching ran thus. Church and state are distinct, each divine in origin and sovereign in its own particular sphere. Whether Christian or pagan, the state derives its sanction from God. Democracy is as tolerable as other forms of government as long as it acknowledges its divine foundation and the special realm of sovereignty of the church. States are bound by the natural law, which requires controls on the expression of moral and religious error. Ideally, in a Christian society, education and the regulation of public morals belong to the church, while the family is, as much as church and state, a sacred institution, also of divine origin, which the state is bound to protect. Voluntary association is a positive good. Leo was hostile to the French Revolution and its successors on the left, for his model of society was based not on class warfare or social equality but on an ideal bodily harmony in which unequal classes in a traditional hierarchy exercise Christian charity and forbearance to one another.

This is conventional Catholic teaching. The original twist was Leo's consistent denunciation of the two rival systems of unregulated liberal *laissez-faire* capitalism and socialism, which he held to be equally wrong in teaching an autonomous secular doctrine of society and the state, placing both beyond religious discipline and the natural law. Capitalism in its monopoly form preaches and practises an economic system simply devoted to making money: it treats persons as atomised individuals and not as creatures in community, and does so without moral reference to the needs of the family, with immoral consequences in the creation of intolerable levels of poverty and suffering.

In his most comprehensive exposition of this theme, the 1891 encyclical *Rerum Novarum*, or 'Workers' Charter' as it was later called, Leo used language which would not have disgraced Karl Marx and sent pious manufacturers fleeing through the church doors: 'a small number of very rich men', he declared, 'have been able to lay upon the teeming masses of the labouring poor a yoke little better than that of slavery itself'.[2]

But the encyclical equally fiercely defended the right to private property, against its socialist detractors, though not to the selfish use of that property: here, as in taxation, there was room for state activity. Moreover families deserve a subsistence wage, and encouragement is given to workers to organise in unions, along with other forms of association intermediate between the state and family, with a backward glance to the medieval guilds.

Leo's teaching shared with conventional socialism its high doctrine of the state, its anti-individualism and its communitarianism. But he thought that property was best protected where it was most widely distributed; hence the word 'distributism' to describe the English version of his doctrine, arising from his reference to a justice distributive to all. His ideal society most closely resembled those of northern Italy, France, Spain and Portugal, and parts of Germany and Austria, with an abundance of small property owners of farms and homes and businesses, whereas socialism and unbridled capitalism both defied social harmony and the natural law.

Catholic electorates and politicians had now been given a fighting practical working guide to Catholicism as a third way which was neither socialist nor liberal. The scheme had its ironies: it was only partly applicable in Italy, where Catholics were forbidden under the *non expedit* of 1867 rule to vote in elections, or to co-operate with the spoliatory Italian state. Leo's hostility to revolution ignored a right affirmed in the Catholic medieval tradition, as some Irish rebels pointed out, and it owed its growth to the extension of the very democracy which, at best, it regarded as one possible system among a number.

The political context of this teaching was Leo's attempt to restore relations with the great European states. This was most successful in Germany, where it was in Bismarck's interest to cultivate relations with the Catholic party, the Zentrum, and bring the *Kulturkampf* to an end. The 1880s, however, saw a new anticlerical attack upon the French church's role in public life, especially in education, and Leo's efforts to 'rally' the monarchist French Catholics to the Third Republic fell foul of the resurgence of anticlericalism over the Dreyfus affair, and could not prevent the dissolution or expulsion of the French religious orders in 1901. Leo also ineffectively intervened at British prompting in Ireland.

This, however, was intelligent conservatism, not liberalism. Leo was bold in giving John Henry Newman a cardinal's hat in 1879, at the behest of Newman's

2 *Ibid.*, p. 325.

tutor, the duke of Norfolk. He was cautious in his encyclical *Providentissimus Deus* of 1893, which welcomed biblical scholarship but placed severe limits upon it, as did his subsequent Biblical Commission of 1902. Nothing happens in Rome which does not begin elsewhere, and he condemned a heresy called 'Americanism' as demanded by conservative American prelates, in a church united in faith but divided by politics. His rejection of the validity of Anglican priestly orders in 1896 as 'absolutely null and utterly void' in his bull *Apostolicae Curae* was at the behest of English Catholics like Cardinal Vaughan and Monsignor Merry del Val, born and partly educated in England, though of Spanish ancestry, who was to become secretary of state to Leo's successor.

Most of Leo's record number of seventy-five encyclicals were purely religious: there were nine on the Rosary alone. They were, however, also global in aspiration and vision, as in his dedication of humanity to the Sacred Heart in 1899. His handsome face and slim, elegant figure, in its white cassock, won hearts, and he even figured, *sine permissu*, in an English advertisement for Bovril. He insisted, however, on the full observance of royal protocol around his person, as pope-king, despite the loss of his dominions, and he lacked the common touch and easy personal charm of his predecessor and successor. His hope was for a European Christendom renewed, with a just social order, under papal guidance, with clear teaching and astute diplomacy for its realisation.

Leo's successor Pius X (1835–1914; ruled 1903–14) was born Giuseppe Melchiorre Sarto at Riese, in the Veneto. His parents were a local *cursore* or municipal messenger and a seamstress, with eight offspring. Sarto was curate for nine years in the Treviso diocese, and only in 1867 became a parish priest. In 1884, he was made bishop of Mantua, and in 1893, cardinal and patriarch of Venice. He died in August 1914, just after the outbreak of the First World War. His body was incorrupt when exhumed in 1944. Pius XII beatified him in 1951, and canonised him in 1954, the first working-class pope and papal saint in modern history.

Pius was typical of his successors in his geographical origin. In the Veneto religious practice was high: in John Pollard's words, 'the strength of the Italian Catholic movement lay in the North: in Venetia, north-eastern Lombardy, and southern Piedmont, in that order. More specifically, it was concentrated in the provinces of Belluno, Padua, Treviso, Vicenza and Verona, Bergamo, Brescia, Como, Sondrio and Cuneo', the so-called 'white areas' of the Christian Democratic party.[3] Sarto, the first of five twentieth-century popes from this

---

3 Pollard, 'Italy', p. 71.

region, was born in Treviso, trained for the priesthood in Padua and became patriarch of Venice. The north Italian church owed much to the educational system established under the Austrians and maintained by the Piedmontese: Sarto received a good free elementary school education. The church was strong among the peasant small-holders, whereas in much of Italy it was overidentified with the greater landowners and disliked by landless labourers.

The north was an area of full churches, where the good works of late nineteenth-century Social Catholicism were numerous, and Catholicism was recast in a modern social mode. He felt himself unfitted to be pope, however, lacking diplomatic experience and foreign languages. Some cardinals wanted a successor to Leo who would continue his policies, and voted for his secretary of state Cardinal Rampolla. Rampolla, however, was obnoxious to the Austrian Emperor Franz Joseph II, who thought him too sympathetic to the nationalist particularisms of his unstable empire, and Rampolla's election was vetoed on the emperor's behalf by Cardinal Puzyna, archbishop of Cracow. One of Pius's first acts as pope was to abolish this veto, though he was unable to publish this until 1909. Rampolla would probably not have been elected even without the imperial veto. The Conclave wanted change, to follow a diplomat with a pastor.

In his hour of need, Sarto turned to the secretary of the Conclave, Rafael Merry del Val, only thirty-seven, and asked him to be his secretary of state. Merry del Val knew the foreign languages, upper classes and diplomacy that the pope did not know. Pius's programme, however, embodied his love of order, tidiness and completeness as a framework for pastoral care, under his motto 'Instaurare omnia in Christo', to restore all things in Christ. The pope began the most thorough reform of the curia in three centuries, and in his constitution *Sapiento Consilio* of 1906 his passion for administrative detail – his 'constructive and simplifying genius' – and his choice of servants to carry it through (Merry del Val, Cardinal Gaetano de Lai and the Spanish Vives y Tuto, known for his industry as Vives fa tutto) restructured the thirty-seven Vatican agencies and dicasteries as eleven congregations, three tribunals and five offices. Churches in largely Protestant countries or under Protestant rule were taken from the administration of the Sacred Congregation of *Propaganda Fide*, where they had been for centuries: Holland, England, Scotland, Ireland, the United States and Canada. These were no longer missionary territories, as their churches were come of age.

With this passion for order, the pope in the Motu Proprio *Arduum Sane Munus* began the codification of canon law largely complete at his death, and issued in 1917 by his successor. Here a genius was to hand in Pietro Gasparri, afterwards secretary of state to Benedict XV and Pius XI. This codification had a vast influence on the church in the twentieth century, especially canon 329, which reserved the appointment of bishops to the Holy See. The changes, moreover, were also pastoral. From 1906, there was a painstaking reform of the education and discipline of the seminaries. Pius reformed the Breviary by reducing the number of psalms for recitation by a quarter, and insisting on the priority of Sundays over saints' days in the calendar. The encyclical *Acerbo Nimis* of 1905 urged the faithful teaching of Christian doctrine through the catechism. The pope issued a new catechism for the province of Rome, later extended elsewhere. In worship, he tried to insist on the use of Gregorian plainchant and polyphony, over the loved modern sub-Mozartian operatic settings for masses, while his support for the Solesmes version of plainchant did away with much local usage. These reforms urged lay participation in the liturgy. Pius rebutted the Jansenist discouragement of frequent reception of the sacrament through a sense of unworthiness, and exhorted the faithful to receive communion often, and even daily: this was a means to holiness and not its reward. The decree *Quam Singulari Christus Amore* of 1910 lowered the age for first communion for children who could recognise the sacrament. Pius created parishes and churches for areas of Rome of increasing population: more than most popes, he was a bishop to the city, less a prince than a pastor, as in his class in catechesis in Christian doctrine on Sunday afternoons in the courtyard of St Damasus.

Pius dined informally with guests, forbade applause when he entered St Peter's, and refused to allow the faithful to kiss his foot. He wore his tiara at a rakish angle. He would not enrich his relatives. There was a grand simplicity in his conception of the pope as the parish priest of Christendom. The Italians loved him as one of them. Born a subject of the Austrian empire, where Italian nationalism was anti-imperial rather than antipapal, he had little of the feeling in the old Papal States that to be a good Catholic was to be a bad Italian. Pius still had to protest at the loss of the States of the church, but told a Catholic layman 'that if Victor Emmanuel were to offer to abandon Rome to him he would at once reply, "Stay where you are"'. 'Members of the Curia were allowed to collaborate publicly with State officials; deputies and senators of the kingdom were received in private audience; more incredible still, the tricolour was seen within the precincts of the Vatican, and delegates from the Italian religious organizations entered to the strains of the Royal March',[4] while the Roman black aristocracy, who had shunned the Italian monarchy, looked on aghast.

4 Binchy, *Church and state in Fascist Italy*, p. 55.

This lessened the antagonism between state and church. So did the weakening of the *non expedit* rule forbidding Catholics to vote in Italian elections. Pius drew on his experience in Venice, where Catholics had acted with liberals to keep out radicals and socialists. He was no democrat. He distrusted the radical Catholic idea for a reforming Christian Democrat Party independent of the clergy and open to non-Catholics, as identifying Catholicism with one political party, outside clerical direction, so that the church would be responsible for its mistakes and get no credit for its successes. Pius instead asserted his authority over the laity by dissolving the lay-run Opera dei Congressi, and regrouping these organisations beneath the banner of Catholic Action. Catholics could then be directed by their clergy to vote for Catholic candidates in any party. Catholic votes now benefited moderate Italian liberals, traditionally opposed to the church, but now more frightened of the socialists, like the pope himself.

The politics of Pius was complicated by the Catholic 'Modernist' movement, as in Italy Modernism was more political than doctrinal, a plea to the church to embrace social and political reform. Yet here, as with Pius IX, it is claimed that Pius X enforced an 'integral' intransigent Catholicism hostile to modernity, in his handling of the French church, and his condemnation of Modernism.

Would Pius, by following Leo's policies, have spared French Catholicism further persecution? The dilemma facing French anticlericals like the prime minister Emile Combes was that abolishing the Napoleonic concordat of 1802 and disestablishing the church would destroy the state's control of her and throw her into the arms of Rome. Combes's fall left the introduction of the law to Aristide Briand, a moderate, surrounded by politicians more anticlerical than himself. His government was united in little except its opposition to the church; by exploiting that opposition it might survive.

The Law of Separation of 1905 abolished long-term state payment of the clergy and transferred all their possessions – cathedrals, churches, seminaries and presbyteries – to the state, to be leased back free to lay-dominated 'cultic associations'. This unilaterally repudiated an international treaty, the concordat, without the agreement of the other partner, Rome. The Law was also founded on a contradiction, claiming to guarantee freedom of worship, while keeping religion under state regulation, by insisting that the church transform herself through the lay 'associations cultuelles', bypassing pope and bishops and clergy. The application of the Law was to lie with the civil Conseil d'Etat. Thus the church was to have the worst of worlds, losing state support while remaining under state control. Although the Law was compatible with the unity of the church, allowing one association to communicate with another, it violated the Catholic conception of a hierarchical authority descending from the pope down. The Law also repudiated Catholic teaching that, ideally, church and state should be allied. Pius condemned the Law of Separation in *Vehementer Nos* and *Gravissimo* in 1906.

Remarkably, the French church, in obedience to Pius, refused to comply with the Law. The bishops surrendered their palaces, the dioceses their offices and seminaries, the parishes their presbyteries and churches, the curés (now pensioned) their salaries. In practice, the Law was applied with leniency: where religious practice was high, the church continued to use the churches for services and the faithful paid the clergy. But where religious practice was low or the commune was hostile to funding repairs, churches became ruinous or were abandoned. On one reading, therefore, the French church suffered for bad papal diplomacy and papal intransigence. It would never have happened under Leo.

As the state had renounced its authority over the appointment of bishops, Rome acquired sole power to name the French Catholic hierarchy, regardless of politicians, for the first time in history: anticlericalism had delivered French Catholicism into papal hands. The Gallican tradition of autonomy from Rome received its final quietus, the state having abandoned it. More favourably, the pope had reasserted the church's freedom as a supernatural society, throwing off the golden chains which the state had laid upon her. On this view, the pope was asserting the spiritual independence of the church, against any sacrifice which the state might require of her. If this was 'integralism', it was also the crown rights of the Redeemer.

The situation in France was not of Pius's making, and the best writing on this subject balances both sides. Not so with Modernism, also in origin French. The most famous of the Catholic Modernists was the priest, professor and biblical scholar Alfred Loisy. Loisy couched his most celebrated book, *The Gospel and the Church*, of 1902, as a reply to the Protestant Harnack. What we have in the Scriptures, said Loisy, is a proclamation of the church's faith in Christ, and Protestants have always been wrong, in separating Christ and the Scriptures from the church. Christ preached the kingdom, and the kingdom came as the church, so that an orthodox Catholic could read Loisy's book as saying with tremendous scholarship what every Catholic believes.

Yet Loisy did not believe that Jesus was divine as well as human or that he had meant to found the church. Loisy's faith was in the contemporary experience of the Catholic Church, which must bring her scholarship up to date, and reinterpret Christianity according to modern ideas, with that development, change and growth which in the past had kept her alive. Also influential in Modernism was the German philosophical tendency to replace God's transcendence with a deity only immanent in this world. A notable exception, the finest Catholic scholar of his generation, Friedrich von Hügel, combined Loisy's biblical radicalism with a profound sense of transcendence, indeed a deep prayer life. Pius and his theologians understood by Modernism Loisy's heretical reinterpretation of Christianity with philosophical immanentism, but they misunderstood both orthodox scholars like Blondel and Laberthonnière, who sought the intellectual renewal of Catholicism through modern biblical study and philosophy and thought, and the socially reforming French Catholic movement Le Sillon, which was unimpeachably orthodox.

On 3 July 1907, sixty-five Modernist propositions were condemned in the papal decree *Lamentabili*, which was followed on 8 September by the encyclical *Pascendi* damning Modernism more generally. Modernism is called a synthesis of all the heresies, implying a consistency of Modernist belief not found in any one thinker or system. Some of the statements are loosely framed, much depending on their interpretation. Loisy was excommunicated in 1908. In 1910, an anti-Modernist oath was introduced, for candidates for higher orders, newly appointed confessors, preachers, parish priests, canons, the beneficed clergy, bishops' staff, Lenten preachers, the officials of the Roman congregations, tribunals, superiors and professors. Meanwhile the 'Sodalitium Pianum', or Sodality of St Pius V, was set up by Monsignor Umberto Benigni with the aim of rooting out Modernists. Merry del Val himself thought by 1911 that it had gone too far. The anti-Modernist movement ceased with the death of Pius in 1914; on his first morning at his desk, the new pope, Benedict XV, is said to have found a letter denouncing him as a Modernist. Benedict promptly censured the Sodalitium Pianum in 1914, and again in 1921. Benigni ended as Mussolini's spy in the Vatican mail room. The anti-Modernist oath, however, remained until the 1960s. The papal condemnation of Modernism isolated the heretics from the great orthodox Catholic scholars, who submitted to papal censure, if resentfully. The application of the anti-Modernist measures varied. *Pascendi* required dioceses to set up Vigilance Committees, but not all did so. Von Hügel was protected in Westminster by Archbishop Bourne.

The enthusiasts for Modernism have now been undermined by the exposure of their dogmatic assumptions by postmodernity. Pius may not have got the balance right, in hunting down Modernists; but from an orthodox viewpoint, he was not as wrong as they claimed. He was a revolutionary about means, a conservative as to ends; and his remoulding of the papacy determined its character for half a century.

Of the seven popes of this period, four – Pius VII, Pius IX, Leo XIII and St Pius X – have claims to greatness. Their choices alienated many Catholics, but they also ushered a growing and thriving church into a new age.

3

Theology and the revolt against the Enlightenment

DOUGLAS HEDLEY

British security, power and imperial expansion between Waterloo and 1914 meant that many English writers saw the period as a golden age. However, even Englishmen were deeply worried throughout this period about radical upheavals. Europe was convulsed and lacerated by revolutions and wars throughout the nineteenth century: the unsatisfactory rule of the reactionary Metternich; the revolutions of 1848, followed by the unification of Germany and Italy; the Prussian-Austrian and Franco-Prussian wars, up to the diplomatic tensions which eventually incited the First World War. The industrial revolution, vast improvements in travel and communication, and the great prosperity of the latter part of the nineteenth century all coincided with a shift in thought towards understanding those natural forces that were being utilised so dramatically. Philosophy and theology moved from an Idealistic-Romantic to a more materialistic and pragmatic ethos: the impact of the pessimistic doctrines and sombre spirit of Charles Darwin upon this development is undeniable. The apocalyptic mood of the early twentieth-century mind has many precedents in the previous century.

Art and theology were more explicitly related in the nineteenth century than ever before in the history of Christianity. Schleiermacher was at the centre of the Romantic movement in Berlin; Tractarianism was forged in the atmosphere imbued with the nostalgia for medieval Christendom in the novels of Walter Scott; and Ruskin and Morris pursued the explicitly religious aesthetic of Novalis, Chateaubriand and Scott. Artistically the beginning of the period is profoundly visionary Romantic – influenced by the noumenal seas, mountains and lakes envisaged in the Romanticism of the *Ancient Mariner*, through the paintings of Caspar David Friedrich, to the *fin de siècle* Impressionists between the cafés of Montmartre and the great boulevards of Proustian Paris. Coleridge's vertiginously speculative *Biographia literaria*, full of German Idealism and speculative neo-Platonism, begins a period which ends with the pragmatic sceptical mood of Loisy's *L'évangile et l'église* and the realism of Zola

30

and Ibsen. The pragmatism of the *fin de siècle* was also linked to the expansion of the industrial revolution within Europe and the evident prosperity of both France and Germany.

Romantic Platonic monism

This visionary element which marks the early period of Romanticism is linked to a revival of speculative Platonism in the early nineteenth century, marked by grand interpretations of nature. Tübingen – the university that produced Hegel, Schelling and Hölderlin – had a long humanistic Platonic tradition cross-fertilised by indigenous south-west German mystical-pietist elements. One of the earliest known works by Schelling was a commentary on Plato's *Timaeus*. The revival of Platonism was not confined to southern Germany. The arch-Romantics Friedrich Schlegel and Schleiermacher conceived together the first German translations of Plato, a huge task that Schleiermacher completed. In England S. T. Coleridge is described in the 1780s as unfolding 'the mysteries of Jamblichus, or Plotinus' as a boy at Christ's Hospital.[1] This 'Platonism' was a syncretistic strand (Spinoza was an important component), often deeply theological in its interests and obsessions, monistic and systematic in its ambitions.

The nerve and tendency of drive of this Platonising monism was towards divine *immanence*. Eighteenth-century theology is often characterised by a strict division between natural and supernatural; nineteenth-century theology blurred the edges between the two. The radically transcendent Deity and a strongly forensic and mechanistic view of Christianity centred around the inerrant oracle of Scripture were replaced with the idea of an immanent divine Spirit shaping the minds of the prophets and the apostles and thus speaking to the souls of those reading the sacred texts.

The impulse to immanence affected both Protestantism and Catholicism. The hostile reaction of the Vatican to Romantic Platonic monism can be seen clearly in the effects of the 1879 encyclical of Leo XIII, *Aeterni Patris*, which established Thomas Aquinas as the normative Catholic philosopher. Equally the critique of 'ontologism' in 1891 tended to repress the Platonic strain. However, such grand speculative Platonising monistic structures gave way to more sceptical and pragmatic approaches to the relationship between philosophy and theology. A more pragmatic approach at the end of the nineteenth century is typified by the Ritschl school and the Catholic Modernists.

---

1 Holmes, *Coleridge*, p. 32 (quoting Lamb).

The Enlightenment legacy: Socinianism and Spiritualism

The Romantics caricatured their religious predecessors as prosaic Philistines, men more content with their sinecures and cosy demonstrations of divine benevolence than with the life of the spirit or true religious experience. In fact bishops Butler and Berkeley, and the non-juror William Law, were Christian apologists of genius who could have adorned any age. Genuinely religious philosophers like Shaftesbury, Burke and Richard Price were just as typical of the Age of Reason as Bentham and Paine. The leading lights of the English Enlightenment, Newton and Locke, were devout Christians, and figures such as Edmund Law, William Paley and Richard Watson were quite justified as seeing themselves in a Christian Lockean–Newtonian tradition. Recent historians such as J. C. D. Clark, J. G. A. Pocock and B. W. Young have tried to correct the false impression that religion was a marginal interest amid a generally monolithic refusal of Christianity in the Enlightenment.[2]

The religious Romantic revolt against the Enlightenment cannot be understood without reference to theological debates which run through the Enlightenment back to the Reformation and Renaissance. Orthodox Protestantism shared a basic doctrinal content with pre- and post-Tridentine Catholicism. The Romantic revolt was in the traditions of radical Protestantism – Socinianism and Spiritualism – in which a climate of radical questioning of tradition and received authority could develop, since here the writers concerned could sincerely appeal to biblical and patristic sources for their Socinianism or Arianism. One of the major challenges of the Enlightenment period was the claim that doctrinal Christianity is not just false but immoral. In Mary Shelley's deeply Romantic novel *Frankenstein* the monster picks up Milton's *Paradise lost* and reads it as the literal depiction of a cruel deity tormenting humanity.[3] Such challenges were often the result of radical movements within Christianity. The two strands which were particularly significant for the nineteenth century are Socinianism and Spiritualism.

Socinianism is rooted in the late Italian Renaissance and in particular the Sienese theologian Faustus Socinus. Arianism is much older as a heresy, being essentially a subordinationist account of the Trinity. Both Socinianism and Arianism agree that strictly only the Father is God, but Socinianism is a more radical form of anti-trinitarianism. Through the Netherlands in particular,

---

2 Clark, *English society*; Pocock, *Barbarism and religion*; Young, *Religion and enlightenment*.
3 Mary Shelley, *Frankenstein or, the modern Prometheus* (1818).

Socinian ideas became very influential in England in the seventeenth century, and often fused with Arianism. Socinianism became the institutional force of Unitarianism, and in this form a very powerful force in the Anglo-Saxon world in the nineteenth century. It bequeathed a determination to submit Christian doctrines to rules of logic and morality. The Trinity was deemed logically incoherent and the atonement declared ethically sub-Christian. Coleridge, who was a Unitarian for some years of his life, felt this challenge very deeply, and in his later intellectual career devoted much attention to the coherence of Christian logical and metaphysical claims (especially by distinguishing 'Reason' from 'Understanding') and the charge that the doctrine of salvation is immoral. Socinianism-Unitarianism was a much more corrosive and dangerous force for orthodox Christianity because it argued from within the Christian tradition. Harnack's programme of *dehellenising* the dogmas of Christianity was a late product of Socinianism.

Spiritualism was a movement within the Reformation that had its roots in German mysticism. In contrast to Socinianism which envisaged the 'evidence' of Christianity as 'outward', i.e. visible proofs of the authenticity of its founder, Spiritualism saw the 'evidence' of Christianity as 'inward'. Its greatest German proponent was Jacob Boehme (1575–1624), and in England it was typically represented by Quakerism. Gotthold Ephraim Lessing (1729–81) was deeply influenced by this tradition, and this explains why he could hold that the (inner) truth of Christianity remained unaffected by the results of biblical criticism. Again, like Socinianism, the challenge of Spiritualism was deeply felt because it had Christian sources. Nor was it confined to Protestantism: the Catholic mystical tradition shaped the thought of Joseph de Maistre in France, and the German Catholic Romantic strand of Franz von Baader and the later Schelling.

Both Socinianism and Spiritualism were products of the Reformation. Socinianism inherited the exclusively biblical concentration, Spiritualism the individualism of the Reformation. Yet both were quite unlike Protestant or Catholic orthodoxy in that together they threatened much of the inherited fabric of belief. Socinianism, combined with Arianism, was intent upon dismantling the dogmas, and Spiritualism tended to corrode the historical foundations, of Christianity. The breezy paganism of Hume and Gibbon so often associated with the Enlightenment is far less significant than is often assumed for the formation of nineteenth-century Christian thought. If one considers the enormous influence of Locke in the eighteenth century – particularly on Law, Paley, Watson, Lessing and Kant – it becomes clear how potent both the

Socinian and Spiritualist legacies were in Enlightenment theology.[4] The real battle was within Christendom, not without.

Lessing, Kant and Spinoza

Goethe and Schiller were at best cool towards Christianity; but Lessing and Kant represent a profound knowledge of, and not uncritical interest in, Christianity. Lessing, the godfather of the German Enlightenment, in his *Uber den Beweis des Geistes und der Kraft* (On the proof of Spirit and power, 1777), criticised the traditional employment of the argument from prophecy and miracle from the testimony of Scripture, whilst his *Das Christentum der Vernunft* (Christianity of reason, 1758) had interpreted the dogmas of Christianity in terms of their rational content. Both in his neo-Spinozism and in his rational interpretation of the dogmas of Christianity, Lessing was both a harbinger of and a decisive formative influence upon nineteenth-century German theology in its Hegelian form.

Kant is also a vital figure. He attacked rationalistic-scholastic arguments for God's existence and the immortality of the soul in the form of his critique of rational psychology and cosmology in the *Critique of pure reason* but rebuilt rational theology upon the basis of his moral theology. The Romantics recognised a profound theological dimension of Kant's thought which has generally been neglected since, and made it the key to his whole enterprise. The fact that Kant became a very important figure at the end of the nineteenth century for theologians like Ritschl and Harnack (and indirectly for the Catholic Modernists) is a testimony to his enduring legacy throughout the nineteenth century.

If Lessing bequeathed an interest in understanding the philosophical and spiritual meaning of the Christian doctrines in a properly critical and historical context and if Kant insisted upon freedom as the key to any proper theology or metaphysics, it was the Janus face of Spinoza that loomed largest over the nineteenth century. Spinoza was widely regarded as an atheist and a sceptic in the seventeenth century, yet his philosophy exerted an immediate appeal to Schleiermacher and also attracted tough-minded followers of Darwin like Nietzsche, Huxley and Haeckel who sought for a metaphysic to correspond to the gloomy doctrine of natural selection. It is intriguing that the two greatest popularisers of Darwin in the nineteenth century, Huxley and Haeckel, were both enthusiasts for Spinoza.

4 Young, *Religion and enlightenment.*

Five responses to the Enlightenment challenge

A traditional and widespread view of the nineteenth century is that Protestantism succumbed to a compromise with secular culture and ideals whereas Catholicism held out robustly but vainly against secular culture with the palladium of unyielding authority. Notwithstanding the evident truth in such a generalisation, there is a subtler picture. It would be more accurate to say that equally within Protestantism and Catholicism we can see both the drive to dialogue and reaction, although in Catholicism political circumstances – the impact of the French Revolution and the often precarious and embattled position of the Vatican in Italy – accentuated the element of reaction. Yet the nineteenth century was a period of revival of Catholic thought – often from converts as brilliant as Friedrich Schlegel or John Henry Newman, and many innovative schools of thought. Even the profoundly conservative Orthodox tradition produced thinkers like Solovyov who engaged with modern culture and thought.

Nevertheless, this period is dominated by the response to the Enlightenment criticism of the dogmas of the Christian religion as unreasonable. The remainder of this chapter will analyse nineteenth-century responses to the Enlightenment according to the following five categories:

1 Ultra-Romantic: Those who rejected the 'Enlightenment' challenge as misguided or resting on false assumptions.
2 Idealistic: Those who accepted the legitimacy of the challenge but denied that the 'Enlightenment' was employing an adequate conception of 'reason', 'religion' or 'Christianity'.
3 Existentialist: Those who attempted to outflank both the Enlightenment and religious Idealism.
4 Rationalistic: Those who accepted the Enlightenment critique and agreed that Christianity as traditionally conceived is an illusion. Usually in this camp some naturalistic or materialistic metaphysics formed the basis of the evaluation. Christianity was either radically modified or rejected.
5 Pragmatic: Those who accepted the validity of the Enlightenment critique but limited its scope to the domain of facts as opposed to values.

Ultra-Romantic refusal of the cultured despisers

Schleiermacher is often thought of as the 'father of modern theology'. One needs to distinguish the early Romantic Schleiermacher of his *Speeches to the cultured despisers* (1799), one of the seminal works of German Romanticism, from the later Schleiermacher of *The Christian faith* (1821–2, 1830–1), his dogmatic great work. His name means literally the 'veil maker'; and indeed Schleiermacher is a complex and contradictory figure. On the one hand he criticises both rationalism and supernaturalism, and develops an intriguing theory of religion that combines elements from Spinoza's speculative pantheism and F. H. Jacobi's philosophy of faith. For Schleiermacher God becomes interchangeable with the universe. Yet rather than postulate any rational cognition of this totality he presents the proper mode of apprehension as a 'feeling' – 'die Anschauung und Gefühl' – and disposes of the theistic idea of God and personal immortality. This is the aspect of Schleiermacher which is developing the radical ideas of the Enlightenment, especially Spinoza.

Schleiermacher represents a reaction to the Enlightenment in so far as he asserted the autonomy of the Christian religion over against both metaphysics and ethics. Religion is precisely the intuition and feeling of the universe rather than cognition (i.e. metaphysics) or action (i.e. ethics). The Enlightenment philosophers (e.g. Locke) assumed that reason can and should criticise revelation. But for Schleiermacher reason is a species of revelation. The entire universe for Schleiermacher is the self-revelation of God. Reason, within this Romantic / neo-Spinozistic context, is dependent upon revelation. Furthermore, religion is not to be understood as the awareness of duty as a divine command, i.e. as the consciousness of the binding and sacral nature of the moral law. On the contrary, religion is defined not as 'autonomy' but as 'dependence'. Whereas religion is essentially *active* for Kant, it is basically *passive* for Schleiermacher.

Schleiermacher was at the centre of the early phase of German Romanticism and one could argue that his early avowal of the autonomy of the Christian religion itself and its irreducibility to some other domain is reinforced by his later definition of theology in *The Christian faith* as the descriptive explication of Christian piety in the self-conscious historical community. Such a view of theology is designed to ward off the Enlightenment or any Hegelian attempt to define Christianity from without. This means that Christianity has no need to try to justify itself according to secular lights. Schleiermacher might well be seen as a forerunner of Karl Barth in his emphasis upon the autonomy of Christianity.

The theocratic and apocalyptic vision of Joseph de Maistre (1753–1821) was very important for the Romantic revolt against the claims of the Enlightenment.[5] His view of the autonomy of Christianity is marked by the experience

---

5 Lebrun, *Joseph de Maistre.*

of the French Revolution as *Terror*. De Maistre is often seen as an anachronism: an Ultramontane Roman Catholic Savoyard critic of the French Revolution.[6] De Maistre's grim vision of sin robbing the human will of real autonomy, demanding, by virtue of its very exigency, strict obedience to the divine representative, leads to an analysis of secularity. He delivers a critique of the terrifyingly destructive reality of secularism and liberalism – despite its claim to liberate it is but a 'déstruction violente de l'espèce humaine'. In the wake of the Revolution Christianity and secular philosophy were at war.[7]

John Henry Newman was explicit in sharing de Maistre's contempt for liberalism: 'liberalism is the mistake of subjecting to human judgement those revealed doctrines which are in their nature beyond and independent of it, and of claiming to determine on intrinsic grounds the truth and value of propositions which rest for their reception simply on the external authority of the Divine Word'.[8]

In some respects the Oxford Movement mirrored the argument of Joseph de Maistre and François-René de Chateaubriand (1768–1848) that occidental culture requires the church as a bulwark against barbarism. John Keble's sermon of 14 July 1833, preached in the wake of sweeping parliamentary reforms of society and ecclesiastical structures, and regarded by John Henry Newman as heralding the advent of the Oxford Movement, was entitled 'National Apostasy'. The primary emphasis of the Oxford Movement was on the objective fact of apostolic succession whereby the church is the continuation of the incarnation, and the vehicle of the Holy Spirit. This could be seen as a refuge in an increasingly secular society. In 1837 Newman produced his *Lectures on the prophetical office of the church* in which he propounded his influential view of 'Anglicanism' (rechristened Anglo-Catholicism in the second edition of the following year) as the *via media* between Roman Catholicism and popular Protestantism.

Yet just as England had avoided the Terror and Revolution, Newman's theology was not merely reactionary. Newman was a fellow of Oriel, quite the most intellectually advanced and innovative college in Oxford. He shared with Coleridge an interest in the spiritual aspect of religion, the heart and the imagination, rather than just rites and ordinances. Sanctification, seen as the necessary expression of justification, was the principle which informed Newman's theology and he shared this with the Broad Church movement of which Coleridge was the *spiritus rector*. Though completely independent in

---

6 Berlin, 'Joseph de Maistre'.
7 J. de Maistre, 'Considérations', in *Œuvres complètes* (Lyons, 1884–6), vol. 1, p. 50.
8 Newman, *Apologia*, p. 387.

origin, there is a parallel between Kant's and Newman's derivation of faith from the sense of obligation to a divine lawgiver and judge in conscience (see the *University sermons*, 1843). Newman's idea of doctrinal development (see his *Essay on the development of Christian doctrine*, 1845), by which Christian doctrine has grown through the organic Spirit-guided unfolding of its original idea down the centuries, has affinities with the thought of the Catholic theologians of the Tübingen school, J. S. von Drey and J. A. Möhler.

Conversely, the idea of the church as the extension of the incarnation came to influence British Hegelians. In the Liberal Catholicism of the *Lux mundi* group of 1889, one can see a movement from the embattled conservatism of Pusey and Liddon: a strain of thought which tried to integrate biblical criticism and evolutionary theory into a self-consciously organic view of the church. Its theology drew much from the Alexandrian-Platonising strand of patristic thought, with much emphasis upon divine immanence and teleology.

Idealistic mediation of philosophy and theology

Georg Wilhelm Friedrich Hegel (1770–1831) was a contemporary of Schleiermacher and is the real father of modern theology. The major developments in nineteenth-century German theology were directly inspired by, or products of, the Hegelian school: the explosive *The life of Jesus* of David Friedrich Strauss, the monumental work in doctrinal history of the founder of the Tübingen school, Ferdinand Christian Baur, and the corrosive criticism of the so-called Left Hegelians such as Bruno Bauer, Ludwig Feuerbach and Karl Marx. Even Kierkegaard and Nietzsche are much more obviously opponents of Hegel than of Schleiermacher. Much of this defining work for nineteenth-century theology came in the wake of Hegel's posthumously published *Lectures on the philosophy of religion* (1832), whereby 'religion' means the finite mind's awareness of itself as absolute mind. This can be seen as an opposition to Schleiermacher, a relation tinged with envy and resentment.

Hegel's thought was much indebted to Schelling, also a product of southwestern Germany (Swabia), and a product of the same cultural and intellectual world as Hegel and Hölderlin – the extraordinary galaxy of genius in the Tübingen *Stift*. As a young man Schelling developed in various drafts a system of absolute Idealism, whereby both the natural realm and the realm of culture and history are the expression of one unfolding absolute spirit. This dynamic monism of Schelling, neither clearly theistic nor pantheistic, became the basis for Hegel's own more rigorous and sophisticated metaphysics in his *Phenomenology of spirit* and *Logic*.

For Hegel philosophy and religion deal with the same object, God. Philosophy considers this object conceptually (*Begriff*) whereas religion grasps religious truths imaginatively (*Vorstellung*). Hegel agreed with the early Schleiermacher that the universe is the self-manifestation of God but there is also an important distinction between man and God in the dialectical process of the divine and finite conscious life which is overcome in religion. God is neither absolutely transcendent nor a purely immanent principle of the universe but a spiritualising progression at work *within* the world, which brings the world to its divine source and goal. Humanity's self-awareness of itself as part of the divine self-consciousness is not a relatively *static* Spinozistic insight into the unified totality of reality but the result of a *process* of mediation of the divine and human. Because God is love and *subject* rather than substance (as in Spinoza) he is himself only in relation to the world and vice versa. Christianity as the absolute religion depicts the finite estrangement from and ultimate reconciliation to God. Hegel's rehabilitation of the doctrines of the Trinity and redemption are part of a bold attempt to employ the doctrines in a philosophical sense.

This contrast between the levels of *Vorstellung* (imagination) and *Begriff* (concept) can be construed in two radically different ways. First, the traditional Christian imagery of doctrinal formulations – 'Father' and 'Son', 'sacrifice', etc. – can be seen as validated by its translation into the conceptual. Hegel can be seen as a great philosophical theologian justifying the Christian religion to its cultured despisers. However, the Hegelian pair *Vorstellung* and *Begriff* can be seen in a very different and inherently reductive manner: the *Begriff* reveals the true meaning of the extravagant and metaphysically otiose language of the *Vorstellung*. Hence the real task of the theologian is radically revisionary. Here we can see the stance of Feuerbach and Strauss.

The rich theological background of Hegel's and Schelling's thought meant that German Catholics could employ these ideas readily. Freiburg, Münster, Würzburg and Vienna were important traditional centres of German Catholic thought, and the Romantic-Idealistic movement led to an enhanced awareness of the positive role of the Catholic Church in medieval Europe and encouraged many leading Protestant intellectuals to convert to Roman Catholicism. Friedrich Schlegel and his wife Dorothea Veit (daughter of the great Enlightenment philosopher Moses Mendelssohn) converted to Catholicism and moved from Protestant Berlin to Catholic Vienna.

The Tübingen School of Johann Sebastian Drey (1777–1853) and Johann Adam Möhler (1796–1838) represents a particularly rich vein of Catholic thought in the nineteenth century. In particular they exploited the Idealistic (and Schleiermacher's) emphasis upon the importance of the social dimension of life and thought to apologetic effect for Catholicism in opposition to Protestantism, and applied this principle to an understanding of church history. Möhler and Drey both saw Catholic dogma in organic terms, and drew upon the Romantic interest in the realm of the symbolic. In many respects they represented the flowering of a tradition that built upon the innovating work of the highly influential figure of Georg Hermes (1775–1831) and the so-called Hermesianism (representing a certain style of Kantianism) of the Viennese Anton Günther (1783–1863), who developed a more explicitly Idealistic and speculative philosophical theology.[9] Two other important figures were the brilliant and eccentric Franz von Baader (1765–1841) – a man who embodies the link between the French mystical tradition in de Maistre and Schelling – and Hegel, who did much to reawaken interest in medieval German mysticism. Von Baader was appointed to a philosophical chair in Munich in 1826. The Bavarian capital also possessed in Johann Josef Görres (1776–1848), appointed to a chair of history in 1827, a vigorous and brilliant polemicist and publicist for Catholicism.

Amidst the birth pangs of the Italian *Risorgimento* the 'ontologism' of Gioberti (1801–52) and Antonio Rosmini-Serbati (1797–1855) belongs to the general nineteenth-century revival of Platonism of the Augustinian-Franciscan kind which stresses the immediacy of the soul's relation to God and hence has affinities with German Idealism and the Platonising strands in the French Restoration thought of de Maistre. The journey of the finite mind to God in philosophy and religion points to the congruity of thought and being in God as absolute subjectivity. Both Gioberti and Rosmini were averse to the strong division between natural and supernatural in traditional textbook Thomism, and stressed the importance of personal judgement. They were doubtful of the apologetic value of crude supernaturalism and critical of an excessive asceticism in ethics and an exaggerated appeal to authority in theology. They were both criticised for excessive immanentism, rationalism and pantheism.

Despite their own internal disagreements, they were both aware of the deep traditions of this strand of Christian thought in the patristic and medieval eras and of the need to restate the Christian faith in credible modern terms. Rosmini

---

9 Oßwald, *Anton Günther*.

was a close friend of the great Italian novelist Manzoni. However, powerful elements in Roman Catholic orthodoxy, not least the Jesuits, were deeply suspicious of such efforts of mediation, and this hostility to modern thought was reinforced by the activity of both men in revolutionary political activity prior to the *Risorgimento* and unification of Italy. In many respects both men were anticipating Catholic Modernism.

Coleridge, like Gioberti and Rosmini, was a liberal conservative who wanted to combine faith with knowledge, tradition and freedom. Mark Pattison in his superbly learned essay 'Tendencies of religious thought in England, 1688–1750' in *Essays and reviews* wrote that 'theology had almost died out when it received a new impulse and a new direction from Coleridge'.[10] Coleridge introduced German critical ideas into England in a moderate and cautious fashion. At the same time he was able to revive the native tradition of the Cambridge Platonists and William Law. He thus inaugurated a shift in English theology that marked much of the nineteenth century. Its temper became more Greek than Latin; the incarnation rather than the atonement was its living centre. Wordsworth's poetry, with its emphasis upon the divine presence and religious experience, helped to reinforce Coleridge's theology of incarnation and sanctification.

J. S. Mill said that 'an enlightened Radical or Liberal' should 'rejoice over such a Conservative as Coleridge'.[11] Coleridge, certainly, had a profound command of German and a wide and detailed knowledge of his German contemporaries. With respect to his theology, Mill observed that the 'new Oxford theologians' – that is to say, the 'rising generation of Tories and High Churchmen' – were likely to 'find him vastly too liberal'.[12] Indeed Newman famously thought that Coleridge indulged a 'liberty of speculation, which no Christian can tolerate, and advocated conclusions which were often heathen rather than Christian'.[13] Coleridge argued in *Aids to reflection* that *Reason* is the organ of wisdom and the source of truth and that the Christian dogmas should be considered in the light of their tendency to improve ethics or mind, an argument that reveals the degree to which Coleridge internalised the ideals of the Enlightenment.

Coleridge developed a political theory which was equally hostile to the authoritarianism of Hobbes and the abstract rationalism of Rousseau. He envisaged the constitution as a dynamic equilibrium of two antagonistic forces,

---

10 *Essays and reviews* (London: John W-Parker and Son, 1860), p. 263.
11 Mill, 'Coleridge', p. 207.
12 *Ibid.*, pp. 211, 225.
13 Newman, *Apologia*, p. 94.

respectively those of permanence and progression: the landowning interest on the one hand, and the mercantile, manufacturing, distributive and professional classes on the other. The 'clerisy' – the broader body of those priests, teachers and scholars – Coleridge thought of as the cultivating force of the nation. Mill noted admiringly that this dynamic concept of the constitution was far more radical than the Whiggish allegiance to the predominance of the landed interest. Mill was correct to point out that Coleridge saw the *ratio essendi* of the church as the cultivation of the nation and its particular communities, rather than the 'performance of religious ceremonies'. The 'bitter error' for Coleridge of the Church of England was its clinging to power and privilege rather than cultivating the people.[14] Education, rather than the apostolic succession or the sacraments, is the key to Coleridge's doctrine of the church.

The question of the harmony, or at least continuity, between Christianity and culture is central for this period. Coleridge's idea of the clerisy exerted its influence upon the great educator Thomas Arnold, with his vision of the Christian gentleman, on Matthew Arnold's espousal of 'culture', and on John Ruskin. Ritschl's rather Kantian view of the Kingdom of God as an ethical and cultural ideal led to the formation of a strong emphasis upon the harmony of Christianity and culture. This *Kulturprotestantismus* provoked the bitter opposition of Franz Overbeck (1837–1905), who insisted upon the radical discontinuity between Christianity and human culture. Overbeck saw Christianity in apocalyptic terms as inherently world-negating and in strident opposition to human culture. Overbeck, a colleague and friend of Nietzsche at Basel, exerted a great influence upon Nietzsche's view of Christianity as inherently ascetic.

It was not until the appearance of *Essays and reviews* in 1860 that many of the critical implications of Coleridge's thought were expounded and widely debated. Coleridge refused to base Christian apologetics upon miracles, and insisted that the words of Scripture were not to be understood as directly dictated, and that crude forensic analogies were not to be foisted upon the Divine. Perhaps the central figure of *Essays and reviews* was Benjamin Jowett (1817–93). He was educated at the great humanistic institution of St Paul's School and was a worthy successor to Dean Colet (who refounded the school) in the tradition of Renaissance Christian Platonism as the Regius Professor of Greek at Oxford and a reforming Master of Balliol. He was a translator, like Schleiermacher, of the works of Plato. For Jowett Christianity was a religion of

---

14 Coleridge, *Table talk*, vol. 1, p. 189.

ultimate spiritual values, whose essence consisted in the imitation of Christ's death and resurrection in the life of the believer: death to sin and separation from God, and rebirth to union with the Divine in the Spirit. Jowett fused Christian, Platonic and Hegelian ideas in a manner that exerted enormous influence in England at the end of the nineteenth century.

The speculative rupture of the later Schelling and Kierkegaard: God, discontinuity, and the priority of existence over essence

The revolt against Hegel in the nineteenth century was deeply indebted to the later Schelling's critique of Hegel. Though Hegel is not usually thought of as a 'Romantic', especially not in Germany, he may be considered as the root of certain anti-Idealistic tendencies or movements in the later part of the period.

Schelling has been called the 'Prince of Romantics' and there is a sense in which this apparently protean philosopher focused upon two themes and obsessions throughout his life which are characteristically Romantic: myth and nature. Schelling consistently reflected on inscrutable or given aspects of these phenomena, regarding them as 'unprethinkable'. From his early development of a philosophy of nature (*Naturphilosophie*) up to his late *Philosophy of mythology*, Schelling was trying to develop a system of Idealism which was able to incorporate these elements that other Idealistic systems would relegate or redescribe. Schelling was concerned that authentic philosophy should describe the reality of existence, as distinct from negative philosophy which is concerned merely with the abstract idea of reality. But he insisted that there can be no deduction of the *that* (*quod* or *Das*) of real experience of *existence* from the merely abstract and sterile *what* (*quid* or *Was*) of conceptual *essence*. Negative philosophy can attain knowledge of formal essences (mere logic), but needs completion in a positive philosophy centred around the idea of God as the 'The Lord of Being' (*Herr des Seins*). This aspect of Schelling led Heidegger and Tillich to regard him as the founder of existentialism.

There is much in Schelling which points to Kierkegaard, especially in the polemic against Hegelianism which starts with *On human freedom* (1809), expressed vividly in the contrast between 'logical' and 'historical' philosophies in the Munich lectures of 1832–3, and his late move to Berlin was heralded as a riposte to the 'dragon's teeth' of Hegelian 'pantheism'. The geography and culture of Munich is perhaps a key. The early Schelling was caught up in the widespread enthusiasm for the French Revolution and Napoleon. Just as Friedrich Schlegel's move to Vienna and conversion to Catholicism marked a shift in his intellectual sympathies, so Schelling's long period in Munich and proximity to Jacobi and van Baader marked a move from the earlier intellectual optimism and revolutionary fervour to a more quietistic and mystical mood. Although there were (false) rumours that Schelling had converted to Catholicism, there is some truth in seeing his thought as having links with the mixture of theosophy and Catholic opposition to Napoleon and sympathy for the feudal-medieval order which came to be characteristic of later German Romanticism. While Hegel remained fascinated by questions of constitutional reform until his early death, Schelling's thought was far less open to the political reforms of the age, and was closer to the aristocratic conservatism of Novalis and de Maistre.

The Whiggish optimism in Hegel can be seen as a form of cultural Protestantism. Christianity, in Hegel's account, has survived the crucible of the Enlightenment and presents the spiritual values of a sophisticated occidental and basically liberal culture long before Harnack or William Temple. Both Schelling and Kierkegaard can be seen as critics of this implicit domestication of Christianity. Whatever else, the paradox of the incarnation and the inscrutable reality of the 'Lord of Being' cannot begin to be identified with the achievements of European civilisation. Hence it is no accident that both Schelling and Kierkegaard attracted such strong interest in the *Katastrophenjahre* after the First World War.

Søren Kierkegaard (1813–55) is an odd figure for at least two reasons. First, he had virtually no influence on the nineteenth century. Intellectually, his legacy was reserved for the following century – especially through Heidegger and Barth. He is also a difficult figure to judge because of his use of pseudonyms. His work represents a link between the counter-Enlightenment polemics of Hamann and the attacks on Protestant liberalism among dialectical theologians via his critique of the Hegelianism of his Danish contemporary Hans Lassen Martensen.

Kierkegaard distinguished between three 'stages' of human existence: the aesthetic, the ethical and the religious. He also insisted upon the Christian doctrine of the Fall as implying the impossibility of the realisation of a truly Christian form of ethical existence. The sinner cannot sustain a genuinely ethical form of existence because of sin. In this sense a move from the merely ethical to the religious sphere is necessary, and Kierkegaard employed the image of Abraham, who vividly demonstrates the incompatibility of the ethical and divine commands in his dilemma over the sacrifice of Isaac.

The exact status of the Abraham and Isaac story within *Fear and trembling* in 1843 is difficult to establish because it remains very unclear to what extent Kierkegaard can be identified with a position proposed by the pseudonym.

The story of Abraham's terrible and haunting predicament is meant to show how the Christian life is almost impossible to live. Kierkegaard saw himself as reintroducing Christianity into a worldly and complacent Christendom, a complacency reinforced by Hegel's view of the state as the divine idea on earth. In this sense the very Protestant Kierkegaard can be seen as the antithesis to those French thinkers from Lamennais to Durkheim who have been interested in religion as an indispensable cohesive force. He mounts a visceral attack on any *domestication* of Christianity.

In his *Philosophical fragments* of 1844 Kierkegaard employed the figure of the Platonic Socrates to exemplify the position that humanity is already in possession of truth and only requires reminiscence. Here the real object of his attack was the Hegelian assumption that the finite has access to the infinite. This, Kierkegaard argued, is quite incompatible with the Christian doctrine of human sinfulness, and that the historical Christ was eternal consciousness that had broken into time. This means that truth is not immanent for humanity but can only be received as a gift from without. In order to bridge the chasm between God and man, God must become man and enter in time. This is fulfilled in the paradox of the incarnation of the eternal Godhead in time. Kierkegaard used the delightful image of the king who must disguise himself in order to woo the humble maiden. The upshot of Kierkegaard's theology is a radical rejection of Hegelian rationalism: discontinuity rather than continuity between finite and infinite, and paradox rather than mediation.

Pessimism and positivism: science, religion and Darwin's legacy

Ludwig Andreas Feuerbach (1804–72) in *Das Wesen des Christentums* (The essence of Christianity, 1841) claimed that anthropology is the secret clue to theology. Rather than seeing man's knowledge of God as itself a part of the dialectical self-knowledge of the divine subject, Feuerbach reduced human knowledge of God into human self-knowledge. What is falsely assumed to be knowledge of a divine subject is, in fact, the projection of facts about the human species considered as a whole: divine and infinite. Bruno Bauer (1809–82) saw this in his *Posaune des jüngsten Gerichts wider Hegel, den Atheisten und Antichristen* (Proclaiming the last judgement against Hegel, atheists and the opponents of Christians, 1841) as the veiled intention of Hegel himself. But Feuerbach saw Hegel's *Logik* as a genuine theology that fell into the same trap as all other forms – the false objectification of an essentially immanent consciousness. Furthermore, Hegel (for Feuerbach) was hamstrung by his Platonising insistence upon the *identity* of Being and Intellect. Feuerbach, by contrast, insisted upon the difference between Intellect and *real*, i.e. material, *Being*. The latter cannot be the object of speculative thought – Being is the opposite of Intellect, and its particularity and individuality cannot be grasped by the Intellect. Hegel represented, for Feuerbach, the neo-Platonic tradition in its supplanting of the real world with the intelligible. Feuerbach saw the new philosophy as a sensualism which maintains the reality of the physical.

The last thirty years of Nietzsche's life was a period of relative sterility in German philosophy after the extraordinary flowering of the early nineteenth century. The mood of German late nineteenth-century philosophy was full of Bismarckian toughness: either philosophy of science (neo-Kantianism or positivism) or vitalism, i.e. some form of a philosophy of life. Nietzsche proposed a version of scientific materialism.

The legacy of Darwin for the question of creation and the origin of man was momentous. The theory of natural selection as the *modus operandi* of biological evolution was a very powerful intellectual force. Not only did this hypothesis appear to challenge the account of human origins in Scripture, but Darwin's deep pessimism reinforced a mood of disenchantment which much weakened the prevailing Romantic immanentist theology. In *The descent of man* (1871) Darwin argued explicitly that the difference between man and the rest of the animal kingdom was one of 'degree' and not of 'kind'.[15] Darwin's influence can be seen, for example, in the thought of Sigmund Freud (1856–1939), which was a mixture of Schopenhauer's metaphysical pessimism, a great admiration for the explanatory scope of science and a vitalistic fascination for a primordial élan or life force which is far more powerful than the veneer of civilisation. This is also a revolt against the Enlightenment, albeit clearly not theological.

In Germany, D. F. Strauss in *Der alte und der neue Glaube* (The old and new Christianity, 1872) presented Darwinism in a very positive light as the fruit of an idealistic conception of progress. However, it was due to the efforts of Ernst Haeckel, following the materialism of Ludwig Büchner's *Kraft und Stoff* (1855), that Darwin was received in an avowedly and radically non-theistic context. In 1889 he published his work *Die Welträtsel* (The riddle of the world) which presented a Spinozistic-monistic naturalism in the form of a pantheistic religion.[16]

---

15 See chapter 11 below.
16 On Haeckel see also chapter 11 below.

George Brandes includes Nietzsche (1844–1900) with the legacy of Kierkegaard.[17] Kierkegaard was opposed to complacent Christendom: Abraham in *Fear and trembling* is in a sense beyond bourgeois 'good and evil'. But Nietzsche relished the breaking of norms and one can see this in his early work *The birth of tragedy*. Nietzsche admired Homeric Greece with its embrace of violence and misery, and his emphasis upon the Dionysian as opposed to Apollonian culture which had attracted German Hellenists since Winckelmann and Schiller. One can see in the opposition between Dionysius and Apollo in Nietszche the world of Schopenhauer as divided between *will* and *representation*. The Dionysian symbolises the irrational will that lies at the basis of all life. Art, according to Nietzsche, had the task of affirming an essentially pointless existence: only art (especially Wagner at this stage) can attain any appropriate articulation of the irrational will beyond appearance. The momentous legacy of Socrates and Plato for the Greeks was their denial of the pessimism of pre-Socratic Hellenic culture and their replacement of this with the optimistic metaphysics of the rational and providential order of Being. Nietzsche's concern with genealogy links him to thinkers like Durkheim and Freud.

Nietzsche was drawing upon the brilliant but eccentric figure of Schopenhauer. In his *Über die vierfache Wurzel des Satzes vom zureichenden Grunde* (The fourfold root of the principle of sufficient causality, 1813) Schopenhauer pursued the Kantian idea of the phenomenal realm generated by the employment of intuitions and categories, which ultimately are reducible to the category of causality. In 1819 with his *Die Welt als Wille und Vorstellung* (The world as will and representation) Schopenhauer replaced the optimistic-teleological idealistic conception of God or the Absolute with a pessimistic view of an absolute blind insatiable Will which produces continual suffering. The central philosophical question is the possibility of escaping this will: philosophy is a doctrine of salvation. Schopenhauer, like Hegel, saw philosophy and religion as having the same metaphysical content. Only Christianity and Buddhism, however, possess a suitably pessimistic anthropology to count as true. The specific Christian doctrines of divine personality, the creation of the world and the immortality of the soul are dismissed.

Nietzsche's attack on truth as the correspondence of intellect and object, degrees of reality and the moral significance of reality was part of his account of the *genealogy* of western thought with its roots in Plato and culminating in

---

17 Brandes, *Friedrich Nietzsche.*

Hegel. This is part of a long debate about Hegel's metaphysics. Nietszche's rejection of morality as a consistent rational structure as well as his rejection of salvation was linked to his admiration for the Dionysian. He employed strongly Darwinistic or vitalistic language, relishing the corrosive impact of such ideas for inherited morality.

Darwin tended to be ignored in France, where the prestige of Jean Baptiste Lamarck worked against the reception of the Englishman. The French tradition exerted an influence through its rich and subtle sociology of religion. Auguste Comte (1798–1857) shared with de Maistre the fear that modern society was marked by a corrosive individualism, rationalism and disregard for authority. His 'religion of humanity' was a bizarre attempt to integrate the importance accorded by de Maistre and Lamennais to religion as a cement of society while dismissing their metaphysical and theological claims, and perpetuating the scientific 'positivism' of his teacher Saint-Simon (1760–1825). Believing that human society progressed from a theological stage of thought in which the major mode of explanation was supernatural on to a metaphysical stage in which abstract concepts replaced supernatural agencies, Comte was convinced that this historical process culminated in the replacement of metaphysics by observational and properly predictive science. Comte developed a complex institutional and ritual replacement for Christianity, which has been wittily described as 'Catholicism minus Christianity'.[18]

One might see the career of Hugues-Félicité Robert de Lamennais (1782–1854) as a bridge between the radical Ultramontanism of de Maistre and the religion of humanity of Comte. Lamennais started his career by being vigorously anti-Enlightenment rationalism, anti-Protestant and anti-Gallican. He produced a theocratic vision of a new Christian order headed by a powerful pope in opposition to a national church enervated by succumbing to the interests of a worldly and decadent state. The battle cry of the early Lamennais was the choice between order or anarchy. As a thinker whose main theoretical interest in the church was social and political, and whose main fear was the corrosive impact of unbelief, Lamennais, in fact, became increasingly disenchanted with the actual ecclesiastical hierarchy. He moved to a more democratic conception of the church and openly encouraged greater liberty and social justice. Eventually his thought drifted into an increasingly deistic mode. What was left was a rather truncated and artificial surrogate Christianity close to the proposal of Comte.

18 Reardon, *Religion in the age of Romanticism*, p. 234.

Developing the work of Comte, Emile Durkheim developed sociology as an autonomous discipline. Like Comte, Durkheim perceived an intimate relation between morality and religion. He saw both from a social perspective: morality is the collective consciousness of society and religion serves to symbolise the unity of society. In his study of aboriginal religion, *The elementary forms of the religious life* (1912), Durkheim argued that religion is a necessary unifying and stabilising force in human society. This would become the basis of functionalistic theories of society such as that of Bronislaw Malinowski.

The pragmatic solution and the revolt against speculation

Albrecht Ritschl of Göttingen in his major work *Die Christliche Lehre von der Rechfertigung und Versöhnung* (The Christian doctrine of justification and reconciliation, 1870–4) argued that Christian theology has to develop a genuine understanding of Christianity by using those documents which originated from the founding period of the church: the New Testament as the sole source of the revelation of God in Christ. Here Ritschl followed the definition of God as love in the Gospel of John. This was seen by Ritschl as the definitive theme of the Christian doctrine of God. Ritschl linked this rejection of natural theology and patristic doctrinal developments with an assimilation of Kantian ethics. Christianity is the perfect spiritual and ethical religion on the basis of the life of its founder which serves as the basis for the Kingdom of God. Like Kant, Ritschl saw the idea of God as a practical rather than as a theoretical object of thought, and in his *Theologie und Metaphysik* (1881) was reliant upon Lotze, his philosophical colleague at Göttingen. The latter distinguished between judgements of 'Being' (*Seinsurteilen*) and judgements of 'Value' (*Werturteilen*). The furious rejection of metaphysics in modern Protestantism has its foundation in Ritschl, even if it found its culmination in Karl Barth.

Adolf von Harnack's *opus maximum*, the magnificent *Lehrbuch der Dogmengeschichte* (History of dogma, 1886–9), was the inversion of the magisterial work of Baur. Whereas Baur saw (in Hegelian terms) a rational and progressive unfolding in the doctrines of Christianity of ideas implicit in the earliest documents, Harnack (1851–1930) perceived a decline from the original insight of primitive Christianity and the effect of the Greek spirit on the soil of the gospel. Harnack saw the link between Christianity and Platonism as essentially a compound of alien elements. The original content of primitive Christianity was described in his famous lecture *Das Wesen des Christentums* (The essence of Christianity, 1900).

The Catholic Modernists were a group largely in France, but there were also distinguished representatives in England and Italy. Dissatisfied with neo-scholasticism and intensely aware of Kant, they were particularly associated with Alfred Loisy (1857–1940) and his work *L'évangile et l'église* (1902) which located itself between neo-Thomism and the Liberal Protestant notion of 'The essence of Christianity': Christianity had to see itself as a part of a dynamic process. The opposition to the Ritschl–Harnack school was in a sense more rhetorical than real, since the neo-Kantian immunisation of Christianity from the intrusions of scientific and historical critique was as radical as anything in the Ritschlian school. With their polemic opposition to 'theoretical' knowledge and 'speculation', Catholic Modernists like Edouard le Roy (1870–1954) shared much in common with liberal Protestants. Lucien Laberthonnière's *Le réalisme chrétien et l'idéalisme grec* (1904), as the title suggests, manifested an anti-Hellenism as pronounced as in Harnack.

But for Catholic Modernism, as with the German Ritschlian school, the compromise with science was inherently untenable. An interesting exception to this was the collection of Oxford essays entitled *Lux mundi* edited by Charles Gore and published in 1889. Here it was argued that evolutionary theory forced the theologian to choose between the omnipresence or the non-existence of the divine: 'In nature everything must be His work or nothing.'[19]

What united the great theological minds of the nineteenth century was the conviction that the inherited orthodoxies required interpretation in an increasingly democratic and industrial context in which natural science was widely seen as the sole path to legitimate knowledge. An unmediated return was impossible. The Enlightenment was correct to dwell upon the ethical dimension of faith – even if it tended to neglect the aesthetic dimensions.

Conclusion

The Christian church could not have predicted the effects of the assaults of historical criticism and natural science upon the fabric of belief that would mark the century after Waterloo. But in the midst of the protracted war with the vast power of France and cruel energy of Napoleon there was a great articulation of artistic, philosophical and religious genius, perhaps unprecedented since the Renaissance, which has enriched and shaken the western mind and life. Germany was the centre of this visionary renewal. Much of this

19 Gore (ed.), *Lux mundi*, p. 99.

spiritual energy was explicitly Christian in inspiration, even if, as in a Caspar David Friedrich landscape, the theological signs were sometimes oblique and muted, based on the principle, unintelligible to the materialist or the hedonist, that through death and suffering comes life renewed. The political dimension of the message for German nationalists of life ensuing out of the death of the Holy Roman Empire is evident. But this Christian theme was echoed in different ways by the French Ultramontanes and by Coleridge and the more religious English Romantic strand.

Many of the visions and proposals were startling for institutional Christianity, but one should not overlook its immense cultural prestige and power at the end of the nineteenth century in England and Germany. In Germany Adolf von Harnack was privy to the inner circle of the emperor, whereas in England the future archbishop of Canterbury William Temple was an honorary chaplain to the king in 1915. This is an indication of the still very close links between theologians and secular power at the end of our period. For a detached observer, the lives of Harnack and Temple might appear to represent the zenith of cultural Protestantism rather than a point of its febrile exhaustion and sterility. Their thought came to be regarded as hopelessly optimistic and anachronistic after the First World War, in the light of the Barthian critique of natural theology and the cultural criticism of the inter-war period. Yet certainly we should not see the nineteenth century as a period of decline and fall of religion through the rise of science and biblical criticism: the effects of both were long delayed. But there is a sense in which Barth's censure of liberal Protestant complacency was close in spirit to the polemics of de Maistre or Lamennais or Newman. Even outside the Protestant German context we can see the recognition of the need for a fresh response to apologetics. Figures such as de Maistre, Lamennais or Newman, three quintessential individualists, were radical in their defence of authority and critique of secular individualism or 'liberalism'; but in fact they soaked up much of the spirit of the age, and felt its concerns keenly. Hence they are more prophetic than anachronistic and Newman and de Maistre in particular were hugely influential figures in the twentieth century.

The great contribution of nineteenth-century theology was its emphasis upon the spiritual dimension of Christianity – the question of self and salvation – and the mediation of these spiritual questions in dialogue with modern science and other religions. This can be seen in such figures at the end of the period as Ernst Troeltsch, William James or Maurice Blondel. Theological orthodoxy was already on the retreat back to Aquinas and medieval scholasticism within Catholicism, or to Protestant orthodoxy within confessional Lutheranism or the Reformed tradition. While the terrible guns of the Great War were about to exact slaughter and mutilation on an unprece-dented scale, and even more terrible tyrants than Napoleon were looming, the creative energy and inquiring spirit of the nineteenth century were about to be replaced by a more intransigent mood of opposition between the Christian religion and its cultured despisers.

4

The growth of voluntary religion

DAVID BEBBINGTON

Charles Haddon Spurgeon epitomised the success of nineteenth-century voluntary religion. From the early 1860s to the beginning of the 1890s the celebrated Baptist preached regularly at his Metropolitan Tabernacle to congregations of around 6,000 people. His vivid, witty and uninhibited approach in the pulpit made him one of the sights of London. By 1865 his sermons had a weekly sale of some 25,000 copies and were syndicated to newspapers throughout the English-speaking world. Although he enjoyed none of the privileges of the established Church of England – and in part because of that circumstance – Spurgeon achieved enormous popularity. The Nonconformists of England whom he championed were at the height of their influence. The descendants of the Puritans, who had left the established church in the seventeenth century and whose ranks had been augmented in the eighteenth by the Methodists, had grown to a position of rough numerical equality with the Church of England. In 1851 whereas some 19.7 per cent of the population attended the Church of England, Nonconformity enjoyed the support of as high a proportion as 18.6 per cent. Dissenters – a term equivalent to 'Nonconformists' – had mushroomed over the previous seventy or eighty years. Between 1773 and 1851 the number of Nonconformist congregations had multiplied tenfold, far exceeding the increase in population.[1] Expansion relative to population, at least as measured by membership, continued after 1851 among the Free Churches for another quarter-century.[2] There were parallel surges of church growth outside the state-supported churches in other parts of the British Isles, in the lands settled from Britain during the century and above all in the United States. Even on the continent of Europe, where state churches were far more persistent in asserting their monopoly of religion, there were the beginnings of the spread of Christian groups similar to those so prominent in England.

---

1 Watts, *Dissenters*, p. 24.
2 Gilbert, *Religion and society*, p. 39.

Voluntary religion became a major feature of the nineteenth-century global landscape.

The parameters of the movement can usefully be appreciated in the first place by a close examination of the scene in England and Wales, much of which was reflected elsewhere. The denominational diversity of English and Welsh Nonconformity was immense. The connexion of Methodist societies formed by John Wesley, organised under a Conference of its leading preachers, was by far the largest Nonconformist body, serving 5.5 per cent of the population in 1851.[3] Like Wesley, its leaders were reluctant to align with Nonconformity against the Church of England, but since 1795 Wesleyan Methodism had been autonomous. The Wesleyans met in weekly classes to discuss the progress of members in the spiritual life; congregations, called 'societies', were served by travelling preachers who changed every two or three years at the direction of Conference; and the affairs of the connexion were watched over by a small group of permanent officials, chief among whom until the early 1850s was the redoubtable Jabez Bunting. The stringency of control from above was probably a necessary check on the extensive authority given to laymen as class leaders, society stewards and local preachers. But the tight discipline was unable to prevent a series of secessions from Wesleyanism: the Methodist New Connexion, asserting greater rights for laypeople in denominational decision-making (with 0.4 per cent of the population in 1851); the Primitive Methodists, practising a more unrestrained revivalism (1.9 per cent); the Bible Christians, largely restricted to the south-west of England (0.3 per cent); and the United Methodist Free Churches, claiming by their very title to be independent of central control (0.7 per cent, though they were still in the process of separating from the Wesleyans in 1851). What the Methodists shared in common was the teaching of John Wesley and the hymnody of his brother Charles. From John they drew their Arminian belief that God gave the freedom to all human beings to accept the gospel, with the corollary that no believer was safe from drifting into sin and so forfeiting salvation. From Charles they received an incomparable legacy of versified spirituality, which, when sung wholeheartedly, constituted the greatest evangelistic asset of Methodism.

The Old Dissenting tradition, deriving from the seventeenth century, included the Unitarians, the Congregationalists, the Baptists and the Quakers. The Unitarians, the heirs of the 'rational Dissenters' of the previous century who were usually Presbyterian by background, insisted that God is one and

---

3 Proportions from the 1851 census relate to England alone and are taken from Watts, *Dissenters*, p. 28.

only one. They held the allegiance of many of the prosperous merchants, industrialists and professionals in the Dissenting community, but their teaching was usually too refined and ratiocinative to attract the multitudes. Accordingly the Unitarians formed one of the few declining sectors of voluntary religion in the nineteenth century: they drew a mere 0.2 per cent of the population at the religious census of 1851. By contrast the Independents, who were increasingly called Congregationalists, expanded greatly to encompass 3.9 per cent in 1851. Beginning the century as moderate Calvinists, upholding the predestination of an elect to salvation, most of them shed this belief during the Victorian years in favour of broader views. They held that each congregation should be self-governing (hence 'Congregationalists') and so free from any external authority (hence 'Independents'). The churches were nevertheless linked by county associations and, from 1831, by a Congregational Union that was entirely voluntary and yet gave a measure of national co-ordination to the denomination. The Baptists were identical in polity to the Independents except that they practised believer's baptism by immersion rather than infant baptism. The Particular Baptists were originally, like the Independents, believers in predestination, but the Calvinism of the majority faded gradually during the century. By 1891 it had thus become possible for them to unite with the New Connexion of General Baptists whose members, like the Methodists, upheld the Arminian belief in the availability of salvation for all. In 1851 the various branches of the Baptists together attracted 2.9 per cent of the population. Unlike the Independents and Baptists, the Quakers, officially known as the Society of Friends, were highly centralised, with local and regional meetings subject to an annual national gathering. Long into the century they professed distinctive teachings, such as belief in guidance by an 'inner light', and maintained archaic practices, such as the use of 'Thou' in conversation. From 1860, however, their declining numbers (they drew only 0.1 per cent of the population in 1851) made them discard some of their more sectarian features such as the rule against marrying outside their ranks. By the later nineteenth century the Quakers were sharing fully in the phase of expansion long enjoyed by the Independents and Baptists.

The two main categories of Methodism and the Old Dissent by no means exhaust the almost infinite variety of Nonconformity. In Wales the preponderant form of Methodism was Calvinistic. Usually worshipping in the Welsh language, the Calvinistic Methodists constituted the second largest denomination in the principality (after the Independents), attracting as many as 15.9 per cent of its people in 1851. In England there was another Calvinist body, the Countess of Huntingdon's Connexion (with 0.1 per cent of the people), which co-operated closely with the Independents but retained its separate organisation. Presbyterians (with 0.3 per cent) who had not trodden the Unitarian road had churches in many cities and were strong in Northumberland, close to the border with Scotland, from where came many of their members. The international Moravian Church had places of worship, some of them in residential communities such as Fulneck near Leeds, that catered for significant numbers, though far less than 0.1 per cent of the population. The only other body to attract a reasonable proportion in 1851, though again far less than 0.1 per cent, was the dynamic group, lay-led and observing the Lord's Supper weekly, that rejected all labels but whose members were known, from one of their early centres, as the Plymouth Brethren. Another new organisation, founded in 1878, was the Salvation Army, which deployed bugles, flags and war cries to mount a strategic assault on the citadels of Satan among the very poor. Many missions, often erected on street corners in working-class districts, were professedly undenominational. There were teeming ranks of Protestant Christianity outside the Church of England.

Beyond these groups, furthermore, was a sectarian fringe. There were bodies – Swedenborgians, Mormons, Christadelphians, Theosophists – whose claims to inclusion within the bounds of the Christian faith would have been challenged by contemporaries on the ground of their heterodoxy. Most of the sects, however, embraced a form of Christian orthodoxy. The Sandemanians, Inghamites and Scotch Baptists were groups inherited from the eighteenth century; the Churches of Christ, the Free Church of England and even a body calling itself the Peculiar People were the fruit of the nineteenth. The Catholic Apostolic Church, as elaborately liturgical as Anglican ritualists, repudiated the label 'Protestant' but was nevertheless part of the sectarian world. Perhaps most intriguing of all, and illustrative of the scope for local initiative in religion, was the Society of Dependants, a group that sprang up in the 1850s on the borders of Sussex and Surrey in the south of England under the preaching of John Sirgood, a former bootmaker. Nicknamed the Cokelers, they grew to around 2,000 people at Sirgood's death in 1885. They formed a holiness body whose theology approximated to that of Wesley, but they had no affiliation to Methodism. They specialised in artless testimonies during their services and composed simple hymns that were transmitted down the generations in manuscript. Believing that union with Christ meant solidarity in economic as well as spiritual life, they ran village stores on the co-operative principle. Union with Christ, however, was also interpreted as discouraging marriage, which goes a long way to explaining why the group soon went into rapid decline.[4] Voluntary religion in England and Wales displayed an enormous variety.

What the great majority of these apparently miscellaneous groupings possessed in common was evangelicalism. The Unitarians wholly rejected evangelical doctrine, sections of the Quakers resisted it and the unorthodox sects dismissed it. Nearly all the others, however, embraced a form of teaching derived from the Evangelical Revival of the eighteenth century. First among its characteristics was a devotion to the Bible. Some Primitive Methodists in a remote village, for example, stuck pins in the family Bible to mark the promises of God until there were two or three thousand pins in the volume.[5] Equally important was the attachment of evangelicals to the cross of Christ as the fulcrum of their theology and the core of their spirituality. It was typical that the 'infinite value of the atonement' was the consolation of a Congregational minister dying in 1852.[6] A third characteristic of evangelical religion was its insistence on the need for conversion. Thus in 1859 a Bible Christian reached 'a happy day when the peace of God first became his blest possession'.[7] Although there was no unanimity on whether a datable experience was imperative, there was agreement that a change of life was essential. And a fourth feature of the evangelical movement was its activism. 'Brethren', Spurgeon urged the ministerial students he trained, 'do something; do something; do something. While committees waste their time over resolutions, do something.'[8] The energy of evangelicals frequently spilled over into organised philanthropy and social reform, but there was eagerness above all to spread the gospel. An evangelicalism displaying these four characteristics – emphases on Bible, cross, conversion and activism – united the great bulk of Nonconformists, partly superseding the formal confessional boundaries.[9]

How is the growth of the style of voluntary religion represented by evangelical Nonconformity to be explained? In the first place there were favourable social circumstances. It was at one time supposed that the urban industrial society being created during the nineteenth century was unreceptive

4 Jerrome, *John Sirgood's way.*
5 Stephenson, J[ohn], *The man of faith and fire: or the life and work of the Rev. G. Warner* (London: Robert Bryant, 1995), p. 184.
6 *Christian Witness*, 1852, p. 256.
7 W. J. Mitchell, *Brief biographical sketches of Bible Christian ministers and laymen*, 2 vols. (Jersey: Beresford Press, 1906), vol. 1, p. 42.
8 C. H. Spurgeon, *Lectures to my students* (London: Marshall, Morgan and Scott, 1954), p. 217.
9 Bebbington, *Evangelicalism in modern Britain*, ch. 1.

to the churches. Incomers to the cities from the countryside, on this account, became alienated from organised religion. It has subsequently been shown that, although working-class people were less likely to attend worship than those of higher social status, many urban congregations consisted largely of workers and their families. All branches of Methodism, for example, had a majority drawn from the working classes throughout the Victorian period.[10] The rapid growth of industrial settlements, especially in the first half of the century, actually benefited voluntary religion at the expense of the established church. Whereas the Church of England was fettered by legal complications in the erection of new places of worship, Nonconformity had no equivalent problem. Meanwhile in the countryside, although there were parishes where it was impossible to persuade Anglican squires to sell land for Dissenting chapels, there were also places such as market towns and new settlements where dispersed landownership made it possible for Nonconformists to find the sites they needed. In urban industrial areas, furthermore, patronage from above could as often be an asset to Nonconformity as a disadvantage. Thus in the textile region of Lancashire around the middle of the century, cotton masters were as likely to be Nonconformists as Anglicans. Businessmen were often known for encouraging their workers to attend chapel. So evangelical Nonconformity was helped to become rooted in town as well as countryside.

Nor was the appeal of voluntary religion restricted to one sex. Women were rarely allowed to serve as ministers outside the Quakers, the Salvation Army and some of the lesser Methodist bodies, but they were normally given a share in the decision-making of Nonconformist communities. Among Congregationalists and Baptists women usually had an equal vote in church meeting and among Methodists they acted as class leaders, often with pastoral responsibility for both sexes. Many roles were predominantly female: ministering to the sick, running bazaars, Sunday school teaching and, perhaps above all, district visiting. The area round the chapels was commonly divided into districts with each assigned to a visitor to maintain regular contact, to offer spiritual support and to solicit financial contributions. Since the chapel was often the chief focus of female sociability in a community, the fact that women were customarily a majority of members, usually by a ratio of something like two to one, is not surprising. Among the attenders who did not assume the responsibilities of membership, however, the proportion of men was consistently higher. Men actually formed a majority in many morning services, even at

10 Field, 'Social structure'.

the end of the period, because at that point in the day wives and domestic servants were often expected to be preparing the Sunday dinner. The male proportion in Nonconformist congregations was regularly higher than that in the parish churches. The chapels projected a virile image. Manliness was a constant theme in the writings of Spurgeon: 'we are men', he declared, 'not slaves'.[11] So there was much less of a gender imbalance in the chapels than in the religious organisations of many other times and places. Men as well as women were attracted to sit in Nonconformist pews.

The success of the chapels was also the result of educational effort. The chief method of providing Christian training for the young was through Sunday school, which normally had two sessions, morning and afternoon. Sunday schools, which at the start of the century were often designed to serve the whole of a community, became increasingly associated with particular places of worship. By the late Victorian period they were overwhelmingly popular. At the end of the queen's reign a single metropolitan Congregational church boasted more than 2,600 pupils together with 284 teachers.[12] Although there was heavy leakage of teenagers out of the chapels, their earlier teaching sowed seed that could subsequently yield a harvest through outreach efforts. Likewise weekday education tended to reinforce the message of the chapels. The chief textbook for learning to read in elementary schools during the early part of the century was the Bible. Although most of the schools built by the British and Foreign School Society, largely Nonconformist in support, and the Wesleyans, who created their own educational network, were handed over to school boards after the Education Act of 1870, the type of religious instruction in the resulting state-sponsored system differed little in content from that offered in chapel Sunday schools. In an age eager for upward social mobility, the Mutual Improvement Societies sponsored by larger Nonconformist congregations drew in young people for lectures and debates. People of all ages had Christian literature available in abundance. In the century after its foundation in 1807, the British and Foreign Bible Society published no fewer than 186 million Bibles, Testaments and Scripture portions.[13] These were supplemented by cheap tracts and, in the later years of the century, Christian novels.

11 Spurgeon, *Lectures*, p. 21.
12 Richard Mudie-Smith (ed.), *The religious life of London* (London: Hodder and Stoughton, 1904), p. 324.
13 William Canton, *A history of the British and Foreign Bible Society*, 5 vols. (London: John Murray, 1904–10), vol. v, p. 377.

The prodigious mass of literature must have exercised a powerful influence in favour of the churches of the day.

Evangelical Nonconformists also threw themselves into direct exertions for the spread of the gospel. In the early years of the century Independents and Baptists copied Methodists in organising itinerant preachers to penetrate areas without places of worship of their own denomination. Nonconformists supported Bible women and literature colporteurs, they held cottage meetings and theatre services, they sponsored city missions and American evangelists. A popular technique towards the end of the century, much favoured by the Salvation Army, was to hold an open-air meeting in the hope of attracting passers-by to a subsequent evening service. The after-meeting, which followed the evening service, was another method of encouraging conversions. Those who were anxious about their souls were invited to stay behind; there would be appeals to those who had been touched to lift a hand; workers would move among the congregation to offer spiritual guidance. Many conversions, furthermore, took place in revivals, which were specially common among Methodists. When a revival broke out in the early years of the century, a whole community might be seized by religious anxiety. These events were often noisy affairs, commonly marked by clapping, screaming and jumping, and sometimes by physical phenomena such as shaking or falling down. Suddenly, ran one Methodist minister's memory of a Cornish revival in 1862, 'the people were roused as though a bomb had fallen. Moans & groans, lamentations & strong cryings & tears burst out on every side.'[14] Although revivalism later turned into a routine procedure planned by visiting evangelists, it was originally a powerful expression of group emotion. Many who professed conversion might fall away, but others were led to enduring commitment.

Mission was by no means confined to evangelism, for Nonconformists believed they had a calling to serve bodies as well as souls. Chapels possessed poor funds, usually collected at communion services, for distribution to the needy of the congregation. Assistance could become a much more elaborately planned affair. When, in 1862, the American Civil War threw men out of work in the Lancashire cotton districts, the Baptist Union set up a special fund to relieve the distress of their families.[15] The chapels increasingly provided a range of activities to train the masses in ways of health, frugality and civilisation. Mission halls at the end of the century offered provident clubs, penny banks, boys'

---

14 Davies *et al.* (eds.), *Methodist Church*, vol. IV, p. 559.
15 *Baptist Magazine*, November 1862, p. 702.

gymnasia, girls' sewing classes and mothers' meetings. Nonconformists also operated directly charitable agencies. They maintained orphanages, financed hospitals and founded deaconesses' institutions to train women for Christian social service. They supported the great interdenominational voluntary societies that held their annual May meetings in the Exeter Hall. And some of their most successful men turned philanthropy into a business. Samuel Morley, a Congregational textile millionaire who became an MP, conducted as large a correspondence on charitable giving as on his commercial affairs.[16] Philanthropy in its various forms was one of the best advertisements for Nonconformity.

It was these factors – favourable social circumstances, an appeal to both sexes, educational provision, insistent evangelism and sustained charitable work – that ensured the growth of Nonconformity in England and Wales. Very similar reasons explain the rise of equivalent forms of voluntary religion in other parts of the world, but there were particular features of other lands that also call for discussion. In Scotland the extent of the similarity has often been obscured by the prevalence of Presbyterianism, so weak a force south of the border. The established Church of Scotland was formally Calvinist in creed and organised in presbyteries where ministers and elders in secular employment sat as equals. Presbyterians, however, were by no means united during the nineteenth century. The previous century had given rise to the Seceders, Presbyterians who believed that the Church of Scotland was not sustaining its doctrinal or behavioural standards with sufficient rigour, and the Relief Church, a haven for those harassed by the church authorities for wishing to call ministers of their own evangelical frame of mind. The two small Seceder denominations split around the opening of the nineteenth century, the more evangelical being called 'New Lights'. These grew rapidly, united with each other in 1820 to form the United Secession Church and eventually merged with the Relief Church to create the United Presbyterian Church in 1847. The Dissenting Presbyterians attracted a substantial following in the Lowland cities, in 1835 enjoying the support of as many as 27 per cent of the churchgoers of Glasgow and 30 per cent of those in Edinburgh.[17] Technically the Scottish Episcopal Church, the equivalent of the Church of England south of the border, was not established and so was a voluntary communion. So were the Independents, Baptists and Methodists, who enjoyed close links with their coreligionists in England, and indigenous bodies such as the Evangelical

16 Edwin Hodder, *Life of Samuel Morley* (London: Hodder and Stoughton, 1888), p. 237.
17 Brown, *Religion and society*, p. 45.

Union, a revivalist body formed in 1843 that repudiated Calvinism. Scotland might be preponderantly Presbyterian, but its religious Dissent was a powerful sector.

The greatest episode in nineteenth-century Scottish history, the Disruption of 1843, added to the religious forces marshalled outside the established church. Evangelicals in the Church of Scotland had long been troubled by the ability of patrons, members of the social elite, to impose (or 'intrude') ministers of their choosing, often far from evangelical in their teaching, on unwilling congregations. In 1834 the highest authority in the church, the General Assembly, passed an act allowing heads of families to veto the appointment of such a minister. In a series of court cases it was established that this measure infringed the secular law of Scotland, but the evangelicals, now called non-intrusionists, would not acquiesce. They demanded that the House of Lords should reverse the ruling of the Scottish courts and then that parliament as a whole should legislate against ecclesiastical patronage, in both cases unsuccessfully. A classic struggle between church and state, additionally fuelled by resentment against the pretensions of the social elite and against the English parliamentary majority that would not provide redress, culminated in the withdrawal from the Church of Scotland of over a third of its ministers under the leadership of Thomas Chalmers. They set up a shadow national church, the Free Church of Scotland, which soon had congregations and schools in nearly every parish. Although support was unevenly distributed over the country, in some parts, notably the Highlands, the great majority of the people joined the Free Church. By the 1851 census it was attracting as many worshippers as the established church. Initially it was in the curious position of maintaining the principle of establishment in theory while repudiating it in practice, but as the century wore on, and especially as the Church of Scotland began to reclaim lost ground, the Free Church became eager to see an end to religious privilege and on that basis was able to combine with the United Presbyterians in 1900 as the United Free Church of Scotland. The existence of the Free Church, however, had ensured that in the second half of the century most Scottish Christians were not in the state church.

In Ireland the Protestant churches, though dwelling in the shadow of the overwhelming Roman Catholic majority, nevertheless grew markedly during the nineteenth century. Among the Presbyterians, who were strong in the north, there was tension in the early years of the century as the unorthodoxy that claimed traditional English Presbyterians made similar headway in their ranks. In 1829 there was schism: those holding these views withdrew to form a Remonstrant Synod, and eleven years later the Synod of Ulster, now wholly evangelical, united with the Seceders to create the vigorous Presbyterian Church in Ireland. Methodism, which was also a major force in parts of Ulster, expanded in a pulsating rhythm that reflected its commitment to revivals. It was the Presbyterians, however, who were caught up most extensively in the Ulster Revival of 1859, an event marked by vast outdoor gatherings, physical phenomena such as prostrations and large numbers of converts. Down to 1869 the Church of Ireland was united with the Church of England, but in that year disestablishment turned it into a voluntary communion. The growing co-operation of its evangelical wing with Presbyterians, Methodists and others was reinforced when, in 1886, the proposal of Home Rule seemed to raise the spectre of Rome Rule. Protestant resistance forged a defensive solidarity that was to mark Ulster religion throughout the twentieth century.

The denominational patterns of the British settler colonies reproduced those of the British Isles, though mingling the distributions of England and Scotland. The balance of Anglicans, Presbyterians, Methodists, Congregationalists and Baptists varied, but it was rare for any of these traditions to be wholly absent. There was even a province, Quebec, where the Catholic dominance of Ireland was replicated. In Nova Scotia the legacy of the revivalist Henry Alline gave the ascendancy to Baptists, but elsewhere in Canada Anglicans, Methodists and Presbyterians vied for pre-eminence. In the earlier part of the century Ontario had set aside clergy reserves as a rudimentary form of establishment for the Church of England, but in new world conditions the system proved impossible to sustain. In the resulting religious free market, the various denominations flourished, turning Toronto into allegedly the most evangelical city on earth. In the Australian colonies of New South Wales and Victoria there were residual features of Anglican establishment, and early settlers from the other denominations exerted themselves for their extinction. By contrast South Australia, founded by the Baptist George Fife Angas in 1836, was designed from the start as a showpiece for religious voluntaryism. It was the first British colony to make a total separation between church and state. New Zealand, which was initially more of a mission field than a settler colony, was fruitful terrain for Methodism, and the Cape, because it bordered the territories occupied by the London Missionary Society, was an area of particular strength for Congregationalism. Even the Dutch Reformed Church in southern Africa was dominated by ministers who were Scottish Presbyterians.[18] The Christianity of all these lands was remarkably similar to that of the homeland because the personnel were overwhelmingly émigrés or their descendants.

The United States showed equivalent features for the same reason. The religious exceptionalism of America has been much exaggerated, for most of its denominations were drawn from Britain. Despite the federal ban on laws for the establishment of religion, two states, Connecticut and Massachusetts, even retained elements of a fusion between church and state down to 1818 and 1833 respectively. The Congregationalists of New England, the heirs of the original Puritan settlers, suffered division in the early nineteenth century as many congregations adopted liberal beliefs. The result, as in England and Ireland, was a sizeable Unitarian community. Methodism, as in England, displayed the greatest capacity for expansion, becoming the largest denomination in the country by 1840. It differed from its English counterpart in being ruled by bishops and the extent of America dictated several Conferences, but otherwise it had the same structure of preachers (though by 1840 more were 'settled' than were travelling 'circuit riders'), societies and classes. The Baptists were second to the Methodists in size, doing specially well in the South, not least among the enslaved African-American population. Methodists and Baptists alike split, in 1844 and 1845, over the issue of whether slave-owning was tolerable, so prefiguring the national conflict of the Civil War. The main divisions among the Presbyterians were over the extent to which doctrinal standards could be relaxed to accommodate revivalism: the Cumberland Presbyterians were most revivalist, the Old School most resistant and the New School in between. Although the Old and New Schools reunited in 1869, a fresh schism between the Northern and Southern sections of Presbyterianism arose from the Civil War. The Catholic presence was regularly augmented from Ireland. The American scene, however, did differ from that in the British Isles in two significant respects. On the one hand immigrants from continental Europe brought their own Christian traditions, especially of the Lutheran and Mennonite families. On the other America proved fertile soil for new religious bodies, generating in particular the Church of Jesus Christ of Latter-Day Saints (the Mormons) and the Seventh-Day Adventists. The common man in America, encouraged to carve out his own path in religion as in politics, ensured that the religion of the republic was even more diverse than in British territories.

Although state churches continued to dominate continental Europe, voluntary religion made inroads there too. There were inherited pockets of

18 Ross, 'Student kaleidoscope', p. 206.

independent Christian witness: French Protestants had persevered in adversity since the revocation of the Edict of Nantes in 1685, Dutch Dissenters had enjoyed religious toleration for longer than their English counterparts and in Italy the Waldensians could claim a lineage extending back before the Reformation. But much of the religion that flowed in separate channels was novel, the result of the Evangelical Revival. Its expression in western Europe, usually called the *Réveil*, was delayed until the early years of the nineteenth century. The *Réveil*, though deeply indebted to the pietist legacy, was often fostered by Moravians or contacts with British evangelicals. Although its chief effect was the revitalisation of the Reformed churches of France and the Netherlands, the *Réveil* in Switzerland generated new bodies that approximated to the 'Plymouth' Brethren in England. In Italy there was a similar indigenous movement, originally centred round Count Guicciardini, that developed into the Free Evangelical Churches. The Dutch Reformed Church eventually, in 1886, suffered a disruption not dissimilar to that in the Church of Scotland, in which many on the more evangelical side followed Abraham Kuyper in setting up the Free Reformed Church.[19] Elsewhere, too, fresh developments were often prompted by Moravians or British evangelicals. In Norway, the Moravians took the lead in creating mission agencies outside the state church; in Denmark a Scot, Ebenezer Henderson, founded the Copenhagen Bible Society; in Sweden it was an English Methodist preacher in Stockholm, George Scott, who gave much of the impetus that led to the eventual creation of Free Church congregations.[20] In parts of Germany, despite the prevailing accommodation of pietism within the state churches, Methodism put down roots and Baptists launched missionary work. The Evangelical Alliance in Britain often provided, particularly in the 1850s, timely intercession with the authorities on behalf of pioneering evangelical groups in German lands. Meanwhile Russia was affected by two very different impulses. In the Ukraine the Stundists represented an indigenous rigorist movement stemming from Russian Orthodoxy; whilst in St Petersburg during the 1870s the elite around the court was touched by the salon evangelism of an English peer, Lord Radstock. Thus the growth of voluntary religion on the continent, though naturally diverse in expression, was frequently intimately associated with the evangelical faith of the British Isles.

In all the lands where Free Churches became a powerful force, growth was challenged by a variety of factors. Many facets of popular culture came into

---

19 See chapter 20 below.
20 See chapter 13 below.

conflict with the stance of those who had adopted an intensely committed form of Christian faith. Although superstition could mesh readily enough with evangelical belief in providence, other aspects of folk belief were condemned by the Free Churches. Such traditions as warding off evil by lucky charms remained strong at the end of the century, even in London. The normal insistence on sabbath observance also clashed with the wish of working people to use the day for other purposes. But the greatest obstacle in popular culture to the progress of voluntary religion was the widespread devotion to strong drink. The consumption of alcohol rose steadily down to late in the century and the number of drink outlets, whether in metropolitan bars or in frontier saloons, was legion. The public house was a centre of male sociability, sustaining a web of values that fostered gambling, tolerated swearing and admired a manliness that could express itself in violence. The temperance movement, though originating outside the churches, was grafted into their life. They banned alcohol from their events, provided organisations such as the Band of Hope to train the young in the dangers of drink and sponsored counter-attractions such as coffee taverns. They also increasingly turned to political measures to restrict the availability of strong drink. The effect was to reinforce the polarisation of society between respectable folk, who went to church, and the rough drinkers, who did not. The endorsement of total abstinence erected a barrier between the Free Churches and many of their potential converts.

The problems faced by the Free Churches multiplied in the last two or three decades of the century. The process of suburbanisation, already underway in the biggest cities of the world, gained fresh impetus as transport became cheaper. Although new places of worship were erected for suburban dwellers, the older congregations near the city centres thinned as former members moved out to homes on the edge of the countryside. The lay leaders on whom voluntary organisations depended were specially likely to possess the initiative to prosper and depart to the suburbs. Meanwhile rural churches, though sometimes flourishing, were often, especially in Britain, hard hit by agricultural depression and so no longer able to pay a minister. The urban workforce, however, enjoyed higher wages than before and so could afford new forms of entertainment. From the 1870s the music hall attracted huge audiences and organised sport took off as a major preoccupation of the masses. So there were new activities competing with the churches for popular favour. On the other hand non-religious reasons for making a connection with the churches declined. The basic training in reading and writing that was often provided in Sunday schools earlier in the century became superfluous as state schools became general. Professional social workers started to appear and welfare services were launched so that philanthropy became less a monopoly of the churches. Politics seemed to offer a surer way of improving the lot of workers than religion. Labour unions began to attract the allegiance of men who would have previously given the whole of their energy to their places of worship. All these trends were to gather force in the early years of the twentieth century, but already in the final decades of the nineteenth century social developments were making the outreach of the Free Churches harder.

There were serious efforts to come to terms with the new situation. One method was to exploit the existing advantage of the Free Churches in the field of music. Well-trained choirs sang regularly and there were special performances of Handel's *Messiah* around Christmas. Another technique was to enter the field of sport, treating it as an ally of the gospel rather than as its foe. Free Churches organised their own teams, competing in local leagues. The most imaginative venture in the strategy of trying to co-opt social trends was the creation by the Wesleyans, from the 1880s, of central halls that provided vast amphitheatres for star preachers and good music together with welfare facilities staffed by trained nurses and other professionals. Associated with the Manchester Central Mission, for example, were a Men's Home and Labour Yard, a Women's Home, a Maternity Home and Hospital and a Cripples' Guild. It also held Popular Saturday Evening Concerts, graced by paid artistes.[21] Some of the preachers at the central halls became exponents of the social gospel, the response of the churches to the ills of industrial society. Hugh Price Hughes, the leader of the West London Mission, claimed in 1887 that Jesus Christ was 'the greatest social Reformer the world has ever seen'.[22] The social gospel, which flourished down to the First World War, especially in America, was an effort to persuade the working men whose minds were turning towards denouncing capitalism that the churches were on their side. It was an attempt to cut with the grain of rising social attitudes, to borrow whatever was good in socialism and show that Christians cared.

There was, however, an undoubted sapping of the fibre of the Free Churches as the nineteenth century wore on. The change was partly intellectual, a result of the milder type of theology that was coming into vogue. The most tangible symptom was the fading of hell from pulpit discourse. Younger ministers tacitly dropped the theme of everlasting punishment from their sermons, and some writers embraced novel theories about the destiny of the unconverted.

21 George Jackson, *Collier of Manchester* (London: Hodder and Stoughton, 1923), pp. 49, 133–5.
22 H. P. Hughes, *Social Christianity* (London: Hodder and Stoughton, 1889), p. 54.

The weighty English Congregationalist R. W. Dale, for instance, adopted the idea of conditional immortality, the notion that only the saved receive the gift of eternal life, so that the unsaved are extinguished rather than punished.[23] For Dale the shift was a matter of intellectual conviction, but for many it was part of a broader tendency to present Christian teaching in a form more palatable to suburban dwellers. The softer form of doctrine went with refined manners, superior taste and, in a word, respectability. It was accompanied by a reluctance to bring sins out into public view and consequently the abandonment of church discipline. No longer was drunkenness or bankruptcy brought before the gathered saints for the church to adjudicate; instead the matter was quietly remitted to the minister for pastoral guidance. Even death became unmentionable. Whereas in the mid-century the denominational magazines were full of the last words of dying Christians, by the 1880s the practice had been dropped because it grated on the feelings. Attendance at the theatre, once shunned, now became acceptable to many. Free Church people, especially those who had prospered, were ceasing to be so distinctive in their ideas or in their behaviour.

There was, nevertheless, a tendency in the contrary direction among a minority of Free Church members. During the last thirty years of the nineteenth century there was a spread of holiness ideals derived from Methodism beyond its ranks. John Wesley's teaching that a state of entire sanctification is available to the believer on earth had declined among ordinary Methodists, but a fresh enthusiasm for this distinctive teaching seized many in the wake of the American Civil War. Holiness camp meetings spread across America, large numbers professed sanctification in an instant and new denominations proclaimed the possibility of a second blessing after conversion. The effect of the holiness teaching was to foster scruples about the avoidance of worldly pastimes as well as to rekindle zeal for dedicated evangelism. Another influence encouraging the same trend was the Welsh Revival of 1904–5, a classic movement of mass conversions in hundreds of chapels. As the enigmatic Evan Roberts, still only a candidate for the ministry, moved from place to place, fervent hymn singing would mingle with spontaneous cries of personal repentance. Together the holiness movement and the Welsh Revival created the context for the beginnings of Pentecostalism. There were expectations of new spiritual power that seemed to be fulfilled when, in a mission that soon moved to Asuza Street in Los Angeles in 1906, speaking in tongues was heard.

23 A. W. W. Dale, *The life of R. W. Dale of Birmingham* (London: Hodder and Stoughton, 1898), pp. 310–16.

There had been comparable occurrences before, but now the news of a fresh Pentecost ran round the world. The foundations were laid for a movement that was to transform global Christianity during the twentieth century.

The voluntary sector of Christianity had expanded hugely over the century since the close of the Napoleonic wars. The primary motor of growth was Methodism, though the sheer variety of the bodies that sprang up outside the state churches was a characteristic of the period. What most, but not all, the growing Free Churches shared was the characteristic dedication of the evangelical movement to spreading the gospel. There were external advantages for the churches in the circumstances of the times, but their advance can be attributed most to their own capacity for appealing to men as well as women, for providing education, for evangelism and for philanthropy. There was a great deal in common between these bodies in England and Wales, in Scotland, Ireland and the British settler colonies and in the United States. Even on the European continent similar churches sprang from the same evangelical impulse. Although the growth of the Free Churches slowed in the later years of the century, they were still capable of adapting to changed circumstances and of generating new forms of spirituality. Perhaps their greatest triumph during the nineteenth century has not previously been mentioned here: the same imperative that induced them to spread the gospel at home also impelled them to undertake missionary effort abroad. The result, as Part III of this volume reveals, was the implanting of Christianity in many lands for the first time. The greatest monument to the dynamic of nineteenth-century voluntary religion was its worldwide profession in the years that followed.

5

Catholic revivalism in worship and devotion

MARY HEIMANN

Over the course of the nineteenth century, there was a widespread change in the way in which religious commitment was expressed and apparently understood by a majority of observant Roman Catholics. For most of the eighteenth century, all that had seemed necessary to lead what was generally considered to be a devout life was to be baptised; to hear Mass on a Sunday; and to take seriously one's duties of going to confession and receiving the Blessed Sacrament at least once a year ('at Easter or thereabouts' according to the catechism, but by convention some eight times a year, on the greater church feasts). Mainstream Catholic sermons, just like mainstream Protestant ones, stressed above all the reasonableness and morality of the central tenets of Christianity; while religious communities which could not prove themselves to be socially 'useful', or which had developed a reputation for excessive attachment to the pope, dwindled in membership and were sometimes forcibly closed down. Biblical miracles, unless considered fundamental to doctrine, tended to be either side-stepped or explained away by Catholic theologians; traditional legends surrounding the lives of the saints were treated with equal fastidiousness, so that St Francis of Assisi, for example, had come to be regarded by the self-consciously enlightened as 'a harmless enthusiast, pious and sincere, but hardly of sane mind, who was much rather accessory to the intellectual than to the moral degradation of mankind'.[1]

In the middle decades of the nineteenth century, during what has come to be known as the Catholic Revival, the tone and presentation of the Catholic message began to change in ways which, within a generation, were to become characteristic of Catholic communities just about everywhere. Catholic churches ceased being designed to look like neo-classical temples, but were built instead in Gothic or Romanesque idiom, the implication being that eternal values

---

[1] Hallam, as cited in T. Okey, introduction to *'The little flowers' and the life of St Francis with the 'Mirror of perfection'*, ed. E. Rhys (London, n.d.), p. xxi; Heimann, 'St Francis and modern English sentiment'.

lay, not in ancient Greece or Rome, still less in the European Enlightenment, but rather in the holiness of medieval Christendom. Going to confession and taking the Blessed Sacrament stopped being treated as fearful privileges to be reserved for the most solemn days of the liturgical calendar, but became a weekly, or even daily, habit for those who aspired to holiness. New hagiographies began to stress, rather than to apologise for, wonders and miracles surrounding the saints' lives; the contemplative orders once again came to be presented as the vanguard of the spiritually advanced; and the clergy, long held in suspicion, came to be widely praised for their perceived self-sacrifice and holiness. Even the papacy, personified in the 'Prisoner in the Vatican' – Pius IX (Pio Nono) – became the object of empathetic prayers, rousing hymns, Peter's pence collections, and special 'devotions to the Pope'.

Together with these changes in the general tone of Catholic preaching and hagiography came a dramatic rise in the provision and popularity of a whole range of voluntary extra-liturgical practices, known in the Catholic Church as 'devotions', many of which had a distinctly medieval flavour. Among the most frequently practised devotions, those which had come to be seen as an inseparable part of Catholic piety by the end of the nineteenth century were Marian devotions such as the Rosary, the thrice-daily recitation of the Angelus and the practice of setting aside the month of May as the 'Month of Mary'; penitential devotions, such as devotions to the Sacred Heart of Jesus and the *via crucis* ('Way of the Cross' or 'Stations of the Cross'); and devotions, or even whole services, which concentrated on the central Catholic mystery of transubstantiation through attention to the Blessed Sacrament, as in Visits to the Blessed Sacrament, the *Quarant'ore* (Forty Hours' Devotion to the Blessed Sacrament) and a variety of special services which shared the name of 'Benediction of the Blessed Sacrament', all of which climaxed with the blessing of the congregation by the Host, framed in an elaborate monstrance.

This marked rise in the use of set devotions among the Catholic laity was an international phenomenon which appears to have left few, if any, nineteenth-century Catholic communities untouched. Its progress can be traced through parish church listings for special services such as Public Rosary and Benediction of the Blessed Sacrament; through visitation reports; through increases in the publication and sale of a wide variety of prayer books, most of which were enlarged in successive nineteenth-century editions to make room for new, or newly promoted, devotional material; and through addenda to catechisms, or short compendia of doctrine, which increasingly taught devout practices, such as genuflexion, the telling of the rosary, the saying of grace before meals, the use of pious exclamations (such as 'Mary, Joseph and Jesus!') during the day and the recitation of prayers 'for a good death' at bedtime, as pious habits recommended for Catholic children preparing to make their first communion.

Devotions were promoted and spread with particular vigour through a host of exclusively Catholic societies, known as confraternities, sodalities or guilds, whose rise was another marked feature of the nineteenth-century religious landscape. Some of these societies, known as Third Orders, offered lay Catholics the opportunity to participate in the religious life of a particular religious order – most commonly the Dominicans or Franciscans – yet without going so far as to become actual novices. Others, such as the sodality for schoolgirls known as the 'Children of Mary', were designed to guide Catholics through particularly tricky stages of life. Still others, such as the Society of St Vincent de Paul, existed primarily to help the poor; or, like the Association of the Cross or Temperance Guild of Our Lady and St John the Baptist, to combat a specific social problem – alcoholism in this case – but from a distinctively Catholic angle. The vast majority of devotional societies, however, which consisted of a bewildering variety of Rosary, Blessed Sacrament, Sacred Heart, Holy Family, Immaculate Conception, Immaculate Heart, Way of the Cross, Precious Blood and other confraternities, sodalities and guilds, were explicitly spiritual in that they sought to focus their members' attention on a particular devotional practice and, through it, to strengthen commitment to a discrete aspect of Catholic doctrine.

At the same time that Catholic expectations of worship and devotion appeared to be becoming more intense and demanding, Catholics were also becoming increasingly segregated from non-Catholics. Educated separately wherever possible, strongly discouraged from marrying outside of the fold, and encouraged to participate more frequently in denominationally specific rites of passage as well as communal events such as retreats, processions and pilgrimages, Catholics found their everyday experience to be increasingly different from that of non-Catholics. Taken together, the changes which swept Catholic worship and devotion from about the middle of the nineteenth century added up to an experience for most observant Catholics which amounted to the adoption of a semi-monastic discipline, albeit one lived in 'the world' rather than in the seclusion of a seminary, convent or monastery.

While the aim of eschewing the 'worldly' in favour of the 'eternal' was nothing new for Catholics – or indeed for any other sort of Christian – the extent to which Catholic spirituality, and ultimately identity, came to be seen as tied to specific services, devotional rituals or quasi-monastic practices increasingly marked Catholics out as different from their neighbours. It was this sense of difference, quite as much as the occasional papal pronouncement reported in the press, which led to increased anti-Catholic prejudice in the second half of the nineteenth century, as shown in the English-speaking world through risqué accounts of convent life and gutter press 'revelations' by ex-priests as well as periodic 'anti-popery' riots; and, on the European continent, through state-sponsored anti-Catholic campaigns of the kind epitomised by Bismarck's *Kulturkampf.*[2]

In the eighteenth century, Catholics who lived in Protestant majority countries had tended on the whole to try to blend in, refraining from proselytising and stressing those points which the Catholic tradition had in common with other Christian, or even non-Christian, denominations. From the mid-nineteenth century, a vocal minority of militant Catholics, often calling themselves 'Ultramontane' (as opposed to 'Gallican'), appeared increasingly to prize precisely those elements of Catholic theology and church history which were least palatable to those outside the fold. Thus, at just the time that democracy and egalitarianism were being promoted as marks of political and social progress, the pope in his Syllabus of Errors (1864) tactlessly condemned 'progress, liberalism and modern civilisation' as among the most pernicious 'errors of the day'; just as 'Science' was beginning to be invoked by liberals as the highest possible authority, a series of claimed apparitions of the Virgin Mary – the most famous of which occurred at La Salette in 1846 and at Lourdes in 1858 – proclaimed the message that the 'materialist' spirit of the age was fundamentally misguided; just when the papacy was finally stripped of its temporal power in 1870, a defiant Pius IX declared papal infallibility to be a doctrine to be held by the whole church. Small wonder that the English convert to Catholicism John Henry, later Cardinal, Newman, felt that 'It is so ordered on high that in our day Holy Church should present just that aspect to my countrymen which is most consonant with their ingrained prejudices against her, most unpromising for their conversion.'[3]

The changes which overtook Catholicism from about the middle of the nineteenth century are often explained as the last, reactionary gasp of a church which had been forced onto the defensive since at least as early as the French Revolution, and arguably since the Protestant Reformation of the sixteenth century. According to this view, the more that the Vatican's political power was challenged by its critics, the more emphatically it insisted upon its spiritual

2 See e.g. Wolffe, *The Protestant crusade in Great Britain* and Sperber, *Popular Catholicism in nineteenth-century Germany.* For a fuller discussion of the *Kulturkampf* see chapter 18 below.
3 As cited in W. Ward, *The life of John Henry Cardinal Newman*, 2 vols. (London: Longmans, Green, 1912), vol. 1, p. 14.

authority. It was thus the fears aroused by the European revolutions of 1830 and 1848 which led Rome, in part by reviving full-blown worship and devotion as a means of attaching Catholics more firmly to the faith, to seek to unify those within the fold; it was the threat presented to the Vatican by the Italian *Risorgimento* that paved the way for the Syllabus of Errors; and it was the crisis over the loss of the Papal States in 1870 which led to the declaration of papal infallibility in faith and morals – popularly misunderstood to mean papal inerrancy in everything – also in 1870.[4]

Historians who favour this sort of institutional interpretation tend to see the whole paraphernalia of changes to nineteenth-century Catholic worship and devotion as little more than an accompaniment to the Vatican's essentially political struggle to close ranks, strengthen internal unity and command obedience throughout the Catholic world, homogenising religious practice for much the same reasons that it sought to tighten ecclesiastical discipline: to mould Catholics everywhere into a single, powerful pro-papal lobby. Although few historians go so far as to claim changes in Catholic piety to have been the result of a 'strategy carefully managed by Rome' in which 'control' was exercised through 'the daily rituals and practices of Catholics',[5] or else linked to a conspiratorial centre based in Geneva,[6] scholars with expertise in nineteenth-century Catholicism in a variety of countries have noted that an increase in devotions usually described as 'Roman', 'Italianate' or 'Ultramontane' coincided with the withdrawal of Catholic communities from non-Catholic society, leading to the creation of what has been called the Catholic 'ghetto'.[7]

To those who believe that the Catholic Revival was primarily about trying to stamp out devotional diversity among Catholic communities in order to increase papal and ecclesiastical authority, its legacy can hardly be viewed otherwise than with distaste and regret. Thus Emmet Larkin has presented us with a picture of a clerically led 'devotional revolution' in mid-century Ireland in which the gradual squeezing out of traditional folk practices, such as the pattern and the wake, went hand in hand with the systematic undermining of a native Gaelic spirituality.[8] John Bossy, too, has noted how traditional English Catholic piety, as encapsulated by the recusant Bishop Challoner's famous prayer book, *The garden of the soul*, came, in the wake of 'Second Spring' propaganda of the 1840s and 1850s, to be increasingly criticised as

---

4 For fuller discussions of the Syllabus and the 1870 definition see chapters 2 and 15.
5 McSweeney, *Roman Catholicism*, p. 38.
6 Lamberts, 'L'Internationale noire'.
7 McLeod, *Religion and the people of western Europe*, p. 36.
8 Larkin, 'The devotional revolution in Ireland'.

'timid', 'apologetic' or 'incomplete',[9] the implication being that only fully 'Roman' Catholicism was true Catholicism. Gérard Cholvy and Yves-Marie Hilaire, many of whose arguments have been presented in English by Ralph Gibson, have likewise written with regret of the replacement of a multitude of idiosyncratic French saints – whose images were often associated with curative and semi-magical powers – with the anodyne, mass-produced plaster and terracotta statues of Counter-Reformation saints for sale near Saint-Sulpice church in Paris.[10] Historians of Australian Catholicism have echoed the refrain in their presentations of the community as having abandoned more ecumenical traditions in order to become, in the infamous words of the English convert Henry Manning, 'more Roman than Rome' and 'more ultramontane than the Pope himself',[11] while historians of American Catholicism remain divided over the extent to which distinctively American Catholic features were replaced by 'Roman' ones.[12]

However compelling arguments for an 'Ultramontane' triumph over 'Liberal Catholicism' or 'Gallicanism' in the nineteenth century may at first appear, their very functionalism ought to put us on our guard: real life is seldom so tidy as to consist merely of the straightforward imposition of 'power' by one group over another. On paper, the Catholic Church may indeed appear as a tightly structured hierarchical organisation with a chain of command not unlike that which exists in an army. In practice, however, the model is highly misleading, since pope, cardinals, bishops and priests can hardly impose their tastes on their flocks, who remain perfectly free to ignore the spiritual recommendations of their clergy; to change churches; to set up their own devotional societies or, ultimately, to cease to be involved in them altogether.

The nineteenth-century Catholic Church, whose missionary endeavour overseas had fallen well behind that of the Protestant churches during the latter half of the eighteenth century, was not likely to make such an elementary mistake as to confuse theoretical authority with actual power. In India, Catholic missionaries who had been sent out with the blessing of the Congregation *de Propaganda Fide* (revived in 1817) were generally met with resistance and suspicion, not only from the Hindu elite, but also from native 'Thomas' Christians, the East India Company and rival, Protestant missionary organisations. Although there were renowned instances in which whole villages

---

9 Bossy, *The English Catholic community*, pp. 297, 364–5.
10 Cholvy and Hilaire, *Histoire religieuse*; Gibson, *Social history of French Catholicism*, pp. 154–6.
11 Cited in Altholz, *The Liberal Catholic movement in England*, p. 212. On the Australian case, see Molony, *The Roman mould of the Australian Catholic Church*.
12 See e.g. 'An American Church' in Morris, *American Catholic*, pp. 134–5, and Taves, *The household of faith*, pp. 113–33.

were persuaded to turn Catholic, overwhelming resistance to the exclusivist claims of Christianity meant that most missionaries, Catholic or Protestant, were forced to lower their sights to the attempted infusion of vaguely defined 'Christian values' into traditional Indian society, and ultimately forced to accept syncretism at the expense of doctrinal rigour.[13]

In western and southern Africa, too, although numerous Catholic missionary societies – among them the Society for African Missions, the Holy Ghost Fathers, the Verona Fathers and the White Fathers – were sent out under the pontificate of Gregory XVI (1831–46) for the specific purpose of 'converting' Africa, they appeared largely unable to compete with native religions, so that Catholic communities could scarcely be said to have existed in most parts of Africa until well after the First World War. Only in East Africa, despite the fierce competition which Catholic missionaries faced from Islamic, Anglican and Ethiopian Orthodox rivals, did they appear to gain something of a foothold; but even there it was only by closing their eyes to many practices considered 'heathen' by European Christians, and by tolerating considerable devotional diversity, that Catholicism, in any form, was able to take root.[14]

The same pattern of failure was even more marked in China, the primary target of Catholic missionary endeavour during the first four decades of the nineteenth century, where the practice of Christianity remained illegal until after the First Opium War (1839–42). Although concessions were afterwards granted to Christian missionaries (in treaties concluded in 1858 and 1860) to allow them to travel and proselytise in the interior, the fiasco of the Taiping rebellion (1851–64), in which a quasi-Christian millennialist sect failed to overthrow the Qing (Manchu) dynasty, widely discredited Christians of every hue, leaving the Chinese Catholic Church almost exclusively in the hands of foreign priests who, as in Africa, all too often found themselves in a white 'ghetto' composed largely of Irish, French, American and Australian priests without *entrée* into local society.[15] In Japan, where Christianity remained proscribed until as late as 1873, relatively few indigenous Christian sects came into being until after the Second World War; even then, Catholicism continued to be generally regarded as an alien creed unsuitable for transplantation into traditional Japanese culture. Only in territories which had been under European control for considerably longer – as in the cases of the northern part

---

13 For a fuller analysis of Catholic missions in nineteenth-century India, see chapter 29 below.
14 Hastings, *African Catholicism*, pp. 75–6.
15 For the Taiping rebellion and its consequences for Christianity in China see chapter 30 below.

of the Philippines, or of the formerly Spanish territories in Latin America – does there appear to have been widespread support for the further spread of Catholicism.

Despite the initially high hopes of some early nineteenth-century missionaries, eager to convert the world to the 'faith of their fathers', by about the middle of the nineteenth century it had become clear, even to the most sanguine, that most non-Christian peoples were either indifferent, or actually hostile, to the 'good news' being brought to them by European missionaries, whether Protestant or Catholic. The 'Catholic Revival' which followed throughout most of Europe and the New World, and which distinguished itself from earlier missionary endeavour by turning its focus almost exclusively on whites, thus came, in practice, to be a movement of significance only in those communities which were already technically Catholic.

It was to these nominally Catholic communities, often held in suspicion by the more rigidly Ultramontane clergy who had been trained in Italy or France to 'missionise' to the infidel, that the sense of a grand mission to 'convert the heathen' and 'restore' Catholicism to its full Tridentine glory was born. The Italian Passionist Fr Dominic Barberi may have dreamed and prayed for the 'conversion' of Protestant Britain, home of what was then the greatest European economic power and the centre of a vast empire; but, despite the headline conversions of prominent Anglican clergymen associated with the Oxford Movement, his successes were mostly confined to winning the allegiance of Irish emigrants who, however patchy their conformity to Catholic doctrine and practice, regarded themselves as Catholics, not Protestants, by birth.[16]

The Catholic Revival of the mid-nineteenth century, for all its disingenuous claims to have 'won' new converts to what it termed 'Christianity', was in practice largely confined to persuading the members of pre-existing Catholic communities to change their habits of devotion and worship. 'Conversion' in this sense could mean little more than going to Mass more often; making more public displays of faith; joining exclusively Catholic societies; and incorporating new or newly recommended devotions and pious practices, both public and private, into one's daily routine. Since Protestant revivalist techniques were having much the same effect on their own communities at just about the same time, it is not clear that this represented much more than a change in religious fashion, a general shift from the more gentlemanly style of piety held to have

16 Connolly, 'Catholicism in Manchester and Salford', vol. III, pp. 5–6; Wilson, *Blessed Dominic Barberi*, p. 262.

been in good taste during the eighteenth century but which, by the middle decades of the nineteenth century, had widely come to be seen as 'cold' or overly 'intellectual' – in short, insufficiently active and enthusiastic – to appear to attest to earnestness of religious conviction. This Romantic or 'evangelical' enthusiasm gave mid to late nineteenth-century Christian worship and spirituality, whether Protestant or Catholic, a kind of broad family resemblance, despite the ever-sharper emphasis being placed, by both communities, on the doctrinal differences which continued to divide them.

Catholicism, as practised in all countries which boasted a substantial Catholic population, came to seem more exclusive and denominationally distinct as Catholics everywhere began to withdraw from what were increasingly perceived to be dangerous, non-Catholic influences by ensuring that they went regularly to church, joined exclusively Catholic societies, had their children educated in Catholic schools, and incorporated pious practices and set prayers into their daily routine. Catholic literature of the day, with its emphasis on the other-worldly, the importance of the saints, the centrality of penance and the holiness of simplicity, gave Catholics a shared sense of values, just as a number of universalised Catholic shrines, saints, images, devotions and places of pilgrimage gave them common points of reference and a shared spiritual vocabulary. But for all the common ground between Catholics of different nationalities, no Catholic was under obligation to feel a sense of attachment or devotion to any one particular devotional or spiritual approach any more than to one particular saint. National differences, although papered over by Ultramontane enthusiasts at the time and by modern historians since, continued to be marked.

Little, as yet, has been published – in English, at any rate – about the transformation of Italian Catholicism in the first decades of the nineteenth century; but traditional Italian devotion, with its concentration on local saints and idiosyncratic tradition of bleeding statues as the objects of local cults, does not appear to have spread to the rest of the Catholic world. Popular French spirituality, with its focus on child visionaries and string of claimed apparitions of the Virgin Mary, led to copycat apparitions over the course of the nineteenth and twentieth centuries, including in places as far afield as Marpingen in Germany (1876), Knock in Ireland (1879) and Fatima in Portugal (1917); but the vast majority of such claimed apparitions remained a distinctively French contribution to Catholic spirituality (La Salette 1846; Lourdes 1858; Pontmain 1870; Tilly-sur-Seulles 1896–9). English and Irish Catholics do not appear to have imported the French and Italian habit of using ex-votos; nor was Belgian spirituality, with its relics of local saints and fashion for miraculous statues of the Holy Child (rather in the Habsburg tradition of the Infant of Prague), the same as German, Dutch or French spirituality, let alone African, Indian or Chinese. Each Catholic community appears, in the main, to have remained attached to its own particular brand of miracle, rather than uncritically to have adopted those of its neighbours.

What was true of claims of the miraculous was equally true of devotional practices, all of which were increasingly available to Catholics, but none of which could be imposed upon them by force. As even the most hard-line or 'Ultramontane' campaigners for papal authority – among them cardinals Henry Manning of England and Paul Cullen of Ireland – were ready to admit, no devotion could be expressly forbidden so long as it did not contradict doctrine; and as even the most irrepressible enthusiasts for the newly emotive style of piety – among them the Brompton Oratorian F. W. Faber – conceded, taste in devotion was idiosyncratic, the 'Holy Ghost', as he put it, leading 'different souls' to 'different devotions' and giving 'various lights upon them'.[17] The charitable requirement to show devotional tolerance for all varieties of Catholic taste, 'low' as well as 'high', was also conceded on the other side of the divide, those who favoured the 'Gallican' or 'liberal' cause when it came to questions of papal authority, and who may have felt unable to respond to many newly promoted devotions, nevertheless acknowledging that not only every individual but 'every nation and age' has 'its own taste'. As Newman of the Birmingham Oratory, unmoved by the sort of schmaltz beloved by his brothers in the London Oratory, counselled one of his more scrupulous correspondents: 'Use your own taste, and let me use mine.'[18]

Changes in devotional taste appear to have had little or nothing to do with papal pronouncements or Vatican guidelines, let alone with the wholesale victory of something vaguely termed 'Ultramontanism' over something equally imprecisely called 'Gallicanism' or 'Liberal Catholicism'. Although a handful of 'Ultramontane' enthusiasts in England, as elsewhere, campaigned hard for the Vatican-approved prayer book, the *Raccolta* or *Collection of indulgenced prayers*, to be translated into English and spread among the local Catholic community, English Catholics continued instead to buy successively enlarged and updated

---

17 F. W. Faber, *Growth in holiness; or the progress of the spiritual life* (London: Burns and Oates, 1854), p. 371.
18 J. H. Newman to Mrs William Froude, 2 Jan. 1855, in C. S. Dessain, *et al.* (eds.), *The letters and diaries of John Henry Newman*, 31 vols. (London: T. Nelson, 1961–77 and Oxford: Clarendon Press, 1978–), vol. XXVI, pp. 342–3.

versions of their own spiritual classic, Challoner's *The garden of the soul*.[19] The same pattern of indifference to Roman imperatives could be seen in Ireland, where the *Key of heaven*, originally known as *The poor man's manual; or, devout Christian's daily companion*, remained the Irish Catholic spiritual classic right up to the First World War, having gone through some thirty-eight editions over the course of the nineteenth century. For all the emphasis on Marian piety characteristic of contemporary French and German Catholic spirituality, in English-speaking countries even the primary Marian devotion of the century, the service of Public Rosary, remained overshadowed by another recusant classic, that version of the service known as Benediction of the Blessed Sacrament which had originally developed in English émigré circles at Douai and found its way into Challoner's *Garden of the soul*, not the service of the same name as practised in contemporary Italy or France.[20]

Faced with such devotional diversity, the Vatican could scarcely have imposed its own preferred brand of Catholic spirituality on all the world – even if it had wanted to – without the risk of losing its appeal altogether. The vehicles through which the Vatican could attempt to control or influence the development of spontaneous cults or devotional practices abroad were just four: the granting of papal indulgences to express approval of particular devotions or sites of pilgrimage; the beatification of persons believed to have special claims to sanctity; the choosing of bishops thought to be especially sound in piety, obedience and administrative competence; and the promotion of particular religious tracts, pamphlets or books. With only these limited tools at its disposal, the Vatican could hardly create beloved saints or manufacture popular devotions; nor, according to its own rules, could it condemn devotional practices, however vulgar or peculiar, providing they did not actually contradict church doctrine. Rome could, in short, choose to send out a particular Italian or French missionary order to India or Africa – or, for that matter, to the 'missionary' territories of Ireland, England or Germany – with instructions to build a perfect replica of a rural church from Tuscany or Brittany: but it could hardly guarantee how such a building would be used, let alone with what degree of orthodoxy or enthusiasm. Similarly, it could advocate and offer to teach the use of rosary beads as an aid to prayer and means of inculcating greater devotion to the Blessed Virgin; but it could not easily prevent rural

19 Heimann, *Catholic devotion in Victorian England*, pp. 72–6.
20 Fr. Herbert Thurston, 'Our English Benediction service', *The Month* 106 (1905), 394–404; 'Benediction of the Blessed Sacrament', *The Month* 97 (1901), 587–97 and 98 (1901), 58–69, 186–93, 264–76; Heimann, *Catholic devotion in Victorian England*, pp. 45–58.

Irish peasants from placing rosaries on the corpses of young girls believed to have lived a life of special piety,[21] any more than it could stop villagers in West Africa from hanging them, like so many charms to ward off evil, on the walls of their homes.[22]

To assume that the changes in devotional taste and practice which characterised the Catholic Revival stemmed from the Vatican is to credit the Catholic Church with a degree of power no human organisation could conceivably possess. Instead of instigating devotional change, the Vatican appears rather to have struggled to keep up with the veritable explosion of new forms of piety which were brought to its attention by bishops and priests from around the globe, attempting where possible to weed out the doctrinally suspect from the doctrinally irreproachable – not always with conspicuous success – but always with the hope of pleasing, and thus retaining, as many of the faithful as possible.

Why so many novel devotions, all jostling for attention and official approval, should have flooded the Catholic market during the latter half of the nineteenth century is a question which has yet to be satisfactorily accounted for by historians. The phenomenon may have had something to do with the world having become 'smaller' through railway travel, lower publishing costs, and the mass manufacture and export of inexpensive devotional kitsch, so that devotees became more eclectic in their tastes, adding selected foreign devotions to their own, more traditional, favourites. It undoubtedly also had something to do with the sharp increase in interdenominational competition, a change which appears to have been sparked by early nineteenth-century missionary endeavours overseas, but was sustained, from about the middle of the century, through the widespread use of revivalist techniques at home, among Protestants and Catholics alike.[23]

Above all, changes in the tone of Catholic devotion and worship in the nineteenth century seem to have been due to the spread of a new mood of devotional inclusiveness which was as much spiritual as it was pragmatic in its aims. Perhaps the most striking feature of this new piety was the degree to which it not only allowed, but positively encouraged, uneducated lay

---

21 Gilley, 'Vulgar piety and the Brompton Oratory', p. 20.
22 Hastings, *African Catholicism*, p. 77.
23 On nineteenth-century British evangelicalism, see especially: David Bebbington, *Evangelicalism in modern Britain: a history from the 1730s to the 1980s* (London: Unwin Hyman, 1989); Richard Carwardine, *Trans-Atlantic revivalism: popular evangelicalism in Britain and America, 1790–1865* (Westport and London: Greenwood Press, 1978); John Kent, *Holding the fort: studies in Victorian revivalism* (London: Epworth Press, 1978).

Catholics – from simple Italian peasants to humble Irish seamstresses or French cowherds – to formulate and express their particular brand of Catholic devotion in their own way and to their own taste. Here the traditional Christian emphasis on the innate holiness of the poor and outcast merged well both with Romantic approval of the simple and childlike and with more prosaic institutional pressures to encourage lapsed Catholics, of whom the majority were thought to be working class, to return to the active practice of the 'faith of their fathers'.

The 'vulgar piety' which resulted tended, unsurprisingly, to be both more 'proletarian' and more 'feminine' than had been the case in the previous century. This was, after all, a time when working-class men – and especially women – took a much more active part in the creation, re-establishment or support of Catholic schools, convents, confraternities, sodalities and other exclusively Catholic societies, and were thus in a good position to promote particular devotions or pious practices.[24] Meanwhile, their social superiors, anxious to show themselves as trusting, childlike and humble, were often quite as eager to emulate the 'simple' piety of peasants and labourers. It was thus no accident that the contemporary figure to arouse the greatest devotion throughout the whole of the Catholic world, Bernadette Soubirous, was a humble peasant girl whose very appeal lay in her reputation for uncalculating simplicity; or that the set devotions taken to be emblematic of the age were those with the direct, sentimental and unsophisticated appeal of 'reparations to the Sacred Heart' or 'devotions to the Holy Family'. As a pious cliché of the day had it, to follow a simple, folksy practice like the rosary was good both for those to whom the devotion naturally appealed and also for those to whom it did not, since it was better than nothing for those who were incapable of a more sophisticated piety and humbling for those who might otherwise suffer from spiritual pride.

What historians have rather loosely called 'Ultramontane' piety consisted of a particular kind of taste, rather sentimental and saccharine to modern sensibilities, but which was aesthetically and emotionally accessible to all, even the most unsophisticated. Characteristic expressions of this brand of Catholic piety, such as pictures of the Sacred Heart, the Immaculate Conception or the Holy Family, have long been assumed to have been imposed upon Catholic communities over the course of the nineteenth century in order to rid national churches of 'Gallicanism' or the avoidance of papal control. Yet devotions

---

24 Gilley, 'Vulgar piety and the Brompton Oratory'; O'Brien, 'Making Catholic spaces'; Gibson, *Social history of French Catholicism*, pp. 158–226.

long assumed by historians to have been 'Roman' often turn out, upon closer inspection, not only not to have been Italian, Italianate, promoted from the Vatican or in any other meaningful sense 'Roman' or 'Ultramontane', but rather – as in the English case – to have been precisely those devotions which had long been prized by the national community.

The devotional evidence suggests that, while Catholic communities everywhere did indeed become more outwardly fervent, demonstrative and showy over the course of the nineteenth century, they did not do so because ordered to do so by the Vatican. Rather than conform blindly to a Roman pattern, nineteenth-century Catholics – just like other sorts of Christians – were strongly affected by what might be thought of as a newly 'evangelical' or 'missionary' tone, a broad shift in taste and mood which affected Catholics and Protestants alike, and which led almost every Christian denomination earnestly to launch its own, distinctive 'revival' while simultaneously redoubling efforts to proselytise among the lapsed or indifferent within its own ranks. While the Catholic Revival made Catholics superficially seem more distinctive and denominationally exclusive than they had during the eighteenth century, it also underlined the degree to which Catholic communities, just like Protestant ones, were becoming more strident, flamboyant and demotic at a time of general interdenominational competition among Christians.

While late nineteenth-century Catholics seemed to be becoming more exclusively Catholic in their social as well as their devotional behaviour, this did not mean that they had lost either their national distinctiveness or their liberty. Although Protestants, liberals, anticlericals and other enemies of the Catholic Church, alarmed by the sight of what seemed to be a newly resurgent and confident Roman Church, leaped easily to the conclusion that every new devotion must have been commanded by the pope, the universal Catholic Church, far from becoming 'more Roman than Rome', was actually becoming more accepting of the low tastes of its poorest and most marginalised members from around the world, making it far more eclectic in its devotional, as well as its aesthetic, tastes.

6

Women preachers and the new Orders

A: Women preachers in the Protestant churches

JANICE HOLMES

Next day, Sunday, July 31 [1763], I told him I had been that morning at a meeting
of the people called Quakers, where I had heard a woman preach. JOHNSON.
'Sir, a woman's preaching is like a dog's walking on his hinder legs. It is not
done well; but you are surprised to find it done at all.'[1]

Samuel Johnson's remark on the Quaker custom of allowing women to preach
has become one of the most famous comments on female ministry in English
literature. Yet his is by no means an isolated opinion. Observers throughout the
history of western Christianity have frequently commented on the 'extraordinary' or 'unusual' sight of a woman preaching to a public, mixed audience,
especially since that activity was meant to be reserved for an ordained clergy,
or at least laymen. However, women have always, if intermittently, held positions of leadership within the Christian tradition. As 'fellow labourers' in the
early church, as medieval nuns and as prophetesses of the radical Reformation,
women have occupied some measure of public religious space.

Women in nineteenth-century Protestantism were no exception. Throughout the transatlantic world, across denominations, regions and decades,
women operated in the public religious sphere and exercised what were often
perceived to be spiritual gifts deemed appropriate only for men. Defining
what this female ministry involved in real terms is a complicated task. It
depends on the observer's theological perspective – how the Scriptures relating to female behaviour ought to be interpreted – and their ecclesiological
assumptions: whether or not women have the right to exercise 'authority' (that
is, to occupy teaching, sacramental and organisational positions) within the
church. At the conservative end of this scale, the Bible does not allow women to
exercise 'headship' over a man, and women should therefore be prohibited

---

1 G. B. Hill (ed.), *Boswell's Life of Johnson*, 6 vols. (Oxford: Clarendon Press, 1934), vol. 1,
p. 463.

from taking on leadership positions within the church. From this perspective, female ministry means service-oriented activity that is rooted within the domestic sphere. At the more liberal end of this scale, the Bible endorses women's spiritual equality with men, and the numerous examples of biblical female leadership give women the right to occupy formal positions within the church hierarchy. From this perspective, female ministry means public leadership activity, such as being an elder or deacon, voting in church assemblies, and in particular, operating as a preacher, evangelist and minister.

For women in nineteenth-century Protestantism, service-oriented ministry was a growth industry. As the number of charitable and philanthropic organisations expanded, women found increased opportunities to exercise their faith in active and useful ways. However, the justification for this activity was often based on restrictive attitudes towards women's 'suitable', 'proper' or 'natural' sphere of influence. In the nineteenth century, women were perceived to be more religious than men and to be the guardians of their family's spiritual and moral development. Charitable work was seen as simply an extension of women's primary role in society, that of mother and wife.

Women's public ministry was another matter. Throughout the nineteenth century, mainline Protestant denominations on both sides of the Atlantic restricted the exercise of public ministry to men. Anglicans, Presbyterians, Baptists and Congregationalists, and to a certain extent Methodists, officially excluded women from the ordained clergy and severely restricted their involvement as lay church leaders. Despite these prohibitions, women throughout the nineteenth century served as itinerant evangelists, deacons, delegates to their denominational conferences, foreign missionaries and temperance speakers. From the mid-1860s American women were being ordained and others were finding greater institutional acceptance of slightly more limited roles. In this respect, and unlike some interpretations, female ministry is not something that 'emerges' in 1800 and 'declines' by 1914. Rather, it should be seen as what Catherine Brekus calls a series of 'discontinuities' and 'reinventions'. Throughout the nineteenth century, women from a diverse range of denominational and social backgrounds sought, at different times and in different places, to forge a tradition of female religious leadership and to take their places alongside men in the exercise of their religious ambitions.[2] What links these women together is their common experience of a divine 'call' to ministry and the informal and vulnerable nature of their authority. For most of them, public ministry

---

2 Brekus, *Strangers and pilgrims*, pp. 15–16.

was only possible in smaller, less sacramentally focused denominations or in congregations far from the centres of denominational power.

This section of the chapter will focus almost exclusively on women's ministry in the transatlantic Protestant world, in particular, the United States and Great Britain. There has been a strong interest in women's ministries in these countries, especially in America, but the availability of similar research for Protestant women in Europe and farther afield is much more limited. The emergence of Protestant women's leadership in the new Christian communities of Africa and Asia has been a very recent development and is outside the timescale of this survey.[3]

Public female ministry in nineteenth-century Britain and the United States can be divided into three rough chronological divisions: the period from 1790 to 1840, when women operated as itinerant evangelists with a degree of denominational approval; the 1840s to 1860s, when female preaching was fragmented and incoherent; and the period from 1870 to the 1920s, when women began to achieve a greater measure of lay and clergy rights within a wider range of denominations.

Public female ministry in early nineteenth-century Protestantism had two important sources, both of which originated in the previous century, if not before. The Society of Friends, which had emerged during the radical days of the English Civil War, had adopted from the outset a distinct spirituality, the 'inward word', that gave women equal authority with men in the spiritual leadership of the sect. Over the course of the eighteenth century, it is estimated that between 1,300 and 1,500 women conducted local and itinerant preaching careers with official approval.[4] Such activity continued throughout the nineteenth century but women increasingly lost ground to men in the control and administration of the denomination.[5]

The second major source of female ministry in the early nineteenth century was the emergence of evangelicalism, a movement of religious ideas that stressed the importance of a personal conversion experience and adopted a pragmatic approach to church growth. Methodism, the most significant outgrowth of the Evangelical Revival, gave women positive roles in its early days. John Wesley encouraged a number of his English female acquaintances to preach, but he only considered it to be 'exceptional' activity.[6] This ambivalence meant that an official female ministry was difficult to sustain. By 1803 Wesleyan

---

3 For a brief overview see Tucker and Liefeld, *Daughters of the church*, pp. 291–327.
4 Larson, *Daughters of light*, pp. 63–4.
5 Plant, '"Subjective testimonies"'.
6 Chilcote, *John Wesley and the women preachers*.

Methodism had moved to prohibit it. It was only within the ambit of breakaway Methodist sects, like the Primitive Methodists (1812) and the Bible Christians (1816), that female preaching was granted an official sanction. Expanding into the 1820s, with a peak in numbers by the 1830s, by the 1860s about ninety Primitive and seventy-five Bible Christian women had served as full-time, paid 'itinerant preachers', the most senior pastoral position within these structurally loose movements.[7]

This rapid growth in female preaching, followed by a steady decline, is a pattern that is repeated in the American denominations influenced by the evangelical revival of the late eighteenth century. The lack of denominational structures and a highly emotional expression of religious feeling combined to create an environment in which female leadership flourished. Young, single women, predominantly from the northern states and from a variety of social backgrounds, could be found leading revival services and preaching to mixed audiences at camp meetings. Freewill Baptists and the Christian Connexion, along with breakaway Methodist groups like the African Methodist Episcopal Church (AME) (1816)[8] and the Methodist Protestants (1830), allowed women to preach from the pulpit and, in some cases, gave them access to decision-making roles in church government.[9]

The status that these women had, with their rustic and spontaneous style of preaching, remained vulnerable to criticism, and in the 1830s and 1840s public hostility towards their activity began to mount. Concerns from mainline denominations about the theological justifications for women's ministry, and the feminist implications of such public preaching, combined with a growing disquiet within the revivalist denominations themselves. Keen to consolidate their numerical expansion, and to inculcate a measure of social respectability, both British and American evangelicals increasingly insisted on an educated clergy and urged women to teach from within the domestic sphere. In response, some female preachers moved into denominations which allowed them to continue their ministry. But by far the larger number simply withdrew from public ministry altogether and accepted their greatly reduced religious roles.[10]

The mid-nineteenth century was not, as has often been portrayed, a period in which women's public ministry ceased. However, there does seem to be a

---

7 Graham, 'Chosen by God', p. 90; Wilson, 'Decline of female itinerant preachers', pp. 17–18.
8 Dodson, *Engendering church*, chs. 1–3.
9 Billington, '"Female labourers"'; Brekus, *Strangers and pilgrims*, pp. 134–6.
10 Brekus, *Strangers and pilgrims*, pp. 284–305.

loss of impetus and a sense of existing privileges being taken away. Women had lost out to growing denominational demands for an educated clergy, but still lacked the access to higher education, both secular and theological, that would have enabled them, potentially, to regain their positions. Within this educational gap, women struggled to find a means of expressing their ministerial talents. As a result, female preaching during these decades appears fragmented and incoherent. Women achieved little more than a grudging acceptance of fairly restrictive ministerial roles.

By the 1840s, the number of women occupying ministerial roles in British Methodism had fallen to single figures. By 1848 there were only three female itinerants within the Bible Christians and by 1850 only one among the Primitive Methodists.[11] However, there is evidence to suggest that within Methodism and in other Nonconformist denominations women's public ministry had not disappeared, it had merely gone underground. Here, at the level of the local circuit or chapel, removed from the reach of denominational regulations, with a sympathetic minister and a congregational tradition of female preaching, women could find an audience that continued to endorse their ministry. Other women appear to have packaged their preaching under the guise of 'Bible teaching' or charitable work. During the mid-nineteenth century, a number of English women set up evangelistic missions to the working classes, and some even established new churches. Accounts suggest that such activity involved public preaching to mixed audiences.[12]

In mid-nineteenth-century Britain it was the emergence of an evangelical sub-culture that provided women with a more favourable environment for their public ambitions. Stimulated by the revival in Ulster in 1859, British evangelicals embraced a more ecumenical approach to gospel work and demonstrated a greater willingness to use lay agents, including women, to achieve their conversionist goals. Throughout the 1860s, female evangelists like Mathilda Bass, Isabella Armstrong and Mrs Col. William Bell featured prominently in the pages of the movement's most influential periodical, *The Revival*. These women were, for the most part, married, middle class and from denominations without a tradition of female ministry, like the Church of England, the Church of Scotland and the Baptists. Their preaching was so

---

11 Graham, 'Chosen by God', p. 90; Wilson, 'Decline of female itinerant preachers', pp. 17–18.
12 Wilson, '"Constrained by zeal"', pp. 193–4. Holmes, *Religious revivals*, pp. 127–31, also suggests there was an underground network of independent Methodist female preaching in the 1880s.

popular that Geraldine Hooper Dening, an Anglican in her mid-twenties, was called 'the female Spurgeon'.[13]

In the United States, public female ministry in the middle decades of the nineteenth century was evident in a variety of different contexts and received support and encouragement from widely diverse theological perspectives. Theological liberalism, in the form of the Unitarian and Universalist churches, acted as a sympathetic and supportive environment for white, middle-class women. Active in the early women's rights movement, these denominations were the first officially to ordain women, calling Olympia Brown to a Universalist pastorate in 1864.[14] Theological orthodoxy, however, in the form of the holiness movement, also proved a fertile breeding ground for public female ministry. By 1864, for example, the radical abolitionist and holiness Wesleyan Methodists (1842) had given local conferences the right to ordain women as elders. One of the leading mid-century female preachers was Phoebe Palmer, a member of the Methodist Episcopal Church and a holiness speaker. In the early twentieth century, women like Aimee Semple McPherson and Alma White founded holiness denominations and conducted highly public preaching ministries. The emphasis of the holiness movement on charismatic leadership, that the Holy Spirit had been 'poured out on all flesh', acted as a powerful justification of women's right to preach.[15]

It is important to remember that the wider social and religious impact of this public female activity should not be overestimated. Middle-class female evangelism, without denominational endorsement, may have gained women some notoriety, but it never functioned as a stepping-stone to ordination, let alone achieving official sanction. The denominations which were endorsing female preaching were, for the most part, marginal players on the American Protestant stage and the recognition which they granted women during this time was quite restrictive and grudgingly given. Official recognition of exceptional individuals, like Olympia Brown, did not indicate a denominational acceptance of female ministry nor did it necessarily pave the way for other women to follow. Female Universalist clergy at the turn of the century still found themselves 'silenced' and 'impotent' within the overwhelmingly male

---

13 Quoted in Anderson, 'Women preachers in mid-Victorian Britain', p. 471.
14 The first woman to be ordained in the United States was the Congregationalist Antoinette Brown in 1853. However, this ministry only lasted a year before Brown moved into suffrage work, the care of her children and the Unitarian faith. She does not seem to have continued her preaching ministry. Cazden, *Antoinette Brown Blackwell*.
15 Tucker and Liefeld, *Daughters of the church*, pp. 261–8, 285–9, 359–74; Dayton and Dayton, '"Your daughters shall prophesy"', pp. 67–92.

hierarchy of their church.[16] Even though Phoebe Palmer wrote a powerful justification of female preaching, *The Promise of the Father* (1860), she based her own ministry on a strongly domestic ideology and did not encourage other women to follow her example.[17] Indeed, once the new holiness sects took on denominational characteristics, roles that women had been encouraged to fill were increasingly closed to them. Women continued to operate on the institutional fringes, despite the appearance of greater acceptance.

The final decades of the nineteenth century can be characterised as a period of growing denominational recognition of official leadership roles for women. Part of the reason for this lay in wider social changes. By the 1880s, women in Britain and the United States were participating in a growing number of protest movements that had increased their visibility as platform speakers and campaigners. Higher education, the vote and the temperance movement all offered women unique opportunities for public speaking. As society moved to accept women in public roles, so denominations found it easier to entertain such participation in the religious sphere.

Women also encountered unprecedented opportunities to exercise their preaching aspirations in the rapidly expanding foreign mission field and took advantage of the freedom and latitude they were given to become not only evangelists, but doctors, administrators and church planters. By 1900, there were over forty female Protestant missionary societies in the United States representing over 1,000 female missionaries.[18] By 1909 approximately 60 per cent of the Church of England's missionaries were women.[19] However, such authority was the result more of racial attitudes, which viewed the 'heathen' as inferior and, therefore, suitable audiences for women's ministry, than of any change in theological opinion concerning women's right to preach.

With women occupying more public roles than ever, it was not surprising that changes began to occur within the wider Protestant community. One of the most significant developments was the formation of the Salvation Army. William and Catherine Booth, deeply influenced by the holiness and revivalist movements of the mid-nineteenth century, in 1865 decided to start their own work, in which women were granted full preaching authority on the same terms as men. This official endorsement of female leadership was unprecedented and extraordinarily successful. As the Army expanded, the

---

16 Tucker, *Prophetic sisterhood*, p. 7.
17 Hovet, 'Phoebe Palmer's "altar phraseology"'.
18 Robert, *American women in mission*, p. 129; Tucker and Liefeld, *Daughters of the church*, p. 301.
19 Gill, *Women and the Church of England*, p. 173.

number of female 'officers' grew; by 1884 there were more than 1,000. When concerns were raised about the propriety of female officers celebrating communion, the Army abandoned the practice rather than restrict women's ministerial functions.[20] The obvious success of these 'Hallalujah Lasses' stimulated other mainline denominations to attempt a similar work. None of them was prepared to give women the same level of ministerial autonomy, but they did see the value of an organised, and trained, body of female evangelists. British Methodists in particular began to experiment with 'female evangelists' homes' and the office of deaconess.[21]

The Salvation Army's decision to abandon the sacraments rather than impede the ministry of its female officers was an indication of how seriously late nineteenth-century Protestants viewed the issue of ecclesiastical authority. Traditionalists believed that a woman celebrating communion bordered on blasphemy and that women in lay offices represented a serious breach of God's holy order. But attitudes were beginning to change and there was a growing recognition that women could occupy some measure of official church leadership without breaching scriptural proscriptions. British denominations were slow to change. It was not until the 1920s that Anglicans and Methodists first started discussing full ordination. In the United States, similarly, mainline denominations remained largely closed to the discussion of female ordination. Many smaller American denominations, however, instituted full ordination rights during this period, like the Freewill Baptists, the Brethren, the United Brethren and the Church of the Nazarene, while others recognised women as local preachers, elders and deacons. Part of the problem for many denominations was turning local practice into official policy. Translating support for ordination in a single congregation into a denominational practice often proved a step too far. As a result, either women were granted more limited ministerial roles, or else existing practices were left alone. In 1907, for example, Free Methodists, despite a tradition of independent female evangelism, the full support of their founder and twenty years of debate, were still unable to achieve a majority in favour of full ordination. Women were still only allowed to become deacons.[22] The vast majority of Protestant denominations did not institute full ordination of women until the 1950s, 1960s and 1970s.

Throughout the nineteenth-century transatlantic Protestant world, women occupied a surprising degree of public leadership. This activity did not decline over the course of the century, but was subject to a series of 'reinventions'

20 Walker, *Pulling the devil's kingdom down*, pp. 105–19.
21 Holmes, *Religious revivals*, ch. 4; Lenton, '"Labouring for the Lord"'.
22 Dayton and Dayton, '"Your daughters shall prophesy"', pp. 86–8.

that saw it lose ground only to gain it in new and diverse areas. Nor was this activity part of a unidirectional, whiggish progression towards the goal of full ordination. In some circles, formal recognition of women's public activity was easily won, in others impossible to achieve.

What does emerge is that nineteenth-century women who were involved in public ministry had fundamentally similar experiences. Women's leadership roles flourished when denominational hierarchies were weak, when there was a strong emphasis on charismatic leadership that did not view education and ordination as prerequisites to public preaching, when there was a 'low' view of the sacraments, and when growth and expansion, rather than consolidation, were denominational priorities. Such features were particularly evident in new religious movements, and throughout the nineteenth century women found that it was within these groups that their leadership skills were most highly valued. However, as these movements became institutionalised they began to focus on sustaining an existing structure rather than forging a new one. The important roles now, those of minister, trustee and treasurer, were all perceived to be male and women were inexorably squeezed out. Where women achieved the greatest measure of acceptance was in the margins and on the edges of institutional religious movements, in the informal environment of religious enthusiasm where gender was disregarded, and 'spirit-filled' was the only educational requirement for religious leadership.

The nineteenth century, more than any other preceding period, did offer women at least limited access to official ministerial positions. Women did achieve a measure of denominational recognition and a number of exceptional individuals conducted highly public ministerial careers. But this was not always the liberating achievement it has been made out to be. The number of women who took up these positions always represented only a small minority of the total female churchgoing population. Their authority, often only locally valid, was vulnerable to future restrictions. Their activity encountered substantial discrimination, both from the wider public and from within their own denominations. Nineteenth-century female ministers were often relegated to rural or struggling congregations, charges that their male colleagues refused to take. And their right to ordination, once granted, did not mean that negative attitudes to women had changed, or that the denomination was suddenly open to female ministry in general. Female ministers often found that they remained exceptions. They rarely became the rule.

With all of this hostility, or at least ambivalence, towards women's ministry it is surprising that so many women actually chose it as a career. What sustained every female preacher, regardless of her background, denomination or region, was her 'call' to preach. With the knowledge that the Holy Spirit had called them to this work, women were prepared to brave both external opposition and hostility and their own internal feelings of inadequacy. Nineteenth-century women, though, did interpret this call in different ways. For some, their ministry was exercised *in spite of* their gender, or *because* they were weak and not naturally suited to a public role. For others, like Catherine Booth, women had the right to preach *regardless* of their sex, and simply because they were children of God.[23]

Throughout the nineteenth century, male-dominated western Protestantism resisted women's desire to exercise a public ministry. It sought to limit and restrict their roles and to deny them access to full rights as church members, believing not only that such roles would contradict Scripture but also that women might seize denominational control for themselves. Yet, the women who sought these roles consistently viewed their ministry in terms of 'service' and argued that they desired ministerial positions only because they wished to serve their God and His people better. With a conception of public ministry that was based more on 'the possession of rank and authority' and less on the exercise of 'servanthood',[24] women were unlikely to achieve their ambitions. That many of their successors have done so in the twentieth century is a testimony to the persistence, determination and faith of these early female pioneers.

23 Walker, *Pulling the devil's kingdom down*, pp. 22–31.
24 Tucker and Liefeld, *Daughters of the church*, p. 441.

B: New religious Orders for women

SUSAN O'BRIEN

In 1794 19-year-old Marie-Claudine Thévenet accompanied her two brothers as they, and a procession of other young men, made their way to the scrubland of 'Les Brotteaux' in Lyons to be executed by the Revolutionary Tribunal of the French Republic. Her brothers were punished for their part in the city's rebellion against the Republic the previous year, for they and their siblings had been brought up in the committed Catholic household of a wealthy Lyonnais silk merchant that openly opposed the Revolution's anticlericalism and anti-Christianity. For more than twenty years after this life-changing experience Marie-Claudine Thévenet lived at home, following a life of prayer and personal charitable activity that was sufficiently striking to be noticed by others. When, in 1816, she worked with a well-known local priest, Fr Andrew Coindre, to establish a 'Pious Union' that would draw together women like herself to increase their outreach, she took the first step in founding a new order or congregation in the Roman Catholic Church. The Daughters of Jesus and Mary, as it became, began life as a teaching congregation in the archdiocese of Lyons running schools and orphanages, but when another proposal was made in 1841 – this time to work in northern India – it did not hesitate to turn itself into an international missionary congregation. As a consequence of going to India the congregation became more widely known among bishops and priests, leading to requests that it establish houses in Spain (1850), Canada (1855) and England (1860). From Spain the congregation undertook missions to Mexico in 1902, making use of Spanish-speaking sisters, and from Canada it expanded into the United States in 1877, following the French Canadians who were migrating to the north-eastern states in search of work. From England a foundation was made in Ireland in 1912, this time not as a mission but in response to the wishes of the many Irish sisters in the congregation and as a way for the congregation to recruit more for its international work. In the same year, the congregation received Vatican permission for its Indian Affiliated Sisters, a group established in the 1860s and canonically incorporated into the congregation in 1909, to be admitted to permanent vows and religious status. This history, particular and complex in its detail, typified the individual elements that made up the general and larger history of new religious orders in the nineteenth and twentieth centuries.

During the hundred years from the end of the Napoleonic wars to the start of the First World War as many as 400,000 women became religious sisters and nuns.[25] At the beginning of this period there had been around 20,000, but the number multiplied rapidly with each decade. Predominantly western European and North American, they lived and worked on all continents by the end of the century, being present in such jurisdictions as China and India as small groups of missionaries and embryonic indigenous groups, and in others, such as Italy and the United States, in large-scale and deeply embedded organisations. A proportion, certainly no more than 10 per cent overall, were contemplative nuns belonging to the long-established Benedictine, Carmelite, Augustinian and other monastic orders that continued to grow steadily throughout this period and to open daughter houses in new places. The vast majority, however, were religious sisters in one of the hundreds of congregations founded or refounded for the active or apostolic religious life in Europe and the New World after 1800. And whilst almost all of these women were Roman Catholics, for the first time since the Reformation conventual foundations, known as sisterhoods, were also made within the Anglican communion. This widespread movement appeared to occur in several countries spontaneously and in parallel, but closer examination shows the existence of a geographic heartland in France and French-speaking Belgium, out of which it spread and from which leaders in other countries took their models, their inspiration and often their training. Although the movement was more powerful in some places and contexts than others, and continued to owe much to its French origins, it proved highly adaptable to differing political, socio-economic and ecclesiological circumstances.

Serious study of this phenomenon did not get underway until the 1980s, when historians began to recognise its significance.[26] Generally accepted as a major force within the Catholic Revival and in its movement to combat the influences of rationalism and the French Revolution, this resurgence of the female religious life has also been described as the single most important source for the feminisation of the Roman Catholic Church in the nineteenth

---

25 This total has been arrived at by adding together known figures for France, Belgium, Canada, Ireland and the United States, with estimates for Britain, Holland, Germany, Italy, Australia and the British and French dependencies in Africa and Asia. As indicative of the proportion of contemplative nuns, where accurate figures are available, the proportion moved between 6 and 8 per cent in the second half of the century. It has been estimated that about 10,000 women spent some time in an Anglican sisterhood in Britain, but that perhaps 5,000 stayed throughout life.

26 See Langlois, *Le catholicisme au féminine*, the seminal work, and De Maeyer, Leplae and Schmieal (eds.), *Religious institutes in western Europe* for a recent historiographical survey of religious life across western Europe.

century.[27] None of this would have been possible without the leadership, often striking in its spiritual confidence, of the individual women and men who made new foundations. Equally, these leaders were effective because they anticipated and responded to the practical needs of the church authorities, of important political and social elites, and of the Catholic community at large in an era of urbanisation, industrialisation and empire. Historians have concluded that the emerging gender ideology of the nineteenth century with its constructs of female moral superiority and separate feminine and masculine spheres of activity provided a cultural environment in which the new orders were able to flourish. This ideology was not without ambivalence, as the repeated and well-documented conflicts between the leaders of the congregations and clergy over control and authority demonstrate, but overall the movement was accommodated within the prevailing culture. Moreover, apostolic congregations were part of the broader nineteenth-century female movement for charitable and evangelical action that in turn helped to develop a sense of professionalism and autonomy in women, and they contributed to it several specifically Catholic features. Foremost among these, at a spiritual level, was the way that the charism of individual women, such as Julie Billiart, Maddalena de Canossa and Katharine Drexel, was articulated in written constitutions and embodied in the life of the congregations they founded. At the practical and professional level their contribution was a wave of institution-building on an unprecedented scale, with its requirement for leadership, organisation and financial management and the opportunity it provided for large numbers of women from powerless sectors of society to combine the pursuit of their own salvation with an effective and sustained collective agency.

Taken together, these developments created a new era in the overall history of the religious life, just as the monastic and mendicant movements had done in earlier centuries. What was novel in the nineteenth century was not so much the idea and practice of an active religious life for women, for this had been pursued persistently, if with great difficulty, through the centuries.[28] Rather, it was the scale of growth of the religious life, the trends that developed within the church's personnel as a consequence, the emergence of a new model of governance for active women's orders and the expansion in missionary activity by Catholic women that made for a distinctive change. All of these developments were closely linked together, but it has been argued that the

---

27 Gibson, *A social history*; McMillan, *France and women*; Magray, *Transforming power*; Wynants, 'Les religieuses de vie active'.
28 Harline, 'Actives and contemplatives' and Rapley, *Les dévotes*.

innovation in governance was a major stimulus to the rest: it was certainly a genuine departure from what had been permitted previously.

Until the nineteenth century, active communities for women in the Roman Catholic Church had been approved within certain constraints. They could either renounce any claim to the canonical (and social) status of religious and be recognised as lay institutes where women took simple annual vows – as had the many *filles séculières* and *sœurs de charité* which developed in France during the seventeenth and eighteenth centuries. In this case they were free to be centrally organised under a superior general like the Daughters of Charity under the general of the Vincentian Fathers. Or, following an important ruling made by Pope Benedict XIV in 1749 concerning the Institute of the Blessed Virgin Mary, they could be recognised as a religious institute with permanent simple vows, but with approval to operate only under obedience to a diocesan bishop, not a superior general. When, for the first time, official approbation was given to female religious institutes governed by an elected superior general with direct responsibility to the Vatican, an historic Gordian knot had been cut. The creation of such pontifical institutes meant that women could lead transnational missionary organisations under the auspices of the Vatican and that members had the recognition and security of religious status through permanent simple vows. By no means all new congregations were of this centralised international type, as can be seen from the proliferation of new diocesan congregations sponsored by bishops that occurred in the nineteenth century, the refounding and revitalisation of the Daughters of Charity as an international lay institute after the Revolution, and the impressive expansion of the Irish Mercy order via the founding of autonomous houses with no central government. However, the trend was increasingly towards the new type of congregation – and with good reason. Its significance for the position, authority, missionary freedom, unity and growth of women's active congregations should not be underestimated, as it was not by Sophie Barat, founder of the Religious of the Society of the Sacred Heart in France, when she explained to Pope Leo XII why she was requesting pontifical status: 'The Society desires to spread devotion to the Sacred Heart over the whole earth and to set everyone on fire with divine love', she wrote. 'But since our Institute embraces various countries where our Society can do good, it is indispensable that we have a uniform rule in the places to which we shall be called, and this uniformity can only result from the will and approbation of your Holiness.' When the approbation was given in 1826, Barat noted that '[it] is of the same nature as that of the Society of Jesus . . . without parallel for nuns without strict enclosure', and she went on to make full use of it, founding houses in twelve countries by her death in 1865.[29] Even so, the degree of change and freedom should be kept in perspective. Barat and many others had to accept a form of semi-enclosure they had not wanted, and the fact that the 'new nuns' mirrored the traditional nun in appearance, in demeanour and in observation of the communal Office says a great deal about the power of conservatism and the need to meet expectations. The latter was also true for the Anglican sisterhoods, although the centrality of the governance issue within Roman Catholicism had no parallel in the Anglican church. Instead, the absence of an established framework or an agreed perspective from the church hierarchy about sisterhoods enabled their founders to appropriate the status of 'ecclesiastical superior' for themselves. Sisterhoods were founded in the spirit of private enterprise, often by upper-class and upper-middle-class women whose class reinforced the independence of their communities and, whilst their relationship with the Church of England was ambivalent and often unhappy, the Anglican movement was not consequently hampered in its development.[30]

In addition to this innovation in governance, the development of religious life in the nineteenth century saw the emergence of several trends that proved to be long-lasting. First, as we have seen, the active rather than the contemplative life became the norm for female religious. It was soon reflected in everyday parlance about 'nuns', and their canonical status as religious was finally confirmed by the promulgation of *Conditio a Christo* in 1900. Second, in place of the practice whereby new groups affiliated themselves to existing traditions or even the amalgamation of kindred initiatives, there was a marked trend for the multiplication and proliferation of fresh foundations. The highest number is known to have been made in France, with more than 200 new or refounded congregations being well established by 1880, but there were large numbers of new foundations elsewhere. The United States saw the creation of almost eighty between 1800 and 1900, in Italy the figure for the same period was 183, and in the Quebec province of Canada alone twenty-six foundations were made between 1837 and 1914. The Church of England, too, experienced this proliferation, with the establishment of ninety separate sisterhoods in the fifty years following 1845. Although the separate foundations had much in common one with another, including the influence of an Ignatian approach to religious life and a model of organisation drawn from France, they remained as hundreds of distinct organisations with specific histories and characteristics. Third, their growth was on such a scale that in many countries the gender balance of the church's *virtuosi* (its professionals) shifted from men to women for

29 Williams, *Society of the Sacred Heart*, pp. 50–1.
30 Mumm, *Stolen daughters*, ch. 5.

the first time, with more women living under vows than the combined totals of priests, monks, friars and brothers. In Ireland, for example, by 1900 women religious comprised 64 per cent of the church's personnel, a pattern repeated in the very different setting of Australia where by 1888 there were around 1,000 sisters but fewer than half that number of priests, brothers and male religious combined.[31] Fourth, as part of its growth the religious life for women underwent a striking degree of democratisation. The new congregations, like the *sœurs de charité* before them, increased the opportunities for women from the lower classes – peasant and working-class women – to enter religious life. In doing so they changed the traditional social profile of women religious. Indeed, working-class and peasant women were themselves founders of new Roman Catholic congregations. As many as one third of French foundations, for example, were made by women from the peasant and lower classes, a phenomenon that was not unique to that country.[32] Finally, the teaching apostolate rapidly outstripped all the other apostolates of the congregations combined, so that the modern period has sometimes been known as the era of the teaching congregations.[33]

By the end of the nineteenth century the social agency of religious sisters was highly visible. The new congregations between them ran or provided staffing for a wide range of institutions, many within the Catholic sub-culture itself, some for the wider community and a growing number within a missionary setting. Across every country where sisters were active the same mix of works in education, health care and social work – with differing emphases and local variations in type – was to be found. Very often congregations specialised in one activity, but rarely to the exclusion of all others. Education embraced not only state elementary schools, and private day and boarding schools, but also special needs, industrial and craft schools, and teacher education colleges. The expansion of elementary education, whether secular as in France, parochial as in the United States, or a blend of state-funded denominational schools as in Ireland, Australia, England and Wales, created a massive demand for teaching sisters. Even before elementary education became compulsory across western societies, Roman Catholic hierarchies gave the highest priority to the creation of a separate Catholic schooling system, an aspiration that could only be

31 Women religious comprised 58 per cent of French church personnel in 1878; in Belgium in 1900 there were some 31,000 women religious and some 6,000 priests, regular and secular; in the United States by 1900, 40,000 women religious and about 10,000 diocesan priests.
32 Langlois, *Le catholicisme au féminine*, pp. 273 and 611–25; O'Brien, 'Religious life for women', pp. 115–18.
33 Wittberg, *The rise and decline of Catholic religious orders*.

realised in the first instance through the support of the congregations, with their low-cost labour and high levels of commitment. The spread of some congregations seems literally like wildfire as groups of two or three sisters were sent by the mother house to set themselves up in small convents and teach in local elementary schools. The Sister Servants of the Immaculate Heart of Mary, an American congregation founded in Michigan in 1845, for example, had sisters teaching in more than a hundred schools across three dioceses by 1914, a pattern that was matched by other congregations in France, Ireland, Belgium, Italy, England and Holland in the middle decades of the century. An involvement in teacher education followed on quite naturally, with congregations such as the German School Sisters of Notre Dame, the French La Sainte Union sisters and the Belgian Sisters of Notre Dame de Namur becoming prominent in teacher training in several countries and playing an important part in the development of new pedagogic methods. Through this work sisters influenced large numbers of Catholic young women who were trained and formed by them, a proportion of whom entered the religious life, and others of whom remained close to the sisters and convent culture when they married and had families. Colleges were particularly significant in the development of the professional life of sisters themselves because of the government accreditation and inspection that was required. Building on their strengths in teacher education, several orders moved into providing more broadly based higher education for degrees, such as Trinity College, Washington, opened by Notre Dame de Namur in 1900, and the affiliation by the same order in England to the newly chartered University of Liverpool in 1903.

In health provision, sisters ran dispensaries, hospitals, nursing and convalescent homes, and mental health institutions. The conduct of nursing sisters, such as the Mercy order, in the American Civil War and the Crimean War was widely reported in the press and had a favourable impact beyond the Catholic community. Likewise Anglican sisters from the All Saints sisterhood and the Nursing Sisters of St John the Divine who provided the nursing staff for several of London's large teaching hospitals, including King's College, Charing Cross and University College Hospitals until the end of the century, won increased respect for sisterhoods in England. One serious limitation on the health service provided by Roman Catholic sisters was the decree from Rome in 1860 that midwifery was incompatible with the vow of chastity, a ruling that they were unable to reverse until 1936. This apart, which was a matter of obedience rather than choice or mission preference, sisters were clearly at the forefront of the development of nursing and allied health care as a semi-professional field for women, at least until the 1880s. Training in health care was of increasing importance to their missionary work in Africa and Asia in the twentieth century, leading to an emphasis on it by existing foundations, and by new congregations founded after 1900. Health services and education were also a part of the evolution of social work as a profession in its own right, and so it is not surprising that the congregations moved easily between these categories of activity. In the field of social care they managed hundreds of homes for children and adults with physical disabilities and for old people; urban hostels for young working women, homes for unmarried pregnant women and those thought to be at risk from predators or their own sexual activity; crèches and temporary or permanent homes for orphans and children unable to be supported by their families. Further activity took place outside specialist institutions in the setting of the parish or in people's own homes, and this too took many different forms. Among the most prominent were the organising of sodalities and gatherings for devotions, sewing circles for church linen and clothes for the needy – all of which involved a social dimension – home nursing, and general home-based support to families affected by illness, death, unemployment or recent childbirth. Many, such as the French Little Sisters of the Assumption and Daughters of Charity of St Vincent de Paul, and the English Little Company of Mary, developed an early form of combined health and social services, providing poor families with a mix of qualified home nursing, health visiting and home help services. The convent too became part of their apostolate since it was in their own space, especially their chapels, that women religious could most readily influence liturgical and devotional practices, including the visual and material culture of Catholicism. Throughout the century congregations adopted new works according to what they and the church hierarchy saw as fruitful.

By 1914 the active congregations were seen as an essential part of the Catholic Church worldwide and had survived the expulsion of religious orders in Germany in the *Kulturkampf* of the 1870s, again in France in 1904 in a massive relocation of sisters to other parts of the world, and in Portugal in 1910. Recruitment of new sisters was very strong, almost systemic, with the peak in membership still lying in the future. On the other hand, the innovative phase lay in the past and the adoption of the New Code of Canon Law (1917) meant much less opportunity for variation and even for the expression of individual charism than previously. There was a more settled expectation at both popular and official levels, and within the congregations themselves, about who and what a religious sister should be, and more centralised control by the church. The uneducated founders, and those founders and founding members with more complex personal histories including marriage, children and conversion, became part of a different past, along with the working-class women who had been made superiors and leaders of mission groups at a young age. The new demands of the twentieth century were already clear: with much greater professionalisation and state regulation in education, health and social care came more inspection, standardisation and cost, and a greater involvement with the state. There was still room for vision, taking risks and new initiatives, but after 1914 these were more often to be found among congregations and sisters who worked with the most socially marginalised, or on the edges of empire.[34]

34 It should be noted that this chapter has employed the terms 'religious order' or 'order' to include religious congregations as well as religious orders in the strict canonical sense. Properly speaking the terms 'religious order' and 'religious congregation' are distinctive in canon law, although not in popular parlance, just as the terms 'nun' and 'sister' are distinctive in canon law but are not commonly distinguished by Catholics or others. Nuns are members of religious orders taking solemn vows and living an enclosed life, sisters are members of the apostolic congregations taking simple vows and whose canonical status as religious was conferred in 1990, as described above.

7

Church architecture and religious art

ANDREW SANDERS

The architecture of two great ecclesiastical monuments of western Christendom can be seen as exemplifying the historicising trend in nineteenth-century art. The first, the Basilica of San Paolo fuori le Mura in Rome, rebuilt from the 1830s onwards, is an expensively confident expression of the last fling of neo-Classicism. The second, Westminster Cathedral in London, completed in 1903 for the newly established Catholic metropolitan diocese, is in the neo-Byzantine style. The architecture of both buildings self-consciously avoids reference to the most commonly employed Christian style of the nineteenth century: the Revived Gothic. Indeed, the two structures are demarcating poles separated by the great mid-century attempt to rival the artistic achievement of the Christian Middle Ages.

The venerable fourth-century Basilica of St Paul was almost entirely destroyed by fire in July 1823. The news of the disaster was kept from the dying Pope Pius VII, who had begun his religious life as a monk in the adjoining monastery, and it was left to his successors, Leo XII, Pius VIII and Gregory XVI, to raise funds for the reconstruction of the church under the Roman architects Pasquale Belli, Pietro Bosio and Giuseppe Camporese. The campaign to rebuild the basilica in a fittingly impressive style was international. Mohammed Ali, the viceroy of Egypt, sent columns of oriental alabaster and Tsar Nicholas I malachite and lapis lazuli for two of its altars. The eastern crossing was reopened for worship in 1840 and the complete church was consecrated by Pope Pius IX in 1854 in the presence of 185 bishops. Despite the grandeur of the eighty granite columns that support its nave, and the richness of its interior, the church has had many detractors. Most mourn the loss of its predecessor and deplore the 'coldness' of its strict neo-classical detail. Augustus Hare even described its exterior as looking 'like a rather ugly railway station'.

The rebuilt San Paolo is a reassertion of the continuity of Christian tradition on the fringes of Catholic Rome. The new cathedral at Westminster, by contrast, asserts an emphatic Catholic presence at the centre of Protestant

England. Catholic dioceses had been re-established in 1850, but the foundation stone of the cathedral of its metropolitan diocese of Westminster was laid only in June 1895. Both the inspirer of the project, Cardinal Vaughan, and the architect John Francis Bentley (1839–1902), were persuaded that the new church should not be in the Gothic style (in order not to replicate Westminster Abbey) or a revived Baroque style (in order not to seem to rival the Anglican St Paul's). Vaughan's insistence that the cathedral should be 'basilican' in form finally determined Bentley's choice of the Byzantine style. To prepare himself for the task, Bentley travelled widely in northern Italy (Milan, Pavia, Lucca, Ravenna and Venice). Vaughan's double insistence on wide-naved basilican form and on an unimpeded view of the sanctuary, and Bentley's first-hand knowledge of Italian sources, rendered the finished building appropriate to Catholic rather than Orthodox worship. The architectural sources for Westminster Cathedral may have been conspicuously un-English, but the building pays homage to the aesthetic principles enunciated by the great English art critic John Ruskin (1819–1900). Ruskin, who so admired the Gothic architecture of Venice in its prime, none the less lovingly described the exotic wonders of San Marco to English readers. Through his advocacy the English had been challenged to understand the effects of colour in architecture. Even in its unfinished state the interior of Westminster Cathedral (which lacks much of its intended mosaic decoration) glows with coloured marble, inlay and sculpture which would have seemed incongruous in a building based on northern European Gothic. The cathedral is a properly 'imperial' structure, possessing an exuberant dignity which testifies to its ancient Mediterranean roots and a noble restraint proper to the heart of the British empire.

Architecture

John Ruskin was the most eloquent and influential apologist for the Gothic Revival. His influence was felt in Europe and America and is discernible in Marcel Proust's translation of *The Bible of Amiens* into French in 1904. Ruskin's advocacy of Gothic forms in both the secular and the religious arts contrasts with the currency of classical, Italianate and, above all, Greek Revival styles in the opening years of the century. This is apparent not only in the reconstruction of San Paolo fuori le Mura in Rome but also in four great publicly financed Catholic churches, each a celebration of restored or reconstituted monarchies. Both San Francesco di Paola in Naples (1817–32, by Pietro Bianchi) and the Gran Madre di Dio in Turin (1818–31, by Ferdinando Bonsignore) were inspired by the Pantheon. Two distinguished Parisian churches, built after the fall of

Napoleon, have more original plans: La Madeleine completed in the form of a Roman temple between 1836 and 1845 by Jean-Jacques Huvé, and the smaller but exquisite Chapelle Expiatoire (1815–26), designed in memory of Louis XVI and Marie Antoinette by Pierre-François-Léonard Fontaine. Two further suburban churches in Paris, both basilican in form, deserve mention: the richly decorated Notre-Dame-de-Lorette (1823–36) was designed by Louis-Hippolyte Lebas while the impressively situated Saint-Vincent-de-Paul, approached by a series of monumental ramps, was begun in 1824 by Jean-Baptiste Lepère but redesigned and completed in the early Christian style in 1848 by his son-in-law Jacques-Ignace Hitorff.

Protestant northern Europe was equally notable for the quality of its state-sponsored churches. The Grand Duchy of Finland had become part of the Russian empire in 1809, and its capital Helsinki was transformed by fine neo-classical public monuments in Senate Square. The sloping square is dominated by the domed, cruciform Lutheran cathedral, which rises above a stately flight of granite steps. The work of the German Johann Carl Ludwig Engel (1778–1840), it was constructed between 1830 and 1851. The principal church in Copenhagen, the Vor Frue Kirke, was handsomely rebuilt from 1811 to 1829 following damage from bombardment by Nelson's navy. The new church, designed by Christian Frederik Hansen (1756–1845), is entered through a severe Doric portico above which rises a boldly unadorned tower. Its interior is notable for its superb coffered barrel vault and its remarkable sculptural decoration, the work of the Rome-based Dane Bertel Thorwaldsen (1770–1844). The nave is lined with statues of the twelve apostles but the altar is dominated by the dignified marble figure of the resurrected Christ, which became a central icon of nineteenth-century art. Thorwaldsen's beautiful font, a shell held by a kneeling angel, was a gift from the artist himself. In Lutheran Prussia the most notable church of the early nineteenth century is the Nikolaikirche in Potsdam, built to the designs of Karl Friedrich Schinkel (1781–1841) between 1830 and 1837. The church was originally intended to be cuboid in form with two low towers at its west end, but these were abandoned and replaced by a high dome rising above the church on a drum of Corinthian columns. The supremely elegant dome, which dominates the town, was completed only in 1849. The church was restored after severe damage in the Second World War.

In Presbyterian Scotland, where prejudice against the 'Catholic' Gothic of the Middle Ages remained strong, three remarkable, and highly original, Classical churches were constructed in Glasgow. All were the work of Alexander 'Greek' Thomson (1817–75). The Caledonia Road Church (1856–7) is now a ruin, while the extraordinary, conically domed Queen's Park United

Presbyterian Church of 1867 was destroyed by bombs in 1943, but the St Vincent Street United Presbyterian Church of 1857 survives intact. It is a structure which refers both to Greek precedent and to the apocalyptic architectural fantasies of the painter John Martin (1789–1854), but behind the design or its tapering sculptural tower and the inventive colour scheme of its altarless interior there also figure highly individual theories which link the mysteries of Solomon's Temple to a Pauline ideal of Christianised Hellenism.

In contrast to the Lutheran north and Presbyterian Scotland, Catholic churches in England and Ireland constructed immediately before or after the Emancipation Act of 1829 tended to be unobtrusive neo-Classical boxes (e.g. St Mary's pro-Cathedral, Dublin, 1815–25, generally accredited to John Sweetman, or St Edmund, Bury St Edmunds, 1837, by Charles Day). The far better endowed Church of England embarked on a campaign of church building following the Church Building Act of 1818 in celebration of the end of the Napoleonic wars and in response to the growing urban population. In London neo-Greek forms predominated (e.g. the 'Waterloo' churches: St Matthew's, Brixton (1822–4, by C. F. Porden), St Mark's, Kennington (1822–4, by D. R. Roper), St Luke's, West Norwood (1822–5, by Francis Bedford) and St John's, Waterloo (1823–4, also by Bedford)). None is particularly distinguished. The finest London church of this period is St Pancras parish church (1819–22), designed by W. and H. W. Inwood with an Ionic portico, a tower derived from the Tower of the Winds in Athens and terracotta caryatids (based on those on the Erechtheion on the Acropolis) supporting projecting side-vestries. At the climax to his scheme for Regent Street, the architect John Nash placed the new church of All Souls, Langham Place (1822–4). The church serves as an eye-catcher and a deft means of linking two major thoroughfares. Its circular Ionic portico and its needle-spire were ridiculed at the time, and the church received sharp criticism in one of the key books of the English Gothic Revival, A. W. N. Pugin's *Contrasts* (1836).

Pugin (1812–52), who converted to Roman Catholicism in 1835, believed that Classical architecture was pagan and that only the Gothic style was appropriate to Christians (though he argued that the term 'Pointed' was preferable to the supposedly pejorative term 'Gothic'). He was the most eloquent polemicist among a growing number of Catholic and Anglican artists who looked back to the Middle Ages when art, and the society which produced it, seemed more ordered and pure. If the Reformation, in its English configuration, stood for an assault on religious art, the Renaissance before it seemed to embody principles contrary to Christian and nationalistic aesthetics. The evolution of English Gothic from the thirteenth century was essentially an expression of the English spirit. But Pugin was not just wedded to the idea of revival. He saw structure as embodying the moral principle that 'there should be no features of a building which are not necessary for convenience, construction, or propriety' and that 'all ornament should consist of enrichment of the essential construction of the building'. Pugin anticipated that the Catholic Church might respond to his calls for a restoration of medieval architectural forms, but he knew that the church was short of funds and that many of its priests hankered after the Classical styles they associated with Rome. Pugin found one rich patron in the Catholic sixteenth earl of Shrewsbury, whose money and encouragement helped to build Pugin's ecclesiastical masterpiece, the church of St Giles, Cheadle, in Staffordshire (1841–6). The church has a superb spire which dominates the surrounding townscape, but its glory is the rich interior glowing with reds, greens and blues and lit by some of the architect's finest stained glass: Pugin actively fostered a new generation of innovative craftsmen working in stone, wood, glass and ceramics. None of Pugin's other churches rivals the splendour of St Giles's. Limited budgets curtailed both decorative experiment and true architectural substance in four of his English Catholic cathedrals built in anticipation of the restoration of the hierarchy: St Chad's, Birmingham (in north Germanic red brick, 1839–41), St Barnabas, Nottingham (1841–4), St Mary's, Newcastle upon Tyne (1842–4) and the largest, St George's, Southwark (1841–8, severely damaged in the Second World War). The construction of his Irish churches, notably St Mary's Cathedral, Killarney (1842–9), also suffered from a lack of funds, here accentuated by the Famine. Pugin's success in proclaiming the potential restoration of the glories of a lost Catholic England went beyond his polemical books (the finest of which is the *Glossary of ecclesiastical ornament and costume* of 1844) and his completed churches. It was particularly evident in the 'Medieval Court' he organised at the Great Exhibition in 1851, a space crammed with examples of his church plate, textiles, sculpture and furniture and dominated by the tabernacle he designed for the church at Ramsgate (now in Southwark Cathedral).

In his autobiography George Gilbert Scott (1811–78) noted that he had been 'awaked' from his 'slumbers by the thunder of Pugin's writings'. Scott, like many of his English contemporaries, had been trained in the use of Classical forms and had merely dabbled with the Gothic. Pugin's 'thunder' alerted a generation to a church architecture drawing directly from medieval forms. This architectural awareness coincided with a new ecclesiology responsive to the latent 'catholicism' of the Anglican liturgy, given prominence by the Oxford

Movement, and fostered by the influential journal *The Ecclesiologist* (1841–68). Although Tractarian principles were generally opposed by senior churchmen, the pervasive culture of Romanticism softened traditional English antipathy to Catholic worship and practice. Hence most churches constructed after the mid-1850s followed the layout of a medieval parish church, with a nave distinguished from a deep chancel. There was a shift from the old Anglican emphasis on a dominant pulpit towards the liturgical significance of the altar. In many churches the revival of church music demanded choir stalls at the east end rather than a western choir-gallery. This new layout is evident in the elaborate reconstruction of Leeds parish church between 1838 and 1841 by the minor architect R. D. Chantrell under the aegis of the vicar, W. F. Hook. To readers of *The Ecclesiologist* the style of the church might have seemed 'impure', but its liturgical ambitions were undoubtedly innovative. Equally creative in its response to Puginian principles was Richard Upjohn's Trinity Church, New York (1839–46), which marked a significant shift in American Gothic Revival design, though with its plaster vault and minimal chancel it remained conservative compared to the churches designed by Upjohn's contemporaries in England. Here the mid-century world of church architecture was to be dominated by three major figures: William Butterfield (1814–1900), George Edmund Street (1824–81) and John Loughborough Pearson (1817–97). Beside their ecclesiastical work, even that of G. G. Scott looks tame and dutifully conventional. Only Scott's finest work, All Souls, Haley Hill, Halifax (1855–9), St Mary's Episcopal Cathedral, Edinburgh (1874–9) and certain of the fittings he designed for the many English medieval cathedrals whose fabric he restored, can stand comparison with the work of his rivals.

The major commissions to Butterfield, Street and Pearson for designs for new churches came from clients sympathetic to the Oxford Movement. Butterfield's early masterpiece, the church of All Saints, Margaret Street (1839–59), was constructed on a cramped site in the West End of London. The church stands to the rear of a tightly designed courtyard containing a rectory and choir school, both contiguous with the church. The site is dominated by a soaring tower crowned by a slate-tiled broach spire which accentuates the horizontal emphasis of the whole composition. What most delights the eye is the strident red brick that Butterfield employed, the surfaces being articulated with stripes, diapers and lozenges of black brick, which originally stood out against the dull and sooty yellow bricks of the surrounding houses. The interior of the church explodes with yet more colour: reds, greens, blues, ochres, blacks and golds. Its materials are suitably rich, but what immediately attracts the visitor is the reredos covering the east wall. All Saints is one of the key buildings of the century, enhancing London with reminiscences of the brick churches of north Germany and the chromatic splendour of Assisi, but habituating them to a Victorian urban context. Butterfield created similarly challenging polychromatic effects in the interiors of his church of All Saints at Babbacombe in Devon (1865–74) and in the chapel of his Keble College at Oxford (1867–83). He designed two further striking London churches, both for Anglo-Catholic worship. St Alban's, Holborn (1856–62) was largely destroyed in the Second World War while the interior of St Augustine's, Queen's Gate, Kensington (1870–7) was whitewashed in the 1920s, its original colour scheme having proved offensive to the refined sensibilities of the period. His compact, but splendidly picturesque Cathedral of the Isles with its adjacent College of the Holy Spirit at Millport, Great Cumbrae, in Scotland (1849–51) stands in contrast to his more restrained design for the Anglican cathedral in Melbourne, Australia (1878–86). Butterfield's delight in the potential of red brick banded with black was shared by George Edmund Street in the design of his fine church of St James-the-Less, Westminster (1859–61). It too is grouped with a school, but its most striking exterior feature is its campanile tower. Although much of the detailing is derived from French and Italian sources, the effect of the church's original interior is of massy richness, enhanced by a remarkable series of fittings (most notably its pulpit and its domed font-cover). Street, the author of *Brick and marble architecture in the Middle Ages* (1855), was determined that the architecture of the Gothic Revival could be invigorated by knowledge of continental, rather than exclusively English, precedent. His taste for Early French Gothic (which the Victorians sometimes called 'muscular') is evident in his fine churches of SS. Philip and James in Oxford (1858–66) and the more compact All Saints, Denstone, in Staffordshire (1860–2). The influence of northern Italian Gothic is clear in the two Anglican churches he designed for Rome, both in the striped or banded manner of Siena Cathedral: All Saints (1882) and the more sumptuous American church of St Paul in the Via Nazionale (1879). The apse of the latter is decorated with a particularly striking mosaic by Edward Burne-Jones. The first major church designed by John Loughborough Pearson, the beautifully proportioned St Peter's, Vauxhall (1859–65), is, like Street's work, based on Early French models. What make it remarkable are its noble stone and brick vault and round apse. Pearson's skill as a designer of vaults marks all of his best churches. St Augustine's, Kilburn (1870–7) is perhaps his finest. Its soaring spire, based on the stone steeples of north-western Normandy, was only completed in 1898, whilst the high interior galleries which rise above the aisles and pierce the buttresses adapt the medieval precedent set by Albi Cathedral in France. Both stone choir screen and chancel are covered in profuse sculptural decoration. Pearson's St Agnes, Sefton Park, Liverpool (1883–5) lacks a tower but has a memorably serene interior. Its ashlar vault is almost playful in its inventive subtlety. Equally distinctive are the tall steeple of St Mary's, South Dalton, Yorkshire (1858–61) and the impressive triple spires of Truro Cathedral (1880–1910). With his son, Frank, Pearson provided the designs for St John's Cathedral, Brisbane, in Australia (from 1887).

The most remarkable nineteenth-century Anglican cathedral outside England is William Burges's St Finn Barre's, Cork, in Ireland (1863–1904). Burges (1827–81) also designed two fine country churches in Yorkshire (Christ-the-Consoler, Skelton-on-Ure, 1870–6 and St Mary's, Studley Royal, 1871–8), but his triple-spired St Finn Barre's is his most ambitious and successful ecclesiastical work. Certain aspects of the Cork cathedral design derive from Burges's success in winning an international competition, with his partner Henry Clutton, to design a new cathedral at Lille in 1856. Although a foundation stone was laid, and prize money was awarded, the cathedral was not finally built to Burges's plans. Burges and Clutton may have been the victims of local chauvinism (being neither French nor Catholic). Certainly in Ireland ecclesiastical commissions were allotted exclusively to Catholic architects. The most talented of these was the Dublin-born James Joseph McCarthy (1817–82), who was responsible for the construction of the new St Patrick's Cathedral in Armagh for the Catholic Primatial See. The building was begun in 1840 as a much-reduced version of York Minster in the English Perpendicular style. Construction was well advanced when McCarthy took over in 1853. He drastically adapted the earlier design, adding spires to the two western towers and crucially changing the style of the building to a severer English Decorated (expressed with a distinctly French accent). McCarthy was also to design Catholic cathedrals for Derry, Monaghan and Thurles, the façade of the last being loosely derived from that of Pisa cathedral. The distinct preference for French over English Gothic precedent, evident in McCarthy's work, determined the architecture of what might be described as the Irish cathedral in exile, the eclectic, twin-towered St Patrick's, New York, designed in 1858 by James Renwick (1818–95). St Patrick's is imposing, and clearly proclaims the Catholic presence in New York, but there is a certain awkwardness about it, in part the consequence of the limited funds available to the architect.

The most distinctive ecclesiastical architect in nineteenth-century America drew his inspiration from Romanesque rather than High Gothic precedent.

Henry Hobson Richardson (1838–86) was a Harvard graduate trained at the Ecole des Beaux-Arts in Paris. His early career was notable for buildings whose plans were not dictated by the demands of an Anglican liturgy: a Baptist Church in Boston (Brattle Square Church, 1871–2) and Unity Church (Unitarian, 1866) and North Congregational Church (1872–3) both at Springfield, Massachussetts. This last structure, an essay in the English Gothic style with neither a chancel nor transepts, has a fine spire. Richardson's reputation as an architectural innovator was established by the construction of the spacious, pyramidically massed Trinity Church, Boston (1874–7). The church, which cost some $800,000, is built of pink granite ashlar trimmed with brownstone and is crowned by an impressive lantern tower which rises over the crossing. Its sumptuous interior is marked by a large semi-circular apse and stained glass windows designed by William Morris, Burne-Jones, Clayton and Bell, and the American artist John La Farge. La Farge also provided the painted decorative scheme for the walls and the handsome double-curved timber roofs.

In France the Gothic Revival was as rooted in precedent, and as fired by Romanticism, as it was in England. It also took on a nationalistic tendency, partly out of concern to proclaim the continuity of modern French Catholicism with that of the Middle Ages. Here the sixteenth-century Reformation was less of an issue than the eighteenth-century Revolution. Nineteenth-century Catholics were readily persuaded that their religious inheritance had been squandered by the aesthetic and philosophical assaults of rationalism and the depredations of the revolutionaries who had profaned churches and demolished the monasteries. In France church building was in part reparation and in part a reassertion of the place of Catholicism at the heart of the nation. The port of Marseilles is, for example, dominated by two substantial churches: the new cathedral of Sainte-Marie-Majeure (1852–93), designed by Léon Vaudoyer (1803–72) and his pupil Henri-Jacques Espérandieu (1829–74), and, on a hill on the other side of the port, Espérandieu's ungainly Notre-Dame-de-la-Garde (1853–64). The spacious cathedral, an admixture of Byzantine, Siennese and Florentine elements, dwarfs its medieval predecessor which was allowed to remain in its shadow.

As in England, the French Gothic Revival went hand-in-hand with a campaign to restore the remaining architectural heritage to its former glory. The most extensive, and prestigious, of such restorations were those of the Sainte-Chapelle in Paris and, from 1844, of the cathedral of Notre-Dame at the hands of the two most prominent and competent Goths in France, Jean-Baptiste-Antoine Lassus (1807–57) and Eugène-Emmanuel Viollet-le-Duc (1814–79). The impressive new chapter house, linked to the south side of the cathedral, is their work. Paris's first full-blown modern Gothic church was, however, Sainte-Clotilde (1846–57), the work of the German architect Franz Christian Gau (1790–1853). The grandly proportioned Sainte-Clotilde is a rich essay in the fourteenth-century style. The design of its high western towers was completed after Gau's death by Théodore Ballu (1817–85). The most distinctive mid-century Gothic churches in France remain those by Lassus, Viollet and their numerous pupils. In 1840 Lassus, who had been responsible for the restoration of Chartres cathedral, took over work on the substantial new church of Saint-Nicholas at Nantes. Here the influence of Chartres is clear, though the façade is dominated by a centrally placed bell-tower surmounted by a complex spire. His church of the Sacré-Cœur at Moulins (1849 onwards) has, like his Paris church of Saint-Jean-Baptiste-de-Belleville (1854–9), a twin-towered façade, though that at Moulins has far finer proportions.

Lassus's colleague and chief collaborator, Viollet-le-Duc, acquired a Europewide reputation through his great scholarly enterprises the *Dictionnaire raisonné de l'architecture française du XIe au XVIe siècle* (1854–68, 1875) and the *Dictionnaire raisonné du mobilier française de l'époque carolingienne à la renaissance* (1858–75). Like Pugin, he was a tireless propagandist. His profusely illustrated volumes became a quarry for generations of architects and designers, both ecclesiastical and secular. The architectural dictionary argued for a rational Gothic style, the construction of a church being defined by a skeletal system of buttresses and flying buttresses which in turn support ribs and vaults. 'All form that is not indicated by structure', Viollet insisted, 'must be repulsed.' One key illustration, in his article on 'The cathedral', defines his 'cathédrale idéale' as being characterised by gabled façades flanked by twin pinnacled flèches to the west, south and north, by a solid central spire rising above the crossing, and by a regular succession of buttresses crowned with protruding gargoyles. The nearest Viollet got to designing a real cathedral was his completion of the thirteenth-century Notre-Dame at Clermont-Ferrand, but his finest non-secular achievement is the church of Saint-Denis-de-l'Estrée, in the Parisian suburb of Saint-Denis (1864–6). The church has a wide nave and is vaulted throughout, though it has lost its original decorative scheme. Amongst the most prominent of Viollet's pupils was Paul Abadie (1812–84). Abadie, who had drastically restored the cathedral of Saint-Front at Périgueux, went on to evolve an eclectic combination of the Romanesque and Byzantine styles which determined the domes of the basilica of the Sacré-Cœur at Montmartre (1876–1919), a distinctive feature of the Paris skyline. The construction of the basilica was intended to be an act of national expiation for the ungodly insurrection of the Communards begun at Montmartre in 1871.

In devoutly Catholic Belgium, with its complex medieval heritage and its tendency to religious conservatism, Pugin's polemics found a ready audience (a French translation of *True principles* was published in Bruges in 1850). When Jean-Baptiste Malou (1806–86) was consecrated bishop of Bruges in 1849 he wore vestments designed by Pugin himself and the bishop later commissioned Pugin's son, Edward, to build him a country retreat. Edward Pugin was also responsible for the design of the manor house at Loppem, built for the prominent van Caloen family, who employed Bishop Malou's nephew, Jean-Baptiste Bethune (1821–94), as an aesthetic adviser and designer of many of the buildings that they patronised. Bethune, a devout disciple of the elder Pugin, exercised a lasting influence on the Gothic Revival in Belgium. Despite a steady campaign of church building and church restoration, Belgium produced no ecclesiastical architect of the first rank. In this it differed from the predominantly Protestant Netherlands. Here, with the advent of full religious toleration in the early nineteenth century and the restoration of the Catholic hierarchy in 1853, the demand for new churches coincided with a mature appreciation of the architectural potential of the revived Gothic style. This appreciation was due to the influence of Pugin and, supremely, of Viollet-le-Duc and it fostered the emergence of a highly original Catholic architect, Petrus (Pierre) Josephus Hubertus Cuijpers (1827–1921). Cuijpers had trained in Antwerp and moved his practice to Amsterdam from his native Roermond in 1865. Like his French counterparts, his early parish churches are often built on a 'cathedralesque' principle (notably the twin-towered St Catherine, Eindhoven, 1859–67, and the now-demolished St Willibrordus-buiten-de-Veste, Amsterdam, 1854–66). The interior of St Catherine's is remarkable for its startling polychromy, though as his career developed Cuijpers's use of coloured brick and tile became both more subdued and more subtle in its effect. He also moved away from the conventional 'cathédrale idéale' plan towards an experiment with central planning. The great church of the Sacred Heart (the 'Vondelkerk') in Amsterdam (1870; now secularised) boldly combines a basilican nave with an octagonal crossing. Its interior is remarkable for the use of banded bricks of differing sizes and textures. His larger Amsterdam church, the Maria Magdalenakerk in the Zaanstraat of 1887, has a brick-vaulted chancel with a wooden vault over its taller nave. Cuijpers's son, Joseph (1861–1949), was responsible for the remarkably eclectic Catholic cathedral of St Bavo in Haarlem (1895–1930), a building which mixes elements of the Gothic, Romanesque and Moorish with an entertaining dash of art nouveau.

In 1872 P. J. H. Cuijpers was appointed architect to the German cathedral of Mainz. Here he rebuilt the eastern tower, replacing an earlier cast-iron Gothic-style dome with a neo-Romanesque octagon and spire. The restoration of Mainz was part of a sequence of German restorations in which Catholics attempted to outbuild and outclass Protestants. The greatest architectural challenge of the period, the completion of the medieval Catholic cathedral at Cologne (1842–80), was rivalled by the construction of the massive western spire of the Protestant minster at Ulm (1843–90), both projects being based on original elevations. After the predominantly Catholic Rhineland had been incorporated into Protestant Prussia in 1815 a struggle developed between representatives of both faiths to claim the prestige of finishing the cathedral at Cologne. The attempt by the Prussian state to take over responsibility for the project was effectively thwarted by the propagandist efforts of a Catholic lawyer, August Reichensperger (1808–95). Both sides regarded the building campaign as an assertion of Germanic nationhood, but for Reichensperger it was also an attempt to claim the Gothic style as exclusively Catholic. As he outlined in his study *Die christlich-germanische Baukunst und ihr Verhältnis zur Gegenwart* (1845), the Gothic style represented the spirit of freedom and independence from the classical ideal of beauty which he associated with Prussian rationalism and Protestant rigidity. Although aware of the French sources for the original design of Cologne cathedral, Reichensperger still regarded it as the key *German* building and successfully raised funds for its construction throughout the still disunited Germany rather than exclusively within Prussia. It was the largest construction project of its type in Europe and was the spur for a series of related, if less ambitious, projects in Catholic Germany and in the Austrian empire (the towers of the cathedral at Regensburg were finished in 1869; the medieval cathedral at Prague was completed in 1892; that at Olomouc was reconstructed between 1883 and 1890, while the cathedral at Brno had its flanking towers rebuilt in 1906; St Matthias, the 'Coronation Church' in Budapest, was transformed by Frigyes Schulek from 1874 to 1896). Perhaps the most significant of the large-scale new Catholic churches is the impressive Cathedral of the Immaculate Conception at Linz (1862–1924) designed by Vincenz Statz (1819–98), the diocesan architect who had worked on the designs for Cologne. The earlier Votivkirche on the Ringstrasse at Vienna (1857–79), designed by Heinrich von Ferstel (1828–83), is a twin-towered essay in the thirteenth-century French manner built to commemorate the Emperor Franz Joseph's survival of an assassination attempt. The construction of the Votivkirche did not please Reichensperger, who, following the principles laid down by Pugin and Viollet, held that its reduced cathedralesque form was inappropriate to a building that was not a cathedral.

In Berlin, after 1870 the capital of the restored German *Reich*, the want of a substantial Lutheran church worthy of the imperial dignity of the Hohenzollerns was keenly felt. A Classical box of a church had been constructed next to the royal palace in 1747–50 which had been adapted and unsuccessfully enhanced according to the designs of Schinkel in 1816–17. A grand new church, now designated a cathedral, was erected in the years 1894–1905 under the direction of Julius Raschdorff (1823–1914). The cathedral, in an ostentateous neo-Renaissance style which complemented the palace, has a prominent central dome flanked by four smaller ones. It was soberly restored after severe bomb damage during the Second World War and remains a significant element in the ravaged townscape of central Berlin. The more subtle Friedrichs-Werderschekirche, also in central Berlin, was completed in 1830 in an austere English Perpendicular Gothic style to the designs of K. F. Schinkel. It long remained a semi-ruin, but was restored as a Schinkel museum in 1987. What is left of the Kaiser-Wilhelm-Gedächtniskirche, built as a memorial to the first kaiser in the years 1891–5, has been retained as a prominent ruin in the Kurfürstendamm. It was built to the designs of Franz Heinrich Schwechten (1841–1924) as an elaborate celebration of the Hohenzollern dynasty and of their defence of Protestantism. It once boasted a prominent west tower in the late Romanesque style which was the highest structure in or near Berlin. Following its partial destruction in 1943, and the division of the capital, the ruins have been turned into a memorial with different connotations from those that first inspired it.

The mid-century idea that the Gothic was a specifically *Christian* style, variously expressed by Pugin in England, Viollet in France and Reichensperger in Germany, became intertwined with the notion that it was also a *national* style evolved in distinctive ways in medieval England, France and the Germanic lands. In the mid-nineteenth century, Gothic became associated not only with neglected national achievement but with the essence of national identity. In later Victorian England church architects such as George Gilbert Scott jun. (1839–97) and George Frederick Bodley (1827–1907) rejected 'muscular' French thirteenth-century models in favour of what was known as 'English Second Pointed' (the 'refined' style of the fourteenth century). It is in this 'national' context that the distinctiveness of the Byzantine Westminster Cathedral should be seen. Early in the century, owing to the persuasive prose of Edward Gibbon's

Decline and fall of the Roman empire (1776–88), the Byzantine achievement in art as much as in politics was generally disparaged. The Gothic Revival had not lost its inventive energy by the 1890s, but the aesthetic climate was more eclectic and open to the idea of an alternative interpretation of Christian architectural history. If the details of Westminster Cathedral are predominantly Mediterranean in inspiration, their translation to a northern European setting is testimony to a more sympathetic reading of a Christian tradition which stretches beyond the confines of the nation-state and the ecclesiology of the western church.

Painting

As with architecture, religious painting remained firmly in the neo-Classical tradition in the early nineteenth century. In Catholic Europe the influence of the academies of Rome remained paramount, giving a conservative artistic focus to the religious revival of the post-Napoleonic years. While Italian religious painters who remained loyal to neo-Classical principles, such as Tommaso Minardi (1787–1871) and Luigi Mussini (1813–88), have largely been wiped from modern histories of art, the work of their French counterparts is often regarded as anomalous. The neglected religious paintings of Jean-Auguste-Dominique Ingres (1780–1867) are a case in point. Ingres, who trained in Italy and had a profound admiration for the work of Raphael, was also influenced by that earlier Rome-based French master, Poussin. These influences are evident in his three major altarpieces: *Christ giving the keys to St Peter*, commissioned for the church of S. Trinità dei Monti in Rome in 1817; *The vow of Louis XIII* (1824) for the cathedral at Montauban (his birthplace); and *The martyrdom of St Symphorian* of 1834 for the cathedral at Autun.

It was, however, in Rome, and among another group of foreign artists, that an artistic revolt against academic convention and neo-Classical forms first became evident. Where German Protestant artists, such as Caspar David Friedrich, found a profound expression of their religious perceptions through landscape, certain of their compatriots, many of them Italian-based Catholics, sought inspiration from artistic sources which pre-dated the High Renaissance. A group of Romantically minded painters formed the 'Lukasbund' (or Guild of St Luke) in Vienna in 1809 under the influence of Wilhelm Wackenroder's *Herzensergiessungen eines kunstliebenden Klosterbrüders*. Wackenroder's short book contained anecdotes from the lives of fifteenth- and sixteenth-century painters and insisted on the essentially spiritual nature of an art that flourished in an age of faith. The group moved to the secularised monastery of S. Isidoro in Rome in 1810, living communally and earning themselves the nickname 'Nazarenes' from their long hair and the eccentric semi-biblical vesture they chose to adopt. Prominent amongst the founders were Franz Pforr (1788–1812) and Johann Friedrich Overbeck (1789–1869). They were later joined by Peter Cornelius (1783–1867), Julius Schnorr von Carolsfeld (1794–1872, who remained a Protestant), Friedrich Olivier (1791–1859), Friedrich Wilhelm Schadow (1788–1862) and Philipp Veit (1793–1877). The early paintings produced by the group were stiffly 'medieval' in character and indicated a rejection of both academic perspective and neo-Classical line. Overbeck's *Entry of Christ into Jerusalem* (1810–24), Cornelius's *Holy Family* (1809–11) and Pforr's *Count Rudolf of Hapsburg and the priest* (1809) are representative. Later explicitly religious works produced in the Rome years include Schadow's *Via crucis* (1817) and *The Holy Family under a portico* (c. 1818) and Schnorr's tender *Annunciation* of 1820. The group's most significant commission came from the Prussian consul in Rome, Salomon Bartholdi, to decorate rooms in his palazzo in the Via Sistina with frescos showing the story of Joseph (the paintings were transferred to Berlin in 1887). The most striking of these are Overbeck's *Joseph sold by his brethren* of 1816–17 and Cornelius's *The reconciliation of Joseph and his brethren* and *Joseph interpreting Pharaoh's dream* (both 1817). A further commission to decorate the Casino Massimo in Rome with scenes from Dante, Tasso and Ariosto (executed 1818–28) saw the gradual dispersal of the Nazarenes as a community. Most returned to Germany. Schnorr and Cornelius settled in Munich and in 1834 Philipp Veit was appointed director of the Art Institute in Frankfurt where he encouraged what he styled 'New German Religious Art'. His most important painting of these years, *Christianity introducing the fine arts to Germany*, remains in Frankfurt. Overbeck, however, kept his base in Rome, beginning work there in 1831 on the picture he considered to be his supreme assertion of faith, *The triumph of religion in the arts*. In his last years he produced drawings for a proposed series of monumental tapestries for Pius IX showing the seven sacraments, which survive in the Vatican Pinacoteca.

The greatest German painter of the early nineteenth century, Caspar David Friedrich (1774–1843), was a Protestant Romantic who offered an expression of his faith through paintings of landscapes permeated by divine light and charged by the presence of overtly Christian symbolism. The scanty remains of the abbey of Eldena, in the suburbs of his native Greifswald, probably inspired the Gothic ruins that appear in his paintings. The pinnacled, mist-swathed churches which loom over such paintings as *The cathedral* (1818), *The cross in the mountains* (1811–12) and *Winter landscape with church* (1811) equally derive from the late medieval monuments of the Baltic coast of Germany. The pictures which place crucifixes against mountain settings (*The cross in the forest*, 1820) or against striking skyscapes (*The cross beside the Baltic*, 1815, and the superb *Morning in the Riesengebirge*, 1810–11) insist most overtly on a Christian reading of landscape. The *Winter landscape* of 1811 shows a man who has thrown away his crutches in the snow as he contemplates the cross. In the distance there rises a church touched by the sun's rays. This Christian context is supremely evident in the so-called 'Teschen Altar' or *The cross in the mountains* (1807–8), which iconises its mountain setting and renders landscape sacred, despite the absence of human figures or any sacred event. Friedrich found patrons in both Protestant and Catholic courts in Germany and in the Russian Orthodox court at St Petersburg.

The early work of the German Nazarene painters had a profound influence on the history of English painting in the nineteenth century. English artists working in Rome expressed a cautious admiration for the novelty of the frescos at the Casa Bartholdi and Casino Massimo, but it was Overbeck who was to benefit from the active promotion of his art by Cardinal Wiseman and who established a mutually sympathetic partnership with the Aberdeen-born painter William Dyce (1806–64). In Rome in 1828 Dyce painted a *Madonna* (now lost) which attracted the attention of German exiles in the city, but his *The dead Christ* (1835) and the later *Madonna* (1838) show most clearly the influence of the work of Raphael and of the Nazarene experiment. The Raphaelesque reference is also evident in his noble fresco *Religion: the vision of Sir Galahad and his companions* (1851) in the Palace of Westminster. Nevertheless, it is Dyce's atmospheric depictions of landscape that give many of his later religious paintings their distinctive quality. This is especially true of *St John leading the Blessed Virgin Mary* (1844–60), of the haunting *Gethsemane* (c. 1853) and of *Christ and the woman of Samaria* (1860). Dyce's dramatic *Joash shooting the arrow of deliverance* (1844), a success when it was shown at the Royal Academy in London, was purchased by a German collector and is now in the Kunsthalle in Hamburg.

The influence of the Nazarenes was also a significant element in the early style of painting adopted by the Pre-Raphaelite Brotherhood. The original Brotherhood, which included the independent-minded young painters Dante Gabriel Rossetti (1828–82), John Everett Millais (1829–96) and William Holman Hunt (1827–1910), set out to present a radical challenge to the received ideas of the Royal Academy and to the excessive contemporary admiration for Raphael and the Bolognese and Roman schools of the seventeenth century. None knew much about the artists who had flourished before the time of Raphael. When the group met in 1848 they drew up a list of those historical 'Immortals' whom they most admired. Most were literary figures, but at the peak of this heroic pyramid stood Jesus. The early exhibited works of the 'P.R.B.' (as they mysteriously signed their paintings) were primarily religious in inspiration. These included Rossetti's *The girlhood of Mary Virgin* (1848–9) and his version of the annunciation *Ecce Ancilla Domini* (1849–50). Chief amongst the models who sat for the figure of the Virgin Mary was Rossetti's sister, the poet Christina. Their pictures were not well received by critics, but the greatest furore connected with the first phase of Pre-Raphaelitism arose when Millais exhibited his *Christ in the carpenter's shop* (1849–50), also known as *Christ in the house of his parents*. The picture's odd perspective, naturalistic setting and use of unidealised models in awkward poses stimulated the fury of critics, among them Charles Dickens. Its symbolic prefigurings of the Passion, however, delighted those sympathetic to the Oxford Movement and Pugin's neo-Gothic propaganda (these loose associations between artistic and religious movements were not lost on the satirical journal *Punch*). Neither Rossetti nor Millais was a particularly devout man and neither pursued the idea of a dedicatedly religious art (though Millais's superbly inventive series of wood-block illustrations for *The parables of our Lord* of 1863 is an exception). Holman Hunt's art retained a more Protestant bias, as in *A converted British family sheltering a Christian missionary from the persecution of the Druids* (1849–50), ironically acquired by one of the prime lay supporters of the Oxford Movement, who later purchased Hunt's symbolic painting of Christ as *The light of the world* (1853–6). This picture was extravagantly praised and painstakingly interpreted by Ruskin, and later assumed quasi-iconic status amongst devout Protestants thanks both to engravings and to the larger version painted by Hunt in 1899 which now hangs in St Paul's Cathedral.

In 1864, after much debate, a scheme of mosaic decoration for the interior of St Paul's Cathedral was initiated. The eight spandrels of the dome were decorated with representations of the four evangelists by George Frederic Watts (1817–1904) and of four major prophets by Alfred Stevens (1817–75). Work was not completed until c. 1891. The stylised, richly toned mosaics of 1892–6 in the cathedral's choir were designed by Sir William Blake Richmond (1842–1921) and are more Byzantine in inspiration, though with art nouveau touches. This belated decoration of St Paul's was rivalled by that of other great European churches in the later nineteenth century, though many of these schemes have been lost to the ravages of war, time and changing fashion. One ambitious scheme of painted murals and mosaics was designed by Cesare Fracassini

(1838–68) and Francesco Grandi (1831–91) for the ancient Basilica of San Lorenzo fuori le Mura in Rome (1869–70). This was severely damaged in the bombardment of 1943 and not restored, though the rich mosaic decoration of the mortuary chapel constructed in 1881 for the remains of Pius IX survives at the east end of the basilica.

8

Musical trends and the western church: a collision of the 'ancient' and 'modern'

JEREMY DIBBLE

To appreciate the part played by church music in the nineteenth century, specifically in continental Europe and Britain, it is vital to acknowledge a number of key issues, most of them inherited from the second half of the eighteenth century. The new secular age, heralded by the philosophical developments of the Enlightenment and major events such as American Independence and the French Revolution, signalled a sea-change in music's function within society, and the church, once the principal patron, and indeed custodian, of musical 'progress', saw its relationship with the art and its diverse profession decline as other musical genres became the foci for creativity and ambition. The opera house replaced the church as the 'cathedral' of the bourgeoisie, while the concert hall became the home of the new cultural intelligentsia and *cognoscenti* as instrumental music assumed a supremacy over vocal. As Julian Rushton has pointed out, 'churches were themselves partly responsible for the fact that their liturgies were no longer the natural home of advanced musical art'.[1]

Eighteenth-century Lutheran music provides an apposite illustration of how the steady growth of pietism and the influence of Calvinism witnessed a decline away from the ornate creations of cantatas, motets and chorale preludes, until, by 1800, the music of German Protestantism consisted of little more than the singing of chorales. No better example of this process can be observed than at Leipzig by the comparison between J. S. Bach's sophisticated sacred works written for his post as cantor at St Thomas's Church, and those of his successor, J. A. Hiller, who wrote little for the liturgy. Though less draconian, the Catholic Church was also driven by a reforming zeal which eschewed the use of instrumental music in the liturgy except as a subordinate role to voices. Such restrictions only served to galvanise a greater polemical distinction between 'old' and 'new' in church music. As evidenced by the works of Mozart, Haydn, Jomelli, Galuppi and Pergolesi, the 'strict' practice of counterpoint,

---

1 Rushton, *Classical music*, p. 118.

demonstrated in fugues and the Palestrina-inspired 'motet' style, stood out in marked contrast to the *style galant* and the imported, florid style of opera. Perhaps the most fertile synthesis of late classical liturgical styles was the symphonic mass – works for four-part choir, orchestra and organ continuo – most prevalent in Catholic Austria and its wealthy monastical tradition. Joseph Haydn's last six masses, composed for the court at Esterházy, are often cited as the most typical examples of the genre, but there was considerable industry throughout the empire with F. X. Brixi in Bohemia (Prague) and K. V. Wratny in Slovenia (Ljubljana and Gorizia) as authors of many works. The greatest and most substantial industry, however, took place in Salzburg where, under the patronage of Archbishop Colloredo, Mozart and Haydn's brother Michael were active. Economic privation, caused by Austria's war with Napoleon, constrained musical activity, and the larger, more ambitious masses (and requiems) were commissioned as *pièces d'occasion*. The tradition of the symphonic mass continued to enjoy popularity into the nineteenth century. Hummel produced an appreciable corpus of masses as concert master to the Esterházy court between 1804 and 1811; Beethoven was commissioned by the Esterházy court to write his Mass in C (1807) and Cherubini's personal fusion of ancient and modern techniques gave rise to two fine requiems, in C minor (1816) and D minor (1836), and several Solemn Masses for the restored Bourbon monarchy in Paris. Even by the middle of the century, Bruckner, then a monastery organist at St Florian, was still wedded to the paradigms of the classical mass, as can be seen in his Requiem (1848–9) and *Missa Solemnis* (1854). With the transformation of Bruckner's style in the late 1860s, his later masses expanded in length and spiritual aspiration to a point where their natural home was the concert hall, a tendency he shared with the earlier conceptions of Beethoven's monumental *Missa Solemnis* (1819–23) and Schubert's late masses in A flat (1819–22) and E flat (1828). Indeed, during the later nineteenth century, the mass and requiem developed into a large-scale choral genre comparable with the oratorio in terms of its dramatic and narrative possibilities, and open to a wide range of heterodox interpretations ranging from those of traditional believers (Dvořák, Liszt, Bruckner, Gounod and Stanford), through the sceptical (Berlioz, Brahms and Fauré), to the outright atheist (Verdi and Delius).

The liberal thought of the Enlightenment and the new aesthetics of Romanticism inevitably provoked debate within the ecclesiastical arena and across denominational barriers, motivated by a desire to restore a sense of traditional religious sentiment, the authority of the church and the imperative of the liturgy, and by a sensibility inspired by the Romantic era itself – a longing for the past and a passion for historicisation. An early eighteenth-century fervour for an 'ideal' church music with little or no instrumental participation gave rise to the establishment of Caecilian-Bündnisse (Cecilian Leagues) in Munich, Passau and Vienna as well as in other cities in Bavaria and Austria, and found endorsement in Pope Benedict XIV's encyclical of 1749, later pronouncements by Leo XII in 1824 and Pius VIII in 1830, and most notably Pope Pius X's *Motu Proprio* in 1903, which, besides giving final enfranchisement to Cecilianism, intended to proscribe perceived aberrant practices in countries such as Italy. The aesthetic principles of a 'true church music' had begun to emerge in the writings of Herder, J. F. Reichardt, K. A. von Mastiaux, Friedrich and August Wilhelm von Schlegel and J. A. P. Schulz, whose ideas chimed with the Fuxian *stile antico* ('the Palestrina style') of composers such as C. P. E. Bach and especially Michael Haydn. The latter, in his sacred works, demonstrated a singular enthusiasm for archaic musical techniques including canon, fugue, imitation, use of cantus firmi, and much effective yet practicably accessible homophonic writing (particularly in the Gradual settings). These works not only made him popular within the nineteenth-century Catholic Church but also ensured his reputation (which, sadly, has not endured to the same extent as his brother's in the province of secular music).

Michael Haydn's sacred output drew the approbation of E. T. A. Hoffmann, whose *Alte und neue Kirchenmusik* (1814) proved to be influential on the Cecilians along with A. F. J. Thibaut's widely read *Über Reinheit der Tonkunst* (1825) and Sailer's *Von dem Bunde der Religion mit der Kunst* (1839). The Cecilian movement sought to re-create a style of sacred music that was equal to the purity, devotion and 'unworldliness' of Palestrina, a composer who enjoyed iconic status among Catholic reformers. Palestrina's pre-eminence was given further impetus by the Italian musicologist and one-time choir member of the papal chapel Giuseppe Baini, who produced an historical study of the composer (1828). In F. S. Kandler's translation, published posthumously and edited by R. G. Kiesewetter (who himself produced a study of the Netherlands composers), Baini's book was widely disseminated and contributed significantly to the extraordinary escalation of Palestrina's standing throughout Europe, not least through the popularity of his *Stabat Mater* and *Missa Papae Marcelli* as concert works. Other important literary and scholarly works followed, with Winterfeld's biography in 1834, Bellerman's theoretical treatise in 1862 and A. W. Ambros's informative commentary in volume IV of his *Geschichte der Musik* (1878); Parry included him in his *Studies of great composers* (1887) and Hans Pfitzner painted a romanticised picture of the composer in his opera, *Palestrina*, of 1915. As for Palestrina's music, Baini's editions (begun in 1841 and completed by Alfieri in 1846) in the *Raccolta di musica sacra* were superseded by a monumental series in thirty-three volumes under the editorial leadership of F. X. Haberl between 1862 and 1903.

As musical Romanticism gathered momentum, so did the fervour and influence of the Cecilian movement which spread outwards from Bavaria. An important symbolic event on Good Friday 1816 was the revival of Gregorio Allegri's setting of Psalm 51 (the *Miserere*) at the service of Tenebrae by Ett and Schmid. Once the exclusive property of the papal choir in Rome, this most famous of penitential works impressed Mozart in 1770 and later both Goethe and Mendelssohn were deeply moved by it. Ett's efforts to revive sacred music of the sixteenth and early seventeenth centuries received the support of King Ludwig I of Bavaria, but much of the significant scholarly work was taken up by Carl Proske at Regensburg. Proske, whose *Denkschrift*, *Die Verbesserung der Domkirchenmusik* of 1829–30 was hugely influential, did much to promote a new musicological rigour as part of the Cecilian ideals. A vast collector of Catholic liturgical works, he began to publish them in the collection *Musica Divina* in 1853; three volumes were published during his lifetime and a fourth posthumously in 1864 (further publications were continued by Franz X. Haberl from 1872). Haberl was even more important in this branch of scholarship. In addition to the work he continued for *Musica Divina* after the death of Proske, he founded a Palestrina society in 1879 and took on the demanding task of editing the complete Palestrina edition begun by Breitkopf and Härtel in 1862. With the musicologist Adolf Sandberger, he worked on the early volumes of the complete edition of Lassus's music, and produced new books of plainchant based on the *Editio Medicaea* of 1614, approved by Rome in 1868. These editions, however, were effectively made redundant when Pius X sanctioned the *Editio Vaticana* (1905–23) prepared by Guéranger, Jausions and Pothier of the Benedictine Abbey at Solesmes. This religious foundation would henceforth find itself at the vanguard of the plainchant revival, with such seminal though controversial publications as Pothier's *Les mélodies grégoriennes* (1880) and *Liber Usualis* (1883).

Haberl was encouraged by Liszt (who remained on the margins of the Cecilian orbit) and Franz X. Witt who, with Michael Haller, composed works for publication (and which came recommended as part of the Cecilian movement's promulgation through their journals). Witt's most important contribution, however, lay in his proselytisation of the Cecilian goals, through his editing of several key Cecilian journals, his seminal publication *Der Zustand der katholischen Kirchenmusik zunächst in Altbayern* (1865), and the founding of the Allgemeiner Deutscher Cäcilienverein in 1868. As a result of the work of Proske, Haberl and Witt, Regensberg became the centre of scholarship, education and *a cappella* performance in the later nineteenth century, and the foundation of the Regensburger Domspatzen (the Regensburg cathedral choir), with boys and men, which was (and remains) well known throughout Catholic Europe.

With the powerful endorsement of successive popes, the Cecilian reforms were also embraced in France (Choron and Niedermeyer), Italy (Basili, Spontini, Baini, Alfieri, Zingarelli and Raimondi), Spain (Eslava), Switzerland (Schubiger) and Belgium (Fétis). In Belgium, the cause of Catholic church music was taken up by the organist, teacher and composer Jaak Nikolaas Lemmens, who, under the auspices of the Belgian bishops, established the Ecole de Musique Religieuse at Mechelen in January 1879. There Lemmens inaugurated the Société de St Grégoire, an organisation devoted to the amelioration of musical standards in church which involved the training of clergy, organists and choirmasters. Lemmens led his new institute until his death in 1881, after which the cause was taken up by his successor and ardent Cecilian, Edgard Tinel. One of the most significant effects of the institute and its training was the number of Flemish organists invited over by the Irish bishops to fill new posts in the cathedrals and larger churches in Ireland, where church building since Emancipation in 1829 had been extremely active. Through the work of Archbishop Cullen, moves to establish a footing for Irish church music were made at the Synod of Thurles in 1850 in which the Cecilian ideals of Palestrina and Gregorian chant were reiterated. Irish church music moved into a higher gear, however, when the German priest and Haberl pupil Heinrich Bewerunge was appointed to the chair of 'Church Chant and Organ' at St Patrick's College, Maynooth in June 1888. Bewerunge, an important scholar and commentator on matters of Catholic church music, proved to be one of the most significant musical forces in Ireland. He was not blind to the merits and cultural contemporaneity of opera in western music, but this admiration was articulated as a means of explicating the need for a distinctive musical voice for the expression of sacred ethics and doctrinal truths.[2] Bewerunge's advocacy of Palestrina and Lassus was later endorsed by Edward Martyn who, emanating from Catholic landed gentry in County Galway, had the means to endow the choir of St Mary's Pro-Cathedral with the princely sum of £10,000 in order to establish its Palestrina Choir. At much the same time, English Catholicism saw the foundation of its own cathedral choir at Westminster Cathedral in 1903 under R. R. Terry. The Westminster choir generated excitement outside Catholic circles for its performances of Palestrina, Victoria and Lassus, which not only spawned a

---

2 See White, *The Keeper's recital*, pp. 74–93.

revival of interest in Britain's Tudor heritage but also encouraged contemporaries such as Stanford, Charles Wood and Holst to write contemporary Latin works in an archaic style.

While many in the Catholic Church welcomed the Cecilians' historicising reforms, there was significant opposition from many quarters to the conservative restraints implied by the movement's search for a 'pure' ecclesiastical style. Moreover, there seemed little scope for aspiring composers to step beyond the limited stylistic parameters laid down by Cecilian values; indeed, much of the original liturgical music written by Cecilian composers was, by dint of its own aesthetic and theological imperatives, artistically modest and often banal. Adherents to the new harmonic progressivism, such as Liszt and Bruckner (and even the more conservative Rheinberger), were scorned for their 'secularism'. Indeed Bruckner's extraordinary corpus of motets, notably 'Ave Maria' (1861), the graduals 'Locus iste' (1869) and 'Christus factus est' (1879), the antiphon 'Ecce sacerdos magnum' (1885) and the Mass in E minor for choir and windband (1866, but revised in 1876 and 1882), shocked many hearers by their shameless chromaticism and tonal dissolution, even though those very constituents of plainchant and strict counterpoint were still active currency in the composer's language. Others such as Johannes Habert spent their lives waging an offensive against the Cecilian proscription of instrumental music in church, and defiantly performed the Viennese symphonic masses in Austrian churches and cathedrals. In Italy, where opera and instrumental *concertato* reigned supreme, congregations were more accustomed to hearing arias, cavatinas, military marches, brilliant organ solos and boisterous choruses. Sacred texts would be adapted to familiar operatic numbers, operatic singers were drafted in to sing for solemn feast days and it was common to hear well-known arias of Rossini, Donizetti, Bellini and Mercadante. It was a stylistic mindset that cut across the growing school of Vatican-based Cecilian musicians such as Baini and Basily, and none other than Spontini, once at the forefront of European opera with works such as *La Vestale* and *Olympie*, denounced the profane demeanour of the music he heard in Italian churches in 1839.[3] The truth was that Italy's churchgoers did not distinguish between the 'sacred' and the 'profane', nor did its foremost composers such as Rossini, who happily juxtaposed 'learned' polyphony and fugues with operatic arias in his *Stabat Mater* (1832, rev. 1841) and *Petite messe solennelle* (1863). Furthermore, Italian church choirs, which suffered a serious decline in numbers during the last third of the nineteenth century, were less well equipped to deal with the

3 Hutchings, *Church music*, pp. 61–2.

demands of polyphony. It was a situation exacerbated by *Motu Proprio* which, in attempting to stem the secular musical practices of many Italian churches, forbade women to sing in church choirs, much to the chagrin of more liberal Catholic organists such as Konrad Swertz (Cork), who resigned and emigrated to the USA in disgust.

In France, church music experienced a major hiatus after the Revolution in 1789. Since 1725, under the aegis of Philidor's *concerts spirituels*, Parisians were familiar with hearing church music performed outside church, and much elaborate church music in the form of the 'grand motet' had become a fashionable feature of concert-going. By the Revolution there is evidence that interest in this genre of sacred music was already in decline, and a more dramatic form of church music, influenced by oratorio, was in the ascendant and led by Jean-François Le Sueur, the director of the choir of Notre-Dame Cathedral between 1786 and 1787. Le Sueur's innovations were censured by the cathedral chapter and he was dismissed, but his appointment later as director of the Tuileries Chapel under Napoleon meant that his ideas could be reintroduced. After the Revolution the choir schools (the *maîtrises*) were abolished and there followed a period of silence for almost twelve years, until the concordat of July 1801, when little or no sacred music was composed or sung publicly. After the signing of the concordat, Napoleon, as first consul, quickly resolved to continue the traditions of former French kings by establishing a chapel in the Tuileries. An admirer of Italian opera, notably the music of Paisiello and Cimarosa, he appointed the Neapolitan composer Paisiello as his new musical director of the chapel. Extremely well paid in his new post and the envy of his jealous French contemporaries, Paisiello composed large quantities of church music for his employer including masses and motets, but failed to succeed at the Grand Opéra, where his own brand of Italian *opera seria* conflicted with the emerging new operatic styles of Méhul, Le Sueur, Cherubini and Spontini. Disenchanted with his artistic predicament in Paris, Paisiello left France in the spring of 1804, having already composed a lavish setting of the Te Deum for Napoleon's coronation in the following December. He was succeeded by Le Sueur, who remained in place until 1830, sharing the position with J. P. E. Martini after the Restoration of the Bourbons in 1816 and with Cherubini after Martini's death in 1816. The Tuileries Chapel was unquestionably the most important focus of French church music for the first thirty years of the nineteenth century, and its surviving payrolls bear witness to an ever-increasing number of singers and instrumentalists and a lavish repertoire of masses, funeral music, settings of the Stabat Mater and other miscellaneous pieces, not only by their directors but also by Plantade, Gossec, Martini, Zingarelli,

Durante, Jomelli, Roze and Persuis.[4] After the 1830 Revolution, however, Le Sueur and Cherubini were made redundant (as were their large retinue of musicians) by the new regime under the 'citizen king', Louis-Philippe, and though Napoleon III revived the Chapelle Royale, the music was never as flamboyant or spectacular.

Many of the large-scale works for Napoleon's chapel and the Chapelle Royale of Louis XVIII and Charles X were composed in an operatic and theatrical style largely devoid of counterpoint and the *style sévère* (the equivalent of the *stile antico*). Of varied quality, it nevertheless stood in stark contrast to the poor state of music in the cathedrals and parishes where little more than plainchant was sung. Some relief came with the restoration of a few *maîtrises* (such as the one at Notre-Dame) which proved to be the only significant agency of musical education during the Monarchy, but the church, impoverished after the Revolution and war, had only meagre funds to support music. Aware of this glaring deficiency, and in contradistinction to the musical trends set by the courts of the head of state, the composer, publisher and teacher Alexandre Choron took up the mantle of promoting sacred works by the Italian masters, and though publication of this music ultimately failed through lack of public subscription, Choron continued to pursue his interest in 'historical' music. After the Restoration he published his *Collection des pièces de musique religieuse qui s'exécutent tous les ans à Rome durant la semaine sainte dans la Chapelle du Souverain Pontife* (1820) which drew broadly on Burney's eponymous collection; it made available a range of Italian *a cappella* works to a French public largely unfamiliar with early church music, a familiarity reinforced by the performance of Renaissance and Baroque music by students of his own school, the Institution Royale de Musique Classique et Religieuse (opened in 1818). With lack of funds, however, Choron's school declined and it was only after public concern was expressed for the low standards of musical attainment in church that the French government agreed financially to support a reopening of the institution in 1853 as the Ecole Niedermeyer, named after its leader Louis Niedermeyer, a Swiss educationist and composer. The mission of Niedermeyer was to revitalise France's atrophying church music tradition and the *maîtrises*. Moreover, in addition to a basic education, pupils at the school were to gain a firm grounding in plainchant and its accompaniment, a broad knowledge of Palestrina, and, at the organ, a thorough understanding of the methods of J. S. Bach. Niedermeyer collaborated with Joseph d'Ortigue in the publication of his *Traité théorique et pratique de l'accompagnement du plainchant* (1857) in

4 See Mongrédien, *French music*, pp. 162–87.

which he attempted to demonstrate how modern harmonic practices and the modality of plainchant could be reconciled; the two men also collaborated in *La Maîtrise*, a periodical devoted to higher standards of musical performance in sacred worship, though it only endured for four years between 1857 and 1861. Though a competent composer himself, Niedermeyer was more influential in his teaching. By all accounts his tolerance of contemporary harmony, with particular emphasis on enharmonic modulation, the use of more distant tonalities, a freer attitude to dissonance and a creative use of modal colour in harmonic progressions, suggests that his methods were more advanced and liberal than those of the Paris Conservatoire. After Niedermeyer's death in 1861, Saint-Saëns was appointed to the school, where he taught until 1865. Though infrequently sung, Saint-Saëns's corpus of sacred works, much of it for organ and a range of soloists, is varied and extensive, added to which his subtle yet conservative harmonic language is well suited to the constraints advocated by Niedermeyer; yet there is also something of the civilised salon in his musical rhetoric and the refined taste of Massenet. Saint-Saëns numbered among his pupils André Messager, Eugène Gigout and Gabriel Fauré, of whom the latter benefited enormously from the atmosphere of the Ecole.[5] Perhaps more than any other composer of his generation, Fauré overtly espoused the modal leanings of his 'harmonic' education which he used with increasing creativity and originality in his output. Although substantially Mendelssohnian in form (a 'song without words') and gesture, the early *Cantique de Jean Racine* Op. 11 of 1865 bears many of the embryonic hallmarks of the composer's intense harmonic vocabulary. The later *Messe basse* (1881, and revised by Fauré in 1906) has more of that individual tonal and modal amalgam so recognisable in the Requiem, first performed at the Madeleine church in 1888 with small orchestra and organ, a boy soprano for the 'Pie Jesu', and the soprano line taken by the children Fauré trained at the church. In this unconventional work (undoubtedly suited best for a liturgical context rather than the concert hall), Fauré was able to merge those distinguishing elements of an 'old' style (in his deployment of modal harmonies and melodic lines) with a 'new' romantic parlance, showing some awareness of Wagner and Liszt, yet also displaying something strikingly modern whether in the stark tritones and austere, imitative counterpoint at the opening of the Offertoire or the chromatic harmonies that accompany quasi-plainchant lines in the Kyrie. Fauré's delicate musical chemistry perfectly embodied the composer's agnostic spirituality which was devoid of all sense of judgement or damnation. A different French sensibility

---

5 Orledge, *Gabriel Fauré*, pp. 6–7.

was manifested in the fifteen masses of Gounod, which reveal a multiplicity of styles, endorsing the purity of Palestrina at one end of the spectrum (such as the *Messe dite de Clovis* of 1895) and the unabashedly emotional and richly operatic at the other (the *Messe solonelle de Sainte Cécile* of 1855). As Alfred Einstein said of the latter: 'This Mass tends towards Catholicism, but it is not itself Catholic. Despite one or another grandiose and orchestrally unified movement like the Credo, it is poetical, subjective, lyric. It is Romanticized church music.'[6] A similar tendency is exhibited in the sacred works of César Franck, Guilmant, Pierné, Widor and the gargantuan *Messe solonelle* of Vierne for choir and two organs written for Saint-Sulpice.

After the decline of Lutheran church music at the end of the eighteenth century, a revival inspired by Frederick William IV of Prussia's unification of the liturgy gave momentum to the churches and cathedrals in Berlin, and provided a creative impetus for composers such as Mendelssohn and musicologists such as J. A. Spitta and R. von Liliencron. As president of the editorial commission of the *Denkmäler deutscher Tonkunst*, Liliencron did much to contribute to the revival of early German masters (notably Senfl, Praetorius, Schütz and Bach), but, unlike the southern German churches, where early music was fulsomely embraced as a liturgical vehicle, the scholarly products of the north Germans were restricted to the more structured liturgies of cathedrals or to the concert halls. Such limitations did not, however, prevent some Palestrina advocates of the 'revival', such as A. E. Grell, from taking a thoroughly dogmatic and didactic position condemning instrumental music as an anathema to church, school and domestic music-making. Mendelssohn's eclectic background, which assimilated Bach and Handel as well as the Classicists, was also open to a Romantic interpretation of Renaissance polyphony and the Gabrielis, a fact evident in his setting of 'Ehre sei Gott in der Höhe', 'Heilig, heilig ist Gott', the brief but sublime 'Kyrie' and the *Sechs Sprüche* Op. 79 written after he was appointed director of Berliner Domchor in 1843. The two psalms Opp. 78 and 91 are altogether more Romantic in deportment, as are the outer sections of the 'Ave Maria' Op. 23 No. 2, though the central section of the latter reveals Mendelssohn's devotion to Bach, one of course reflected in his all-important revival of Bach's *St Matthew Passion* at the Singakademie in 1829. The amalgam of Mendelssohn's Protestant sacred style was later promoted by Grell's pupil, Arnold Mendelssohn, by two Catholics, Herzogenberg and Reger, Kiel and, most substantial of all, Brahms,

---

6 Einstein, *Romantic music*, p. 166.

whose study of Schütz, Gabrieli and Lotti profoundly influenced his *a cappella* motets (notably the *Fest- und Gedenksprüche* Op. 109), while his Lutheran background in the chorale, combined with his worship of Bach, emerged in motets such as *Es is das Heil* Op. 29 No. 1 and *Warum ist das Licht gegeben den Mühseligen* Op. 74 No. 1.

The debate about 'ancient' and 'modern' emerged in the English theological and musical press during the 1830s and 1840s at a time when questions were being posed about the poor standards of choral singing of cathedral foundations, depleted numbers of boys, indisciplined men and restricted repertoire. Various reformist factors effected a transformation over the next thirty years, though it was from the parish and educational establishments, not the cathedral, that these reforms were led. Ecclesiastical reform, spearheaded by the Tractarian revival, ignited a huge improvement in standards of worship and greater emphasis was placed on externals such as choir demeanour, dress and attendance. In fact the greatest enthusiasts for reform came from the Ecclesiologists, who believed in a return to plainchant, the 'motet' style, new works composed in a sixteenth- and seventeenth-century manner and the general avoidance of contemporary church music. Examples of this more polemic reaction could be seen at Margaret Chapel (later All Saints, Margaret Street) and St Mark's College, Chelsea under Thomas Helmore.[7] For most parishes and collegiate institutions with musical aspirations (and latterly cathedrals), there was much less enthusiasm for chant and 'old' music; rather there was a desire to see higher standards in singing, musicianship and the composition of new liturgical works. In this regard, the appointments of E. J. Hopkins at the Temple Church in London and T. A. Walmisley at Trinity College, Cambridge became a focus for change, as did E. G. Monk's choral services at Radley College, and Ouseley's self-financed establishment of St Michael's College, Tenbury, intended as a model of the cathedral ideal, was perhaps the most remarkable. The most strident cry from the cathedral quarter, however, came from S. S. Wesley with his tract *A few words on cathedral music* (1849) written in response to the suggestions by parliament that cathedral choirs should be downgraded even further.

The Cathedrals Commission of 1852 marked a sea-change for cathedral music in England, in that, after much stagnation and indifference, cathedrals became central to diocesan life and, with the impetus provided by many

---

7 See Zon, *The English plainchant revival*, and Adelmann, *The contribution of Cambridge ecclesiologists*.

amateur parish choirs, began to invest in their choirs with a fresh vigour and professional idealism. This is perhaps best signified by the appointment of John Stainer as organist of St Paul's Cathedral in 1872. Building on the reforms already under way, Stainer (once Ouseley's assistant at Tenbury) honed and enlarged the St Paul's choir, ill-disciplined under the regime of his predecessor John Goss, into a well-regimented choral instrument which rapidly became the paradigm for other cathedral institutions. Reforms, under Ouseley and Sterndale Bennett, also took place in the ancient university music degrees whose musical aspirations – ultimately to train cathedral organists – were closely intertwined with the Anglican church.

The genres of cathedral music at the beginning of the nineteenth century – the *verse* anthem (for soloists and chorus), the *full* anthem (for full choir, sometimes with a central verse) and the service (settings of the morning and evening canticles and the ordinary of the mass) – showed little change from those practised in the sixteenth and seventeenth centuries. Moreover the style of early nineteenth-century church music was one largely formed during the Baroque, and this only showed signs of change with Thomas Attwood, a Mozart pupil, and his classical anthems 'Turn thee again' (1817), 'Come, Holy Ghost' (1831) and 'Turn thy face from my sins' (1835), the latter very much influenced by Mozart's 'Ave verum';[8] John Goss's anthems in abridged sonata style, namely the dignified 'If we believe that Jesus died' for Wellington's state funeral (1852) and 'O Saviour of the world' (1869), also reveal classical thinking. The 'learned' contrapuntal style also enjoyed some currency among English ecclesiastical composers of this period, notably William Crotch, Samuel Wesley and Thomas Attwood Walmisley, whose Evening Service in D minor (1855), replete with modal harmony, counterpoint and *cantus firmus* (based on quasi-plainchant), reveals an archaic style popular since the 1830s. Classicism yielded to an appetite for Mendelssohn and Spohr in the music of Samuel Sebastian Wesley, undoubtedly England's most gifted composer of the early Victorian era. Wesley agitated vigorously against those who advocated the appropriateness of an 'old style' in favour of modernism and the full assimilation of Romanticism, a view manifested in his anthems 'Blessed be the God and Father' (1834), 'To my request and earnest cry' (c.1835), 'Let us lift up our heart' (c.1836) and 'Wash me throughly' (1840) as well as the influential Service in E major (1845). Wesley's service in particular articulated a brand of diatonic harmony, a thoroughly modern fusion of sixteenth- and seventeenth-century archaisms, Bachian counterpoint and contemporary dissonance, that would have a

---

8 See Temperley, 'Mozart's influence on English music'.

far-reaching effect on both his contemporaries and his successors. The opening of 'Drop down, ye heavens, from above' (1866) by Stainer shows this harmonic predisposition, but also prevalent in Stainer's style, more typical of the mid-nineteenth century, is a greater sense of theatricality and emotionalism often linked with 'High Victorianism'. This is most characteristically portrayed in his early anthem 'I saw the Lord' (1858), in 'Lead, kindly light' (1868) and in his universally popular setting of Christ's Passion, *The Crucifixion* (1887). In the 1870s a reaction to Stainer's 'emotional' style emerged in the church music of Irish-born and Leipzig-educated Charles Villiers Stanford. Full of Brahms and Schumann, and a fervent believer in the merits of instrumental composition, Stanford brought a symphonic and cyclic dimension to his Morning, Communion and Evening Service in B flat Op. 10 in which choir and organ are fully integrated. The avoidance of cadence, the integral role of key, the sense of continuing variation, and the seminal role of the organ are all features that set it apart from the more episodic settings of Wesley and Stainer. Indeed, the most striking attribute of Stanford's new style is the emphasis placed on musical issues – syntax, continuity and coherence – which take priority over the detail of word illustration and the portrayal of theological meaning. The famous Magnificat, perhaps Stanford's most enduring composition for the church, further extends the analogy of 'dance'. As a scherzo, in a clear-cut ternary design, it provides a thoroughly original interpretation of the 'Song of Mary' with its strong differentiation of two robust thematic ideas. However, the concept of a scherzo formed part of a wider scheme in which the composer attempted to create movements more analogous to those of the symphony. This is evident in the Nunc Dimittis, a 'slow movement' full of pathos, the Te Deum, a 'first movement', and the Jubilate, another dance movement. A further dimension of the service is its series of cyclic references to early Gregorian fragments such as the plainsong intonation of the Ambrosian Te Deum and the Dresden Amen. Use of this material was designed to create a larger sense of cohesion across the entire service and opened up the opportunity of hearing the service as a more expansive symphonic work as part of the Sunday liturgy. More significant still, this scheme enabled Stanford's involuted musical strata of organicism, analogy, and thematic and tonal symbols to form a more complex ecclesiastical *Gesamtkunstwerk* in which elements of time, architectural space, liturgy, music and words coalesced into an artistic entity greater than the sum of its parts. Stanford repeated this with his even more symphonically conceived Evening Service in A Op. 10, written for St Paul's Cathedral in 1880, but his masterpieces are his Service in G Op. 81 (1902), drawing on the German lieder tradition, and the elusively complex Service in C Op. 115 (1909) which transforms the 'High Victorianism' of Stainer and the dissonance of Wesley into a wholly new vision of faith.

Anglicanism led the way in English choir music, but it was tardy in recognising the value of hymnody, though when it did, it fostered arguably the richest and most popular tradition in the world. One important source of hymn-singing was the revival of the extensive Lutheran chorale literature which took place alongside the scholarship of early music throughout northern Germany (notably Wackernagel's *Das deutsche Kirchenlied von der ältesten Zeit bis zu Anfang des 17. Jahrhunderts* of 1864) and Scandinavia. This tradition, vibrant under pietist influence in the eighteenth century, inspired John Wesley and the Methodists in England and (especially) Wales, with the result that dissenting congregations began to reject the established metrical psalmody still practised in Anglican parish churches, and hymns became increasingly popular at Sunday worship and at open-air meetings. As the use of hymnody spread, two of its most seminal exponents, Isaac Watts and Charles Wesley, emerged as pioneers of the literary art. More importantly, John Wesley's *Collection of hymns for the use of people called Methodists* was published as the first denominational hymn book in 1780, indicating how quintessential hymnody had become to Nonconformist worship. In Anglican worship metrical psalmody, invariably sung unaccompanied, dominated parish worship, though 'west gallery music' performed by singers and instrumentalists (where the congregation would turn round to face the choir and musicians at the rear of the church) was also prevalent in some country parishes, especially in the west country; but after a tentative beginning, with localised, parochial hymn publications, a wider range of hymn books for high church and evangelical persuasions began to appear by the 1850s led by J. M. Neale's *The hymnal noted* (1851–4), a collection of translations of Latin hymns with music drawn mainly from plainchant, Edward Mercer's *Church psalter and hymn book* (1854), Edward Bickersteth's *Psalms and hymns based on the Christian Psalmody* (1858) and Catherine Winkworth's *Chorale book of England* (1863, with music edited by Sterndale Bennett). The culmination of this trend, in which there was now a major commercial interest, was *Hymns ancient & modern* (1861) edited by Henry Baker with W. H. Monk as musical editor. This publication, more than any other, sold thousands of copies, was soon expanded in further editions of 1868 and 1875 and helped to promulgate the 'Victorian' hymn (now led by the choir and organ) as a universally admired, fashionable and distinctive artistic genre. Moreover, its success encouraged other denominations to publish their own 'official' hymn books with musical editors of stature to give their publications a sense of prestige, as revealed by the *Church hymns* (1871, edited by Sullivan), the High Anglican *Hymnary*

(1872, edited by Barnby), the *Congregational Church hymnal* (1887, edited by E. J. Hopkins) and the Presbyterian *Church hymnary* (1898, edited by Stainer).[9] It was, however, *Hymns ancient & modern* that had the widest audience, appealing to all branches of the church with its combination of Gregorian melodies, chorales, eighteenth-century psalm tunes and hymns specially written for the collection, though it was the latter that caught the contemporary imagination.

Of the many composers who contributed tunes – Gauntlett, Barnby, S. S. Wesley, Sullivan, Goss, E. J. Hopkins, H. Smart, Stainer and Dykes – it was Dykes above all who seemed to encapsulate the archetypal art form and whose contributions were more abundant than any of his contemporaries. Melodies such as 'Dominus regit me' ('The King of love my shepherd is') were attractive for their yearning contours and sequential phrases, but what truly distinguished Dykes's work was the quality of his harmony, part-writing and bold structure. Dykes had been a keen Cambridge musician, a founder of the University Musical Society, and numbered Walmisley and Ouseley among his friends. His innate musicality drew him to contemporary Romantics such as Mendelssohn, Spohr, Schumann, Chopin and Weber. It was an assimilation of these continentals that found its way into the chromatic emotionalism of tunes such as 'Melita' ('Eternal Father, strong to save'), 'Strength and Stay' ('O strength and stay') and the little known 'Charitas' ('Lord of glory, Who hast bought us'), and it was Dykes's strong bass lines, suspensions, striking modulations, deft tonal recoveries and variation structures in microcosm that raised his art form to a higher level. Perhaps more significantly, Dykes's expressive style of hymn established a norm, which, though it provoked violent reactions in the next generation of hymn book editors (such as Vaughan Williams in the *English hymnal* of 1906) who either bowdlerised their chromaticisms or omitted them altogether, still remains one of the most widely sung examples of the genre.

9 See Bradley, *Abide with me* and Watson, *The English hymn.*

Christianity and literature in English

ANDREW SANDERS

In a letter written the day before he died Charles Dickens insisted that he had 'always striven in [his] writings to express veneration for the life and lessons of Our Saviour'. He felt constrained to add, however, that he had 'never made proclamation of this from the house tops'.[1] Dickens was responding to a correspondent's complaint that he had made a flippant reference to Scripture in a passage in *Edwin Drood*. His forceful response is two-edged. He protests that his religious faith is implicit in what he had written, but that he had been disinclined to express that faith *explicitly*. Not a regular churchgoer, he attended a Unitarian chapel occasionally in the 1840s. Dickens's response can be seen as typical of a great deal of the literature in English produced in the first two-thirds of the nineteenth century. It is a literature that can best be described as Christian in its broad cultural context and Christian in its moral ethos, but rarely is it specifically propagandist in intent, confessional in inspiration or dogmatically defined. This is particularly true of the dominant genre in nineteenth-century literature, the novel. Dickens's description of the implicit Christian moral base of his work could equally be applied to that of Jane Austen, the daughter and sister of clergymen, Charlotte Brontë, the daughter and wife of clergymen, Mrs Gaskell, the wife of a Unitarian minister, and Nathaniel Hawthorne. It could even describe much of the work of that devout agnostic among the mid-Victorian novelists, George Eliot. Explicit religious conviction often fared badly, especially Protestant Nonconformity, which was 'everywhere spoken against' in fiction, nowhere more so than in Dickens, with a figure like Mr Chadband. It should, however, come as no surprise that two great Russian novelists, Tolstoy and Dostoevsky, would admire Dickens as a popular disseminator of the gospel and that Dostoevsky would recognise in Mr Pickwick a type of the 'absolute beauty' he saw as supremely embodied in Christ.

1 Letter to John Makham, 8 June 1870, in G. Storey (ed.), *Letters of Charles Dickens*, vol. XII (Oxford: Clarendon Press, 2002), pp. 547–8.

The century did, however, produce certain prominent propagandist and/or confessional novelists who had a considerable impact on the beliefs of their time. Out of a general unworldliness which encompassed a rigid sabbatarianism, a fear of wasting time on idle pursuits and an unremitting hostility to the theatre, many evangelical Protestants disapproved of fiction altogether at the beginning of the period, apart from explicitly religious tales like those of Miss Hannah More (*Coelebs in search of a wife*, 1809). Novel reading, however, became respectable for all but the strictest sects, and Protestant denominations produced their own favourite novelists, such as the long-lived Methodist ministers Silas and Joseph Hocking, still writing in the 1930s. An 'improving' favourite for Protestant children was Mary Martha Sherwood's *The history of the Fairchild family* (3 parts, 1818–47). Much of this literature was ephemeral, as in the large body of fiction which appeared as serials for Christian family journals, and the innumerable publications of the Religious Tract Society which were given away as Sunday School prizes, and included vast quantities of popular history and science as well as fiction. Christian biography, usually hagiographical, was another important genre, ranging from improving brief lives to solid three-volume works by the wives or children of the subject deceased, encompassing their letters and literary 'remains'. Protestantism also strongly influenced books of adventure with a patriotic dimension for boys, such as those of the Scottish Free Church elder R. M. Ballantyne, author of *The coral island* (1858) and *Martin Rattler* (1858). The righteous anger which inspired Harriet Beecher Stowe's *Uncle Tom's cabin* (1852), which sold some 300,000 copies in its first year of publication, rendered the novel a vital element in the moral campaign against American slavery, a campaign fought with evangelical vigour on both sides of the Atlantic.

The Oxford Movement and the Roman Catholic Revival in England also stimulated a very distinctive kind of propaganda which took the form of historical fiction. The nineteenth-century interest in the Middle Ages was fed by the historical poetry and novels of Sir Walter Scott, himself a Protestant Scottish Episcopalian, and contributed to a popular fascination with the externals of Catholicism which gave it a new cultural cachet, even if this was sometimes accompanied with a frisson of Protestant horror. Certain novels argued for a Catholic view of early Christian history (e.g. Cardinal Nicholas Wiseman's *Fabiola, or the Church of the Catacombs* of 1854, or J. H. Newman's *Callista, a sketch of the third century* of 1855), and others for a liberal Protestant one (e.g. Charles Kingsley's *Hypatia, or New foes with an old face* of 1853).

Two Catholic literary canons, the Irish Patrick Augustine Sheehan, author of *The graves at Kilmorna* (1915), a novel about the Fenian rising of 1867, and the English William Barry, who wrote *The new Antigone* (1887), about Victorian feminism, reflected contemporary political and social concerns in works which won a readership outside their churches. So also did the finest Catholic convert fictional writers, John Oliver Hobbes (Mrs Craigie), author of *Some emotions and a moral* (1891) and *The sinner's comedy* (1892), and R. H. Benson, the son of an archbishop of Canterbury, who wrote the spiritual ghost stories in the collection *The light invisible* (1903) and historical fiction such as *By what authority?* (1904) and *Come rack! Come rope!* (1912). In a class of its own is a work about a fantasy pope, Frederick Rolfe's *Hadrian the Seventh* (1904), Rolfe belonging to the decadent school which produced a number of Catholic converts.

The leading ideas of the Oxford Movement were variously to inform Newman's fictional account of an Oxford conversion to Catholicism in *Loss and gain* of 1848, and the Anglo-Catholic cleric John Mason Neale's oriental novels like *Theodora Phranza* (serialised 1853–4; separately published 1857), implying the kinship between the Church of England and Eastern Orthodoxy. Neale was the translator of Latin medieval and Orthodox hymnody as well as the historian of the Orthodox churches. There was a domestic setting for the refined moral and theological arguments of *The heir of Redclyffe* (1853) and *The daisy chain* (1856) by the loyally Anglican Charlotte Mary Yonge (1823–1901). In contrast to Yonge's work, Anthony Trollope's very secular novels of church life, notably *The warden* (1855) and *Barchester Towers* (1857), offer a gently satirical picture of clergy in a highly politicised and factionalised cathedral city rather than an account of spiritual crises or ethical aspirations. Such dilemmas and aspirations are, however, central to the argument of Thomas Hughes's *Tom Brown's schooldays* (1857), a book written explicitly for boys and shaped by Hughes's own understanding – which was probably a misunderstanding – of the moral principles of his mentor, Thomas Arnold. The immensely popular Canon Frederic William Farrar's *Eric, or Little by little* (1858) tried to claim the school story for Christianity. Indeed school stories in general became a vehicle for the inculcation of the muscular Christianity, rather different from Eric's, of the cold shower and the straight bat. A major Victorian literary influence on twentieth-century Christian writers was the visionary ex-Congregational minister George MacDonald, who in *The princess and the goblin* (1872) and *The princess and Curdie* (1883) could be said to have created the modern genre of fantasy.

Charlotte Brontë's *Jane Eyre* (1847) can be seen as a study of conscience in an explicitly Protestant, Christian context. The late-century agnostic reaction against the explicitly devout fiction of a Newman, a Yonge or a Hughes appears in such novels as William Hale White's *The autobiography of Mark Rutherford* (1881), a tale of de-conversion, Walter Pater's *Marius the Epicurean* (1885), on the aesthetic alternative to Christianity, Mary Ward's *Robert Elsmere* (1888), with its progress to agnosticism, and Thomas Hardy's *Jude the obscure* (1895), attacking what Hardy perceived to be the Christian hypocrisy about marriage.

A good deal of 'canonical' nineteenth-century poetry is more explicitly religious than the mainstream fiction of the period. To strictly orthodox minds the poetry of William Blake (1757–1827) might seem radically individualistic, but the profound spirituality of Blake's work (neglected in its own time) has found many committedly devout admirers since. The eclectic Blake delighted in and redeployed elements of biblical prophecy, the moralising verse of Isaac Watts, the mysticism of Swedenborg and the epic visions of Dante and Milton. Having emerged from the margins, Blake's work now seems central to the English poetic canon. One poem from the *Songs of innocence* has found its way into Anglican hymnals and, in Sir Hubert Parry's setting, the lyric 'Jerusalem' has assumed something of the role of an alternative Christian national anthem for England. Blake's contemporary, William Wordsworth (1770–1850), moved steadily from a broad pantheism to a conventionally Anglican viewpoint. Some ten years after declaring that he 'felt no need of a Redeemer',[2] Wordsworth published the sequence of 102 sonnets which make up his *Ecclesiastical sketches* (1822), and which contain a notably sympathetic verse on the Immaculate Conception of the Virgin. These poems, which trace the history of Christianity in England, are testimony to the poet's faith in a developing, various and continuing Christian presence at the centre of national life. They were to have a considerable influence on Wordsworth's successors. The work of two clergyman poets, Henry Francis Lyte (1793–1847 – the author of 'Abide with me') and John Keble (1792–1866), can be seen to parallel Wordsworth's historical retrospect. Both poets looked back to the tradition of religious verse established in the seventeenth century and notably to the model established by the enduringly popular George Herbert. Keble's much reprinted collection of poems, *The Christian year* (1827), was intended to be a verse companion to the *Book of Common Prayer*, offering meditations for the Sundays and major feast days of the Church of England. It served to stimulate a renewed interest in the calendar and its distinctive seasonal patterning of the year. Keble's essentially placid, but consistently lucid, verse was to find echoes in the work of one minor Tractarian poet, Isaac Williams (1802–65, the author of *The cathedral*

---

2 Recorded in shorthand note in Morley (ed.), *Henry Crabbe Robinson*, vol. 1, p. 87.

of 1838), and of one major one, Christina Rossetti (1830–94). Rossetti, who is perhaps best known as the author of 'In the bleak midwinter', published a wide range of religious writing, in both verse and prose. Although her secular writing has attracted more critical attention, her specifically Christian poetry is marked by a delicacy, an observation and a challenging directness. John Henry Newman's *Dream of Gerontius* (1864), most of which was later set to music by Edward Elgar, contained two hymns which joined the enormous popular canon of Victorian sacred song, 'Firmly I believe and truly' and 'Praise to the Holiest in the height', where they found a place with his youthful hymn of hope and aspiration, 'Lead, kindly light'.

The rhythms of the seasons and the celebration of Christian feasts mark the longest and perhaps the greatest religious poem of the nineteenth century, Alfred Lord Tennyson's *In memoriam AHH* of 1850. Tennyson (1809–92), the son of a Lincolnshire clergyman, was moved to write his great elegy by the premature death in 1833 of his close friend and mentor Arthur Hallam. It grew from a series of lyrics expressive of acute and seemingly inconsolable grief (lyrics which Tennyson characterises as 'The sad mechanic exercise / Like dull narcotics, numbing pain'). These lyrics were gradually subsumed into a larger structure which explores the nature of mourning and which seeks to place Hallam's death in the context of an evolutionary process which links human love and human aspiration to the wonder of the Divine Incarnation and the Resurrection. The poem's opening addresses the 'Strong Son of God, immortal Love'; despite a sceptical aspect to it, reflecting the anxiety about evolution before Darwin, it concludes with a confident reference to a God who is all in all:

> That God, which ever lives and loves,
> One God, one law, one element,
> And one far off event,
> To which the whole creation moves.

The power, the potential for consolation and the ready accessibility of *In memoriam* are witnessed in the fact that it is the poem most commonly quoted on the headstones of those who fell in the First World War.

The most innovative and lexically idiosyncratic religious poet of the English nineteenth century is Gerard Manley Hopkins (1844–89). Hopkins was received into the Roman Catholic Church in 1866 by J. H. Newman and entered the Jesuit novitiate in 1868. His first great poetic achievement, 'The wreck of the Deutschland' (which celebrates the piously heroic death of five Franciscan nuns) was rejected by the Jesuit periodical, *The Month*, in 1875 and it, like the rest of Hopkins's verse, remained unpublished until long after his death. The poems found a ready audience in the years following the Great War, when they seemed more in tune with the spirit of modernism than with the world of Victorian Catholic piety that produced them. Hopkins's feeling both for God and for God in Nature are, however, informed by a strict theology and by an eye trained to observe natural detail by Ruskin. His linguistic daring and his radically distinct use of rhythm variously express an intensity of wonder and an agony of spiritual discomposure which lesser poets might have considered to be inexpressible.

American Christian poetry in the nineteenth century has little to match the doctrinal definition and the European, Catholic passion of Hopkins. If anything, the spirit of that poetry was defined by the individualist spirit of Protestant New England but it was also reflective of the insistently democratic spirit of the new republic and of the wide, wild, seemingly empty landscapes which lay beyond the cities of the eastern seaboard. Romanticism had, however, served to temper the predominantly Unitarian intellectualism of Boston in the 1830s, giving rise to the Transcendental movement which characterises so much of the art of the mid-century. Ralph Waldo Emerson (1803–82) proclaimed Nature 'the incarnation of thought' and declared of himself: 'I am nothing, I see all; the currents of the Universal Being circulate through me; I am part and parcel of God.' The liberal philosopho-theology which asserted that man was 'conscious of a universal soul within or behind his individual life' and which saw natural phenomena as the actuality of God would variously touch writers as diverse as Henry David Thoreau (1817–62), the Quaker John Greenleaf Whittier (1807–92) and that quintessentially gnomic delineator of the scintilla of nature, Emily Dickinson (1830–86).

10

Christian social thought

A: Catholic social teaching

JOHN MOLONY

In the Catholic tradition, the contours of Christian social thought in the nineteenth century were increasingly defined by the content of papal encyclicals. An encyclical is a letter, usually addressed to the Catholic bishops of the world, by which a pope attempts to strengthen the unity of the church in its belief and discipline. He may also apply that belief to the day-to-day affairs of the human race and therefore pronounce on social, economic and political problems. The first pope to revive the ancient practice of issuing encyclicals was Benedict XIV (1740–58), but, before *Rerum Novarum* in 1891, the papal encyclicals contained no social teaching as such.[1] When the popes dealt with matters such as the state and the family, they usually looked to Revelation as their authority and spoke to Catholics, or to transgressors of the rights of the church.

Divine Revelation, formally speaking, is the source from which the church draws its teaching. None the less, for the development of its social teachings, the church increasingly turned to the natural law, sometimes referred to as the moral law, and saw it as a handmaiden of Revelation. The church could do so because it believed that the natural law is written in the human heart by God and can be known by the use of reason. Therefore, when the popes began to teach on the rights of the family, and on the right to possess private property and to association, the basis for the existence of the state, they claimed that reason could deduce such rights from the natural law. This appeal to the natural law is vital to the cogency of the papal encyclicals, because the church argues that its social teachings are valid for everyone, irrespective of belief in Revelation. The popes hoped that anyone of good will, with no knowledge or acceptance of Revelation, would none the less heed, and weigh solemnly,

---

1 For the English text of the encyclicals see Carlen's two volumes, *The papal encyclicals 1740–1878* and *The papal encyclicals 1878–1903*. From Benedict XIV in 1740 to Pius VII in 1800, the popes issued twenty-six encyclicals. During the nineteenth century, 125 were issued.

their social teaching precisely because the truths contained in the encyclicals could be known by human reason.

In the turbulent years that led to the loss of the Papal States, the popes were principally concerned to argue against those whom they regarded as responsible for the woes of the church. Thus Pius VII (1800–23), in his encyclical *Diu Satis* (1800), reminded such transgressors that all attempts made to overthrow the 'House of God' would be in vain.[2] Leo XII (1823–9) argued against religious indifferentism in his *Ubi Primum* (1824) and Pius VIII (1829–30) promised to work against indifferentism in his first encyclical *Traditi Humiliati* (1829).[3] In *Cum Primum* (1832), Gregory XVI (1831–46) came closer to social teaching in insisting on civil obedience to higher authority because all authority comes from God, and with another encyclical, *Mirari Vos* (1832), he set the stage for Pius IX's Syllabus of Errors. Gregory rejected the possibility of gaining salvation 'by the profession of any kind of religion so long as morality is maintained' and condemned those who held themselves free to publish any writing whatsoever. Lamennais's *Paroles d'un croyant* was rejected with fervour in *Singulari Nos* (1834). It was judged as 'small in size', but 'enormous in wickedness' because it threw all human and divine affairs 'into confusion'. Finally, Gregory's *Commissum Divinitatis* (1835), on the church and the state, denied the state's right to meddle in church affairs by attempting to control church teaching, its disciplinary laws, clerical formation and episcopal synods.[4]

In *Qui Pluribus* (1846), Pius IX (1846–78) condemned those who wanted to 'import the doctrine of human progress into the Catholic religion', deplored indifferentism and asserted that 'the unspeakable doctrine of *Communism*' would destroy all law, the structures of government, the possession of private property and, finally, human society itself.[5] In *Quanta Cura* (1864), the pope stated that the source of contemporary errors was the rejection of right reason and of the natural law 'engraved by God in men's hearts'. He repeated the strictures on freedom of conscience in *Mirari Vos*, again condemned both communism and socialism and rejected the proposition that ecclesiastical power is not 'by divine right distinct from, and independent of, the civil power'. A mournful litany called the Syllabus of Errors was attached to *Quanta Cura*. The Syllabus detailed the church's rejection of those elements in modern society it regarded as baneful, principally the proposition that 'Moral laws lack Divine

---

2 Carlen, *The papal encyclicals 1740–1878*, p. 190.
3 *Ibid.*, pp. 201, 222.
4 *Ibid.*, pp. 234, 237–8, 249–50, 254.
5 *Ibid.*, pp. 278, 280. In his *Nostis et Nobiscum* in 1849 Pius IX repeated the condemnation of socialism and communism. See p. 296 in the same volume.

sanction, and there is no need for human laws to conform to the Natural Law or to receive obligatory force from God.' The rejection of the idea that 'the Roman Pontiff can and should reconcile himself and reach agreement with progress, Liberalism and recent departures in civil society' caused widespread unease, then and since, despite the attempt by John Henry Newman and others to explain the temporary and localised nature of the concerns addressed by the Syllabus.[6]

The struggle to unify Italy had been decisive for the papacy. When Leo XIII succeeded Pius IX in 1878 he reluctantly accepted his situation as the 'prisoner in the Vatican' and constantly expressed his disapproval of the loss of his states in Italy, but changed circumstances freed him to use his authority unfettered by temporal affairs. Moreover, the new doctrine of papal infallibility immeasurably increased papal power yet was so overwhelming in its implications that it has been used only once since its definition in 1870. Yet, even without its use, infallibility added an indefinable dimension to papal teaching. When the pope spoke to the bishops and their flocks through an encyclical, both clergy and laity were expected to accept its contents as so weighty that disagreement or rejection bordered on the unthinkable. Once the papacy began to enunciate principles on the social question, the material itself and its diffusion within the church took on a magisterial aspect. Catholic social teaching, rather than individual expressions of social thought, was now possible.

Nevertheless Leo, inheritor of a mindset in which a hierarchical model for church and state was dominant, was as committed as his predecessors to maintaining the *status quo* and he declared in *Diuturnum* (1881) that 'those who refuse honor (*sic*) to rulers refuse it to God', but reaffirmed that the purpose of the state is the good of the people, rather than of its rulers.[7] Soon after his election he issued an encyclical, *Quod Apostolici Muneris* (1878), in which he lumped socialists, communists and nihilists together as striving for 'the overthrow of all civil society' and said that, if these tendencies were not checked, 'the greater portion of the human race will fall into the vile condition of slavery'. He appealed to 'Catholic wisdom, sustained by the precepts of natural and divine law' to lead from this pitfall and added freemasonry as another peril, eventually calling it a 'vile sect' in *Inimica Vis* (1892).[8]

By 1885 Leo had widened his horizons with an encyclical, *Immortale Dei*, on 'The Christian constitution of states' in which he insisted that, while the right

6 For *Quanta Cura* see Carlen, *The papal encyclicals 1740–1878*, pp. 382–3 and for the Syllabus of Errors see Ehler and Morrall (eds.), *Church and state through the centuries*, pp. 281–2.
7 Carlen, *The papal encyclicals 1878–1903*, pp. 52–4.
8 *Ibid.*, pp. 52–4, 11–16, 91–105.

to rule was not connected with any specific form of government, all must rule with 'even-handed justice'. Catholics were exhorted to 'take a role in the conduct of public affairs', but to remember that 'the origin of the public power is to be sought for in God Himself, and not in the multitude'. This stricture was not necessarily anti-democratic: Leo was simply restating the fundamental principle of the divine origin of power, rather than denying its earthly source. In 1890 he returned to these themes with *Sapientiae Christianae* and restated the principle that it was not the province of the church to decide on which is 'the best amongst many diverse forms of government', but that Catholic citizens must love and defend their nation as they do the church. In undertaking these tasks he asked them to avoid two 'criminal excesses' – 'so-called prudence and false courage'. *In Plurimis* (1888) and *Catholicae Ecclesiae* (1890) both insisted that slavery was a system contrary to 'religion and human dignity' as well as wholly opposed to that freedom which was 'originally ordained by God and nature'. Leo rejoiced that the slaves had been set free in Brazil to honour the golden jubilee of his priesthood in 1888 and asked for common action to end slavery in Africa.[9]

Leo's principal encyclical before *Rerum Novarum* (1891) was *Libertas* (1888) which dealt with the nature of human freedom. Although he held that 'natural freedom is the fountainhead from which liberty of any kind whatsoever flows', he denied the alleged principle of liberalism that 'man is the law to himself' and insisted that law, in particular the natural law 'engraved in us all', commands us to do right and avoid sin. To Leo the natural law was the eternal law, and even human law had its origin in God, which meant that civil society had to be deeply rooted in the transcendent. He made one concession to the contemporary scene by saying that freedom of speech and of the press were both valid provided they remained 'true and honourable'.[10]

Meanwhile some laymen and bishops had begun to raise their voices on the problems of the toiling masses. Vast numbers of men, women and children bartered their labour for a wage and toiled in grimy factories, mines and other workplaces. Control of their working conditions was minimal, and the concept of a just wage was a mere ideal. Grinding poverty was everywhere apparent, while the owners of capital accumulated riches, often immense riches based on capital rather than on land. Gradually, workers realised their potential strength when united in organisations of their own, and signs of upheaval increasingly caused alarm among the self-satisfied and comfortable, and in government circles.

9 *Ibid.*, pp. 108–16, 212–19, 298, 160, 232.
10 *Ibid.*, pp. 170–6.

The church had a long tradition to call on regarding the social question that dated back to Aquinas, who had touched on the issue of labour and wages in the thirteenth century. Others followed Aquinas, and in the seventeenth century the Spanish theologians Il Corduba, Vasquez and De Lugo held that a just wage must contain an element that provided for the family of the worker. Despite sporadic attempts to formulate social thought in the church, only in the nineteenth century did a true flowering take place and the foundations of Catholic social teaching were laid. Austria, Germany, France and Belgium were to the forefront, while England, as the anvil on which industrialisation was shaped, made a precious contribution. North America did likewise, but chiefly as a reaction to novel ideas on land ownership.

On a practical level, the Sorbonne university professor and learned historian of the middle ages Frédéric Ozanam left an enduring legacy to the church by taking an 'option' to work among the Parisian poor in the 1830s. His students followed his example and, although Ozanam never developed any cohesive body of social teaching, his work lives on in the St Vincent de Paul Society and he would have accepted all that *Rerum Novarum* contained. Many new communities of nuns in the Catholic world, whether as teachers or nurses, gave their lives for the poor, while Edmund Rice, at Waterford, Ireland, founded the Christian Brothers to educate the male children of those numerous Catholics whose circumstances made their sons' education virtually impossible.

Surprisingly, Marx and Engels had little influence on the development of Catholic thinking on the social question, as did the growth of the early socialist movement, although there were reactions to socialist doctrines and especially to that of inexorable class conflict. Writing in the Vatican, where he had taken refuge from Mussolini, Alcide De Gasperi looked back in 1928 and decided that Vienna was the birthplace of the Catholic social movement and that Baron Karl von Vogelsang was its master. Vogelsang was convinced that the divisions within society could only be solved on a vertical level, which meant that owners and workers must be united in corporations serving their mutual interests and resolving their differences. Furthermore, he was convinced that the vitals of capitalism had to be cut by prohibiting usury. These ideas were rooted in the guilds of the Middle Ages and in the church's insistence until the eighteenth century on the evil of usury. The question of usury, however, was incapable of resurrection without the abolition of capitalism. It was difficult to envisage what would take its place except socialism, which Leo had repeatedly rejected in his previous encyclicals.[11]

11 De Gasperi, *I tempi*, p. 27.

The concept of a corporate society had some appeal to traditionalists, and especially in France where Leon Harmel set up a mixed corporation of owners and workers in the early 1870s. It was an admirable, but paternalistic, venture accepted by the right-wing La Tour du Pin and Albert de Mun, who saw in it the germ of a corporate regime which would become the state. They failed to recognise that a corporate state would be a sham democracy in which a powerful few would suppress deviation in a spurious desire to bring about a harmonious society.[12]

Theoretical considerations aside, it was rather the conditions of the workers witnessed by Catholics such as Franz von Baader, professor of philosophy at Munich from 1826, that inspired some of them to respond. A foundry manager in England, he had observed at close quarters 'the abyss of the physical and moral misery of the Proletariat'. This led him to condemn Manchester *laissez-faire* liberalism and call for the workers' right to form trade unions. Wilhelm Emmanuel von Ketteler, bishop of Mainz since 1850, saw Manchester liberalism as 'a form of State absolutism masquerading under liberal phraseology and administered by a bourgeoisie whose guiding ideal was that of rampant egoism'. Leo looked on Ketteler as his 'great predecessor', and *Rerum Novarum* elaborated on Ketteler's idea that the worker question could only be solved by combining state intervention and workers' associations.[13]

The relationship of the church to the state had long been a vexed question wherever the church had to struggle to maintain its rights in the face of absolutist states. This was especially so in France since the Revolution, and in Germany where Bismarck with his *Kulturkampf* had attempted to Prussianise the church and make it subordinate to his will. Understandably any talk of welcoming, or fostering, state intervention was mistrusted in Catholic circles, arousing anxieties expressed forcibly at the Catholic Congress of Liège in 1890. Conversely, Henry Edward Manning, archbishop of Westminster since 1865, insistently taught that, when masters violated the rights of their workers who were unable to defend themselves, the state had to intervene or there would never be a just outcome for the working classes: he regarded it as self-evident that 'between a capitalist and a working man there can be no true freedom of contract' and that capital would remain invulnerable as long as the worker had to continue to labour at a price decided by the employer. The Congress timidly called for an international convention to limit working hours. Manning called

---

12 Calvez and Perrin, *The church and social justice*, pp. 404–6.
13 Molony, *The worker question*, pp. 18–20.

for the pope to speak, thus echoing the expectation of the Union of Fribourg in 1888, which had said to Leo, 'Everyone is now looking to the Vatican for a word.'[14]

Meanwhile, Vatican circles were agitated about the teachings of the American populist Henry George on the private ownership of land. His ideas had been praised and disseminated by Edward McGlynn, a Roman-trained priest based in New York. McGlynn was more forthright than George and asserted that 'land is legitimately the property of the people in general and its private ownership is contrary to natural justice'. Cardinal Camillo Mazella, having read George's works, recommended that a pontifical document should address the 'censurable teachings' of George and 'others like them'.[15] McGlynn was excommunicated and George's works put on the Index of Prohibited Books, despite the appeal for prudence by Cardinal James Gibbons of Baltimore. In the event, their opposition to land ownership was as much at the basis of the papal teaching on private property as anything that socialists taught.

Listening to the diverse pleas addressed to him, Leo concluded that so pressing a problem required a pithy title, 'The Worker Question', and on 1 May 1891 issued his lapidary encyclical entitled *Rerum Novarum*. The encyclical was composed entirely in the Vatican by Jesuit and Dominican scholars working under the constant supervision of the pope. The principal author, an elderly Jesuit, Matteo Liberatore, had lectured and published in Rome extensively on economics and social principles. *Rerum Novarum* began with the proposition that the 'Worker Question' was of such importance that beside it stood 'no other question of greater moment in the world today' and that it was 'one of great concern to the well-being of the State'.[16]

After eight laborious drafts and various translations from Italian into Latin, the encyclical was published on 15 May 1891. The first sentence, beginning with the words '*Rerum Novarum*', was capable of a grave misunderstanding in translation and was rendered into English as 'the spirit of revolutionary change which has long been disturbing the nations of the world'.[17] Students of the late

---

14 See H. E. Manning, *A pope on capital and labour: the significance of the encyclical Rerum Novarum*, new edn (London: Catholic Truth Society, 1931), pp. 21–37; De Gasperi, *I tempi*, pp. 83–105; Molony, *The worker question*, p. 48.

15 Molony, *The worker question*, pp. 54–8.

16 *Ibid.*, pp. 165, 201. (The author's translation of the encyclical is used here and throughout.) For the drafts of *Rerum Novarum* in Italian and Latin, see Antonazzi, *L'enciclica Rerum Novarum*; Molony, 'The making of *Rerum Novarum*', pp. 27–39.

17 See the sentence in Fremantle (ed.), *The papal encyclicals*, p. 166; Molony, *The worker question*, pp. 101–3.

Roman republic had often come across the words 'rerum novarum cupidine' in the writings of Cicero, Sallust and Caesar, where they invariably meant that the 'mob' was often stirred up by a determination to overthrow the existing order. None of the authors of the encyclical had intended to conjure up visions of ugly mobs rising in revolutionary action, but the widespread impression persisted in hostile circles that *Rerum Novarum* was little more than a diatribe against socialism and communism. A translation closer to the original Italian and the official Latin texts is 'The burning desire for change, which for so long has begun to stir up the masses'.[18]

Like previous popes, Leo rejected socialism as a solution to the ills of the working class, but its condemnation is not the burden of the encyclical, although the inevitability of class conflict is portrayed as 'a concept so contrary to reason and truth that it flies in the face of reality'. Mindful of Henry George, several pages are devoted to defending the right to private property which stands beside an elaborate and careful analysis of the excesses of capitalism summed up in the trenchant words 'a monopoly of production and commerce has fallen into the hands of a small number of tycoons who have laid upon the teeming masses of the labouring poor a yoke little better than that imposed by slavery itself'.[19] Leo objected to the manifold excesses of capitalism rather than to the system itself, but the reader is entitled to wonder what means were available, apart from the trade unions, then in their infancy, to civilise a system that often descended into heartless barbarism.

Throughout the encyclical, the misery of the poor, the disadvantaged and the oppressed is constantly before the reader. In a marked departure from previous popes and well aware that he was speaking to a wider audience, Leo regularly turned to the natural law when he pleaded that justice, combined with the teachings of the New Testament, be taken as the yardstick by which all people of good will must act in the interests of the disadvantaged. The pope and his collaborators were conscious of the need to lay down firm and abiding principles, so that *Rerum Novarum* is a moderate, prudent document revealing a reluctance to relinquish old forms of thought or to launch out too far into uncharted waters. To that end neo-Thomistic thinking, a development that had been led in Rome by Liberatore and greatly favoured by Leo, was easily adapted. Despite its innate caution, the burden of the encyclical demanded innovative teaching and Leo and Liberatore were equal to the task.

18 Molony, *The worker question*, p. 165.
19 *Ibid.*, pp. 174, 166.

The inviolable right to the innate dignity of the individual person was the principle underlying the whole encyclical. In magisterial tones Leo claimed that 'No one may outrage that human dignity which God himself treats *with great reverence*' and insisted that 'man himself can never renounce his right to be treated according to his nature or to surrender himself to any form of slavery of the spirit'.[20] With that principle, the church assumed the mandate to champion the oppressed and reject the pretensions of the oppressor. Perhaps more importantly, it could demand that those subject to oppression were not merely entitled to protest, but were obliged by their very nature to do so. To that extent Leo spoke to, and on behalf of, the entire human race.

As a corollary to the intrinsic rights of the individual, Leo insisted that the family is the basic unit of society. 'It is a great and pernicious error, therefore, to propose that the State can interfere at will in the sanctuary of the family.' He accepted that, in case of dire need or of 'a grave violation of mutual rights' within a family, the public authority should intervene, but he rejected that child care should be taken from parents by the state, because it is '*against natural justice* and destroy[s] the structure of the home'. Leo furthermore insisted that the church had a special obligation to care for those for whom 'God himself has reserved a special love', namely the 'less fortunate and the poor', among whom the pope included the great mass of the workers in their 'depressed state'.[21]

When it came to the central thesis of the worker question, *Rerum Novarum* strongly asserted the right of the worker to humane labour conditions, especially for women and children. Although the encyclical accepted that the workers had a just cause to withdraw their labour when their hours of work were too long, their labour excessive or they judged their wages insufficient, the state should use its authority and influence to 'forestall and prevent' strikes. Liberatore had initially toyed with the possibility of a reversion to some form of guild system, or at least the development of corporate bodies comprising workers and employers. Ultimately an explicit decision was made in favour of trade unions, but the text, whether in Latin or Italian, fell short of using direct terminology. None the less, that trade unions were endorsed gradually becomes clear as the argument develops, and especially when their freedom from state intervention is demanded. It is evident that common sense prevailed in light of the fact that trade unions were already a widely accepted

20 *Ibid.*, p. 189.
21 *Ibid.*, pp. 171–2, 179, 188.

element of working-class organisation, even if individual capitalists and some governments opposed them.[22]

A more serious problem arose with the question of a just wage. In his first draft Liberatore said that it had to be sufficient to meet the simple needs of a worker and his family. The text was reworked by the Dominican theologian Cardinal Zigliara, who refused to go so far because a just wage had to be paid principally for work done, without reference to the social status of the worker. In the event the question remained clouded, because the encyclical also stated that 'a wage ought to be sufficient to support a frugal and well-behaved worker' and further spoke of the worker receiving 'a wage sufficient to support himself and his wife and children in moderate comfort'. After the publication of *Rerum Novarum*, Cardinal Goosens, archbishop of Malines, put the question to Rome as to whether natural justice was violated if an employer did not pay a family wage. The carefully elaborated answer, vetted by Leo, said that in a just wage there was an inherent and exact balance between the wage paid and the work done. This ruled out the inclusion of the family on the grounds of justice, leaving it to the charity of employers, or to state intervention, to include the needs of the family in the wage.[23] Few idealists, and certainly not Liberatore, would have imagined that employers would feel obliged to pay a family wage as a matter of charity.

The elaboration of the concept of social justice was, of necessity, merely foreshadowed in the pages of *Rerum Novarum*, and its further development awaited the twentieth century. Indeed in one country, Australia, the ferment created by the encyclical was already reflected in legislation by 1907 where a 'fair and reasonable' wage was judged to be one that provided for a man, his wife and his children so that they might live in 'a condition of frugal comfort estimated by current human standards'.[24] That the words used by Leo became part of the ethos of some legislators indicates the widespread influence of the encyclical in the decades after its publication. In parts of Europe there was considerable opposition among large industrialists, including Catholics, to those sections of *Rerum Novarum* that set down the proper relations between capital and labour. This does not mean that the encyclical was premature but, given the widespread opposition, the true wonder is that it was not stillborn. Although Leo was not formally its author, *Rerum Novarum* could never have been written and published without his steely determination.

22 *Ibid.*, pp. 175–200.
23 *Ibid.*, pp. 85–7, 192, 117–23.
24 See Rickard, *H. B. Higgins*, pp. 171–5.

The other element of the encyclical that heralded the future development of the relations between the church and the world was the acceptance of the absolute necessity of the direct involvement of the state for any genuine resolution of the worker question. That this acceptance took place in Italy, where the curia still looked out across the Tiber with resentment at the new Italian state, was a further tribute to the leadership of Leo XIII, who saw far beyond the Vatican in his determination to make the voice of the church heard among the world's working masses. It was no longer a question of concentrating on the problems of the old European heartland of the church, but one of also facing the situation in America and Australia. That the masses of Asia and Africa were not addressed in the contemporary context of the worker question is explained by the lack of industrial development among them, as well as their subservience to the colonial powers.

It would be as naive to imagine that Leo and Liberatore were not conscious of the intimate link between free trade unions and a democratic state, as it would be to imagine that they were unaware of the danger to which the church would expose the workers were she to promote the intervention of totalitarian states on their behalf. To this extent it could be said that *Rerum Novarum* speaks of democracies when it speaks of the state. This opening to a positive relationship between the church and the democratic state made possible the use of terminology such as Christian Democracy which, a decade after *Rerum Novarum*, had brought about a strong reaction in parts of Europe. Leo was forced to issue his *Graves de Communi Re* in 1901 in which he said that there were two objections to the use of the title 'Christian Democracy'. It seemed, first, to disparage other methods of political administration and, second, to belittle religion by restricting its scope to the care of the poor. The pope warned that it would be a crime to apply Christian Democracy to political action and asked that it be used 'to mean nothing else than beneficent Christian action in behalf of the people'. Yet he castigated those 'who criticise Christian Democrats [for] wanting to better the lot of the worker' and asserted that such action was 'in keeping with the spirit of the Church'. Finally, he insisted that the rich also have a 'strict duty' to engage in the task of helping the disadvantaged, because 'no one lives only for his personal advantage in a community, he lives for the common good as well'.[25]

By 1919 the way was clear in Italy for a political party imbued with the ideals of *Rerum Novarum*, but its founder, Luigi Sturzo, carefully avoided the title

---

25 *Graves de Communi Re* (1901) in Carlen, *The papal encyclicals 1878–1903*, pp. 480–3.

Christian Democracy and named it the 'Partito Popolare Italiano'.[26] Many whose ideals and impetus were shaped in their youth by *Rerum Novarum* – Alcide De Gasperi, Konrad Adenauer, Robert Schuman, Carlo Sforza and Luigi Einaudi – took part in the making of a new Europe in the twentieth century. Leo's encyclical had become part of the history of modern Europe.

26 See Molony, *The emergence of political Catholicism*, pp. 22–7, 46.

B: The social thought of the Protestant churches

DAVID M. THOMPSON

Any consideration of social thought in the Protestant churches in the nineteenth century immediately raises the question of whose thought is under discussion. The traditional Protestant confessions of faith usually contained some reference to the church's relationship to civil authority, marriage and the obligations of the moral law. But they did not touch on forms of government or questions of poverty. Most Protestant churches did not claim to teach on these matters, unlike the papacy. For established churches there was a question of whether they could take a position different from that of the state, and if so, by what procedure this could be expressed; for non-established churches, whilst it was easier, at least in principle, to challenge positions taken by the civil government, the procedure for doing so still had to be clear. Thus in Great Britain, whilst the various Methodist Conferences had a clear procedure for expressing their mind, they also all had a 'no politics' rule, which was a self-denying ordinance in this area; the Congregational and Baptist Unions, on the other hand, felt freer to pass resolutions on such matters, but they did not bind local congregations. The alternative strategy is to consider the thought of individual theologians or groups within the churches. Here it is easier to find clearly articulated positions; it is more difficult to estimate how representative such views might be of the broader Protestant constituency.

Two issues were inherited from the eighteenth century. The first was the question of slavery, particularly in the United Kingdom. Here evangelical Christians were to the fore in campaigning against the slave trade and later slavery itself. The second was the French Revolution and democracy. Established Protestant churches showed little sympathy for the Revolution, but among Nonconformists there was more support for radical politics. However, once again this was a minority movement rather than formal support. Jabez Bunting's famous remark that 'Methodism is as much opposed to democracy as it is to sin'[27] may not have been typical of many working-class Methodists but it did represent the leadership's view. The new issue in the nineteenth century was industrialisation, and more particularly the question of poverty, although this may be better articulated as a consequence of rapid population growth and urban expansion, which strained traditional structures of workshop labour and poor relief to breaking point.

27 T. P. Bunting and G. S. Rowe, *The life of Jabez Bunting* (London: Longman, 1887), p. 472.

The antislavery issue was important in Britain in a way in which it was not elsewhere in Protestant Europe. It was also important because it involved taking a stand against something not explicitly condemned in Scripture. Later in the century the disputes in the United States over the issue led some Christians to argue that Scripture supported slavery. This did not happen in Britain, but the fact that the antislavery campaign was led by evangelicals – notably William Wilberforce, but also others of the so-called 'Clapham sect' – meant that the appeal to Divine Providence by these Christian campaigners was particularly significant. Legislation to abolish the slave trade in British ships was passed in 1807, and slavery was abolished in the British empire in 1833, news of this reaching Wilberforce a few days before he died. However, the system of indentured labour in the Caribbean which replaced slavery had several problems, and was partly responsible for some of the civil unrest in the 1830s. In South Africa the abolition of slavery was one of the reasons for the Great Trek in 1836, when a number of Boer farmers left the Cape Colony and founded two new states – the Transvaal and the Orange Free State. Britain secured a commitment from the other European powers to abolish the slave trade at the Congress of Vienna in 1815, but slavery was abolished in the French colonies only in 1848 and not in the Dutch colonies until the 1860s.

The democratic implications of the French Revolution were overtaken by the consequences of the French war in Europe which followed in the 1790s. Protestant churches in continental Europe did not hesitate to defend the political independence of the states of which they were a part. Furthermore in so far as the Revolution had moved towards a 'religion of reason' it was understandable that the churches should be concerned about the threat this might pose to Christian faith. Thus the more significant issues surrounding democracy had to be tackled in the period after 1815, when Napoleon had been defeated. The number of German states was reduced from over three hundred to just over thirty; several acquired new liberal constitutions; and new legal arrangements were made for the recognition both of Roman Catholics and of the Reformed (or occasionally Lutherans). Protestant churches found themselves in a new kind of legal world. In Great Britain the Toleration Act of 1812, the legalisation of Unitarianism in 1813, the Repeal of the Test and Corporation Acts in 1828 and Roman Catholic Emancipation in 1829 represented similar developments. The Belgian Revolution of 1830 also marked a significant change for Dutch Protestants: perhaps more than any other event in the century it illustrates a reversal of traditional roles, with Catholics supporting liberalism and Protestants taking a very conservative position.

In Great Britain the bishops in the House of Lords found themselves blamed for the defeat of the first Reform Bill because they were an identifiable group, even though they were no more to blame than any other group of thirty or so opposition peers. There were some hopes that after the 1832 Reform Act was law, the position of the Church of England would be changed; certainly there were significant political demands by Nonconformists, though few were met in full. Only a few British Christians were to be found backing the most radical political demands of the People's Charter, though there were sufficient to form a Christian Chartist movement. Yet even the Primitive Methodist Church, which probably had a higher proportion of working-class members than any other Nonconformist group, applied its 'no politics' rule consistently. The 'Tolpuddle martyrs', six men sentenced to transportation in 1834 for forming a branch of the Grand National Consolidated Trade Union in Dorset, included five Primitive Methodists, three of them local preachers, yet they never received any kind of official church backing for their action. Nevertheless, the secretary of the union, George Romaine, who was not prosecuted, was owner of one of the local chapels and also a local preacher.[28]

The new fact of the nineteenth century was industrialisation, though even in England many places were not significantly affected until after 1850. In particular the increase in the scale of production represented by the change from workshop to factory meant that workers were now selling their labour, rather than finished or semi-finished goods, and with this the balance of economic power shifted to the advantage of the manufacturer. With workers in towns increasingly dependent on wage labour without any agricultural fall-back, the effects of the trade cycle led to sharp movements of wages and periods of unemployment. This changed the nature and extent of poverty. The churches had traditionally been to the fore in providing assistance for the poor, with the parish as the usual unit of support. In the 1820s Thomas Chalmers in Glasgow tried to develop church structures as the primary source of poor relief; this attempt eventually collapsed after the Disruption of 1843 and secular poor relief agencies were established by an Act of 1845. To a large extent these followed the model established in England by the New Poor Law of 1834. Significantly, bishops like J. B. Sumner (bishop of Chester and later archbishop of Canterbury) and C. J. Blomfield (bishop of London) had been members of the Royal Commission on the Poor Law, whose recommendations were embodied in that legislation. Sumner sought to put a more optimistic interpretation upon T. R. Malthus's influential *Essay on population* (1798).

28 Wearmouth, *Methodism and the working-class movements of England*, pp. 217–21.

Alongside these legal structures, which after 1834 were very much intended to be a last resort, the British churches supported a host of charitable activities at a local level to assist those in need. Historically many parish churches had charities for the local poor. The new developments ranged from soup kitchens, and the provision of linen for pregnant women and new mothers, to church schools for the children of the poor. By the mid-century many urban Anglican (particularly evangelical) parishes had a range of such organisations which remained important for the rest of the century. The larger urban Nonconformist churches developed the same pattern, though this was mainly after 1850. The Church of Scotland, the Free Church of Scotland and the United Presbyterian church also had similar structures.

At the Wittenberg church Congress of 1848 Johann Heinrich Wichern (1808–81) from Hamburg declared that the church should be involved in resolving social problems; and he founded the Inner Mission in Germany, which provided many crèches, kindergartens, children's homes, and homes for prostitutes, drunkards, epileptics and the mentally handicapped. Through this movement deaconesses served the church in a variety of ways. A similar movement began in Denmark in September 1853, founded by a small group of laymen, and led by a former smith, Jens Larsen (1804–74), who became a paid missionary. It took off in the 1860s, when the lay majority on the organising committee were replaced by clergy, led by Vilhelm Beck (1829–1901), growing from four missionaries in 1862 to forty-four in 1867, and 158 by the end of the century.[29] In both Germany and Denmark the tension between a relatively conservative revivalist programme and a potentially more radical social policy rapidly became clear.

The standard criticism of such efforts is that they were primarily 'ambulance work'; they left the underlying causes of the social problems untouched. But Christians were aware of the alternative secular socialist solutions put forward by men like Robert Owen in Britain, Louis Blanc in France, or Karl Marx and Friedrich Engels in Germany. In England F. D. Maurice, Charles Kingsley and J. M. Ludlow were the nucleus of a group of 'Christian socialists', who sought to provide an alternative programme to Chartism in 1848. As a result of the work of Ludlow in particular a stimulus was given to co-operative production, and the Friendly Societies Act of 1855 provided the necessary legal basis for such developments in Britain.

In Germany Victor Huber (a university professor in Rostock, Marburg and Berlin and a firm believer in absolute rather than constitutional monarchy) also regarded co-operative organisations for handicrafts, commerce, manufacture,

---

29 Lausten, *A church history of Denmark*, pp. 242ff.

agriculture, buildings loan societies, etc. as the only way to overcome social and economic disaster. His writings were most read in the decade before his death in 1869. Rudolf Todt, minister in Barenthin and Brandenburg until his early death in 1887, published *Radical German socialism and Christian society* in 1877. He examined the work of Lassalle and Marx, concluding that the New Testament endorsed the principles of socialism, but not atheism. Whereas Wichern and Huber had not called for state action, Todt believed that the only remedy for current problems was state intervention.

In England B. F. Westcott (1825–1901), Regius Professor of Divinity at Cambridge from 1870 until he became bishop of Durham in 1889, was particularly influenced by Auguste Comte's positivism. He rejected the atheism but affirmed the social emphasis. From 1884 he was a canon of Westminster, and preached the 'social gospel' instead of a disproportionate emphasis on the individual.[30] In 1889 he became president of the new Christian Social Union (CSU) in the Church of England: other key figures were Charles Gore, a former pupil of Westcott at Harrow, and later bishop of Worcester, Birmingham and Oxford, and Henry Scott Holland. The CSU involved a large number of Anglican clergy. More radical was the Guild of St Matthew, formed in 1883 by Stewart Headlam; it was smaller, with a higher proportion of lay members, and was more ready to identify itself with workers' protest movements, such as the London Match Girls' Strike of 1889.

English Nonconformist attitudes to social questions tended to be dominated by the issue of alcoholic drink. The temperance movement, which effectively meant total abstinence, came to be almost synonymous with English Nonconformity in the second half of the century, even though Jabez Bunting had regarded temperance societies with suspicion, emphasising the importance of using proper wine in the Lord's Supper at the 1841 Wesleyan Conference.[31] The United Kingdom Alliance brought members of many different churches together. However, from the 1860s ministers in London and other large industrial towns developed the same kind of temperance groups within their congregations as the Church of England. They were also prepared to campaign for various kinds of social legislation in parliament. The preoccupation with temperance assisted this, because only by legislation could the availability

---

30 Westcott spent the summer of 1867 studying Comte's *Politique positive*, and his essay 'Aspects of positivism in relation to Christianity', published in the *Contemporary Review* for 1868, was included as an Appendix to the 3rd edition of his *Gospel of the Resurrection* (London: Macmillan, 1874, pp. 249–76). See also his *Social aspects of Christianity* (London: Macmillan, 1887, p. XII).

31 B. Gregory, *Side lights on the conflicts of Methodism . . . 1827–1852* (London: Cassell, 1898), p. 318.

of alcohol be limited; in the event it was the First World War rather than Nonconformist pressure that led to restricted licensing hours.

The Congregational minister J. B. Paton, first principal of the Congregational Institute, Nottingham (1863–98), was a regular visitor to Germany and an admirer of the Inner Mission, who spent his life emphasising the social significance of Christianity. As a consulting editor to the *Contemporary Review* for many years, he made that periodical the vehicle for the publication of such ideas. R. W. Dale, minister of Carrs Lane Congregational Church, Birmingham from 1859 to 1895, criticised John Bright's narrow view of the state in an obituary in the *Review* in 1889; he himself had been active in what was often called 'municipal socialism' in the last third of the century, when municipal corporations took over the provision of many public services. Andrew Mearns's *The bitter cry of outcast London* (1883) put the spotlight on the extent to which the working classes suffered from poor housing conditions, such that those living on immoral earnings were able to afford better rooms than honest labourers. The outcry of Nonconformists and others led to the establishment of a Royal Commission on the Housing of the Working Classes. John Clifford, minister of Praed Street, later Westbourne Park Baptist church, London (1859–1915), was the first president of the predominantly Nonconformist Christian Socialist League (later Brotherhood), founded in 1894; as early as 1872 he had spoken of the need to go beyond poor relief, to improve wages and education, and to moralise the relations between masters and men in commerce and industry.

The emergence of an explicit German Christian socialist movement took place at about the same time, but with a more decisively conservative tone. Adolf Stöcker, a court chaplain to William I from 1874, shared with Todt in the founding of the Central Union for Social Reform in 1877, and a few weeks later founded his own Christian Social Labour Party. This was essentially a conservative opposition to the Social Democrats, and initially it drew recruits from Social Democrats among working men. However, after the Anti-Socialist Law of 1878, the party tended to attract artisans, small shopkeepers and small officials rather than factory operatives and it increasingly based its policies on anti-Semitism; Stöcker himself became a member of the Prussian House of Deputies in 1879 and the Reichstag in 1881. In 1882 a rather different development began in Rhineland-Westphalia, when a miner named Ludwig Fischer founded the first evangelical workmen's union as a reaction against the Roman Catholic unions, which were tending to proselytise among Protestants. By 1887 there were forty-four unions with 11,700 members. Their anti-Catholicism tended to be a defining characteristic, but they were also educational and provided the usual mutual funds, benefit clubs, savings banks, etc. Initially they were essentially non-political, but from 1888 they spread to the whole of the *Reich*; by 1896 there were 350 unions with 80,000 members. The emphasis shifted to opposition to Social Democrat unions, and anti-Catholicism receded. In 1890 a new body, the Evangelical Social Congress, was initiated to meet annually as an attempt to draw all strands of the Christian social movement together. Nevertheless, there remained a difference between the older and the younger leaders, especially Friedrich Naumann, a pastor in Langenberg, who was more prepared to preach loyalty to both Jesus and Marx. In 1896 he formed a Nationalsozialer Verein, seeking to combine social reform at home with an aggressive nationalist foreign policy; but he dissolved it in 1903, feeling that the Social Democrats were prepared to work for reform rather than revolution.

In Denmark Bishop H. L. Martensen in *The Christian ethic* (1871–8) noted that liberalism and free competition had brought misery to many as well as wealth to some, and whilst rejecting revolutionary socialism proposed 'an ethical socialism, namely the Christian variety'.[32] Although in most respects he was a political conservative, Martensen's book attracted attention because of the positive views of socialism it contained. Professor Harald Westergaard and Henry Ussing, a minister in the Church of Our Lady in Copenhagen, both gave lectures in the late 1880s suggesting that Christianity could and should tackle the social problem; both were involved in a group to build new churches in Copenhagen in order to reduce the size of parishes to 10,000 inhabitants; twelve new churches were built in less than ten years from 1890. Fernando Linderberg (1854–1914), founder of the Danish Workers' Union, wanted to show that Christianity and socialism were compatible; in 1898 the first Christian socialist movement was organised in Denmark, and several of its organisers had been influenced by Anglican Christian socialism. Although it did not last long, in 1906 a new Christian Social Committee was founded by a group which included Westergaard; and eventually in 1913 the Christian Socialist Union was founded, with Linderberg as secretary.

Sweden was in many respects more conservative than Denmark. Only in the 1850s and 1860s was there a relaxation of the legislation which restricted religious freedom and punished those who left the state church. The evangelical revival in Sweden from the early nineteenth century began to undermine the dominance of the established church. The first Swedish Baptists from 1848 supported universal suffrage, before becoming more politically conservative

---

32 Lausten, *A church history of Denmark*, p. 262.

later in the century. The revivalists were influenced by contacts with Germany, Britain and the United States; the last was particularly important because of the levels of Swedish emigration, which reached a peak in the thirty years after 1880. Full religious freedom was guaranteed by a law of 1873. However, the effects of the revival were generally socially conservative, providing some kind of consolation for the break-up of traditional agricultural communities, and to some extent it broke down barriers between classes. Swedish towns were more widely dispersed than in Britain, Belgium or Germany, and tended to be smaller; but the new sawmills, metalworking towns or old iron-mill towns still had sharply demarcated social areas, in which revivalists struggled to make an impact. The Social Democratic party in Sweden was founded in 1889, based on the German and Danish precedents, but in almost every respect it was more moderate; in the first decade of the twentieth century political co-operation with the Liberals brought a number of measures of social reform, such as pensions, social insurance and unemployment benefits. Although the party officially worked for the disestablishment of the Church of Sweden, in practice its members locally did not distance themselves from the church. Church leaders generally emphasised their opposition to the atheism of socialism – one of the few who took a more positive attitude was Nathan Söderblom (1866–1931), later archbishop of Uppsala. In fact, Christian socialism never really took root in Sweden.

Holland also provided a generally conservative picture. The most liberal social ideas in the early nineteenth century were found among the Roman Catholics (who were the majority in the united kingdom after 1814), and after the Revolution of 1830 these ceased to be relevant in the northern provinces. The generally liberal pattern of government in the mid-nineteenth century meant that the Ministries of Worship for Catholics and Protestants established in 1814 were abolished in 1862. The so-called 'Ethical' movement became dominant in the Dutch Reformed Church, emphasising personal religious experience (almost in a pietist way) and in the 1870s and 1880s began to acknowledge the importance of social and political problems for the churches. Then a striking shift took place under the leadership of Abraham Kuyper (1837–1920), who underwent an evangelical conversion which led him to a more conservative theology.[33] Kuyper not only preached a return to Calvinism; he was also a highly successful politician and was prime minister from 1901 to 1905. Kuyper's Anti-Revolutionary Party, based on Protestant artisans, tradesmen, small farmers and the aristocracy of labour, was prepared to offer an alternative

---

33 On Kuyper see also chapter 20 below.

programme to modern society. Despite the fact that in his earlier days he had not hesitated to voice strong anti-Catholic views, in 1889 Kuyper allied with Roman Catholics to provide state support for confessional, as well as state, schools. The result of this was a *de facto* pluralism, in which the essentially conservative voices of Protestantism and Catholicism allied together. Ironically it was Kuyper's allies, the Roman Catholics under H. J. A. M. Schaepman (1844–1903), who developed a system of Catholic trade unions, despite episcopal opposition, after Leo XIII's *Rerum Novarum* in 1891. The 1912 Poor Law still gave the churches pride of place in the provision of poor relief, and it was not superseded until 1963. Calvinist Christian Democrat proposals for old age pensions, invalidity pensions and health insurance were passed in 1913, though not implemented until 1919.

One point which has emerged from this description is the extent to which there were common emphases on the importance of Sunday schools and other education for children, and also the frequent provision of orphanages and other refuges for children in distress. In several countries the churches were to the fore in campaigning for legislation to restrict the hours of work for children (and women) in factories. Nevertheless while there was a general emphasis on education (and often the provision of church schools), there was not in the period before 1914 any concerted feeling that the age limit for compulsory education should be raised. The inevitable fact of children's employment was taken for granted.

Similarly it was generally assumed that a woman's place was in the home. This lay behind much of the concern to rescue women from prostitution, and to ensure that they were not exploited economically. Perhaps the most positive development was that of deaconesses in Germany from quite early on in the nineteenth century, which provided an opportunity for single women to commit themselves to the work of the church. Florence Nightingale's experience of this inspired her to develop a new approach to nursing in England. From the 1880s opportunities were provided for single women as missionaries overseas. The Salvation Army from its foundation in the 1860s recognised the equality of women and men among its officers, largely through the example of Catherine Booth herself. The Society of Friends also retained a traditional commitment to the equality of women in public ministry. But there was no real suggestion in the period before 1914 among either the established Protestant churches or the larger Free Churches that women might be eligible for ordination to the ministry, notwithstanding the experience of a generation of women preachers among Methodists at the beginning of the nineteenth century.

Between all the countries discussed there was regular interchange. People from Germany, Scandinavia and the Low Countries visited Great Britain and vice versa; and the influence of Germany on Scandinavia and Holland was considerable. Furthermore, the extent of European emigration to the United States established links there also. This is a significant part of the background to the campaigning on the question of peace. Mid-nineteenth-century liberals tended to be somewhat complacent on this because they believed that free trade guaranteed that it was in no country's interest to go to war. However, the wars of the 1860s and 1870s, and the development of competition for empire, changed attitudes. The churches generally supported the Hague Peace Conferences of 1899 and 1907. In July 1914 a meeting of the World Alliance for Promoting International Friendship among the Churches was brought to an abrupt end by the outbreak of war, and its members returned to their countries in sealed trains. Although the churchmen involved in this enterprise may be criticised for their naivety, it has to be remembered that they were no less surprised than many of the population of Europe at the turn of events that month. But it is a reminder of the real distance that separated church leaders from influence on the outcome of political events. It is also a reminder that the most obvious example of a church leader we have discussed exercising political power is Abraham Kuyper, a clear conservative in politics. In none of the countries discussed can it be claimed that church involvement was decisive in moving social attitudes in a new direction. This does not mean that those Christians who were involved in thinking out new ways of expressing their faith in contemporary society were merely following the general political mood, as some have argued, but it does reflect the fact that by 1914 there was no European country in which Protestant thinking on social questions determined the political agenda.

Christianity and the sciences

NICOLAAS A. RUPKE

Cognitive dissonance about cosmogony

Among the different possible approaches to Christianity and the sciences is that of the Christian conduct of science, involving a study of Christian scientists, their scientific accomplishments, and the importance of religious upbringing and beliefs for the character of scientific subjects and theories. This approach was followed as early as the closing decades of the period 1815–1914, when a Lutheran theologian at the University of Greifswald, Otto Zöckler (1833–1906), produced his two-volume *Gottes Zeugen im Reich der Natur* (1881), and when from the Catholic side *Das Christentum und die Vertreter der neueren Naturwissenschaft* (1903; English trans. 1911; new edition 1995), by the Jesuit church historian Karl Alois Kneller (1857–1942), was published. Yet apart from a number of biographical studies of individual Christian scientists, 'few attempts to pursue this link between religion and science'[1] have been made since. The majority of studies of 'Christianity and the sciences' have focused on the converse, namely the impact of scientific discoveries and theories on Christian beliefs, in particular on biblical hermeneutics and the question of the historicity, inerrancy and literal-versus-symbolic meaning of Genesis. Nearly all the primary sources of the period of this chapter as well as the secondary ones, up to the present day, have been preoccupied with what James Moore – following Leon Festinger – has called the 'cognitive dissonance'[2] that developed between the 'Mosaic cosmogony' and the scientific study of origins – of the universe, of life and of humankind.

Harmonisation schemata of Genesis and geology

Many of the scientists who contributed to these developments were Christians, and Charles Gillispie long ago pointed out that the debate over 'Genesis and geology' in the period 1790–1850 was a matter not of religion versus science

---

1 Numbers, 'Science and religion', p. 70.
2 Moore, *The post-Darwinian controversies*, pp. 14, 111–13.

but of religion within science.[3] The opposite tendency, that is the workings of science within religion, also helped shape the discourse, theologians taking account of geology in their commentaries on Genesis. Both groups – leading Christian scientists and theologians – were concerned that the book of nature should not be at variance with Scripture and, in coming to terms with the apparent 'cognitive dissonance', a variety of harmonisation schemata were put forward. A genre of literature developed that exclusively or primarily concerned the harmony of the Bible and science. Across the western world, many dozens of monographs on the subject were produced and thousands of articles, pamphlets and similar smaller publications. Not uncommonly, geological textbooks would include a chapter on how to reconcile the new earth history with the biblical accounts of creation and deluge.[4] Catholics as well as Protestants, of various denominational shades, participated in the effort to devise reconciliatory outlines. During the early part of the nineteenth century, much of this literature was produced by English-language scientists – experts for the most part in comparative anatomy, palaeontology and stratigraphy, such as the Anglican divine and geologist William Buckland (1784–1856) at Oxford – whereas during the century's second half the genre was enriched with a number of monographs by theologians, mainly in Germany where, moreover, entire magazines were devoted to the issues, such as the Catholic *Natur und Offenbarung* (1855–1910) and the Protestant *Natur und Glaube* (1897–1906). The high point of the reconciliation literature was reached with the formidable scholarship of Zöckler, renowned also for his work in the areas of Old and New Testament studies, dogmatics and church history. His *Geschichte der Beziehungen zwischen Theologie und Naturwissenschaft, mit besondrer Rücksicht auf Schöpfungsgeschichte* (2 vols., 1877–9) is a classic of the genre and remains valuable as a source book on the subject, along with his *Gottes Zeugen im Reich der Natur*.[5] But also in France, Italy, the Netherlands, Sweden and other continental countries, a variety of publications on Christian belief and modern science saw the light. The bibliographical documentation of this body of literature, which is essential for a balanced study of the subject, remains to date fragmentary at best.[6]

3 Gillispie, *Genesis and geology*.

4 Benjamin Silliman added a substantial reconciliation 'Supplement' to his edition of R. Bakewell, *An introduction to geology* (New Haven: H. Howe, 1833). J. Trimmer, *Practical geology and mineralogy* (London: J. W. Parker, 1841), ch. 3; J. Anderson, *The course of creation* (London: Longman, 1850), ch. 6.

5 Gregory, *Nature lost?*, pp. 112–59.

6 Further examples of scientists who produced important reconciliation treatises are: the Catholic magistrate and geologist Marcel Pierre Toussaint de Serres de Mesplès

In the meantime, the New York chemist and historian John William Draper (1811–82), who was intimately familiar with religious issues from his Methodist upbringing, presented a diametrically opposed view to that of the 'Gottes Zeugen' (God's witnesses) literature, attacking the Catholic Church for its alleged traditional hostility towards science and scientists. Religion and science had fought a continual battle in an effort by Christianity, 'steeped in blood', to attain and retain political power over and against 'the expansive force of the human intellect'.[7] The general drift of Draper's argument was continued by the Cornell University historian Andrew Dickson White, brought up as a high church Episcopalian, who characterised the engagement of Christianity and the sciences as a perennial war between 'Dogmatic Theology' and 'untrammelled scientific investigation'.[8] The warfare model in describing the relationship of religion and science has bedevilled the historiography of the subject ever since, and for much of the twentieth century it was fashionable to speak of 'the warfare waged by traditional religion against scientific knowledge'.[9] That interpretation has now given way to major revisionist scholarship by, among others – for the period of this chapter – John Hedley Brooke, David Livingstone, James Moore and Ronald Numbers, who have produced a fuller understanding of the remarkable diversity of Christian engagements with the sciences.[10]

The nineteenth-century harmonisation schemata were first and foremost a reaction to the then new perspective of geological time and history, and centred on the meaning of the Genesis stories of creation and deluge. As a Catholic theologian at Maynooth, Gerald Molloy (1834–1906), commented: 'The rapid progress of Physical Science, in modern times, has given rise to not a few objections against the truths of Revelation. Of these objections there is none which seems to have taken such a firm hold of the public mind in

(1780–1862) at Montpellier; the Lutheran zoologist Johann Andreas Wagner (1797–1861) at Munich; the Congregationalist president of Amherst College, Edward Hitchcock (1793–1864); Hitchcock's teacher Benjamin Silliman (1816–85), Professor of Chemistry and Natural History at Yale University; the latter's pupil and Yale colleague, the geologist James Dwight Dana (1813–95); and the Calvinist geographer at Princeton, Arnold Guyot (1807–84). Among the theologians were such Catholics as the later archbishop of Westminster Nicholas Patrick Stephen Wiseman (1802–65), the Professor of Old Testament Studies at Bonn and active supporter of the Old Catholics Franz Heinrich Reusch (1825–1900), and the Italian scientist-theologian and Jesuit Giambattista Pianciani (1784–1862).

7 J. W. Draper, *History of the conflict between religion and science* (London: Henry S. King, 1875), pp. vi, xi.

8 A. D. White, *A history of the warfare of science with theology in Christendom*, 2 vols. (New York: Dover republication, 1960), vol. 1, pp. viii–ix.

9 Russell, *Religion and science*, p. 7.

10 Brooke, *Science and religion*; Lindberg and Numbers, *God and nature* and *When science and Christianity meet*; Ferngren (ed.), *The history of science and religion*.

England, and, indeed, throughout Europe generally, as that which is derived from the interesting and startling discoveries of Geology.'[11] There were three basic reconciliatory exegeses of the hexaemeron, namely the concordist or 'day–age' interpretation, the restitution or 'gap interpretation' and the idealist version. The first of these saw a concordance between the Mosaic days of creation and the major periods of earth history, giving the word 'day' the meaning of 'age'. This view had been authoritatively expressed well before 1815, by Jean André Deluc (1727–1817), a Genevan Calvinist who had moved to London. In one of a series of published letters, he pointed out that the days of creation could not have been periods of twenty-four hours, because the sun and other celestial bodies were not created until the fourth 'day'.[12] Georges Cuvier (1769–1832), a life-long Protestant who worked at the world's largest research establishment at the time, the Muséum d'Histoire Naturelle in Paris, and who was the greatest scientific authority in opening up the new view of the geological past, was influenced by Deluc's schema and himself wrote a kind of treatise of reconciliation in the form of a *Discours préliminaire* (1811) to his major work on the osteology of fossil vertebrates (1812), arguing that the principal periods of earth history had been determined by global catastrophes.[13] Many other naturalists with an interest in geology and palaeontology followed suit, especially in Britain – Joseph Townsend (1739–1816), James Parkinson (1755–1824), John Kidd (1775–1851), Gideon Algernon Mantell (1790–1852), Hugh Miller (1802–56) – all suggesting that the days of the creation week of Genesis should be understood as periods of geological time.[14] Also Serres, in his *De la cosmogonie de Moïse* (1838; 3rd edn 1859), and initially Wagner as well, in his *Geschichte der Urwelt* (1845), adopted Deluc's stance. The 'day–age' exegesis received authoritative support from Franz Delitzsch (1813–90), a Lutheran theologian at Leipzig, Rostock and Erlangen, a great exegete who opposed the relativistic approach of higher criticism and who in his *Commentar über die Genesis* (1852) argued for the historicity of the hexaemeron, which was 'Schöpfungsgeschichte' (history of creation), not 'Schöpfungsdichtung' (creation fiction) nor visionary prophecy, yet in accommodating the geological need for millions of years he interpreted the days of creation as periods.[15] Variations on the 'day–age' theme were suggested by, among others, another 'biblical realist', the Dorpat professor of

11 G. Molloy, *Geology and revelation*, 2nd edn (London: Burns and Oates, 1873), p. 7.
12 J. A. Deluc, *Lettres physiques et morales sur l'histoire de la terre et de l'homme*, 5 vols. (The Hague: Detune, and Paris: Duchesne, 1779), vol. v, p. 636.
13 Rudwick, 'The shape and meaning of earth history', p. 313.
14 Rupke, *The great chain of history*, p. 205.
15 F. Delitzsch, *Commentar über die Genesis*, 4th edn (Leipzig: Dörffling and Franke, 1872), p. 87.

church history and Old Testament studies, Johann Heinrich Kurtz (1809–90).[16] Among the problems of the concordist approach were that, first, it limited the freedom of stratigraphy, because the sequence of geological periods had to be identical with that of the creation days; and, second, a literal meaning of the word 'day' had to give way to a symbolic one. Nevertheless, the 'day–age' view was widely adopted by the diluvialists, as it accommodated their belief that the historic deluge of Noah and the most recent of Cuvier's geological cataclysms had been one and the same event.

The second schema – the exegesis of restitution or 'ruin and restoration' – focused on the first two verses of the Mosaic hexaemeron. The first verse, 'In the beginning God created the heaven and the earth', is not a prospective summary of the creation week described in the verses that follow, but a retrospective reference to the primeval creation of matter, the stars, the planetary system and the earth. The second verse, 'And the earth was without form and void', takes up the history of the earth after an indefinite and possibly very long interval at the moment of the last geological revolution, as a preparatory statement to the creation of the human world. Thus there existed a time gap that could accommodate all of geological history, which had taken place before the six days of creation. Through the early decades of the nineteenth century, the gap interpretation grew increasingly popular with geologists, and was prominently advocated by Buckland in his Bridgewater Treatise of 1836, giving the schema a gloss of religious and scientific credibility.[17] Wagner, in the second edition of his Geschichte der Urwelt (1857–8), adopted Buckland's 'gap exegesis'. It had the sanction of leading Anglican theologians, including the evangelical John Bird Sumner (1780–1862), bishop of Chester and later archbishop of Canterbury, and Edward Bouverie Pusey (1800–82), Regius Professor of Hebrew at Oxford and Tractarian leader; the same exegesis had previously been put forward by the Scottish Presbyterian Thomas Chalmers (1780–1847), in his Evidence and authority of the Christian Revelation (1814). Buckland was supported and followed by a large number of scientists and theologians, among them the Nonconformist divine and naturalist John Pye Smith (1775–1851).[18] Placing geological history before the hexaemeron presented a theological problem, however, in that carnivorousness and death – traditionally seen as

---

16 J. H. Kurtz, *Bibel und Astronomie*, 5th edn (Berlin: Wohlgemuth, 1865), p. 82.
17 W. Buckland, *Geology and mineralogy considered with reference to natural theology*, 3rd edn, 2 vols. (London: George Routledge, 1858), vol. 1, pp. 13–31.
18 J. P. Smith, *The relation between the Holy Scriptures and some parts of geological science*, 5th edn (London: Henry Bohn, 1839); Greene, 'Genesis and geology', pp. 139–59.

the consequence of human sin – had entered the world long before the fall of man.

The restitutionary exegesis – just as the concordist one – was not new; it had been approvingly discussed by eighteenth-century theosophists and attained a strong following during the 1820s and 1830s among nature philosophers of the school of Friedrich Wilhelm Joseph Schelling (1775–1854). Henrik Steffens (1773–1845), for example, in his *Anthropologie* (1822), imaginatively combined it with the 'day–age' interpretation. The notion of restitution accommodated the dualism, demonology and Satanology of their developmental view of the world in which constructive forces appeared interlocked with destructive, and the 'tohu wabohu' of Genesis 1 verse 2 referred to one of a series of ruinous upheavals through which the earth had passed in a struggle between good and evil.[19]

The 'gap interpretation' gave geology all the time it needed and a literal interpretation of the Genesis days of creation was left intact. Noah's deluge might well have been a historical event, but had left no appreciable geological traces. The last global cataclysm had taken place just before the human world was created. This exegesis seemed corroborated by Cuvier's observation that human fossil bones do not occur, and by Buckland's failed attempt to find human remnants in prehistoric, diluvial deposits. Yet a further reconciliatory adjustment became necessary when by the end of the 1850s the discovery of primitive tools made of chipped flint mingled with the bones of extinct Pleistocene mammals made it undeniable that humans had been contemporaneous with extinct mammals and, as the Scottish geologist Charles Lyell (1797–1875) showed in his *Geological evidences of the antiquity of Man* (1863), were of much greater age than allowed for by traditional biblical chronology.[20]

The third and least literal exegesis was the idealist, which stated that the creation days represent 'moments' rather than consecutive periods: 'the six days do not signify six consecutive periods but six moments of God's creative activity which can be logically distinguished from one another, six divine thoughts or ideas realized in the creation'.[21] The hexaemeron did not represent a chronology of events, the creation days were neither actual days nor periods but a logical list of aspects of divine creation – the sequence was ideal,

19 Otto Zöckler, *Geschichte der Beziehungen zwischen Theologie und Naturwissenschaft: mit besondrer Rücksicht auf Schöpfungsgeschichte*, 2 vols. (Gütersloh: C. Bertelsmann, 1877–79), vol. 11, pp. 516–29.

20 Riper, *Men among the mammoths*.

21 F. H. Reusch, *Nature and the Bible*, 2 vols. (Edinburgh: Clark, 1886), vol. 11, p. 356.

not real. This schema was advocated by several Catholics, the Braunsberg theologian Friedrich Michelis (1815–86), editor of *Natur und Offenbarung*, and the theology professor Johann Baptist Baltzer (1803–71), in his *Die biblische Schöpfungsgeschichte* (2 vols., 1867, 1872),[22] as well as Reusch.

In addition to the harmonisers, there were those who opposed the results of modern science, and insisted on a traditional, literal interpretation of Genesis. The entire geological column as well as the palaeontological record had accumulated after the six days of creation or, more precisely, after the fall of man, and was generally attributed to the deluge.[23] The publications by this group of literalists formed the intellectual roots of twentieth-century fundamentalist creationism.[24]

The reconciliatory schemata provided science with considerable freedom to pursue its investigations of the physical world. Simultaneously, biblical literalism was weakened, to which, from the theological side, textual and higher criticism contributed. The reinterpretation of the Mosaic accounts of creation and flood, triggered by geology, linked up with results from the historical study of the Pentateuch, the archaeological study of Israel and the Near East, and the anthropological study of Old and New Testament religion. More radical than the revisions that were forced on many believers by science was this critical tradition within theology, leaders of which ranged from Johann Gottfried Eichhorn (1752–1827) to Julius Wellhausen (1844–1918), both Göttingen orientalist-theologians. The documentary hypothesis of the historical school in biblical studies, especially Old Testament studies, reduced the entire Pentateuch from a unitary record of divine revelation to a product of historical change, cobbled together from a variety of other sources and repeatedly altered in a process of editorial changes.[25] Higher criticism did not become a topic of major public debate in Britain before the 1860s, with the appearance of *Essays and reviews* (1860), written by members of the Church of England, and *The Pentateuch and the Book of Joshua critically examined* (1862), by the bishop of Natal, John William Colenso (1814–83), which questioned the Mosaic authorship and with that the authenticity of the Pentateuch as a divinely inspired account of history. A protest by fellows – some eminent – of the Royal

22 J. B. Baltzer, *Die biblische Schöpfungsgeschichte*, 2 vols. (Leipzig: Teubner, 1867, 1872), vol. I, pp. 322–54, table ii.
23 Rupke, *The great chain of history*, pp. 42–50; Reusch, *Nature and the Bible*, vol. I, pp. 294–310; Zöckler, *Theologie und Naturwissenschaft*, vol. II, pp. 470–83.
24 Numbers, *The creationists*.
25 Kraus, *Geschichte der historisch-kritischen Erforschung*, pp. 120–264.

Society followed, who declared that revealed religion and science are not in conflict.

More fundamental yet in taking down Scripture from its elevated level of divinely inspired purity was the scholarship that turned the Christian religion with its textual sources, ritual practices and context of historical origins into a subject of comparative scientific research.[26] The decipherment of tablets with Sumerian parallels to the Old Testament stories of creation and deluge – *Enuma Elish* and the *Gilgamesh Epic* respectively – strengthened Friedrich Delitzsch (1850–1922), son of Franz Delitzsch, and other Assyriologists, in the belief that the Bible was not an original source, but that 'Bible' had to be traced back to 'Babel'. More comprehensively, the history of religions approach, inspired by the work of the Oxford philologist Max Müller (1823–1900) and adopted at Göttingen by a group of young theologians whose *primus inter pares* was Albert Eichhorn (1856–1926), made all religions part of a relativising process of evolution in which Christianity as well as more 'primitive' systems of worship go back to a form of pre-religious magic – as argued by the Cambridge social anthropologist James George Frazer (1854–1941).[27] In this way, the non-essentialism of the 'Leben-Jesu-Forschung' (quest for the historical Jesus), from David Friedrich Strauss (1808–74) to Albert Schweitzer (1875–1965), was amplified.[28]

Natural theology in decline

The cognitive dissonance which developed with revealed religion did not exist to the same extent in relation to natural religion. However searching the criticisms of the design argument by David Hume (1711–76) or by Immanuel Kant (1724–1804) had been, natural theology continued to flourish, especially in the English-speaking world, and the high point of the tradition occurred during the early decades of the nineteenth century. A new phase of the tradition's popularity began with William Paley's *Natural theology* (1802), cresting during the 1830s when the so-called Bridgewater Treatises on the 'Power, Wisdom and Goodness of God, as manifested in the Creation' were published. The majority of studies of design belonged to the category of special teleology, in that they demonstrated functionalism, the adaptation of plants, animals

---

26 Kippenberg, *Entdeckung der Religionsgeschichte*.
27 Kraus, *Geschichte der historisch-kritischen Erforschung*, pp. 265–308.
28 A. Schweitzer, *Geschichte der Leben-Jesu-Forschung*, 2nd edn (Tübingen: J. C. B. Mohr, 1913). See below, chapter 12.

and human beings to the external conditions of existence. The Bridgewater Treatise on *The hand*, written by the surgeon Charles Bell, was a brilliant exposition of special teleology. The most frequently reprinted and most widely translated Bridgewater monograph was William Buckland's. Paley had made the human body the main source of evidence for design, though he also used plants and animals. Geology now provided a new range of facts that exemplified adaptation and contrivance. In particular palaeontology, with its extinct and unfamiliar forms of life, enriched the canon of design examples by adding new, in some instances bizarre, organic forms from the geological past.

Yet the close relationship between religion and science that had existed in natural theology dissolved in stages, and the language of providential design disappeared from scientific discourse in a process of the secularisation of the study of nature. The period 1815–1914 saw the disappearance of natural theology as a genre of scientific literature. To attribute this decline to Darwinism is probably inadequate as an explanation. Admittedly, Darwin's notion of natural selection turned the argument from design (special teleology) inside out by stating that anything not well adapted (not properly designed) simply will not survive in the struggle for life: 'in one sense Darwinism is Paleyism inverted'.[29] Design in the sense of special teleology is therefore not proof of intent but merely the chance result of the struggle for life. Yet as repeatedly urged by Peter Bowler, Darwinism – defined in terms of natural selection – never became widely accepted among biologists and palaeontologists of the second half of the nineteenth century, and a 'Darwinian revolution' in this sense never occurred. *The origin of species* proved compelling, but not in converting the scientific community to evolution by natural selection – only to evolution by natural means. Many scientists incorporated general teleology in models of orthogenetic or more specifically also of theistic evolution, the Christians among them grafting evolutionism onto one of the several, existing harmonisation schemata.[30]

A more significant factor in the decline of the scientific discourse of design may have been that its social functions were taken over by Darwinism. Robert Young, in pointing to the contiguity between theological and scientific belief systems, has contended that the argument from design helped maintain the socio-political status quo, and that Darwinism could be appealed to for the same purpose. Both parties were in agreement with the Malthusian population

29 Gillispie, *Genesis and geology*, p. 219.
30 Bowler, *The eclipse of Darwinism* and *The non-Darwinian revolution*.

doctrine. The social order with its class hierarchy and privileges could be ratified by natural selection just as well as by natural theology. In the latter the inequalities of wealth and poverty were expressions of divine laws, in the former of the laws of nature.[31]

A further significant factor may have been that Cuvierian functionalism, which was at the root of the argument from design in Buckland's and other Bridgewater Treatises, lost its scientific currency. Special teleology – the core of the natural theological discourse – was by and large replaced by general teleology in giving meaning to the organic form, in particular the fossilised instances. The use of form rather than function in explaining organic diversity had been promoted by Cuvier's adversary at the Muséum d'Histoire Naturelle, Etienne Geoffroy Saint-Hilaire (1772–1844), as well as by the Jena zoologist Lorenz Oken (1779–1851) and the multi-talented Carl Gustav Carus (1789–1869). In the English-speaking world, the approach was followed by Richard Owen (1804–92) and carried to perfection in his *On the archetype and homologies of the vertebrate skeleton* (1848). The vertebrate archetype represented a generalised and simplified skeleton of all backboned animals, to which the many parts of real skeletons of fishes, amphibians, reptiles, birds and mammals could be reduced on the basis of their homological relations. The meaning of a particular organ was to be determined not by its function but by its homological relations. With this demotion of special teleology, a compensatory effort was made by Owen and his circle of Anglican patrons to retain the perception of providential design, not in concrete, functional adaptations but at an abstract, general level, by interpreting the archetype in terms of a Platonic idea – a blueprint in the mind of the Creator that had produced unity of design in nature, as well as through geological time, from the earliest and lowest creature up to 'man'.[32]

The disappearance of the language of design from scientific discourse furthermore reflected the fact that such language had become unfashionable. Admittedly, it survived in some of the popular treatises in Germany and France, such as *Die Wunder der Urwelt* (1853) by Carl Gottfried Wilhelm Vollmer (1797–1864) who wrote under the pseudonym W. F. A. Zimmermann. Far more trend-setting, however, among the popular science books was Alexander von Humboldt's *Kosmos* (1845–62), which may well have been the scientific text that most contributed to the removal throughout Europe from scientific discourse of the language of natural theology. In none of its five volumes was the

31 Young, *Darwin's metaphor*, pp. 23–55.
32 Rupke, *Richard Owen*, pp. 161–219.

argument from design developed or even mentioned, causing a stir across the western world. The British reviews of *Kosmos* noted with dismay the absence from this book of 'proofs of divine design' and of even just the word 'God'. Whereas in France the positivistically inclined orientalist-theologian Ernest Renan (1823–92), in his review of *Kosmos* for *La Liberté de Penser*, explicitly praised Humboldt for having avoided the language of natural theology 'as it is understood in England', the Tory *Quarterly Review*, the Benthamite *Westminster Review* and the Congregational *British Quarterly Review* all sorely missed references to 'the power, wisdom and goodness of God as manifested in the creation'. To many of Humboldt's British critics, it was inconceivable that a popular exposition of science should be without the stated aim that the study of nature leads up to nature's God.

Science and the soul

One reason for Humboldt's avoidance of the language of natural theology may have been that teleology, and especially general teleology, was a central tenet of nature philosophy, from which Humboldt believed science should keep its distance. His critics, by contrast, were concerned that *Kosmos* should not provide additional impetus to philosophical materialism, which was drawing considerable new strength from nineteenth-century science, as described by the Kantian philosopher Friedrich Albert Lange (1828–75).[33] Belief in miracles, for example, came under renewed criticism from the sciences. It was critically discussed within Christianity by the Savilian Professor of Geometry at Oxford, Baden Powell (1796–1860),[34] and its evidential objective nature was denied by the physicist and enthusiastic supporter of Darwin, John Tyndall (1820–93). In the decades that followed, many religious writers in the English-speaking world 'recast their language about miracles to meet these objections', admitting that the concept of a miracle was ultimately a religious category.[35]

Most heatedly debated was the issue of an immaterial soul and whether or not humans occupy a unique place in nature. In this matter, the military metaphor of Draper and White would seem to apply, although the battle lines were drawn differently from those of their warfare models, namely between Christian scientists and theologians on the one hand and materialist scientists

---

33 F. A. Lange, *Geschichte des Materialismus*, 2nd edn, 2 vols. (Iserlohn: J. Baedeker, 1875), vol. II, pp. 139–452.
34 Corsi, *Science and religion*.
35 Mullin, 'Science, miracles', p. 210.

and philosophers on the other. Two epic clashes in this war occurred, the first initiated at Göttingen, the second at Oxford. Comparative anatomy was the battlefield and in particular the physical anthropology of skulls and brains. Christian anthropologists such as Johann Friedrich Blumenbach (1752–1840) and James Prichard (1786–1848) upheld the unity of mankind, which to many implied that differences between human races are small as compared to those between humans and the anthropoid apes. A search continued for anatomical differences that would set *Homo sapiens* apart from the animal world and that might prove to be 'organs of the soul'. At Göttingen, Rudolph Wagner (1805–64), who was professor of anatomy in succession to Blumenbach, curated and augmented the famous collection of human skulls which his predecessor had amassed. Like his namesake and friend Andreas Wagner, Rudolph Wagner was concerned with the origin and distribution of human races across the surface of the globe.[36] Both Wagners followed Blumenbach as well as the Heidelberg anatomist Friedrich Tiedemann (1781–1861) in arguing for the biblical belief in the unity of the human race, to which Rudolph Wagner added his conviction that there is a life after death, and that humans differ from animals in that they have a soul – a direct gift from God.

Controversy over the issue flared up in Germany in the context of the so-called 'Materialismusstreit', engendered by attempts to put science before the cart of materialist and positivist philosophy. The soul has no independent reality from the brain – it was famously asserted – and is as much its product as are the various bodily fluids of other organs. In 1854 the Versammlung deutscher Naturforscher und Ärzte (on which organisation the British Association for the Advancement of Science was modelled) met in Göttingen, when Rudolph Wagner addressed the assembly on 'Menschenschöpfung und Seelensubstanz' (creation of mankind and the soul's substance). He argued that there are no physiological grounds for denying the existence of an independent, immaterial soul, and that the moral order of society requires us to assume the soul's existence. This address was published, and republished, Wagner adding among other things that in matters of faith he preferred the simple 'Köhlerglauben' (the faith of a charcoal-burner). This expression provided Carl Vogt (1817–95), known for his scientific materialism and political radicalism, with the title of a scathing counter-booklet, *Köhlerglauben und Wissenschaft* (1856), in which he denounced Wagner's Christian piety. Wagner countered with his *Der Kampf um die Seele* (1857) and subsequently made capital out of the fact that he had in

36 Soulimani, *Naturkunde*, pp. 224–353.

his collection of human brains the prize specimen of his Göttingen colleague Carl Friedrich Gauss (1777–1855), one of the greatest mathematicians of all time, with whom he had conducted pious deathbed conversations about the immortality of the soul in which Gauss deeply believed. A careful study of this and other brains carried the promise that a uniquely human feature might be found – if not a specific anatomical part then the architecture of brain convolutions – possibly an 'organ of the soul'.[37]

The classic controversy initiated at Göttingen was now followed by another, at Oxford, pitching the aggressive advocate of Darwinism Thomas Henry Huxley (1825–95) against Owen and his supporters. The Huxley–Owen clash, which continued during the annual British Association meetings of 1861 and 1862, must rank as one of the fiercest, most bitter and most publicly sensational battles between scientific rivals of the nineteenth century. It was known as the hippocampus controversy, as Owen had identified several anatomical features of the human brain and in particular the hippocampus minor – an elevation at the rear of the brain's lateral ventricles – as 'peculiar' to the human brain, associated with special mental powers, by means of which humans rise above animality, representing the image of God.

Huxley denied that an anatomical chasm exists between animals and humans, arguing, in *Evidence as to man's place in nature* (1863), that, on the contrary, there is a close animal–human proximity, supporting the theory that mankind and the higher apes are related by descent. The use of Gauss's brain was turned into its opposite by Huxley's followers, who argued that its large size and intricate convolutions showed that he was further removed from a Hottentot than a Hottentot from a chimpanzee or gorilla, thus demonstrating the closeness of 'man and monkey'.[38] Another strategy in establishing the essential animality of humans was to argue against the unity of mankind and for polygenesis. To Vogt and many others, polygenesis was an integral part of a materialist, evolutionary theory of human origins.[39] It had links with the theologically heterodox view of pre-Adamites which went back to the French Calvinist Isaac de la Peyrère (1596–1676), but in the USA polygenesis was championed by Christian scientists such as Harvard University's Louis Agassiz (1807–73), to whom it provided a means of legitimising slavery or at

37 R. Wagner, *Vorstudien zu einer wissenschaftlichen Morphologie und Physiologie des menschlichen Gehirns als Seelenorgan*, 2 vols. (Göttingen: Verlag der Dieterichschen Buchhandlung, 1860–2); Rupke, *Richard Owen*, pp. 303–9.

38 E. Haeckel, *Anthropogenie oder Entwickelungsgeschichte des Menschen* (Leipzig: Engelmann, 1874), pp. 489, 697; C. Flammarion, *Le monde avant la création de l'homme* (Paris: Marpon and Flammarion, 1886), pp. 752–3.

39 C. Vogt, *Vorlesungen über den Menschen*, 2 vols. (Giessen: I. Ricker, 1863), vol. ii, pp. 283–7.

least the emplacement of a social divide between white settlers and coloured groups.[40]

Darwin himself, who in the *Origin of species* had circumnavigated the contentious issue of human origins and had restricted himself to a terse 'Light will be thrown on the origin of man and his history',[41] at long last came out with *The descent of man* (1871), extending the mechanism of natural selection to the origins of humans and human society and providing further material for Herbert Spencer (1820–1903), who coined the phrase 'survival of the fittest', substituting a natural for a divine basis of morality.[42]

The attempt by Wagner, Owen and others to set humans fundamentally apart on the basis of cerebral characteristics failed. Dana argued that our upright position – the 'cephalisation of the body' – separates us from the rest of the mammalian world; others emphasised the criterion of speech, reason or imagination. To great acclaim across the USA, the New York University professor of medicine Martyn Paine (1794–1877) affirmed that the human soul is an independent, immortal, spiritual entity, adding an essay on the 'physiology of the soul' to a major, creationist reconciliation schema of 'Genesis and geology'.[43] Literature on the issue was abundant, not only because of the religious aspects, but also because the questions of mind and soul impinged on the emerging field of psychology. Yet the combined authority of Owen, Wagner and other Christian scientists failed to win the day. The materialists declared themselves the winners, and like the language of providential design and of miracles, that of an immortal soul disappeared from public, scientific discourse, finding a place of refuge in the sphere of private belief or of such fringe or pseudo-sciences as spiritualism.

Situating the issues institutionally

The major treatises on the issue of religion and science enjoyed an international readership. Of Buckland's *Geology and mineralogy*, for example, there were, in addition to four London editions, a Philadelphia one, as well as translations into French and German. The treatise was discussed in detail by Reusch, whose *Bibel und Natur* in turn came out in an English edition. Yet it would be wrong to assume that the debates were part of an international, unitary

---

40 Nelson, '"Men before Adam!"', pp. 161–81.

41 C. Darwin, *The origin of species* (London: John Murray, 1859), p. 488.

42 H. Spencer, *The principles of ethics*, 2 vols. (London: Williams and Norgate, 1892–3).

43 M. Paine, *Physiology of the soul and instinct, as distinguished from materialism* (New York: Harper and Bros., 1872).

discourse. Quite the contrary was true. After all, both Christianity and the sciences have not merely a cognitive side, but a concrete existence as well in the form of people, careers and institutions, part of the rough and tumble of distinct networks of power. This banal fact takes on significance if we want to deepen our understanding of the forces that drove the debates. A single text or a particular argument might have different and even contradictory meanings depending on 'geography', including ideological geography, as compellingly argued by David Livingstone.[44] This emphasis helps reveal the embeddedness of the religion–science literature in the many and various vested interests that were circumscribed by the institutions of nation-states, churches, denominations or political parties. Buckland's Bridgewater Treatise as well as his earlier *Vindiciae geologicae* (1820), for example, must be institutionally situated in order adequately to grasp the meaning of these texts. At the Muséum d'Histoire Naturelle in Paris, the explicitness of concern with deluge and design in these texts represented an instance of antiquated theory, yet 'on the ground' – Anglican Oxbridge – it meant quite the opposite, being part of a latitudinarian, broad church reform movement to establish the natural sciences at England's ancient universities.[45] Robert Young and others have contended that natural theology in Britain provided a 'common context' for debate and co-operation among the social and scientific elite. Different religious denominations could come together under the umbrella of a teleological world-view in the cultivation of science.[46] For this very reason, John Henry Newman (1801–90), his Tractarian followers and various other traditionalists regarded Buckland's teleology as a form of dangerous interdenominational libertarianism. What is more, its arguments for the existence of a divine power did not extend to the elements of Christianity: 'It cannot tell us anything of Christianity at all.'[47]

The reception of Darwin's theory of evolution was equally multi-levelled, as Alvar Ellegård long ago documented in impressive detail.[48] The creation–evolution issue could function as a vehicle of modernisation and church reform, and accordingly was instrumentalised by the liberal wings of denominations. Scottish and American Calvinists form a case in point. James Moore has shown in his *The post-Darwinian controversies* that Darwinism, in spite of the problems it raised for many Victorian intellectuals, could be accommodated by orthodox Protestants, in particular Calvinists – Asa Gray being

44 Livingstone, *Putting science in its place.*
45 Rupke, *The great chain of history*, pp. 21–6, 51–63.
46 Young, *Darwin's metaphor*, pp. 126–63.
47 Rupke, *The great chain of history*, p. 271.
48 Ellegård, *Darwin and the general reader.*

one of them. The Calvinist context has been explored further by David Livingstone – for Northern Ireland, Scotland and the USA – arguing, too, that Presbyterians had little trouble reconciling their orthodox theology to Darwin's theory in the form of theistic evolution.[49] The American location with its various sub-locations has recently become the subject of flourishing research.[50]

For the European continent, the situatedness of Christianity-and-science literature is by and large an uncultivated field of study, yet equally suggestive. The Protestant authors of major treatises, from Kurtz to Zöckler, were close to the nineteenth-century movement of neo-Lutheranism with its ecumenical programme and openness to contemporary currents of thought, including scientific thought. The Catholic theologians in Germany, cited above, who addressed the issues of Bible and science all belonged to the movement of Old Catholicism and were, because of their disobedience to the Vatican, excommunicated by their bishops – Baltzer in Breslau, Michelis in Braunsberg and Reusch in Bonn. It is likely that an understanding of their interest in the issue of Bible and science as well as their promotion of the idealist interpretation of the creation days of Genesis 1 will be deepened by exploring these as an integral part of internal church politics.

Thus the discourse over Christianity and science was anchored in particular socio-political programmes within the institutional enclosures of different churches and church groups. The situation was further concretised by the fact that the sciences went through a process of institutionalisation and professionalisation, accompanied by a growing resentment about the pervasiveness of the ecclesiastical hold over the nation's institutions. Not just 'cognitive dissonance' but 'institutional dissonance' produced tensions which led to border clashes of science with traditional estates of cultural authority, including the churches. Many scientists strove for a fundamental redistribution of this authority in society, so as to acquire for themselves a major share of it. Frank Turner has highlighted the importance of the professional dimension in the Victorian religion–science controversies of the English-speaking world. It was less a question of a fight between Christian belief and scientific theory than of professional rivalries between theologians and scientists.[51] Among the latter were Christians as well as non-Christians. The devoutly religious and church-going Anglican Owen, for example, the most formidable figure of British

---

49 Livingstone, *Darwin's forgotten defenders*.
50 Numbers, *Darwinism comes to America*; Roberts, *Darwinism and the divine in America*.
51 Turner, 'The Victorian conflict between science and religion', and *Contesting cultural authority*.

science of the middle of the nineteenth century, claimed for himself and his scientific colleagues a truth mission and a scientific priesthood – no less than his non-Christian rival Huxley did. Scientific discovery – he maintained – was a form of divine revelation. The scientific institution founded by Owen, the British Museum (Natural History), was seen by many of his supporters as a 'cathedral of nature', and some of its architectural features gave expression to such ecclesiastical pretensions.[52]

The institutional tug-of-war, in extreme cases, divided the scientific community, with Christian scientists founding bulwarks against anti-ecclesiastical colleagues. For example, in 1907 the Lutheran biologist Eberhard Dennert (1861–1942), supported by the botanist and Darwin-critic Johannes Reinke (1843–1921) and many other scientific as well as non-scientific academics, founded the Kepler Union, to counteract the Monist League, established in 1906 at the instigation of Ernst Haeckel (1834–1919). For decades, the monist movement had gathered strength in Germany, claiming to replace the churches and appropriating Christian ritual. Science was put forward as a secular religion, Darwin as its saviour and redeemer, Humboldt as one of its saints; scientists were priests or high priests, monistic Sunday sermons were preached, and hymns of scientism composed and sung during the Sunday services.[53] Haeckel wrote a widely translated confession of scientific faith under the title *Der Monismus als Band zwischen Religion und Naturwissenschaft* (1892). When the monists founded the periodical *Der Monismus*, the Kepler Union countered with *Unsere Welt*, and when Haeckel built his monist temple, the Phyletic Museum in Jena, the Kepler Union established its Museum for Popular Science. Organisational initiatives were matched, blow for blow, and the Catholics followed suit with the founding of the Albert Union (1912–13) and its periodical *Die Schöpfung*. Many local branches were established, linking the religion–science discourse to a range of national, provincial and local issues.[54] Such situated studies help show the extent to which the cognitive dissonance was part of institutional power politics, and more of these studies are needed. Yet the most urgent desideratum of secondary scholarship remains a comprehensive critical documentation of the primary literature, combining and comparing the Anglo-American with the continental, Protestant with Catholic, scientific with theological, and building on the encyclopaedic approach by Zöckler.

52 Rupke, *Richard Owen*, pp. 323–52.
53 W. Bölsche, *Alexander v. Humboldt* (Berlin: Rubenow, 1891).
54 Daum, *Wissenschaftspopularisierung*, pp. 220–4.

12

History and the Bible

JOHN ROGERSON

The defeat of Napoleon in 1815 marked the end, from a British point of view, of a significant episode in world history that had apparently been foretold in the Bible. According to Daniel 7:23-7, a fourth kingdom would arise which would war against the saints of the Most High for 'a time, two times, and half a time', after which it would be destroyed and be replaced by the everlasting kingdom of the saints of the Most High. British Protestant interpretation of Daniel 7 identified the fourth kingdom with the papacy, and its war against the saints of the Most High with the persecution of movements such as the Waldensians and the Hussites. On the view that 'time' meant a year of 360 days, the period of domination of the fourth kingdom would be 1,260 years, and depending on when it was believed that papal power began to be exercised in an anti-Christian way, the ending of the period of 1,260 years could be seen as 1798, when the French republican army took possession of the city of Rome.[1] The events of the French Revolution and the defeat of Napoleon gave rise in Britain to intense speculation that biblical prophecies had been fulfilled and that the second advent of Jesus was imminent. Such speculation had several consequences. First, there was renewed interest in missionary work among Jews and in assisting the return of Jews to Palestine. Second, conferences were convened by Henry Drummond in 1826-9 at his home at Albury Park in Surrey, whose purpose was to identify biblical prophecies that were yet to be fulfilled. Third, adventist speculations and in some cases charismatic phenomena marked the formation of new churches such as the Catholic Apostolic Church and the so-called Plymouth or Christian Brethren.[2] These developments had the effect of creating an atmosphere that was hostile

1 A. Clarke, *The Holy Bible with a commentary and critical notes*, vol. v (London, 1825) on Daniel 7:25. A similar calculation could be made on the basis of Daniel 12:6–7. At Daniel 12:11, a period of 1,290 days (i.e. years) is mentioned from the time that the 'abomination that makes desolate' is set up. Clarke considered the possibility that the beginning of Islam in AD 612 was meant.

2 See Clements, 'George Stanley Faber'; Flegg, *'Gathered under apostles'*, pp. 33–68.

to the development of biblical criticism in Britain, and which lasted until the 1870s. At the same time, however, it was recognised in some circles that the Bible contained apparent contradictions and inconsistencies, which needed to be explained.

T. H. Horne's *Introduction to the critical study and knowledge of the Holy Scriptures*, of which several editions appeared in the 1820s, was frank in its admission of difficulties in the biblical texts.[3] The Book of Joshua had suffered 'accidental derangement of the order of the chapters',[4] as had 1 Samuel 16–18. Some events, such as the creation of male and female in Genesis 1:27, anticipated the fuller accounts at Genesis 2:7, 21–3, while Abram's departure from Haran in Genesis 11.31 preceded God's call to him to depart at 12:1.[5] Apparent contradictions that critical scholarship explained by assigning material to different sources were noted by Horne. They included the discrepancies between the accounts of creation in Genesis 1:1–2.4a and in 2:4b–25, the taking into the ark of two pairs of animals at Genesis 6:19–21 as opposed to taking seven pairs of clean animals in 7:2, and the problem that Egyptian cattle were mentioned as existing in Exodus 9:20 whereas they had all been destroyed at Exodus 9:6. In all these cases Horne found ways of defending the unity and accuracy of the text, but by resorting to explanations such as that chapters or sections had become accidentally deranged, he was using critical methods to solve problems of historical criticism.

An event that caused a considerable stir in ecclesiastical circles was the publication, in 1829–30, of Henry Milman's *The history of the Jews*.[6] Its appearance reflected the interest in the Jews which the conclusion of the Napoleonic wars had engendered in Britain, and its three volumes covered Jewish history from its Old Testament beginnings to Napoleonic times. As a piece of critical scholarship, it was innocent of the historical criticism that was developing in Germany, and given that it never questioned the historical accuracy of the Old Testament it should not have aroused controversy. Yet its first volume, dealing with the Old Testament period, caused a storm because it described the history of ancient Israel in a way that equated it with the history of any other nation. This did not mean that Milman thought that Israel's history was like that of any other nation. He believed, and endeavoured to show in his account, that divine providence had guided and sustained the people of

3 T. H. Horne, *An introduction to the critical study and knowledge of the Holy Scriptures*, 4 vols. (London: Longman, 1825).
4 *Ibid.*, vol. II, p. 36.
5 *Ibid.*, vol. I, pp. 545–6.
6 H. H. Milman, *The history of the Jews* (London: John Murray, 1829–30). See Clements, 'The intellectual background of H. H. Milman's *The history of the Jews*'.

Israel in order to vouchsafe the revelation of God to the world through the chosen nation. What Milman's critics seemed to take exception to was the idea that the Bible's own account of its history could be put into other words, and be accompanied by observation and reflection, so that the human narrator appeared to be in charge of the exercise. The reception of *The history of the Jews* showed the extent of the conservatism of the ecclesiastical establishment, and what the emerging discipline of biblical criticism was faced with.[7]

If 1815 brought adventist hopes to the fore in Britain, the German states were preoccupied with the question of their political future and possible unity. The approach, in 1817, of the three-hundredth anniversary of the beginning of the Reformation led radical groups, especially among students, to demand democratic reforms in state and church. A student demonstration in 1817 at the Wartburg near Eisenach, where Luther had translated the New Testament into German in 1521, was looked on unfavourably by the authorities in Prussia. The assassination of the playwright August Kotzebue by a theological student, Karl Ludwig Sand, in March 1819 on suspicion of lack of patriotism led to a closing of the ranks by the German states which had formed a German Confederation in 1815. A meeting in August 1819 led to the issuing of the Carlsbad decrees which imposed restrictions upon universities and their teachers.[8] This political clampdown also enabled some theological scores to be settled, especially by the conservative and pietistic circles that held sway at the Prussian court. In September 1819, W. M. L de Wette was dismissed from his chair in Berlin. The official reason was that he had written a letter of sympathy to the mother of the student who had assassinated Kotzebue. The underlying reason was that de Wette's radical critical work on the Bible and theology was viewed with deep suspicion in influential conservative and pietistic circles.[9] In pioneering works published from 1805 to 1807, de Wette had turned upside down the version of the history of Israelite religion and sacrifice contained in the Old Testament. According to that version, Moses had instituted the system of Israelite priesthood and sacrifice at the beginning of the nation's history, during the wilderness wanderings that followed the exodus. According to de Wette, the fully fledged Mosaic system had developed over many centuries and had been preceded by a period in which there was no centralised priesthood or fixed ritual for sacrifices. A decisive stage in this process had been Josiah's reforms in 622 BC which had centralised worship in Jerusalem and closed down the many local sanctuaries. The Book of Deuteronomy, or parts of it, dated from

---

7 See Rogerson, *Old Testament criticism*, pp. 184–8.
8 See Sheehan, *German history*; McClelland, *State, society and university in Germany*.
9 Rogerson, *W. M. L. de Wette*, pp. 145–57.

this time. As well as advocating a revolutionary view of the history of Israelite sacrifice and religion, de Wette had argued that much of the material in the Pentateuch was unhistorical, and that its main value was that it expressed the religious beliefs of the period in which it was written, namely, the tenth to ninth centuries BC.

De Wette's dismissal was a victory for the conservative and pietistic forces in Prussia (after a period of unemployment he went to Basel in 1821 where he remained until his death in 1849), but it did not stop other scholars such as Wilhelm Gesenius, C. P. W. Gramberg and J. F. L. George from developing de Wette's ideas.[10] However, in 1835 two books appeared in Germany which enabled the authorities to take stern action against the rising tide of biblical criticism. The works were Wilhelm Vatke's *Biblische Theologie* and D. F. Strauss's *Leben Jesu*. Vatke followed de Wette in presenting a very minimal account of what could be known about Moses and the early years of Israelite history, but he also reconstructed Israelite history along the lines of Hegel's philosophy in a manner that seemed to rob the Old Testament of its unique status as divine revelation. Strauss's book attacked the trustworthiness of John's Gospel as a source for the life of Jesus, and regarded much of the gospel material as 'mythical', that is, as presenting what were essentially 'ideas' in narrative form. The Prussian authorities responded by blocking the academic careers of Vatke and Strauss and by ensuring the appointment of orthodox scholars in universities under their control.[11]

If biblical criticism was to make progress against the conservatisms of Britain and Germany, it would be by way of moderate criticism that did not over-turn accepted belief so radically, and a work that provided the inspiration for such an approach was B. G. Niebuhr's *History of Rome*.[12] In Britain it inspired Thomas Arnold, headmaster of Rugby School, to learn German in order to read and review it. In Germany it became the model for Heinrich Ewald's *History of Israel*.[13] Niebuhr demonstrated how classical legends and other lit-erature could provide a solid basis for the writing of history; but he also believed that history written in this way contained evidence of the workings of divine providence in human affairs. Arnold did not attempt to write a history of Israel, but he was emboldened by Niebuhr's work to preach and write about the Old Testament in a way that showed how Israel's history

10 See Rogerson, *Old Testament criticism*, pp. 50–68.
11 *Ibid.*, pp. 79–90; Kümmel, *The New Testament*, pp. 120–6.
12 B. G. Niebuhr, *Römische Geschichte*, 2 vols. (Berlin, 1811–12).
13 H. Ewald, *Geschichte des Volkes Israel* (Göttingen, 1843–59).

exhibited divine providence, and constantly confronted the people with moral choices. It was the prophetic traditions that exhibited the moral challenges most clearly, and although these traditions originated in specific historical and cultural circumstances, they had a universal significance which meant that they could challenge modern readers to decide for or against what was good and true. This was a far cry from the attempts of the Albury conferences to discover which Old Testament prophecies remained to be fulfilled and was a step along the road to a proper historical treatment of prophecy.[14]

Ewald's *History* was a monument of critical scholarship, which drew together work on the sources and fragments of which the Pentateuch, Joshua to 2 Kings, and Chronicles and Ezra and Nehemiah were made up, work which had begun in the eighteenth century. He identified six 'narrators' or editors who had added material to existing editions of the Pentateuch and Joshua over a period of six or seven centuries, and proposed similarly complex solutions to the composition of the 'Great Book of Kings' (Judges to 2 Kings) and the 'Great Book of Universal History to Greek Times' (Chronicles, Ezra and Nehemiah). He identified many problems that were recognised in subsequent scholarship and although his own solutions were often too idiosyncratic to gain acceptance he anticipated theories that were later to hold sway in critical scholarship.[15]

On the face of it, Ewald's *History* was not a likely candidate for furthering the critical cause, yet it did so because its reconstruction of Israel's earliest history was much more positive than what was found in de Wette and Vatke. For the former, the stories in Genesis about Abraham, Isaac and Jacob yielded little historical information. Ewald recognised that, in their present form, the stories about the Patriarchs presented them as types of heroes, but he also maintained that they contained information about the migrations of peoples who were the forebears of the Hebrews, whose religion could also be reconstructed. Ewald also wrote much more fully and positively than de Wette about the person and work of Moses. The result was that Ewald's *History*, in spite of all its elaborate theorising about the compositional processes of the Old Testament – theorising that put it light years away from traditional views that ascribed the Pentateuch to Moses, Joshua to Joshua, etc. – basically upheld the outline of history that the Old Testament contained. Indeed, it

---

14 T. Arnold, 'Two sermons on the interpretation of prophecy', in *Sermons by Thomas Arnold, D.D.*, 4th edn (London, 1844), vol. 1, pp. 365–449; Rogerson, *Old Testament criticism*, pp. 188–91.

15 See Rogerson, *Old Testament criticism*, pp. 91–103.

provided comfort to traditionalists that such a great critical scholar as Ewald could produce a reconstruction that seemed to vindicate the Old Testament in opposition to what was regarded as the negative criticism of de Wette and his followers.

The impact of Ewald's *History* was, in fact, greater in Britain than in Germany, and it was the main inspiration for A. P. Stanley's *Lectures on the history of the Jewish church*, of which the first two series were published in 1863 and 1865.[16] While omitting any reference to the complex source and compositional theories on which Ewald's work was based, Stanley gratefully accepted Ewald's results when it suited him, and provided readers with a straightforward account of Old Testament history in which all the Israelites from Abraham onwards were treated as fully historical figures. This did not mean that Stanley shirked facing up to difficulties. How, for example, could the prophetic denials that Israel offered sacrifices to God in the wilderness (Amos 5:25, Jeremiah 7:22) be reconciled with the accounts in the Pentateuch of the institution of the sacrificial system in the wilderness? Stanley's view was that sacrifices had been offered in the wilderness, but that the laws regarding sacrifice and priesthood had assumed their final shape at a later period. Priesthood and sacrifice (for which Stanley had a lower regard than prophecy) had, indeed, enabled the 'Jewish church' to endure when the monarchy and prophecy were no more. In 1867 English readers were able to begin to have access to Ewald's *History* themselves, thanks to the initiative of a Unitarian woman, Charlotte Lupton, who financed and assisted in the translation.[17] The effect of this, and of Stanley's lectures, was to assure liberal-minded people that biblical criticism could yield results that were sufficiently traditional not to cause great anxiety. Such reassurance was necessary in view of developments that were taking place in several countries, and which would result in something like the rehabilitation of the radical views of de Wette.[18]

De Wette, it will be remembered, had argued that the system of priesthood and sacrifice described in the Pentateuch was a late development, and that it had been preceded by a period in which there were many sanctuaries and no centralised priesthood or sacrificial regulations. To sum up the matter crudely, did the law (including the regulations about priesthood or sacrifice) precede the prophets, or did the prophets precede the law? Ewald's approach favoured

16 A. P. Stanley, *Lectures on the history of the Jewish church*, 3 vols. (London: John Murray, 1st ser. 1863, 2nd ser. 1865, 3rd ser. 1876).

17 H. Ewald, *The History of Israel* (London: Longmans, Green and Co., 1867–86).

18 See Rogerson, *Old Testament criticism*, pp. 238–42.

the Old Testament's precedence of the law, de Wette's the precedence of the prophets. From a number of quarters support began to gather for the priority of the prophets, together with the radical implications this had for the history of Israel.

An early advocate of the priority of the prophets was the Alsace scholar Edouard Reuss, who taught in the Protestant Theological Faculty in Strasbourg. His opinions dated from 1834, but he had declined to publish them because of the outcry over Vatke's *Biblical theology* the following year. Among his theses was the proposition that the prophets of the eighth and seventh centuries had no knowledge of the Mosaic law.[19] In Britain, the 1860s saw the publication of the first five parts of J. W. Colenso's *The Pentateuch and Book of Joshua critically examined*, and while they did not address the relation of the law and the prophets directly, they had an effect on the thinking of the Dutch scholar Abraham Kuenen, whose publications in the 1860s played a major part in the development of biblical scholarship.

The first volume of Colenso's *The Pentateuch and Joshua* was a crude attack on the historicity of the biblical account of the exodus and wilderness wanderings, making much of the improbability that some 2 million Hebrews together with their sheep and cattle crossed the Red Sea and journeyed through the wilderness.[20] It raised an outcry not only because of its lack of respect for the biblical text but because the author was the Anglican bishop of Natal. Such was the hostility that it provoked that a project called the *Speaker's commentary* (named after J. E. Denison, Viscount Ossington, Speaker of the House of Commons from 1857 to 1872) was organised to rebut the results of the biblical researches that Colenso published with increasing competence during the 1860s. Colenso was, in fact, in conflict with the ecclesiastical establishment in Britain for a number of reasons. He had been accused of following F. D. Maurice in denying that there was eternal punishment for unbelievers[21] and he was invited to dine with scientists such as Charles Lyell, T. H. Huxley, Herbert Spencer and Joseph Hooker.[22] Later he would support the rights of the Zulu people against the colonial policies of the white settlers in Natal.[23] From 1863 Colenso was in contact with Kuenen by letter, the two men

19 *Ibid.*, p. 259 n. 8.
20 J. W. Colenso, *The Pentateuch and book of Joshua critically examined*, Part 1 (London: Longmans, Green, 1862). See Rogerson, *Old Testament criticism*, pp. 220–37.
21 Guy, *The heretic*, pp. 43–5.
22 L. Huxley, *Life and letters of Thomas Henry Huxley*, 3 vols. (London: Macmillan, 1900), vol. 1, pp. 256–8.
23 Guy, *The heretic*, pp. 193–214.

met several times during Colenso's visits to Britain and Europe, and Colenso translated and published volume 1 of Kuenen's *Historisch-kritisch onderzoek* in 1865.[24] Colenso convinced Kuenen that what was called the Book of Origins (roughly what has come to be known as the Priestly source or document, and containing narratives and the Mosaic legislation in Exodus, Leviticus and Numbers) was post-exilic, a view that Colenso later partly embraced himself as far as the sacrificial and priestly regulations were concerned, and which confirmed his antagonism to the high church ritualists whom he opposed in South Africa and Britain. This post-exilic dating decisively placed the law after the prophets. Similar conclusions were being reached by two students of the Alsatian Edouard Reuss, Karl Heinrich Graf (in 1866) and August Kayser (in 1874),[25] and the way was being prepared for the publication of two classic versions of what was to become known as the Graf-Wellhausen hypothesis, Julius Wellhausen's *History of Israel* (1878) and William Robertson Smith's *The Old Testament in the Jewish church* (1881).[26]

The so-called Graf-Wellhausen hypothesis linked a documentary theory of the composition of the Pentateuch with a reconstruction of the history of Israelite religion that had been anticipated by de Wette over seventy years earlier. Four sources, or documents, were proposed. The J source (so called because it primarily used the name Yahweh for God), probably written in Judah in the ninth century, and the E source (so called because it used the Hebrew word *Elohim*, meaning God), probably written in the northern kingdom, Israel, in the eighth century, reflected a period when God was worshipped at many sanctuaries and there was no centralised priesthood or sacrificial legislation. The reforms of Josiah in 622 in response to the preaching of the prophets against social injustice and Canaanite religious practices found their legal justification in Deuteronomy (D), which was written in the seventh century. These reforms closed the local sanctuaries and made Jerusalem the sole legitimate sanctuary. The destruction of Jerusalem by the Babylonians in 587 BC and the subsequent exile of the Jews led to a concern for atoning sacrifices and the practice of ritual purity. Following the return from exile after 540 BC, the Priestly source (P) was composed to set out the requirements for ritual purity

---

24 A. Kuenen, *The Pentateuch and book of Joshua critically examined, translated from the Dutch and edited with notes by the Right Rev. J. W. Colenso, D.D. Bishop of Natal* (London: Longmans, Green, 1865). See Rogerson, 'British responses to Kuenen's pentateuchal studies'.

25 See Rogerson, *Old Testament criticism*, pp. 258–9.

26 J. Wellhausen, *Geschichte Israels*, 2 vols. (Berlin: G. Reimer, 1878), more familiar from its second edition *Prolegomena zur Geschichte Israels* (Berlin: G. Reimer, 1883); W. Robertson Smith, *The Old Testament in the Jewish church: twelve lectures on biblical criticism* (Edinburgh: A. and C. Black, 1881).

backed by a system of priesthood and sacrifice, which were projected back into the time of Moses following the exodus. An implication of the scheme was that the prophets of the eighth century played a decisive role in the development of Israel's ethical monotheism, while the post-exilic religion centred on Jerusalem and, dominated by ritual purity and atoning sacrifices, fell below the achievements of the earlier prophetic religion.

If Wellhausen presented his case with forceful logic and overwhelming evidence, Robertson Smith's no less logically presented case was marked by Christian evangelical fervour. It is true that Smith's book was the published version of public lectures delivered to large audiences while he was on trial for heresy before the General Assembly of the Free Church of Scotland (he eventually lost his case and was dismissed from his post in Aberdeen); but Smith believed passionately that biblical criticism was a continuation and completion of what was begun at the Reformation. The fact that the new criticism produced a version of Old Testament religion and history at variance with that presented in the Bible was not a problem for Smith. Rather, it enabled the Old Testament to regain the respect of intelligent readers, and it confirmed Smith's belief that 'the Bible history [was] no profane history, but the story of God's saving self-manifestation'.[27] It was, incidentally, also Colenso's faith rather than his scepticism that made him become such a fearsome biblical critic. As a missionary to the Zulu people, biblical criticism, along with recent scientific discoveries, meant that he did not have to make his converts believe that the world had been created in 4004 BC, that woman was created from the rib of a man, that there had been a universal flood, that an ass had spoken and that the sun had stood still. The abandonment of such literalism left the way open to concentrate on what the Bible was really about, which was about the Living Word which spoke through the Bible to bring a clearer knowledge of the Living God.[28]

The mention of the literalism that Colenso opposed is a reminder that while orthodox churchmen in Britain were reeling from the shock of his attacks on the historicity of parts of the Pentateuch, they were also having to respond to the implications of works such as Lyell's *Principles of geology* (1830) which showed that the earth was much older than the 6,000 years of Ussher's chronology based on the Bible, and Darwin's *Origin of species* (1859) which

27 W. Robertson Smith, *Lectures and essays of William Robertson Smith* (London: A. and C. Black, 1912), p. 233.

28 J. W. Colenso, 'On missions to the Zulus in Natal and Zululand', reprinted in *Bringing forth light: five tracts on Bishop Colenso's Zulu mission* (Pietermaritzburg: University of Natal Press; Durban: Killie Campbell Africana Library, 1982), pp. 205–38.

gave a natural explanation for the development of the human race.[29] In the earlier part of the century various efforts had been made to reconcile the newly emerging sciences such as geology with traditional interpretations of the Bible and the 'design theology' of William Paley, which deduced the existence of God as designer from the alleged perfection of the natural world as a designer's artefact.[30] Paley's view was based upon belief in the fixity of species, a view that was directly challenged by Darwin. While liberal members of the church were not greatly bothered by Darwin's theories – and even some Calvinist theologians believed that he had simply described the processes through which God had worked to create the human race – there were still many who regarded Darwin as a threat to the Bible and the whole edifice of Christian theology.[31] An excellent example of a response to Darwin from the traditional side can be found in Christopher Wordsworth's commentary on Genesis of 1865.[32] Wordsworth, who would become bishop of Lincoln (1869–85), produced a very thorough and scholarly piece of work which, while it paid attention to Colenso, Darwin and German biblical criticism, was uncompromisingly apologetic and traditional. Fundamental to Wordsworth's approach was the decisive authority of the New Testament, and in particular the teaching of Jesus, in matters of criticism. The truth of Jonah's having been swallowed by a whale was confirmed by Jesus's reference to it as prefiguring his death and resurrection (Matthew 12:40), while 2 Peter 2:16, which referred to Baalam's speaking ass, guaranteed the truth of that story from Numbers 22:28–30.[33] On the age of the earth, Wordsworth accepted that geology showed it to be much older than 6,000 years. However, what geology had discovered was the state of the earth *before* the six days of creation in Genesis 1, when the earth was 'without form and void' (Genesis 1:2). Somehow, but with divine permission, a hostile agency had distorted this creation and the six-day account in Genesis was the description of a re-creation. Darwin's view that the human race had evolved from a barbarous state was contradicted, among other things, by the biblical teaching that the first humans were created in the image and likeness of God, and that this image had been restored in Christ following its

---

29 C. Lyell, *Principles of geology*, 3 vols. (London: John Murray, 1830–3); C. Darwin, *On the origin of species by means of natural selection, or the preservation of favoured races in the struggle for life* (London: John Murray, 1859).

30 Addinall, *Philosophy and biblical interpretation*.

31 For a fuller discussion of the impact of Darwin and geological science see chapter 11 above.

32 C. Wordsworth, *Genesis and Exodus: with notes and introduction* (London: Rivingtons, 1865).

33 Wordsworth, *Genesis*, 2nd edn (London: Rivingtons, 1866), p. xxxii.

loss by Adam. When it is considered that a highly intelligent and competent churchman with such views would be an influential bishop until 1885, it is easy to see how hard biblical criticism had to battle in order to gain any headway.

So far, nothing has been said in this chapter about the New Testament, and this must now be remedied. At the beginning of the nineteenth century New Testament scholarship had recognised the so-called synoptic problem – the striking similarities between the first three Gospels – and had solved it by adopting the so-called Griesbach hypothesis, after J. J. Griesbach (1745–1812). This supposed that Mark's Gospel was an abbreviation of Matthew (in fact a view that went back at least to Augustine) but had also drawn on Luke. For the purposes of reconstructing the life of Jesus, the two primary sources were the 'eye-witness' Gospels of Matthew and John. As mentioned above, Strauss's *Life of Jesus* (1835) contained a sustained attack on the credibility of John's Gospel as a source for the life of Jesus and the same year saw the publication of an article by Karl Lachmann which argued for the priority of Mark, and that there must also have been another source for the synoptic gospels. Lachmann's work began a line of research which ended with the publication in 1863 of H. J. Holtzmann's *The Synoptic Gospels* which put the classic case for the priority of Mark and for the existence of another source.[34] However, a radical alternative for the origins of the New Testament had been proposed by F. C. Baur, in a series of articles and books beginning in 1831 and culminating in *Christianity and the Christian church of the first three centuries* (1853).[35] Baur believed that early Christianity was formed out of a conflict between Paul on the one hand, who accurately understood the implications of the teaching of Jesus, and Peter on the other, who represented a Jewish understanding of Christianity. This division, which split the church grievously, was healed only in the second century when writings such as Acts and the Epistles (with the exception of the four genuine Pauline letters, Romans, 1 and 2 Corinthians and Galatians) were composed, with the process culminating in John's Gospel, which was dated by Baur to AD 170. The earliest Gospel was that of Matthew.[36]

Such a radical challenge to the dating of the New Testament was bound to provoke opposition, and it has become almost legendary to write of how

---

34 H. J. Holtzmann, *Die synoptischen Evangelien, ihr Ursprung und geschichtliche Charakter* (Leipzig, W. Engelmann, 1863). See Kümmel, *New Testament*, pp. 146–55.

35 F. C. Baur, *Das Christentum und die christliche Kirche der drei ersten Jahrhunderte* (Tübingen: Fues, 1853).

36 See Kümmel, *New Testament*, pp. 127–43.

Baur provoked the famous Cambridge triumvirate of J. B. Lightfoot, B. F. Westcott and F. J. A. Hort to refute him on behalf of British scholarship.[37] They, and others, succeeded, to the extent that no competent scholar today would accept a second-century dating for any part of the New Testament, and Paul would be accorded more than the four letters allowed to him by Baur. On the other hand, the importance of the division between Paul and 'Jewish' Christianity in the formation of the early church cannot be denied. In practice Lightfoot, and later Westcott, defended the authorship of John's Gospel by the disciple John the son of Zebedee, with obvious implications for reconstructing the life of Jesus.[38] A more radical contribution to scholarship was the work of Westcott and Hort on the textual criticism of the New Testament, work which drew on such things as the discovery of Codex Sinaiticus by Constantin Tischendorf in 1844.[39] Their *The New Testament in the original Greek* (1881) broke new ground and significantly affected the readings adopted by the scholars who produced the Revised Version of the New Testament in the same year (1881). Lightfoot's main contribution to the modification of Baur's position lay in the field of patristic rather than biblical scholarship, in that his work on the Apostolic Fathers demonstrated that works such as the letters of Ignatius (c. AD 110–15) and the first Letter of Clement (c. AD 96) were genuine, whereas Baur's position argued and demanded that they were forgeries.[40]

The last two decades of the nineteenth century saw the spread and consolidation of the critical positions that had been painstakingly established during the preceding decades. In England, E. B. Pusey, who had consistently rejected critical developments in Old Testament scholarship, was succeeded in 1883 as Regius Professor of Hebrew in Oxford by S. R. Driver, whose *Old Testament introduction* of 1891 provided a critical, lucid and positive advocacy of the 'Wellhausen' theory.[41] This became a standard work and went through many editions well into the following century. A joint Anglo-American project which similarly spearheaded the critical approach was the International Critical Commentary series, begun in 1895, and edited on the Old Testament side by Driver and by C. A. Briggs of Union Theological Seminary, New York. The cause of Old Testament criticism in America had been well served by the Unitarian

37 For a critical review of this position see Treloar, *Lightfoot*.
38 See Treloar, *Lightfoot*, pp. 295–302.
39 See Parker, 'The New Testament'.
40 Treloar, *Lightfoot*, pp. 336–71.
41 S. R. Driver, *An introduction to the literature of the Old Testament* (Edinburgh: T. and T. Clark, 1891).

scholar Theodore Parker, who was a follower of de Wette, and who published an English version of the latter's Old Testament Introduction with extensive notes of his own.[42] In Sweden Otto Myrberg strongly resisted the tide of Old Testament criticism, and in particular S. A. Fries's *History of Israel* (1894), which advocated the 'Wellhausen' view.[43] Myrberg's successor in Uppsala in 1892, Waldemar Rudin, was more open to critical scholarship although shaken by Fries's *History*. He played a leading part in blocking Fries's appointment to a lectureship in Uppsala. It was left to Erik Stave, who succeeded Rudin as Ordinary Professor in 1900, to initiate the acceptance of the results of Old Testament criticism.

An important development in French Roman Catholic scholarship was the founding, in 1890, of the Ecole Pratique d' Etudes Bibliques in Jerusalem and of its journal, the *Revue Biblique*, in 1892. The scholar behind this development was the Dominican priest Marie-Joseph Lagrange who, in the 1890s, undertook an expedition to Sinai, where he became convinced that this wilderness could not have supported the 2 million Israelites who left Egypt at the exodus, as implied by Exodus 12:37 and other passages. Lagrange realised that these figures were an idealisation, a projection back from a later age, as argued by Wellhausen and those who had preceded and followed him. Although such a view could not be openly expressed at that time in the Roman Catholic Church, the encyclical *Providentissimus Deus*, issued by Leo XIII in November 1893, gave qualified encouragement to critical scholarship. Catholic scholars were encouraged to master the Semitic languages and to utilise the discoveries of archaeology. The main purpose of the Bible was to disclose the way of salvation and not to be a handbook of scientific knowledge. Unfortunately, the Biblical Commission that the encyclical established took a very conservative line, partly in response to the views of another Catholic scholar, Alfred Loisy, who argued in 1903 that the Pentateuch was not composed by Moses and that the opening chapters of Genesis were not reliable history.[44] Loisy was excommunicated in 1908 and Lagrange's work came under suspicion, and had to be modified accordingly. Five years after his death in 1938, the encyclical *Divino Afflante Spiritu* (1943) gave renewed official encouragement for Catholic scholars to engage in historical-critical research on the Bible. It has

---

42 W. M. L. de Wette, *A critical and historical introduction to the canonical scriptures of the Old Testament, translated and enlarged by Theodore Parker*, 2nd edn (Boston: Little, Brown, 1858).

43 S. A. Fries, *Israels Historia* (Uppsala, 1894). See Idestrom, *From biblical theology to biblical criticism*.

44 Cook, 'Loisy'.

been said that much of the substance of this was based upon Lagrange's early work.[45]

Another important factor during this period was the development of Assyriology, which not only contributed vastly to knowledge of the world of the Old Testament in the form of the history and religion of Babylon, Assyria and Persia, but also demonstrated that the biblical accounts of the creation and the flood had older, Babylonian parallels. The claim, by the German Assyriologist Friedrich Delitzsch in 1901, that everything in the Old Testament derived from Babylon caused a storm which died down when it became clear that such assertions were grossly exaggerated. However, that there was an element of truth in these claims was supported by further discoveries, such as of the laws of Hammurabi in 1901. Hammurabi had been king of Babylon in the eighteenth century and some of his laws resembled those in Exodus 21–23.

The discovery of extra-biblical material similar to material contained in the Bible had the effect of shifting attention away from the documentary sources that had been identified with so much scholarly effort during the nineteenth century, to what lay behind them. This, in turn, focused attention upon the social milieux in which the basic units that underlay the biblical tradition had their origin. On the Old Testament side pioneering work was done by Hermann Gunkel in the three editions of his commentary on Genesis (1901, 1902, 1910) which moved progressively to the view that the stories of the Patriarchs had their origin in Hebrew folk tales (Märchen), which in their turn had much in common with the folk tales of all nations. Earlier, Gunkel's *Creation and chaos* (1890) had drawn attention to the importance of Jewish apocalyptic as the milieu which had preserved the biblical traditions about the beginning and end of time, traditions which owed much to Babylonian influence.[46]

Gunkel was a member of what became known as the 'history of religions' school ('die religionsgeschichtliche Schule'), a group of scholars based originally in Göttingen who, without giving up their commitment to the uniqueness of the Bible, believed that it should be investigated from the standpoint of the emergence of the Jewish and Christian faith communities from their particular historical and religious settings. In the case of the Old Testament this meant the cultures of Babylon and Persia as disclosed by the Assyriological discoveries. For the New Testament it meant Jewish apocalyptic and, towards the end of

---

45 See De Vaux, *The Bible and the Ancient Near East*, p. 276 n. 2; also Lagrange, *Père Lagrange*.
46 See Klatt, *Hermann Gunkel*.

the period covered by this chapter, the exotic world of the Hellenistic-Oriental mystery religions.[47]

The assessment of the figure and mission of Jesus was radically affected by this new orientation. Whereas Jesus had been presented as a moral teacher of this-worldly values by the so-called liberal theology of the late nineteenth century, the history of religions approach saw Jesus as an eschatological prophet, warning his generation about the imminent arrival of the kingdom of God, an event that would bring history to an end. Albert Schweitzer's *The quest of the historical Jesus* (1906) put the case for understanding Jesus and his mission in this way with classic power. The form that Christianity took owed much to the non-fulfilment of this expectation, according to the apocalyptic approach.[48]

It is no exaggeration to say that in the period 1815 to 1914 the study of the Bible experienced the biggest changes that had ever occurred in its history. This is particularly striking in the case of Britain. The period began with the Albury conferences trying to ascertain which biblical prophecies remained to be fulfilled. It ended with almost complete acceptance in academic circles of the view of the history of Israelite history and religion classically expressed by Wellhausen. Change was inevitably much less on the New Testament front, but it is noteworthy that some British scholars gave a guarded welcome to the eschatological interpretation advocated by Schweitzer.[49] What had been achieved in academic scholarship hardly penetrated to the general or churchgoing public, the only noteworthy exception being the commentary on Genesis published by S. R. Driver in 1904.[50] This argued that there was no fundamental disagreement between the findings of science and biblical scholarship, and that the value and importance of Genesis for the Christian church was enhanced rather than diminished by the discoveries of science and the broader study of religion. On the New Testament front the acceptance of the priority of Mark's Gospel led to the view that it was possible to reconstruct a non-ecclesiastical Jesus along traditional lines, who could be presented in simple terms alike in church and school as a figure to be admired and followed. It would not be until after the Second World War that Rudolf Bultmann's pioneering and

---

47 See Kümmel, *The New Testament*, pp. 245–80.
48 A. Schweitzer, *Von Reimarus zu Wrede: eine Geschichte der Leben-Jesu Forschung* (Tübingen: J. C. B. Mohr, 1906), English trans. *The quest of the historical Jesus* (London: Adam and Charles Black, 1910).
49 See the preface to the English edition of Schweitzer's *Quest* by F. C. Burkitt.
50 S. R. Driver, *The Book of Genesis with introduction and notes*, Westminster Commentaries (London: Methuen, 1904).

radical *History of the synoptic tradition* (1922) would become available in English translation. In 1914 the practical implications of the advances made in biblical scholarship in the previous hundred years had yet to be confronted seriously by the churches in Britain and in most other Christian countries, with the exception, perhaps, of Germany.

13

Popular religion and irreligion in countryside and town

DAVID M. THOMPSON

Christianity spread in the Roman empire as an urban religion, and the term 'pagan' originally meant a country-dweller. In the second millennium of the church's history in Europe popular Christian practice became the norm in the countryside, and such difficulties as there were tended to be found in the towns. The nineteenth century proved to be a much more testing time for the church than before, and the urban population grew very rapidly. In 1800 only the Netherlands had more than a quarter of its population living in towns of more than 10,000 inhabitants. By 1890 Great Britain had a predominantly urban population, and the proportion in towns of over 10,000 exceeded 30 per cent in Belgium, Prussia and Saxony as well as the Netherlands.[1] The main reason for this change was industrialisation, though not all new industry developed in towns.

Population growth posed significant problems for the church, particularly when associated with urbanisation, because of the need for new churches and more clergy. Notwithstanding significant efforts made by the church – sometimes with active assistance from government, sometimes by raising funds from benefactors – levels of religious practice were not sustained. It became possible to argue, as one contemporary, Karl Marx, did, that industrialisation exposed the essential flaws in religion. Against this background sociologists developed a cluster of theories of secularisation to describe or explain the changes in the modern period; the extent to which they have explanatory force has remained controversial.

Nevertheless, whilst the significance of population growth and urbanisation cannot be denied, the extent to which the changes at the end of the eighteenth century were underlying causes rather than presenting causes remains open for discussion. The French Revolution, for example, made it possible for the

---

1 McLeod, *Religion and the people of western Europe*, p. 75.

population to neglect their duty to take communion at the major Christian festivals with much less chance of investigation and accusation. The religious changes of 1790–4 represented a violent upheaval from the past; and the religious scene in France has never been the same since. However, although before the Revolution it was rare for the population absent from Easter Communion to be more than 10 per cent, the variations from place to place in regular Sunday mass attendance were very much greater. Although it is probably true, as Professor Gabriel Le Bras declared, 'that religious practice was never more widespread than between 1650 and 1789', there was evidence before the Revolution (and industrialisation) of significant regional variations in practice; furthermore the same variations emerged much more clearly in the nineteenth century. The west, the east, the Massif Central and the western Pyrenees were the most fervent; the centre, the south-west and the Mediterranean south were much less so; and Paris was much the least practising.[2]

Arguably Spain was the most religious country in Europe; even in the twentieth century levels of religious practice in some northern Spanish valleys approached 100 per cent.[3] Yet there were wide variations in the level of religious practice in Spain as elsewhere in Europe: whereas in the north there was not only regular attendance at Sunday mass by men as well as women but also regular attendance at weekday mass, in the southern provinces of Andalusia, Extremadura and Las Manchas, where the parishes were much larger and the majority of the rural population were landless labourers rather than peasant proprietors, regular mass attendance was much lower. Frances Lannon's summary is true for many countries: 'Catholic practice was affected by the following factors: region, size of settlement, the ownership of property, occupation, age, and sex'.[4] Spain also had a high number of priests, but although it was overwhelmingly rural, the clergy were concentrated in the towns, not least because of the relatively high number in cathedral and associated appointments – only a little more than a third of the secular clergy were involved in parish work. So rural parishes still found it difficult to secure a priest, and rural stipends were very low. In the late eighteenth century a number of reforming bishops sought a better distribution of priests and an emphasis on interior faith rather than simply outward observance. Significant

---

2 Boulard, *Introduction to religious sociology*, pp. 12–40; the quotation is from Le Bras, *Etudes de sociologie religieuse*, vol. I, p. 275.
3 Christian, *Person and God in a Spanish valley*.
4 Lannon, *Privilege, persecution, and prophecy*, p. 10.

use was made of the regular clergy to organise parish missions, almost along evangelical lines.[5]

However, from the Napoleonic era reform became primarily associated with secular criticism of the church, and the clergy became sharply more conservative. The Napoleonic era was the first disruption in the unquestioned position of the Roman Catholic Church in Mediterranean Europe, with some dioceses remaining vacant for several years. It was also the first opportunity for anticlerical voices to be heard in force; thereafter in the nineteenth century it proved impossible to quell them. This was first apparent at the time of the Cortes of 1812, though their reforms were short-lived. The Revolution of 1820, which abolished the Inquisition for a second time and once more removed the Jesuits from the scene, began the process of reforming the monasteries; about half of them were suppressed. This was carried further in the Liberal period of 1833–43, when the remaining contemplative monasteries were suppressed from 1835. This had more drastic effects on male congregations than female: about 800 out of nearly 1,100 women's communities survived at the mid-century.[6] Sales of monastic property lasted until 1860. Tithes were abolished in 1837 and the state took over responsibility for payment of the clergy. Clerical incomes fell drastically – nearly half the parishes of the archdiocese of Tarragona lacked priests by 1840, and by 1843 effective clerical numbers were one third of that under the *ancien régime*.[7] 'The parish clergy, profoundly conservative, devoted to Rome, and concentrated in an isolated countryside became the dominant group within clerical ranks.'[8] In 1846 nearly half the dioceses of Spain were vacant. In the Revolution of 1854–6 the process of amortising other church property began, which reduced the ability of the church to support itself and created a group with a vested interest against any revival of its position.[9]

There is no evidence of a mass desertion from the church in the 1830s, but the old variations in religious practice remained. It proved increasingly difficult for the church to keep pace with industrial and urban development in the later nineteenth century, though there was some recovery. The church of 1860 was poorer than that of 1760 but better off than that of 1830.

5 Callahan, *Church, politics and society in Spain*, pp. 6–31.
6 Lannon, *Privilege, persecution, and prophecy*, p. 59. On the suppressions, see pp. 383–4 below.
7 Callahan, *Church, politics and society*, pp. 165–77.
8 *Ibid.*, p. 178.
9 Kiernan, *The revolution of 1854*, pp. 2–3, 18, 121–34. For a fuller account of church and politics in Spain and Portugal see chapter 23 below.

Popular devotions, especially that of the Sacred Heart, intensified, overtaking the simple interior faith of the eighteenth century reformers. Also there was no attempt in Spain to eliminate religion from the schools as new education laws were passed. The new religious congregations of the later nineteenth century founded orphanages, hospitals, reformatories and schools. The 2,000 men and 20,000 women of 1868 had grown to 11,000 men and 40,000 women by 1904. By contrast the number of diocesan priests almost halved between 1867 and 1951.[10] But the regular clergy ceased to be involved in home missionary activity, and ironically as urbanisation and industrialisation developed the church became more concentrated in the countryside than the towns. The state refused to create new parishes in the towns from the 1880s.[11] Lannon regards the religious revival in later nineteenth century Spain as 'a mainly bourgeois phenomenon, not a popular one'.[12] Certainly the church became more exclusively identified with right-wing politics. The freedom of religious worship permitted under article 11 of the 1876 constitution provoked traditional cries that this permitted error. Leo XIII appealed to the church in Spain in 1882 to accept the new constitutional situation, as he was to do in France ten years later; but efforts to form a Catholic Union which might represent a more moderate position in politics failed.[13]

Portugal escaped the Napoleonic period more lightly, but had a nineteenth-century history very similar to that of Spain. Religious practice was much stronger in the north than the south, and the majority of monasteries were dissolved in 1833–4. Subsequently the religious orders reappeared and developed in ways very comparable to Spain and France. The state abolished tithes in 1832 and took over parochial endowments in the 1860s, resulting in a significant loss of income for the parochial clergy. Religious toleration was introduced in 1864 despite the strong opposition of the church, but Roman Catholicism was recognised as the official religion of the state until 1911, when it was separated after the revolution of 1910. This legislation was very similar to the Law of Separation in France of 1905, and also involved the suppression of the religious orders again.[14]

Italy too in the late eighteenth century was well provided with clergy – in the Kingdom of Naples there was probably one priest for every hundred people,

---

10 Lannon, *Privilege, persecution, and prophecy*, pp. 59, 61, 89.
11 Callahan, *Church, politics and society*, p. 245.
12 Lannon, *Privilege, persecution, and prophecy*, p. 149.
13 *Ibid.*, pp. 122–3, 133–6.
14 Chadwick, *A history of the popes*, pp. 469–83.

and monasteries and convents were well filled.[15] However, the Napoleonic era had a more drastic effect on Italy than on Iberia. Monks and nuns were driven from their monasteries and convents, and many never returned, though some former monks became secular priests. This enabled the popes to reorganise religious orders in Italy after 1814. Similarly the number of dioceses in southern Italy was reduced from 131 to 50 between 1818 and 1834. Many churches fell into disrepair and needed restoration. There was a sharp decline in recruitment to the priesthood in the early nineteenth century, particularly in the north, where religious practice was generally less strong than in the south. The disappearance of brotherhoods removed one previously significant aspect of lay religion. The number of canons in cathedrals and collegiate churches also reduced, because of fewer resources. Both these developments made the parish priest more significant.[16] In Piedmont contemplative religious orders were dissolved in 1855, and this legislation was extended to other parts of Italy as Piedmont unified the country after 1859–60. Church property in Italy was sufficient to support clerical stipends.

There were similar regional variations in religious practice in northern Europe. In Great Britain the difference between areas was less than in France. Professor McLeod noted that few, if any, areas of England could match the overwhelmingly high levels of religious practice found in parts of Brittany, and England certainly had no dechristianised areas to match the Limousin.[17] However, the situation was more complicated because of the existence of Protestant Nonconformists, as well as Roman Catholics, alongside the established churches of England and Scotland. Roman Catholics, for example, had a traditional strength in north-west England, before their geography was changed profoundly by Irish immigration, particularly after 1840. The pattern of distribution of Methodism, in its various forms, was different from that of the Old Dissent of Presbyterians, Independents and Baptists, partly because Methodists had concentrated on areas where Dissent was weak, and partly because they appealed to rather different social groups. As emphasised in chapter 4, the period after 1815 saw a significant expansion of Protestant Nonconformity of all types.[18] Nevertheless not all villages in a given area were the same. There is a correlation between the presence of Nonconformity and patterns of landholding, such that it was most often found when there was a large

---

15 Chadwick, *The popes and European revolution*, pp. 96ff.
16 Chadwick, *A history of the popes*, pp. 578–608.
17 McLeod, *Religion and society in England*, p. 2.
18 See above, pp. 53–69.

number of small landowners and rarely found when the land belonged mainly to a single landowner.[19] Moreover, the religious dynamics of a place were different when there were three or more places of worship, rather than simply the parish church and a Nonconformist chapel. In the latter the difference between the Church of England and Nonconformity was likely to be foremost in the perceived identity of the two groups, whereas in the former there were often subtle social differences between the various Nonconformist chapels – farmers and their labourers, for example, or farmers and artisans. The presence of a Roman Catholic church immediately made the difference between Protestant and Roman Catholic important.

A survey of (Protestant) parishes in Germany in 1862 showed that very few had populations of more than 3,000: most were between 1,000 and 2,000 in size, and the largest parishes were in Prussia. However, the German population grew by 11.2 million in the thirty years after 1871, and there was significant church building after 1880. By the end of the century the number of new parishes had nearly kept pace with the growth of population. Statistics for churchgoing in 1891 showed that it was generally worst in those places where the distance to the parish church was greatest – east Prussia, parts of Franconia and Bavaria east of the Rhine, Schleswig-Holstein, the Hansa cities, Hanover, Frankfurt and other industrial towns. Berlin, however, was almost unique; the legal difficulties in dividing parishes resulted in around eight parishes with populations of more than 20,000 in 1871, with consequently low rates of churchgoing, up to a third of children unbaptised, and a significant increase in marriages outside the church.[20]

The difference between Catholic and Protestant was also primary in Germany. In some states the parish church in one village might be Lutheran and in the next village Roman Catholic; and in some towns, for example Landau in the Palatinate, the parish church was shared between Protestants and Catholics until the twentieth century, when a new Catholic church was built. More often, the post-Westphalia conditions required Catholics and Protestants to live side by side. The presence of the Roman Catholic Church was much more apparent in the west of Germany than in Prussia, apart from that part of East Prussia that had originally been Poland. Another reason for the change in the balance of Catholic and Protestant was the high level of Protestant emigration from Germany: between 1871 and 1897 2.2 million Protestants

---

19 Everitt, *The pattern of rural dissent*; Thompson, 'The churches and society in nineteenth-century England'.
20 Hope, *German and Scandinavian Protestantism*, pp. 497–508, 524.

emigrated, mainly to North America.[21] By contrast in Italy and the Iberian peninsula Protestant churches were very rare: the Waldensians in the Alpine valleys hung on to a precarious existence in the early nineteenth century, and Protestants only appeared in Spain from the 1830s as a result of the influence of the British and Foreign Bible Society. In France the areas with a significant Protestant presence were few after the Revocation of the Edict of Nantes in 1685, though the Reformed Church began to grow again after the Revolution introduced religious toleration.

The Netherlands also contained a mixed Catholic and Protestant population. There was a Catholic majority in Belgium, and after the revolution of 1830 it became the centre of liberal Catholicism. Roman Catholics were also increasing in numbers in Holland. They had become full citizens as a result of the reforms during the French occupation, and politically they supported Liberal policies, since the Conservative party claimed that the Netherlands was a Calvinist state. On the opposite side was the Groningen movement, which sought to overcome religious divisions on the basis of the Dutch traditions of Erasmus and the Brethren of the Common Life. Johan Rudolf Thorbecke was a Lutheran prime minister, who because of his support for 'Christianity beyond religious division' did not resist the restoration of the Roman Catholic hierarchy in Holland in 1853, which led to his political downfall. Education led the Roman Catholics to change sides politically. Whereas the Groningen movement supported state schools where teaching was not based on Calvinist or Catholic dogma, in 1857 an Education Law permitted the establishment of denominational schools; so Catholics, who were moving steadily in an Ultramontane direction, sought public funds for their schools. Eventually they allied with Abraham Kuyper's Anti-Revolutionary Party.[22]

The membership of the Dutch Reformed Church had fallen to 48.5 per cent of the population by 1899 (though the combined total of the Reformed Church and the Gereformeerde Kerken had been around 56 per cent for fifty years); the Roman Catholic Church was the largest church in Holland by 1930. The number of those with no explicit religious affiliation was very slow to grow and was only 2.3 per cent in 1899.[23] Given that the balance between agricultural and industrial population had reached an 'economically advanced' level by 1700 (rather than 1820 as in the United Kingdom), Holland, with a high level

---

21 *Ibid.*, p. 504.
22 Vlekke, *Evolution of the Dutch nation*, pp. 309–20; Kossmann, *The Low Countries*, pp. 289–96, 302–7; Bornewasser, 'Thorbecke and the churches', pp. 146–69. On Kuyper, see below, pp. 334, 337–8.
23 Wintle, *An economic and social history of the Netherlands*, p. 28. See p. 335 below.

of urbanisation and of religious practice, obviously represents an exception to any general theory of secularisation. Indeed the process of 'pillarisation', or the differentiation of the population into distinct religious groupings in the nineteenth century, might almost be seen as an alternative to secularisation.[24] The level of migration from Holland was more like Denmark and Sweden than Germany, Scotland, Ireland and Norway; and it was not religiously skewed.[25]

Scandinavia illustrates population growth without significant urbanisation – at least in the nineteenth century. In 1800 Stockholm's population was 75,000 (by comparison with 960,000 in London, 600,000 in Paris or 104,000 in Copenhagen) and only two other towns in Sweden had a population of 10,000. By 1900 the population of Stockholm was 300,000 and Gothenburg 130,600, with ten towns over 10,000. The Swedish population more than doubled in the nineteenth century, but in 1900 nearly 80 per cent of them still lived on farms or in villages. The rural growth was sustained by a more intensive agriculture of subdivided farms, often growing potatoes (not unlike Ireland). The result was the development of a rural proletariat, and the disappearance of many communal festivals with magical overtones and fertility rites, leaving only the national festivals of Midsummer, Walpurgis Night (the eve of 1 May), both with some witchcraft associations, and Christmas, which was still half pagan.[26] In the diocese of Skara customary attendance at parish communion dropped from four times a year to once after 1830.[27] The new rural poor, especially young men and female domestics, were no longer attending the parish church. There was not a significant increase in the number of clergy but, since Scandinavia had enjoyed very favourable ratios of clergy to people in the eighteenth century, the ratio was still comparable to that in Germany by the end of the century. However, in northern Sweden and Norway parishes were very large and the difference between those and parishes in the south and in Denmark was very great.[28]

Despite the local variations in religious practice and the development of anticlericalism which have dominated the historiography, the nineteenth century was also a period of religious revival. Existing religious orders, particularly for women, grew rapidly in Mediterranean Europe, such as the Daughters of Charity (1617) and the Daughters of Wisdom (1703), and new ones were

24 Ibid., pp. 167, 317–19. For a full discussion of pillarisation see pp. 333–4 below.
25 Ibid., pp. 34–6.
26 Scott, Sweden, pp. 338–51.
27 Hope, German and Scandinavian Protestantism, p. 376.
28 Ibid., pp. 508–12.

founded, for example the Sisters of the Good Shepherd (1835).[29] New men's orders were founded as well, for example the Salesians by John Bosco in 1859. Moreover, although attendance at mass probably declined in percentage terms by comparison with the previous century, especially in industrial and urban areas, it remained a significant part of the weekly routine, particularly for women. The various religious festivals, which were usually the main holidays, also remained significant. Devotion to particular saints and shrines remained important locally, though perhaps the most significant development here was the increasing dominance of devotion to the Blessed Virgin, particularly as reflected in the dogma of the Immaculate Conception, proclaimed by Pius IX in 1854.

What was popular religion, or indeed irreligion? The answer to this question often seems more straightforward for Roman Catholics. An emphasis upon the saints, particularly local images of saints, or the Blessed Virgin, and the festivals associated with them, could be more important for many than attendance at mass. One of the interesting features of the Roman Catholic Church in the nineteenth century was the extent to which it was prepared to embrace a popular Catholicism that it had tended to be officially cautious about in the past.[30] Even in Lourdes the local priest, the Abbé Peyremale, was initially sceptical about Bernadette's visions in 1858, not least because of the variety of local Pyreneean cults to which they bore similarities; he demanded evidence, but subsequently became one of her chief protectors.[31] In Spain the various processions at religious festivals were a distinct culture. Popular religiosity within its own cultural structures was a phenomenon quite distinct from conventional Catholic practice.[32] Lannon observed that Holy Week processions belong to the streets not the churches, the people not the priests, the lay singers of saetas and noisy bands not the church choirs, just as the brotherhoods themselves are essentially lay in organisation, composition and leadership.[33]

The urge to restrain the popular was not confined to Roman Catholics. In Scotland the traditional summer communion seasons had been occasions which were widely attended, not just from the village concerned; indeed there is some evidence that people travelled from village to village. They were often contexts for religious revival; but they could also be occasions for rather

---

29 See chapter 6 above, pp. 94-102.
30 See chapter 5 above, pp. 70–83.
31 Harris, *Lourdes*, pp. 6–8, 68–71, 151–3; compare Blackbourn, *Marpingen*.
32 Lannon, *Privilege, persecution, and prophecy*, p. 25.
33 *Ibid.*, p. 28.

wild behaviour and some sexual promiscuity. In the early nineteenth century there was a concerted effort by evangelical clergy in the Church of Scotland to rein in the traditional celebrations and make them much more parochial occasions.[34] Consequently the notion of reform in religion, which characterised all churches in all countries in rather different ways, is somewhat ambiguous. The increased number of clergy, usually more systematically trained, tended not to be sympathetic to traditional customs, and sought to eliminate them. An English example would be the removal of the village singers from many parish churches, and their replacement by boys' choirs, often in surplices. This often meant refurnishing the chancels of parish churches with choir stalls (modelled on cathedral or collegiate churches), which was presented as restoration but was actually innovation. The revival of church music in Germany and Sweden in the first half of the nineteenth century parallels that in England, and also drew on fifteenth- and sixteenth-century precedents; most of all there was a rediscovery of the music of Bach.[35]

Particularly among Protestants there was a change in the pattern of congregational worship. Whereas in the Roman Catholic Church the weekly celebration of mass remained the norm (though the extent of preaching varied), among Anglicans and some other Protestants there was a shift away from the post-Reformation pattern of celebrating Holy Communion only three or four times a year. Evangelicals introduced monthly communions in the early nineteenth century, and the weekly communion later appeared in many places under the influence of the Oxford Movement, even though it tended to be at 8.00 a.m. and did not usually displace Mattins as the normal morning service.[36] A new liturgy was introduced in Sweden in 1811, and in Bavaria (including the Palatinate) in 1818. The new liturgy of the Evangelical Union Church in Prussia in 1822 exposed the liturgical diversity which already existed: it was revised in 1856 and 1895.[37] By contrast with the Church of England, where suggestions for any modification of the Book of Common Prayer were suspect in the nineteenth century, in Germany and Sweden liturgical revision was not only possible but took place; and several revisions moved in a more Catholic direction. In some parts of Germany any liturgical reform was resisted or regarded with suspicion – Silesia, Thuringia and Saxony, for example – and in other parts the new liturgies did not penetrate rural parishes. Franconian Bavaria, especially the University of Erlangen, provided the

---

34 Schmidt, *Holy fairs*, pp. 192–212.
35 Hope, *German and Scandinavian Protestantism*, pp. 420–7.
36 Davies, *Worship and theology in England*, vol. III, pp. 223–7.
37 Hope, *German and Scandinavian Protestantism*, pp. 293–4, 344–5, 347, 351–3.

leadership for more traditional Lutheran revival in both Germany and Scandinavia after 1840.[38]

One key question is what level of religious practice might be assumed to be normal, and how far this changed in the course of the nineteenth century. Clearly this depends on local or regional factors as much as on any national tradition. There were countries with one dominant church, where high levels of attachment were combined with low levels of practice. This was as true for Scandinavian Protestant churches like those in Denmark and Sweden as it was for southern European Catholic churches such as those in Portugal or Italy. France, Holland, Germany and Great Britain provided a rather different picture, with subtly different variations: in Great Britain the established churches of England and Scotland were increasingly challenged by varieties of Protestant Nonconformity, particularly in the period up to 1875; in Holland and Germany there was a balance between Reformed or Lutheran churches and the Roman Catholic Church, which varied from state to state; whereas in France the dominant position of the Roman Catholic Church increasingly had to contend with anticlericalism, which tended to prevail in government after 1875.

This is the context in which revivalism should be understood. The original revivalist movements of the late seventeenth and early eighteenth centuries clearly arose from within the existing churches. Indeed the use of the term revival represented the conviction of the original pioneers that the aim was to revive the faith of those who for various reasons were not living up to expectations. This was as true of German pietism as it was of Jonathan Edwards's American Congregationalism; it was also true initially of John Wesley's Methodism in the Church of England. However, from an early stage there were also those who were sufficiently critical of the existing churches that they set up alternative structures, for example the Moravian Brotherhood under Count Zinzendorf. What was increasingly discovered, even by Wesley's Methodists, was that there were certain areas where people were hearing the gospel for the first time. Almost inevitably, though gradually, this led to the gathering of such people into separate churches. Thus the followers of Wesley and Whitefield were effectively separated from the Church of England before the nineteenth century began; and the stimulus that Methodist revivalism gave to Congregationalists and Baptists led to rapid Nonconformist growth in the early nineteenth century.

38 *Ibid.*, pp. 445–9.

The dynamics of religious revival in Britain came from Germany, through the pietism associated with the University of Halle at the end of the seventeenth century and the growth of the Moravians in the mid-eighteenth century. Both pietists and Moravians also exercised significant influence at the Prussian court in the early nineteenth century. But the influence went beyond the court. In the Reformed parishes of the Lower Rhine and Westphalia there was a significant pastoral awakening in the 1820s, especially in Elberfeld and Barmen. G. D. Krummacher (1774–1837) and his son F. W. Krummacher (1796–1868) filled their churches in Elberfeld, Ruhrort and Barmen on Sundays and weekdays, with extensive distribution of Bibles and tracts. A similar movement was found in Pomerania and Lutheran provinces east of the Elbe.[39]

Revivalism in Scandinavia was lay in origin. In eastern Jutland and western Norway there was a rural lay movement from the 1790s which converted several thousand. Hans Nielsen Hauge (1771–1824) was a popular Norwegian lay preacher. In Copenhagen the Bible Society was founded in 1814 by a Scot, Ebenezer Henderson (1784–1858). By the 1830s this became a national religious revival, which linked with Danish and Norwegian cultural nationalism, though the rural awakening was rather different from the pattern followed by liberal townspeople.[40] In Sweden a similar movement was represented initially by the Readers, who read religious tracts in house groups, again inspired by pietism and the Moravians. They were involved in mission work in the far north of Sweden. Methodism was established in Stockholm by George Scott, an Edinburgh-born preacher in 1830, and subsequently led by Carl O. Rosenius (1816–68), some of whose followers later formed the Swedish Covenant Church. Hence in Sweden some of those influenced by revival remained within the established Lutheran Church, but others in effect left.[41] The Swedish state church lost influence in the more divided villages and towns, and the new free churches acquired a distinctive social character; in some of the growing towns this reflected the social differences between different housing areas. Methodists and Baptists doubled their numbers in the 1880s and, with the other free churches, continued to grow until about 1930.[42]

Freedom of religion did not exist in Denmark before the adoption of the Danish constitution in 1849; all inhabitants had to belong to the Lutheran Church in order to qualify as citizens. The new constitution turned the state

---

39 *Ibid.*, pp. 388–99.
40 *Ibid.*, pp. 369–72.
41 On Rosenius, see p. 348 below.
42 Scott, *Sweden*, pp. 355–61, 573; Samuelsson, *From great power to welfare state*, pp. 168–70, 182–4.

church into a people's church, though the promised constitution for the church never materialised. Membership of the people's church remained at nearly 90 per cent of the population until the 1990s, with 80 per cent of children being baptised; but church attendance on a weekly basis was less than 5 per cent. Nevertheless more than half the population attended church from time to time, so that formally there has been no large-scale drift from the church. Lay revivalism developed from the 1790s, and after being opposed by ministers educated on Enlightenment principles, it was drawn back into the mainstream in the 1830s and 1840s by ministers influenced by the more sympathetic teaching of N. F. S. Grundtvig (1783–1872).[43] There has been much discussion of the extent to which the revivals reflected or were assisted by agrarian economic change, as farmers came to own their own land, but without any clear conclusion, since the revival affected large and small farmers in both wealthy and poor regions. The Danish Inner Mission, founded by laymen in 1853 but under clerical control from 1861, spread from Zealand to the whole country; under the influence of Vilhelm Beck it moved in a steadily conservative direction, eventually separating from the more socially radical Copenhagen Inner Mission in the 1890s.[44]

One of the chief characteristics of revivalist movements was the expectation that there would be weekly attendance at church, perhaps even twice on a Sunday. There is little evidence to suggest that this had been normal in the eighteenth century, or even earlier. The Roman Catholic, Lutheran and Anglican churches specified the laity's obligations of church attendance in different ways, but all gave particular emphasis to attendance at communion at Easter. Weekly attendance reflected a particular devotion. Of course, in estate villages, dominated by a single large landowner, estate employees might be expected to attend regularly on Sundays; and this did happen. But in England these villages were always a minority; and there were problems where the clergy were non-resident, even if services were conducted by a curate. Thus the competition between churches could lead to high levels of church attendance. At the time of the 1851 Census of Religious Worship in Britain, for example, the highest proportions of church attendance in England were to be found in Bedfordshire and Huntingdonshire, where both the Church of England and Nonconformity were strong. Similar patterns have been observed in other countries, in both northern and southern Europe. The contrast between the piety of peasant smallholders in northern Spain and landless

---

43 On Grundtvig and Danish revivalism, see pp. 345–7 below.
44 Lausten, *A church history of Denmark*, pp. 200–57, 315–16.

labourers in the latifundia areas of southern Spain is perhaps the most obvious example.

The most important point is the great range of variation in the levels of religious practice both within and between different countries. The explanation for these variations may be on the supply side as much as on the demand side. In other words, the shortage of clergy and church buildings in rapidly growing areas, whether towns or industrial villages, certainly created conditions in which the proportion of the population attending church fell dramatically. This explains the emphasis on church building in the Church of England in the middle third of the nineteenth century and the significance of the rise in clerical recruitment in that period; the same happened in the Nonconformist churches. Yet in recent years it has been argued that the major churches engaged in over-building in the mid- to late-nineteenth century, so it is not surprising that some of the new churches were less than half-full.[45] Nevertheless, there is evidence of a falling away from religious practice altogether, particularly though not exclusively in towns. This became apparent through a failure to respond to the emphasis on more regular church attendance; but even the number of those attending for festivals in the lifecycle – baptisms, weddings, funerals – began to decline, though non-Christian funerals were the most difficult to arrange.

As significant as the level of religious practice, however, is how it was understood. Any detailed examination of popular religion shows that there is a mixture of orthodox and unorthodox conceptions of what religious duty involves. For example, popular conceptions of baptism often included what religious people would regard as superstition – that it was almost a kind of lucky charm or spell. Systematic evidence of this is often hard to secure, since the dominating interpretation of the meaning of religious festivals comes from official sources. At the end of his career Gabriel Le Bras stated that religious practice had 'social rather than properly and profoundly religious meaning'; he even rejected the term 'dechristianisation' because he thought that the 'ages of faith' were a myth, and he distinguished between social custom and personal conviction.[46]

The social institutions of Roman Catholic countries changed in the nineteenth century. Lay brotherhoods declined in influence after the French Revolution in France and Germany; in some places they became almost exclusively

---

45 E.g. Gill, *The myth of the empty church*; Green, *Religion in the age of decline.*
46 Le Bras, *L'église et la village*, pp. 186, 191–2, quoted in Devlin, *The superstitious mind*, p. 4.

mutual benefit societies and lost their religious functions at members' burials and on the festival of their patron saint's day.[47] Similarly traditional pilgrimages and processions, which had been as much for worldly amusement as for religious inspiration, were almost defunct by 1850. They were replaced by Marianic sodalities and congregations, firmly under priestly control, and new kinds of pilgrimage with a much more exclusively religious emphasis.[48] Nevertheless healing was as much a purpose of pilgrimage as religious devotion; and although Lourdes overtook other places in popularity, it did not displace them.[49] This was part of the 'compromise' which the official church made with popular religion in the nineteenth century.

Although Enlightenment rationalism has tended to regard both religious ideas and earlier superstitious attitudes as outdated, the evidence does not suggest that superstitious ideas died very quickly. Stories of witches, fairies, spells, etc. were actually written down and printed in the nineteenth century, rather than simply being told by one generation to the next. Does this mean that they are less or more significant? There is plenty of evidence that such stories were widely believed, and even that central figures in Christianity, particularly the saints, were often understood in similar ways by many people. For example, Dr Devlin challenges the view that the superstitious mind is incompatible with 'the reasonable pragmatism of modernity' and she also argues that popular religion was based on simple ideas of healing and justice to the poor, with priests almost redundant.[50]

A key element therefore was education. Schools, whether dominated by clergy or by secular-minded teachers, were the main means for diminishing superstition, though it did not disappear completely. The nature of irreligion changed, particularly in urban areas. Medical improvements reduced the reliance on traditional cures. The mechanised industrial world was more obviously under human control than the world of nature which determined agricultural prosperity, and did not require supernatural remedies.[51] Furthermore the more intense timetable of industrial work, by comparison with the seasonal variations in agriculture, put greater pressure on people's use of their small amount of leisure time; and freedom not to go to church was often exploited. Secular political gospels, such as those of positivism or socialism,

47 Sperber, *Popular Catholicism*, pp. 30–5.
48 *Ibid.*, pp. 63–77.
49 *Ibid.*, p. 70.
50 Devlin, *The superstitious mind*, pp. xii, 42.
51 McLeod, *Religion and the people of western Europe*, p. 93.

became as attractive as the Christian gospel – indeed Christian and political radicalism could be combined, as in teetotalism. It was not only in Britain that the tavern was seen as the natural rival to the church for the attention of the mass of the population. Owenite Halls of Science developed into Secular Societies in mid-nineteenth-century Britain, under the influence of men like G. J. Holyoake and Charles Bradlaugh. Their 'activist' approach led to regular meetings and rallies of their members, not unlike religious services. Secularist activists tended to come from the same social groups as Christians, whereas many ordinary folk who ignored the churches ignored secularism as well.

Thus there is a difference between popular irreligion and that of the more educated classes. Some evidence suggests that nineteenth-century interest in paganism came more from academics or other professional people seeking to revive something they regarded as past, than from the survival of pagan groups. Orders of Druids, for example, were instituted in the nineteenth century as part of an attempt to revive tradition, particularly in Wales. The questions of how 'popular' such developments were, and how far what happened was the 'invention of tradition', need further research.

There were also various eccentric religious movements in the nineteenth century. Indeed it is not easy to know quite where to draw the line between, for example, Joanna Southcott, Joseph Smith and William Miller. Had Joanna Southcott been a Roman Catholic, who articulated her religious visions in terms of the Blessed Virgin Mary, she might have been regarded as one of a number of significant lowly religious figures who, though unusual, were definitely in the fold. William Miller was one of several people who made predictions about the second coming of Christ, which turned out to be false; but in significant respects the Adventist movement gained a kind of respectability within the nineteenth-century church. Joseph Smith, on the other hand, by claiming to have had visions of biblical stories transferred to a New World setting, lost more in terms of orthodoxy than he gained in relevance; yet the subsequent success of the Church of Jesus Christ of Latter-Day Saints makes it still a puzzle to classify in relation to orthodox Christianity. Moreover, the emigration of the majority of English Mormons to the USA in the early 1850s when the state of Utah was being established means that it is easy to overlook how successful they were in the England of the 1840s.

One obvious point about popular religion (and indeed not only popular religion) is the significance of gender in religious observance. Women were generally significantly more observant than men – the only possible exception to this is male practice in the most devout northern Spanish valleys. The extent of difference between men and women varied greatly between and within countries. The nineteenth century was particularly significant for the development of women's religious orders – not only in Roman Catholic countries, but in the Church of England and the Lutheran churches. In part it may be related to different patterns of population balance and changes in the family as a result of increased women's employment. It is also seen in the development of nursing as a career, and ultimately in the development of women doctors and teachers. The latter two occupations became the entry point for women into overseas missions.

A final reflection concerns anticlericalism. In many ways this was concentrated in predominantly Roman Catholic countries. It was initially inspired by revolutionary ideas, and it became a staple of secularising political programmes, based on the assumption that the church in general and the clergy in particular were opposed to enlightened thinking. In predominantly Protestant countries anticlericalism does not seem to have been so strong. This may partly reflect the fact that generally in such countries the clergy had already lost significant political power during the Reformation, and were firmly subordinate to lay leadership, either locally among landowners and political hierarchies or in a wider national scene, as in Denmark, for example. In countries such as Britain the legal existence of several churches meant that it was possible to be religious without being attached to a clerically dominated national church. In Nonconformist churches the relative balance of power between clergy and laity was different from that in the Church of England – Wesleyan Methodists perhaps being the group among whom the position of the clergy was strongest. But another point needs to be made. In Roman Catholic countries the massive reduction in the numbers of male regular clergy as a result of the French Revolutionary era profoundly changed the balance of power in favour of the parochial clergy. When this is combined with the reduction of the significance of many lay brotherhoods, it can be seen that there was a significant change in the way in which religion was perceived at the local level. The parish priest's loyalty to Rome immediately became much more important. Sperber's verdict on western Germany that 'the growing centrality, prestige, and authority of the local priest was apparent in all aspects of Catholic religious life' was true of Catholic Europe more generally.[52] It is also significant that the way in which the lives of the local church, whether Roman Catholic or Protestant, were reformed in different European countries in the

---

52 Sperber, *Popular Catholicism*, p. 94.

nineteenth century generally placed more significance on the role of the local minister. In this way the world of religion became more localised. At the same time the increasing dependence on the local minister meant that any slackening in recruitment for the ministry was the seed for a future crisis. In different ways and over different periods this was realised in the twentieth century.

PART II

*

THE CHURCHES AND
NATIONAL IDENTITIES

14

Catholic Christianity in France from the Restoration to the separation of church and state, 1815–1905

JAMES F. McMILLAN

Introduction

The relationship between church, state and nation in nineteenth-century France was shaped in large measure by the legacy of the preceding revolutionary era. The French Revolution had begun with the blessing of the church but it ended in a seismic rupture. Whereas the *clergé patriote* of 1789 had looked to religion to bind the nation together, within a few years religion had developed into the single greatest source of national discord. The Jacobins proclaimed the Republic one and indivisible, but their onslaught on Catholic Christianity in effect turned France into not one nation, but two.

On one side of the fault-line lay those who continued to identify with the revolutionary idea of the sovereignty of the people, to be realised in the construction of a new kind of polity, the liberal or democratic nation-state. On the other were those who refused to embrace a social order which did not rest on religious foundations and who still thought of France as the Christian nation *par excellence*, the eldest daughter of the church, the creation of a Christian monarchy best exemplified by St Louis. The Revolution thus bequeathed to the nineteenth century a mythic vision of a 'culture war' between *les deux France* which would last throughout the nineteenth century, and even beyond, though only after 1879 would it once again involve hostile action on the part of a republican state against the forces of organised religion.

Of course, to highlight the persistence of the culture war is by no means to deny that there were people on both sides of the divide, Catholics and liberals, who regretted the conflict over religion and who continued to work for reconciliation between the church and a modern polity. Still less would one wish to imply that there was any inevitability about the eventual outcome of the war of the two Frances: the Separation, when it came in 1905, owed much to accident and circumstances.

The fact remains, however, that the ending of the revolutionary era in 1815 did not close the question of the place which religion should occupy in national life. The concordat of 1802 restored order in the religious field after the turbulence of the 1790s and provided the legal basis for relations between church and state until 1905, but it did not of itself end all religious conflict, since Bonaparte was soon embroiled in a titanic struggle with the papacy after his annexation of the Papal States in 1809. Thus, when the revolutionary era was finally over and the Bourbons were restored definitively to the throne of France in 1815, the French church was confronted with a formidable task of reconstruction. To the surprise of many, it achieved a phenomenal success, though it was a success purchased at a high price.

The Catholic Revival and the rise of Ultramontanism

If, as has already been shown elsewhere in this volume, the nineteenth century was an age of religious revival as much as the age of 'the secularisation of the European mind', French Catholicism was a notable case in point. Between 1815 and 1880 Catholic Christianity in France was completely transformed from the ruinous state to which the Revolution had reduced it. The entire infrastructure was rebuilt, starting with the diocesan clergy, who were recruited in impressive numbers from the Restoration period onwards. By 1830 there were some 40,600 priests, and 58,000 by 1878. This meant that (if we exclude the religious orders) there was one priest active for every 814 inhabitants in 1821 but by 1848 one priest active for every 752 inhabitants, a figure which fell to 657 in 1877. By 1901, it is true, the corresponding figure was 690, but this still represented a much better situation than in 1815. Moreover, especially in the first half of the nineteenth century, this was a youthful and vigorous clergy.

Still more spectacular was the progress in recruitment to the religious orders, and in particular to the female religious orders: between 1800 and 1880 almost 400 new female orders were founded and some 200,000 women took religious vows. These were overwhelmingly *congréganistes* rather than *religieuses*, that is members not of enclosed orders like the Carmelites but active professional women engaged in teaching, nursing and social work (the archetype being the Little Sisters of the Poor, founded by Jeanne Jugan in the 1840s). Male recruits were fewer, but it remains significant nevertheless that in addition to the return of former well-established orders such as the Jesuits, Trappists, Benedictines and Dominicans, there appeared a crop of new foundations for men such as the Oblates of Mary Immaculate, founded by

Eugène Mazenod in 1815, and the Assumptionists, founded by Emmanuel d'Alzon in 1845.

The reconstitution of the French clerical cohorts was only one manifestation of a Europe-wide Catholic Revival which owed much to the change in the intellectual climate produced by the rise of the Romantic movement. Chateaubriand's *The genius of Christianity* (1802) did more than any other single work to restore the credibility and prestige of Christianity in intellectual circles and launched a fashionable rediscovery of the Middle Ages and their Christian civilisation. The revival was by no means confined to an intellectual elite, however, but was evident in the real, if uneven, rechristianisation of the French countryside. Coming on top of an already significant decline in religious practice towards the end of the *ancien régime*, the French Revolution had created a situation in which entire generations had reached adulthood without exposure to any kind of religious formation (a typical case in point being François-Brice Veuillot, the artisan father of the Catholic journalist and polemicist Louis Veuillot). By the calculations of Gérard Cholvy and Yves-Marie Hilaire, the ignorance in religious matters of the great mass of the French population was probably at its peak around 1830. But as clerical numbers expanded and the church began to put down roots in the villages and communes of France clear signs of a return to religious practice could be discerned, particularly in the period 1830 to 1880. Mass attendance rose, as did the number of Easter communicants, though under the impact of the anticlerical policies of the Third Republic after 1879 there was some serious, though by no means universal, backsliding, which may have been partially compensated for by greater commitment on the part of the *pratiquants*.

Especially in the first half of the nineteenth century, the Catholic Revival owed much to missionary activity, conducted mainly by the religious orders and often directed at children. During the Restoration period (1814–30), missions to adults took spectacular form, with rousing sermons accompanied by lavish ceremonies – including processions, hymn-singing and, most notably, the erection of huge missionary crosses – all of which were calculated to make a deep impression on the popular imagination (though they succeeded also in offending the secular sensibilities of the liberal bourgeoisie). Under the July Monarchy (1830–48) the internal missions lost some of their more provocatively ostentatious character but they continued to be employed by parish priests to reinforce their work of evangelisation. The orders – including the female orders, the *bonnes sœurs* – played a crucial role in the consolidation of the reawakened faith through schooling. With the blessing of the state, irrespective of the regime (for, until the anticlerical initiatives of the Third Republic after 1879, the ruling classes in France held firmly to the view that religion was 'good for the people', if not for the educated bourgeoisie) religion was assigned a prominent place in the primary curriculum and teaching orders like the Marist Brothers seized the opportunity to develop new techniques of religious instruction to reach out to the children of some of the most remote and backward rural areas. For the church, this obligation to educate and socialise the faithful was fundamental to its sense of mission and was defended as a non-negotiable right. Inevitably, therefore, when the state once again dared to challenge the hegemony of the church in this sphere, education immediately became the principal theatre of a renewed culture war between the church and the Republic.

A further factor in the Catholic Revival was what has aptly been called a clerical recuperation of popular religion (the latter term being understood as the mix of animist and heterodox Christian beliefs which held sway in much of the countryside, having survived in the face of efforts down the centuries to convert them into the tenets of Counter-Reformation Catholicism). In the nineteenth century, the church succeeded as never before in narrowing the gap between the religion of the people and the religion of the clergy, largely by embracing beliefs and practices which had powerful resonances with the religious impulses of the rural masses: the cult of saints, the veneration of shrines, the organisation of pilgrimages and enthusiasm for miracles. All of these elements were combined in the promotion (from the pope downwards) of the cult of Mary, the Virgin Mother of God, who famously appeared to the peasant girl Bernadette Soubirous at Lourdes in the Pyrenees in 1858 and who was reputed to have been seen at other sites such as La Salette in the French Alps in 1846 and at a convent in Paris in 1830. Pilgrims came to Lourdes in their hundreds of thousands, testifying to the mass appeal of the new, revitalised Catholicism.

There was, however, a price to pay for the narrowing of the gap between learned and popular religion, namely an immense widening of the gap between believers and non-believers, the more so because some of the newer forms of religious enthusiasm appeared to have close links with reactionary politics. The cult of the Sacred Heart, long a favourite of the Jesuits and a banner of royalist and Catholic resistance to the Revolution in the Vendée in the 1790s, was explicitly adopted by militant Catholics as their symbol of a Catholic, as opposed to a Republican, vision of the nation. The building of the massive votive church of the Sacré Cœur in Montmartre after the Paris Commune of 1871 was – and still is – resented by many on the left as a provocation. Rightly or wrongly, the new forms of piety have been labelled together as 'Ultramontane piety' – a new, more brazen and more militant manifestation of Catholicism that went hand in hand with the inexorable rise of Ultramontanism in the matter of church government that, as has been explained in chapter 1, transformed and reinvigorated the papacy in the nineteenth century, especially during the long reign of Pius IX (1846–78). In France, as elsewhere, the rise of militant Ultramontane Catholicism stoked the fires of anticlericalism, but it should be appreciated also that it was not accomplished without a great deal of internal controversy and conflict within the ranks of French Catholics themselves.

In the period 1815–48, the Gallican tradition remained deeply entrenched in French culture, both at the Ministry of Ecclesiastical Affairs where, as Napoleon had intended, ministers and officials, true to the precepts of the parlements of the Old Order, upheld the right of the state to regulate the external aspects of religious practice, and also within the church establishment itself. Ecclesiastical Gallicanism was expounded in the seminaries, notably by the Sulpicians and the Lazarists, and in conformity with its traditional ecclesiology it rejected the notion of papal infallibility and argued for the centrality of the role of the individual bishop. 'In France, the Pope reigns but does not govern', quipped Mgr Affre, archbishop of Paris (1840–8).

Most of his confrères agreed, and had no difficulty in accommodating themselves to the concordat and in establishing a good working relationship with the Ministry of Ecclesiastical Affairs. The best of them were skilled administrators, possessed of finely honed diplomatic skills, men of tact and judgement who could mingle easily with the social and political elite of their day: zealots they were not. As late as 1850 Ultramontanes were a distinct (if active) minority (seventeen out of eighty) on the bench of bishops, and after 1830 the church also numbered few bishops who united their Gallican ecclesiology to a commitment to ultra-royalist politics: Bishop Clausel de Montals of Chartres (1769–1857) was the last of a dying breed. Indeed, the Gallican establishment was increasingly sympathetic to liberalism, whether religious or political, above all in the key episcopal see of Paris.

In the era of a resurgent papacy, however, the days of Gallicanism were numbered. The future lay with the new, militant, and above all Roman, Catholicism of Pius IX. From the outset of the nineteenth century, powerful arguments against Gallicanism gained currency in intellectual circles as a result of the writings of the likes of Joseph de Maistre and, in his first incarnation, the abbé Félicité de Lamennais (1782–1854). The latter's *Essai sur l'indifférence en matière de religion* (1817) was a particularly influential text, refuting the notion of religious pluralism and defending the church's right to support from the state to uphold divine truth (as expounded by the church) in the face of 'error'. A romantic and charismatic figure, Lamennais established a kind of counter-seminary at La Chenaie in Brittany which between the 1820s and the early 1830s acted as a powerful magnet for some of the brightest and most idealistic of the younger clergy.

Though Lamennais would personally undergo an extraordinary intellectual and political evolution, and eventually leave the church altogether, none of his disciples followed him into the wilderness. On the contrary, most remained more committed than ever to his original vision of a Catholic Christianity centred on Rome rather than on Paris and became leading activists in a dynamic Ultramontane network that by the middle decades of the nineteenth century had dealt a mortal blow to the Gallican tradition. Lamennais's followers included both clerics and laymen. Among the former, none was more influential than Dom Prosper Guéranger, who re-established the Benedictine Order at Solesmes in the 1830s. At La Chenaie, his specialism was the history of the liturgy and in the 1840s he spearheaded a campaign to impose the Roman liturgy on the dioceses of France that was brought to a triumphal conclusion by the decree *Inter Multiplices* issued by Pius IX in 1853.

Among the lay followers of Lamennais, the outstanding figure was the count of Montalembert, who with the count of Falloux and others in the 1840s formed themselves into a pressure group, the *parti catholique*, to seek to end the state's monopoly rights in the sphere of education, particularly at the secondary school level. As political liberals, however, these Ultramontanes increasingly found themselves at odds with the predominant tendency in the Ultramontane movement, notably on the clerical side, to identify with legitimism, all the more so after 1836 when the new Pretender, the count of Chambord, sought to unite his own cause with that of the papacy in a crusade designed explicitly to restore a Christian social order in France. By the advent of the Second Empire, Ultramontanism and political and religious liberalism had parted company and, like many of the bishops, liberal Catholics like Montalembert increasingly adhered to a neo-Gallican ecclesiology, promoted in the pages of the journal *Le Correspondant*, which was destined to remain a distinguished but undeniably minor current alongside the Ultramontane mainstream.

By far the most decisive factor in assuring the victory of the Ultramontanes in France was the role played by the Catholic press, and in particular by *L'Univers*, the Catholic daily directed by Louis Veuillot (1813–83). An autodidact and a journalist of genius, Veuillot declared himself independent of all political factions and a *catholique avant tout*. For almost forty years between roughly 1840 and 1880 his was the voice of intransigent, Ultramontane Catholicism with a French accent, much to the delight of the humble parish clergy for whom he became a hero on account of his vitriolic broadsides against the enemies of religion. What appealed to them most was Veuillot's strenuous defence of the idea of France as an overwhelmingly Catholic country in the face of the efforts of secular liberals to represent France as the heir of the French Revolution. For Veuillot – as indeed for the adepts of the revolutionary tradition – the Revolution was not over, and France was a battleground between the champions of the eldest daughter of the church and the apologists for a secular world in which the church would be entitled to no say in public life. In this conflict of good versus evil, there could be no compromise, as liberal Catholics (and many moderate republicans) believed. Compromise, according to Veuillot, was 'the liberal illusion': the fight had to be fought to the finish.[1]

Thus, by 1880, the Catholic Church had made a remarkable recovery from the ruinous condition in which it had found itself on the morrow of the revolutionary era. In the process, however, it had become a much more militant and intransigent organisation, still haunted by the wrongs it had suffered in the past and ready to resist any future attempts to relegate it to only a marginal social role. The stage was set for a renewal of hostilities with a republican state which, by that time, was willing to nail its colours to the mast of the *idée laïque*, the realisation of a completely secular polity and society.

Religion and politics: the rise of anticlericalism

Discontent with the clergy was hardly new in the 1870s. On the contrary, irrespective of relations between government and the church, conflicts between priests and their parishioners were a hardy perennial of life in the communes of rural France. *Le bon curé*, the village priest who lived harmoniously as the good shepherd of his flock, was by no means an entirely mythical figure – witness Jean Vianney, the celebrated *curé d'Ars* – but all too often villagers found cause to grumble about their clergy, as the archives of the Ministère des Cultes testify. Popular anticlericalism was fuelled by perceived abuses of clerical authority – humiliating families by a public refusal of communion, charging too much for a funeral mass, trying to curb dancing and drinking, and a host of other grievances which were inevitable in the face-to-face interchanges of community life. Significantly, from the 1840s, these conflicts increasingly involved the mayor and the local schoolmaster as figures willing to contest the authority of the priest and to assist with the drawing up of formal complaints to be laid before the minister. By the 1860s, in the context of a very different political

---

1 L. Veuillot, *L'illusion libérale* (Paris: Palmé, 1866; reprinted privately, 1969).

and intellectual climate at the national level, the everyday clashes between the *parti du maire* and the *parti du curé* became increasingly politicised, and anticlericalism emerged as the one banner under which the burgeoning but disparate republican movement could unite.

For, if the triumph of Ultramontanism in the French church was an affront to the liberal mind, so too was the church's consistent identification with the forces of political reaction. Time and again – under the Restoration, after the June Days of 1848, during the Second Empire and under the 'Moral Order' of the 1870s – the church sided with the enemies of liberalism and republicanism. Anticlericalism, at one level, was a response to what the French left, self-conscious heirs of the revolutionary tradition, came to view as an aggressive and unacceptable 'clericalism'. At another and deeper level, however, anticlericalism needs to be understood as far more than a direct and legitimate reaction to clericalism. There is a real sense in which 'clericalism' was an invention of anticlericals, and anticlericalism, certainly in its most extreme forms as expounded by the likes of Proudhon, Paul Bert and Emile Combes, a mythic and fanatical ideology based on a highly partial interpretation of French history. Anticlericalism had a dynamic all of its own which owed little or nothing to the actual behaviour of churchmen. Mythic anticlericalism, in short, was a continuation of the 'culture war' started under the Revolution – a refusal to accept that the Revolution was over while there remained unfinished business with the church.

As a word, the term 'clericalism' only came into common usage in the 1870s. Before then, opponents of the clergy spoke of their 'tyranny' or 'despotism' or 'contempt for the civil authorities'. What is clear, however, is that throughout the nineteenth century priests were confronted both at village level and at the level of national politics by opponents who, usually in the name of popular sovereignty and an essentially republican idea of the nation, were determined to set limits to ecclesiastical authority. The clergy, on the other hand, rejected any interference in their mission to save the souls of the faithful. From popes to humble parish priests, while always recognising the legitimate authority of the established power, the church categorically refused to renounce a public role for religion on the grounds that religion was a social, not an individual phenomenon. It was the church's business to reconstruct a Christian social order and the church therefore claimed the right to exercise influence on national life. Increasingly, however, and especially from the 1860s, republicans advocated a completely secular vision of the social order and affirmed their adhesion to the *idée laïque* – the organisation of society on a totally secular basis. By 1880, the ground had been prepared for a renewal of open hostilities between the church and a republican state.

It should be stressed that the breach was a long time in the making and that it was not necessarily destined to end in the separation of church and state. Nevertheless, tensions were apparent from the Restoration, which renewed the alliance of throne and altar, especially after Charles X – the chief Ultra – was crowned king at Rheims in 1824 with medieval pomp and ceremony to symbolise the indissoluble bond between church and state. The Sacrilege Law of 1825, by which sacrilege was made a crime punishable by death, was another spectacular symbolic gesture guaranteed to affront the liberal conscience of the age. (The rationale for the law was that desecration of the sacred Host equated to the murder of the body of Christ, which, as the liberal Royer-Collard observed, effectively wrote the doctrine of the Real Presence into the Constitution.) But nowhere was the influence of the church more apparent – or resented – than in the field of education. A leading ecclesiastic, Mgr Frayssinous, was appointed minister of education and of ecclesiastical affairs, with a remit to give a distinctly Catholic bias to education at all levels. Bishops were empowered to appoint all teachers in primary schools and they also acquired new rights of supervision in secondary schools. In the higher sector, Frayssinous shamelessly appointed priests to key posts and brought sanctions against dissident professors at the Sorbonne such as François Guizot and Victor Cousin. He was even prepared to shut the Ecole Normale Supérieure and the Medical School. In view of such measures, the anticlerical backlash which accompanied the Revolution of 1830 was entirely predictable.

Ironically, the advent of the liberal July Monarchy in 1830 gradually effected a marked improvement in church–state relations. The new regime distanced itself from any overt support for the church, but in the face of mounting social unrest and political opposition it increasingly appreciated the church as a bastion of social order: for the Protestant François Guizot, the towering ministerial figure of the age, the church was 'the greatest, the holiest school of respect which the world has ever seen'.[2] What eventually disturbed the harmony which had been achieved by 1840 was the launch of Montalembert's campaign for 'freedom of education', a liberal ideal enshrined in the 1830 Charter but one which militant lay Catholics (the church hierarchy was much less enthusiastic) interpreted as the right to establish their own schools and universities entirely free from state controls. Opposition to the *monopole de*

2 P. Thureau-Dangin, *L'église et l'état sous la monarchie de juillet* (Paris: Plon, 1880), p. 93.

l'état throughout the 1840s appeared to place the church on the side of the opponents of the regime who, much to their own surprise, found themselves in power after the revolution of 1848 which ushered in the Second Republic.

For a brief moment, the revolution of February 1848 appeared to hold out the tantalising prospect of reconciliation between the church and a Republic that was not unsympathetic to religious sensibilities. Many on the republican left preached a social gospel in which the image of 'Christ the revolutionary' featured prominently. On the Catholic side, even Louis Veuillot was prepared to give the new regime the benefit of the doubt, as was the liberal Catholic Montalembert, while there was even a Christian democrat circle headed by Frédéric Ozanam, the abbé Maret and the Dominican Henri Lacordaire which expressed its enthusiasm for the Republic in its newspaper *L'Ere Nouvelle*. Harmony was short-lived, however. In the wake of the violence of the June Days (which claimed the archbishop of Paris, Mgr Affre, as one of its 2,000 victims) Catholics of all shades (apart from the *Ere Nouvelle* group) rallied to the 'party of order' – essentially the former Orleanist elite – which took control of the Republic.

In return, the regime gratefully conceded many of the demands which the *parti catholique* had been seeking in the field of education throughout the 1840s. The Falloux Law of May 1850 (named after the liberal Catholic minister of education who sponsored the bill in parliament) gave the church the freedom to expand its secondary school provision, though the state preserved the *monopole universitaire* at the tertiary level – a concession which went too far for intransigent Ultramontanes like Louis Veuillot, who split the *parti catholique* by demanding nothing less than complete *liberté d'enseignement* for the church throughout the educational sector.[3] And, as we have seen, it was the *veuillotiste* current that increasingly dominated French Catholicism in the 1850s and 1860s.

Under the Second Empire of Napoleon III, the emperor was keen to retain the support of the church as an agent of social control. Much to the satisfaction of the clergy and the likes of Veuillot, he initially provided tangible evidence of his good will, helping to defeat the Roman Republic and to restore Pius IX to his throne in 1849. He also raised clerical salaries and encouraged the proliferation of church schools, especially those run by female religious orders. If liberal Catholics such as Montalembert were soon disillusioned – the latter's brochure *Catholic interests in the nineteenth century* (1852) denounced the perils of absolute power for spiritual as much as political freedom[4] – the church hierarchy and

3 Cf. A. de Falloux, *Le parti catholique: ce qu'il a été, ce qu'il est devenu* (Paris: A. Bray, 1856).
4 C. de Montalembert, *Les intérêts catholiques au dix-neuvième siècle* (Paris: J. Lecoffre, 1852).

Ultramontanes like Veuillot remained enthusiastic supporters until 1859, when the emperor reversed his Italian policy in favour of the Italian nationalists rather than the papacy. The 'Roman Question' was a matter of indifference to most voters, but it drove hardline Ultramontanes like Veuillot into the opposition camp, all the more so when in 1863 the emperor appointed the anticlerical Victor Duruy as his education minister with a remit to promote state rather than church schools (Duruy's attempts to establish secondary courses for girls taught by members of the Sorbonne were denounced in vitriolic terms, even by the so-called liberal Bishop Dupanloup). By the end of the Second Empire, tensions between church and state were already mounting.

At the same time, a change in the intellectual climate in France as in Europe as a whole exacerbated divisions between Catholics and sections of the educated classes. If romanticism had helped to rehabilitate religion in the first half of the nineteenth ceentury, positivism – the favourite philosophic creed of mid-nineteenth-century intellectuals, popularised in France by Emile Littré – encouraged scepticism about the truths of revealed religion. Modern science – epitomised by Charles Darwin, whose *Origin of species* was translated into French in 1862 – and German biblical criticism confronted Ultramontane Catholics with more formidable enemies than the sons of Voltaire. Ernest Renan's *Vie de Jésus*, published in 1863, was a sensation, depicting Christ as an extraordinary human being but not the son of God. In the burgeoning free-thought societies of the Second Empire era, militant atheists – many of them disciples of Pierre-Joseph Proudhon – called for a war against God and the complete extirpation of religion from society.

True, such hard-liners were a minority, even in the free-thought community: the majority of the adepts of the *idée laïque* – liberal Protestants, freemasons and republicans – retained a residual respect for religion. There were even spectacular deathbed conversions, like that of Littré in 1881. Nevertheless, under the impetus of the Roman Question, the anticlerical press, spearheaded by organs like *L'Avenir Nationale* and *L'Opinion Nationale* but also including the more moderate *Le Temps*, increasingly demanded the separation of church and state in the 1860s. By the end of the Second Empire a new generation of republican politicians which included men of markedly different temperament like Jules Ferry and Léon Gambetta, were convinced that, in the interests of national unity, a choice had to be made between the church and a modern polity.[5] Their conviction only hardened in the early 1870s following the experience of the

---

5 Cf. J. Ferry, *Discours sur l'éducation: l'égalité de l'éducation* (Paris: Société pour l'Instruction Elémentaire, 1870).

'moral order' regime of Marshal MacMahon, which to the republican mind offered evidence that attempts to rechistianise French society went hand in hand with the goal of trying to effect a monarchist restoration. By 1879, when republicans finally emerged in undisputed control of their own creation, the Third Republic, they were ready to reopen a legislative culture war to bring the church to heel.

The French culture war, 1879–1905

For moderate republicans such as Jules Ferry who were now the masters of the French state, the key to implementation of the *idée laïque* was education. A law of 1879, aimed primarily at the Jesuits, banned unauthorised religious orders from teaching in secondary schools. Legislation in 1881 and 1882 made primary education free, compulsory and non-denominational for both sexes. Religious instruction now had to be provided outside of the classroom for those children whose parents wanted it and its place in the curriculum was taken by new classes on 'moral and civic education'. A further law of 1886 provided for the progressive laicisation of the teaching profession itself: around half of the nuns and brothers who taught in the nation's primary schools were removed by the early 1890s.

The education of girls was a particular target of the republicans, who were convinced that women's greater allegiance to organised religion was both a source of division in families and a barrier to the spread of the republican ideal. Accordingly, legislation of 1879–80 established teacher training colleges for women teachers and a network of state secondary schools for girls. Other measures designed to take forward the secularising agenda included the divorce law of 1884, which ended the ban on divorce imposed by the restored Bourbons in 1816, and a conscription law which obliged seminary students to do their military service like everyone else.

The legislative culture war unleashed in 1879, however, stopped well short of a full-scale assault on religion. Ferry and his fellow opportunist republicans retained a profound respect for the rights of the individual conscience and were also wary of offending the religious sensibilities of voters. Notwithstanding the availability of free state schooling, around 20 per cent of parents preferred to send their children to Catholic primary schools. A higher percentage – nearer 50 per cent – continued to opt for private (mainly Catholic) secondary schools, as much for social as for religious reasons (the Jesuits had a particularly good track record in preparing their pupils for the elite *grandes écoles* which were the passport to success in both the public and private sectors). Only the extreme left wanted to abolish the concordat altogether: the moderate republicans appreciated the hold which it allowed them to exercise over the clergy, notably by suspending the salaries of priests who stepped out of line. The separation of church and state was not a republican priority in the 1880s in the first phase of the French culture war.

Indeed, for a brief moment there were signs of détente. The new pope, Leo XIII (1878–1903), was anxious to stay on good terms with the moderate leaders of the Third Republic. Convinced that there was no viable royalist alternative to the republican regime, he was anxious to see French Catholics join forces with conservative republicans in the face of a mounting challenge from the left. In his encyclical of February 1892, *Au milieu des solicitudes*, he explicitly exhorted French Catholics to rally to the Republic. Traditionalists were dismayed, and refused to heed the pope's call. The majority of the French episcopate was likewise less than enthusiastic. But some laymen, headed by Albert de Mun, Jacques Piou and Etienne Lamy, reacted positively and worked for the construction of a broad-based Catholic–republican conservative alliance. At the same time, and largely in response to Leo XIII's celebrated encyclical on social justice *Rerum Novarum* (1891), there emerged a second generation of Christian Democrats – some of them priests like the abbés Garnier, Naudet, Six and Lemire, others laymen like Georges Fonsegrive, founder of the influential journal *La Quinzaine* in 1894, and Marc Sangnier, founder of *Le Sillon* (the Furrow) in 1899 – who concerned themselves above all with the plight of the industrial working class.

Though Rome soon grew alarmed at the divergent tendencies which marked the second Christian Democracy and forbade social Catholics to engage directly in political action in the encyclical *Graves de Communi* of 1901, both the *Ralliement* and social Catholicism helped to prepare the ground for new initiatives which would move French Catholics on from their traditional attachment to the alliance of throne and altar. In Lower Brittany, supposedly one of the most backward and 'clerical' regions in France, social Catholics championed a regionalist but non-separatist version of the republican ideal against the secular, 'Jacobin' and unitary conception of the nation. Elsewhere, in other strongly Catholic regions, such as the southern Massif Central, Savoy, Franche-Comté and Lorraine, it was eminently clear that the predominantly Catholic electors were prepared to endorse the Republic, despite its anticlerical overtones. Separation of church and state, as has been said, was not inevitable.

On the other hand, it is misleading to give the impression that the culture war existed only in the minds of crusading Catholics and anticlerical intellectuals. It was fought also on the ground, nowhere more so than in Brittany, where the school war, or *guerre scolaire*, as described by Michel Lagrée, was 'the continuation of *la chouannerie* by other means', a kind of action replay of the conflicts of the revolutionary era.[6] At the height of the *Ralliement*, in the mid-1890s, many of the Breton clergy refused to follow the lead of either Leo XIII or their bishops in their search for accommodation with the Republic and resorted to all kinds of devices – including pressure in the confessional – to prevail on their parishioners to support Catholic schools against state schools. Even before the *Ralliement* was scuppered by the reverberations of the Dreyfus Affair, it failed to make much headway at grassroots level. Prominent *ralliés* like de Mun, Piou and Lamy were all defeated in the elections of 1893, while on the republican side moderates were reluctant to make any concessions to the church, lest they be seen as the dupes of a clerical manoeuvre, as radical republicans alleged the *Ralliement* to be.

The fall-out from the Dreyfus Affair sealed the fate of the *Ralliement*. Once again Catholics were seen to be on the wrong side of the political divide, largely because of the high-profile role played by the Assumptionist order and its widely read, and rabidly anti-Semitic, newspaper *La Croix* in the campaign against the Jewish army captain Alfred Dreyfus, falsely convicted of treason. In the face of mounting evidence that the conviction was unsafe (enough to convince Leo XIII, for one, that revision was essential) many republicans, spearheaded by Radicals like Georges Clemenceau, came to see in Dreyfus a symbol of the need to vindicate a secular and republican conception of justice and the nation against a *raison d'état* that ultimately derived from the Old Regime. Rumours of a clerical–militarist plot were absurd, but there was no denying that most Catholic spokesmen defended the army and its honour against what they saw as the political machinations of the left. At the turn of the century, the culture war moved into a new and hotter phase which led to the severing of the ties between church and state which had endured for over a century.

The government of René Waldeck-Rousseau, formed in June 1899, brought together a broad coalition of the left which agreed that the church should pay for its anti-Dreyfusard connections. The Assumptionists were dissolved in 1900, and in 1901 a law on associations was passed which required religious congregations to receive authorisation from parliament. But it was Waldeck-Rousseau's successor, Emile Combes, who was to use the new law as an instrument for a general attack on the church. A visceral anticlerical, he systematically denied

---

6 M. Lagrée in J. Delumeau (ed.), *Le diocèse de Rennes. Histoire des diocèses de France* vol. x (Paris: Beauchesne, 1979), p. 221.

authorisation to the vast majority of religious communities and sought to close down their schools. His persecution culminated in the passing of a new law in July 1904 which banned even authorised orders from teaching. At the same time he encouraged discrimination against practising Catholics in certain sectors of the bureaucracy and, infamously, as the *affaire des fiches* revealed, sought to prevent them from being promoted in the army.

Yet not even Combes wanted to dispense with the concordat, which he valued as a tool to keep the clergy under control. On the other hand, he was rash enough to threaten the Vatican with its abolition when the new pope, Pius X (1903–14), proved a much more intractable opponent than his predecessor over the question of episcopal appointments. Anticlerical parliamentarians, including the leading socialist Jean Jaurès, took Combes at his word and seized the opportunity to force through a Separation Bill which became law on 9 December 1905. It was a unilateral act on the part of the state, motivated primarily by a desire to break the power of the church as a political force.

By the terms of the Separation Law, the state ceased to pay the salaries of the clergy (and of pastors and rabbis). Church property was to be transferred to *associations cultuelles*, representative bodies made up of parishioners from each parish in France. The chief architect of the law, Aristide Briand, intended not to suppress the Catholic religion but rather to free Catholic laypeople from the domination of the hierarchy. Nor was the law aimed at the expropriation of the church (as under the Revolution): the intention was rather to place church buildings under the care of the faithful provided they set up the stipulated religious associations in each parish to guarantee their upkeep. However reluctantly, most French bishops and lay Catholics accepted the law and wanted to comply with the obligation to establish *associations cultuelles*. Rome, however, had other ideas. Pius X, egged on by his equally intransigent secretary of state Cardinal Merry del Val, was convinced that the law would undermine the hierarchical basis of the church and also feared that a tame surrender before the French state would encourage similar anticlerical legislation in other countries. Accordingly, he forbade the formation of *associations cultuelles*, with the consequence that until 1924 the church did not exist as a legal entity capable of taking ownership of its own property. In the interim, much of that property was converted to other use: many episcopal palaces became museums, libraries or other municipal buildings. Rome's intransigence on the matter of *associations cultuelles* proved highly costly for the French church.

The influence of Rome continued to shape the French church up to 1914, and beyond. Unrestrained by the French state, Pius X and Merry del Val took full advantage of their freedom to appoint bishops who shared their reactionary outlook, many of them sympathetic to the extreme right-wing nationalist organisation Action Française. At the same time, Rome vetoed the formation of a national assembly of French bishops and thus deprived them of the opportunity to develop a national forum in which to address the particular challenges facing the church in their own country. Finally, the Vatican cracked down hard on intellectual tendencies within the French church which it regarded with suspicion, condemning as heretical so-called 'modernism'.

All told, the church was undoubtedly the loser in the French culture war. Deprived of the financial support of the state, the clergy now had to be paid for by contributions from the faithful themselves. Income fell, and so too did clerical recruitment (though arguably the calibre of the priesthood rose, given the commitment required from men who often faced lives of real hardship). Above all, the republican state had forever denied the church the central place which it aspired to occupy in national life. Nevertheless, the dream of recatholicising France did not die in the early 1900s: it lived on, for instance, in the ranks of militant social Catholics, who would make considerable headway in the Catholic Action movements of the inter-war period. Catholic nationalists, too, still cherished a Catholic vision of the nation and, as the strongest adherents to the *union sacrée*, were loud in its defence during the Great War. Even at the height of the anticlerical onslaught on the church, most French people continued to receive a Christian burial: in the cemeteries, Thomas Kselman has suggested, 'the French eventually worked out an understanding of death that accommodated Christian belief and symbol with a devotion to family, village and nation'.[7] Not even Vichy, however, would undo the undoubted triumph of *laïcité*.

7 Kselman, 'The dechristianisation of death in modern France', p. 156.

15

Italy: the church and the *Risorgimento*

FRANK COPPA

The *Risorgimento*, culminating in the creation of the Italian Kingdom and the collapse of the temporal power, sparked a papal Counter-*Risorgimento*. The clash between Italian nationalism and the Catholic Church from the restoration of 1815 to the seizure of Rome in 1870 was threefold: ideological, political and religious. This chapter probes into the roots and the flowering of all three from the pontificate of Pius VII (1800–23) to that of Pius IX (1846–78). It explores the confrontation between the national *Risorgimento* and the Catholic Counter-*Risorgimento* – and the far-reaching consequences for both.

The conflict between the papacy and patriots in Italy had deep roots, as Lorenzo Valla in the fifteenth century and Niccolò Machiavelli in the sixteenth both challenged the temporal power. Nationalist suspicion of Rome transcended the *literati* during the course of the Napoleonic wars, when patriots confronted a church aligned to the conservative order. Although Pius VII rejected the invitation of Tsar Alexander of Russia (1801–25) to join his 'Holy Alliance', he adhered to much of its conservative, antinationalist programme. In turn, the allied powers viewed the pope as a fellow victim of Napoleonic aggression, returning most of his territory, with the exception of one part of Ferrara that was transferred to Austria, and Avignon and the Venaissan which were retained by Paris. Despite these favourable terms, in June 1815 Cardinal Ercole Consalvi, the papal secretary of state, issued a formal protest against these minor losses, seconded by Pius in September.[1] It represented a precursor of Rome's unyielding stance in the ensuing nationalist age.

When the Spanish revolution of 1820 inspired upheaval elsewhere, the ultra-conservative party in the curia, the *zelanti*, pointed to the papacy as the antidote to revolution. Following the outbreak of a *carbonari* revolution in Naples early in July 1820, Consalvi opted for pragmatism rather than conservative solidarity.

---

1 Erasmo Pistolesi, *Vita del Sommo Pontefice Pio VII*, 4 vols. (Rome: F. Bourlie, 1824), vol. IV, pp. 106–16; Edward Hertslet, *The map of Europe by treaty*, 4 vols. (London: Butterworths, 1875–91), vol. I, pp. 267–8.

Announcing his obligation to protect the Faith, he accorded the constitutional regime in Naples *de facto* recognition.[2] Metternich urged Rome to condemn the *carbonari*, considering it complementary to Austria's military intervention against the Neapolitan revolution. The pope and his secretary of state insisted that spiritual strictures were reserved for those societies manifestly opposed to the Catholic religion. Only when the Austrians uncovered the sect's initiation ceremonies, which ridiculed church ritual, did Rome act. In mid-September, Pius VII launched an excommunication against the *carbonari* for their blasphemous misuse of Roman ritual. Justified on spiritual grounds, its motivation was political, and as such proved a failure. While it did little to suppress the unrest or undermine the sects, it alienated Italian nationalists by identifying the papacy with Austria and reaction.[3] Pius VII, assisted by Consalvi, balanced his religious responsibilities with political reality to the end of his pontificate in 1823.

The 1823 conclave was dominated by the *zelanti* cardinals who disparaged the political realism of Consalvi and Pius VII. Austria's Metternich, on the other hand, invoked a moderate successor. When the election of the intransigent Cardinal Gabriele Severoli appeared certain, Metternich authorised Cardinal Giuseppe Albani, representing Austrian interests in the conclave, to exercise its veto. The frustrated cardinals lined up behind another *zelanti*, securing the election of Cardinal Annibale della Genga, who assumed the name Leo XII.[4] The new pope shared the *zelanti* views on church–state relations, and in his first encyclical (May 1824) condemned dechristianisation, indifferentism, toleration and freemasonry, tracing contemporary problems to the contempt for church authority.[5] He warned the bishops of the sects and railed against the indifferent, who under the pretext of toleration undermined the faith. Leo proved a jealous guardian of the Holy See's prerogatives, continuing the centralising tendencies of his predecessor while abandoning his political moderation.

Pope Leo initially sought to safeguard the papacy by invoking the support of the faithful. During the course of 1826, he moved away from Lamennais's idealistic notion of relying on the devotion of the Catholic masses towards the more realistic support of the armies of the conservative powers. In mid-March, he denounced the masons and other secret societies, renewing the decrees of his predecessors against them. Cardinal Tommaso Bernetti ventured to Vienna, St Petersburg, Paris and Berlin, assuring these governments that Leo renounced

2 Brady, *Rome and the Neapolitan revolution*, p. 13.
3 Reinerman, 'Metternich and the papal condemnation', pp. 60–9.
4 Colapietra, 'Il diario Brunelli', pp. 76–146.
5 *Ubi Primum* in Carlen (ed.), *Papal pronouncements*, p. 21.

Ultramontanism, while placating the powers by removing Father Ventura, a disciple of Lamennais, from his teaching position. Metternich was perturbed by the death of Leo in February 1829, urging his successor to continue to collaborate with Austria.

The Austrian ambassador sought the election of a moderate pope. On 31 March 1829, the 68-year-old Francesco Saverio Castiglioni, supported by both the French and the Austrians, was elected. The new pope showed himself well disposed towards antinationalist Austria. Devoting himself to the renewal of the church, he left the task of governing the Papal States to Cardinal Giuseppe Albani. In his first encyclical (May 1829), Pius VIII denounced its enemies. Commencing with a condemnation of those who attacked the church's spiritual mission, he condemned indifferentism as a contrivance of contemporary sophists. The encyclical censured the growing menace of the secret societies, which opposed God and princes, denouncing them as a threat to church and state.[6] Pius thus tied the papacy to the restoration regimes, and the price paid for their moral and military support was the animosity of their enemies.

Pius VIII was distressed that the July 1830 revolution in France struck at the church as well as the monarchy, but shied from sanctioning Lamennais's call for the separation of church and state. To make matters worse, at the end of August a revolution erupted in Belgium, in which Catholics co-operated with liberals in overturning the regime created by the Powers at Vienna. Only after Vienna extended formal diplomatic recognition to Louis-Philippe in early September did Rome follow suit. Although Pius belatedly displayed the pragmatism earlier shown by Pius VII, Rome's reliance on the restoration order made it a target for patriots in the Italian peninsula. The July Revolution inspired the *carbonari* in Italy to prepare for another insurrection. The new pope, Gregory XVI (1831–46), protected the temporal and spiritual power of the papacy by aligning his state if not the church with the conservative powers in Europe, and above all Austria. Austrian intervention proved decisive in the suppression of the Italian revolution, but aggravated rather than mitigated nationalist resentment.

When Giovanni Maria Mastai Ferretti assumed the chair of Peter in June 1846 as Pius IX, the Papal States remained on the verge of revolution. Little had been done in Rome to eliminate the discontent festering since the revolutionary upheaval of 1830–1. The major powers – England, France, Austria, Russia

---

6 Carlen (ed.), *The papal encyclicals*, vol. 1, pp. 221–4; Fremantle (ed.), *The papal encyclicals*, p. 123.

and Prussia – had proposed a series of reforms, including the creation of a consultative assembly to provide advice on governmental matters. Their suggestions were ignored as Pope Gregory condemned liberal Catholicism and nationalism in his *Mirari Vos* of 1832,[7] and later denounced the false idols of 'modern civilisation'.[8] Gregory resisted even technical innovations such as the railways, provoking resentment throughout his state. In 1837, Viterbo was stricken, while in 1843 and 1844 the Legations exploded.[9] Moderates believed revolution imminent and considered reform the antidote to an impending catastrophe.[10]

The new pope appreciated the need for change. As bishop of Imola (1832–46), he had explored the prospect of conciliation between Catholicism and liberal-national principles. Although far from a revolutionary, Mastai proved critical of the ponderous Roman administration which provoked the constant round of revolt and repression. He suggested that the condition of the Papal States could be improved by infusing a bit of common sense and Christian justice in the government. Theology, Mastai observed, was not opposed to the development of science and industry.[11] He catalogued his suggestions in a work entitled 'Thoughts on the administration of the Papal States' (1845), which saw the need for some collegiate body to advise and co-ordinate the administration.[12]

Once pope, Pius proposed a series of innovations encouraging liberals and nationalists such as Minghetti and Cavour, while inspiring the revolutionary Mazzini. Pio Nono's July amnesty of political prisoners electrified Rome and Italy. To the delight of liberals extraordinary tribunals were abolished, while railway lines were projected and telegraph companies chartered. The pope reformed the collection of revenue and the management of finances, while opening a number of offices to laypeople. Unlike his predecessor, Pio Nono allowed his subjects to participate in the scientific congresses that were convoked in Italy. To reduce unemployment he urged the provinces to provide public work projects for his subjects.[13] He relieved the burdens imposed on

---

7 Momigliano (ed.), *Tutte le encicliche*, pp. 186–95.
8 *E Principio certo*, in Carlen (ed.), *Papal pronouncements*, vol. 1, pp. 25–6.
9 Archivio di Stato di Roma (ASR), Fondo Famiglia Antonelli (FFA), busta 1, fascicolo 125.
10 Metternich-Winneburg (ed.), *Memoirs*, vol. vii, p. 246; *British and Foreign State Papers* (*BFSP*) vol. xxxvi (1847–8), p. 1195.
11 P. D. Pasolini (ed.), *Giuseppe Pasolini, Memorie. 1815–1876* (Turin: Bocca, 1887), p. 57.
12 Serafini, *Pio Nono*, vol. 1, pp. 1397–1406.
13 *Atti del sommo pontefice Pio IX, felicemente regnante. Parte seconda che comprende I Motu-proprii, chirografi editti, notificazioni, ec. per lo stato pontificio*, 2 vols. (Rome: Tipografia delle Belle Arti, 1857), vol. 1, pp. 8–10, 15.

the Jews of Rome and even proposed the creation of a Council of State.[14] News of his reforms was facilitated by a revised press law which tolerated the expression of liberal and nationalist sentiments.

These changes delighted liberals and nationalists such as Massimo D'Azeglio, and Leopoldo Galeotti.[15] From Montevideo, Garibaldi proclaimed Pius the political messiah of the peninsula, while in Turin, Gioberti prophesied that Pius had opened a new age for Italy.[16] His reforms were enthusiastically received, provoking manifestations of public gratitude. Wherever he appeared, the pope was greeted as the father of his people. Pius perceived no danger when the Romans applauded their prince, who was also head of the church.[17] Others saw things differently. The pope had a responsibility to transfer full sovereignty to his successor, Metternich warned, and should not barter any of it away. The Austrian minister predicted that if he continued pandering to the radicals and nationalists, he would be forced out of Rome.[18]

Initially Pius did not share the conservative fears, preferring reform to reaction. His optimism was not shared by his own secretary of state, Pasquale Gizzi, who, like Metternich, appreciated the danger that Italian nationalism posed to the Papal States and the papacy. Gizzi had reservations about both the national and constitutional goals of the reformist party. Pius believed that the creation of a tariff league to co-ordinate economic activity in the peninsula would address its economic problems while quelling the growing national sentiment in Italy. To satisfy those who called for some form of representative body, he announced the intention of forming an advisory council. Gizzi accepted both proposals with the understanding that the tariff league would not assume a political dimension, while the consultative chamber would not become a legislative chamber. Assured by the pope, in April 1847, Gizzi published the edict on the *Consulta di Stato*.[19]

At the end of 1847, Pius introduced a measure of ministerial responsibility while granting laymen access to several ministerial posts. However, he had reservations about granting liberty of conscience to all inhabitants of the Papal States and balked at the laicisation of the administration. 'I have done enough', he exclaimed, 'I will do no more.'[20] It was easier said than done. He

14 ASR, FFA, busta 3.
15 Coppa, '*Realpolitik* and conviction', p. 582.
16 Archivio Segreto del Vaticano (ASV), Archivio Particolare Pio IX, oggetti vari, 412; Maiolo (ed.), *Pio IX*, p. 59.
17 ASV, Archivio Particolare Pio IX, Sardegna, Sovrani.
18 Metternich-Winneburg (ed.), *Memoirs*, vol. VII, p. 572.
19 *Atti del Sommo Pontefice Pio IX*, vol. I, pp. 47–8.
20 Nielsen, *History of the papacy*, vol. II, p. 142.

responded to the cries for a constitution by warning that his subjects should not make requests which he could not, ought not and did not mean to grant. He was equally adamant about creating a civic guard. Finally, he resisted the call to champion the liberation of the peninsula, considering the creation of an Italian league presided over by the pope a utopian scheme. None the less, he found it hard to resist the popular clamour and eventually persuaded Gizzi to authorise the controversial guard, but the cardinal, fearing the consequences, resigned a few days later.

Pius reconsidered his stance on constitutionalism following the outbreak of revolution in Palermo and Paris early in 1848, warning he could not violate his obligations as head of the universal church. Only when a special commission of ecclesiastics saw no theological hindrances to the introduction of constitutionalism in the political realm did the pope proceed. Pressured by events, the pope also changed course on the question of the league, and in 1848 moved beyond the commercial league he had originally sanctioned to accept the political and national one earlier deemed inadmissible.[21]

The pope's subjects demanded more, calling upon him to launch a war of national liberation against Austria. In response, Pius allowed his ministers to appeal to the Turin government to provide a military man to organise a papal military force. 'The events which these two months have seen succeeding and pressing on each other with so rapid change are not the work of man', Pius announced to the people of Italy in an address of 30 March.[22] These words appeared to foreshadow an active papal involvement in the national crusade to liberate Italy, seemingly confirmed by the movement of his troops northward. Inwardly, Pius had reservations about declaring war on part of his flock and resented the proclamation of General Giovanni Durando, which labelled the war not only national but Christian. These words created consternation in Austria, where Princess Metternich lamented that the pope blessed the troops dispatched to conquer their provinces.[23] Deeming his first responsibility to the church, Pius feared that his association with the war of liberation might provoke a schism in Germany. He was stunned by the April 1848 dispatch from his nuncio in Vienna, which reported that Catholics there held him responsible for the war. Although he understood that Italian nationalism was sweeping the peninsula, Pius proclaimed that he could not declare war against anyone.

---

21 ASV, Archivio Particolare Pio IX, Oggetti Vari, n. 368.
22 *BFSP* vol. xxxvii (1848–9), p. 981.
23 Metternich-Winneburg (ed.), *Memoirs*, vol. viii, p. 15.

Pius considered himself a priest first, and only secondly a temporal ruler, and acted accordingly. When his ministers urged him to enter the war of national liberation, he consulted a number of theologians to determine if this would be legitimate.[24] A majority considered it improper, and he followed their advice rather than that of his cabinet. His reluctance to enter the war, announced in an allocution of 29 April 1848, provoked a revolution in Rome and his flight from the capital at the end of November 1848. It was a flight from his subjects and his earlier reformism. Patriots denounced the papal refusal to declare war a betrayal, and perceived his flight as an abdication.

These events turned Pius against constitutionalism, liberalism and nationalism and those states identified with these movements. Liberalism he branded a dangerous delusion.[25] The theory of nationalism he found as criminal as that of socialism. Pius defended his decision not to assume leadership of the national movement. 'Who can doubt that the Pope must follow a path which extols the honour of God and never that sought by the major demagogues of Europe?', he asked, adding, 'And with what conscience could the Pope have supported such a national movement, knowing . . . it would only lead to the profound abyss of religious incredulity and social dissolution?'[26]

Papal abandonment of the national crusade provoked resentment among liberals and patriots. The Piedmontese, distraught by their defeat, tended to blame Rome for the catastrophe. Count Cavour's newspaper *Il Risorgimento* reported that the pope's 'betrayal' proved crucial, and Italians could only conclude that the national movement and the papal temporal power were incompatible.[27] The hostility was mutual. Pius proved suspicious of the Piedmontese, who urged him to negotiate with the 'rebels', and assumed leadership of the national movement. In mid-February, the acting secretary of state invoked the intervention of the Catholic powers: Austria, France, Spain and the Kingdom of the Two Sicilies, to restore the states of the church. Piedmont and France, seeking reconciliation rather than revenge, urged the pope to retain his earlier reforms, but Rome balked. Pius cited the incompatibility of constitutionalism with the free exercise of his spiritual power. While the Austrians defeated the Piedmontese at the battle of Novara (23 March 1849), the French Republic authorised an expedition to Rome. Louis Napoleon claimed he sought to

24 ASV, Archivio Particolare Pio IX, Oggetti Vari, n. 415.
25 A. Rosmini, *Della missione a Roma* (Turin: Paravia, 1854), pp. 143–4; ASV, Archivio Particolare Pio IX, Francia, Particolari, n. 18; Segreteria di Stato Esteri [SSE], corrispondenza da Gaeta e Portici, 1848–50, rubrica 248, fascicolo 2, sottofascicolo 4.
26 ASV, Archivio Particolare Pio IX, Particolare, n. 30.
27 *Il Risorgimento*, 23 November 1848.

re-establish constitutional government, and pressed the pope to do so.[28] The French catalogued the essential reforms, including an amnesty, a law code patterned on their own, abolition of the tribunal of the Holy Office, modification of the rights of ecclesiastical tribunals in civilian jurisdiction, and granting the Consulta a veto on financial issues.[29] These suggestions were coldly received by Antonelli.

The papal retreat from the national programme spawned anticlericalism. In national circles in Turin, clericalism was denounced as the vanguard of absolutism and the enemy of Italian nationalism. By this time, even Gioberti concluded that the union of the temporal and spiritual power of the papacy was disastrous for both, as well as national unification. The parties of the left charged that Pius had conspired with the Austrians to annul their constitutional regime.[30] In Turin, Agostino Depretis insisted on curbing Catholic privileges and clerical abuses. Among other things he proposed that the ministry appropriate ecclesiastical benefices, suppress some of the religious orders, sequester convents and introduce legislation to provide civil matrimony.[31]

Depretis's programme was partially implemented by the Siccardi Laws of 1850, which included nine measures. The first five abrogated various forms of ecclesiastical jurisdiction enjoyed by the church in Piedmont; the sixth eliminated the church's right of asylum; the seventh limited punishment of non-observance of religious solemnity to six Catholic holidays and Sundays. Proposal VIII stipulated that ecclesiastical corporations could no longer acquire real property without the state's consent. Finally, the last proposal called for legislation regulating marriage as a civil contract.[32] In the interim, measures were taken to wrest control of education from clerical domination. Following the expulsion of the Sisters of the Sacred Heart from Piedmontese territory, the school law of 1848 stipulated that direction of the schools was a civil rather than an ecclesiastical function, so that bishops could no longer prevent individuals from teaching as they had under the regulation of 1822. Thus, by the end of 1848, the Turin government had restricted church control over education, deepening the divide between church and state. Cavour, the architect of Italian consolidation, desired an educational system open to all, and eventually invoked a separation of church and state. This infuriated Pio Nono, who branded this programme demonic.

28 *Hansard's Parliamentary Debates*, vol. CV (1849), p. 376.
29 ASV, SSE, corrispondenza da Gaeta e Portici, 1849, rubrica 242, sottofascicolo 76.
30 Coppa, '*Realpolitik* and conviction', pp. 590–3.
31 Archivio Centrale dello Stato, Archivio Depretis, Serie I, busta 10, fascicolo 29.
32 *Legge Siccardi sull'abolizione del foro e delle immunià ecclesiastiche tornate del Parlamento Subalpino* (Turin: Pomba Editori, 1850), p. 77.

Pius had come to the conclusion that the Turin government was dominated by antireligious sentiments; its mania for expansion in Italy was perceived as a threat to the pope's temporal and spiritual power. The pope complained that the foes of Catholicism used nationalism to wage a war against the Apostolic See. His denunciations were ignored by Cavour. 'With us the Court of Rome has lost every sort of moral authority', he wrote to one of his English friends; 'it might launch against us all the thunderbolts it keeps in reserve in the cellars of the Vatican and would fail to produce any great agitation in these parts'.[33] Papal complaints and calls for assurance of church interests found a more receptive audience elsewhere. In 1850, the Madrid government concluded an agreement which pronounced Catholicism the religion of state, while the clergy was invested with broad powers, including the supervision of education. Negotiations were also opened with the Vienna government, which resulted in an accord which made broad concessions to the church, as Franz Joseph proclaimed his devotion to the Holy See.[34]

The deference showed Rome by Madrid and Vienna highlighted the ecclesiastical policies of the Turin government, as well as its nationalist policy in Italy, which Pius found objectionable. In September 1851, Pius rejected the Piedmontese contention that their school administration had to be under exclusive civil authority. The recently formed journal of the Jesuits, *Civiltà Cattolica*, seconded his stance. To further widen the rift, the *connubio* or marriage of the centre-right led by Cavour and the centre-left led by Urbano Rattazzi in 1852 provided the parliamentary basis for additional anti-ecclesiastical legislation and the downfall of the D'Azeglio government, which proved unable fully to implement the Siccardi legislation. At the end of 1852, Cavour assumed the presidency of the Council of Ministers. His government, to the pope's displeasure, assumed a more radical position on ecclesiastical and national issues than the D'Azeglio government. Pius believed Italian nationalists threatened both his temporal and spiritual power, perceiving the *Risorgimento* as doubly damnable. He preferred antinationalist Austria, which sought to preserve the status quo, to revisionist Piedmont, which aimed to unite the peninsula under its banner.

Since its defeat in the first war of Italian unification (1848–9), Turin had sought to restrict the role of the church in its territory. The pope resented the Piedmontese legislation and its appeal to Protestant Britain for approval of what London dubbed a 'second Reformation'. In Austria, the official gazette

---

33 Count Nigra (ed.), *Count Cavour and Madame de Circourt: some unpublished correspondence*, trans. A. J. Butler (London: Cassell, 1894), p. 98.

34 ASV, Archivio Particolare Pio IX, Sovrani, Austria.

observed that Turin wished to differentiate herself from Catholic Austria by persecuting the papacy, which had wounded national sentiment during the abortive war of liberation. Vienna, in turn, determined to show herself persistently Catholic as Piedmont betrayed her 'heretical' sentiments. Pius was scandalised by the works published in Turin and their permissive philosophy, which he denounced as detrimental to the faith. He considered the Sardinian ecclesiastical legislation contrary to the rights of the church, accusing that state of interfering in the administration of the sacraments.[35] In the spring of 1854, Rattazzi, Cavour's political ally, proposed a law (the Law of Convents) which envisioned the suppression of a number of Piedmont's religious orders. To make matters worse, the pope feared that the Turin government would export its power and policies to the other states of the peninsula.

Rumour spread that Louis Napoleon had promised the Piedmontese that he would eventually champion their cause, a commitment he later confirmed. Antonelli was convinced that so long as things remained quiet in Europe, Habsburg arms could preserve the status quo.[36] Rome feared that Napoleon III envisioned a war against Russia as a means of reorganising Europe along national lines. Despite the pleas of Pope Pius IX for peace, by the spring of 1854 the British and French were ranged against the Russians in the Crimean War. Cavour, who joined the anti-Russian coalition, hoped that the Habsburg monarchy would aid its conservative ally, so that the liberal bloc of London, Paris and Turin might co-operate to push the Austrians out of Italy.

Cavour's dream was the pope's nightmare. He feared that Austrian involvement in the war would lead to a relaxation of her efforts in Italy, encouraging the revolutionaries to unleash another wave of terror. Rome was likewise troubled by Piedmont's efforts to ingratiate herself with the British by denouncing the temporal power.[37] The pope urged the faithful to pray for peace, lamenting the injuries threatened by bellicose afflictions.[38] His words were wasted on the 'Piedmontese Machiavelli', who was frustrated by the unwillingness of the French and British to make any tangible concession to his country to bring her into the war, and the unwillingness of his political ally, Urbano Rattazzi, to support Piedmont's entry without compensation. Cavour resolved the issue by promising his support for Rattazzi's Law of Convents in return for Rattazzi's

---

35 ASR, Miscellanea di Carte Politiche o Riservate, busta 121, fascicolo 4214; memorandum of 23 June 1852.
36 ASV, SSE, corrispondenza da Gaeta e Portici, rubrica 247, sottofascicolo 222.
37 Prela to Antonelli, 9 and 14 June 1853, ASV, SSE, 1853, rubrica 242, fascicolo 3, sottofascicoli 19, 24.
38 Carlen (ed.), *The papal encyclicals*, vol. 1, pp. 331–3.

unconditional commitment to bring Piedmont into the Crimean War. This cynical compromise confirmed Pio Nono's conviction that nationalism and anticlericalism were synonymous, and he opposed both.

In February 1856, when the congress ending the Crimean War convened, Pius implored Napoleon's protection for the church, asking the French to prevent the congress from addressing papal affairs.[39] His intentions were thwarted by Cavour. In April, after the terms of peace had been settled, Waleski, at Napoleon's bidding, proposed discussing problems that might disturb the peace. Cavour addressed the powers and the tribunal of public opinion, denouncing the irregular state of affairs in the Papal States, and suggesting that its problems burdened the entire peninsula. Pius was exasperated by Cavour's tactics, lamenting that he had even charmed the Russians. Perhaps it was because a big dog does not notice the barking of a small one, he confided to his brother, adding that he had certainly followed the Piedmontese antics.[40]

Rome wondered why the study Napoleon had commissioned on the papal government and its finances (the Rayneval report) was not released. That report contended that the 'abuses' of the Roman regime were neither qualitatively nor quantitatively different from those elsewhere. Antonelli released this positive report to the courts of Europe. However, the goodwill it generated was squandered by Pio Nono's stance during the Mortara affair of 1858. The Hebrew child, Edgardo Levi Mortara, secretly baptised by a Christian servant of the household during a childhood illness, was taken from his parents in June 1858, to assure his salvation. There were protests from the family, the Jews of Italy and Napoleon, but Pius refused to relent. Despite the condemnation of world opinion and the unfortunate publicity it generated, Pius would not budge.[41] Cavour utilised the Mortara affair to discredit Rome, and secretly schemed with Napoleon to reorganise Italy. At Plombières, in late July 1858, the two plotted war against Austria and a diminution of the Papal States. The nuncio in Paris, Sacconi, reported that the French empire had little good to say about the papal government, proposing that the pope have a smaller state so he would be less embarrassed by the burdens of power.[42]

---

39 ASV, Archivio Particolare Pio IX, Francia, Sovrani, nn. 30 and 32.
40 Monti, *Pio IX*, p. 260.
41 Gabriele (ed.), *Il carteggio Antonelli-Sacconi*, vol. 1, p. xiii; ASV, Archivio Particolare Pio IX, Oggetti Vari, n. 1433.
42 Gabriele (ed.), *Il carteggio Antonelli-Sacconi*, vol. 1, p. 5; Massari, *Diario*, pp. 84, 93.

Pius, regretting the prospect of war, invoked prayer to avoid the catastrophe. His prayers were not answered, and on 29 April 1859 the Austrians declared war. Napoleon, who cast his lot with Piedmont, promised to protect the pope. The pledge was violated under the pressure of events.[43] Following the battle of Magenta on 4 June 1859, the Austrian garrisons were withdrawn from Pavia, Piacenza, Ancona and Ferrara, encouraging revolutionaries in Bologna to move against the legate, who fled to Ferrara. The provisional government which ensued called for Piedmontese protection, and Victor Emmanuel dispatched 2,000 troops, appointing Massimo D'Azeglio his representative in the Romagna. Pius decried the conspiracy in his dominions, excommunicating all those involved in the rebellion. There was a call for the papal government to mediate the Franco-Austrian dispute and restore peace, but Pius realised that Vienna's call for a return to the status quo would be unacceptable in Paris.[44]

The Second War of Italian Liberation, seizure of papal territory, and the legislation of the Turin government hardened the pope's heart against the Piedmontese. In November 1859 the government approved the Casati education law, soon extended to the Kingdom of Italy, which stipulated that the ministry of public education would supervise all schools – including religious ones. Following the papal lead, the bishops protested against the laicisation of education and the attempt to place seminaries under state control. Convinced that a war was being waged against the church, in the decade between the second restoration and the proclamation of the Italian Kingdom in 1861, Pio Nono issued more than a dozen condemnations of Cavour and his colleagues responsible for unification. He did more than denounce the Piedmontese aggression and extension of their anticlerical legislation to other parts of the peninsula, assailing the modern doctrines which encouraged non-Catholic cults, and permitted the press to subvert the faith and undermine the church.[45] Trusting in divine providence, the diplomacy of Antonelli and the troops of Napoleon III, Pio Nono remained in the eternal city while the greater part of his state was merged into the Kingdom of Italy.

The spoliation of his temporal power took a toll on the pope's health, and in April 1861, fever-stricken, he collapsed in the Sistine Chapel. However in

43 ASV, Archivio Particolare Pio IX, Sovrani, Francia, n. 42; 'Proclamation L'Empereur au peuple français', *Le Moniteur Universel*, 3 May 1859; Victor Emmanuel to Pius IX, 25 May 1859, ASV, Archivio Particolare Pio IX, Sovrani, Sardegna, n. 52.
44 ASV, Archivio Particolare Pio IX, Sovrani, Sardegna, n. 53; Gabriele (ed.), *Il carteggio Antonelli-Sacconi*, vol. I, pp. 136–8.
45 ASV, Archivio Particolare Pio IX, Sovrani, Austria, n. 35; 'Allocuzione di N.S. Papa Pio IX', 18 Mar. 1861, *Civiltà Cattolica*, ser. IV, 10 (1861), 17.

1861, the Angel of Death bypassed the aged and ailing pontiff, who would live to 1878, removing Cavour, who had just become Italy's first prime minister. The pope was scandalised by the extension of the Piedmontese Casati Law of 1859 to the other provinces in a quest to create a national consciousness and restrict the influence of the church on the young. The Italian scholastic policy challenged the clergy's role in education, seeking by means of lay teachers and secular curricula a non-confessional culture. Pius considered these measures an insidious attack upon the faith, which he contrasted to the more open attempt by Garibaldi and his supporters to seize Rome in the summer of 1862.

The pope resented French pressure upon him to come to terms with modern civilisation in general, and the Turin regime in particular, decrying the threats to remove French troops from Rome unless it reached some accommodation. On 15 September 1864, the Minghetti government signed an accord with the French empire to regulate the Roman question without consulting Pius IX. It provided that Napoleon would withdraw his forces from Rome within two years, while the Italian government promised not to attack the patrimony of St Peter and to prevent others from launching an attack from its territory. Pius, still smarting from the Turin government's insistence in 1863 on the *exequatur*, requiring its consent to have papal bulls, briefs or other documents approved in the Kingdom, as well as the *placet*, requiring approval for ecclesiastical acts, was anxious to speak out. There had been talk of tying the condemnation of modern errors to the Proclamation of the Immaculate Conception in 1854, but this was deemed inappropriate. The pope returned to the need for a forthright condemnation following the seizure of the greater part of the Papal States. He catalogued many of the errors later listed in the Syllabus.[46]

The September Convention encouraged Pius to unleash the spiritual weapons in his arsenal, issuing the encyclical *Quanta Cura* on 8 December 1864, to which was appended the Syllabus of Errors, listing eighty errors drawn from previous papal documents, condemning various movements and beliefs. The encyclical reaffirmed the church's right to educate, the plenitude of papal authority, and the absolute independence of the church *vis-à-vis* civil authority. Under ten headings the Syllabus condemned pantheism, naturalism, materialism, absolute as well as moderate rationalism, indifferentism, and false tolerance in religious matters, finding them incompatible with the Catholic faith. In addition, socialism and communism, as well as secret and Bible societies, were denounced. Likewise condemned were errors regarding marriage,

---

46 Report of the Congregation of the Holy Office on the seventy principal errors of the time, ASV, Archivio Particolare Pio IX, Oggetti Vari, n. 1779.

as well as those on the temporal power of the pope. The secular system of education advocated by the Piedmontese and Italians was condemned in errors 45 and 47. The critique of the errors of the liberalism of the day caused the greatest controversy, and especially the condemnation of the final error, which called for the Roman pontiff to reconcile himself with progress, liberalism and recent civilisation.[47]

Pius considered convoking a council to deal with the contemporary dilemma, and on 6 December 1864, two days before issuing the Syllabus of Errors, asked the cardinals in curia to weigh the possibility. Encouraged by their response, he proceeded. In June of 1867, Pius publicly revealed his decision to convoke a council. He had hoped to have it open shortly, but difficulties at home and abroad conspired against an early convocation, including Garibaldi's incursion into the Papal States in 1867, before he was halted by a Franco-papal military force at Mentana. As a result, French forces were again stationed in Rome.

On 29 June 1868, the papal bull of convocation explained its purposes: the combating of error, the definition of doctrine and the upholding of ecclesiastical discipline. The opening was set for 8 December 1869, the feast of the Immaculate Conception. Prior to its opening, Pius implored remedies for the numerous evils afflicting church and society. Considering the Holy See to be the centre of unity in the church, the pope revealed his determination to play a key role in the council's proceedings. The bull of November 1869 providing its guidelines allowed him to propose questions for discussion and to nominate the cardinals, who presided over the committees of the council, as well as its secretary.[48] The committees devised fifty-one *Schemata* for consideration, but eventually only two were discussed: *Dei Filius* and *De Ecclesia*. The former, adopted by a unanimous vote on 24 April 1870, aimed not simply to condemn rationalism, modern naturalism, pantheism, materialism and atheism, but to elaborate the positive doctrines which these 'errors' violated. Reason was not rejected, but its limitations were exposed in the natural order, and more so, in the spiritual sphere. It reaffirmed the reasonableness of the supernatural character of Christian revelation, deeming faith an assent of the intellect, moved by will, and elevated by divine grace.

De Ecclesia, which contained three chapters on the pope's primacy and one on his infallibility, created greater controversy. Bishop Ullathorne of

---

47 For *Quanta Cura* see Carlen (ed.), *The Papal encyclicals*, vol. 1, pp. 381–6, and for the Syllabus Kertesz (ed.), *Documents*, pp. 233–41.

48 Carlen (ed.), *Papal pronouncements*, vol. 1, p. 40; Coppa, *Pope Pius IX*, pp. 159–61.

Birmingham reported that Pius had strong opinions on both issues, and claimed that the pope constantly supported the majority in favour of infallibility. Thus not many were surprised, at the end of April, when he agreed to give precedence to the section on the powers of the pope, removing it from its order in the face of the opposition of the minority, and the reservations of part of the majority. In mid-May, the chapters on the papacy were placed before the general assembly. On the final vote on 18 July 1870, 535 assented to infallibility while only two opposed. The dogma declared that the Roman pontiff, when he speaks *ex cathedra* and defines a doctrine regarding faith or morals to be held by the universal church, is infallible. Controversy surrounded it, even after the outbreak of the Franco-Prussian war and the close of the council.

Pius sought to mediate between the French and the Prussians, but his efforts proved abortive,[49] rendering Rome vulnerable to the vagaries of war. When the French evacuated their troops from Civitavecchia in early August, Pius hoped that some other power might step into the breach, but found no volunteers. The Italians, in turn, fielded an 'army of observation' in central Italy, and sent dispatches on 29 August informing their representatives abroad of their decision to take Rome.[50] The intransigent element in the eternal city urged Pius to flee from the impending Italian occupation, and the Empress Eugénie, the regent, sent the man-of-war *Orenoque* to Civitavecchia to evacuate Pius to France. However, the 78-year-old pope wanted to die at home. On 8 September Victor Emmanuel sent an envoy to the pope, justifying the necessity of occupying what remained of the Papal States. 'Nice words, but ugly deeds', the pope muttered as he read the king's letter, responding with a firm refusal.[51] On 19 September, Pius instructed his forces to offer token resistance to the impending Italian intrusion, letting the world know that while they could not prevent the thief from coming, he entered by violence.

Early in October, the occupiers held an election on whether the citizens of Rome and its environs wished union with the constitutional monarchy of Victor Emmanuel. The vote overwhelmingly favoured inclusion in the Italian Kingdom. On 9 October 1870, Rome and its provinces were incorporated into Italy, while the pope was promised inviolability and the personal prerogatives of a sovereign. Pius withdrew into the Vatican, considering himself a prisoner therein. On 20 October, he suspended the Vatican Council. Rejecting all offers

---

49 ASV, Archivio Particolare Pio IX, Sovrani, Francia, n. 86.
50 Commissione per la Pubblicazione dei Documenti Diplomatici, *I documenti diplomatici Italiani. Prime serie (1861–1870)* (Rome: La Libreria dello Stato, 1952), vol. XIII, n. 580.
51 ASV, Archivio Particolare Pio IX, Sovrani, Sardegna, n. 82; Coppa, *Pope Pius IX*, p. 170.

of asylum, he pledged to defend his rights. In a November encyclical, Pius condemned the 'sacrilegious' seizure, invoking the major excommunication for all those who had perpetrated the invasion, the usurpation and the occupation of the papal domain, as well as those who had aided or counselled this 'pernicious' action.[52]

To reassure Catholics, as well as the Powers, in December 1870 the Italians introduced a Law of Guarantees which recognised the inviolability of the pope, while investing him with the attributes of a sovereign. As financial compensation for the loss of his territory, he was pledged annually and in perpetuity the sum of 3,225,000 lire, not subject to taxation. Regarding church–state relations the *exequatur* and *placet* were abolished, along with other government mechanisms for controlling the publication and execution of ecclesiastical acts, in accordance with Cavour's notion of a separation of church and state. It became effective in May. Pius repudiated it, refusing to accept any agreement diminishing his rights, which were those of God and the Apostolic See.[53] In his view, truth and lies, light and darkness, could not be conciliated. Attacking the laws as inspired by atheism, indifference in religious matters and pernicious maxims, he repeated his condemnation in a series of subsequent encyclicals, warning the bishops of impending difficulties and hardships.[54]

The plight of the church in Italy worsened following the 'parliamentary revolution' of 1876, which saw the party of the Destra (right) replaced by the more anticlerical Sinistra (left). The new minister of education, Michele Coppino, replaced religious education in the schools with the study of 'the duties of man and the citizen'.[55] Distressed by developments in Italy, Pius galvanised the church to fight the 'poison' of the revolution, abandoning himself to the hands of God, certain that He would ultimately resolve matters in favour of the faithful.[56] For his part, he saw the need to strengthen Catholic ideology and safeguard the pontifical magistracy, which was threatened by the revisionist, heretical and liberal-national currents which had overtaken Italy.

Pius openly condemned whatever and whomever he deemed in error, regardless of rank, popularity or power. He perceived himself the agent of truth and justice, which had been outraged and offended. His assertion that

---

52 Carlen (ed.), *The papal encyclicals*, vol. 1, pp. 393–7.
53 *Ibid.*, vol. 1, pp. 399–402.
54 Carlen (ed.), *Papal pronouncements*, vol. 1, p. 41; P. De Franciscis (ed.), *Discorsi del sommo pontefice Pio IX pronunziati in Vaticano ai fedeli di Roma e dell'orbe dal principio della sua prigionia fino al presente*, 4 vols. (Rome: G. Aureli, 1872–8), vol. 1, pp. 89, 137–40.
55 Ministero della Pubblica Istruzione, *Testo unico delle leggi sull'istruzione superiore* (Rome: Tipografia Romana Cooperativa, 1919), p. 2.
56 ASV, Archivio Particolare Pio IX, Francia, Particolari.

the church had to instruct, direct and govern the Christian world clashed with the liberal demand for popular sovereignty, and the nationalist call for the omnipotence of the state. Pius's traditionalism and Ultramontanism left little room for compromise with the liberal and national notions which prevailed in Italy. Liberal Catholics came in for a special condemnation from this pope, who charged they undermined the spiritual unity of the church while championing a false liberty. In their efforts to reconcile 'human progress' with the gospel, light with darkness, Christ with Satan, they did more harm than good.[57] The conflict between church and state in Italy which emerged during the *Risorgimento* would not be resolved until 1929.

57 Pius to a delegation from the Catholic Clubs of Belgium, 8 May 1873, *Dublin Review* [new series] 26 (1876), 489.

16

Catholicism, Ireland and the Irish diaspora

SHERIDAN GILLEY

Some seventy bishops of Irish birth and 150 of Irish descent are said to have attended the First Vatican Council in 1869–70. This reflected a great international phenomenon, the emigration of Irish Catholics to the United States and the four corners of the British empire in the century from 1815, in a river of people which became a flood during the Great Famine of 1846–9. The Irish ecclesiastical control of most of this emigration, outside Britain itself, was asserted by the Rome-trained and Rome-trusted Paul Cullen, archbishop of Armagh (1849–52) and then of Dublin (1852–78), apostolic delegate in Ireland with full authority from Rome, and from 1865 the first Irish cardinal. Cullen came to recommend the appointment of most of the bishops of the Irish diaspora, as it is now commonly known, and a stream of priests and religious also left Ireland to minister to their countrymen abroad, as the new territories slowly developed native Catholic institutions of their own.

This Irish empire of the spirit, compared by Catholics to the British Empire of the flesh, was rooted in the nineteenth-century Catholic Revival in Ireland itself, where despite the Penal Laws against the faith from the 1690s, four-fifths of the population had remained Catholic. The leading light of the revival was not a priest but the quintessential Irish Catholic layman, Daniel O'Connell (1775–1847), a utilitarian-minded lawyer, of Irish-speaking gentry stock, educated by English Catholics and at the English bar, and called the Liberator by his people. O'Connell reacted against the failure of the Irish rising of 1798 and against the union of the parliaments and established Protestant churches of England and Ireland to espouse the cause of a non-violent constitutional Catholic nationalism. He found a peasant following, the first of its type as a mass democratic body, in his Catholic Association of 1823, which drew its income from a monthly penny rent. O'Connell achieved his first principal aim, the Catholic Relief Act of 1829, which admitted Catholics to the parliament of the United Kingdom. He was less successful in his Repeal Association of

1840, which sought to end the union of the parliaments, but by the time of his death in 1847, he had, despite his non-sectarian attitude to Irish Protestants of like political views, so fused together the loyalties to the Catholic faith and the Irish Fatherland that they would endure for another 150 years, giving most ordinary Irish Catholics at home and abroad an unshakeable sense of the interchangeability of Catholicity and Irishness.

This union of church and nation was cemented by the failure of attempts by the British government to achieve with Rome a veto over the appointment of Catholic bishops or to endow the Catholic clergy. The only official state patronage came through its grant to the chief Irish seminary at Maynooth, founded in 1795, which was made permanent in 1845 but was abolished when the Protestant Church of Ireland was disestablished by W. E. Gladstone's Liberal administration in 1869–71, leaving Ireland as almost unique in Europe without a state church. The popularity of the Irish Catholic Church as a voluntary institution was not even disturbed by its general opposition to the minor revolution against British rule by the 'Young Irelanders' of 1848 and to the more serious Fenian rising of 1867, both of which were condemned by leading churchmen, including Cullen, who also acted to prevent the involvement of his clergy in the Tenant League for land reform. The reasons for the failure of Catholic anticlericalism to take root in Ireland had to do with the patriotism both of most of those clerics who were opposed to violence, including Cullen – the so-called 'Castle Catholic' who favoured full-blown rule from Westminster was rare – and of the minority of clerics who supported rebellion, at least by seeming wild rhetoric, like Cullen's enemy and rival in the Catholic hierarchy John MacHale, archbishop of Tuam (1834–81), christened by O'Connell 'the Lion of the Fold of Judah'. The rise of the Home Rule movement in the 1870s, led from 1880 by a Protestant landowner, Charles Stewart Parnell (1846–91), accompanied the appointment of nationalist clerics like William Walsh, archbishop of Dublin (1885–1921) and Thomas Croke, archbishop of Cashel (1875–1902), who supported the revival of Irish sport, language and culture and the Land War for the rights of tenant farmers. Even the falling out of Walsh and Croke with Parnell in 1890 over his adultery, essentially out of embarrassment over the indignation of British Nonconformists, did not fundamentally disturb the union of the church with an emerging Irish state, yet to achieve Home Rule, which was coming into existence before the First World War. Only the events of the Great War seem to explain why a small minority of devout Catholics like Patrick Pearse persuaded church and nation to accept a violent resolution to the problem of British rule by dying as Christian martyrs in the quixotic Easter Rising of 1916.

If politics worked in the long term in the church's favour, its mission was even, arguably, assisted by the Famine, in which more than a million people died, and more than a million emigrated. This last phenomenon produced in turn further emigration and a declining population, which fell from a recorded peak in 1841 of over 8 million to under $4\frac{1}{2}$ million by 1921, turning a worsening ratio of religious professionals to people into an improving one, while less seriously affecting the better-off farming families who were the principal sources of recruitment for the fast-expanding convents and the clergy. Few results were achieved by the small number of Protestant ministers in the phenomenon called 'souperism', to convert starving Catholics by offering them food.

The Catholic Revival also, however, had a more purely religious dimension in improving regular Sunday mass attendance which, David Miller has estimated for 1835, was a matter of as little as 20 to 40 per cent of population in rural parishes with numerous Irish speakers, especially in the west with few priests and churches. The rates were up to 70 per cent in the towns, but this was well below the rates of 90 per cent which prevailed for most of the twentieth century.[1] Indeed Sean Connolly has argued that much rural religious practice before the Famine, for large numbers, was of a premodern kind, being lay and family controlled, and based upon the home, the holy well, weddings, wakes and the 'patterns' or pilgrimages to a local saint, which could be rowdy occasions sometimes degenerating into drunkenness and violence.[2] Emmet Larkin, the most prolific historian of the Irish Catholic Church, has suggested that with the eclipse of the Irish-speaking culture which was strongest among the victims of the Famine, a traumatised population was susceptible to a 'Devotional Revolution' encouraged by Archbishop Cullen, through the celebration of the cults of the Virgin and saints and popular devotions in English, and by an elaborate ritual in new richly decorated and appointed shrine churches, fed by new service books, prayer cards and English Catholic hymnody, and exploring the senses through candles and flowers, elaborate marble altars and precious altar furniture, coloured vestments and frontals, and the odours of beeswax and incense.[3] Cullen was a strong Ultramontane, in favour of improving clerical discipline under episcopal and papal authority, and his determination to root out the ill-defined Gallican tradition in the Irish church made the institution look more Roman than Rome in the eyes of Protestants and encouraged the solidarity of Catholics against Protestants both abroad and in Ireland.

1 Miller, 'Irish Catholicism and the Great Famine'.
2 Connolly, *Priests and people in pre-Famine Ireland*.
3 Larkin, 'Devotional revolution'.

It is a paradox that as the Irish became better churchgoers, indeed the 'most practising' Catholics in the world, they corresponded more closely to the British Protestant churchgoing mid-Victorian norm, as did their sexual *mores*, though this may have had less to do with formal religion than with the postponement of marriage for the inheritance of property by the eldest son and the dearth of dowries for women. The 'Devotional Revolution' is also associated with what Joseph Lee has called the modernisation of Irish society, through the Church's provision of popular as well as middle-class education, assisted by the state, though not without controversy, with an improving if still modest standard of living to sustain a more orderly and stable life.[4]

In fact, as Desmond Keenan has suggested, the 'Devotional Revolution' needs a longer timescale: Ireland had its full complement of dioceses and parishes in the eighteenth and early nineteenth centuries, with hard-working archbishops like Troy and Murray in Dublin before Cullen, in what was a fairly well-disciplined church; town churches in the east had their full range of 'Italianate' devotions before 1850, when most church building took place.[5] The movement towards a more Puritan, Victorian set of *mores* can be seen in the 1840s in the rhetoric of the temperance crusade of the Capuchin friar, Fr Theobald Mathew. Yet the creation of a respectable and well-behaved body of worshippers in urban shrine chapels was essential to sustaining the new Irish church of the diaspora, in the slums of Liverpool, Boston and Sydney. The underchurched character of a good deal of the older Irish Catholicism and the drunkenness and disorganisation of Irish rural life before 1850 may partly explain why so many emigrants in their new, mainly urban, settings abroad failed to make the transition to the Tridentine norm of Sunday mass-going, and lost their connection with their religion, which had been bound up with traditional folklore and folk practice in a sacred landscape in Ireland, now abandoned forever.

The foundation of All Hallows College by Fr John Hand in Ireland in 1842 to provide priests for the diaspora helped to confirm the Irish character of the new church, as did the new Irish religious orders, especially the Christian Brothers and the Sisters of Mercy, which founded hospitals and schools. All Hallows alone had sent out 1,500 priests by 1902.

The largest body of emigrants went to North America, predominantly to the United States, in all between $5\frac{1}{2}$ and 6 million people from 1776, with perhaps 40 million present-day descendants. A substantial minority of these

---

4 Lee, *The modernisation of Irish society*.
5 Keenan, *The Catholic Church in nineteenth-century Ireland*.

were Protestants, who probably formed a majority of the emigrants before 1830. The first Catholic bishops in what was to become the United States presided in the colonies of France and Spain, and French clergy, who remained numerous, only gradually lost their dominance of the North American church. The first diocese in the newly independent country, created in 1789, with an Irish-American bishop, John Carroll (consecrated 1790; archbishop 1808–15), was Baltimore, originally founded as a colony by English Catholics. The huge post-Famine Irish Catholic populations of the great eastern cities like New York, which had more than 200,000 Irish-born by 1860, and in the Midwest, Chicago, acquired powerful prelates like John Hughes of New York (bishop 1838–50; archbishop 1850–64), who were the architects of massive building programmes of new churches, presbyteries and parochial schools, the last not funded by the state, a cause of lasting grievance, for neighbourhoods in which an expatriate ethnic and religious identity survived the often traumatic uprooting to the New World.

After 1860, the Roman Catholic Church became the largest religious body in the United States. By 1910, it claimed more than 12 million communicants, compared with 22 million communicants for all the Protestant churches combined. The body of believers or more casual adherents was, of course, much larger in both cases. Rome's policy was an expansive one of erecting vicariates and dioceses where virtually no church existed. As the bishops set out to establish their monarchic authority, they faced the problem of missionary orders sometimes stronger than themselves, or confronted priests and congregations who demanded either lay trusteeship or the election of the clergy by an ecclesiastical democracy. There was also sometimes conflict between the Irish 'hibernarchy' and other immigrant groups, first the Germans, who were the largest Catholic immigrant group between 1865 and 1900, then the Italians and Poles, Hungarians and Czechs. A lack of Irish sympathy resulted in Polish and Uniate schisms from the Catholic Church. Germans alone came to constitute about a seventh of the Catholic population, in what remained an Irish-dominated but otherwise an increasingly multiethnic church with numerous 'national parishes' catering to particular communities, in which continental priests ministered to their coreligionists from Europe.

In an overwhelmingly Protestant nation, the church had to face discrimination and popular persecution, most spectacularly from the 'Know-Nothing' movement; Protestant nativists burnt down two churches and the diocesan seminary in Philadelphia in 1844. Prejudice against the Irish was exacerbated by their poverty, and the first attempt to create a national trades union, the Knights of Labor, led from 1878 by a Catholic, Terence Powderly, with millions of Catholic members, confronted the church with the problem of the poor in its modern industrial form. Elzéar Taschereau, archbishop of Quebec, with his predominantly rural flock, had Rome condemn the Canadian Knights, but the ban was successfully opposed in the United States by James Gibbons, archbishop of Baltimore (1877–1921), the effective primate, though not in name, of the United States. With John Ireland, archbishop of St Paul, and John Keane, bishop of Richmond and first rector of the Catholic University of America, Gibbons led the liberal arm of the American church. A more conservative strategy was offered by Michael Corrigan, archbishop of New York; he was strongly sympathetic to the city's famous Tammany Hall political machine and provoked popular demonstrations by suspending the pastor Fr Edward McGlynn, whose social gospel drew on the ideas of the land reformer Henry George. The division between liberals and conservatives reflected a wider tension over the accommodation of the church to American liberal democratic ideals, pioneered by the convert Isaac Hecker, and resulted in the papal condemnation of the heresy of 'Americanism' in the encyclical *Testem Benevolentiae* in 1899.

There was an appreciable emigration to Canada, with its open border with its greater neighbour, which supplemented the French church of Quebec with an Anglophone church of Irish and Scottish Catholics. A majority of emigrants from Ireland to Canada were Protestant, who did much to confirm the power of Canadian anti-Catholicism. The major Irish Catholic settlement of Newfoundland, of fisherfolk largely from Waterford and New Ross, had six successive Irish-born bishops, the first James Louis O'Donel (1796–1807), who carefully conformed to English colonial rule. Very different was the fiery Franciscan bishop Michael Anthony Fleming (1829–50), a priest formed on the model of O'Connellite nationalism, who championed the poor against the elite of his own flock as well as against British authority. The Irish also dominated the Catholic Church in Nova Scotia, most notably through Thomas Louis Connolly (archbishop 1859–76), a champion of Canadian Federation. The first bishop of New Brunswick, William Dollard (1843–51), was also Irish, as were his two successors. The province of Ontario could claim fourteen Irish-born bishops in the nineteenth century, the most distinguished being John Joseph Lynch, archbishop of Toronto, from County Monaghan (bishop 1860–70; archbishop 1870–88), who succeeded a French aristocrat, the comte de Charbonnel; at one point Ontario had five Irish-born bishops. In Quebec, the Irish sometimes formed their own parishes, islands in the larger sea of French Catholicism. Most of the missionary work in western Canada was the work of the French.

The United States illustrates most of the oddities of Irish emigration, but the Catholic immigration into England and Scotland also vastly increased the numbers of Catholics in Britain, especially in four great urban centres, London, Liverpool, Glasgow and Manchester. The Irish-born population peaked in 1861. The first cardinal archbishop of Westminster in the hierarchy restored in 1850, Nicholas Patrick Wiseman (1802–65), was born in Spain of an Irish merchant family, but he had nothing much that was Irish about him, having been educated for the priesthood in England and Rome. His successor, Henry Edward Manning, archbishop of Westminster (1865–92), an Anglican convert, cultivated both his Irish pauper flock and the Irish nationalist leadership in the House of Commons. His first great social work was the temperance crusade, a revival of Fr Mathew's pioneering work in the 1840s. His mediation in the London Dock Strike of 1889 was assisted by his friendships with leading trades unionists, as well as the support of the Irish Catholics among the dock workers themselves, earning himself an appearance on a trade union banner in the first May Day demonstration of 1890. Manning's strategy, to place the church at the headship of popular opinion in England as in Ireland, was also intended to distance his flock from the appeal of secular socialism. His Hibernophile views were abandoned by his successor, Herbert Vaughan, archbishop of Westminster (1892–1903), who came from an English gentry family. As in Scotland, where the hierarchy of bishops was restored in 1878, and the Irish membership of the church was in an even larger majority, the leadership of the Catholic Church in England remained in the hands of native Catholics, blunting the edge of the kind of identification of faith and fatherland which occurred in Irish communities elsewhere.

The original convict settlement in the colony in Sydney, Australia, included a good number of Irish, including the first priests, transported after the 1798 rebellion. While Australia received only 5 per cent of the Irish emigration, these constituted a hefty 25 per cent of the population in 1861, comprising the only significant white minority in an otherwise overwhelmingly British and Protestant people. Conflict between Catholicism, Protestantism and the Enlightenment has been identified by the Australian historian Manning Clark as the most enduring theme of Australian history.[6] The first Catholic bishop, John Bede Polding (vicar apostolic 1835; archbishop and primate 1842–77), was an English Benedictine, who dreamed of creating a vast new diocese for his order, but his English successor, Roger Bede Vaughan, archbishop of Sydney (1877–83), brother to the cardinal archbishop of Westminster Herbert Vaughan,

---

6 Clark, *A history of Australia*, chs. I–III.

was succeeded in turn as archbishop (1884–1911) by Patrick Francis Moran, Cullen's nephew, the first cardinal in Australia (from 1885), in a hierarchy which under Cullen's influence had become overwhelmingly Irish. A steady flow of priests and religious from Ireland confirmed the Hibernian character of the Australian church, with the impressive expansion of parishes and schools chronicled by Moran in his massive celebratory *History of the Catholic Church in Australasia*. Moran also offered the sort of welcome to the more moderate elements in the labour movement afforded by Gibbons in the United States, Lynch in Canada and Manning in Britain, and supported the aims of the strike of 1890. James Quinn, the first bishop of Brisbane (1859–81), who renamed himself O'Quinn in honour of the Liberator, and his brother Matthew, first bishop of Bathurst (1865–85), were militantly nationalist prelates who combined the loyalties to faith and fatherland in a manner exploited by the greatest of the Irish bishops of Australia, Daniel Mannix of Melbourne (born 1864; coadjutor-archbishop of Melbourne 1912; archbishop 1917–63), to oppose conscription in Australia during the First World War, and rally the Irish by birth or descent in Britain in 1920 after his arrest on the high seas by an English destroyer.

In New Zealand, in which the church was founded by a French missionary bishop, the Irish formed only about 14 per cent of the population. In both Australia and New Zealand, sectarian politics was dominated by the largely ineffective Catholic claim for public funding for their schools. These were only founded and maintained by the self-sacrifice of religious orders of Irish origin, though there were also new indigenous orders, most notably the Sisters of St Joseph, founded by the first Antipodean canonised saint, the Scots St Mary MacKillop.

Other areas of some Irish settlement within the empire include South Africa. The small number of early Irish immigrants, especially those who arrived in the colony in 1820, were largely lost to the church, whose growth dates from the appointment of an Irish Dominican, Patrick Raymond Griffith, as vicar apostolic of the Cape Colony in 1837. He had to establish his authority by deposing the churchwarden directors of the vicariate. A second vicariate in the eastern Cape was created in 1847, and was administered by Irish bishops. Its great expansion came in the twentieth century. In Argentina, a unique Irish community was formed by Fr Anthony Fahy, and about 300,000 Argentinians claim Irish ancestry. Irish Catholics made up a large if varying proportion of the British army, with their own chaplains; Kipling's Kim in India was the son of such a soldier. The appointment of Irish bishops in India had as its outcome the opening of schools and orphanages by the Loreto Sisters and the Christian Brothers. The Society of African Missions and Holy Ghost Fathers contributed to the missionary effort in Africa which, with the Maynooth Mission to China, was to become much more substantial after 1914. The half-century to 1960 was to be the golden age of Irish missions.

The religious energies of the Irish church at home and abroad came essentially from the neo-Ultramontane movement to exalt papal authority over the Catholic Church, with a strong devotional life and with a high doctrine of church, priest and sacrament, though a minority of Irish bishops, MacHale and Morarty of Kerry in Ireland and most of the Americans, were technically inopportunists opposed to the definition of papal infallibility at the First Vatican Council in 1870. Edward Fitzgerald, of Little Rock, Arkansas, was one of only two bishops to vote against the definition at the session when it was finally resolved. But even inopportunism was generally loyal to Rome, and it was the international solidarity supplied by Ultramontanism that gave the church unity and coherence against what were, for most Irish emigrants, informal but hostile and predominantly Protestant establishments in all their privilege and power. Only in Ireland to 1869, and in Britain itself, were impressive Protestant churches actually established; prejudice took more subtle forms which were just as insidious, and tended to make Catholics enthusiastic voluntarists, committed to the separation of church and state, except in the matter of state subsidies to their schools.

It is now generally accepted that while there were large concentrations of emigrants in particular places, as in the eastern cities of North America, they tended not to form exclusive geographical 'ghettos' or 'Little Irelands' of the sort described in 1844 by Engels in Manchester. Indeed in spite of considerable 'leakage' or 'seepage' from the faith, which varied greatly from one setting to another, and was probably most acute among the very poorest, and more common among men than women, it is remarkable how many found their religion strengthened in new and alien surroundings.

This Irish Catholic appeal to a sense of traditional, local and international community was reflected in their initial generally low rates of intermarriage with non-Catholics. Indeed the enormous effort of creating a separate Catholic world within and against a largely Protestant one was fed by memories of ancestral wrong and sustained by both continuing disadvantage and new-found prosperity, and also conferred and reinforced a definite sense of unity and identity, drawing on family and institutional loyalties, and binding past and present in one, in a view of things which for the children and grandchildren of the expatriates endured long after the disappearance of any first-hand knowledge of Ireland itself. The vast and expanding historiography of the subject is now somewhat bedevilled by the modern tendency to interpret religious behaviour in purely secular terms, when what is required is a much more subtle demonstration of the interaction of religious energies with the social and political needs of the diaspora in the varied environments in which it found a home. The Catholic Church was quite the most striking legacy of the Irish emigration to the United States and the British empire, and while other Catholics also made their contribution to the church's growth, the nineteenth-century Irish determined much in its shape and structure to the present day.

17

Catholic nationalism in Greater Hungary and Poland

A: Hungary

GABRIEL ADRIÁNYI

The Hungary which became a co-equal partner with Austria in the Austro-Hungarian empire in 1867 was more than three times larger than the truncated modern state which emerged from the First World War, and which excluded 3 million Hungarians. Hungary before 1918 included Slovakia (which became part of Czechoslovakia) and Transylvania, which was transferred in 1918 to Romania. Croatia-Slavonia, which was 70 per cent Catholic and a little over a quarter Orthodox, and was to become a part of Yugoslavia, had its own institutions, but was subordinate to Hungary, with representation in the Hungarian government and parliament. Hungary was very diverse religiously. Where the Austrian half of the empire in 1900 was 91 per cent Roman Catholic (including 3 million Uniates), Hungary (excluding Croatia) was only just under half Roman Catholic (8,200,000 people) and another 10 per cent Uniate (over 1,800,000), mostly Romanian and Ruthenian. The remaining 40 per cent of the population included just under $2\frac{1}{2}$ million Hungarian Calvinists (14 per cent of the population), $1\frac{1}{4}$ million German Lutherans, and over 2 million Greek Orthodox, most of them Romanians in Transylvania. There was a substantial minority of more than 800,000 Jews and an historic body of nearly 70,000 Unitarians.

This mosaic of minorities, the consequence of the absence of Habsburg power during the era of Ottoman occupation and its limitations after the subsequent Habsburg reconquest, left the Roman Catholic Church a diverse, rich and privileged institution, by far the largest in the country. It bore a special relation to the Hungarian state and nation, but without the kind of historic monopoly it enjoyed in most countries with a predominantly Catholic tradition. The church's difficulties arose partly from its wealth and privilege, and partly from its need to co-exist with other traditions.

During the first half of the nineteenth century, there were few outstanding figures amongst the Hungarian episcopate. From 1819 to 1831 Cardinal Sándor Rudnay stood at the head of the hierarchy. His name is linked with the national synod of 1822, the most recent to date, which was a dismal failure despite the best efforts of the primate and the bishops. This was due to the fact that the synod's resolutions, which, though they were at least in part informed by Josephinist thinking and gave serious consideration to internal ecclesiastical reform, were not forwarded from Vienna to Rome. It was only in 1827 that Franz I gave permission to the bishops to comment on a draft that had been completely distorted by the authorities and have it sent on to Rome. The Hungarian bishops declined to do so.

Thoroughgoing reforms in the church were all the more necessary because the powerful current of liberalism had already swept across western Europe in the early decades of the nineteenth century, and soon reached Hungary as well. In the wake of the new spirit of the age, the Hungarian parliament, after a delay of thirteen years, embarked upon the so-called 'age of reform' (1825–48), which inevitably affected relations between the state and the church. The new liberal ideas were not consonant with the existing character of the church, which was closely identified with the state. This was particularly apparent in the laws on marriage, and their implementation in the matter of marriages between members of different denominations ('mixed marriages'). Hungary followed the lead given by the archbishop of Cologne, Clemens von Droste zu Vischering, in Germany in 1830. The bishop of Nagyvárad prohibited the blessing of a marriage unless the children were to be guaranteed a Catholic baptism and upbringing. The ensuing fury in the parliament forced the Habsburg court to send a bishop as an emissary to Rome, and after tough negotiations Bishop József Lonovics succeeded in persuading Pope Gregory XVI to alter the ruling of the Council of Trent (the *Instructio Lambruschiniana*) with respect to Hungary, to permit the so-called 'passiva assistencia' of blessing mixed marriages, and to recognise the validity ('illicitum sed validum') of mixed marriages solemnised in the presence of Protestant clergy. These papal concessions did not, however, calm the tense situation, and the issue of religion continued to dominate parliamentary proceedings until 1844.

The liberals in Hungary were of a radical bent, and embarked upon a battle against the church, which they considered antiquated; however, they did not wish to give up their control of it. The bishops, meanwhile, could understand the need for reform, but were afraid that this would radically alter the existing relationship between state and church. They did not want a confrontation, and could not embark on one in the absence of popular support. Thus the last parliament of estates (1847–8) began a new chapter in the life of the church. As a result of the introduction of the Hungarian ministerial administration, the so-called 'royal right of patronage' was transferred to the control of the ministry. Political events snowballed. Article xx of 1848 on the equality of the received religions could not be altered even by the newly elected parliament (*Reichstag*) or the hierarchy's proposal to establish an autonomous church. The situation was not improved by the episcopal appointments proposed by the government and implemented by the imperial court in Vienna without, however, being confirmed by the pope. On the contrary, the spirit of the revolution had a good many supporters among both the secular clergy and the members of religious orders. There was no alternative but to consider the possibility of holding a national synod; but it never took place, owing to the outbreak of war ('the War of Independence'). However, the new, revolutionary minister for cults, bishop-elect Mihaly Horvath, attempted to pass a new set of regulations for the church by convening a church assembly, but his objective was to create a national church based on extremely liberal principles.

During the Hungarian War of Independence (1848–9) the bishops made attempts at mediation both in Vienna and in conversation with the Hungarian government. However, their efforts achieved quite the opposite: they lost the trust of both. Worst of all, the hierarchy itself was split. While the grassroots / lower echelons of the clergy aligned themselves wholeheartedly with the revolution and the ensuing war, a substantial proportion of the bishops maintained their allegiance to the old system. Both parties in the conflict, the Hungarian government and the Viennese court, demanded huge material and moral support from the bishops. Partly unwilling and partly unable to supply it, the chief pastors fell out of favour with both sides. After the revolution had been suppressed with the help of Russian military intervention, the court of Vienna found a scapegoat for the rebellion in the Hungarian hierarchy and clergy. Five bishops were forced to resign, several hundred Catholic priests went to prison, and six of them were executed. The situation was chaotic: the church's financial situation was in tatters, church institutions and buildings had been looted or taken over by the military, and normal church administration was all but impossible. The new primate, János Scitovszky, tried in vain to soften the measures imposed by the court, for Hungary was now to become part of a unified overall monarchy, politically via the enforced constitution of Olmütz, and ecclesially by means of an agreement (concordat) with Rome. Hungary's national and religious (ecclesial) sovereignty was doomed to disappear.

The Hungarian nation reacted to these attempts with passive resistance. Primate Scitovszky opposed the abolition of the distinctive features and special privileges of the Hungarian Catholic Church by convening bishops' conferences, and eventually, in 1854, he personally presented a *Promemoria* to Pius IX in Rome, in which he put forward arguments against extending the negotiated concordat to cover Hungary. However, it became clear that Emperor Franz Joseph I was only prepared to ratify the concordat (which would dispose of the last remnants of Josephinism) on condition that the agreement be extended to cover all the lands of his realm, including Hungary. The pope backed down, and the Hungarian bishops had to accept the concordat. However, since the concordat had been concluded illegally because of the suspension of the Hungarian constitution, the Hungarian bishops allowed it to lapse from the church's side after the political settlement with Austria in 1867. Until that time, Cardinal Scitovszky successfully resisted the abolition or restriction of his rights as primate.

During the 1850s, the church was at last in a position to consider internal reforms. Two provincial councils – at Esztergom in 1859 and at Kalocsa in 1860 – and two diocesan synods took place, and passed numerous regulations dealing with various measures for reform, notably concerning the sacraments, worship and the mode of life of clergy and religious, as well as church discipline. The dioceses introduced retreats for priests, the theological formation of candidates for the priesthood was modernised, support was provided for the theological faculty of Budapest University, the first Catholic publishing house was founded and the first Catholic societies were established. The religious orders, particularly women's orders, flourished. The Jesuits returned. But there were also political problems, as was demonstrated in 1864 by the case of Bishop Lajos Haynald of Transylvania, who had to resign because of his support for the incorporation of Transylvania into Hungary.

The suppression of the Hungarian revolution and of the constitution, together with the centralising tendencies that came from Vienna, all caused a great many problems for the church, but they did temporarily banish the threat of liberalism. Until the settlement in 1867 there was no liberal movement worth mentioning within Hungarian Catholicism. But the old problems re-emerged in the wake of the settlement and the restoration of the 1848 constitution. The main liberal 'Deak party' was moderately liberal, demanding reforms in the area of interdenominational issues such as marriage law, education, church property and registration, but with the objective of achieving peace between the denominations. By contrast, the radical left-wing liberals demanded the 'democratisation' of the Catholic Church, and the abolition of religious orders, of celibacy and of ecclesiastical privileges, together with the nationalisation of church property. The bishops therefore cautiously aligned themselves with the Deák party's policies and suppressed both the Ultramontane and radical liberal tendencies among the clergy. The bishops and leading Catholics envisaged the creation of 'Catholic autonomy' as the solution to these problems. This was to be a kind of self-administration for the church, in the shape of an organisation of clergy and laypeople that would regulate all the church's affairs including schools, societies, property, etc., with the exception of strictly ecclesiastical and dogmatic matters. After lengthy deliberations, which were accompanied by strongly worded campaigns in the press both for and against, a draft was finally completed in 1869. However, a parliamentary committee put it on hold (*ad acta*), and it was only taken up again in 1893. The failure of the attempt at autonomy was due to a number of reasons, above all the aversion of the Roman curia and the hierarchy to strong lay involvement in church affairs. The First Vatican Council (1869–70) also did nothing to encourage the idea of ecclesial autonomy. With just one exception, the Hungarian bishops rejected the proclamation of papal infallibility as a dogma, as they clung firmly to the notion of the 'magisterium petro-apostolicum', the infallibility of the teaching of the whole church as represented by the pope and the bishops. They, together with the other opponents of the dogma, left Rome a day before the final vote, as they were of the opinion that a valid definition could not be reached in the absence of the necessary *consensus moralis unanimis*. Although their objections failed, the contributions of the fifteen Hungarian attendees at the Council were not a wasted effort. The Hungarian government's approach to its bishops in Rome, threatening the sequestration of the church's entire wealth, achieved nothing, but the government did reinstate the 'right of placet': the bishops could not promulgate any announcements from Rome – including the resolutions of the Council – without state permission. On two occasions this led to clashes in parliament, but the Hungarian bishops behaved circumspectly towards both Rome and the government, and thereby ensured that the Old Catholic movement did not take root in Hungary.

One consequence of the entrenched and turbulent relationship between parliament and the Catholic Church was the drafting of a bill that included a whole set of new administrative measures, amongst others the introduction of obligatory civil wedding ceremonies, the abolition of several church holidays, the change of legal status of religious orders from that of a single 'person' to that of a private society, and absolute state control over church schools. At the same time, the bill maintained the royal rights of patronage, including the 'right of placet'. Fortunately for the church, the government did not obtain a majority, and the new Protestant prime minister, Kálmán Tisza, altered the course that had been taken, as he needed the support of the Catholic clergy against the left wing of his liberal party. Throughout his long period of office (1875–90) he therefore avoided anything that might have provoked a conflict with the Catholic Church. Using skilful tactics he ensured that parliamentary questions and petitions which might have disturbed the interdenominational peace disappeared from the agenda, and he even granted more protection for religion by means of several new laws. The bishops were content with this tactic of letting sleeping dogs lie (*quieta non movere*), as they themselves were of a moderate liberal persuasion, and in any case they had no other option. However, despite the basic agreement between Tisza and the bishops, there were some conflicts, particularly in the areas of education and finance. When the government introduced a bill in parliament to permit marriages between Jews and Christians, and the bishops caused its defeat, Tisza retaliated by reforming the 'panel of magnates' (*Magnatentafel*): the so-called 'chosen bishops' lost their seats and were replaced by representatives of the Protestant and Orthodox churches who were loyal supporters of the government. Moreover, the new law made it possible for the monarch to appoint batches of fifty new members of the upper house as and when required (known in Hungarian as *Pair-Schub*, or batches of peers). Ten years later, these new members of the upper house decided the fate of the so-called 'interdenominational laws'.

Despite many problems, the bishops remained loyal to the government. As a result, the church was allowed to maintain its social influence, its institutions and its property, and even to develop them further. There was no question of founding a Catholic political party on the model of the German 'Centre Party'; the church even allowed the government to extend the royal 'right of patronage' ever more widely, and saw politically active, pro-government prelates become bishops, mainly as a result of the government's right to nominate candidates. The bishops lived and behaved like aristocrats; they paid no official visitations to their dioceses, and delegated administrative matters and confirmations to their vicars-general and suffragans. The lower orders of the clergy lived as they pleased. They chased better benefices, did scarcely any pastoral work, and preferred to devote their energy to managing their parish estates and participating in the life of high society. The bourgeoisie was either indifferent to religion or Protestant. Under the leadership of the Protestants, the extremely liberal spirit of the age pervaded every national institution, the press, and even the academy.

In the circumstances it was not surprising that the government once again took up the old and repeatedly postponed plan to enact new marriage laws. First, the minister for cults issued a ruling in which he added an enforcement clause to the existing legal prescription that boys were to follow their father's religion and girls their mother's. If Catholic priests ignored this regulation and accepted children into their denomination contrary to the terms of the legislation, they were punished. This stirred up severe unrest both in society as a whole and among the Catholic clergy, which led to heated debates in parliament and the public arena, as well as to an exchange of letters between Pope Leo XIII and the Emperor Franz Joseph I, and finally to a governmental crisis. In the end, Franz Joseph I, as constitutional monarch, was forced to allow the bills to be passed by parliament after two infusions of *Pair-Schub*, and even to give his assent to them. The laws that were passed (GA xxxi, xxxii, xxxiii of 1894, and xlii of 1895) related to the introduction of obligatory civil marriage and the maintenance of registers, the possibility of divorce, and the promise of Catholic baptism and upbringing for children of mixed marriages (*Reversale*), together with the official proclamation of Judaism as a recognised religion.

This great defeat suffered by the Catholic Church in parliament and in society when the interdenominational laws were passed finally shook the remnant of the Catholic camp out of its lethargy. Political events convinced Count Nándor Zichy that a political party was needed in order to defend Catholic interests, and so, in 1895, a Catholic People's Party ('Neppart') was founded on the model of the German Bavarian People's Party. In 1896 it already had seventeen MPs, and in 1901 the number rose to twenty-five. The party's manifesto included not only the revision of the interdenominational laws, but also a number of social laws in the spirit of the encyclical *Rerum Novarum* (1891), the establishment of true Catholic autonomy, and the recognition of the legitimate claims of ethnic minorities within the country. However, the manifesto failed to address the most fundamental problem facing Hungary, the long overdue land reforms. Unfortunately the party disintegrated after it became involved in constitutional wrangling. It officially ceased to exist in 1918, when it merged with the Christian Socialist Party.

The complicated question of ethnic minorities also affected the Catholic Church in Hungary. After the War of Independence, the government in Vienna had, without Hungary's participation, established two ecclesiastical provinces – Zagreb for the Croats in 1852 and Fogaras for the Uniate Romanians in 1853 – in order to build up a counterbalance to the troublesome Hungarians, and Vienna also appointed several bishops who proceeded to promote Slovak and German interests. At the same time as the settlement in 1867, Law xliv was passed, which promised the ethnic minorities equality, independent administration and cultural autonomy. However, pan-Slavic or pan-Germanic propaganda was no longer tolerated. The law was repeatedly broken from 1880 onwards, and an ill-advised wave of Magyarisation spread across the country. International public opinion was outraged, and considered the best solution to the problem would be to split up the ancient Kingdom of Hungary.

After 1867 the bishops were still sympathetic to the provision of pastoral care for their congregations in their native languages. Unfortunately, however, those Hungarian bishops in the hierarchy who were close to the government supported the short-sighted government policy of forcible Magyarisation, which led to unrest in Upper Hungary (present-day Slovakia) and in 1907 even to bloodshed during police action in the diocese of Besztercebánya (present-day Banska Bistrica).

The most difficult ethnic problem for the Catholic Church was in Transylvania. In 1900, some 1.8 million Romanians lived there, of whom 1,719,336 were Orthodox Christians, administratively structured as a metropolitan see and three eparchies (dioceses). In addition, there were 1,658,298 Catholic Romanians of the Byzantine rite ('Uniates'), who also had a metropolitan see and three eparchies. Besides these communities, there were also Jews, a large number of Catholics of the Armenian rite, and over 1.3 million Catholics of the Roman rite, resulting in an extremely diverse ethnic and religious mix in the population. The Romanians were not satisfied with Law IX of 1868, despite the fact that it promised autonomy to the Romanian Orthodox Church. They wanted Transylvania to be separated from Hungary and incorporated into the Kingdom of Romania.

The disputes and tensions between Hungary and Romania with regard to policy on ethnic affairs (literally, nationalities policy, referring to groups within a multinational state) came to a head when a separate Uniate diocese was established for Hungarian congregations. Up to then, these Hungarian Uniates, numbering approximately 335,000, had been integrated into four Romanian and two Ruthenian eparchies, so when the Holy See established the diocese of Hajdudorog in 1912, the Romanian National Party and the Romanian Uniate church regarded this as a blatant infringement of their rights, and began an international campaign against it.

At the end of the nineteenth century, Hungary was still predominantly an agrarian society. Industrial development only began in 1890, in Budapest, and as a result the capital city also became the centre of the workers' movement, which was supported by the Hungarian Social Democratic Party. The Social Democrats' manifesto included plans for the nationalisation of church property and religious schools, and extensive laicisation of the state. Church leaders reacted to this development far too late and indecisively. Bishop Ottókar Prohászka (1858–1927) became a champion of social justice, and a noteworthy organiser was Sándor Giesswein, a canon of Győr diocese, the founder of the Christian-Social Union, which in 1906 already had 20,000 members and which soon developed into a political party. The party's co-operation with the Catholic People's Alliance ('Katolikus Nepszovetseg') increased its membership to 300,000, and it was active in ninety-eight working men's associations and forty-five regional branches.

A further contribution to the defence of the church's interests and the deepening of religious life was made by the twelve Catholic congresses that were held between 1894 and 1918, mostly in Budapest. During these three-day conventions, there was a public session each day, usually with three lectures; the rest of the days were given over to work by specialist panels charged with formulating wishes and demands relating to religious-charitable and social issues. Amongst the problems discussed, the questions of the Catholic press, Christian socialism and social issues (charity, the status of apprentices, male and female workers, prison chaplaincy, etc.) were given special attention. In this way the Catholic congresses – despite defamatory attacks from the anticlerical and liberal press – contributed to directing the attention of society and the church to developments which until then had gone more or less unnoticed. As for the bishops, who in 1900 were still living like aristocrats, changes began to take place in 1906, when the new minister for cults, Albert Apponyi, assumed office. He was instrumental in the appointment of truly apostolic, energetic senior bishops, of whom Ottókar Prohászka was one example. A man of many talents, Prohászka used both the written and the spoken word to arouse Hungarian Catholicism from its slumbers. He gave fresh impetus to the formation of priests and to pastoral work, attended to social issues and the relationship between theology and science, and led the ascetic life of a saint. Although he was the most noteworthy figure in Hungarian Catholicism since the death of Cardinal Péter Pázmány (d. 1637), he had opponents who in 1911 saw to it that three of his works were – completely undeservedly and misguidedly – placed on the Roman Index.

The training of clergy in diocesan seminaries continued to follow a Josephinist-mechanical pattern, beginning to change only around 1900 with the introduction of academic subjects including scholastic philosophy, catechesis, homiletics, sociology and pastoral care for the sick, as well as aids to spiritual formation including retreats, frequent confession and daily communion. Towards the end of the nineteenth century a slow but steady process of reform of the religious orders also took place. Along with the Dominicans, Carmelites,

Brothers of Charity and Franciscans, the Jesuits in particular recorded an upturn, and in 1900 the Hungarian Jesuit province was established. Women's religious orders grew rapidly: whereas in 1877 there had been eighty-two religious communities in Hungary, with a total of 993 nuns, by 1917 the number of convents had risen to 463, and there were 7,060 nuns.

Although church activity was restricted during the period of neo-absolutism (1849–67), academic theology was nevertheless able to develop. Several professors at the Theological Faculty of Budapest University became well known throughout Europe, high-quality, ambitious new journals helped develop theology and pastoral work, and every area of theology could boast outstanding scholars. Particularly remarkable were the church historians, who attracted considerable attention both at home and abroad as a result of distinguished serial publications such as *Monumenta Ecclesiae Strigoniensis*, *Monumenta Vaticana Dioecesis Vesprimiensis* and *Monumenta Vaticana Hungariae*. At the end of the nineteenth century Catholic societies and the Catholic press blossomed. However, the country's total of sixty-two Catholic newspapers could not compete with the liberal Hungarian press: in 1886, the Catholic press still only accounted for 3.6 per cent of the media output in the capital city alone. This meant that a Catholic press apostolate was needed. The Jesuit Béla Bangha achieved this objective when, in 1908, he founded a Catholic news agency, a publishing house, and a famous newspaper (*Magyar Kultura*) with the help of an endowment.

In 1896 Hungary celebrated its millennium, a thousand years of the nation's existence. The festivities for this and for the coronation of Karl IV (Emperor Karl I of Austria) in 1916 showed the whole world the power and splendour of the Hungarian Catholic Church. However, a serious crisis lurked behind the magnificent exterior, and one reason for it was that those forces within society that questioned the existing relationship between church and state were gaining ground ever more rapidly.

Despite this, a renewal movement from within the Catholic Church slowly set itself in motion. By the early twentieth century, priests and religious of an apostolic spirit had emerged, who did outstanding work especially in the capital. Some of the bishops, however, remained as immovable as ever, and were still closely allied to the ruling political factions, primarily in order to protect the church's property, wealth and estates (latifundia).

The warnings and wake-up calls of individual bishops, priests and Catholic politicians went unheeded, and as a result, in 1914, Hungarian Catholicism was inwardly completely unprepared as it slid into World War I and thence into defeat, chaos and, in 1919, a communist dictatorship.

B: Poland

JERZY KŁOCZOWSKI

General introduction

The history of Polish Catholicism and of the Catholic Church in Poland in the years 1815–1914 is inseparably linked with the history of the Poles and the Polish nation. It is a deeply dramatic history, because Poland, divided among three great powers, Russia, Prussia and Austria, was deprived of its own state and independence. The struggle for this independence in different forms dominated the minds of generations of the Polish elites, and influenced the whole of Polish culture and religious life. The remembrance of a great federal Polish-Lithuanian state, which had existed until 1795 and which was increasingly idealised in the memories of the people, reinforced this struggle, and merged with the more recent memories of sacrifices and battles against oppression.

This history must be considered within the more general framework of the history of the national groupings of central-eastern Europe. The territory is that of the three great states formed in the Middle Ages – Hungary, Bohemia and Poland – the last named being linked from the end of the fourteenth century, and formally joined in 1569, with the Grand Duchy of Lithuania, including Belorussia and almost all the Ukraine. This entire area was dominated in the nineteenth century by the three empires mentioned above: Tsarist Russia, Prussia, which would succeed in dominating Germany, and the Austria of the Habsburgs which would become Austria-Hungary.

These three powers had an assured place in the European order of the time, which was one of relative peace and increasing prosperity. But they were profoundly undermined by the aspirations of other nations occupying the space corresponding to the three historic monarchies. The history of the rise of these aspirations in the course of the nineteenth century is complicated and diverse. It was a question not only of the pressures from the dominant empires, but also of the tensions between the oppressed nationalities, their various demands, and their mistrust or even fear of neighbouring peoples. For historical reasons that were still visible in the nineteenth century, the ethnic, cultural and religious map of central-eastern Europe is a rich and exceptionally diverse mosaic that made it difficult to find solutions for the future, but all too easy for empires to play their traditional game of divide and rule.

The importance of the national question in central Europe became obvious in 1848 in the 'springtime of the European peoples'. But it was only the collapse of the three ruling empires in the years 1917–18 that demonstrated the profound strength of national movements and at the same time the difficulties of constructing a new order. In fact, only after the paroxysms of the twentieth century, culminating in the events of 1989, has a new map of the nation-states of central-eastern Europe emerged, together with aspirations to find a place in the European Union. With our long perspective, we can better understand the weakness of the great powers of the nineteenth century, and appreciate the importance of the national movements, including their fundamental religious elements.

The originality of the Polish experience

In the context of central-eastern Europe, it is necessary to recall the originality of the Polish national movement, involving the very notion of Poland and the Poles. The legacy of the 'political nation' of the Polish-Lithuanian federation remained alive throughout the nineteenth century. This idea embraced the very numerous multi-ethnic nobility – at least a million people, including their families. The Lithuanian political nation of the Grand Duchy was to be distinguished from that of the crown of Poland in a more limited sense. Less frequently, the word 'Polish' was used for all the Poles of the federated states, the more so because the cultural Polonisation of this nobility, of varied ethnic origin, was well advanced in the eighteenth century. The elites of the nineteenth century liked to call 'Polish' all the inhabitants of the former state (*Rzeczpospolita*). A great historian and one of the leaders of the Polish democrats, Joachim Lelewel, said before 1850: 'Do not distinguish among the sons of Poland, because they speak Ruthenian, Polish or Lithuanian, or because they are of such or such confession.' He added that there was no difference among the peoples who formed this Poland: Poles, Lithuanians, Germans, Ruthenians (Ukrainians and Belorussians in the twentieth century), and the others, such as Polish Jews and Muslims. There was here a significant democratic programme for the extension of the Polish nation to the wider population, a process of ennoblement of different ethnic groups from their 'inferior' status. The question of the consciousness of the masses who made up the majority of the population was at the centre of this question, recognised as crucial for the very survival of the Polish nation.

Before going into the details of religious history, it is useful to chart the effects of the Poles' great struggle for independence in the years 1815–1914.

The deep 'ethnic base' determined the outcome. Polish-speaking peasants freed from serfdom found in the course of the first decades of the twentieth century a well-established and self-conscious place within the ancient Polish nation. The Lithuanians, Ukrainians and some of the Belorussians formed their own nations, led by intellectuals of peasant origin. The example of the Polish national movement played an important role in the formation of their consciousness, but at the same time it awakened the fear of Polonisation, as in the case of the nobles of the former Respublica. Thus a social factor (the great Polish lords were proprietors of half the land on these territories before 1914) also decided their choice of their own national consciousness.

Towards the end of the nineteenth century, in the atmosphere of the strengthening and radicalisation of national movements, a strand of aggressive nationalism developed. In its programme, which soon became popular, a new peasant-based ethnic society of 'true Poles' invented a new Poland, by rejecting all the weaknesses of the former nobility. All the defects and disasters of Poland were attributed to the tolerance of the nobility, their utopian ideas of the brotherhood of peoples and their relations with the powerful and dangerous Jews.

Thus two deeply contradictory ideas of 'Polishness' must be carefully distinguished in the nineteenth century, and they were bequeathed to the twentieth century. The case of the political Polish nation is comparable with that of Hungary, which not only had kept its traditional position up to the nineteenth century, but by the 1860s, after the accords with Vienna, had achieved the status of a virtual independent state, though some nations were now in revolt against its authority. The case of the Slovaks is comparable to that of the Lithuanians, while the Croats and Romanians of Transylvania were in an intermediate situation between the two types of nationalism in this area of Europe.

The Catholic Church faces three confessional absolutisms

In the Polish-Lithuanian federation, the Roman Catholic (Latin) Church enjoyed quite exceptional freedom in this period of almost omnipresent confessional absolutism, and of state control of ecclesiastical structures and their functioning. The bishops were members of the senate, with an important position in matters decisive for the state. Because of the monarchy's weakness relative to the aristocracy and the regional assemblies of nobles, all difficult problems had to be taken to the local or regional nobility and compromises sought. But the relations between the clergy and the nobility were in general very good in the age of the Enlightenment, when ecclesiastical elites played an important role.

The shock of encountering the three absolutisms which divided up the federation was enormous. Their governments organised a strict control over the whole of ecclesiastical life. They changed the borders of dioceses to fit the new frontiers, and tried to place the maximum restraint upon links with Rome. The nomination of docile bishops was a crucial factor in the politics of subjugation. Because of protests from Rome, dioceses sometimes lacked bishops in ordinary for decades. Loyalty towards the civil power, presented as coming from God, was everywhere imposed upon the clergy, with public prayers for the king-emperor and his family. The confiscation of the church's lands by the state and the system of state payment of priests were effective instruments of control, as was the suppression of convents considered to be too independent and linked to the native population. The state's intentions were very clear: the Catholic Church – like any other church – was obliged to enforce a new order and to persuade the population to accept their new regimes as being according to the will of God. Those who took part in resistance, above all in armed insurrections, were regularly denounced to the papacy as revolutionaries seeking to destroy the divine order of things. It is interesting to observe the similarities in the practice of the three absolutisms, despite the differences between Orthodox Russia, Protestant Prussia and Catholic Austria.

In Russia, the Orthodox Church was governed by the state and was prepared to further the state's imperial goals. The suppression of the powerful Uniate Catholic Church before the dismemberment of the Ukrainian and Belorussian lands of the federation was a primary objective in 1772. Before 1772, this church had the most numerous network of parishes in the federation – almost 10,000 compared to 5,000 Latin parishes. It was energetically attacked before 1795, then again, after a pause due to liberal Tsars, after 1825. The last Uniate network was suppressed around 1875. The statistics are revealing: before 1772 in the Ukrainian–Belorussian area of the federation there were a few hundred Orthodox parishes in a diocese numbering 250,000 faithful. By the early twentieth century, on the same territory, there were nine Orthodox bishoprics, more than 6,000 parishes, and more than 10 million faithful. This touches on the problem of central importance for the national history of the Belorussians and Ukrainians, the clear role of Russification linked to the Orthodox Church.

The situation of the Catholic Church was different in the Kingdom of Poland, with the Tsar as king, and in the territories of the federation directly annexed to the Russian empire. These western 'goubernias' for a long time retained a special status in the empire, including legal provisions; for example, the very numerous Jews in this area did not have the right to leave and settle in other regions of the empire. At the time of the Tsar Alexander I (1801–25) and his liberal politics towards the Catholics, there was even talk of reuniting the Polish-Lithuanian federation, with the Tsar as king.

Under Tsar Nicholas I after 1825, politics changed profoundly, with ever greater pressure to identify Orthodoxy with Russia and its empire; forced Russification and the struggle against Catholicism, identified with the Poles, was the rule to the beginning of the twentieth century. The Polish insurrections of 1830–1 and 1864 provided useful pretexts for brutal repression and severe restrictions. The autonomy of the kingdom was restricted and abolished, and Russification affected the Poles as well as Belorussians, Ukrainians and even Jews.

In Lutheran Prussia, the Poles preserved some autonomy after 1815 only in the region of Poznań; in the other provinces, the Germanisation of the churches was a latent threat. The first conflicts of a simultaneously religious and national character broke out in the 1830s, but the great Polish/German conflict began with the *Kulturkampf* in the 1870s and lasted until the First World War. In the eastern provinces of Prussia, the anti-Catholic struggle was linked from its beginning with the politics of Germanisation, provoking both religious and national opposition; the conflict lasted even after the end of the *Kulturkampf* because Berlin would not abandon its systematic anti-Polish politics. At the height of the conflict, the Polish archbishop of Gniezno, Mieczyslaw Ledochowski, was arrested in 1874 and then expelled; hundreds of priests followed him, and fifty convents were closed. The constant pressure from Berlin provoked fierce resistance in the Polish Catholic population.

In the Habsburg empire, Catholic absolutism probably had greater success in the Catholic churches than in the Russian and Prussian zones. The position of the Uniate Church – called from then to now Greek Catholic – was reinforced in east Galicia among the majority of the Ukrainian population, and in time this church achieved an extremely important position in the Ukrainian national movement. The Polish clergy of the Latin rite were strongly imbued with the Josephinist respect for the state.

In the 1860s Galicia, as the Austrian part of the former federation was called, acquired a considerable degree of autonomy within Austria-Hungary. The province then quickly became a sort of Polish Piedmont, with a degree of freedom affecting the church and religious life. Thus the last decades of the nineteenth century and the beginning of the twentieth century were characterised by severe national and religious oppression in the Russian and Prussian zones and great liberty in the Austrian.

Resistance

One can understand the force of social resistance to the pressures imposed by such powerful states only by recognising the strength of the links of Polish society with traditional Catholicity and with customs on the margins of folklore and popular religion. There were no traces of significant dechristianisation at this time. The overwhelming majority of Poles, up to 90–95 per cent, followed obligatory practice: mass on Sunday, confession once a year, etc. The peasant masses and the rural nobility, rich and poor, everywhere laid claim to at least an outward or intended fidelity in spite of a daily morality which was often not very edifying. When they moved into towns, people now liberated from their peasant state and traditional serfdom tried to maintain their religious traditions. There are striking examples from certain towns in the United States, above all Chicago, to which millions of Polish peasants came at the end of the nineteenth century. As they began to earn money, they first constructed their parishes with Polish clergy in order to be 'at home'. The dozens of churches in the centre of Chicago still bear witness to this striking and very important phenomenon. Chicago quickly became the largest centre of Polish Catholic life in the United States. In the 'old country' of the Russian zone, state authority prevented the creation of new parishes. A new industrial town, Łódź, with 142,000 inhabitants in 1906, of whom 90,000 were Catholics (the others were Jews and Germans), had two parishes, but at the same time, two of the biggest parishes in Warsaw included 82,000 and 65,000 faithful respectively.

Real confrontation, a religious war involving the masses, broke out when the dominant states undertook operations in a new spirit of national aggression. This began in the Russian and Prussian zones in the 1830s, but the great decisive battles occurred from the 1860s and 1870s. Language was everywhere one of the most difficult issues, the language of the catechism, sermons and chant. Everywhere, the Latin Catholic churches of the federation kept the same liturgy, with Polish saints and ceremonies and religious customs. Ecclesiastical buildings were full of the splendid memories of the glorious past. For Poles acutely conscious of their national identity, the interiors of Polish churches represented a zone of public liberty; private houses symbolised the zone of family liberty and friendship which were equally important, and where religious symbols naturally held their place of honour.

The overconfident authorities did not recognise the strength of this world of profound values or the resilience of the culture, in which many customs and convictions coalesced to form a very effective resistance. The national factor in the pressures for systematic Germanising and Russifying often produced contradictory outcomes. Among Polish peasants, there was a new consciousness of their Polish identity, which was now considered, thanks to its persecutors, to be inseparable from traditional religiosity. The Polish national movement, strongly supported in society but incapable of defeating the occupying powers by force, profited from this situation by organising a national education for all, with very different means adapted to the needs of the different zones of occupation and particular regions.

National solidarity played an extremely important role in these efforts. The enormous differences in the living conditions and regimes across the three zones, Russian, Prussian and Austrian, became more and more obvious (they remain so even at the beginning of the twenty-first century) but, at the same time, the elites at least were very conscious of a national unity transcending political frontiers. The freedom of Galicia was especially exploited to disseminate information about the persecutions and difficulties which Polish compatriots encountered in the Prussian and Russian zones, where censorship prevented publication. Works printed in Galicia, including religious books and manuals, for example historical ones, circulated clandestinely in the other two zones among Poles.

At the end of the nineteenth century, Polish Catholic resistance took a mature and well-organised form, above all in the Prussian zone centred around the city of Poznań. It profited from the great progress on all levels in the Prussian state: a prosperous economy, illiteracy abolished and the rule of law respected. A movement for national solidarity was organised around the parishes and Polish clergy, who were able to profit from the lessons of German social Catholicism. Priests were often the natural leaders of the masses. Above all, there was a fierce legal struggle to teach the catechism in Polish – schooling was only in German – which by the beginning of the twentieth century found favour not only in Polish opinion. One achievement inspired by this dynamic movement was the Polonisation of a considerable part of the population of the industrial region of Upper Silesia. This area had been outside the Polish state from the fourteenth century, but had kept a Polish dialect; conflicts concerning the language reawakened the people's national consciousness. There were similar phenomena in the other eastern Prussian provinces.

In the two Russian zones, the 'Kingdom of the Congress' (Vienna 1815 or Kongresowka in Polish) and the 'western goubernias' of the empire, the situation was very different. The anti-Polish strategy of the 1830s and 1840s implied the marginalisation of these territories on all possible levels. The network of schools, Russian exclusively from the last decade of the century, further dwindled, and increasingly illiteracy prevailed. Outside some progressive industrial towns such as Łódź or Warsaw traditional poverty was dominant. Force reigned in the place of law, and widespread corruption often gave opportunity to buy a favourable decision from the authorities. Parishes were strictly controlled; a parish priest did not, for example, have the right to leave his place of residence without the permission of the Russian police. Resistance was obliged to take a more or less hidden, even clandestine, form, very different from official declarations.

The problems of elites

The existence of important social and intellectual elites was a great strength of the national Polish movement in the nineteenth century, compared with other movements in central-east Europe. The social elites, the aristocracy and numerous and diversified nobility, were in process of slowly losing their privileged position, but remained generally faithful to Polish allegiance; they kept their place throughout the national movement, sometimes even, among the rich, against the interests of their class. Marx and Engels wrote in high praise of the Polish nobles in struggling for the people's freedom against the forces of reaction. This large, impoverished nobility formed the basis of a new class, the intelligentsia, which from the second half of the century aspired to guide the Polish spirit. This democratic intelligentsia, open to individuals from the lower classes and to the general elevation of these classes, entered into both partnership and competition with the Polish clergy, who were much weakened but still accustomed to rule the Polish soul. From the end of the nineteenth century, this would become a grave problem in Polish religious life and culture.

The difficulties of forming Polish universities against the strategies of three dominant countries naturally caused repercussions in all. At the beginning of the nineteenth century, it was thanks to Russian politics that the university of Vilnius (now the capital of Lithuania) became for several years probably the most dynamic intellectual centre in central-eastern or eastern Europe. The intellectual aristocracy of Vilnius now played an extremely important and sustained role in Polish high culture, but also in the culture of the other nations born from the former federation. The closure of the university was a catastrophe, born of a new Russian strategy that was both anti-Polish and anti-western.

Not until forty years later did new dynamic Polish university centres come into existence in Austrian Galicia. Cracow and Lvov (today Lviv in the Ukraine) played extremely important roles for the Polish elites in all three zones. At the same time, the Academy of Sciences at Cracow became a national centre for Polish science and thought.

The universities also possessed faculties of theology, and the crucial issue of the formation of priests became for several reasons a very difficult and delicate matter in the nineteenth century. The seminaries, strictly controlled by the states, often offered a mediocre practical formation, particularly in the largest Russian zone. In the Prussian one, advantage was taken of the German theological faculties, often at a high level, but there were no centres for specifically Polish theological reflection. It was only with the universities of Cracow and Lvov that centres of this type were created, though not outstanding ones. The deeper influence on the formation of Polish priests was probably through adaptations of new western theological thought in practical theology and social and pastoral reflection from the end of the nineteenth century.

Given the relative intellectual weakness of the priests engaged in pastoral service, the religious reflection of the cultural and intellectual elites became more important. The 'Great Emigration' after the insurrection of 1830–1 valued and idealised Poland in Romantic fashion in the works of eminent poets and original thinkers. The Messianism of this generation – Poland was portrayed as the 'Christ of the nations' – exalted the religious vocation of Poles as forever faithful to their religion. The great poet Adam Mickiewicz – recognised as a 'national prophet' by successive generations – published in 1832 *A book of the Polish nation on pilgrimage* in the form of a biblical book of piety. It is a sort of catechism of Christian and fraternal liberty, opposed to all oppression, and deeply ecumenical in spirit. Long popular in Poland, the work was translated into nearly all the languages of central-eastern Europe. The Polish Messianism of Mickiewicz visibly expressed universal values, but his ardent patriotism was fundamentally contrary to the aggressive nationalism of later generations. In spite of a positivist current which was very fashionable in the second half of the nineteenth century, with a scientism often much attenuated in the setting of a country inhabited by the Catholic masses, Romantic ideas, embodied especially in great literature, remained very popular in the wider ranks of

Polish society among the young, and would return again at the beginning of the twentieth century.

From the point of view of religious history, an important phenomenon at the end of the nineteenth century was the formation of a Catholic intelligentsia that was capable both of entering into dialogue with different intellectual currents, even those hostile to religion, and of mounting a profound and sympathetic critique of Polish Catholicism and its weaknesses – in intellect, morality, and the quality of popular religion. Certain priests – intellectuals formed chiefly at Louvain in Belgium and Fribourg in Switzerland – began their activity in Poland from the beginning of the century, with crucial consequences for the evolution of Catholic society. A Dominican, Jacek Woroniecki, and two priests, Wladyslaw Kornilowicz and Idi Radziszewsk (the latter was from 1918 the first rector of the Catholic university created at Lublin), were particularly notable in reinforcing the Catholicism of the Polish intelligentsia.

It became quite widely accepted that a moral and even a religious renaissance was an indispensable condition for the independence of the country. The great success of the Polish scouting movement in the service of 'God and country' stems from this idea; the formula proved extremely appealing to successive generations of young Poles in the twentieth century.

The religious elites: men and women in the religious orders

The religious orders which had been so important in the religious and cultural life of the Polish-Lithuanian federation before its dismemberment were practically annihilated in the course of the successive suppressions ordered by the states. One exceptional case was Cracow, where several convents active without interruption from the Middle Ages survive to this day. Nevertheless, the recovery of this tradition despite numerous obstacles is one of the most striking phenomena of the Christian dynamism of Polish society.

From within the heart of the Great Emigration into France in the 1830s there was formed – with the help among others of Mickiewicz – a congregation of Resurrectionists, whose idea of the resurrection embraced Poland itself. They created a centre in Rome to train Polish priests and inform the papacy of the true religious situation in Poland falsified by the representatives of the dominant states, who had even succeeded in getting Gregory XVI to condemn the Polish insurrection of 1830–1, which shocked not only Poles, but liberal Catholics throughout Europe. The restoration of the orders in Galicia made greatest progress in the 1860s under the leadership of the Jesuits. They were particularly prominent in the publication of works of popular devotion for the Poles in the three zones of occupation. Their review, *Prezglad Powszechny*, became from 1884 the most important intellectual organ for Polish Catholics. A great artist and national hero, St Albert Chmielowski, organised a fraternity of men and women in the service of the poorest.

Among the numerous initiatives that characterised this movement, a major innovation compared with the older tradition was the leading place of women. There were some remarkable personalities, sensitive to the needs of the time, and dozens of congregations of Polish and foreign origin, which developed structures most notably for education and social assistance.

Female action even succeeded in implanting itself clandestinely in the Russian zone. A movement of Franciscan tertiaries was organised in some twenty-five specialist congregations under the direction of a Capuchin, Honorat Kozminski, who was confined and controlled by the police in a small provincial convent without permission to leave it. He communicated with his collaborators through the confessional, directing the activities of the sisters (also of the brothers, who were apparently less numerous) towards the urgent needs of society, notably the workers, female servants, and peasants. Some thousands of people organised in little groups dispersed throughout the country and several tens of thousands of associates (perhaps as many as 100,000), most of them women, succeeded in escaping the surveillance of the Russian police and quietly developed religious devotion and effective social work under the guise of officially sanctioned activities.

The situation at the beginning of the twentieth century

An important change occurred at the beginning of the twentieth century, the Russian Revolution of 1905, which created much greater freedom for the church in the zone comprising the greater part of the former federation – which was never forgotten – and of the Polish population. The social context was in any case very different after the profound transformation of the nineteenth century. The population had doubled since 1860, and now comprised some 20 million Poles in place of 1 million in 1800. This was the second generation of people free from serfdom and with rising aspirations. National consciousness increased enormously. But at the same time, difficulties of every sort and social and national discontent increased considerably. There was also growing tension between the peoples of the former federation: between Poles and Jews, between Lithuanians and Ukrainians, and to some extent with the Belorussians. Polish political parties that had been organised from the end of the nineteenth century in Galicia tried to widen their activities in all the zones. The expectation of a world war also increased both hopes and fear of new demands.

The Catholic Church preserved its deep social bases, notably in the peasant world. It was from there that the priests now came, and increasingly even the bishops who replaced the nobles. Tension rose nevertheless between the clergy and the new peasant parties, and above all the Polish socialism of the working classes. It was chiefly, however, a matter of popular anticlericalism and rarely – even among the workers – of a truly antireligious attitude.

The Catholic social movement was, moreover, preponderant in several regions, notably Upper Silesia, the most industrial area, among Polish workers, and in all the Prussian zone. Polish nationalism sought to integrate Catholicism inasmuch as it was an element in the Polish tradition and achieved some success, but also aroused opposition.

Another cause of increasing tension was the relationship between Polish and Lithuanian Catholics, as well as between Greek Catholics (Uniates) and Roman Catholics in east Galicia. This situation corresponded closely with that in the whole of central-eastern Europe on the eve of the First World War.

A summary of religious change in Polish society during the century from 1815 to 1914 must first take account of the strength of a traditional religiosity that was profoundly linked with cultural and national consciousness. The originality of the Polish experience in the special context of relations with the three Great Powers is extremely important on the confessional level, and requires deeper comparative study. The socio-religious history of central-eastern Europe still has enormous gaps. This chapter has proposed a provisional synthesis which raises important questions for future research.

18

Christianity and the creation of Germany

ANTHONY J. STEINHOFF

Shortly after the proclamation of the Second German empire in 1871, the future Prussian court preacher Adolf Stoecker rejoiced, remarking: 'The holy, Protestant empire of the German nation is now completed.'[1] This statement exemplifies the important, if often overlooked, contribution that Christianity made to the construction of modern Germany. The phrase itself recalls the 'Holy Roman Empire of the German Nation' that perished in 1806 and demonstrates the ongoing resonance of the imperial idea for conceptualising the nation throughout the nineteenth century. But by substituting the word 'Protestant' (*evangelisch*) for the word 'Roman', Stoecker also asserted that creating this new Germany was not simply a matter of 'blood and iron' or even of establishing acceptable constitutional relationships among the member states. In a very fundamental way it entailed resolving a question left open since the Reformation: what kind of Christian nation would Germany be?

Christianity exercised a telling influence on the creation of modern Germany. After 1815 confessional pluralism existed in most of the major German states, compelling each one to develop new legal and social policies to deal with the reality of religious co-existence. The redrawing of state boundaries also necessitated alterations in ecclesiastical organisation and the clarification of church–state relations. Such measures were intended to promote interconfessional peace, but as religious revivals renewed a sense of confessional particularity among Catholics and Protestants, state policies increasingly touched off dissent and socio-political conflict. By mid-century, the heightened sense of confessional difference had constructed a minefield for German politicians that affected domestic politics, church–state relations and, above all, public discussions of the 'German question'. Christian concepts and symbols permeated the discourse of nationalism and understanding of the state, but Protestants and Catholics constructed discrete, rival visions of this nation. Prussian might

---

1 As cited in Nowak, *Geschichte des Christentums in Deutschland*, p. 158.

resolved the closely related questions of Germany's territorial and confessional definition in favour of Protestantism in 1870. Yet, despite the strong Protestant bias in German national rhetoric between 1870 and 1914, Germany never stopped being at heart a Christian state. On this basis, even Catholics could claim membership in the nation, which distinguished their experience both from German Jews and socialists and from French and Italian Catholics.

The Christian state

With Napoleon Bonaparte's defeat in 1815, the question of German Europe's future organisation loomed over the Congress of Vienna. During the Wars of Liberation (1813–14), nationally minded intellectuals like Ernst Moritz Arndt, Joseph Görres and Friedrich Jahn called for the creation of a state to unite and protect the Christian people of Germany. Instead, the statesmen at Vienna recognised thirty-eight German sovereign states and grouped them loosely together as the German Confederation (*Bund*). The *Bund* was an even weaker expression of German political identity than the old empire had been. It also preserved many of the empire's shortcomings as a German nation-state. Many ethnic Germans still lived outside of the Confederation's borders, three states had foreign sovereigns (Luxemburg, Hanover, Schleswig), and the *Bund*'s two largest members, Austria and Prussia, ruled considerable territories outside the Confederation. The Vienna Settlement did appreciably alter the relationship of these two states to 'Germany'. Prussia became more closely tied to German Europe through its acquisition of the Rhineland and Westphalia. Conversely, Austria's gains in central Europe and Italy diminished her status as a German state, the possession of the *Bund* presidency notwithstanding.

The return of peace, however, did not fully extinguish nationalist yearnings. At universities across German Europe, student fraternities (*Burschenschaften*) arose to champion German nationalism and resist the politics of reaction promoted by the Austrian minister and dominant personality of post-Napoleonic German Europe, Clemens von Metternich. The student movement peaked in October 1817 with a festival at the Wartburg castle where, exactly 300 years before, Martin Luther had defied imperial (Habsburg) and papal authority. By making this reference to the Reformation and framing the German national struggle in religious and confessional terms, the students did more than just make a powerful political statement. They established a precedent for nationalist discourse that became especially prominent in later years. In the end, however, Metternich prevailed. Taking advantage of the public outcry against former fraternity student Karl Sand's murder of the reactionary playwright August von Kotzebue in 1819, Metternich compelled the German Diet to pass the Carlsbad Decrees and the Vienna Final Act. With the first measure, Metternich shut down the *Burschenschaften* and imposed a confederation-wide regime of censorship. The second empowered the *Bund* to act against any political changes that would threaten either monarchical power or particularism.

Mounting hostility towards nationalism helps to explain another facet of the 1815 agreements: the absence of Confederation-wide solutions to the complex ecclesiastical problems ensuing from the Holy Roman Empire's collapse. Chief among these was how to define the Catholic Church's legal status in the new German states. Certain prominent Catholic churchmen, notably Heinrich Ignaz von Wessenberg of Constance and Karl von Dalberg, the last imperial chancellor, strove to establish a national Catholic Church. Wary of an overly independent German church, however, the papal secretary, Cardinal Consalvi, preferred that the Congress only proclaim a concordat that fixed uniformly the legal relationship between church and state throughout the *Bund*. The German princes liked neither idea. They felt that a national concordat would impinge upon their sovereignty, whereas the existence of a national Catholic Church might foster unwanted nationalist movements.

In fact, the princes made only one Confederation-wide statement on religious policy, but it was significant. Because the territorial reorganisations of 1815 had made the major German states denominationally pluralistic, Article Eleven of the 1815 Act of Confederation decreed: 'In the states and territories of the Confederation, confessional differences among Christians may not justify any distinction in the enjoyment of civil and political rights.' In this manner, confessional parity became a fundamental principle of German administration and law, guaranteed by the Confederation's Diet and, more appreciably, by the respective political might of Protestant Prussia and Catholic Austria. Yet parity also restricted full citizenship to German Christians. For while states could not use religion to discriminate among Christians, they could use religious beliefs to deny non-Christians (e.g. Jews) civil and political rights.[2]

The other major ecclesiastical questions found resolution on a state-by-state basis. With respect to Catholicism, two tasks remained: delineating diocesan boundaries and fixing the relations between church and state. The settlement of the first issue itself broke new ground: as far as possible diocesan boundaries would coincide with state borders. The borders of Fulda (Hesse-Kassel), Hildesheim (Hanover) and Limburg (Nassau) were thus redrawn, the old

---

2 Clark, 'German Jews', p. 127.

bishopric of Constance divided into the dioceses of Freiburg (for Baden) and Rottenburg (Württemberg), and the former electoral diocese of Mainz restored as the see for Hesse-Darmstadt. At the same time, the Vatican strove to create mutually favourable agreements with the states on such issues as ecclesiastical pay, clerical nominations, education and the Catholic Church's general ability to manage its internal affairs. This resulted in the Bavarian concordat in 1817, a Prussian convention in 1821, and more informal arrangements with Hanover and Württemberg. In Austria, however, Metternich held firm to the policy of Josephinism, whereby the clergy functioned as state agents of religion, morality and public order. Taken together, the post-Vienna settlements put the Catholic Church in a position *vis-à-vis* the state remarkably similar to that which the Protestant churches had known since the Reformation: subject to close state regulation and supervision.

German Protestantism was also affected by the new political geography, for several states now found themselves home to a variety of Protestant traditions. Propelled by a sense that the old reasons for intraconfessional division were no longer valid, Protestants in Baden, Nassau and the Hesses created new, united state churches. King Frederick William III adopted a similar strategy, but in fusing the Lutheran and Reformed churches in old (pre-1815) Prussia by royal fiat, he aroused the ire of many churchmen, above all Berlin's leading theologian, Friedrich Schleiermacher. The predominantly Reformed Prussian Rhineland and Westphalia, however, remained outside the union, receiving their own church constitution in 1835. In Bavaria too multiple models of Protestant church organisation co-existed: union in the Palatinate and a confessional Lutheran church for the rest of the kingdom.

The same factors that encouraged the development of united Protestant churches also promoted peaceful relations between church and state and among the Christian churches. Rulers desired an alliance between throne and altar. They regarded the churches as necessary pillars of order and authority, and relied on clergy to serve as local agents of state power. Churches likewise lent the princes their support, seeing the latter's conservative policies as complementary to their own efforts to root out religious rationalism and promote the rechristianisation of German Europe. The Holy Alliance between Catholic Austria, Protestant Prussia and Orthodox Russia stands as one of the clearest expressions of this Romantic ecumenism. But it also appears in the contributions of Ernst Ludwig von Gerlach, the founder of the influential Protestant *Evangelische Kirchenzeitung*, to the Catholic *Politisches Wochenblatt*, and in the intellectual exchanges between Protestant and Catholic theologians at the University of Tübingen.

The post-1815 religious revivals would undermine this socio-confessional harmony. Within both Catholicism and Protestantism a strong sense of denominational particularism emerged, and increasingly the 'awakened' felt called to stand up against what they regarded as distortions of true ecclesiastical and doctrinal practice. In eastern Prussia and Silesia, orthodox Lutherans not only criticised the United church's deviation from Lutheran theology, but refused to use the required liturgy. Faced with such open resistance, the Prussian state arrested non-compliant ministers and laymen after 1830 and sent troops to occupy recalcitrant parishes. In 1837 King Frederick William finally allowed the 'old Lutherans' to emigrate, but the underlying problem of religious conscience remained unresolved.

By contrast, the conflicts that arose in western Prussia and Bavaria were touchstones for gauging the true extent of confessional parity and religious freedom in the *Bund*. In the overwhelmingly Catholic Rhineland and Westphalia, anxiety mounted steadily in the face of the Prussian state's anti-Catholic actions. It brought Protestants from old Prussia to fill government positions, keeping local Catholics out of public employ. Then in 1825, the old Prussian ordinance on mixed marriages was introduced. Accordingly all children from such marriages were to be raised in the religion of the father. This not only conflicted with the Catholic practice of raising all such children as Catholics but clearly favoured the immigrant Protestants. An uneasy peace held until 1836 when the new, Ultramontane bishop of Cologne, Clemens von Droste zu Vischering, insisted on applying canonical norms strictly. The Prussian government demanded the bishop's resignation and, when he refused, it suspended him from office and forced him from the diocese. This 'Cologne Incident' galvanised Catholic opinion throughout Germany, fanned by the publication of hundreds of leaflets pro and contra. It also led Catholic leaders to cease co-operation with conservative Protestants, who defended the Prussian state's policies, and develop their own, confessional political programme. Similarly provocative and conducive to confessional conscience-raising was the Bavarian 'Genuflection Edict' of 1838, by which every soldier, regardless of denomination, had to kneel when the Holy Sacrament passed during a religious procession. Protestants now railed against this affront to their religious sensibilities; nevertheless, seven years passed before Ludwig I rescinded the order.

The noisy responses to the Cologne Incident and the Genuflection Edict were symptoms of the heightening of confessional tension in Germany. But like the 1844 pilgrimage to Trier, which brought roughly half a million Catholics from across Germany to view the Holy Robe, these affairs also fostered a sense of national Catholic and Protestant community, thereby contributing to the revival of German nationalism. Still, the lines of confessional division were hardly cast in stone. In Prussia, Frederick William IV strove to heal the rifts that occurred during the reign of his father. Upon ascending the throne in 1840, he ended the persecution of the Orthodox Lutherans and made peace with the Catholics. He also supported the completion of Cologne cathedral, celebrating it in 1842 as a great German, Christian monument. This spirit of reconciliation, however, stopped short of outright religious tolerance. In 1845, a Prussian cabinet order authorised the repression of the liberal Protestant 'Friends of Light' (*Lichtfreunde*) movement. Furthermore, at a joint meeting of the Prussian provincial assemblies in 1847 the influential conservative Protestant theologian Friedrich Julius Stahl successfully argued that Prussia should not grant Jews full civil rights, for 'it would violate the principles of a Christian state, if non-Christians were allowed to hold public offices'.[3]

Forging the German nation-state

Well into the 1840s, German conservatives emphasised the Christian character of monarchical rule to hinder political and social change. Dissatisfaction with the status quo, however, was rising. The industrial and cultured middle class resented existing economic regulations, censorship, and the enduring restrictions on political activity. Peasants were suffering from a series of bad harvests and rising indebtedness. These tensions exploded in 1848 as word spread of the latest Parisian uprisings. In March, rural revolts shook Baden, Hesse and Thuringia. Popular unrest forced Frederick William from Berlin and Metternich from Vienna. Then in May, representatives from across German Europe assembled at St Paul's Church in Frankfurt am Main to give birth to a German nation.

The Frankfurt Assembly was the brainchild of German liberals, a predominantly bourgeois Protestant group. Since the late 1810s they had actively fostered the development of Germany's identity as a cultural nation (*Kulturnation*). The Grimm brothers' grammars and folk tale collections called attention to a shared linguistic culture that transcended state boundaries. The humanistic *Gymnasium* provided a common educational experience for the middle class and nurtured in them an appreciation of German literature, language and music. A national consciousness developed too, in the networks of middle-class gymnastic societies, singing clubs and shooting associations, particularly at events like the 1847 Lübeck all-German choral festival. And as liberals came

---

3 *Evangelische Kirchenzeitung* (1847), p. 657.

to view the establishment of a national state as the only way to save Germany from its political, legal and economic backwardness, these organisations served as a quasi-public space in which liberals elaborated and advanced a political programme.

Even among liberals, defining this Germany at Frankfurt proved difficult. Yet, early on in the discussions a consensus did emerge to de-emphasise religion's role in public life. This certainly reflected the influence of the liberal majority, who felt that the existing system of church–state relations (*Staatskirchentum*) thwarted political and social progress. But it also came about because Catholics and liberal-moderate Protestants wished to escape from the heavy hand of state tutelage in ecclesiastical affairs. Hence, Catholic deputies voted *en bloc* for most of the liberal proposals concerning religion in the 'Basic Rights of the German People' (*Grundrechte*), even though Catholics never endorsed the liberals' sense of what 'religious liberty' meant. As approved in January 1849 and incorporated into the Imperial Constitution that March, the *Grundrechte* guaranteed Germans freedom of belief and conscience. It also separated church and state to an important degree. Religious institutions would organise their affairs without state interference. Conversely, churches would lose their status as state institutions. They would forfeit their educational privileges, and the maintenance of birth, marriage and death records would devolve to the state. The constitution, however, did not make all religious organisations equal: only recognised churches would enjoy complete freedom of religious assembly.

In the meantime, the parliamentarians struggled to set Germany's territorial boundaries. As late as December 1848, a considerable majority favoured the so-called 'greater Germany' (*großdeutsch*) approach. This meant that all the *Bund*'s existing members, including Austria, would be part of the new nation-state. Political and confessional concerns spoke in favour of this arrangement. Smaller and medium-sized states (e.g. Baden, Hanover, Saxony) wanted to counterbalance Prussia's might. Catholics viewed Austria's inclusion as the best way to protect Catholic interests. Yet, since most of the Habsburg empire's subjects were not ethnically German, many nationalists opposed incorporating all of Austria into Germany. The Austrian government itself resolved the Assembly's dilemma. When the Habsburgs returned to power in December, Prince Schwarzenberg announced that Austria would have nothing of the Assembly's nationalist schemes. By default, the Assembly embraced the 'small German' (*kleindeutsch*) solution (Germany without Austria), and in April 1849 it offered the imperial crown to Frederick William of Prussia.

Frederick William's rejection of the imperial distinction effectively wrecked the National Assembly's plans. By June the delegates had been dispersed from Frankfurt, ending the experiment in popular nation-building. None the less, Prussia continued to explore the possibilities of forming a *kleindeutsch* state with the other German princes, over Austria's stated objections. Only upon learning late in 1850 that Russia would support Austria should war break out did Frederick William back down. At the Bohemian town of Olmütz, he agreed to restore the German confederation as it had existed before the upheavals of 1848. Austria regained its pre-eminence within German Europe, Germany remained divided, and the politics of reaction returned.

Yet, it was too late to turn back the clock. With the exception of Austria, most German princes – including Frederick William – ruled constitutionally after 1850. Significantly, the constitutional provisions for legislative institutions and elections opened up German political life as never before. Long term, this also undermined rulers' efforts to revive censorship and restrictions on political associations. Moreover, the princes granted the Christian churches much of the freedom promised by the stillborn imperial constitution of 1849. The Prussian constitution of 1850 gave the Catholic and the Protestant churches significant autonomy to run their internal affairs. Frederick William even placed the direction of the Protestant church in a new organisation, the Superior Church Council (*Oberkirchenrat*), which no longer reported to the Prussian ministry for church affairs (although it remained responsible to the king as *summus episcopus*). To gain Catholic support for their conservative policies, several states signed new agreements with the Vatican. The most generous of these was the Austrian concordat of 1855, which not only freed the church from state control over clerical nominations and internal administration, but effectively subordinated civil society to the church. The church gained extensive rights over the public schools, and the state pledged to uphold canon law as civil law, particularly with respect to marriage. But even in Württemberg, Hesse-Darmstadt and Baden, the new concordats reduced state influence over episcopal and priestly appointments, gave the churches a freer hand in exercising church discipline and organising religious services, and enhanced the church's role in public schooling.

The years after 1848 also witnessed important changes in the complexion of German Protestantism and Catholicism. The return to reaction strengthened the conservative-orthodox position in many Protestant state churches, particularly in Mecklenburg, Bavaria, Hesse-Kassel and Prussia. Once more, the princes looked to the church to help guard against sinful revolution. But now conservative churchmen used this support to undercut liberal theologians and silence advocates of synodal government. Liberal Protestantism remained prominent in Baden and the Rhineland. Elsewhere it struggled to survive against the conservatives, who largely controlled clerical appointments and nominations of university theology professors.

Rivalry within the Protestant fold, however, did not check the growing desire to co-ordinate policies among the state churches. A first attempt in this direction had been made at the 1846 Eisenach Congress; it foundered in the face of the princes' refusal to cede any measure of their ecclesiastical prerogatives. More fruitful were the Evangelical Church Conferences, which from 1852 on also met regularly at Eisenach. The brainchild of the Württemberg court preacher Karl von Grüneisen, the 'Eisenach Conference' became an important forum where representatives of the state churches discussed questions of ecclesiastical organisation and religious practice. Its resolutions did not bind the member churches, but they had enormous influence on German Protestantism's development. Most of the state churches adopted the Conference's policies for regulating mixed marriages, its revision of the Luther Bible, and its standards for church design and construction. The Conference also published the first national Protestant paper, the *Allgemeines Kirchenblatt für das evangelische Deutschland*, and collected annual statistics of religious practice from its member churches. The Eisenach Conference's activities greatly contributed to the creation of a national Protestant consciousness, even if church leaders themselves were generally unsympathetic to the rising chorus of *kleindeutsch* nationalism.

In Catholicism, the pivotal development was the triumph of Ultramontanism. Ultramontanes disdained the episcopal, tolerant and pluralist traditions within German Catholicism, which intellectuals like Ignaz von Döllinger still championed from Munich and Bonn. The Ultramontane model stressed instead hierarchy, discipline and absolute obedience to the church's spiritual head: the pope. The Ultramontanes also fought states' efforts to push the church out of public life. Instead of the Church compromising with secular trends, they felt that political, social and cultural life should conform to Catholic teaching. Mainz was the initial home of German Ultramontanism. But as Pope Gregory XVI succeeded in making loyalty to Rome the precondition of being a German bishop and as German seminaries came under the influence of priests trained at the Jesuit Collegium Germanicum in Rome, Ultramontane sympathies spread quickly. Indeed, so advanced was the Ultramontane movement among the German clergy, that when Pius IX indicated his opposition to the plan to establish a national bishop and synod at the first conference of German bishops at Würzburg (1848), the bishops quickly dropped it. Public outcry over Pius IX's treatment during the 1848 Revolution had the further consequence of transforming the pope into an icon of lay adoration. Hence, by 1850 Ultramontanism had become as much a popular as a clerical force in Catholic Germany, with the significant exception of Austria. There it remained blocked by Josephinism.

Closely associated with the Ultramontane movement was a revitalisation of Catholic religious practices and sensibilities.[4] Priests revived devotions to the Virgin Mary and the Immaculate Conception, and established new ones to the Sacred Heart and St Joseph. The church promoted pilgrimages. It organised missions. Women and men flocked to the religious brotherhoods and congregations that were (re-)established in growing numbers after 1850. With its emphasis on sentiment, emotion and the miraculous, this renewal appears at first glance to be a mere restoration of Counter-Reformation and Baroque piety. In fact, it was quite innovative and modern. Priests gradually brought public religious life under their supervision and control. They carefully scripted pilgrimages and processions. They used voluntary associations and newspapers to mobilise the masses and place them more closely under clerical oversight. But these organisations also opened up new spheres of Catholic activity. Local chapters of the Borromeo Society (named after the influential Italian prelate whom Pope Pius IV declared 'Protector of Lower Germany' in 1560) disseminated Catholic religious literature and set up lending libraries. Associations like the St Vincent and Kolping societies extended the church's social mission, and the Boniface Society defended the interests of the Catholic diaspora.

Ultramontanism's achievements also fuelled an increase in interconfessional polemic during the 1850s and 1860s. Although many Protestant churchmen longed for a similar increase in devotion among their own flocks, they were sceptical of what passed for piety among Catholics. Individual pastors as well as many laymen with only weak ties to the organised churches (often called 'secular' or 'cultural' Protestants (*Kulturprotestanten*)) took a dimmer view of the situation. Pointing to the Westphalian Protestants who attended Jesuit missions and the Boniface Society's proselytising activities, they charged the Catholic Church with trying to destroy Protestantism. To fend off the attack, such Protestants unleashed a torrent of sermons and popular literature that glorified the Protestant past and belittled Catholicism as emotional, superstitious, feminine and foreign. Liberal politicians and middle-class intellectuals, including the noted historian Heinrich von Sybel, broadened the

---

4 For a fuller account see chapter 5 above.

scope of anti-Catholic rhetoric by declaring Catholicism intellectually and morally backward, a view that Pius IX duly reinforced with the 1864 Syllabus of Errors.

This anti-Catholicism became even more significant after 1859 with the onset of the 'New Era' in German politics. Capitalising on public dissatisfaction with clericalism, liberals throughout the *Bund* took power in the state parliaments and strove to reverse the previous decades' concessions to the churches. In Prussia, the Chamber of Deputies protected liberal Protestants like Adolf Harnack and the adherents of the *Protestantenverein*. In Baden, anticonservative protests triggered the elaboration of a new Protestant church constitution in 1861. But the main concern was the Catholic Church. In Austria, liberals campaigned to abrogate the 1855 concordat, which they felt not only blocked social and cultural progress, but undercut Habsburg claims to lead Germany. Over the strenuous protests of Catholic groups, Baden passed a law in 1864 that made local school councils, and not the clergy (Protestant or Catholic), responsible for school oversight. Bavarian liberals also hoped to curtail the church's educational privileges, but the reforms were ultimately blocked by the parliament's upper house.

The confessional name-calling that accompanied these disputes also spilled over into discussions of the German question, which was reinvigorated by Piedmont's defeat of Austria and the declaration of an Italian nation-state in 1859. Liberal groups like the German National Association (*Nationalverein*) advanced their *kleindeutsch* programme by asserting that Austria's enthralment to Catholicism made it incapable of uniting, much less leading Germany. Similarly, Protestant publicists, reviving the nationalist rhetoric of the early 1800s, asserted that German culture was a particularly Protestant creation. Thus Germany would have to have a Protestant head. Otto von Bismarck, who became Prussian minister-president in 1862, only encouraged this undermining of Austria's position as he plotted to make Prussia the master of German Europe. Not surprisingly, given this constellation of forces and Prussia's support for the antipapal Italian state, German Catholics in the 1860s backed Austria and the *großdeutsch* nation-state. But as conflict between Prussia and Austria loomed after 1864, the medium and smaller states and even most of the Protestant state churches joined the *großdeutsch* ranks. The German princes continued to fear Prussia, and the churches regarded as sacrilege secular Protestants' portrayals of *kleindeutsch* nationalism as a religious, and specifically Protestant cause.

Prussia's quick defeat of Austria in 1866 greatly clarified the German question. The German Confederation was dissolved and Austria excluded from

Germany. Although Prussia made no territorial demands on Austria, it annexed Frankfurt am Main, Nassau, Hanover and Hesse-Kassel and forced the remaining German states north of the Main into a North German Confederation. Prussia dominated this new Confederation, but because it did not encompass the southern German states, German unification remained unfinished. The events of 1866 also altered the balance of confessional relations in Germany. With the omission of Austria and the southern German states, the proto-German nation became overwhelmingly Protestant, making Prussia's victory at Königgrätz seem the confessional triumph of which nationalists later boasted. More critically in this time of heightened religious tension, the *Bund's* demise meant that the German states were now free to alter their policies on confessional parity.

For this very reason, the Catholic deputies to the North German parliament wanted the new constitution to guarantee religious freedom. The liberal majority, however, branded this plea for toleration as disloyalty to the nation and voted down the Catholics' motions. Although Catholics held a more pluralist sense of German identity, their acceptance of the new Germany really was not at issue, as events soon showed. When relations between France and Prussia worsened after 1867, leading Catholic opposition figures such as August and Peter Reichensperger publicly endorsed Prussia's position. As war broke out in 1870, Catholics joined their Protestant neighbours in justifying it and sanctioning war aims like the 'return' of Alsace. Nevertheless, the Franco-Prussian war effectively established Germany's identity as a Protestant nation. Journalists, politicians, academics and pastors on both sides of the Rhine framed the war as a clash between Protestant Germany and Catholic France. Germans and French interpreted the German alliance's easy victory as evidence of Protestantism's and German *Kultur's* moral superiority. Finally, since Prussia's triumph gave birth to a German Empire (*Kaiserreich*) that included the southern German states, Protestantism was even given credit for consummating German unification.

The Christian German empire

There was a fair amount of truth behind Adolf Stoecker's glorification of the new *Kaiserreich* as a 'Protestant empire'. Protestants comprised roughly two-thirds of Germany's population. Protestant religious and cultural values figured prominently in statements of German national identity. The state Protestant churches abandoned their former resistance to the nation and actively propagated nationalist symbols and rhetoric. Bismarck and liberal politicians even tried to force Catholics to assimilate into this Protestant nation. But this *Kulturkampf* (literally: culture war) actually strengthened Catholic solidarity and deepened the Catholic–Protestant divide. Nevertheless, because imperial Germany remained a fundamentally Christian state, even Catholics found meaningful ways to claim citizenship in the nation. In Austria-Hungary, too, Christianity played a critical symbolic role in keeping the fragile, multinational dual monarchy together.

The Franco-Prussian war completed the territorial dimension of German nation-building, but internally the process had just begun. The *Kulturkampf* represented a pivotal, if ultimately unsuccessful facet of this effort. It was triggered by two developments: the declaration of papal infallibility at the First Vatican Council, which raised new questions about Catholics' political loyalties, and Catholic successes in the 1871 *Reichstag* elections, which created a major Catholic bloc in the new parliament. Faced with this potential oppositional force, Bismarck decided to launch a pre-emptive strike. A pious man himself, the chancellor had no problems with Catholicism *per se*. But Bismarck fervently believed that churches should not meddle in politics. Indeed, since coming to power, he had tried to reduce the Protestant church's influence over Prussian politics, and thus had no intention now of permitting Catholicism to establish itself as a political force. Bismarck's plan to disarm political Catholicism delighted liberal politicians, who provided the parliamentary backing for the crusade. Yet, the phrase the left-liberal Rudolf Virchow coined for this struggle, the *Kulturkampf*, suggests that the liberals wanted to do more than prevent Catholicism from becoming a political force. They wanted victory over Catholicism itself, the long-delayed conclusion of the Reformation.

Because the 1871 imperial constitution made ecclesiastical affairs the prerogative of the individual states and not the imperial government, only a few of the *Kulturkampf* measures applied empire-wide. The *Kanzelparagraph*, inserted into the Imperial Penal Code on 10 December 1871, banned priests from discussing political matters from the pulpit. In 1872 the *Reichstag* also expelled the Jesuit, Redemptorist and Lazarist orders from Germany. At the state level, noteworthy clashes erupted in Baden, Bavaria and Hesse-Darmstadt, but the primary theatre for the *Kulturkampf* drama was Prussia. The stage for conflict was set with Bismarck's appointment of the liberal Adalbert Falk as minister for education and cultural affairs in February 1872. That March, the Prussian parliament placed the supervision of all schools under state instead of clerical control. One year later, it passed the 'May Laws', giving the state extensive control over priests' training and appointment.

Widespread resistance to these measures compelled Bismarck and his allies to escalate the attack. New legislation allowed the state to suspend or exile priests who refused to obey the May Laws. Government officials could also seize church property and, after 1875, suspend financial support from recalcitrant clergy (the 'bread-basket' law). The toll of these measures was considerable. As of 1878, only three of eight Prussian dioceses still had bishops, some 1,125 of 4,600 parishes were vacant, and nearly 1,800 priests ended up in jail or in exile. Approximately 16 million Reichsmarks appropriated to the Catholic Church went unspent. Finally, between 1872 and 1878, numerous Catholic newspapers were confiscated, Catholic associations and assemblies were dissolved, and Catholic civil servants were dismissed merely on the pretence of having Ultramontane sympathies.

Nevertheless, the *Kulturkampf* ultimately failed. Why? In part, state officials and liberal politicians underestimated the degree to which Ultramontanism had integrated the clergy into Catholic society. Thus, when the state moved against the priests, the laity – and especially laywomen – took it personally. They staged demonstrations to protest against the arrest of clergy and auctions of church property. They collected money to cover for the funds withheld by the state, helped loyal priests escape to non-Prussian territories, and even organised an underground church. The persecutions also galvanised the Catholics politically, which translated into massive support for the pro-Catholic Centre Party. But the *Kulturkampf* also foundered because conservative politicians and the Protestant churches refused to endorse it. Indeed, the school inspection laws and the 1873 law that transferred their traditional registration of births, marriages and deaths to civil authorities affected Catholic and Protestant church alike, to the consternation of the latter. Thus, when Pope Pius IX died in 1878, Bismarck decided to reverse course. By the time he resigned from office in 1890, almost all of the *Kulturkampf* legislation had been either repealed or disabled.

The *Kulturkampf* was supposed to integrate Catholics into Protestant Germany. Instead, it widened the gulf between Catholics and Protestants. Accused of being national enemies (*Reichsfeinde*) and vilified as disturbers of the peace, German Catholics increasingly severed their ties with their Protestant neighbours, creating a socio-cultural world of their own that scholars have alternatively described as a Catholic ghetto or milieu. They bought from Catholic-owned shops and read newspapers published by and oriented towards Catholics. Distinctly Catholic approaches to folk literature, church architecture, art, and even historical writing and scholarship also emerged after 1870, all of which the Protestant middle class roundly disparaged. Most significantly,

Catholics created an ever-widening array of social, cultural, charitable and economic organisations to meet their special, confessional needs: from literary and sporting societies to teachers' organisations, credit unions and women's clubs.

Significantly, this 'ghettoisation' also encouraged a nationalisation of Catholicism. Catholics abandoned their *großdeutsch* and particularist mentalities, thinking and acting instead in terms of the *kleindeutsch* nation. This posture was already apparent in the moral and material assistance that Catholics across Germany provided to the Prussian faithful during the *Kulturkampf*. The empire's leading Catholic newspapers, especially the *Kölnische Volkszeitung* and the Berlin-based *Germania*, had a national readership, and the regular conferences of German bishops at Fulda promoted unity within the entirety of German Catholicism. Catholic associational life also had a manifestly national character. Hiking, gymnastic and music clubs were organised into empire-wide confederations. Furthermore, groups from the Görres Society for the Promotion of Knowledge in Catholic Germany to the twin pillars of Catholic social action in the Wilhelmine period – the Volksverein für das Katholische Deutschland (the Popular Association for Catholic Germany) and the German Caritas Bund – explicitly defined themselves in national terms.

After 1900 Munich-based intellectuals and younger clergy sought to lower the ghetto walls. But until 1914 the most effective agent of Catholic integration was the Centre Party, the very organisation Bismarck meant to cripple. The Centre not only defended Catholic interests in the state and federal legislatures, but also provided them with a way to participate actively in political life. The Centre gained a crucial measure of respectability with its decision to back conservative tariff legislation in 1879. And by 1890, Centre Party leaders were using their solid and remarkably stable block of votes to lend critical support to successive German chancellors, thereby becoming a major party of government. They also backed fiscal and legal reforms, such as the new civil code of 1900, in exchange for concessions on religious issues and better employment prospects for Catholic civil servants. Indeed, the Centre gave pre-war German Catholics a respectability and sense of membership in the nation-state of which their Italian and French counterparts could only dream.

The interplay between Catholicism and politics followed an altogether different course in Austria between 1866 and 1914. Austria's loss at Königgrätz precipitated a political crisis, resulting in the creation of the Dual Monarchy and the definitive introduction of constitutional government in 1867. It also brought the liberals to power, who quickly moved to restore the upper hand to the state in church–state relations. Between 1868 and 1874 they passed laws to guarantee religious freedom, end the church's educational monopoly and separate civil from canon law. In 1870 the concordat itself was declared void. There was, however, no Austrian *Kulturkampf*. After fifteen years under the concordat, the Catholic Church was thoroughly discredited. The bishops themselves were in no position to resist effectively had they so desired (and most did not). Finally, in contrast with their German counterparts, Austrian liberals wanted to divest the church of its political authority and public power, not destroy it. Hence, they allowed the church to continue to benefit from state patronage and support, albeit only as a privileged public corporation.

Under the leadership of Karl Lueger, a political organisation rooted in Austrian Catholic culture did emerge to challenge the liberals after 1882: the Christian Social Party. But while Christian Socials defended Catholicism against liberalism and social democracy and exploited parish and church networks to build their organisation, theirs was never a church or confessional party. Lueger won over the lower middle classes by downplaying clericalism and embracing petty bourgeois anti-Semitism, all of which made his movement suspect in the eyes of the church hierarchy. Lueger's confirmation as lord mayor of Vienna in 1897 marked the end of the liberal era. It also established the Christian Socials as an official ruling party, an honour regularly denied the German Centre before 1914.

Austrian discussions about religion and politics were also unique because, with the exception of Georg von Schönerer's abortive Free from Rome movement, they lacked a nationalist dimension. In Habsburg Austria state and emperor served as the objects of patriotism, not a confessionalised nation-state, and the dynasty remained resolutely Christian throughout the liberal campaign to de-emphasise the state's religious character. Symbolic of this link between religion and dynasty was the emperor's participation in Vienna's annual Corpus Christi procession, which recalled the legendary sanctification of the Habsburgs' right to rule through the Eucharist. Indeed, the more nationalist rivalries threatened to dissolve the empire, the more Emperor Franz Joseph turned to religion to inspire patriotism based on loyalty to the crown. This explains both his recognition of the pro-dynasty Christian Socials and his prominent participation in the activities of the Eucharistic Congress, which Vienna hosted in 1912.

In fact, Austrian and German Catholic efforts to downplay the confessional dimension of citizenship were astonishingly consonant with Bismarck's own efforts to found the German empire on a secular basis. He intentionally established both of the two principal imperial institutions – emperor and constitution – without any reference to religion or divine grace. Nevertheless, over the course of the *Kulturkampf*, the equation of Protestantism with German nationalism became routine not just for cultural Protestants, but for Protestant Germany in general. The anti-Catholic legislation did not itself change the minds of church authorities and conservatives. Rather, the shift stemmed principally from German Protestantism's status as a state religion (*Staatsreligion*), where the head of the state was also the head of the church. With the *Kaiserreich* legitimately established, church authorities transferred obedience to king and state to the new emperor and nation. Pastors celebrated the emperor's birthday and the anniversary of the German victory at Sedan as religious events. Church leaders, like *Oberkirchenrat* President Herrmann, proclaimed the church's duty to help the nation develop its most noble powers and overcome its gravest weaknesses. Protestant ministers also joined in the attacks on Catholicism, which now appeared as unrepentant foe of both Protestantism and the nation-state.

So strong was the ecclesiastical and conservative investment in the idea of the Protestant empire that Protestants became alarmed at Catholic efforts at reconciliation with the German national state, particularly the repeal of major elements of *Kulturkampf* legislation. Thus in 1887 Willibald Beyschlag organised the 'Protestant League for the Defence of German-Protestant Interests' (*Evangelischer Bund*) to prevent further appeasement of Catholic interests and counter political Catholicism's rising influence. In the 1890s, other ultra-nationalist organisations, including the Agrarian, Colonial and Navy Leagues, took up this cause, openly opposing efforts to repeal the anti-Jesuit laws and vigorously protesting against decisions like the 1901 appointment of Martin Spahn, the son of a major Centre Party official, to the University of Strasbourg's history faculty.

Still, many Germans bemoaned the nation's confessional divisions. In the final decades of the century, men like Paul de Lagarde, Julius Langbehn and Arthur Bonus called for healing the rift by 'Germanising' Christianity. They advocated stripping Christianity of its foreign influences so that it expressed the healthy values and virtues of the German people (*Volk*), a sentiment that also infused Richard Wagner's final opera, *Parsifal*. Extreme as these notions were, they indicate that the basic understanding of Germany as a Christian nation remained intact, despite the era's confessional polemics. Thus, in its founding charter of 1876, the German Conservative Party noted that, although the dominant religion of the German nation was Lutheran Protestantism, the party strove, more generally, to preserve 'the religious life of the German people, maintain and strengthen the Christian ecclesiastical traditions . . . and, above all, [to preserve] the Christian confessional school'.[5] Bismarck too conceived of the state's duties in largely Christian terms, even characterising the social insurance legislation of the 1880s as 'practical Christianity' (*praktisches Christentum*). For their part, Christian organisations, from the Protestant Inner Mission to the Catholic *Volksverein*, turned to the state to protect Christian standards of morality, as exemplified in their campaigns for new obscenity and prostitution laws.

The *Kaiserreich*'s Christian orientation also manifested itself in colonial politics. For such prominent advocates of the German imperial mission as Friedrich Fabri, director of the Rhenish Mission in Barmen (Germany's largest Protestant mission), the acquisition of colonies was a moral necessity and a Christian duty. Both the Catholic and the Protestant communities had a significant missionary presence overseas and received state assistance for this work. Representatives of these missions, Catholic and Protestant, also had seats in the *Kolonialrat*, the council Kaiser Wilhelm II created in 1890 to co-ordinate German colonial policy. In other words, colonial policy was notably 'confession-blind', even if the most zealous advocates of imperialism, the Colonial and the Pan-German Leagues, were essentially Protestant organisations.

Ultimately, it was this underlying idea of a Christian Germany that distinguished Catholics from the two other major groups with contested claims on German citizenship after 1871: Jews and socialists. Because Catholics were Christians, nationalists could countenance their participation in such institutions as the civil service and the army, whereas they rejected that of Jews and 'godless' socialists. Catholics and Protestants also agreed that socialist materialism and irreligion posed a major threat to German society. However, they preferred to fight socialism separately. Because of the *Kulturkampf*, Catholics were loath to support particularist legislation like the 1878 anti-socialist law. Instead they expanded their activities among the working classes, organising trade unions and expanding the range of Catholic charity. When the anti-socialist measures expired in 1890, Catholics decided to meet the socialist challenge head on by founding their own mass-based social and cultural organisation: the *Volksverein*. Catholics and Protestants, however, closed ranks when socialists attacked the state's Christian foundations, rebuffing socialist efforts to end obligatory religious education and public support for the churches. Catholics and Protestants also shared anti-Semitic sympathies. But in contrast to Austria, where anti-Semitism was an integral part of Christian socialism's *raison d'être*, it had little appreciable role in constituting or maintaining the German Catholic

5 Cited in Tal, *Christians and Jews in Germany*, p. 125.

milieu. Rather, the main challenge to Jews' Germanness in the *Kaiserreich* came from Protestant circles, from high-profile pastors like Adolf Stoecker and from integralist nationalist organisations like the Pan-German League.

When war broke out in early August 1914, Kaiser Wilhelm II urged his subjects to defend the fatherland 'without difference of race or religion'. In one stroke, he sought to set aside the divisions that almost forty years of exclusivist, Protestant nationalism had sown. Nevertheless, the speech left little doubt that Germany would still fight the war as a Christian nation. 'Following the example of our fathers, staunch and true . . . humble before God, but with the joy of battle in the face of the enemy, we trust in the Almighty to strengthen our defence and guide us to good issue.'[6] It was this image of a Christian Germany that chaplains and ministers, at home and at the front, repeated and maintained down to the end of the conflict – and of the *Kaiserreich* – in 1918.

6 *Verhandlungen des Reichstags*, no. 1, 4 August 1914, pp. 1–2.

19

Anglicanism, Presbyterianism and the religious identities of the United Kingdom

JOHN WOLFFE

On 21 July 1815 a large crowd assembled to witness the admission of a celebrated new parish minister to the charge of the Tron Church in the centre of Glasgow.[1] Thomas Chalmers (1780–1847) was already one of the leading figures in the evangelical party in the Church of Scotland and was destined to play a central role in events and movements that had a profound impact on religious life and identities, in Scotland above all, but also throughout the United Kingdom. Chalmers's move to Glasgow in the month after Waterloo symbolises and illustrates, moreover, the great challenge of rapid urban growth facing both the Church of Scotland and the Church of England in 1815. His previous parish, Kilmany, in Fife, was rural and predominantly agricultural with a declining population, amounting to only 787 in 1811. In such an environment it remained relatively easy for an energetic pastor like Chalmers to develop a ministry that brought him and the Church of Scotland into meaningful contact with all his parishioners.[2] Glasgow on the other hand had tripled in population – from 40,000 to over 120,000 – during Chalmers's own lifetime, and his own parish had a population of approximately 11,000, many of them Dissenters from the national church, and many others lacking any contact with organised Christianity.[3] Such was Chalmers's concern at these unchurched multitudes that in November 1817 he turned a memorial sermon on the tragically early death of the king's granddaughter, Princess Charlotte, into an appeal for efforts 'to bring this enormous physical strength under the controul of Christian and humanized principle'.[4] In Glasgow, as in other burgeoning towns of the British industrial revolution, the national Anglican and Presbyterian churches appeared in imminent danger of losing any tangible

---

1 Brown, *Thomas Chalmers*, pp. 93–4.
2 *Ibid.*, pp. 73–84.
3 *Ibid.*, p. 95; Roxborogh, *Thomas Chalmers*, pp. 67–8.
4 T. Chalmers, *A sermon delivered in the Tron Church Glasgow, on . . . November 19, 1817* (Glasgow, 1817), p. 31.

identification with the people as a whole. In Ireland, they faced the different but equally pressing challenge of living alongside each other as a Protestant minority in a predominantly Roman Catholic country.

The United Kingdom was created by the Acts of Union between England (and Wales) and Scotland in 1707 and between Great Britain and Ireland in 1800. In 1815 the constitutional position of the national churches had changed little since 1688. In England, Ireland and Wales the established church was Anglican; in Scotland it was Presbyterian. In terms both of numbers and of effective power, Anglicanism was the dominant religious tradition in the United Kingdom as a whole. The four Welsh dioceses were fully part of the Church of England, and as a corollary of the Union of the Dublin and Westminster parliaments implemented on 1 January 1801, the Church of England and the Church of Ireland were brought into closer association. Convocation, the church's own assembly, had been suspended since the early eighteenth century, and parliament legislated for the church alongside its other more secular business. The church's interest in parliament was represented by the presence in the Lords of all the English and Welsh bishops and four elected Irish ones. In the Commons until 1828 all members (except Scottish Presbyterians) were in theory nominally Anglican, although in practice indemnity acts allowed Protestant Nonconformists to take seats. Hence the Commons was perceived as a representative assembly of Anglican laymen, and the legitimate body for overseeing the church's affairs. Similarly intermingled roles were evident at local level, where the parish, run by the vestry meeting, was the basic unit of civil as well as ecclesiastical government, and numerous clergy served as magistrates.[5] These arrangements were reflected in the constitutional theory that, as Edmund Burke said in 1792, 'in a Christian commonwealth the Church and the State are one and the same thing, being different integral parts of the same whole'.[6] Above all national religious identity was perceived as embodied in the monarch, 'in whom', according to a preacher on the death of George III in 1820, 'was centered the well-being both of Church and State'.[7] It was a patriotic consensus with which even Protestant Dissenters could identify, provided they themselves were accorded toleration and freedom of worship.[8] In Ireland, on the other hand, such definition of state and nation in Anglican terms was inevitably divisive, given the minority status of

5 Cf. Brown, *The national churches*, pp. 1–15.
6 Quoted in Clark, *English society*, p. 250.
7 W. Carus-Wilson, A *sermon* . . . *on occasion of the death of* . . . *George III* (Preston, 1820), pp. 5–6.
8 See for example J. Morison, *Patriotic regrets for the loss of a good king* (London, 1820), p. 20.

the Church of Ireland, which in 1834 was supported by only 10.7 per cent of the people, while Roman Catholics made up four-fifths of the population.[9] Here the logic of the church–state connection was translated into the spirit of Protestant ascendancy, which maintained that Ireland must continue to be ruled by Protestants if it was to maintain its Union with Britain. Initial plans after the Union to emancipate Catholics, giving them the same civil rights as Protestants, including crucially entitlement to sit in parliament, were thwarted by the opposition of King George III, who believed that such a concession would have been a violation of his coronation oath to maintain the Protestant religion.

The Church of Scotland lacked the same sense of organic connection with the structures of the United Kingdom state. Indeed it had historically seen itself as a separate spiritual kingdom, in partnership with the state, but distinct from it, and under the headship of Christ, not the monarch. Nevertheless as in England its ministers were appointed by lay patrons. This system was uncontentious south of the border, but in Scotland was a matter of ongoing grievance and tension because it appeared to compromise the spiritual integrity of the church. The Church of Scotland lacked any presence in parliament other than the voices of individual Scottish MPs and peers, who were in a small minority relative to their English and Anglican counterparts. Its organisation was presbyterian rather than episcopal, and its doctrinal standards, unlike those of the Church of England, were unambiguously Reformed. It also differed from the Church of England in having retained a national representative body, the General Assembly, but without effective legal powers. At the local level, however, civil and ecclesiastical structures were even more seamlessly interwoven than in England: the board of heritors (landowners) supported education as well as the church; the kirk session (minister and elders) was responsible for poor relief and the moral regulation of the parish in addition to specifically religious functions.[10] Presbyterianism was also a major religious force in the north of Ireland, having been brought by Scottish settlers in the seventeenth century. Although Presbyterians only made up 8.1 per cent of the total population of Ireland, 96 per cent of them were concentrated in the province of Ulster, and in counties Antrim and Down they were the largest single religious group.[11] While they lacked the legal primacy accorded to the Church of Ireland they were therefore a major social and political influence.

9 Connolly, *Religion and society*, p. 3.
10 Brown, *The national churches*, pp. 22–31; Brown, 'The myth of the established church', pp. 51–63.
11 Connolly, *Religion and society*, pp. 3–4.

Whatever the appearances of continuity and stability, by the early nineteenth century this structure was under severe strain, owing in part to rapid population growth and social change, in part to the increasing numerical strength and self-confidence of religious alternatives to the national churches. The population of the United Kingdom grew from 15.9 million in 1801 to 21.01 million in 1821 and to 26.75 million in 1841, an increase of 68 per cent over the first four decades of the century.[12] Moreover, as the case of Glasgow well illustrates, this growth was particularly problematic for church organisation because it was geographically concentrated. Agricultural parishes such as Kilmany could well have stagnant or even declining population at the very time that urban and industrial ones were seeing overwhelmingly rapid expansion in numbers. At least for Chalmers his numerous Glasgow parishioners were all accessible to him in a compact overcrowded area. Elsewhere substantial new industrial settlements, their location determined by proximity to water power or to a mine, developed several miles away from any existing churches and accordingly were initially without any organised religious provision. The urgent needs were recognised in 1818 when parliament passed a Church Building Act which provided £1 million of public money for the Church of England, supplemented with a further grant of £500,000 in 1824. Voluntary subscriptions yielded a further £1.5 million by 1832.[13] Between 1821 and 1830 235 new churches were built, a notable upturn from the twenty-eight between 1801 and 1810 and the seventy between 1811 and 1820.[14] Nevertheless it was a belated and insufficient response: in many places a generation had already grown up without a sense of church connection.

The consequent religious vacuum and indifference was partially being filled by Dissent. As described in chapter 4, this period saw an enormous expansion in evangelical voluntary religion, which with its more flexible structures and capacity to harness lay congregational energies could rapidly establish a presence in hitherto unchurched or poorly churched locations. The result though was an increasing awareness that the national churches were no longer virtual monopoly providers of religious services, and hence that existing constitutional arrangements and assumptions were overdue for adjustment. Such a situation was even more acute in Ireland, where the rapid growth of the Roman Catholic population, and its increasing politicisation during the 1820s (see chapter 16), represented a serious challenge to the status of the Church of Ireland. It responded from 1822 onwards in the 'Second Reformation'

12 Mathias, *The first industrial nation*, p. 449.
13 Machin, *Politics and the churches*, p. 17.
14 Gilbert, *Religion and society*, p. 130.

movement which sought large-scale conversions to Protestantism, but bore very limited fruit, although reinforcing further the trend to sectarian polarisation.[15] In Britain meanwhile there was also a revival in Catholicism, assisted by growing immigration from Ireland (see chapter 16).

These tensions came to a head from 1828 onwards with changes that have been perceived as 'revolutionary'[16] in their implications for the relations of church, state and society. These developments and their aftermath will first be examined. The remainder of the chapter will then provide a survey of continuing potent interactions between religious and national identities in the various countries of the United Kingdom.

In the spring of 1828 parliament somewhat unexpectedly voted to repeal the Test and Corporation Acts that had hitherto theoretically excluded Protestant Dissenters from sitting in parliament or holding other civil office. At one level this decision looked like an uncontroversial adjustment of a constitutional anomaly, as in practice the provisions of this seventeenth-century legislation had long since been relaxed, but at a symbolic level it substantially weakened the principle of identification between Anglicanism and the state.[17] Then, at the end of June 1828, Daniel O'Connell's victory at the County Clare by-election served notice to the duke of Wellington's Tory government that the Catholic Association and its campaign for political equality in Ireland was now irresistible. It was probable that at the next general election the Clare result would be replicated across southern Ireland, with Catholic electors returning a large cohort of Catholic MPs precluded from taking their seats at Westminster and hence likely to lead a movement to civil war and secession. Rather than risk such outcomes, the government decided that it had to reverse its previous stance and concede Catholic Emancipation, which was duly enacted in April 1829. Although the measure was passed primarily in order to resolve a crisis in Ireland, its implications for Britain were also profound, as it compromised the 'Protestant constitution', seen as a cornerstone of the settlement following the 1688 Revolution and as a defining feature of national identity throughout the eighteenth century. It was a decisive step towards a more religiously pluralist concept of the British state.

After the fall in November 1830 of the Wellington government, deserted by many of its own diehard backbenchers who could never forgive it for Catholic Emancipation, the Whigs, led by Earl Grey, came to power with a clear reforming agenda. The struggle for parliamentary reform heightened

15 Bowen, *The Protestant crusade*; Brown, *The national churches*, pp. 93–136.
16 Cf. Clark, *English society*, pp. 393–408.
17 Brown, *The national churches*, pp. 138–9.

popular antagonism to the church, because when in October 1831 the House of Lords rejected the measure the negative votes of twenty-one bishops had determined the outcome. When it was eventually passed, the 'Great' Reform Act of 1832 had important implications for religion, because the expansion of the parliamentary franchise and the reshaping of constituencies to provide greater representation for the growing industrial towns also gave increased electoral and political influence to Dissenters. Church reform followed quickly. The liberal aristocrats who dominated the government, notably Lord John Russell, differed from some of their own Dissenting and radical supporters in that they were not hostile to the principle of a state church as such. Indeed they saw it as a vital source of non-dogmatic Christian instruction, morality and social harmony. They were, however, at odds with the traditional high church Tory vision of an organic equal partnership between church and state. The Whigs were Erastians who saw the state as fully justified in changing the nature of the church establishment if it could thereby be made better to serve its essential purposes as they perceived them. In particular they wanted to make it more comprehensive in its appeal and more acceptable to those who conscientiously differed from it.[18] Such views were also shared by some leading liberal Anglican clergymen, notably Richard Whately, whom Grey appointed archbishop of Dublin in 1831, and by Thomas Arnold, headmaster of Rugby School. In his pamphlet *Principles of church reform*, published in January 1833, Arnold argued for a radically expanded national church. Given that it was 'both wicked and impossible' 'to extinguish Dissent by persecution', the effort should be made to 'extinguish it by comprehension'.[19] He believed that, with good will, all groups except Quakers, Roman Catholics and Unitarians could reach sufficient agreement on the essentials of Christianity to join such a body, and that even these exceptions might gradually become reconciled to it.[20] Underlying Arnold's vision was a strong English nationalism founded in a close identification between church, state and people.[21] He believed that 'of all human ties, that to our country is the highest and most sacred' and that 'unnatural' divisions among Christians risked the destruction of the church establishment and consequent national moral degradation.[22]

Ireland, however, was the initial focus of Whig reforms. Here the inherent vulnerability of the minority Anglican state church was further exposed from

---

18 Brent, *Liberal Anglican politics*, p. 63.
19 T. Arnold, *Principles of church reform* (London, 1833), pp. iii–iv.
20 *Ibid.*, pp. 31–7.
21 Forbes, *The Liberal Anglican idea of history*, pp. 94–5.
22 Arnold, *Principles*, pp. 83–4.

1830 onwards by extensive popular resistance to the collection of tithes, leading to some violent confrontations and loss of life.[23] In 1832, in the face of protests from many Protestants but with the support of Archbishop Whately, the government set up a national scheme of education in Ireland, which sought to mitigate sectarian animosities through mixed schooling.[24] Then in February 1833 the Irish Church Temporalities Bill was brought forward. This measure proposed to reduce the hierarchy from four archbishops and eighteen bishops to two archbishops and ten bishops and to abolish or suspend cathedral and parochial appointments that lacked active pastoral responsibilities. The incomes of the two wealthiest sees were to be cut, and the richer parish clergy taxed. Reforms in the tenure of church lands were expected to raise extra income. The net financial result of the measure was expected to be a substantial surplus which the government envisaged would be appropriated for the general welfare of the Irish people rather than for the specific support of the Anglican church. The Bill amounted to an acceptance that the Church of Ireland was not, and never would become, the church of the Irish people, and that it therefore needed to be resourced in a manner more commensurate with its minority position and less offensive to the Catholic majority. For those committed to the maintenance of a uniform dominant Anglican religious settlement throughout England, Wales and Ireland it was therefore a very bitter pill to swallow. It conceded the principles both that the legitimacy of religious establishments was derived from popular acceptance rather than a conviction of the truth of their teachings, and that religious diversity in the constituent parts of the United Kingdom should be recognised by varying constitutional and organisational arrangements. It therefore stirred considerable controversy and strong opposition from the Tories in Parliament. The government eventually had to drop the appropriation clause in order to get it through the House of Lord, but its other provisions became law.[25]

A counterattack from the church was already under way. In a sermon in the University Church at Oxford on 14 July 1833 the leading High Churchman John Keble addressed the theme of 'national apostasy', with clear implicit reference to current events. When the Act passed he saw it as a ratification by the legislature of the principle 'that the Apostolical Church in this realm is henceforth only to stand in the eye of the State, as *one sect among many*, depending for any pre-eminence she may still appear to retain, merely upon the accident of her

---

23 Brown, *The national churches*, pp. 150–4.
24 *Ibid.*, pp. 154–9.
25 *Ibid.*, pp. 160–7; Machin, *Politics and the churches*, pp. 32–6.

having a strong party in the country'.[26] Keble's sermon was seen as a rallying cry by others, notably John Henry Newman, and has traditionally been seen as marking the beginning of the Oxford Movement, which in the ensuing years did much both to revive and to divide the Church of England. Keble himself was already contemplating disestablishment as likely to be necessary to preserve the spiritual integrity of the church, and for Newman and others alarm at state interference was eventually to contribute to their conversion to Roman Catholicism. For more conservative churchmen, however, such radical options were unthinkable, and their energies rather were directed towards defending the continuing establishment of the Church of England. They were encouraged by events in 1834, when the government was first weakened by the resignations of four ministers, who would not countenance continued discussion of appropriating the Irish church surplus, and was then, in November, dismissed by King William IV, who saw himself as committed to the defence of the Protestant church. During late 1834 and 1835 there was a strong campaign of agitation in Britain in defence of the Church of Ireland, presenting it as an essential bulwark against the perceived corrupt religion and subversive politics of Roman Catholicism. Under these circumstances the evangelical Ulster Presbyterian leader Henry Cooke also gave notable support to the established church.[27]

After the king's dismissal of the Whigs, Wellington and Sir Robert Peel formed a minority Conservative government, and made significant gains in a general election in early 1835. Although their administration was nevertheless short-lived, and fell in April 1835, it had a substantial impact in steering the stream of church reform into a substantially more moderate course. In particular Peel set up a Royal Commission to reform the Church of England, with five bishops among its membership of twelve, thus giving the church the opportunity to reform itself, and escape the more radical treatment already given to its Irish counterpart.[28] The Ecclesiastical Commission, as it came to be known, was to be responsible for a sequence of recommendations implemented by the subsequent Whig government, which reorganised dioceses, redistributed resources from cathedrals to parishes, and controlled the abuses of pluralism and non-residence. It strengthened the church in the industrialising regions by creating new dioceses of Ripon (for western Yorkshire) and Manchester (for Lancashire), although the latter was not implemented until

---

26 J. Keble, *National apostasy considered* (Oxford, 1833), p. iii.
27 Wolffe, *The Protestant crusade*, pp. 77–91; Holmes, *Henry Cooke*, pp. 115–20.
28 Best, *Temporal pillars*, pp. 296–300.

1847. These were substantial reforms, but they left the fundamental structures and constitutional status of the church unchanged.

The reforms initiated by the Ecclesiastical Commission were effective because they worked in parallel with a widespread grass-roots movement of renewal of institutions at the regional and local level, which was already well under way by the 1830s.[29] This 'diocesan revival' saw increasingly energetic activity by bishops such as Charles James Blomfield (Chester 1824–8, London 1828–56), John Bird Sumner (Chester 1828–48, Canterbury 1848–62), Henry Phillpotts (Exeter 1830–69) and Samuel Wilberforce (Oxford 1845–69, Winchester 1869–73). Subordinate dignitaries such as archdeacons and rural deans also became much more effective. A particular focus of revived Anglican effort was church extension, the building of new churches and the creation of new parishes to meet the spiritual needs of the rapidly growing population. Numerous diocesan church-building societies were founded in the late 1830s, prominent among them Bishop Blomfield's Metropolis Churches Fund, directed to the pressing needs of London.[30] As we have seen, there was a rising trend in the building of new churches even before 1830, but thereafter there was rapid acceleration, with 514 constructed between 1831 and 1840, and 759 between 1841 and 1850. There was a slight drop to 654 between 1851 and 1860, but a peak of 791 between 1861 and 1870. Many hundreds of existing churches were also rebuilt.[31] The very substantial resources required all came from voluntary donations, an indication of warm support for the church among the wealthier classes, although in 1840 a Commons motion calling for state support was only narrowly defeated. In 1843, during Peel's second ministry, legislation was passed which greatly simplified the creation of new ecclesiastical parishes, thus further stimulating and facilitating the process of church extension.

For the Church of Ireland, too, there was a period of stabilisation. Although there was continued radical pressure for appropriation of its alleged surplus revenues, no proposal was implemented, and in 1838 parliament passed an Act that took much of the sting out of popular opposition to tithes, by converting them to a levy on rents, payable by the landlords (who were usually Protestant) rather than by the predominantly Catholic tenants.[32] Moreover the church has been perceived both by its contemporary advocates and by recent scholars as

---

29 Burns, *The diocesan revival*.
30 Brown, *The national churches*, pp. 208–9.
31 Gilbert, *Religion and society*, p. 130.
32 Akenson, *The Church of Ireland*, pp. 189–94.

responding to the severe challenges it faced with a measure of spiritual revival and increased pastoral efficiency.[33]

Meanwhile the Church of Scotland had its own difficulties. In Edinburgh in 1833 Dissenters began a campaign of non-payment of the Annuity Tax, which financed the stipends of the city ministers. The town council attempted to resolve the problem by reducing the number of clergy, but, led by Thomas Chalmers and the other evangelicals who gained control of the ruling General Assembly in 1834, the church responded with a vigorous campaign to promote extension, building churches and creating new *quoad sacra* (ecclesiastical) parishes. Between 1834 and 1841 £305,000 was raised by voluntary subscriptions and 222 new churches were erected in Scotland, a noteworthy achievement. Like its English counterpart, however, the campaign was in 1838 in effect refused state support.[34]

For Chalmers and his supporters the church extension campaign was not merely an endeavour to gain additional resources, but a matter of sustaining the perceived historic identity of the Church of Scotland as the spiritual foundation for the 'godly commonwealth' of the Scottish people.[35] He responded to the government's rebuff by delivering in London a series of 'Lectures on the establishment and extension of national churches'. For Chalmers the central purpose of religious establishments was to preach the gospel to every human being.[36] He argued that on its own the voluntary support of religion could never Christianise Britain because the poor would never know their need of Christianity, let alone be prepared to pay for the provision of Christian ministry, until an awareness of their spiritual need had been awakened in them.[37] Moreover the clergy of the established churches served and spoke for 'the unfranchised multitude', seeking 'the moral well-being of that mighty host who swarm and overspread the ground-floor of our commonwealth'.[38] Despite fashionable interest in Chalmers's lectures, his appeal for state assistance continued to fall on deaf ears. A further major setback occurred in 1842 when the Court of Session (the highest legal authority within Scotland) ruled that the *quoad sacra* parishes were illegal. In the context of the ongoing non-intrusion crisis (see p. 62), this decision reinforced the conviction of evangelicals that

---

33 Brown, *The national churches*, p. 190; H. McNeile, *Nationalism in religion* (London, 1839), p. 16; Akenson, *The Church of Ireland*, pp. 215–25.
34 Brown, *The national churches*, pp. 179–80, 190–7, 217–27.
35 Brown, *Thomas Chalmers*, pp. xv–xvii.
36 T. Chalmers, 'Lectures on the establishment and extension of national churches', in W. Hanna (ed.), *Select works of Thomas Chalmers* (Edinburgh, 1857), vol. XI, p. 121.
37 *Ibid.*, vol. XI, pp. 136–55.
38 *Ibid.*, quoted in Brown, *The national churches*, p. 226.

the terms on which the Church of Scotland was currently founded were fundamentally flawed and that secession was their only viable option. When the now inevitable Disruption came in May 1843, the Free Church, led by Thomas Chalmers, carried with it much of the impetus of the church extension movement, together with over a third of the Church of Scotland's ministers.

Elsewhere in the United Kingdom 1843 was also a climactic year. Whereas the events of 1834 and 1835 saw the checking of the impetus to radical reform of the state churches, those of 1843 showed that there could be no return to the pre-1828 confessional state.[39] In England, provision for the education of child workers in the 1843 Factory Act had to be withdrawn in the face of protest from Dissenters because they felt it gave too much control to the Church of England. In September, John Henry Newman resigned his living of St Mary the Virgin, Oxford, believing that the Church of England could never fulfil his aspirations for the spiritual regeneration of the nation. His conversion to Roman Catholicism in 1845 was now merely a matter of time. In Ireland the climax of the campaign for the repeal of the Union, led by Daniel O'Connell, was a striking demonstration of the political importance of the Roman Catholic Church and its growing identification with the cause of Irish nationalism. In such a context the situation of the Church of Ireland looked ever more marginal and perilous. There is room for pondering the parallel between the repeal movement in Ireland and the Disruption in Scotland, as proto-nationalist movements, drawing much of their inspiration from organised Christianity.[40] Moreover all these developments in 1843 pointed, in different ways, to widespread resistance to close association between church and state.

Thus by the 1840s there had already been substantial weakening in the constitutional linkages between church, state and nation as they had existed before 1828. At the same time, however, the considerable energy shown by both Anglicans and Presbyterians in renewing and expanding their churches ensured that they retained a strong presence at the grass-roots in England, Scotland and the north of Ireland. The context though was now usually one not of monopoly but of competition, sometimes with each other, sometimes with other varieties of Protestantism, notably Methodism, sometimes with Roman Catholicism. In Scotland, although the Disruption proved a body blow to the association of church and state in its historic form, the Presbyterian tradition was invigorated through the energy and commitment of

39 Gash, *Reaction and reconstruction*, pp. 88–9.
40 Wolffe, *God and greater Britain*, p. 105; Brown, *The national churches*, p. 367.

the new Free Church of Scotland, with its distinctive aspirations to cast off the oppressive state connection, while continuing to be national in its vision and coverage.

The continuing conflict between church and Dissent in the mid-nineteenth century needs to be set in the context of a widespread sense of common Protestant identity. It has been argued that during the eighteenth century 'Protestantism was the foundation that made the invention of Great Britain possible'.[41] Although Catholic Emancipation undermined Protestantism on the level of defining constitutional principle, it helped to galvanise its reassertion on the level of popular and political sentiment. Such Protestantism was, in the words of Hugh McNeile, one of its leading advocates, a matter of 'nationalism in religion'.[42] Further factors here were the influence of evangelicalism, which at this period developed a more explicitly anti-Catholic strand, and a rising tide of Irish migration to Britain in the 1830s and 1840s, all of which caused anti-Catholic movements to become more organised and assertive. The Protestant Association was formed in 1835, the National Club, to promote Protestant interests in parliament, in 1845, the Scottish Reformation Society in 1850 and the Protestant Alliance in 1851.[43] Events too fuelled Protestant feeling: the defence of the Irish church in the 1830s was followed in 1845 by a campaign of resistance to Peel's plan to provide a permanent state endowment for the Roman Catholic seminary at Maynooth near Dublin. Although the protesters could not prevent parliamentary approval of the Maynooth grant, they did show that they were a political force to be reckoned with, and knowledge of the likely Protestant outcry held governments back from pro-Catholic measures. A notable example of this restraint occurred in the late 1840s when Lord John Russell, now prime minister, had to conclude that plans he personally favoured for the wider state support of the Irish Roman Catholic Church would be politically unacceptable in Britain.[44] Against this background, when in the autumn of 1850 Pope Pius IX restored the English Roman Catholic hierarchy, and the newly elevated Cardinal Nicholas Wiseman flamboyantly announced that he was to 'govern . . . the counties of Middlesex, Hertford and Essex . . . Surrey, Sussex, Kent, Berkshire and Hampshire, with the islands annexed',[45] this perceived 'Papal Aggression' was a red rag to the British Protestant bull.

41 Colley, *Britons*, p. 54.
42 McNeile, *Nationalism*.
43 Wolffe, *The Protestant crusade*, pp. 318–19.
44 *Ibid.*, pp. 198–246.
45 Young and Handcock, *English historical documents*, p. 365.

Russell identified himself with the storm of popular protest, complaining publicly of the pope's 'pretension of supremacy over the realm of England'. Hostility to pope and 'popery' was confirmed as a central attribute of British national identity. The inevitable other side of the coin was the further political and religious alienation of Roman Catholic Ireland.

While Protestantism thus reasserted itself, it overlaid and was to some extent in conflict with a variety of other religious aspirations to express national identity. Alongside an internally diverse Anglicanism and a divided Presbyterianism was an increasingly self-conscious Nonconformity, which, in Wales above all, was challenging the traditional role of the state church as the religious expression of national identity. In the remainder of this chapter these various strands will be more systematically identified and explored, by considering the component nations of the United Kingdom in the period between 1850 and 1914.

Ireland

The reforms of the 1830s proved sufficient to maintain the link between the Church of Ireland and the state for another three decades. Despite the failure of the 'Second Reformation' movement of the 1820s, these years saw further efforts by evangelicals to secure large-scale conversions among the nominally Roman Catholic population. In 1834 the Rev. Edward Nangle established a Protestant mission on Achill Island, off the coast of County Mayo, which enjoyed some success until it stirred vigorous resistance from the Roman Catholic Church. Another Protestant colony was established on the Dingle peninsula in County Kerry.[46] A wider movement was launched in 1849 with the formation of the Irish Church Missions to Roman Catholics. It had some limited impact, as indicated for example by the claim of the bishop of Tuam in 1852 that he had confirmed 837 converts during the preceding three years,[47] but this was in a diocese where there were more than 300,000 Catholics.[48] In reality such movements were significant much more in reinforcing a sense of polarised confrontation with the Roman Catholic Church than in shifting the denominational arithmetic. In the context of serious overall population decline as a result of the Great Famine of the late 1840s and of emigration, the

---

46 Bowen, *The Protestant crusade*, pp. 204–5.
47 *Ibid.*, p. 238.
48 Akenson, *The church of Ireland*, p. 210.

proportion of Anglicans only increased slightly from 10.7 per cent in 1834 to 11.9 per cent in 1861.[49]

In the late 1860s pressure for disestablishment was building, but it only became inevitable when in March 1868 the Liberal leader W. E. Gladstone placed it at the centre of his attack on the Conservative government and won the subsequent general election on that basis. Although, thirty years before, Gladstone had written a book affirming the duty of the state to recognise and support religious truth as taught by one church, he now openly admitted that this position had become untenable, at least in relation to Ireland.[50] Moreover disestablishment of the Church of Ireland could be viewed as a strategic retreat, giving up something indefensible to preserve wider interests, the establishment of the Church of England itself and British rule in Ireland. The complex legislation required passed through parliament in 1869 and became law on 1 January 1871. Disestablishment was initially devastating for Irish churchmen, who suffered not only the loss of considerable financial resources, but also their sense of identity founded in the linking of church and nation: as the hymnwriter Mrs C. F. Alexander put it, 'Fallen, fallen, fallen is now our Country's crown.'[51] In the longer term though, it was tacitly accepted as an adjustment to the reality of their minority status.

In the period after disestablishment, a minority of Irish Anglicans, particularly in the south, supported the nationalist cause: successive leaders of the Home Rule party, Isaac Butt and Charles Stewart Parnell, were members of the Church of Ireland. The dominant trend, however, especially in Ulster, was for Anglicans and Presbyterians to develop a sense of shared Protestant identity. Now that the establishment issue no longer divided them, for both minority groups this was a natural response to the challenge presented to them by Catholic Irish nationalism. It also reflected the powerful impact of a cross-denominational evangelicalism which, to a greater extent than in other parts of the United Kingdom, came to dominate the religious culture of the non-Catholic churches in Ireland. It was further boosted by the Ulster Revival of 1859. Alongside this powerful spiritual dimension, Ulster Protestantism developed during the nineteenth century a strong communal culture expressed in the Orange Order, with its lodge structure and colourful parades. A sense of militant sectarianism was reinforced by extensive Catholic migration into Belfast, transformed in this period from a small predominantly Protestant

---

49 *Ibid.*
50 Bell, *Disestablishment*, pp. 76–8.
51 Quoted in Bell, *Disestablishment*, p. 158.

town into a major industrial city, in which Catholics, although still a minority, numbered over 40,000 in 1861, 33.9 per cent of the total population.[52]

In 1886 Gladstone, again prime minister, brought forward in parliament proposals for Home Rule for Ireland. Fierce and prolonged opposition to this step both consolidated the gathering together of Protestant forces in Ulster, and reinforced their consciousness of themselves as an embattled religious minority that would never surrender to Rome. This state of mind was sustained both by theological hostility to Roman Catholicism, derived from a polemical reading of the evangelical and reformed traditions, and by vigorous keeping alive of the memory of historic confrontations.[53] In particular there was celebration of the successful Protestant defiance of the besieging forces of James II at Londonderry in 1688–9, which served as a legitimation of the siege mentality developed by Ulster Protestants three centuries later.[54] Successive Home Rule Bills failed in parliament, largely because of the opposition of the Conservative-controlled House of Lords, but the Parliament Act of 1911 removed their ability to frustrate the will of the Commons indefinitely. It therefore seemed probable that the Liberal government of H. H. Asquith would eventually be able to force through a Home Rule measure. In 1912, Ulster Protestant resistance accordingly took a new turn with the signing of the Covenant. This document, with a format resonant with biblical and Presbyterian tradition, along with a parallel Declaration for women, was signed by nearly half a million people, over a quarter of the population of the province. It contained a commitment to refuse to recognise a Home Rule parliament, and an ominous statement of intent to use 'all means which may be found necessary' to defeat it.[55] Thus on the eve of the First World War, the British government faced the very real prospect that in its endeavours to accommodate the nationalist aspirations of Catholic Ireland it would provoke civil war with the Protestants in the north. The seemingly irreconcilable national identities of Catholic and Protestant Ireland led in 1921 to the partition of Ulster, with the six counties making up Northern Ireland remaining under British rule, while the reminder of the island formed the Irish Free State. This step, however, while inevitable in the circumstances of the early twentieth century, left an enduring legacy of confrontation between the Protestant majority and

---

52 Hempton, *Religion and political culture*, pp. 103–6; Hempton and Hill, *Evangelical Protestantism*, p. 106.
53 Hempton, *Religion and political culture*, pp. 106–13.
54 McBride, *The siege of Derry*, pp. 66–9.
55 Stewart, *The Ulster crisis*, pp. 62–6.

the Catholic minority in the North in which polarised religious identities have continued to dominate politics.

Wales

During the first half of the nineteenth century Wales saw the most striking advances by evangelical voluntary religion in any part of the United Kingdom. Here the Church of England's general problem with inadequate and poorly allocated resources was especially acute in the face of the rapid industrialisation of the south, while its hostile, or at best indifferent, attitude to the Welsh language meant it was alienated from the mainstream of Welsh popular culture. Nonconformity on the other hand had the flexibility rapidly to develop a strong presence in industrialising settlements and a readiness not only to adopt the medium of Welsh but to become a central channel for the maintenance and diffusion of Welsh culture in the Victorian era. The centrality of Nonconformity to Welsh national identity was reinforced in 1847, by outraged reaction to a royal commission report on the state of education in the principality which had attacked both Dissent and the language for allegedly giving rise to backwardness and immorality.[56] In the religious census of 1851, only 18.6 per cent of attendances were at Anglican churches, with all the remainder, apart from a tiny proportion of Roman Catholics, at Nonconformist chapels.[57]

From the middle of the century onwards the Church of England developed an increasingly effective response. A symbolic turning point came in 1846 when it was decided not to proceed with a merger of the North Wales bishoprics of Bangor and St Asaph, which had been recommended by the Ecclesiastical Commissioners.[58] A further key development was the appointment in 1850 of an energetic new bishop, Alfred Ollivant, to Llandaff, the diocese which included many of the most industrialised districts. He recognised that 'our Church, if it would be a national Church, should provide for the instruction of the people in the tongue not only in which they speak, but in which they think and feel'.[59] Although Ollivant himself was not a native Welsh speaker, both he and his contemporary at St David's, Connop Thirlwall, struggled to learn and use the language. In 1870, with the appointment of Joshua Hughes to St Asaph, Wales had its first native Welsh-speaking bishop since the early

---

56 Morgan, 'From a death to a view', pp. 92–4.
57 Currie, Gilbert and Horsley, *Churches and churchgoers*, p. 218.
58 Brown, 'In pursuit of a Welsh episcopate', p. 91.
59 Quoted in Davies, *Religion in the industrial revolution of South Wales*, p. 102.

eighteenth century.[60] Meanwhile substantial achievements were underway in terms of church extension: for example in part of the ironworking districts of the South Wales valleys there was an increase from 21 to 108 churches between the mid-nineteenth and the early twentieth centuries with a corresponding growth in clergy numbers and of numbers of services.[61] Similar expansion was apparent in other parts of the country, notably Carmarthenshire. By the end of the nineteenth century the Anglican church was again the largest single religious body in Wales and 'had a real and increasing role in the spiritual lives of Welsh people'.[62]

This revival came, however, too late to avert an eventually successful campaign for disestablishment. Once the Church of Ireland had been disestablished, the four Welsh dioceses of the Church of England appeared the most vulnerable part of the remaining state churches and hence were a natural target for Liberals and Nonconformists in England as well as Wales. In Wales itself a tithe war raged in the 1880s and 1890s. The demand for disestablishment also became a politically defining cause for Welsh nationalism, as despite its efforts the Anglican church was unable to overcome the perception that it was an alien institution. Disestablishment, though, was resisted until legislation was passed in 1914, with implementation delayed until 1920 as a consequence of the First World War. The effect of disestablishment was to strengthen the Welsh identity of the church, by making it the 'Church in Wales', a separate ecclesiastical province with its own archbishop. The interwar years were to see a continuation of a steady upward trend in communicant numbers that had begun in the late nineteenth century.

Scotland

The Church of Scotland split in 1843 as a result of the paradoxical conviction of the founders of the Free Church that integrity of witness as a national church required, under then current circumstances, the renunciation of formal connections with the state. Presbyterianism north of the Border had, however, already been divided before 1843, by the departure of those in the United Secession Church and the Relief Church who felt unable to accept state connections under any terms. In 1847 these two groups came together to form the United Presbyterian Church. In 1881 the Church of Scotland had 528,475

---

60 Brown, 'In pursuit of a Welsh episcopate', pp. 84–92, 97–8.
61 Davies, *Religion in the industrial revolution of South Wales*, pp. 139–40.
62 Cragoe, *An Anglican aristocracy*, p. 246.

members, the Free Church 312,160, and the United Presbyterian Church 174,557 communicants.[63]

The Scottish situation differed fundamentally from the Irish and the Welsh ones in that, although there was initially intense rivalry between the divided Presbyterian churches, there was no privileged alien religious establishment to stir religious nationalist feelings. Spurned though it was by the founders of the Free Church, the Church of Scotland was an undeniably Scottish institution, while Episcopalians in Scotland were a small minority, who in any case also had an indigenous tradition behind them. Certainly the Free Church was to some extent a cradle for proto-nationalism: under the editorship of Hugh Miller its newspaper, *The Witness*, was prominent in stating national grievances against England, while James Begg, one of its leading ministers, was a prominent member of the National Association for the Vindication of Scottish Rights, founded in 1853.[64] In general, however, Scottish political nationalism in the Victorian era was both more secular and, for that very reason, less powerful than its Irish or Welsh counterparts. Presbyterianism though remained an important force in Scottish culture and society, and despite the Disruption the Church of Scotland parish remained central to civil as well as ecclesiastical government, particularly in relation to education and poor relief.[65]

From the later nineteenth century onwards there was a gradual movement towards Presbyterian reunion, associated with changes in the relationship between the Church of Scotland and the state. The Patronage Act of 1874 abolished lay patronage, the key grievance that had given rise to the Disruption, and thus in the longer term cleared the way towards reunion, although in the short term demands for disestablishment intensified. In 1900 the Free Church and the United Presbyterians came together to form the United Free Church. A small rump of the Free Church (popularly known as the 'Wee Frees') refused to join the united church, feeling that this merger with an avowedly voluntaryist denomination was a betrayal of the national church principles on which the Disruption had occurred. In 1929 the United Free Church rejoined the Church of Scotland in the context of a sequence of legislation between 1921 and 1933 that removed most of the remaining practical civil functions of the Church of Scotland, leaving establishment as merely a matter of symbolic and ceremonial function.[66]

---

63 Currie, Gilbert and Horsley, *Churches and churchgoers*, p. 132.
64 Hanham, 'Mid-century Scottish nationalism', pp. 150–6.
65 Brown, 'The myth of the established church', pp. 60–70.
66 *Ibid.*, pp. 70–3.

England

The Victorian Church of England was internally diverse and at times bitterly divided between the three main party groupings of high church / ritualist, broad church / liberal and evangelical. The intensity of church party rivalries reflected a state of mind in which there was a struggle for the essential character of the church, which was a matter of national as well as theological identity. Thus for High Churchmen, increasingly influenced by the Oxford Movement, there was a necessity to assert the Catholic (though not Roman) character of church and nation through highly visible liturgy and architecture and church furnishings that maintained a continuity with the supposed religious culture of the Middle Ages. For evangelicals there was the converse necessity to maintain the Protestant identity of the Church of England through emphasis on the Reformation heritage and simplicity in both the content and environment of worship. For them the established church was the providential means for the evangelisation of the nation, calling individuals to personal conversion. The Broad Church tradition associated with Thomas Arnold emphasised above all the comprehensiveness of the national church, and for that very reason played down the importance of the theological and liturgical issues that were crucial for the other two parties.[67]

These tensions came to a head in a series of celebrated legal actions around the middle of the century. In 1848, the bishop of Exeter, Henry Phillpotts, refused to institute an evangelical clergyman, George Gorham, to a parish on the grounds that he held unsound doctrine in not teaching the unconditional regeneration of a baptised infant, a theological issue at the heart of differences between evangelicals and High Churchmen. Gorham pursued the bishop through the courts, and in 1850 secured judgement in his favour from the Judicial Committee of the Privy Council (JCPC), the highest court of appeal in ecclesiastical matters. The court did not attempt specifically to define correct Anglican doctrine, but held that Gorham's position was not inconsistent with the church's published standards, the Thirty-Nine Articles and the Prayer Book.[68] Consequent protests from High Churchmen were founded not merely on the specific doctrinal point, but on the conviction that the involvement of a civil court, the JCPC, compromised the church's Catholic and apostolic identity. Such an outlook led to a number of prominent conversions to Roman Catholicism, notably that of Henry Manning,

---

67 For a classic contemporary survey reviewed in the light of recent scholarship, see Conybeare (ed. Burns), 'Church parties'.
68 Chadwick, *The Victorian church*, vol. 1, pp. 250–71.

later second archbishop of Westminster. Despite the differences in theology, the underlying principle of objection to perceived state interference with the spiritual nature of the church was the same as that which had led the Free Church to leave the Church of Scotland in 1843. On the other hand, in 1858 the JCPC ruled, albeit only on a technicality, that the prosecution by evangelicals of the High Churchman George Denison, who had taught the real presence in the Eucharist, was invalid.[69] Then in 1864 the JCPC decided that the liberal teachings of *Essays and reviews*, published in 1860, were not inconsistent with the formularies of the Church of England. The collective implication of these judgements was that, whatever many of its clergy might want, the future of the Church of England lay in the acceptance of considerable internal theological and liturgical diversity. The trend was confirmed after the passing in 1874 of the Public Worship Regulation Act, intended to control ritualism. In practice, however, prosecutions of ritualists under this measure proved too divisive and counterproductive for bishops to continue to allow them.[70]

The internal variety, and hence multifaceted appeal, of the Church of England was one key reason for its success in averting the disestablishment that overtook its Irish and Welsh counterparts. Two further factors were also important. First there was the success of the ongoing process of reform and pastoral renewal, at the grass-roots as well as at the legislative level. The late Victorian church was substantially more effective in meeting the spiritual needs of its congregations than its Georgian predecessor had been. The creation of six new dioceses in the 1870s and 1880s helped to strengthen a sense of local and regional identification with the church, notably in relation to the dioceses of Liverpool, Truro (Cornwall) and Newcastle upon Tyne (Northumberland). Second, a succession of concessions to Nonconformists helped gradually to take the sting out of their hostility to the Church of England. Legislation in 1854 for Oxford and 1856 for Cambridge allowed them to graduate at the ancient universities. At the other end of the educational scale, the 1870 Elementary Education Act, while continuing support to church schools, provided that religious instruction in board (state) schools would be non-denominational in character. In 1868 church rates, a long-standing Nonconformist grievance, were made voluntary, and the 1880 Burials Act allowed Nonconformist ministers to conduct funerals in parish churchyards.[71] There was still potential for Nonconformists to protest about perceived Anglican privilege, as notably

---

69 Machin, *Politics and the churches*, pp. 255–6.
70 Bentley, *Ritualism and politics*.
71 Marsh, *The Victorian church*, pp. 72–81, 137, 256–63.

in their resistance to the 1902 Education Act, but the occasions for such conflict were much reduced by the end of the nineteenth century. The state also adopted a more inclusive attitude to non-Christian minorities, with Jewish Emancipation in 1858 and the admission of atheists to the House of Commons in 1886.

The last third of the nineteenth century thus saw the Church of England consolidating a changed role, no longer enjoying the exclusive constitutional status accorded to it prior to 1828, but still acknowledged as the leading religious expression of national consciousness. It retained some important attributes of establishment, notably the presence of bishops in the House of Lords, and its historic endowments, although these were now deployed in a manner very different from that operative before the 1830s. Important in developing the national role of the church was Arthur Penrhyn Stanley, dean of Westminster from 1864 to 1881, a Broad Churchman and pupil of Thomas Arnold, who sought to make the abbey accessible to people of diverse religious opinions, as symbolised by his readiness to bury the heterodox Charles Dickens in 1870 and the Nonconformist David Livingstone in 1874.[72] Charles Darwin was also interred in the abbey in 1882. Meanwhile the Church of England also remained closely linked to the royal family. This was an important association both in enabling the church to benefit from an upsurge in the popularity of the monarchy in the later years of Victoria's reign, and also in according it a wider United Kingdom ceremonial role, as it participated in the 'invention of tradition' associated with such events.[73] The tone was set in February 1872 by a thanksgiving service at St Paul's Cathedral in London to mark the recent recovery of the Prince of Wales from serious illness, an Anglican service, but one attended by numerous invited Nonconformist representatives.[74] Subsequent important events of this kind included the jubilees of 1887 and 1897, the coronation of Edward VII in 1902, and the funerals of the duke of Clarence in 1892, Victoria in 1901 and Edward VII in 1910. On such occasions the Church of England not only played a prominent role in central national ceremonial, but also provided services that were a focal point for local observance.[75] In general, in the Edwardian years of imperial self-confidence and militaristic nationalism, the church served more to endorse than to question these prevalent states of mind.[76]

72 Wolffe, *Great deaths*, pp. 72–3.
73 Cannadine, 'The context, performance and meaning of ritual', pp. 120–38.
74 Wolffe, 'National occasions at St Paul's', pp. 384–5.
75 Wolffe, *Great deaths*, pp. 94–135.
76 Wolffe, *God and greater Britain*, pp. 215–35.

A suggestive cameo of relationships between church, state and nation at the turn of the twentieth century is provided by a conversation between King Edward VII, and Randall Davidson, then bishop of Winchester, soon to be archbishop of Canterbury, regarding the funeral arrangements for Queen Victoria. Davidson was alarmed at plans by the royal family to include in the service the Russian Kontakion 'Give rest O Christ to thy servant with thy saints', an implied prayer for the dead that would outrage many. He thought that on such 'a great national occasion' controversy should be avoided. When Davidson went to Edward VII to voice his concerns:

> The King said repeatedly, 'I see. What you want to protect is the Noncon-formist conscience.' I said he might put it so without being far wrong. Anyhow, it was a near shave, and the blunder might have turned out to be a real mis-fortune for the Protestant and oldfashioned outcry would have set back the hopes of our getting such prayers generally used.[77]

What is interesting about this incident is Davidson's acknowledgement of the continuing 'old-fashioned' strength of Protestantism, alongside a personal preference that pointed to the advance of Catholic and Orthodox devotional influences. Both king and bishop, however, recognised that the 'Nonconformist conscience' had to be accommodated, and that religious comprehensiveness and avoidance of controversy were ends to be served above personal preference.

Such ready accommodation to the reality of diversity links the English experience to the wider United Kingdom one. Davidson's pragmatism would have shocked early nineteenth-century churchmen such as Keble and Chalmers, and their more exclusive and doctrinally specific visions of national churches still had their advocates in Davidson's day. Nevertheless the overall trend was towards internal pluralism within the Church of England, towards acceptance of a diversity of Christian belief and practice outside the national churches, and to recognition of the diverse religious circumstances of the different nations of the United Kingdom. Only in Ireland were religious differences so profound and entrenched as to remain irreconcilable, a situation which had profound political consequences. Conversely Anglican and Presbyterian churches had a crucial role in supporting national cohesion in Britain, and in ensuring that the eighteenth-century confessional state gave way not to a secular state, but to a pluralistically Christian one.

77 Lambeth Palace Library, Davidson Papers, vol. XIX, 101, pp. 26–7; Wolffe, *Great deaths*, pp. 79–80.

20

Protestant dominance and confessional politics: Switzerland and the Netherlands

A: Switzerland. Religion, politics and the nation: competing and overlapping identities

URS ALTERMATT AND FRANZISKA METZGER

In nineteenth-century Europe, the nation became one of the dominant factors in the construction of collective identities and social organisation. However, in denominationally mixed countries, such as Switzerland, religion remained a significant element in the construction of identity.[1] In nineteenth-century Switzerland, religion was one of the most important forces in the creation of competing conceptions of the nation. By creating a multi-cultural network of ideological and political loyalties, which cut across the linguistic frontiers and assured the cohesion of the multi-lingual state, the *Kulturkämpfe* of the middle decades of the nineteenth century reduced the importance of the linguistic factor. Although the *Kulturkämpfe* had weakened by the 1880s, ideological solidarities had assumed such fundamental discursive and organisational structures that they remained constitutive of the Swiss party system until the second half of the twentieth century.

Stability of confessional distribution and regional changes

In the confessional era of the sixteenth and seventeenth centuries, the Swiss *Eidgenossenschaft* generated a model of religious co-existence in which the

---

1 See for Switzerland: Altermatt, 'Religion und Nation'; Zimmer, *A contested nation*; Metzger, 'Die Reformation in der Schweiz'; Vischer, Schenker and Dellsperger (eds.), *Ökumenische Kirchengeschichte der Schweiz*. For more general treatments of this theme see: Heinz-Gerhard Haupt and Dieter Langewiesche (eds.), *Nation und Religion in Europa: Mehrkonfessionelle Gesellschaften im 19. und 20. Jahrhundert* (Frankfurt and New York: Campus Verlag, 2004); Michael Geyer and Hartmut Lehmann (eds.), *Religion und Nation. Nation und Religion. Beiträge zu einer unbewältigten Geschichte* (Göttingen: Wallstein Verlag, 2004).

principle of territoriality – *cuius regio eius religio* – guaranteed confessional homogeneity within precisely defined areas.[2] However, this right of existence was not applied to the small Jewish minority.[3]

Unlike the older predominantly mono-confessional cantons, most of those established by the Mediation Act in 1803 were denominationally mixed. After the foundation of the modern nation-state in 1848, fourteen of the twenty-five cantons were more or less mono-confessional (Protestant: Zurich, Schaffhausen, Appenzell Outer-Rhodes, Vaud and Neuchâtel; Catholic: Lucerne, Uri, Schwyz, Nidwalden, Obwalden, Zug, Appenzell Inner-Rhodes, Ticino and Valais). Moreover, Fribourg and Solothurn had Catholic majorities, and Berne, Glarus and Basel Protestant majorities, all of between 80 and 90 per cent.[4] In the mixed cantons of St Gall, Grisons, Argovia and Geneva the Protestant and Catholic populations varied between 38 and 62 per cent either way.

Between 1850 and 1900, the percentage of Protestants and Catholics in the whole of Switzerland remained very stable, with a Catholic population of 40.6 to 41.9 per cent. Census returns indicate that there were 971,809 Catholics and 1,417,786 Protestants in 1850 and 1,379,664 Catholics and 1,916,157 Protestants in 1900. The number of Jews was 3,145 in 1850 and 12,264 in 1900. Owing to migration within Switzerland and immigration in the wake of industrialisation, especially from Germany and Italy, the cantons of Zurich, Geneva and Basel – and especially the towns of the same name – experienced a significant growth in the Catholic population. Whereas in 1850 there were 6,690 Catholics living in the canton of Zurich, their number had increased to 40,402 by 1888 and 80,752 by 1900. More than 90 per cent of these were labourers, workmen and domestic servants.[5] In contrast, in Solothurn, immigration from Berne brought about an increase in the number of Protestants from 11.6 per cent in 1850 to 25.6 per cent in 1888 and 30.9 per cent in 1900. Between 1850 and 1888 the Catholic population in the Protestant cantons of Zurich, Berne, Glarus,

2 See Kaspar von Greyerz, *Religion und Kultur: Europa 1500–1800* (Göttingen: Vandenhoeck and Ruprecht, 2000).

3 See Florence Guggenheim-Grünberg, 'Vom Scheiterhaufen zur Emanzipation. Die Juden in der Schweiz vom 6. bis 19. Jahrhundert', in Willy Guggenheim, *Juden in der Schweiz. Glaube – Geschichte – Gegenwart* (Küsnacht and Zurich: Kürz, 2nd edn, 1983), pp. 10–53; Augusta Weldler-Steinberg, *Geschichte der Juden in der Schweiz vom 16. Jahrhundert bis nach der Emanzipation*, 2 vols. (Zurich: Schweizerischer Israelitischer Gemeindebund, 1966, 1970); *Jüdische Lebenswelt Schweiz: 100 Jahre Schweizerischer Israelitischer Gemeindebund (SIG)* (Zurich: Chronos, 2004).

4 See for the following figures: *Statistisches Jahrbuch der Schweiz*, ed. by the Statistisches Bureau des eidgenössischen Departementes des Innern, Berne, vol. I (1891), pp. 14–15; and XII (1903), p. 7.

5 See Altermatt, *Katholizismus und Moderne*, pp. 239–40, 181–202.

Basel, Schaffhausen, Appenzell Outer-Rhodes, Vaud, Neuchâtel and Geneva doubled: by 1888, almost as many Catholics lived in these cantons as in Catholic central Switzerland; by 1900 their numbers exceeded those in the latter region. The increasingly bi-confessional situation in many regions, and especially in some towns, caused social and political friction, but, not least through inter-marriage, was leading also to an increasing ecumenism in everyday life and a decline in prejudices and resulting conflicts.

Conflicts between church and state

Whereas after the Helvetic Revolution of 1798 the new elites had aimed at sec-ularising the central state while maintaining state sovereignty over the church, in the Mediation Act of 1803 the regulation of freedom of belief and worship was transferred to the cantons. The Federal Treaty of 1815 did not mention religious freedom, but affirmed the preservation of the monasteries, whilst declaring state sovereignty over religious orders and congregations, whose situation varied according to the different cantonal constitutions. Whereas in some cantonal constitutions of the Regeneration Era of the 1830s, freedom of belief and conscience was guaranteed to the Christian confessions, a number of cantons recognised only one church.[6]

In the 1830s, the Liberals and Radicals were eager to subjugate the Catholic Church to secular state power. The abolition of the monasteries in the can-ton of Argovia by the anticlerical Radicals and the appointment of Jesuits to institutions of higher education by Catholic ultras in Lucerne brought about a further radicalisation of the conflicts, leading to the civil war of 1847 (the *Sonderbundskrieg*). These actions were an expression of the politicisation of reli-gion and the confessionalisation of politics characteristic of the *Kulturkämpfe* between the 1830s and the 1880s. These were, above all, conflicts about the demarcation of spheres of influence, cultural hegemony and conceptions of political and social order.[7]

In the 1830s, the Catholic movement was not completely homogeneous in its ideology; a reactionary ultra-Catholic traditionalist direction can be differentiated from a more moderate conservative one. The leaders of the ultras, Josef Leu von Ebersol and Constantin Siegwart-Müller, reflected the

6 See Alfred Kölz, *Neuere schweizerische Verfassungsgeschichte: ihre Grundlinien vom Ende der alten Eidgenossenschaft bis 1848* (Berne: Verlag Stämpfli, 1992), vol. 1, pp. 337–9.

7 See Urs Altermatt, 'L'engagement des intellectuels catholiques suisses au sein de l'Internationale noire', in Emiel Lamberts (ed.), *The Black International 1870–1878: the Holy See and militant Catholicism in Europe* (Leuven: Leuven University Press, 2002), pp. 409–26; Metzger, 'The legal situation of religious institutes'.

politicisation of religion very explicitly. In 1841, they imposed a Catholic-exclusionist constitution in Lucerne, which made the right to vote dependent on belonging to the Catholic Church. They promoted the appointment of Jesuits in order to ensure the Ultramontane orientation of the new generations of Catholics.

From the early nineteenth century onwards, Protestant theologians, such as Johann Kaspar Lavater and Johann Jakob Hess from Zurich, also found themselves among the antirevolutionary conservatives. Parallel to Catholic traditionalism, a Protestant revivalist movement arose. In 1839, the conservative rural population of Protestant Zurich overthrew the liberal government after the appointment of the controversial theologian David Friedrich Strauss, author of *Das Leben Jesu* (1835–6), to a post at the University of Zurich. However, an alliance between Catholic and Protestant conservatives did not take shape because of the confessionalisation of political conflicts.[8]

The constitution of the Swiss Confederation of 1848 declared freedom of religion and belief to be an individual affair, not linked to territoriality, and assigned church matters to the cantons. However, with their discriminatory articles against the Catholic Church and religious congregations, the constitutions of 1848 and 1874 remained expressions of the politicisation of religion and anticlerical intrusions by the liberal state into the sphere of religion. The ban on the Jesuits lasted for more than a century.[9]

In the 1870s the conflicts surfaced once more, especially in the large diocese of Basel. Bishop Eugène Lachat, who had openly declared himself in favour of the dogma of papal infallibility, was dismissed by the diocesan conference of the cantons in 1873 and, despite demonstrations in his support by Catholics, was exiled from liberal-radical Solothurn to Catholic-conservative Lucerne. After a protest from the pope, the Swiss government broke off its relations with the nuncio in Lucerne. In 1873 Pius IX designated Gaspard Mermillod apostolic vicar of Geneva, trying to re-establish a diocese without consulting the cantonal or national government. As a consequence, Mermillod was exiled from Switzerland, becoming, for Catholics, the martyr of the *Kulturkampf* in Geneva.[10]

The incomplete character of religious freedom in the constitution of the modern Swiss nation-state is especially apparent with regard to the Jewish

---

8 See Altermatt, 'Conservatism in Switzerland'; Olivier Fatio, 'Die protestantischen Kirchen', in Vischer *et al.* (eds.), *Ökumemische Kirkengeschichte*, pp. 215–19.
9 See Urs Josef Cavelti, *Kirchenrecht im demokratischen Umfeld* (Fribourg: Universitätsverlag, 1999).
10 See Stadler, *Der Kulturkampf*, pp. 260–316, 586–94.

population. Freedom of worship, freedom of settlement and legal equality were accorded solely to Christians. It was only in the context of a trade treaty with France that a partial revision of the Swiss constitution in 1866 granted the Swiss Jews the right of free settlement and legal equality. Freedom of belief and conscience was not extended to all Swiss until the revision of 1874. In 1893, a discriminatory law against kosher slaughter was added to the constitution. Central to the double exclusion of the Jews, political and cultural, was the idea of the so-called 'Christian state', often linked to anti-Semitic discourse.[11]

Protestantism between revivalism and liberalism

At the beginning of the nineteenth century, a Protestant revivalist movement arose in reaction to liberal theology. This brought about a heterogenisation of Protestantism. In addition to the cantonal churches, the Landeskirchen, and the Schweizerische reformierte Kirchenkonferenz founded in 1858, a variety of evangelical churches and communities were established, centred in Basel and Geneva. Here an Evangelical Free Church was founded in 1849 as a church independent of the state. From the mid-nineteenth century, revivalism became part of the conservative Protestant movement. It also gave rise to a number of pious, missionary and welfare societies, which were ambivalent in their attitudes to modern society. Since the diffusion of the Bible was a central concern of the revivalist movement, in several cantons so-called Bible associations were established. Among the foreign missionary societies, the Basler Mission (founded in 1815) became the most prominent. Controlled by an influential and tightly knit social elite, and with its own missionary seminary in Basel, it was especially oriented towards West Africa and south-west India.[12]

Liberal Protestant theology was influenced by the rational theology of the Tübingen School. One of the most renowned Protestant theologians in Switzerland was Alexandre Vinet in Lausanne, a vehement warrior for religious freedom and the separation of church and state. Under his influence, the Free Church of Vaud was set up. From the mid-nineteenth century, liberal theology became the dominant strain in Swiss Protestantism, aiming

---

11 See Altermatt, 'Religion, Staat und Gesellschaft in der Schweiz'; Mattioli (ed.), *Antisemitismus*, especially: Mattioli, 'Die Schweiz und die jüdische Emanzipation 1798–1874', pp. 61–82; Pascal Krauthammer, *Das Schächtverbot in der Schweiz 1854–2000: die Schächtfrage zwischen Tierschutz, Politik und Fremdenfeindlichkeit* (Zurich: Schulthess, 2000).

12 See Fatio, 'Die protestantischen Kirchen', pp. 215–19; Olivier Fatio, 'Auseinandersetzungen und Aufbrüche', in Vischer *et al.* (eds.), *Ökumenische Kirkengeschichte*, pp. 236–46; Pfister, *Kirchengeschichte*, pp. 251–9; Gäbler, 'Erweckungsbewegungen'.

at the integration of new religious perspectives with modernity. Within this reformist tradition of theology, Zurich and Berne became the predominant centres. In Zurich, influenced by Schleiermacher and Hegel, the two systematic theologians Alexander Schweizer and Alois Emanuel Biedermann became the leaders. In 1871 liberal Protestant associations were united in the Schweizerischer Verein für freies Christentum and, influenced by the liberal movement, a number of other social and pedagogical institutions were established, including the International Red Cross, founded by Henry Dunant in 1863. Between the two poles represented by the traditionalist and the reformist theologians, intermediary positions, such as that held by the Basel church historian Karl Rudolf Hagenbach, remained in a minority.[13]

Whereas mainstream liberal Protestantism found itself represented by political liberalism and integrated in the nation-state and its culture, the conservative Protestant minority time and again took a political stand against the new nation-state. The writer and pastor Jeremias Gotthelf belonged to this line of thought. After 1875 the Eidgenössische Verein mobilised Protestant conservatives, and in the canton of Berne the Protestant opposition movement was led by the Bernische Volkspartei of Ulrich Dürrenmatt. Conservative alliances for popular votes were not merged into a common party; different confessionally defined identities played a much more important role in the conservative movement than in the liberal-radical one. Towards the end of the nineteenth century, some individual conservative Protestant intellectuals, such as the Basel historian Jacob Burckhardt, remained prominent. Most of the members of the Protestant wing of conservatism now supported the liberal party (Freisinnig-Demokratische Partei), which had become more moderate. After World War I, some of the Berne conservatives joined the newly founded agrarian Bauern-, Gewerbe- and Bürgerpartei.[14]

The Catholic milieu

The confessionalisation of politics and the politicisation of religion were intensified by the increasingly Ultramontane and socially organised character of Catholicism. As a result of their interaction with modernity, new social forms of Catholicism as a sub-culture or socio-cultural milieu emerged in the second half of the nineteenth century.[15]

13 See Fatio, 'Auseinandersetzungen und Aufbrüche', p. 237; Pfister, *Kirchengeschichte*.
14 See Altermatt, 'Conservatism in Switzerland'.
15 See Altermatt, *Katholizismus und Moderne*.

On the level of ideology and *Weltanschauung*, Catholic identity was characterised by an antimodernist cultural code based on antiliberalism, antisocialism and antifreemasonry. Such anti-positions also found expression in rites and religious practices, such as anti-Judaism in the Passion plays. Mass pilgrimages to the statue of Our Lady of Einsiedeln, or the veneration of Pius IX, were manifestations of the transformation of Catholicism from a traditional religion into a mass one.[16]

The centralisation of church authority, which reached a climax in 1870 with the definition of the dogma of papal infallibility, led to resistance from 'liberal' Catholics. Between 1871 and 1876, in the wake of the *Kulturkampf*, some of these Catholics went on to found the Christ-Catholic Church. This movement initially also had a political character, bringing together politically liberal Catholics. The central figure in the constitutional phase of Christian Catholic theology was Eduard Herzog, Professor of New Testament at the University of Berne and the first Christian Catholic bishop.[17]

Clerical and lay elites played a crucial role, and occupied positions of power in the Catholic milieu, producing and mediating cultural codes and descriptions of society. The only Catholic associational structure which had survived the civil war, the Schweizerische Studentenverein, founded in 1841, became a central network for Catholic elites. In the second half of the nineteenth century a number of more or less interrelated networks can be observed which differed in their attitudes towards the liberal state and Ultramontanism. Whereas in homogeneously Protestant cantons Catholic organisations were rare, in regions affected by the *Kulturkampf*, such as Solothurn, St Gall and Argovia and the diaspora, a strong milieu was constituted, and in predominantly Catholic regions loose structures dominated by the Church were prevalent. Among the elites we can identify an Ultramontane network predominant in Fribourg, in the *Kulturkampf* regions and in the diaspora and a more moderate conservative one developing out of the Catholic cantons of central Switzerland.[18]

Ultramontane elites created associations on a national level. For more than a quarter of a century, the publicist Theodor Scherer-Boccard was one of their leaders. From 1857 to his death in 1885, he presided over the first nationwide Catholic association, the Piusverein. In Fribourg the young priest Joseph

16 Altermatt, 'Ambivalence of Catholic modernisation'; Altermatt, *Katholizismus und Antisemitismus*, pp. 59–96. For this trend elsewhere in Catholic Europe see chapter 5 above.
17 See Arx, 'Christkatholische Kirche'; Conzemius, *Katholizismus ohne Rom*.
18 See Altermatt and Metzger, 'Milieu, Teilmilieus und Netzwerke'; Altermatt, *Der Weg der Schweizer Katholiken ins Ghetto*; Altermatt (ed.), 'Den Riesenkampf mit dieser Zeit zu wagen . . .'.

Schorderet was a dominant influence, establishing in the 1870s a network of associations and newspapers in the French-speaking part of Switzerland, the most important of which was *La Liberté*.[19]

Representatives of the Ultramontane line of thought were also the main promoters of social reform. From the 1830s a number of charitable organisations were established, whose networks increased in the second half of the century and were united in the Schweizerische Caritasverband in 1901. In 1887, the Verband der katholischen Männer- und Arbeitervereine was founded by Joseph Beck, Caspar Decurtins and Ernst Feigenwinter. They proclaimed corporatist models aiming at an antimodernist restructuring of society as a whole, and their idea of self-help resulted in the foundation of Catholic health insurances and savings banks. At the beginning of the twentieth century, the old social movement was replaced by the Christian social labour movement.[20]

The Catholic networks were also essential for the foundation of the University of Fribourg in 1889. From its beginnings, the state university had the function of an international Catholic centre, which became manifest not least in the conferences of the Union de Fribourg which played an important role in the formulation of the encyclical *Rerum Novarum* of Pope Leo XIII in 1891.[21]

During the first forty years of the new Switzerland, the historian and publicist Philipp Anton Segesser was the leader of conservative political Catholicism and its grouping in the Swiss parliament.[22] This was the predecessor of the Christian-Democratic Party, one of the oldest Christian-Democratic parties in Europe. Although the Catholic Church only developed a positive attitude to democracy at a late stage, the majority of Swiss Catholics already took the democratic form of government for granted. Between 1874 and 1884, they frequently used the direct democratic instrument of the referendum to obstruct the politics of the national government. In 1891 Joseph Zemp was elected the first Christian-Democratic member of the Swiss government. In addition to the party, the Katholische Volksverein and media networks, especially the newspaper *Vaterland*, were important pillars of political Catholicism. After 1891, the Christian-Democrats were continuously represented in the Swiss government. However, internal opposition to mainstream conservative Catholicism from

---

19 See Alois Steiner, *Der Piusverein der Schweiz: von seiner Gründung bis zum Vorabend des Kulturkampfes 1857–1870* (Stans: Kommissions-Verlag Josef von Matt, 1961).
20 See Altermatt and Metzger, 'Katholische Arbeiter und Milieuidentität'; Ruffieux, *Le mouvement chrétien-social; Von der katholischen Milieuorganisation zum sozialen Hilfswerk*.
21 See Ruffieux et al. (eds.), *Geschichte der Universität Freiburg Schweiz*.
22 See Conzemius, *Philipp Anton von Segesser, 1817–1888*.

a grouping of ultra-Catholics continued into the twentieth century, especially around the integrist networks of the weekly *Schildwache*.[23]

Nation and religion

Unlike the Catholics, the Protestants saw themselves as the dominant confession in Switzerland. They were integrated within the *freisinnige* liberal-radical party which dominated political culture well into the twentieth century. The nation was a central strand in their sense of identity, which was the main reason why Protestantism did not constitute structures similar to the Catholic milieu. As a political and cultural minority, Catholics stood in opposition to the new liberal nation-state and its political system, while identifying more or less closely with the old nation (the old *Eidgenossenschaft*). Since Catholics created conceptions of the nation of their own, two competing, partially overlapping communicative communities can be observed – a national one dominated by liberal and Protestant conceptions, and a Catholic one.[24]

These mechanisms become apparent in the constructions of history and memory. The nation on the one hand, and political and social Catholicism on the other, can each be described as communities of memory, with parallel and partially overlapping narratives. Competing conceptions of the nation were created, especially where contemporary conflicts seemed to reflect historical conflicts, which applied especially to the history of the Reformation period. There, the confessional factor became an instance of difference in the construction of a Swiss national history. National-liberal and Protestant discourses described the sixteenth-century reformer Huldrych Zwingli as the prototype of a 'real' Christian and republican Swiss, defining the confessional factor as part of a dominant national narrative directly related to conceptions of the modern nation-state. In contrast, Catholics brought counter-reformers such as Cardinal Carlo Borromeo into their national narratives, and confessionalised the prominent medieval politician Bruder Klaus von Flüe, who formerly had been an integrative historical character. The Catholic historical journal *Zeitschrift für Schweizerische Kirchengeschichte* was established in 1907 as a counterpart to the Protestant *Zwingliana*, founded in 1897.[25]

---

23 See Metzger, *Die 'Schildwache'*.
24 See Altermatt, 'Religion und Nation'; Metzger, 'Die Reformation in der Schweiz'; Urs Altermatt, 'Das Bundesjubiläum 1891, das Wallis und die katholische Schweiz', *Blätter aus der Walliser Geschichte* 21 (1989), 89–106.
25 See the contributions in *Zeitschrift für Schweizerische Kirchengeschichte* 90 (1996).

In spite of these differences, the national celebrations of the 600th anniversary of the Swiss *Eidgenossenschaft* in 1891 expressed the increasing integration of the Catholic population, who participated in the foundational myth of 1291. Politically and socially, Catholic self-definition through segregation led to the integration of Catholics into Swiss society, both through political participation and through shared or differing narratives of the nation. In spite of this integration, however, Protestantism remained more formative for Switzerland's national culture.

B: The Netherlands

MICHAEL WINTLE

The role played by the Calvinist faith in the Revolt against Spain has ensured that Dutch religious history in the time of the Republic is relatively familiar outside its borders; the same is not true of the nineteenth century. None the less, two features stand out in the period between the defeat of Napoleon and the First World War: the complex variety of denominations which existed, especially amongst the orthodox Calvinists, and the growth of a system of 'pillarisation' or *verzuiling*, which involved the institutionalisation of those denominations in a plethora of civil society organisations. This half of the chapter will provide an account of developments in church history and theology in the Netherlands in the nineteenth century, against a trend towards secularisation and an increasing separation of church and state. A framework will be sought in which to locate all the different sects and denominations, and to explain how religion contributed to the famed Dutch 'pillarisation', linked to a consideration of the relationship between religion and national identity. In accordance with the complexity and diversity of religious experience, there was no single national identity or process of nation formation in the nineteenth century in the Netherlands, but several. These separate but parallel paths towards a multiple national identity were themselves part and parcel of the particularly Dutch process of vertical pluralism, or 'pillarisation'.

'Pillarisation' requires careful definition. Strictly speaking, it refers to a condition found in many countries where vertical, ideological divisions dominate more than socio-economic (class) ones, and where those ideologies are 'pillarised' in the form of institutions formed on ideological or denominational lines, such as social clubs, schools, welfare agencies, churches and political parties.[26] The Netherlands had become extensively 'pillar*ised*' in that sense by the 1920s, and remained so until the 1950s; the nineteenth century was therefore formative, while pillar*isation* was taking place, into four pillars, of Catholics, orthodox Calvinists, Socialists and liberals. Two features distinguished these pillars. First, they had their own organisations in every conceivable arena, which succeeded in ensuring that it was possible to lead more or less separate Socialist, Calvinist or Catholic lives inside the pillars of society. Just as important for the Dutch version of pillarisation, although it has received very much less attention, was the system which held the pillars in place, namely

---

26 Righart, *De katholieke zuil.*

the network of mechanisms, formal and informal, for negotiation, conciliation and compromise, which linked the highest levels of the pillars together. The leaders or elite of each pillar met each other in all kinds of committees and working groups in order to run the country, while ordinary people could be permitted to live out their lives within the pillars. This vision of Dutch society in the first half of the twentieth century, often symbolised by four great pillars in a classical pediment, supporting a common roof or superstructure (the governmental apparatus), was presented most famously by Arend Lijphart in 1968.[27] Its roots are in large measure to be found in the nineteenth century, not so much in terms of the long-standing ideological conflicts, but rather in the growth of the various ideology-based organisations and of the negotiating system which made it all work: these were the crucial nineteenth-century contributions to the creation of *verzuiling*. Moreover, they played an essential part in the reformulation and crystallisation of Dutch national identity before the First World War.

While religious groups in other countries experienced pillarisation in the sense of vertically integrated institutions, only the Netherlands developed such a complete set of negotiating mechanisms between the pillars, and remained so long a segregated society, until the 1960s. The confessional groups used their increasing electoral power towards the end of the nineteenth century, fuelled by the enfranchisement of the lower middle classes, in order to protect their position against the power of the secular state. While Dutch Calvinist leaders before the 1870s strove towards a Christianisation, or re-Christianisation, of the whole of Dutch society, later ones such as Abraham Kuyper (1837–1920) did not expect total victory. By the last decade of the nineteenth century, he was working for a safe and protected place within a broader society in which various groups would lead their own, pillarised lives. Kuyper proclaimed, 'I exalt multiformity, and hail in it a higher stage of development.'[28]

The religious affiliation of the Dutch population towards the end of the nineteenth century, according to the census of 1899, is shown in Table 20.1. The figures make clear that the Calvinists of the Dutch Reformed Church dominated, especially if the orthodox Calvinists are added to them. However, within most of the officially recognised denominational groups, there was to be found a wide range of religious and theological opinion. In order to rationalise some of the complexity, the following account will employ a distinction between 'progressive' and 'orthodox-conservative'. It would be a simplification to suggest

27 Lijphart, *The politics of accommodation*.
28 A. Kuyper, *Calvinism: six Stone lectures* (Amsterdam: Höveker and Wormser [1899]), p. 268.

Table 20.1. *Religious affiliation, 1899*

Dutch Reformed Church	48.6 %
Roman Catholic	35.2 %
Orthodox Calvinist	8.2%
Agnostic / Atheist	2.3%
Jewish	2.0%
Lutheran	1.8%
Baptist	1.1%
Remonstrant	0.4%

Source: From De Kok, *Nederland*, pp. 292–3.

that this was the only criterion which divided religious thought, but it was an underlying factor in many of the disputes in most of the groups.[29] Conservatives tended to see the root of most evil in the French Revolution, with its fruits of rationalism, anthropocentrism, individualism and the power of the secular state. Indeed the two most important Calvinist leaders of the century, Guillaume Groen van Prinsterer (1801–76) and Abraham Kuyper, immortalised their personal opposition to the Revolution, first when Groen entitled his 1847 magnum opus *Unbelief and revolution*,[30] and then when both of them referred to their political group as the 'Anti-Revolutionaries', and eventually as the Anti-Revolutionary Party, founded in 1879. In theology the progressive trends were represented by humanistic and individualistic tendencies, and in church politics by a desire on the part of the state to distance itself from any one religion or established church. The state also wished to break down religious resistance to liberal reforms and, in the early stages at least, to use church structures as hierarchies for carrying out state reforms and programmes, for example in education. Much of the history of religion in nineteenth-century Europe can be construed as the response of the churches to such attempts at change: the way in which the Dutch in particular dealt with the challenge is what gave their experience its unique, national qualities.

In theology, the infiltration of rationalism into the Dutch Reformed Church came about through a movement known as 'Supranaturalism', based on a tolerant compromise between the demands of a questing and rational intellectual

---

29 Wintle, *Pillars of Piety*, pp. 1–10 and *passim*. See also Kossmann, *The Low Countries*; Van Rooden, *Religieuze regimes*; and Bank and Van Buuren, *1900*, chapters 9 and 10.
30 G. Groen van Prinsterer, *Ongeloof en revolutie: een reeks van historische voorlezingen*, 4th edn (Amsterdam: Van Bottenburg, 1940) (original edition 1847; abridged English translation by Harry van Dyke, *Groen Van Prinsterer: lectures on unbelief and revolution* (Jordan Station, Ontario: Wedge Publishing Foundation, 1989)).

Enlightenment and the revealed truths of the church confessions.[31] There were a number of ecumenical initiatives, and the 'Spirit of the Age' celebrated the enlightened virtue of tolerance. According to such values, the external forms of the churches had to be made as rational and hierarchical as possible, and where necessary should be available for use by the enlightened state in order to promote the advantage and felicity of the people. Reaction was widespread against these manifestations of progressive religion. A nostalgic Romanticism was an important part of the *Réveil*, a literary-religious movement looking back to a pre-Enlightenment world. Rationalistic and cerebral theology was rejected by the 'Groninger Movement' from the late 1820s onwards with their 'theology of feeling' and Christian Humanism; meanwhile the orthodox Calvinists rejected all these new initiatives *en masse*. Amongst the Catholics, powerful elements opposed the attempts of the government to reform them, and Ultramontanism evolved in reaction to the Enlightenment.

Later on in the century, the rise of modernism in Dutch Reformed theology, led first by J. H. Scholten (1811–85), and later renowned as the 'Dutch Radical School', represented the increasing influence of rationalism in religion. Meanwhile, the liberal governments after 1848 dismantled the bonds between church and state, while the Synodal Committee of the Dutch Reformed Church regularly launched innovative schemes like new hymn books, Bible translations and liturgical forms. In reaction to this, there were orthodox theological developments as well, such as the 'Ethical Movement', and orthodox Calvinists also left the Reformed Church in protest. The Catholics built up their own episcopal hierarchy, and with it laid the foundations of their own Catholic world. In the second half of the nineteenth century, then, those who opposed the influence of rationalistic progress, of the Enlightenment and of liberalism began to organise themselves in a struggle which Kuyper represented as the 'antithesis between Christendom and Humanism', or between true Christians and those who placed their trust in such things as human reason and progress, or in mankind itself.[32]

The Dutch Reformed Church (*Nederlandse Hervormde Kerk*) was the mainstream Calvinist church, and was descended from the Calvinism of the Dutch Revolt. In 1795 French Revolutionary troops had invaded the Netherlands and removed its privileges, making it just one church among equals; following the new ideas of statecraft manifested in the policies of Joseph II of Austria and then of Napoleon, a new Regulation (*Algemene Reglement*) was provided by

---

31 See Rasker, *De Nederlandse Hervormde Kerk*; and Bos, *In dienst*.
32 Lipschits, *De protestants-christelijke stroming*, p. 34.

the secular state in 1816, streamlining the church, making it at least in part a department of state for carrying out the policies of the king and his government. Within the church itself, the traditional Presbyterian organisation was replaced by a top-down corporate structure where the Synod ran the regional church assemblies (*classes*), while they in turn were in charge of the local congregations. It left a structure very unlike the Calvinist church of the seventeenth century. From the 1840s onwards the governments were led by the 'doctrinaire' liberals under Johan Rudolf Thorbecke (1798–1872), true heirs of the Enlightenment in politics, and they continued the secularisation of the Dutch state. Having been dictated to by Erastian governments in the first half of the century, the Reformed Church was now being cut off from the state in the second half.

In opposition to these changes were first and foremost the strict orthodox Calvinist groups, organised in congregations which wanted little to do with a church hierarchy or indeed with other parts of society in general. They were known as the 'blackstockings', the 'weighty' or 'heavy' ones. Their numbers were very small, but they were at the heart of a major schism or *Afscheiding* of 1834, and they were often persecuted in the Erastian state of the 1830s. By 1850 they had become a small but recognised group in Dutch religious life.

A larger and less inflexible group was formed by those orthodox Calvinists who were not as severe in their doctrine as the strict orthodox, but who were determined to keep to the principles, if not every single letter, of the church of Calvin and the Dutch Revolt. Often they were reluctant to leave the Dutch Reformed Church, preferring to try and work from within, although in 1886 there was another large schism, called the *Doleantie* or 'Protest': 180,000 left in three years. They formed the *Gereformeerde Kerken*, reverting to the more traditional word for Reformed (*gereformeerd*, as opposed to *hervormd*), and rejecting all the innovations associated with the new church structure since 1816. In 1892 they joined forces with the *Afscheiding* of 1834.

Much of this orthodox religious dissent was brought together after 1870 by the imposing figure of Abraham Kuyper. He has been called the Dutch Gladstone, indicating his importance to both religion and politics. He was a major leader of church, party and government, an important theologian whose Princeton lectures on Calvinism in 1899 had a global impact,[33] a leading academic and co-founder of the Calvinist Free University of Amsterdam, a prolific homilist, a journalist of legendary energy and influence, and an indefatigable organiser. He bound his orthodox Calvinist following into a modern political

---

33 Kuyper, *Calvinism*; see Heslam, *Creating a Christian worldview*.

force, with a party manifesto (the first in the Netherlands) in 1878,[34] dedicated party newspapers in the *Standaard* and *Heraut*, and in 1879 the first modern political party in the country, the Anti-Revolutionary Party. Its platform was suffrage for the lower middle classes, and state funding for confessional education. Kuyper's theology was orthodox Calvinist in its temper, and strongly against the elevation of mankind and human reason favoured by the Enlightenment. His doctrine of 'sphere sovereignty' was a version of subsidiarity, holding that the various levels in society, like the family, the business, the church, the school and the community, should be answerable, like the Calvinist congregation, to no absolute authority but that of God.[35] This formed the kernel of the ideology which Kuyper developed to protect the rights and interests of his followers to worship and live as they saw fit in the orthodox Calvinist tradition, although without the rejection of the modern world shown by the ultra-orthodox. It was also to be one of the cornerstones of pillarisation, or *verzuiling*, in Dutch society.

Apart from the Calvinists, there were other Protestant sects in the Netherlands, including the Remonstrants, the Lutherans and the Mennonites or Baptists (see Table 20.1). These groups were small – 1 or 2 per cent each of the population in 1899, often urban, and (with some exceptions) more wealthy than other groups. They too had their internal struggles, splits and reunions in the course of the nineteenth century – just as did the Calvinists.[36] The battle lines were drawn up on very similar issues, namely in the first place church order and relations with the state; and secondly, new ideas based in human reason and the Enlightenment.

If the century began with Protestant dominance, the other major denomination in the country, the Roman Catholics, was considerably less marginalised by the end of it. There were no new schisms here, but in 1723, the low church Jansenists in the Dutch Roman Church had set up their own episcopal hierarchy, called the Old Catholic Church. Rome was constantly concerned about them in the nineteenth century, fearing a revival of Dutch Gallicanism, but they never amounted to more than 0.2 per cent of the population. Dutch Catholics were used to centuries of suppression in varying degrees, but having achieved theoretically equal status under the law in 1795, they suddenly found themselves the majority church in the country, for between 1816 and 1830 the Netherlands was joined to the Catholic Belgian provinces under the rule of the Dutch king, Willem I. His government imagined it could use the Roman

34 A. Kuyper, *Ons program*, 2 vols. (Amsterdam: Kruyt, 1879).
35 A. Kuyper, *Souvereiniteit in eigen kring* (Amsterdam: Kruyt, 1880).
36 For a brief account, see Wintle, *Pillars of piety*.

Church, as it was using the Reformed Church in the North, as an extension of its power structure, especially when it wanted to reform education, much of which was run by the clergy in the southern provinces. Resistance to such policies became one of the main reasons for the Revolution of 1830, which separated the present-day countries of Belgium and the Netherlands. In the 1830s Dutch Catholics were obliged to keep a low profile because of their association with the southern rebels, but with the accession in 1840 of King Willem II they began to reassert their identity, with the help of publicists such as J. le Sage ten Broek (1775–1847), and later J. A. Alberdink Thijm (1820–89). Since the Reformation there had been no Roman Catholic episcopal hierarchy in the Netherlands – the faithful were served by clergy answerable to the *Propaganda Fide* in Rome, and formed a 'mission area'. A succession of concordats between Rome and the Dutch government were tortuously arranged, but before the mid-century the organisation of Roman Catholicism in the Netherlands was both weak and complicated.

In 1848 the Dutch underwent their version of the European liberal revolution (more or less bloodless in the Netherlands). Armed with a new constitution designed by Thorbecke, the new liberal government let it be known that it would not oppose the reintroduction of a formal hierarchy, and in March 1853 Pope Pius IX issued an apostolic brief announcing five new sees in the Netherlands, with the archbishop's seat at Utrecht.[37] This provoked one of the more unsavoury incidents in the generally respectable, bourgeois history of the nineteenth century, known as the Great Protestant or April Movement. It unleashed antipopery riots and bigotry at all levels of society, and led to the fall of the liberal government. However, the combination of the hierarchy with the new constitution of 1848, which made all the churches equal and gave more votes to the Roman Catholics, provided the legal basis for a Roman Catholic emancipation movement in the second half of the nineteenth century. There was a boom in recruitment for monasteries and seminaries, Roman Catholic clubs sprang up everywhere, and (like the other pillars in the making) the institutions of Catholicism contributed to a burgeoning Dutch civil society. The Catholics felt their way towards a political alliance with the orthodox Protestants under Kuyper: despite their antipathies, the two groups often desired the same things in politics, like state subsidies for religious education, the extension of the suffrage to include their lower-middle-class supporters, and protection against the growing, intrusive power of the secular state. The political alliance with the orthodox Calvinists was constructed on the Catholic side by Herman

---

37 Vis and Janse (eds.), *Staf en storm*.

Schaepman (1844–1903), who was the first Catholic priest to enter parliament. He had to pacify the traditional conservative Catholic elite, but at the same time mobilise political support for Catholic aims. As with the Protestants, this meant a party organisation, with a political programme, and recruiting the votes of the masses. *Rerum Novarum* in 1891 was a vindication of Schaepman's efforts, and by the end of the century he had won most Catholics over to his approach. In 1901 the Roman Catholic and orthodox Protestant political parties formed a coalition under the premiership of Abraham Kuyper, and the emancipation of those groups had been largely achieved. The structure of pillarisation, with its ideological divisions and its system of negotiation at elite level, was in place; moreover its realisation also made a defining contribution to the ways in which the Dutch national consciousness emerged in the heyday of European nation formation.

It was, after all, the century of secularisation, as well as the century of religious revival,[38] and organised religion was being challenged. A secular professionalisation of medicine, poor relief and social work meant that several church functions were being eroded. However, improvements in transport and communication allowed the mobilisation at national level of the emerging confessional organisations: Kuyper reckoned the advent of the affordable daily newspaper to have been critical to his success.[39] The internal integration of religious groups escalated, and they began to take on a new, nation-wide identity, the Calvinists assisted by an idea of their mission in the world, for example in South Africa or the Dutch East Indies.[40] This specifically Calvinist national identity was not valid for the whole nation, but along with others was an essential part of the maturing of Dutch nationalism around 1900.[41]

The Catholics followed a similar though separate path. Their revival or emancipation allowed a whole process of identity reconstruction and self-awareness which saw them take their place, after centuries of subjection, alongside the orthodox Calvinists, as an equal part of the nation. Thus Catholics also created a national identity for themselves,[42] for example in their architecture, in their revived processions, and in their participation in debates like those addressed in *Rerum Novarum*. But these identities were specifically Catholic or

---

38 Van Sas, 'De mythe Nederland', p. 24.
39 'De rede van dr. Kuyper (1897)', in J. C. Boogman and C. A. Tamse (eds.), *Emancipatie in Nederland: de ontvoogding van burgerij en confessionelen in de negentiende eeuw* (The Hague: Nijhoff, 1978), pp. 179–81.
40 Van Koppen, *De geuzen*, pp. 232–3.
41 Kossmann, 'Some questions', p. 12.
42 Raedts, 'Katholieken op zoek', p. 720.

Calvinist, going to make up a multiple rather than a single shared national identity.[43]

At first glance it might seem that these different nationalisms were pulling in different directions. However, nationalism is seldom unified, but at best a force which integrates very different sub-nationalisms. Nation-building efforts were creating a location for the various groups within the framework of the nation at large; it was a search for legitimation, for a just and recognised place for themselves as an active, important, but unique part of the Dutch nation, past, present and future.[44] National identity assisted the process of *verzuiling* by providing a common concept, even if the content of the concept differed considerably from group to group. The growth of the various group national identities in the nineteenth century, often centred around the issues of religion and education, not only contributed to *verzuiling* but itself benefited from the culture of integration and accommodation. Thus religious pillarisation and the evolution of Dutch national identity were mutually complementary, part of the same process, and indeed two sides of the same coin.

43 Wintle, *An economic and social history*, chapter 11.
44 Van Sas, 'De mythe Nederland', pp. 18–19; Van Miert, 'Confessionelen en de natie'.

21

Scandinavia: Lutheranism and national identity

DAG THORKILDSEN

Nation, nationalism and national identity

Nationalism is an ideology or a principle, in which the political and the cultural parts should agree. The political ambition of a nation is independence or domestic self-government, while its cultural aspiration is moral and national regeneration on the basis of a national and historical distinctive character.[1] The main problem when nationalism became a strong political force during the nineteenth century, altering the map of Europe, was, however, that almost no European state matched such goals, because they were composite states. Another obstacle was that the cultural unit called the nation was defined in different ways. The definitions combined language, history, culture, religion and ethnicity in all kinds of permutations. Such was the case in nineteenth-century Scandinavia.

The nation is first of all an imagined community,[2] but it is not an invented community. It is based on historical raw material, which the intellectual elite shapes to form the concept of the nation. The nation as an imagined community means that it depends on people's consciousness of belonging to a national community characterised by certain features. These features create national identity, which becomes an important part also of individual identity. For this reason a national system of education is a central part of nation building. Furthermore, national identity describes that condition in which a mass of people have internalised the symbols of the nation, so that they may act as one psychological group when there is a threat to, or the possibility of enhancement of, nation and national identity.[3]

---

1 Hutchinson, *The dynamics of cultural nationalism*.
2 Anderson, *Imagined communities*.
3 Bloom, *Personal identity*, p. 52.

Scandinavia, Norden and Lutheranism

Literally, Scandinavia is a peninsula consisting of Sweden and Norway, but Denmark is usually also included. 'Norden', however, also includes Finland, the Åland Islands, Iceland and the Faeroe Islands.[4] Even Greenland is sometimes called a Nordic nation, but in the period from 1815 to 1914 it was a Danish colony, closed to the rest of the world.

From the age of Reformation to the time of the Napoleonic wars, Norden was divided into West- and East-Norden. West-Norden consisted of Denmark-Norway, a kingdom including Iceland, the Faeroe Islands and the duchy of Schleswig-Holstein, while East-Norden consisted of the kingdom of Sweden including Finland, and since the treaty of Westphalia (1648) the western part of Pomerania. Thus Sweden-Finland and Denmark-Norway were multi-national states, and for geopolitical reasons they were sworn enemies, fighting a string of inter-Nordic battles.

The churches in the Nordic states were organised as state churches with a Lutheran confession. Since the sixteenth century, the government of these churches – with certain variations – had been an integral part of the government of the state. Furthermore, religious confession and church order were an important part of legislation. The church had not only a religious, but also a political aim. Till the nineteenth century, Lutheran Christianity gave legitimacy to the authorities, and religious confession corresponded to the territorial divisions between states. For this reason, the Nordic churches are often called national churches. This description is, however, more applicable to the period from the nineteenth century, when the Nordic nation-states were established. Prior to that, it is more correct to describe them as territorial churches. For the same reasons contacts between these churches were sporadic, and we find few traces of a consciousness of a religious unity in the Nordic region, though there was a consciousness of belonging to the wider Protestant world.

From the end of the sixteenth century Lutheranism was the only faith that was allowed, with the exception of foreign visitors. However, there was a clear distinction between West- and East-Norden, since these two blocs represented different types of Lutheranism. In Sweden-Finland, the whole Book of Concord was the basis of the Lutheran confession, while in West-Norden only the *Confessio Augustana* and Luther's Minor Catechism were included. Furthermore, liturgies, hymns and church order were different. This distinction between west and east also had consequences for the relationship between

4 Sørensen and Stråth, *The cultural construction of Norden.*

church and state. The West-Nordic tradition was to a certain degree low church Lutheran with a strong integration of church and state. The once mighty bishops had, as a consequence of the Reformation, been replaced by the king's superintendents. But the East-Nordic tradition was high church and confessionally orthodox, with a weaker degree of integration with the state. In Sweden, for example, there was a certain, recognised, ecclesiastical realm, and the archbishop's office had continued through the Reformation. In Finland a similar see was established after the separation from Sweden in 1809. These western and eastern traditions lived in almost total isolation from each other. But such patterns and traditions were challenged and altered during the nineteenth century.

Geopolitical changes and pan-Scandinavianism

The geopolitical map of Norden has changed dramatically since the beginning of the nineteenth century, with a resulting impact on the churches and church life. Sweden lost Swedish Pomerania in 1807. Finland, the eastern part of Lutheran Sweden, was separated from Sweden in 1809 and became an autonomous Russian Grand Duchy, a traumatic loss for Sweden. But the Tsar, Alexander I, promised the Finnish Diet in Porvoo in 1809 to uphold the Lutheran religion of Finland. After the Russian Revolution and a terrible civil war during which the Lutheran Church and the revivalist movement became involved with the war of 'the whites' against 'the reds', Finland became an independent nation-state in 1917–18 with a Lutheran majority church and a small Finnish Orthodox Church (representing some 1 per cent of the population) as established churches.

Denmark became involved in the Napoleonic wars on the French side, went bankrupt in 1813 and had to give up all rights to Norway in the Treaty of Kiel (January 1814). After an important interlude in the spring of 1814 that led to a liberal Norwegian constitution, and a short war against Sweden, a new union between Norway and Sweden under one monarchy and with a common foreign policy was established. This lasted until 1905, when it was dissolved. While the former union with Denmark had made a strong impact on Norwegian society, culture and church life, the union with Sweden was loose. Each country had its own ecclesiastical administration, and owing to an awakening national consciousness there was no wish for any unification of the churches and their separate traditions.

In 1864 Denmark lost Schleswig-Holstein and the island of Als after two German–Danish wars about Schleswig's national identity. The conflict was solved by a referendum after World War I, which fixed the present border between Denmark and Germany. Denmark was, however, further reduced to a small-state nation,[5] and in East-Norden the geopolitical situation remained tense.[6]

At the beginning of the nineteenth century a new political configuration emerged, which superseded the former bitter enmity of Sweden and Denmark. Now the threat to the Nordic region came from Russia in the east and Germany in the south. At the same time, there was a growing consciousness of a common Scandinavian or Nordic identity, based on cultural heritage and history. In this concept the idea of a common Lutheran identity became one of the pillars, and in the 1850s and 1860s the first Scandinavian church assemblies were arranged. From around 1830 a pan-Scandinavian movement emerged, supported originally by students, who arranged spectacular assemblies with hundreds of participants from the whole of Scandinavia. This pan-Scandinavianism was a sort of nationalism with cultural and political goals. Its cultural goal was closer cultural exchange and co-operation between Denmark, Sweden and Norway, while the political goal was union under the same king or a military alliance. Finland, however, stood on the sidelines because of its relations to Russia. Owing to the national conflict with Germany over Schleswig-Holstein, the Danes were strongly united upon an agreed political goal. For this reason and owing to the lack of support from Sweden-Norway, political pan-Scandinavianism came to an end with Denmark's defeat in 1864. But a cultural and practical Scandinavianism or Nordism survived and flourished in the twentieth century, although the break-up of the Swedish–Norwegian union in 1905 led to a brief break in it.

One of the key persons in this Scandinavian awakening was the Danish theologian, minister, poet, historian and politician N. F. S. Grundtvig (1783–1872). While studying theology in Copenhagen, he was influenced by rationalism and the rise of Romanticism. As an ordained chaplain, however, he returned to an historical and biblical Lutheranism. But he continued to search for a kernel

---

5 Iceland was granted partial home-rule in 1918, and declared itself an independent nation-state in 1944. The Faeroe Islands received home-rule in 1948 and Greenland likewise in 1979.

6 In 1920 there was a harsh conflict between Finland and Sweden over the national identity of the Åland Islands, which ended with the islands remaining Finnish, but with home rule and Swedish language and culture. During World War II Finland lost a large part of its core territory, Karelia, to the Soviet Union.

of essential Christianity which would be impervious to rationalistic biblical criticism. In 1825 he found it in the Apostles' Creed. As long as Christianity had existed, people had been baptised and the faith in the Trinitarian God confessed. For this reason the church did not rest upon the Bible, but upon the Creed. At the same time, a basic concept in Grundtvig's religious, cultural and political activities from the beginning of the nineteenth century till his death was the idea of awakening the sleeping and almost forgotten Nordic spirit, which he found expressed in Norse literature and poetry. This Nordic spirit, according to Grundtvig, represented a Nordic and national identity. Since nationality was the expression of the character of the people, Christianity had to become Nordic and national in order to influence the average person. Grundtvig claimed that the Spirit of the Creator manifests itself in the spirit of a people. For this reason creation (nature and culture) stands not merely in contrast to Christian belief and life as in pietism, but has its own value. Likewise a national people has a value in itself, not only as the people of God.

Although pan-Scandinavianism did not succeed politically, it illustrates that there were different concepts of nation-building and national identity in Norden during the nineteenth century, which in the end led to a system of individual Nordic nation-states and churches, as we know them today. The relationship between Lutheranism and national identity varied in these nation-states, but the tradition of being territorial churches was carried on into the nineteenth century with each nation's confession of faith defined in the new constitutions.

Revivalism and nationalism

Religious, national and social revivalism was a characteristic feature of the Nordic nations in the nineteenth century. Revivalist movements played an important role in the transformation of these societies into modern societies. Religious revivalism was generally the predominant strain, with the exception of Iceland, where national revivalism functionally replaced religious revivalism.[7]

Religious revivalism, a phenomenon not easy to classify, occurred not only in the Nordic region, but also in most of the Protestant world in the eighteenth and nineteenth centuries. However, it made an even larger impact on the Nordic societies, especially in Norway and Finland, than in the rest of

---

7 Peturson, 'Väckelser på Island'.

Europe. It created an active and productive ethos, combined with self-discipline and self-constraint, which often led to an improvement in living conditions. Some revivalists became rather wealthy, and revivalism was important in the formation of a middle class. Thus the revivalists were early modernisers and represented an ethos that has been regarded as a prerequisite for a liberal democracy.

This religious revivalism has often been interpreted as a popular reaction to the Enlightenment and rationalism, and the continuity between the pietism of the early eighteenth century and the religious revivalism of the nineteenth century has been stressed. An obvious reason is that the authorities used eighteenth-century legislation dealing with pietistic group assemblies in private homes in an attempt to curb revivalist meetings. In Sweden a low church revivalism in the north and a Free Church movement in other parts had roots going back to eighteenth-century pietism and Moravianism. But at the same time such movements of 'awakening' represented something new. Religious revivalism challenged the unity of premodern agrarian society, created new social forms and mobility, promoted a claim for individual authenticity and thus represented an early modernity.[8]

The early religious revivalist groups emerged around the same time and they had a charismatic leadership. In Denmark radical groups of religious revivalism arose in the area of Vejle and Horsens in the 1790s and an ecstatic group in Korning around 1800.[9] From the mid-1830s, the young theologian Jacob Christian Lindberg (1797–1857) introduced Grundtvigian ideas among the revivalists. The farmer Ole Larsen Skræppenborg (1802–73), a popular preacher and key figure among these groups, managed to reconcile pietistic revivalism with Grundtvig's emphasis on creed, church and sacraments. Thus there was a Grundtvigian wing of Danish revivalism that was national and pro-congregational, and a more apolitical pietistic wing leaning towards separatism and home mission.

In contrast to Grundtvig's emphasis on community and collective life in Church and nation stood his contemporary Søren Kierkegaard (1813–55), the most famous Danish philosopher and theologian of the nineteenth century. He promoted existential individuality, subjectivity and authenticity. In his writings he referred to Christianity as an 'impossibility', and he ended his life forcefully attacking the established church and its leaders for betraying Christ. Thus he gave impulses to both cultural radicalism and religious individualism.

---

8 For a more general discussion of the social roots of evangelicalism see chapter 4 above.
9 Lausten, *A church history of Denmark*, p. 209.

In Norway an influential revival movement occurred at the same time as in Denmark. Hans Nielsen Hauge (1771–1824) had a mystical experience in 1796 which gave him a vocation to preach to others. He was arrested in 1804 accused of serious crimes, and was kept in prison for almost ten years. The imprisonment broke his health and made him more co-operative with the established church. In the longer term his plight gave him mythical status as the martyr of the Norwegian laity, and the patron saint of what has been called a Norwegian national counter-culture. For this reason it was important that in his last will he asked his followers to remain in the established church and to respect the clergy. His followers were eventually totally integrated into the Norwegian Lutheran Church. Some of the second generation (among them Hauge's son) began to study theology to become ordained. Thus revival Christianity with its traces of Moravianism infused the Christianity of the established church, and the pietistic preaching of awakening and personal improvement became the pastoral ideal.

In Finland an ecstatic revival movement started in Savojärvi in 1796, and a few years later the well-known Paavo Ruotsalainen (1777–1852) became its undisputed leader. Although in Sweden and Finland we find religious revivalism in connection with some ministers like Henrik Schartau (1757–1825), canon of Lund cathedral, it is striking that its leaders often had no education and no formal position in the local community. Compared with an earlier pietism, this new religious revivalism was dominated primarily by the laity and expressed a new self-confidence. Furthermore, it represented a challenge to traditional Christian social theory with its 'status hierarchicus triplex' of the three estates of the nobility, clergy and peasantry. The laity no longer wished to remain loyal subjects taught by the clergy. Instead they usurped the right to preach. The political and ecclesiastical authorities treated these revival movements severely and arrested the leaders, because they were interpreted as a type of social rebellion. But the politics of religious unity was not maintained as rigorously in Norway and Denmark as in Sweden, where it led to a brusque polarisation between the established church and religious revivalism and to the establishment of regular Free Churches. The undisputed leader of Swedish revivalism in the nineteenth century was Carl O. Rosenius (1816–68), a lay preacher influenced by Methodism and representing what was called Neo-Evangelism. He published a widespread periodical (*The pietist*), and in 1856 directed a large part of the revival movement into the Swedish Evangelical Mission, a sort of home mission within the Church of Sweden. But as early as the 1870s, a large fraction broke away and established a Congregationalist Free Church (Swedish Covenant Church). In Finland, Denmark and Norway, however, revivalism remained mainly within the established churches and became 'free churches' within the boundaries of the state church. These were also important in the founding of home and overseas missionary societies in the second half of the nineteenth century, which became a distinctive feature of Nordic church life, and gave women a 'public arena' in which to express themselves.

Revivalism was not usually nationalistic. It was often locally based and had inter-Nordic and international links, as in the case of Swedish Roseni-anism (after Rosenius), which also made an impact in Finland, Norway and Denmark. An inter-Nordic ethnic revivalism occurred among the indigenous Saami population in northern Sweden, Norway and Finland, originating with the preaching of the Swedish minister Lars Levi Læstadius (1800–61). Its follow-ers experienced ecstatic phenomena such as jumping, clapping and sighing, and in 1852 a small group caused an uproar in Kautokeino in Norway by slaughtering the local sheriff and tradesman and flogging the pastor. Two of its leaders were executed.

Although the Nordic countries responded to religious revivalism in different ways, the attempts to repress such movements led to claims to political rights such as freedom of assembly and freedom of religion. For this reason we find an interaction between religious revivalism and political liberalism, which meant that the clergy lost control over the religious activity of the laity, and that freedom of religion was gradually realised. This development took place first in Norway and in Denmark in the 1840s, when the laws regulating lay assemblies were abolished in 1842 (in Norway) and 1849 (in Denmark). In Sweden and in Finland, however, the politics of religious unity were sustained through the nineteenth century. Here the main issue was not freedom of religion but the freedom of the church to govern itself. In Sweden full religious freedom was not guaranteed to everyone by law until 1951. It is important to stress that the development of revival movements implied an end to the religious unity of the state, and opened society to modern pluralism. In this way religious revivalism made an important contribution to the secularisation of the Nordic nations. Outside a smaller elite of radical intellectuals this secularisation, however, consisted not in dechristianisation, but rather in a religious and ideological individualisation, differentiation and pluralism.

Church, state and nation

While religious revivalism actualised the question of individual identity, the modernisation of the Nordic societies challenged the traditional identity of the church. As mentioned above, the Nordic churches before the nineteenth century could be accurately described as territorial churches. The concepts of 'state churches', 'folk churches' and 'national churches' were comparatively new, as they presupposed the idea of a church as something different from a state and its government. Together with the concept of Free Churches, which replaced old terms like sects and separatism, all these concepts expressed changes in the understanding of the church which occurred in nineteenth-century Europe. At the same time they expressed new relations between state, people and church. As a simplification, one may say that 'Free Church' and 'state church' are contradictory concepts which refer to different conceptions of the organisation of the church, whilst the terms 'folk church' and 'national church' also have a qualitative dimension.

Among the more recent concepts, that of 'state church' expressed most clearly a continuity with premodern society. Although the concept was new, its content had roots going back to the age of Constantine. In the post-Reformation centuries, however, it was fully displayed in Protestant Europe, especially in the Nordic states during the age of absolutism, when monarchy became hereditary, and the monarch was considered as God's anointed. For this reason, the monarch was obliged to ensure that only the true religion was taught and preached in his realm and to decide all religious questions. The local clergyman represented both God and king, and from the pulpit preached the word of God and proclaimed royal decrees. It was this type of church order, continued in the system of state churches, that gave Lutheranism a privileged position in the Nordic nations. Nevertheless, the concept of a church as a state church meant something new. It implied that state and church were different units with distinct purposes: respectively the *salus publica* and eternal values. But to realise its purpose the state needed the church, because it gave reasons for morality. These views actualised two problems: freedom of religion and church government.

In Norway, for example, the new concept of a state church arose in the period between the liberal constitution of 1814 and the liberalisation of religious legislation in the 1840s. The constitution had made the Evangelical-Lutheran faith the official religion of the Norwegian state, and thus carried on the religious politics of absolutism. But in 1845, an Act allowing Dissenters to practise their faith passed the parliament. From this year it became possible to be a Norwegian citizen without being a member of the Lutheran Church. This was the first occasion on which the expression 'state church' was used in Norwegian history, though the phrase had appeared in Sweden in 1837 and in Denmark in 1842. The new legislation rested upon the modern idea that religious faith is a voluntary and personal matter. For this reason religious affiliation could not be linked to citizenship. Freedom of religion was gradually extended during the second part of the nineteenth century, and during the first two decades of the following century the legislation that made baptism, confirmation and participation in communion compulsory was abolished. A similar development took place in Denmark after the constitution of 1849, though the politics of religious unity continued for longer in Sweden and in Finland. Swedish citizens were not allowed to leave the Church of Sweden before 1860. In Finland Protestant Dissent was not legalised until 1889 and full freedom of religion was granted only in 1922. In this East-Nordic region the changing understanding of the church found its initial expression through the establishment of new church bodies and extended self-government. Sweden received its Church Assembly in 1863 and Finland in 1869.

To simplify, in Denmark and in Norway religious toleration came as a result of an interaction between liberalism and revivalism, while a high church and conservative political line held the field in Sweden. Despite these variations, one may conclude that in Scandinavia, as in the United Kingdom, a distinctive northern European pattern was created during the religious modernisation of the nineteenth century. It consisted in combining a state church with freedom of religion.

Freedom of religion expressed also a new understanding of the people. At the beginning of the nineteenth century the people were understood primarily as Christian subjects. At the end of the century the concept of the people had become far more complex. They had become responsible citizens, an authoritative laity, an organised people, a national people, a people consisting of classes. These changes affected the system of state churches. At the same rate as government of the state was democratised, so was the government of the church. Democratic government by the people superseded absolutist government by the prince, which also had consequences for an understanding of what the church was. It should be a church for and of the people, a democratically governed 'folk church'.

The concept of 'folk church' came to the Nordic nations from the German *Volkskirche*. The German theologian and philosopher Friedrich Schleiermacher (1768–1834) was allegedly the first to use this concept in the early 1820s. He used it in opposition to the coercive religious politics in Prussia, where Fredrick William III was attempting to enforce a union between the Lutheran and Reformed Churches and introduce a new liturgy. In this situation Schleiermacher used *Volkskirche* to describe a church ideal, which was as remote from the coercive and bureaucratic government of the state church as the powerless and non-influential Free Church. A 'folk church' implied to Schleiermacher an alliance between people and church against a repressive state, and in a *Volkskirche* full freedom of individual faith should rule.

Later *Volkskirche* was reshaped in the programme for home mission which Johann Hinrich Wichern (1808–81) presented in 1848 to rechristianise the people through evangelism and Christian social welfare. The regenerate Christians in the German 'folk church' were to carry on missionary work among the unregenerate, in order that the national people and the true church should ultimately become identical bodies.

In addition to these two concepts of 'folk church', the Nordic 'folk church' had similar ambiguity to the concepts of 'people' and 'nation'. The term was used both in a 'democratic' and in an 'ethnic cultural' sense, and these were often mixed together. On the one hand 'folk church' described an inclusive church which comprised the whole, or at least a majority, of the people, and which was governed by the people. On the other hand it was used in the same sense as a 'national church', i.e. it was one of the national characteristics to belong to a certain church, which expressed the history and spirit of the nation.

The concept of a national church became particularly strong in Denmark. The followers of Grundtvig used 'folk church' synonymously with 'national church'. In Grundtvig's paradigm of a universal history based on the seven letters in the book of Revelation, the Nordic 'folk church' was the sixth. For this reason the Nordic nation was to have a tremendously important mission in history, and he saw the Nordic nation in terms of 'a New Jerusalem'.

In Sweden the concept of a national church did not have the same Nordic orientation and framework, and it was not combined with the same measure of freedom as in Denmark. It was rather attached to a defence of the old politics of religious unity. The important church historian and conservative politician Henrik Reuterdahl (1795–1870), later archbishop of Uppsala, used the concept of a national church two years before Grundtvig. Later, as minister of ecclesiastical affairs he claimed that a church which wanted to be united with civil society for that reason could not allow apostasy, and could not possibly accept any kind of private religious assemblies. A similar conservative, but Hegelian, comprehensive idea of state, nation, people and religion is found among other Swedish theologians in the middle of the nineteenth century. But they also met liberal opposition advocated by Johan H. Thomander (1798–1865), professor and later bishop of Lund, who wanted church reforms and ecclesiastical self-government. At the turn of the twentieth century, Swedish national religiousness was strengthened by the crisis and break of the Union with Norway. The Young Church Movement, with its base in student circles in

Uppsala, made the Swedish people the object of a national religious mission, summed up in the slogan 'the Swedish people a people of God'.

The difference between the Danish and Swedish concepts of a national church is an illustration of the problem of using the modern concepts of 'state church', 'folk church' and 'national church' to describe the Nordic churches. Their meaning and function differ in the various nations. The Church of Denmark may be called a state church, since the Danish parliament deals with ecclesiastical legislation and a government ministry takes care of the administration of the church. But the term 'state church' is also used to describe the Danish church before 1849, before the free constitution put an end to it. After 1849 it is preferable to use the expression the 'Danish folk church', although the content of this concept has been disputed. During the debate which preceded the 1849 constitution, 'folk church' was mainly used in a democratic sense. It was, in historical fact, the church of the Danish people, and therefore the people should govern it. At the same time 'folk church' was an important concept to the followers of Grundtvig, although, as already mentioned, they used it in the sense of a national church. Furthermore, their point was that the 'Danish folk church' was only an external civil institution, while the true faithful could reconcile themselves to it, if there was sufficient freedom for both laity and clergy.

In Norway the concept of a 'state church' was used to describe the state's government of the church, and the privileged position of the Church of Norway. The alternative was usually not a free church, but ecclesiastical self-determination within the boundaries of a state church. Yet the concept of a 'folk church' never had the same importance as in Denmark, and was often used synonymously with state church.

The idea of a national church was, however, rather weak in Norway during the nineteenth century. The reason was tension and conflict between confessional orthodox revivalism and the Norwegian followers of Grundtvig in the second half of the century. While the latter represented a liberal and national church ideology, a religious revival movement under the leadership of Gisle Johnson (1824–92), a professor of theology, represented political conservatism and traditional Lutheran loyalty to the authorities, which to Johnson meant loyalty to the Swedish-Norwegian king. On account of the Union, cultural nationalism could easily come into conflict with the authorities if it developed into a political nationalism with demands for national self-government. That was exactly what happened from the 1860s. During a constitutional battle in the 1870s and 1880s, where the issue was a parliamentary system, the king engaged himself on the conservative side and made plans for a *coup d'état*. The conflict ended in 1884 with the impeachment of a conservative government, which meant a victory for the middle-class counter-cultural coalition which gathered around the Liberal Party, and its democratic and national politics.

At the beginning of 1883, when the situation was very tense, Professor Johnson published an appeal to the friends of Christianity in Norway, attacking the Liberal Party and its democratic politics; 450 prominent men in church and society, among them all the bishops, signed it. This appeal scandalised the Norwegian church for decades and made the gap between the church and the political, democratic and national movement obvious. At the turn of the century religious revivalism first began to issue in national revivalism, and during the conflict with Sweden in 1905 sentiments of religious nationalism arose, interpreting national history as an expression of the will of God. The prime minister, Christian Michelsen, deliberately used the Church of Norway to give legitimacy to his secessionist government and to gain support in the two referendums for the break-up of the Union and the acceptance of a new monarchy.

After the ending of the Union, the Young Church Movement in Sweden used 'folk church' to mean a national church, rediscovering the historical roots of church and nation and describing the vital role of the church for people and society. The Church of Sweden could be characterised as 'national church' or 'folk church', but not as 'state church', because the independence of the church was expressed by the establishment of a Church Assembly in 1863. That happened also in Finland, but the Finnish Lutheran Church did not have the same aversion to being characterised as a state church, because the links between state and church concerning administration and economy continued after 1869. It is, however, more common to talk about the two 'folk churches' of Finland since the legislation gives both the Lutheran and the Orthodox churches the same position, and both churches identify themselves qualitatively with the people.

In conclusion, one may say that the 'folk church' was stronger in Denmark and in Sweden than in the other Nordic nations. While 'folk church' in Denmark assumed a liberal low church form in which the church had few administrative bodies of its own, the Swedish tradition of a 'folk church' was conservative high church, stressing ecclesiastical independence. In Norway and in Finland, revivalist influence ensured that the pietistic tradition of Wichern dominated the concept of 'folk church'. Here a 'folk church' with ties to the state was understood as an outer framework, where all the baptised were members. The kernel, however, i.e. the true Christians, were the 'awakened' Christians.

National education

Even before the Reformation, education was the business of the church. In Denmark-Norway attendance at a church school became compulsory for everybody in the eighteenth century as a part of a state pietistic programme to make all subjects pious Christians, and as a preparation for a reintroduced confirmation (1736). In order to know the basic Christian truths the children had to learn to read, which led to the beginning of public schooling. In Sweden-Finland the households were responsible for the religious upbringing of children, and the ministers visited households regularly to hold examinations and ensure the members had the expected knowledge of the Christian truths. The whole of Norden Luther's Minor Catechism and various explanations of it, including numerous Bible quotations, formed the basis of religious education as a summary of the Bible and Christian faith. But the nineteenth century's nation-building and modernisation required another type of education of the population. People needed a new type of knowledge to participate in the progress of society, and society needed a new 'glue' to replace religion. For this reason reform of the educational systems played an important role in the growth of nationalism in the nineteenth century. Through these systems the national myth was spread to the mass of the population. Religion had given legitimacy to premodern society. The prince had symbolised the state and kept it together through the local authorities, which Christians should obey in accordance with the will of God, as commanded by St Paul in Romans 13. Modern society, however, needed another and more functional 'glue' that could keep it together. Legitimacy came not from God, but from the people themselves, and in the same way the primary obligation of the individual became the nation and the people, not the prince and the will of God.

As a result, the ties between public schooling and the Lutheran Church were loosened in all the Nordic countries. Religion was still an important subject in school, but only one among others like national culture, history, language and geography. The education of professional teachers was also improved, their salaries were raised, schoolhouses were built, and the school year was prolonged. School administration was gradually transferred from church to state bodies and local counties. These changes represented a gradual secularisation of public schools, but one which theologians and other churchmen often promoted.

In West-Norden, Grundtvig and his disciples played an important role in the modernisation and nationalisation of education. In Norway, for example, a younger generation including many followers of Grundtvig started a public debate about schooling and suggested fundamental reforms, and they succeeded when a new law passed the parliament in 1860. First, secular subjects became an important part of education, and the vicar's absolute power came to an end with the new boards. The purpose of schools should be to support the parents in raising children, giving them a Christian enlightenment and a general cultural education, together with the knowledge and skills which each member of the society ought to have.

In order to break with the old orthodox and pietistic educational system, Grundtvig developed the idea of the Folk High School, which would give the youth a 'historical-poetical' education, emphasising the people's character and identity. The nation's history, the mother tongue, the ancient Nordic myths and knowledge of the country became the main subjects. In this way these schools became a nursery of nationalism, and the idea was also spread to other nations.

In Sweden it took some time to establish a public school system, and to replace the religious education given in the household on the basis of the catechism, examined by the local vicar. The first school law legislation was introduced in 1842, but in the second half of the nineteenth century liberals, rationalists and members of the Free Churches, especially the Baptists, increasingly opposed the teaching of Lutheranism. The tensions and conflicts ended in 1919, when religious subject matter was reduced, and teaching was made non-confessional. In Finland, where the tradition that religious education should take place in the household was carried on after 1809, the first school law came in 1866, while school administration was separated from the church in 1870. But the basis of religious education remained the catechism.

National language

A part of the legacy of the Lutheran Reformation was the use of the vernacular language in worship, liturgy, hymns, translations of the Bible and catechism. But under the influence of Romanticism, the national language acquired a new function. It now expressed the heart of national identity and became a necessity in the education and unification of the people. School and church were key institutions in promoting such a language to the broad mass of the people and to give it official legitimacy. But most states were composite states with more than one vernacular language. Linked with nationalism, this easily led to conflicts. In Schleswig-Holstein, for example, German language and culture mainly dominated Holstein. The same could be said about southern Schleswig, while the northern part had a Danish-speaking population. Middle

Schleswig, however, had a mixed Danish and German culture and an almost bilingual population. In the west on the coast of the North Sea there lived a Friesian-speaking minority. This situation led to tensions in the 1830s, and the national conflict of Schleswig reached a peak when P. Hiort Lorenzen (1791–1845) insisted on speaking Danish, not German, in the duchy's consulting assembly of estates, but was stopped. That event engaged even Grundtvig. To him the Danish mother tongue, which was spoken first by the peasants, expressed the very heart of Danishness. For this reason he resented the lethal Latin and the non-spiritual German. Grundtvigianism and Folk High Schools became important measures in upholding Danish language and identity in southern Jutland, and after the defeat in 1864 in the whole of Denmark.

In Iceland and the Faeroe Islands the union with Denmark was decisive for the development in the churches, since they were united with the Danish folk church. Before World War I a movement to separate church and state grew in Iceland and several free congregations were established. The confessional basis was, however, Lutheran, and the liturgy the same as in other Icelandic parishes. The motivation, therefore, seems to have been purely national, and after 1944 most of them were reunited with the Church of Iceland. For the same reason it was decided in 1909 that the bishop of Iceland in future should be inaugurated in Iceland. But since there was only one bishop in these islands, a special solution was introduced to secure autonomy. There were always two ministers who were invested as bishops, so that they could act as inaugurating bishops.

In the Faeroe Islands, the vernacular language became the main issue of the national movement, since it was about to be extinguished. One of Grundtvig's sons and even Grundtvig himself took an interest, and in 1888 a claim for using the mother tongue in church was raised. But the struggle for the use of national language in school and church did not succeed until after World War II.

More successful was the strong cultural nationalism in Finland, with the national language as the main issue. It was rooted in the Finnish geopolitical situation after the separation of Finland from Sweden and expressed in the following saying: 'Swedes we are no more, Russians we do not want to become, so let us be Finnish.' Only 13 per cent of the population were primarily Swedish-speaking. Since they were also a privileged class, this prepared the soil for the growth of Finnish nationalism. In the 1840s Johan Snellman (1806–81), philosopher and statesman, formulated a Fennomanic programme to protect Finland's culture and autonomy against Russification, a programme that was further developed by Y. S. Yrjö-Koskinen (1830–1903), an historian and politician. The scholar Elias Lönnrot (1802–84) expressed what it meant to be Finnish, when in 1835 he published Finland's national poem, *Kalevala*, which described the first Finns as a heroic, brave and wise people. Furthermore in the second part of the nineteenth century we find a close interaction between Finnish nationalism, the clergy and religious revivalism. For this reason some have considered Finnish religious and national revivalism to be two sides of the same coin.[10] However, since there are two vernacular languages, Finnish and Swedish, the formula became 'one state, but two nations'.

In Norway the situation was complicated. Danish had been the official administrative and ecclesiastical language for centuries. Nationalist scholars, however, searched for the surviving remains of an Old Norwegian or Norse culture. They examined the dialects spoken in the rural regions of the country. The goal was to change the literary language from Danish into a more Norwegian style, or to construct a New Norwegian literary language on the basis of the rural dialects, one not 'polluted' by the Danish language. In 1869 a Norwegianised hymn book was introduced, but at the same time the first leaflet with hymns in New Norwegian was published. Gradually the Bible was translated into New Norwegian, and the hymns became popular, especially during the dramatic year of 1905. In 1908 New Norwegian was authorised as the liturgical language, but it remained a minority language.

During the nineteenth century, Scandinavia changed from unionism with two blocs to a separatist nationalism, creating a new pattern of nation-states that is called Norden. As a part of these changes the former Lutheran territorial churches became national and folk churches. At the same time religious unity was gradually superseded by freedom of religion and pluralism, a process in which religious revivalism played an important role. In these processes, the individuality of the Nordic churches was further developed, although the division between West- and East-Norden remained.

10 Eino Murtorinne, 'Den fennomanska rörelsen'.

22

'Christian America' and 'Christian Canada'

MARK A. NOLL

In the century from 1815 to 1914, the churches of North America experienced an expansion all but unprecedented in the modern history of Christianity. In an era of break-neck population growth (United States, from 8,400,000 to 99,100,000; Canada, from about 600,000 to about 8,000,000), rates of church adherence increased even more rapidly – in the United States from under one-fourth of the population to over two-fifths, and in Canada from an even smaller proportion at the start of the period to an even higher proportion at the end. Yet this era was just as noteworthy for how innovatively religion was being organised as for how rapidly the churches were growing. Christian believers in the United States gloried in their 'freedom', by which they meant they neither enjoyed nor sought the protection of establishment. In Canada, there was less enthusiasm about disestablishment, but by the second half of the century a similar state of affairs prevailed there. The self-starting efforts of denominations and the mobilisation of voluntary societies had taken the place of formal church–state ties, but the result was a more thorough Christianisation of the population than in Europe and an exertion of social influence at least as powerful as in the old world. In 1854 the learned Swiss émigré Philip Schaff returned to Europe and reported on his new land. Schaff granted that Americans had taken an unprecedented step in separating the churches from 'the temporal power', but insisted none the less that 'Christianity, as the free expression of personal conviction and of the national character, has even greater power over the mind, than when enjoined by civil laws and upheld by police regulations.' To Schaff, the proof could be discerned in practice:

> the strict observance of the Sabbath, the countless church and religious schools, the zealous support of Bible and Tract societies, of domestic and foreign missions, the numerous revivals, the general attendance on divine worship, and the custom of family devotion – all expressions of the general

Christian character of the people, in which the Americans are already in advance of most of the old Christian nations of Europe.[1]

For all its dynamism, the course of Christianity in North America throughout this period was never tranquil. If there were triumphs of democratic churchmanship, there were also moral failures like the continuation of slavery in the United States to the 1860s or the destitution of urban populations at the end of the century. If both the United States and Canada opened settlement to many kinds of Christians, the mere expanse of geography could not entirely eliminate ongoing religious antagonism that sometimes flared into violence. If liberating the churches from European dependence on the state gave them extraordinary influence in constructing two national cultures, that same condition left churches fragmented and confused in responding to the challenges confronting religion in the latter part of the nineteenth century. In both the United States and Canada, the churches succeeded in fashioning what may genuinely be regarded as 'Christian societies'. But that fashioning always mingled tragedy with triumph, irony with achievement, ambiguity with advance.

The construction of 'Christian America', 1815–1844

The driving force in the religious history of the United States during the first half of the nineteenth century was evangelical Christianity. Following the War for Independence (1776–83), religious uncertainty had proceeded in tandem with political uncertainty. After the revival fires of the colonial Great Awakening cooled in the 1750s, church growth for a half-century lagged behind the general rise in population. The authority of the colonies' two established churches – Congregational in New England, Anglican in the South – drained away in the face of the free market in religion defined by the first amendment to the United States Constitution (1791): 'Congress shall make no law respecting an establishment of religion, or prohibiting the free exercise thereof.' With only a few exceptions the religious faith of the founding fathers was far closer to the fashionable Deism of the Age of Enlightenment than to the white heat of revival. Into this parlous situation burst evangelical renewal.

The Christianity that prevailed was best exemplified by Francis Asbury (1745–1816), whom John Wesley in 1771 dispatched to America to help plant Methodism in the new world. As Asbury travelled annually through the United

---

1 Schaff, *America*, p. 76.

States, he preached the new birth, recruited young men to join him as itinerants, organised class meetings for converts and seekers, appointed elders to oversee local activities, conducted quarterly and annual conferences, managed the publication of hymnals, pamphlets and devotional manuals, carried on an extensive correspondence, counselled local Methodists as they began to construct church buildings, and fended off any who would divert the Methodists from their spiritual concerns. Although somewhat more open to tradition than many of their American contemporaries, Methodists, like the other key leaders of early national religion, innovated ceaselessly in order to improvise organisational and ideological forms appropriate for a thinly spread, freedom-obsessed and market-oriented population. The normal pattern for Methodist itinerants was to preach on the move for three or five or ten years and then to marry and 'locate' as unpaid exhorters or preachers. The main support for itinerants came from sympathetic women, sometimes joined by their husbands, who responded to the message and opened their homes to the wayfarers.

From these exertions there were spectacular results. In 1776, Asbury was assisted by twenty-four itinerants; at his death in 1816 there were 695; that number by 1844 had risen to 4,479 (with another 8,101 Methodists settled as preachers in localities). By comparison, the active duty roster of the United States army in 1844 numbered only 8,730. At the outbreak of the Civil War in 1861, there were almost 20,000 Methodist churches and over 1.7 million full members; about a third of American church adherents were Methodists.[2]

But Methodists were far from the only energetic revivalists. Baptist success depended upon the labours of laymen who plied their trades during the week and turned to preaching on Sunday. As intense localists, Baptists usually required a public profession of faith before allowing participation in the ordinances of baptism and the Lord's Supper. The commitment to believers' baptism, which had marked Baptists as sectarian in Britain, worked much more effectively in the mobile, expanding, and traditionless spaces of the new American nation. By the mid-1840s, there were more than three times the number of Baptist churches (over 11,000) as Congregational and Episcopal combined (respectively, about 1,500 and 2,000).

A full roster of others contributed to the evangelical surge. Alexander Campbell (1788–1866), who immigrated from Northern Ireland, and Barton W. Stone (1772–1844), who had trained for the Presbyterian ministry before helping with a memorable revival at Cane Ridge, Kentucky, in August 1801, led a

---

2 *Minutes of the annual conferences of the Methodist Episcopal Church* (New York: T. Mason and G. Lane, 1840–61).

'Restoration' movement that turned in exasperation away from confessions, synods and inherited traditions in order to follow 'no creed but the Bible'. Their programme of antidenominational ecumenism led, in typical American fashion, to the creation in 1831 of a denominational-like fellowship known simply as the Christian Church (Disciples of Christ). By 1860 there were nearly 2,100 Disciples churches concentrated in the upper South and the new states of the Midwest.

Among the older churches, Presbyterians did best at adjusting to the helter-skelter realities of the new nation. Their main contribution to organisational innovation was the free-standing theological seminary, a distinctly American institution pioneered by Congregationalists at Andover, Massachusetts, in 1808. By 1860 there were at least fifty such schools existing to prepare college graduates for the ministry. One-fourth were Presbyterian, with Princeton in New Jersey as the leader. Presbyterians, by insisting on an educated ministry, could not respond as rapidly as Methodists, Baptists and Disciples to the swiftly opening new frontier. But their strenuous efforts at melding old world churchly standards to new world sectarian realities paid off – over 2,000 churches by 1830, over 6,400 by 1860.

In the absence of formal church establishments, voluntary societies provided the most effective means to address problems requiring more than a local response. The most widely supported, like the American Board of Commissioners for Foreign Missions (1810) and the American Bible Society (1816), reached their peak effectiveness in the 1830s, by which time they had inspired the formation of many others, including the American Sunday-School Union (1824) and the American Anti-Slavery Society (1833). Voluntary agencies co-ordinated programmes of social welfare, promoted higher education, encouraged literacy and advanced foreign contacts through missions when no other national organisations, governmental or private, were taking up such tasks.

Inadvertently, the expanding evangelical denominations and the burgeoning voluntary agencies served a secular purpose by creating national infrastructures. In 1838 Nathan Bangs (1778–1862) – tireless itinerant, pioneer publisher, historian and theologian – averred that the Methodists had never intended to exercise political influence. Yet because of 'its extensive spread in this country, the hallowing influence it has exerted in society in uniting in one compact body so many members, through the medium of an itinerant ministry, interchanging from north and south, and from east to west', Methodism had contributed substantially 'to the union and prosperity of the nation'.[3] America's republican, independent and antiauthoritarian experiment – especially when riven by sharp economic, political and racial differences – was hardly capable of putting together a national culture. Evangelical Protestants, because they adapted so well to the new nation's republican values and to the circumstances of a far-flung population, did the job.

They also opened the door to public service by women. The sisters Sarah (1792–1873) and Angelina Grimké (1805–79) became active advocates against slavery after they moved from their native South Carolina to Philadelphia. Angelina's tract, *An appeal to the Christian women of the South* (1836), won recognition in the abolitionist movement but also caused conservatives to worry about the dissolution of family order. When such public advocacy came under fire, Sarah responded with biblical, political and philosophical arguments in *Letters on the equality of the sexes, and the condition of women* (1838). Other women, like the revivalist Harriet Livermore, who in 1827 was the first woman to preach a sermon before the United States Congress, innovated as public speakers. Still others won recognition for service alongside their husbands, such as Ann Hasseltine Judson (1789–1826), Sarah Boardman Judson (1803–45) and Emily Chubbuck Judson (1817–54), successive wives of Adoniram Judson, pioneer Baptist missionary to Burma; their labours as translators and their fortitude in suffering and death made them well-publicised icons of evangelical faithfulness.

The driving force of Methodist expansion also exerted a considerable impact on American theology. Varieties of Calvinism that had dominated the colonial period remained alive in the new republic, especially through the works of Jonathan Edwards (1703–58). Against such views, Methodists urged a stronger sense of human ability, both in appropriating salvation and in exercising the rights of the redeemed to advance towards Christian perfection. Methodists at first did most of their theologising through sermons, hymns and personal exhortations. But by the 1830s more formal presentations came from scholars like Wilbur Fisk (1792–1839), who explained Methodist reliance on divine grace in terms of the era's popular faculty psychology, and from authors like Phoebe Palmer (1807–74), who stressed the immediate availability of holiness to the earnest biblical seeker.

American theology was affected even more directly when traditional Calvinists adjusted their convictions to fit the ideological certainties of the new

---

3 Nathan Bangs, *A history of the Methodist Episcopal Church*, 4 vols. (New York: T. Mason and G. Lane, 1838–41), vol. 1, p. 46.

nation. By making peace with republican political reasoning, which still scandalised orthodox believers in Europe, the American churches were able to influence the common polity. In turn, republican wariness of arbitrary power and republican trust in the capacities of self-directed citizens nudged hereditary Calvinism towards accepting a self-determining power of the human will and de-emphasising total divine sovereignty. Similarly, popular forms of common-sense philosophy that had supported political revolution also pushed theologians towards conceding a universal validity to human ethical intuitions and so to weakening the Augustinian character of much earlier American theology.

The leading proponent of this 'modified Calvinism' was N. W. Taylor (1786–1858), professor at Yale College who taught 'the moral government of God' as a way of fending off both Unitarians on his left and conservative Presbyterians on his right. Charles Finney (1792–1875), the era's most effective revivalist, was also an earnest advocate of the new theology, especially through his *Lectures on revival* (1835), which depicted evangelism as a science to be programmed for definite results, if only believers would exert themselves appropriately. Conservatives who challenged the wisdom of such theological adjustments were led by Charles Hodge (1797–1878) of Princeton Seminary, whose writings conceded only a little to the spirit of the new American age. In the late 1840s, Horace Bushnell (1802–72) of Hartford abandoned 'common-sense' theology for an alternative at once both more evangelical and more liberal.

When Alexis de Tocqueville visited the United States in the early 1830s, he was most struck by the indirect influence of the churches, and he thought he knew why such influence was possible: 'On my arrival in the United States it was the religious aspect of the country that first struck my eye . . . Among us, I had seen the spirit of religion and the spirit of freedom almost always move in contrary directions. Here I found them united intimately with one another: they reigned together on the same soil.'[4]

The unravelling of 'Christian America', 1844–1865

There were complications as revivalistic Protestants set about winning the new nation for Christ. For one, Native Americans had to be shunted aside, even when, as in the case of the Cherokee, they fully embraced the vision of a free and Christian future. Guided by energetic leaders like Elias Boudinot (1802–39), the Cherokee of Georgia were well advanced in building their own miniature

---

4 Tocqueville, *Democracy in America*, p. 282.

Christian republic when in the mid-1830s land hunger, racial antagonism and the connivance of President Andrew Jackson drove them onto 'a trail of tears' to barren reservations in the trans-Mississippi West. The contradictions of 'Christian America' were felt even more strongly by African Americans whose story is told in chapter 26 of this volume.

Aspirations for a 'Christian America' defined by evangelical Protestants of British background also collided with the reality of religious pluralism. Protestant bodies that wanted to maintain old world forms – first the Dutch and German Reformed and then the Lutherans – vacillated over whether to join the evangelical phalanx. Sectarians like Mennonites, Moravians and the Church of the Brethren tried hard to maintain their peace testimony in distinction from 'Yankee' religion. Quakers divided in this period between more evangelical 'Gurneyites' (after the Englishman J. J. Gurney) and more rationalistic 'Hicksites' (after the Long Island farmer Elias Hicks), but all debated how far they should go in aligning themselves with the era's dominant Protestants. From early in the nineteenth century, a high church Episcopal movement led by John Henry Hobart (1775–1830) of New York defended tradition and criticised revivalism, and so set itself at cross-purposes with popular evangelicalism. Further removed from convention were followers of William Miller (1782–1849), who predicted the Second Coming of Christ for around 1843. After the 'Great Disappointment', Miller's ex-disciples went on to establish the Seventh-day Adventist and Advent Christian churches. Joseph Smith (1805–44), founder of the Church of Jesus Christ of Latter-Day Saints, proclaimed a new revelation in *The Book of Mormon* that represented even further protest against the norm. But the most important exception to a Protestant evangelical construction of 'Christian America' came from the burgeoning presence of Roman Catholics.

At the time of the nation's founding in 1776 there were only 25,000 Catholics served by only twenty-three priests. Eighty-five years later the census of 1860 counted 2,550 Catholic churches with a constituency of close to 3 million (about 10 per cent of the national population). This spectacular expansion continued – in 1916 the census counted 15,120 churches and a membership of almost 16 million (or 16 per cent of the population).

For Catholics, the manifest opportunities of the new world were accompanied by a full range of problems, among which the antagonism of Protestants was prominent. Lyman Beecher (1775–1863), the tireless Congregational reformer, exemplified that antagonism in 1835 with a widely circulated tract, *A plea for the west*, that targeted the Roman Catholic Church as the greatest danger to the expansion of both American freedom and true Christianity. The year before, a Boston mob had torched an Ursuline Convent school in

Charlestown, Massachusetts, under the erroneous suspicion that the nuns were corrupting their charges. In 1840, the Irish-born Catholic bishop of New York, John Hughes, asked the city's Public School Society to provide money for Catholic schools to balance its support for Protestant-run establishments. The resulting quarrel flared close to violence and earned Hughes his nickname of 'Dagger John' for his vigorous defence of Catholic churches. The antebellum climax of anti-Catholicism was the formation in 1854 of the American Party, which held that immigrants, especially Roman Catholics, were corrupting America's Anglo-Saxon stock and subverting American liberties.

The most pressing religious difficulties for an immigrant church were the strains created by immigration itself, especially with the multiplication of ethnic origins. Early came Irish and Germans, later large numbers were added from Poland, Lithuania, Hungary, Croatia, Czechoslovakia and Italy. The organisation of parishes, and of ecclesiastical thinking, around ethnic loyalties maintained the centrality of the church for uprooted populations, but also created internal friction. Meanwhile, great sacrifices by local communities built churches. Dedicated priests, lay brothers and nuns staffed these churches, even as they oversaw the development of schools, insurance societies, youth organisations, newspapers and other accoutrements of civilisation.

The second generation of American bishops included leaders like Irish-born John England (1786–1842) of Charleston, South Carolina, who directly addressed the persistent Protestant charge that no church owing allegiance to the pope could ever be truly loyal to the United States. While eager to maintain traditional spiritual authority, England assured his fellow Americans that the pope did not have 'any power or right to interfere with the allegiance that we owe to our state; nor to interfere in or with the concerns of the civil policy or the temporal government thereof, or of the United States of America'.[5] Other adjustments required mediation between ancient church practice and habits of American democracy. Trustees of local congregations often desired to follow the practice of American Protestants and vest ownership of churches in themselves. With an American environment enthusiastic for the rights of the common man, it took more than fifty years to bring American Catholics in line with historic Catholic practice.

To meet the multiple challenges of American life, a Catholic form of voluntary activity also emerged as, following European examples, Americans began to establish their own religious orders. The former Episcopalian Elizabeth Ann Seton (1776–1821) was the most notable of early pioneers, founding a new

5 Carey (ed.), *American Catholic religious thought*, p. 81.

order in Baltimore, the Sisters of Charity, whose members gave themselves to education as well as the care of orphans.

Growing religious diversity undercut aspirations for a 'Christian America' defined in evangelical terms. But stresses within the dominant Protestant movements were just as corrosive. The social promise of evangelical revival early in the century was that, by converting individuals, society could be transformed. By the 1830s, the persistence of many social problems, especially slavery, belied this facile assumption. For their part, the voluntary agencies were also beset by mounting difficulties. Temperance societies hesitated over whether to seek all-out prohibition of alcohol, and then found that prohibition laws could not deliver all the social benefits they had seemed to offer.

But the greatest difficulty was slavery. The American Colonization Society, which tried to raise money to send blacks to Africa, never could reach its funding goals and was roundly criticised by African Americans. The American Anti-Slavery Society faltered when its demands for immediate emancipation generated ever stronger defences of slavery, the most powerful of which drew on the same biblical resources that abolitionists used to appeal for reform. In 1840 the Anti-Slavery Society itself divided between those who wanted to extend reforms to include women's rights and those who wanted to remain focused on slavery.

Schism among the national Protestant denominations was an even stronger blow. In 1837, questions over slavery played a small part in dividing the Presbyterian church between a New School and an Old School. More extensive was the schism that divided the Baptist mission agency into southern and northern parts in 1844–5. Out of this breach, which resulted from northern complaints about the appointment of slave-holding missionaries, arose the Southern Baptist Convention, which would by the early twentieth century become the largest Protestant denomination. Most serious was the schism of the Methodists, also in 1844–5, and over virtually the same issue – in this case, whether bishops should hold slaves. Leaders at the time looked upon the Baptist and Methodist schisms with great trepidation. Words from the last public speech in 1850 of the Southern statesman John C. Calhoun were long remembered: when the national bonds represented by the great Protestant denominations would all be broken, 'nothing will be left to hold the States together except force'.[6]

---

6 John C. Calhoun, *The works of John C. Calhoun*, vol. IV: *Speeches of John C. Calhoun, delivered in the House of Representatives and the Senate of the United States*, ed. Richard K. Crallé (New York: D. Appleton, 1854), pp. 557–8.

After the revolutionary era, American churches promoting reasonably orthodox beliefs flourished, precisely *because* they adapted so energetically to the republican freedoms won by the War for Independence. But by 1860 the mixture of religious and political freedom had taken on a sobering aspect. In both the North and the South, evangelical Christians, who held that the Bible was true and who trusted their own understandings of Scripture above all other religious authorities, constituted the most influential religious presence. Religion was now at a higher point of public influence than at any time in American history. Yet these Protestants recognised no authority greater than the Bible for adjudicating disagreements over interpretations of Scripture. In 1860 such fundamental disagreement existed on what the Bible had to say about slavery that the churches were no help when the nation tore itself apart over the issue.

The Civil War itself offered great practical challenges to the churches, which were well met through the North's Christian Commission and, especially in the South, by a powerful surge of revival in the camps. The disintegration of 'Christian America' caused by competing claims about what it meant for a nation to be Christianised was a different matter. As a demographic indication of broader change, it was during the 1860s, while Baptists, Presbyterians, Methodists and other Protestants were caught up in the civil strife, that the Roman Catholic Church became the largest Christian denomination in the United States.

Dilemmas of 'Christian America', 1865–1914

Significant changes in American Christianity arose directly from the Civil War itself. In the victorious North concern for containing slavery gave way to a fixation on inner spirituality and to coping with industrialisation, the creation of large bureaucracies in government and industry, and the movement of people from farms to cities. For the defeated South, religion grew stronger, but at a price. In the wake of the War's economic and cultural devastation, evangelical denominations offered profound consolation. Yet they were also complicit in the passage of Jim Crow laws against blacks and the dreadful wave of lynchings that began in the 1870s and lasted for more than fifty years.

The Civil War also affected the way in which the West was incorporated into national religious life. Protestants soon found that the influence they had exerted east of the Mississippi would not extend much beyond the Mississippi, where a large Hispanic Catholic population already existed in the Southwest, Mormon settlements had spread over Utah and Idaho, Indian reservations (with a mixture of indigenous and Christian faiths) were in place, immigrants from Asia were entering the region, and traditional resistance to religion of all kinds was widespread.

In the half-century after the war, religious diversification also intensified. Most important were Roman Catholics who began to exert a significant political impact in many northern cities. Protestants of non-British background, especially Lutherans from Germany and Scandinavia, proliferated. By 1900 substantial numbers of Eastern Orthodox from Greece and Russia were joining the nation's older Orthodox communities in Alaska and California. And soon a growing number of Americans, particularly Jews, were not connected to Christianity in any form. Protestants of the older sort continued to promote a full circle of activity, but a United States where Protestants enjoyed universal supremacy was steadily passing away.

Sharp intellectual challenges worked to the same end. The biggest was the growing confidence in science, exemplified by the great reputation of Charles Darwin's *On the origin of species* (1859). The problem was not evolution as such, since many traditional Christians held that God may have used evolutionary processes to shape the natural order. As an example, the conservative Presbyterian Benjamin B. Warfield (1851–1921) of Princeton Theological Seminary championed the inerrancy of Scripture but also held that biblical faith could accommodate evolution. The problem was rather that more and more well-known intellectuals were using evolution as a grand idea to replace traditional views of God and his design of the world. They embraced instead the vision of a future guided by science, but a science triumphant in what an early president of Cornell University, Andrew Dickson White, called *A history of the warfare of science with theology* (1896).[7]

New views of the Bible also upset inherited religious opinions. In the years 1881–3 Presbyterians introduced American readers to European critical Bible scholarship through an extensive debate in the *Presbyterian Review*. Within decades, the relatively small differences reflected in this intra-Presbyterian debate had become chasms that divided most professional students of the Bible, who argued that Scripture should be interpreted as any other ancient text, from many people in the pews, who continued to trust in the Scriptures as the divinely inspired and divinely preserved Word of God.

In popular venues, Protestants found their most notable champion in Dwight Lyman Moody (1837–99), a native New Englander transplanted to Chicago, where during the Civil War he was active in the work of the Young

---

7 For a fuller discussion see chapter 11 above.

Men's Christian Association (YMCA). Later he teamed up with the musician and publisher Ira Sankey (1840–1908) to mount large public meetings. Moody's great popularity as an urban evangelist did not make him callous to the needs of society, but his focus was on the soul. His broader significance lay in the institutions he founded, including a Bible training centre for lay workers in Chicago (later the Moody Bible Institute) and the Student Volunteer Movement (1876) that encouraged thousands of students to dedicate their lives to service as foreign missionaries.

While Moody's solution to the problems of a rapidly industrialising America was primarily preaching, many others addressed social and political issues directly. The Salvation Army, founded in London by William and Catherine Booth in the 1860s, was one of the most successful. The Booths' daughter, Evangeline (1865–1950), eventually came to direct the work of the Army in the United States, where she promoted the same range of activities that her parents had advanced in England – provision of food, shelter and medical assistance; vocational training, elementary schooling and internships in manufacturing and farming; visits to prisons, legal aid for the indigent and inexpensive coal in the winter.

Better known at the time was an informal movement called the Social Gospel. Its early leaders included Washington Gladden (1836–1918), a minister in Springfield, Massachusetts, and Columbus, Ohio, who in 1876 published *Working people and their employers*, an appeal for fairness towards labour, and who later acted for a national Congregational organisation in rejecting a gift from oil magnate John D. Rockefeller as tainted money. The most important voice in the American Social Gospel belonged to Walter Rauschenbusch (1861–1918), a German-American Baptist whose friendship with the New York City socialist Henry George led him to propose governmental actions for repairing the wounds of industrialisation. The Bible was an even stronger influence, as illustrated by his *Christianity and the social crisis* (1907), which drew on the Old Testament prophets as well as New Testament warnings about the dangers of money.

Social concern of a different sort drove large-scale efforts to control the production and use of alcoholic beverages. The most successful agency working for this reform was the Women's Christian Temperance Union (WCTU), which was guided by the able Frances Willard (1839–98), a Methodist teacher and collaborator with D. L. Moody, who looked upon temperance as the most important means of protecting women, children and the urban poor from the vagaries of modern industrial society.

In the face of the rapid social, intellectual and demographic change, earlier tensions in American Protestantism developed into broad fissures. Along with the growing presence of Lutherans and other newer Protestant groups, the evangelicals who had dominated nineteenth-century society fell apart into quarrels among themselves. Self-conscious modernists, like Arthur Cushman McGiffert (1861–1933) of Union Theological Seminary in New York and Shailer Mathews (1863–1941) at the University of Chicago, tried to adjust Christianity to new science, new economic expansion, and new ideals of human progress. For McGiffert, the apostle Paul was a villain who had undercut the simple teaching of the peace-loving Jesus. Mathews's *The faith of modernism* (1924) summarised what he had been teaching for many years about the need to move beyond immature supernaturalism in order to secure the morality necessary for peace in the modern world.

Fundamentalists offered the counterpart to modernists. A few were intellectuals, like J. Gresham Machen (1881–1937), whose major polemic, *Christianity and liberalism* (1923), defined the religion of McGiffert and Mathews as antithetical to the genuine article. More typical were popular presentations like those in a series of booklets, *The Fundamentals: a testimony to the truth* (1910–15), which mixed sophisticated argument and testimonial exhortation to defend the reality of the Bible as the inspired Word of God, the Virgin Birth of Christ, his substitutionary death on the cross and the promise of his literal Second Coming. The prominence of apocalyptic belief among fundamentalists owed much to a new theology of premillennial dispensationalism that had risen to popularity at prophecy conferences from the late 1880s. The dispensational emphasis on a mostly literal interpretation of Scripture focused on biblical prophecy received its most influential formulation in a Bible annotated by a lawyer turned minister, C. I. Scofield (1843–1921).

A third important strand of American Protestantism was associated with themes of holiness as defined by Phoebe Palmer and, with some variation, the revivalist Charles G. Finney. Free Methodists, Wesleyan Methodists and the National Campmeeting Association for the Promotion of Christian Holiness (1867) had kept those emphases alive and nurtured a resurgence of interest at the end of the century. In pursuit of holiness as a goal of Christian life and organising principle for Christian fellowship, Daniel Sidney Warner in 1881 led a group out of the national Methodist denominations to form the Church of God (Anderson, Indiana). A few years later Phineas F. Bresee (1838–1916) started a new congregation in Los Angeles, which proved to be a precipitate for others who in 1907 organised the Church of the Nazarene.

From the holiness movement, as an extrapolation with worldwide significance, arose modern Pentecostalism. Soon after William J. Seymour (1870–
1922), an African-American preacher, founded the Apostolic Faith Gospel Mission in 1906 at an abandoned Methodist church on Azusa Street in Los Angeles,
the message he had learned about the sign gifts of the Holy Spirit from Charles
Fox Parham (1873–1929) and other holiness evangelists created a local sensation.
Hispanics, blacks and Caucasians streamed to Azusa Street, and they were soon
joined by a wide array of international visitors, who were eager to experience
physical healing, ecstatic worship and the gift of tongues. Out of the sanctified
chaos of early Pentecostalism eventually arose several major denominations,
including the Church of God in Christ, organised by C. H. Mason (1866–1961),
which served a mostly black constituency, and the Assemblies of God, which
was established in 1914 to serve mostly white churches.

Also responding to the shifting contours of a rapidly changing America were
Roman Catholics, especially in what came to be known as the 'Americanist'
controversy. The flash point was the publication in 1897 of a French translation
of a biography of Isaac Hecker (1819–88), an adult convert who had founded
the Paulists as a preaching, educational and publishing order designed especially for reaching other Americans. Attention to this book exacerbated an
ongoing debate in the American hierarchy between those who favoured as
much accommodation to American ways as possible and conservatives who
wanted to protect American Catholics from the corrosion of democracy.

The upshot from a tangle of intra-American and European-American con-
tentions was a pair of documents from Pope Leo XIII. In 1895, an encyclical,
Longinqua Oceani, praised American Catholics for heroic efforts on behalf of the
church, but also warned them about too easily accepting American notions like
the separation of church and state as universal norms. This letter was followed
in 1899 by an encyclical, *Testem Benevolentiae*, which condemned 'Americanism' by name as the mistaken desire for the church to conform to the shape
of liberal, individualistic culture. American reactions were mixed, with some
conservative bishops hailing the vindication of their cause, while other leaders
of the American church like James Cardinal Gibbons (1834–1921) of Baltimore
remained unfazed. Gibbons agreed that it was wrong to change the church's
faith but avowed that teaching such as the pope condemned was not permitted
in the American church.

Unlike their Protestant contemporaries, Catholics did not have a tradition of
proprietary ownership of American culture. But with all American believers at
the start of the twentieth century, they realised that intentional effort was now
required to sustain historical Christianity – whether Catholic, Protestant or

Orthodox, whether pietistic, communal or institutional – amid the economic, political and demographic challenges of a modern era.

The alternative 'Christian America': Canada

The nineteenth-century history of Christianity in Canada looks strikingly similar to what took place in the United States. Like their American contemporaries, Canadian believers faced a vast sub-continent where great dedication was required to build churches and the institutions of Christian civilisation. As in the United States, public life reflected the endeavours of numerous believers, nowhere more obviously than at the creation of the Canadian confederation in 1867. Following the suggestion of a Methodist politician, Leonard Tilley of New Brunswick, Canada became a 'Dominion' rather than a 'Kingdom', in direct application of Psalm 72:8 – 'He shall have dominion also from sea to sea.'

But if there was much in common between the histories of Christianity in the United States and Canada, there was also much that differed. Most importantly, Roman Catholicism was the first Christian presence and Protestantism in several varieties only a later addition. When in the nineteenth century Protestant numbers in Upper Canada (later Ontario) caught up to the Catholics in Quebec, the result was a delicate negotiated balance. Canadians of all kinds, including residents in the Atlantic Maritime provinces, also remained closer to French, English, Scottish and Irish church practices than their peers in the United States. Canada's most significant political developments from 1815 to 1914 were reactive: resisting American invasion and incorporation during the War of 1812, rejecting armed attempts in 1837 and 1838 to turn Upper Canada and Lower Canada (Quebec) into republican imitations of the United States, and embracing confederation in 1867 as, in part, a cautionary move against the great military might displayed by the Union in the American Civil War. The prime factors of public life – ongoing French–English bilateralism, the rejection of republican revolution in favour of loyalty to Britain, and a persistent dialectic of attraction cum aversion to the United States – were also prime factors in shaping the churches.

Each of the three original Canadian regions faced significant religious challenges during the first part of the nineteenth century. After a spurt of growth with the arrival of American Loyalists in the 1780s, and a liminal period of revival in the 'New Light stir' under the charismatic Henry Alline (1748–84), the Maritimes dropped back into the settled patterns that prevailed for the rest of the century. Religious leadership was supplied by vigorous contingents of Scottish Presbyterians, Methodists influenced by British Wesleyanism, con-servative Anglicans, increasingly Calvinistic Baptists and significant numbers of active Catholics (especially the Acadians of New Brunswick). The minis-terial and educational labours of Thomas McCulloch (1776–1843), founder of Nova Scotia's Pictou Academy, helped define what historians have called the region's 'evangelical creed'. But a stagnating economy, the slowing of immi-gration and a sense of regional isolation soon settled in over the provinces as well. In this setting, well-disciplined and socially influential churches pro-vided the critical structure for Maritime life and a strong anchor for Maritime identity.

In Lower Canada the Constitutional Act of 1791 left in place the legal and social structures of New France, including an established status for the Roman Catholic Church. Half-hearted British efforts at transforming Quebec into an English Protestant province were almost entirely abandoned after Bishop Joseph-Octave Plessis (1763–1825) rallied support for the British during the War of 1812. By 1819, when Lower Canada was divided into two dioceses, with about 200,000 Catholics each in Quebec and Montreal, religious orders had taken responsibility for most of the province's schools as well as its hospitals and social services. None the less, a rising professional class of doctors, lawyers and small businessmen resisted episcopal authority. When Louis-Joseph Papineau (1786–1871) began to agitate for republican political reform, he put himself at odds with both British governors and the church. The armed revolt that followed in 1837 was quickly put down; its leaders were executed or, like Papineau, fled to the United States.

During the early 1840s, events centred in Montreal promoted a more homo-geneous Catholic presence. In December 1840 and January 1841, Mgr Charles de Forbin-Janson, co-founder of the Missionaires de France (later known as the Fathers of Mercy), conducted a well-attended mission that stressed the virtues of the sacraments. The most important local support for Forbin-Janson was offered by Mgr Ignace Bourget (1799–1885), soon to be Montreal's second bishop. Over the next few years, revulsion against revolution, a widespread renewal of devotion and Bourget's dedicated leadership combined to create a powerful Catholic presence. Bourget stabilised the recruitment of priests, organised religious orders to staff Quebec's schools and hospitals, and encour-aged a distinctly Catholic literary life among the province's intellectuals. Such efforts could never win over all opposition, yet they established what would be for more than a century one of the strongest organic Christian societies anywhere in the world.

Upper Canada was virtually without permanent European settlement until after the Revolutionary War and the immigration of several thousand United Empire Loyalists. Once settlement began, however, a rush of land-hungry immigrants from the new United States threatened to overrun the province. In the Constitution Act of 1791 public lands (the Clergy Reserves) were set aside for the support of Protestant ministers, and two years later Jacob Mountain (1749–1825) was appointed the first Anglican bishop. Mountain assumed that the Clergy Reserves would be used to create a replica of the English state church system, but was disappointed when new world religious pluralism proved intractable. At the start of the War of 1812, there were only forty-four clergymen ministering to the 75,000 inhabitants of Upper Canada. That war had a momentous effect in solidifying loyalty to Britain, weaning Upper Canadians from their American connections and energising Protestants for the great work of taming the Canadian frontier. The conflict also set the stage for a surprising *rapprochement* between a conservative, establishmentarian vision for Canadian Protestant life and a more individualistic, entrepreneurial one – represented, respectively, by the Scottish-born Anglican John Strachan (1778–1867) and the Methodist itinerant Egerton Ryerson (1803–82). Strachan, who eventually became bishop of Toronto where he contended that an Anglican establishment was the necessary basis for Christian civilisation, used his funeral sermon for Jacob Mountain in 1826 to blast Methodists and other Dissenters as uneducated louts threatening the body politic. Ryerson responded vigorously to criticise Anglican ritual as pompous formalism and to urge passionate gospel preaching as the secret to creating a Christian society.

Yet as the Methodists grew rapidly and as a never-ending series of complications impeded Strachan's push for an Anglican establishment, tempers cooled and former antagonists began to drift closer to each other. Increasingly, Methodists worked at shoring up society directly, as indicated by Ryerson's move from the Methodist ministry to become director of public education in Ontario. Anglicans came gradually to give up pretensions to establishment and sought informal ways to promote their vision of a Christian society. By mid-century, Methodists and Anglicans had begun to co-operate with Presbyterians in using education, informal suasion with government, frequently affirmed loyalty to the crown and diligent religious exertions to build a non-establishmentarian version of British Christendom.

By the time of Confederation in 1867, English Canada was well on the way to becoming nearly as thoroughly Christianised as French Canada. The Clergy Reserves were distributed to all qualifying Protestant denominations,

Methodist and Presbyterian splinters consolidated into powerful denominations, and in many Ontario towns the churches and a wide range of voluntary societies were creating a strong Protestant culture. By 1900, up to half of Toronto's population was in church every Sunday, and Ontario's smaller towns and rural areas often witnessed even more faithful religious practice. This degree of Christianisation fell well below the levels in Quebec, where mass attendance was often as high as 90 per cent, but it was considerably more than in the United States.

By the last third of the century, Canada West was also opening to settlement. Early incursions by traders and trappers into the Red River Valley had left a hardy population of *métis*, mixed French and Indian, who resented the fact that they had not been consulted when in 1869 the Hudson Bay Company ceded the Red River region to the Canadian Dominion. Under the leadership of Louis 'David' Riel (1844–85), a messianic and earnestly Catholic leader, the *métis* resisted. After years of negotiation, increasing settlement from the east, the execution of a Protestant by Riel's military court and deployment of an armed Dominion force, Riel in 1885 was himself tried, convicted and executed. For Catholics throughout Canada, Riel became a symbol of overweening Protestantism and for many in Quebec a symbol of English cultural imperialism.

The practical political issue spotlighted by debate over Riel was the funding of provincial schools. Wilfrid Laurier, a Quebec leader of the Liberal Party, became Canada's first Catholic prime minister in 1896, in part because of his ability to defuse that issue. The compromise was to grant public money for minority Protestant (and English) schools in Quebec, to fund Catholic schools alongside the provincial schools of Ontario (still self-consciously Protestant), and to allow some support for Catholic (and French) schools in Manitoba, and then also Alberta and Saskatchewan when these provinces joined the Dominion in 1905. The strength of Catholic culture in Quebec and the successful activity of political leaders like Laurier meant that Canada never developed the strict separation between tax-supported public education and privately funded religious schools that came to characterise primary education in the United States.

Another significant difference was the broader influence in Canada of social Christianity as a response to the crises of industrialisation and urbanisation. Catholic Ultramontane corporatism resisted anything labelled as socialism, but did encourage an intensely communal attitude towards public life. In English Canada, traditions of Anglican conservatism, practical efforts by churchmen (and more often churchwomen) to meet the needs of immigrants, occasional radicalism as with the Methodist minister J. S. Woodsworth (1874–1941) and a general Protestant acceptance of the Social Gospel prepared the ground for different varieties of religiously inspired social concern that flourished in the early and mid-twentieth century.

The Canadian willingness to modify religious individualism by communal thinking, along with the practical difficulties of maintaining competitive Protestant denominations in the lightly populated West, were factors in moving towards church union, which was proposed by various Methodists, Presbyterians and Congregationalists in the years before World War I. One of the leaders of that move was Nathanael Burwash (1839–1910), the foremost Methodist theologian and educator of his era, who in his last years helped craft the broadly evangelical platform that led after his death to the creation of the United Church of Canada in 1925.

Practices of North American Christianity

Christian practice in North America often resembled that in Europe, whether because of common Protestant ancestry, immigrant ties linking Catholics and Lutherans to the old world, or a general adaptation to western Victorian culture. Yet the American environment also made a difference in several spheres.

Scripture

Of the ancient religious authorities carried to the new world, only the Bible was exempted from America's profound suspicion of the past. Historic allegiance to Scripture merged easily with the new democratic ethos, and literacy became the only requirement for harvesting the Bible's spiritual fruit. The explosion of cheap print in the United States' early national period meant that the means were at hand for putting the Bible, and all manner of biblical interpretations, into the hands of the people at large. The result was a distinctly American attachment to Scripture.

The American Bible Society, founded in 1816, by 1830 was distributing annually over 300,000 copies of the Bible (in whole or parts). Throughout the nineteenth century, American settlers regularly named their communities after biblical places, like Zoar, Ohio (Genesis 13:10) or Mount Tirzah, North Carolina (Joshua 12:24), as well as forty-seven variations on Bethel, sixty-one on Eden and ninety-five on Salem.[8] When in 1844 the Roman Catholic bishop of Philadelphia, Francis Patrick Kenrick, petitioned city officials to allow school

---

8 Leighly, 'Biblical place-names'.

children of his faith to hear readings from the Douay-Rheims translation of the Bible instead of the King James Version (KJV) sacred to Protestants, the city's Protestants rioted and tried to burn down Philadelphia's Catholic churches. Abraham Lincoln, in his sublime second inaugural address of 1865, put the Civil War into perspective by quoting Matthew 18:7 and Psalm 19:9 and by noting that 'Both [sides] read the same Bible.' In 1881, American publication of the Revised Version, produced by noted biblical scholars from Britain, for the first time provided a serious alternative to the KJV as 'America's Bible'. Throughout this period, a huge number of foreign-language editions of the Bible were also printed in the United States (for example, at least a hundred different German editions between 1860 and 1925). In 1898, two travelling sales-men, John H. Nicholson and Samuel Hill, who met by chance at the Central Hotel in Boscobel, Wisconsin, formed a society to provide easy access to Scrip-ture that came to be called the 'Gideons' and that has distributed hundreds of millions of Bibles all over the world.

Fiction, hymns and poetry employing biblical themes were staples of pop-ular publishing. In the visual arts, biblical materials provided inspiration for German immigrants embellishing needlework with *Fraktur* print, nineteenth-century lithographers like Currier and Ives, countless painters at countless levels of ability along with a few masters (like Edward Hicks who in the mid-nineteenth century painted several versions of *The Peaceable Kingdom*). After the mass-marketing of religious objects began after the Civil War, both Catholics and Protestants purchased immense quantities of pictures, statues, games, children's toys, greeting cards, calendars and business cards decorated with biblical motifs.

The Victorian era was the great age of the decorative family Bible whose massive size, graphic illustrations, blank pages for recording family births, deaths and marriages, and considerable expense illustrated the domestic force of religious values. For Catholics, an equivalent to the Bible-centred ritual of Protestants could be the celebratory street festival where images and folk practices sometimes enlisted more enthusiastic support than was given to the church's ordinary ministrations. Yet Catholics also remained loyal to the Douay-Rheims translation of Scripture, and also sponsored several new translations, including one prepared by Francis Patrick Kenrick in the late 1840s.

The Bible was the focus of private meditations, regular reading by families, informal study in Methodist cell groups, Catholic retreats and a multitude of other gatherings. In addition, millions of Americans regularly listened to sermons, a nearly universal vehicle through which biblical phrases, values and culture worked their way into the fabric of daily life – though often in tellingly diverse forms.

Reading and Singing

In the nineteenth century, basic statements of Christian belief by notable theologians, but aimed at popular audiences, often gained a very wide distribution. Such volumes included Charles Hodge's *The way of life* (1841), and *The faith of our fathers: being a plain exposition and vindication of the church founded by our Lord Jesus Christ* (1876) by James Cardinal Gibbons, Catholic archbishop of Baltimore, which sold more than 2 million copies in more than a hundred editions during its first forty years in print.

Although descendants of the Puritans had opposed the reading of fiction, by the nineteenth century the religious novel had more than overcome that uneasiness. Biblical content contributed to the masters of nineteenth-century fiction, including Nathaniel Hawthorne's *The scarlet letter* of 1850 (the letter being an 'A' for adultery worn by Hester Prynne in a drama playing off biblical narratives at every point) and Herman Melville's *Moby Dick* of 1851 (which begins, 'Call me Ishmael'). Better read at the time was popular fiction inspired directly by Scripture. The first important novel of this kind was William Ware's *Julian: or, scenes in Judea* (1856), which described gospel events through the letters of its fictional protagonist. Later titles, with even greater success, included General Lew Wallace's *Ben Hur* (1880) and Henryk Sienkiewicz's *Quo Vadis?* (1896).

The paradigmatic author of religious fiction in the nineteenth century was Harriet Beecher Stowe (1811–96), whose *Uncle Tom's cabin* (1852) constructed a polemic against slavery by focusing on the Christian integrity of its African-American characters. Stowe had many imitators, including Orestes Brownson, who wrote several novels for appreciative Catholic audiences. In the late nineteenth century the Social Gospel was fictionalised in the work of a clergyman from Topeka, Kansas, Charles Sheldon, whose best-selling *In his steps* (1897) presented a picture of Christians who approached life by asking themselves at every moment, 'What would Jesus do?' Charles Gordon (1860–1937), a Canadian Presbyterian minister writing under the name Ralph Connor, parlayed similar themes, set in Western Canada, into great successes, like *The sky pilot* of 1899.

The centrality of hymn-singing in American Protestantism was rooted in the evangelical revivals of the eighteenth century. At the start of the nineteenth century, Americans, particularly in the South, developed shape-note singing from tune books as an indigenous, democratic way of putting to use the work of Isaac Watts, Charles Wesley, John Newton and other stalwarts. Newton's 'Amazing Grace' was first paired with the tune 'New Britain' in the *Southern Harmony* of 1835, later picked up a last verse home-grown in America ('when we've been there ten thousand years'), and then went on to become the most widely used hymn in all of American public life.

In the middle decades of the century, Lowell Mason (1792–1872), first president of Boston's Handel and Haydn Society, returned from European study to compose a number of popular settings for earlier melodies, like 'Hamburg' from Gregorian chant (for Isaac Watts' 'When I survey the wondrous cross') and 'Azmon' from Carl Gläser (for Charles Wesley's 'O, for a thousand tongues to sing'). With his own compositions, like 'Missionary Hymn' (for Reginald Heber's 'From Greenland's icy mountains'), these adaptations made Mason's work as widely used as any other contribution to American religious life.

A hymn by the Canadian Joseph Scriven (1819–86) represented a more popular type of gospel song that became immensely popular in America. Scriven wrote 'What a Friend we have in Jesus, / All our sins and griefs to bear' after enduring several personal tragedies; it became well known after it was included by Ira L. Sankey in the first of his *Gospel hymns* (1875), which inaugurated a series that included many of Sankey's own compositions, like 'The ninety and nine'. But Sankey's most popular author was Fanny J. Crosby (1820–1915), who had become blind as a child. Her more than 8,000 hymns and religious verses offered a perfect complement to the themes of Christian sentiment emphasised in the campaigns of Moody and Sankey.

The religious practices that in home, church and public expressed the faith of North American believers drew on many strands of traditional Christianity. But they also reflected prominent aspects of North American experience by growing more from individual spirituality – and individual morality – than from corporate responsibility, by deferring to authority achieved rather than authority inherited, by trusting in personal appropriation of Scripture more than in respectful acceptance of tradition, and by favouring entrepreneurial innovation over theological depth. As the inner forces paralleling the external organisation of churches, voluntary agencies and educational institutions, spiritual practices constituted the heart of what made the United States and Canada into distinctly Christian, if far from perfect, societies in the century from 1815 to 1914.

23

Spain and Portugal: the challenge to the church

WILLIAM J. CALLAHAN

The transition from royal absolutism to liberalism in nineteenth-century Spain and Portugal was turbulent and diverse.[1] Civil wars between defenders of absolute monarchy and liberalism, periodic revolutions, military interventions, popular rioting and passionate constitutional debates produced chronic political instability, especially between 1820 and 1850. Throughout these upheavals, the Catholic Church remained the established church in both Iberian countries. The republican revolution of 1910 in Portugal finally led to the separation of church and state, an example imitated by the Second Republic in Spain in 1931. In the officially Catholic states of the nineteenth and early twentieth centuries, there were periods when the church appeared on the verge of disintegration. During the 1830s liberal governments in Madrid and Lisbon suppressed the regular clergy, ordered the sale of their property, forbade ordinations to the priesthood, exiled bishops and abolished the tithes on which diocesan priests depended. At other times, conservative liberals sought an accommodation with the church. Portugal and the Holy See concluded a *convenio* in 1848 and concordats in 1857 and 1886, while Spain agreed to a concordat in 1851 that governed civil–ecclesiastical relations until 1931, save for two periods.

The shifting balance between aggressive and moderate approaches to relations with the church reflected the divisions of liberal opinion. For the Moderate and Progressive parties of mid-nineteenth-century Spain and the Regenerator and Historical parties of Portugal, the question of the church and the degree of state control over its affairs remained a central concern. At the end of the day, the changes imposed by Spanish and Portuguese liberalism, whether in an aggressive or a moderate version, undermined the ecclesiastical establishment of the eighteenth century. Identified with absolute monarchy,

---

1 Although there were differences between Spain and Portugal, there was also 'a strong parallelism' in their respective histories during the nineteenth century. See Halpern Pereira, 'Del Antiguo Régimen al liberalismo', p. 39.

an essential part of a hierarchical society and possessor of immense riches used to sustain a numerous body of priests and religious, the imposing church of the past staggered before the liberal offensive. Moreover, the ecclesiastical changes associated with liberalism posed a religious challenge for the church. The disappearance of the male religious orders during the 1830s, until their reintroduction later in the century, deprived the church of an important instrument of popular evangelisation, while the controls imposed on the parochial clergy during the civil wars of the period disrupted parish life significantly in many regions.

With few exceptions, clerical and lay defenders of the church saw liberal ecclesiastical policies as the fatal result of corrosive, secular ideas bent on the destruction of religion. The reformers of the Cortes of Cádiz (1810–13), Spain's first modern parliamentary assembly, were accused of passing legislation 'under the cover of every kind of insult to religion and its dogmas'.[2] In fact, every Spanish and Portuguese constitution of the nineteenth century affirmed Catholicism as the state's religion. With the exception of the Spanish constitution of 1869, none authorised the introduction of religious liberty, although the Portuguese constitution of 1822 and the constitutional charter of 1826 allowed the private practice of other religions, as did the Spanish constitution of 1876. Legislation ordering religious instruction in primary schools (Portugal, 1832, 1836; Spain, 1838) remained on the books into the early twentieth century. Moreover, no liberal governments in Spain and Portugal ever contemplated abandoning the crown's historic patronage rights over episcopal appointments. The issue at stake was never Catholicism or anti-Catholicism. Liberals sought to redefine the church's place in a political and social order radically different from that of the eighteenth century in the interests of a 'pure, peaceful and perfect religion' practised through a church working harmoniously within the new liberal society and its political and social institutions.[3]

Fulfilling this expectation proved impossible. Spanish and Portuguese liberals carried out a political revolution, but their ideas on civil–ecclesiastical relations fell within the regalist tradition of eighteenth-century absolute monarchy. This was not only a question of control over episcopal appointments and ecclesiastical resources, it also involved the direct involvement of the state in virtually every sphere of the church's activities, even those of a pastoral nature. In Spain, for example, the Cortes of 1820 proposed a radical parochial

---

2 Quoted in Cuenca Toribio, 'La Iglesia sevillana', pp. 155–6.
3 Longares Alonso, *Política y religión en Barcelona*, p. 207.

reorganisation to create parishes in accord with the size of local populations and recommended that in non-Spanish-speaking areas, such as Catalonia and the Basque Provinces, parish priests should be fluent in the language of their parishioners.[4] At least until the mid-nineteenth century, liberals believed that their task was to carry out a broad programme of ecclesiastical reform. There was no question of papal participation in the process, nor were the clergy consulted, save for a small clerical minority disposed to co-operate with the authorities.

The commitment of bishops and priests to a return to absolutism, expressed in Spain by support for King Ferdinand VII between 1814 and 1820 and 1823 and 1833, and in Portugal for King Miguel between 1828 and 1834, left a legacy of mistrust and suspicion towards the church that quickly surfaced following the death of Ferdinand VII (1833) and the exile of Miguel (1834) after years of civil war. Portuguese liberals acted even before defeating absolutists on the mainland by suppressing friaries and monasteries in the Azores in 1832.[5] In 1834, the government of Queen Maria II (1833–53) ordered a general dissolution of the male regulars and the appropriation of their property by the state for eventual sale. Spanish legislation (1835–6) under the ministry of Juan Álvárez Mendizábal visited the same fate upon that country's male religious, while ordering the sale of their property for the benefit of the public treasury.[6] In both countries, the female orders survived, although legislation prohibiting the reception of new entrants sought to assure their eventual disappearance.

The closure of about 2,000 monasteries and friaries in Spain and 448 in Portugal undermined a centuries-old clerical infrastructure. At the time of dissolution, the orders were scarcely models of religious vitality. For years, even under absolute monarchy, critics accused them of failing to observe the austerity and discipline intended by their founders. Liberal reformers shared these concerns and argued that the number of religious was far in excess of that required to meet pastoral needs. Liberal hostility towards the regulars rested also on economic grounds. Monasteries and friaries, declared the Spanish disentailment decree of 1835, were 'useless and unnecessary . . . for the spiritual

---

4 *Proyecto de decreto de nueva demarcación de parroquías y dotación de párrocos* (Madrid, 1821), pp. 115–22.
5 There were precedents for the suppression of the regulars and the sale of their property. Following the liberal revolutions of 1820 in Spain and Portugal, a partial suppression and disentailment was carried out in each country, although the process was reversed in 1823. Rueda and Siliveira, 'Dos experiencias: España y Portugal', pp. 20–1.
6 Almeida, *História da Igreja em Portugal*, vol. III, pp. 133–4; Simón Segura, *La desamortización española*, pp. 84–9.

assistance of the faithful'. The sale of their property would serve 'the public convenience' by increasing 'the resources of the state and opening new sources of wealth'.[7]

The sale of the regulars' property during the 1830s did not end the confiscation and sale of ecclesiastical property. It continued, albeit episodically, in Spain until 1859 and in Portugal until 1869. By the time it was over, the church had lost the vast endowments, including those of the diocesan clergy, that had sustained it for centuries. It also saw the other bedrock of ecclesiastical finances, the tithe, abolished. In return for the loss of ecclesiastical property and the tithe, liberal governments undertook to sustain the diocesan clergy, although such support was stingy at best. In Spain, following the 1851 concordat, priests received their incomes directly from the national budget; in Portugal, they depended on what was in effect a parochial tax paid by their parishioners under government supervision. Whatever the formula used, the clergy became dependent on the state for their financial survival.

This dependency was reinforced by liberal policies with respect to the ecclesiastical organisation. In Portugal, the constitution of 1822, the constitutional charter of 1826 and legislation of 1833 saw regalism in full blood by asserting the state's absolute right of control over the appointment of bishops, canons and parish priests. A Historical Party ministry in 1862 went even further by creating a selection process for parish priests that virtually excluded diocesan prelates, who declared that they had been reduced to mere 'shadows of bishops' by the civil authorities, a view shared by Pope Pius IX (1846–78) in a vigorous protest against the government's action.[8] Spanish liberal governments did not go this far. After 1843, they interfered less in the church's internal affairs, even during the revolutionary periods 1854–6 and 1868–73, although they insisted on retaining the state's rights over episcopal appointments. In both countries, however, moderate and aggressive liberals agreed on the necessity of reforming the ecclesiastical organisation by reducing the number of dioceses and parishes. The Spanish concordat of 1851 provided for a consolidation joining small dioceses to larger ones and a reduction in parish numbers. This plan was never realised because of clerical resistance and government reluctance to promote changes certain to arouse strong local opposition. Portuguese governments were more successful, although a parochial consolidation carried

---

7 Quoted in Simón Segura, *La desamortización española*, p. 85. The Reverend W. M. Kinsey noted in 1829 that 'the enlightened classes' in Portugal desired a 'change in the monastic system with the view of unlocking vast means and resources for the benefit of the nation': *Portugal illustrated* (London: Treuttel and Wurtz, 1829), p. 196.

8 Almeida, *História da Igreja*, vol. III, p. 38, cited in Oliveira, *História eclesiástica de Portugal*, p. 259.

out between 1837 and 1850, when 203 of the country's approximately 4,000 parishes were closed, fell short of what liberal ecclesiastical reformers had in mind. The long quest for a diocesan reorganisation finally produced results in 1882 when the government and Pope Leo XIII agreed to suppress five of the kingdom's nineteen dioceses.[9]

The regalism of liberal governments proved especially disruptive for the church between 1834 and 1843 in Spain and between 1833 and 1840 in Portugal. For the first time in Spain, a violent urban anticlericalism moved by hostility towards the religious orders emerged during the summer of 1834. In Madrid, crowds murdered seventy-eight religious, some of whom were stabbed to death, while others were hanged and still others hurled from the rooftops of their residences.[10] The anticlerical wave hit Barcelona a year later when religious houses were set ablaze, although the number of victims was less than in Madrid during the previous year. The civil authorities lamented the violence but did little to stop it, seeing the *matanza de los frailes* primarily as a regrettable but understandable lapse from the norms of civilised behaviour.

Popular hostility directed against the regulars in the cities arose in part from the belief, largely inaccurate, that monks and friars stood in the front line of the movements to restore absolutism by working on behalf of Fernando VII's reactionary brother, Don Carlos, against the king's young daughter, Queen Isabella II (1833–68), who enjoyed liberal support.[11] The movement known as Carlism remained a nagging danger for liberal governments until the 1870s, but it was at its most threatening during the mid-1830s. In fact, disoriented and disorganised priests and religious were in no position to provide effective support to Carlism, but a few did so, thereby provoking reprisals. In 1836–7, the authorities deprived bishops absent from their dioceses for 'political' motives of their incomes and regarded priests accused of Carlist sympathies as conspirators against the state. In 1837, the government prohibited ordinations, while it prepared a radical reorganisation of the diocesan clergy. Bishops either fled into exile or abandoned their dioceses. By 1840, only eleven of the kingdom's sixty dioceses were being administered by their prelates. In the archdiocese of Tarragona, where battle raged between the supporters of liberalism and Carlism, nearly half of the clergy had abandoned their parishes by 1840.[12]

9 Neto, *O Estado, a Igreja*, p. 55; Almeida, *História da Igreja*, vol. III, p. 14.
10 Revuelta González, *La exclaustración*, pp. 207–21.
11 Revuelta González, *La exclaustración*, p. 132, maintains that, although sympathetic to Carlism, 'the great majority' of religious were 'resigned and silent' when it came to practical support for the movement.
12 Callahan, *Church, politics and society in Spain*, p. 165.

Worse was to come. Liberal regalism reached its high point during the regency (1840–3) of General Baldomero Espartero, who was associated with the Progressive Party. Before the refusal of Pope Gregory XVI to approve the government's episcopal nominations, the authorities forced the appointment of diocesan administrators, sometimes at gunpoint. In 1841, the government proposed a radical reorganisation of the church involving the suppression of seventeen dioceses and 4,000 of the country's approximately 19,000 parishes. A later proposal in 1842 exalted the authority of the bishops at the expense of the papacy and reduced the pope's authority over the Spanish church to the purely ceremonial. The Revolution of 1843 and the beginnings of a long period of rule by conservative liberals gathered in the Moderate Party ended these radical projects. In fact, no liberal government ever again attempted the kind of sweeping unilateral reform of the church attempted by the Espartero government.

The Portuguese church fared little better during the 1830s, although spared the violent assaults against the regular clergy that occurred in Spain. Liberal governments followed a policy of rigorous ecclesiastical centralisation, which in some respects went beyond that pursued in Spain. Decrees in 1830 and 1832, for example, created parish committees (juntas de paróquia) which drastically reduced the authority of parish priests.[13] Moreover, the support of bishops and the rural clergy for the absolutist King Miguel during the civil war of 1828–34 left a score that liberal governments were determined to settle.[14] They refused to recognise the episcopal appointments made by Miguel, while a series of 1833 decrees declared that priests and religious who abandoned their posts upon the proclamation of María II as queen were nothing less than rebels and traitors.[15] Pope Gregory XVI protested against these measures to no avail in 1834. The impasse between the liberal state and the clergy resulted in many priests abandoning their parishes. By 1840, only one bishop, the patriarch of Lisbon, Patricio da Silva, remained to administer his diocese.[16] The so-called 'schism' (cisma) of the 1830s created a deep division between the papacy and the Portuguese state, divided the clergy into two camps and threw pastoral activities into disarray.[17]

13 Carmo Reis, O liberalismo em Portugal e a Igreja católica, p. 97.
14 See, for example, the strong attack by a liberal supporter against the archbishop of Evora for defending the cause of King Miguel. Francisco Freire de Melo, Reposta á infame pastoral, que escreveu o ex-arcebispo d'Évora . . . contra o senhor Dom Pedro, Regente em nome da Reinha e senhora Dona María II (Lisbon: Imprensa Nacional, 1834), pp. 1–18.
15 Oliveira, História eclesiástica, p. 232.
16 Almeida, História da Igreja, vol. III, p. 39.
17 By 1835, half of the parishes of the Evora diocese lacked parish priests: Neto, O Estado, a Igreja, p. 59. In the town of Vila do Conde (diocese of Braga), twenty priests supported

The dramatic ecclesiastical changes imposed by liberalism and the turbulence associated with them appeared to leave the church with few options. 'Observing the furious interferences of the revolution', declared Bishop Romo Gamboa of the Canaries in 1840, prelates could not see 'how they could salvage the ship of the church in the midst of such shocks'.[18] The suppression of the regular clergy, the collapse of the church's role in education and charity, so essential to its social role in the eighteenth century, and the disorientation of a parish clergy left virtually without episcopal direction appeared to offer a gloomy future. But all was not lost. There is no evidence that the turmoil of these years undermined the faith in either Spain or Portugal, at least in northern regions where a dense infrastructure of rural parishes intimately connected to the concerns of peasant communities survived. Conditions in the large cities, whether Madrid, Barcelona, Lisbon or Oporto, were less promising, for there were already signs of the religious alienation of urban populations. Moreover, the cities were strongholds of liberalisation both politically and ideologically.

The church managed to recover from the catastrophic situation of the early liberal period. By the early and mid-1840s, the growing influence of conservative liberals, who saw an accommodation with the papacy and the clergy as necessary for the stability of the liberal system, moved the civil authorities to seek a compromise with Rome. In Portugal under the Chartist Party governments of the 1840s (committed to the restoration of the moderate 1826 constitutional charter), Costa Cabral, minister of justice and ecclesiastical affairs, promoted negotiations with the papacy and sought to end the *cisma* of the 1830s by allowing bishops and priests excluded from their positions for political reasons to return to their posts.[19] In Spain, the Moderate Party, in control of the government between 1843 and 1854, ended the radical ecclesiastical schemes of General Espartero and opened negotiations with Pope Pius IX, which culminated in the 1851 concordat. This shift in the political winds should be kept in perspective. The moderate liberals, the Moderate Party in Spain and the Regenerator Party in Portugal, by no means abandoned regalism as a principle of government, although they tempered it considerably. Nor did they have any intention of restoring to the church its former property holdings and endowments. Moreover, the opposition parties of the mid-nineteenth century,

the absolutist cause. Thirteen were identified as *cismáticos*. Franquelims (ed.), *O Concelho de Vila do Conde*, p. 17.

18 Judás José Romo Gamboa, *Independencia constante de la Iglesia hispana y necesidad de un nuevo concordato* (Madrid: Aguado, 1843), p. 341.

19 Neto, *O Estado, a Igreja*, pp. 86–9.

the Progressives in Spain and the Historicals in Portugal, took a much tougher stance towards the church when they were in power. By the last quarter of the century, a political consensus of sorts had emerged in both countries that gave the church breathing space. There were tensions among the parties over the so-called 'religious question', but there was no return to the radical ecclesiastical policies of the past, a change symbolised by the presence of bishops as senators in the parliaments of both countries.[20]

Support for Carlism in Spain and hostility towards liberalism in Portugal remained strong among priests and some bishops throughout the nineteenth century. But as early as the 1840s, the recognition dawned among more pragmatic clerics that the church needed to redefine its position in view of liberalism's political dominance and to adapt religious activities to the new realities of liberal society. 'Reason dictates that prescinding from the rights which have been swept away forever, and submerged at the bottom of the sea, we should content ourselves with saving those which, floating to the beaches, are still capable of being saved', declared Bishop Romo Gamboa in 1843.[21] In 1841, a proposal to create a Catholic association of a million members 'to defend the Catholic religion . . . by the means authorised by law' surfaced in the confessional press.[22] This attempt to create a modern organisation enlisting the Catholic masses to work for the church within the liberal system did not prosper, although it anticipated similar efforts later in the century.

Portuguese Catholic leaders were more successful over the short term. In 1843, they created the Sociedade Católica Promotora da Moral Evangélica to engage in campaigns of religious propaganda through a membership open to all Catholics, whatever their dynastic or political loyalties, and operating within the established political order. Although the new organisation, approved by Costa Cabral and Gregory XVI, survived until 1853, it was not successful. It failed to take root over the country as a whole, while supporters of absolutism rejected it as a Trojan horse designed to integrate Catholics into the liberal system.[23] Later attempts to forge unity among Catholics, the Union Católica in Spain (1881) and Uniao Católica Portuguesa (1882) encountered

---

20 In both countries by the mid-1870s a system of alternating power between the principal parties, now the Conservatives and Liberals in Spain, the Regenerators and the Progressives in Portugal, had come into being. Although constitutional and parliamentary in form, these governments were scarcely democratic. Elections were manipulated to produce the results desired by the politicians.
21 Romo Gamboa, *Independencia constante de la Iglesia hispana*, p. 329.
22 *El Católico* (Madrid), 26 Feb. 1841.
23 Neto, *O Estado, a Igreja*, pp. 401–6.

similar resistance, thereby frustrating a cherished dream of some bishops and laymen, the creation of a mass party similar to the Catholic parties of Belgium and Germany.

The pragmatism of the papacy and the clerical leadership which led to a workable, although grudging, accommodation with the liberal state did not extend to religion. In Spain and Portugal, bishops and priests viewed the impact of the liberal social and political order on religion as catastrophic. A Spanish preacher declared in 1847: 'Faith nearly extinguished, charity frozen or deadened offers nothing more to our eyes than Christians without souls and without life. The times are obscured by clouds of vice and the dark mists of error.'[24] In 1870, a Portuguese religious journal censured bishops and priests for not living up to their pastoral responsibilities in a period when the very foundations of religious belief appeared threatened. Parish priests stood accused of abandoning the cure of souls by neglecting the teaching of the catechism and by failing to instruct the faithful properly in their preaching. 'In the majority of churches', the report declared, 'confessionals and the eucharistic table' were left 'deserted'.[25]

These pessimistic assessments fell short of the mark, although assessing the religious condition of nineteenth- and early twentieth-century Spain and Portugal is difficult. There are few statistical studies of religious observance such as those available for both countries after 1950. But the gloom and doom of nineteenth-century clerics failed to take into account the regional character of Spanish and Portuguese Catholicism. In Spain (Old Castile, Galicia, Santander, Asturias, Navarra and the Basque Provinces) and in Portugal (north of the Tagus River), the church was able to rely on a dense network of small parishes intimately linked to the concerns of the peasantry.[26] This religious world had little of the theological about it. It revolved around local shrines, pilgrimages and traditional devotions designed to ward off earthly disasters, bring the faithful good fortune in this life and secure a holy intercessor in the quest for salvation. The strength of northern rural Catholicism in Spain and Portugal provided the church with a solid religious base, although

---

24 Santiago José Garcia Mazo, *Sermones predicados por el licenciado Don Santiago José Mazo*, 3 vols. (Valladolid: Manuel Aparicio, 1847), vol. I, pp. 1389–91.

25 Quoted in Almeida, *História da Igreja*, vol. III, pp. 258–9.

26 The Portuguese archdiocese for Braga, for example, had 1,270 parishes in the mid-nineteenth century; the archdiocese of Evora in the south only 145. Similarly, the Old Castilian archdiocese of Burgos had 1,500 parishes in 1842 but the archdiocese of Seville, with a far larger population, only 172. Neto, *O Estado, a Igreja*, pp. 55–6; Sáez Marín, *Datos sobre la Iglesia española contemporánea*, pp. 139–40.

as time passed agricultural modernisation and emigration to the cities and Latin America led to rural depopulation that undermined the vitality of village life.

Conditions in southern regions, such as Andalusia and Extremadura in Spain and the Baixo Alentejo in Portugal, were less promising. Parishes were few compared to the north, while in districts of large estates worked by landless day labourers religious indifference took root. The indefatigable Redemptorist missionary Ramón Sarabia, who worked extensively in rural Andalusia and Extremadura early in the twentieth century, saw a pattern of low religious observance, the massive abstention of men from religious services and widespread ignorance of elementary doctrinal knowledge as characteristic of southern Catholicism.[27] Although there is less evidence for Portugal, it is reasonable to assume that the low levels of practice observed by religious sociologists for the twentieth century in certain regions can be traced in part to earlier times.[28] The situation in the cities experiencing industrialisation was little better. A Catalan priest commenting on religious observance in Barcelona in the 1850s believed that it once was 'a Christian town' in which 'our churches were filled with men in their workers' shirts'. But 'the day arrived when this people, who until then appeared Catholic, abandoned religious practices little by little'.[29] In Lisbon and Oporto towards the end of the nineteenth century, workers 'lived totally at the margins of the church'.[30]

In spite of the loyalty of the northern peasantry to the church, clergy and activist laity faced daunting challenges. How they were to be met caused controversy and, at times, confusion among bishops, priests and laymen seeking to 'rechristianise' that part of the population that had become indifferent or even hostile to religion. But by the last quarter of the nineteenth century, numerous initiatives on a broad front were underway, although this 'Catholic revival' produced mixed results. Liberal governments permitted the reintroduction of the male religious orders, although their precise legal status remained ambiguous. The expansion of the orders provided the church with an invaluable means of expanding its religious, social and educational activities. In Spain, the number of male religious increased from 1,683 in 1860 to 13,359 by 1910, the number of nuns from 18,819 to 46,357 during the same period. In Portugal, the ten

---

27 Callahan, *The Catholic Church in Spain*, p. 245.
28 See, for example, França, *Comportamento religioso da população portuguesa*.
29 Cited in Benet and Martí, *Barcelona a mitjans segle XIX*, vol. 1, pp. 203–4.
30 Rodrigues, 'Le Portugal', p. 413.

Jesuits of 1860 increased to 359 by 1910, while the number of religious orders operating in the country, insignificant in 1860, reached thirty-four by this date.[31] For the first time under liberalism, the regulars' expansion allowed the church to establish an important presence in education, largely through fee-paying schools serving middle- and upper-class students. The female orders provided personnel for work in a wide range of charitable institutions, a field of activity where the church's involvement had been minimal for years.

Expansion of the male orders intensified domestic missionary activity that had disappeared during the 1830s and 1840s and then reappeared sporadically during the 1850s and 1860s. Spanish Redemptorists calculated that between 1879 and 1931 they had conducted nearly 6,305 popular missions in rural and urban areas across the length and breadth of the country.[32] In spite of their tireless energy, missionaries were most successful in those areas where one would have expected them to be, the still observant villages of the north. In the southern estate lands, they encountered opposition at worst, indifference at best. In Portugal, Jesuit missionaries made little headway as they worked in southern dioceses, while the Spanish Jesuit Francisco de Tarin, known as the 'Apostle of Andalusia', declared in one of his rare moments of depression, 'Everything is lost. All the zeal of a saint would be dashed to pieces', before the indifference that he encountered in the towns and villages where he conducted missions towards the close of the nineteenth century.[33]

Members of the religious orders were also prominent in the devotional resurgence that occurred from the mid-nineteenth century onward. Traditional devotions anchored in the patterns of village life continued, of course. But they were supplanted to some extent by the spread of devotions that were less oriented to the cohesive village community than to the cultivation of individual piety among rural and urban populations. Proclamation of the dogma of the Immaculate Conception by Pope Pius IX in 1854 reinvigorated Marian devotions. Pious associations devoted to the cult of Mary multiplied, such as the Court of Mary in Spain with 50,000 members by 1865, or the Archconfraternity of the Sacred Heart of Mary in Portugal with 100,000 members by the mid-1880s. By the early twentieth century, certain devotional associations, such as the Apostolate of Prayer, promoted by the Jesuits in Portugal, had enrolled a million members, while in Spain, the Association of Three Marys and

31 Callahan, *The Catholic Church in Spain*, p. 190; Neto, *O Estado, a Igreja*, pp. 313–14.
32 Tellería, *Un instituto misionero*, p. 436.
33 Neto, *O Estado, a Igreja*, p. 316, cited in Callahan, *The Catholic Church in Spain*, p. 260.

Saint John, committed to the eucharistic devotion, had enlisted 2 million.[34] These membership figures show that the church was successful in recasting its devotional arsenal towards personal acts of piety, which reflected the individualist orientation of liberal society. This devotional resurgence may have established the church's influence among those already committed to the faith. There are few indications that it made headway against the religious indifference prevailing in the southern estate lands or among workers in industrial towns. According to a Portuguese observer in 1906: 'excepting some regions of the north, where the people conserve the custom of daily mass . . . in the rest of the country churches are nearly empty'.[35] In one town of the Alentejo with 11,000 inhabitants, he noted, scarcely anyone attended Sunday mass, a situation that in his judgement also prevailed in Lisbon.

The need to reach out to the religiously alienated gradually and fitfully moved the church into the realm of social action. The 'social questions' began to attract the attention of some clerics and laymen during the 1870s. Pope Leo XIII's 1891 encyclical, *Rerum Novarum*, stimulated further interest and encouraged the creation of workers' associations. These took the form of Workers' Circles following the model of Count Albert de Mun in France. In Spain by the early twentieth century, the circles numbered 257, with a membership of 180,000; in Portugal by 1910, they numbered twenty-five, with a membership of 10,000.[36] But membership comprised only a small minority of industrial workers. Moreover, their 'mixed' character as joint associations of workers and employers left them open to the charge that they were little more than tools of capitalism. Later, 'pure' Catholic labour syndicates emerged, although they proved only marginally more successful. In Spain after 1906, Catholic agricultural syndicates began to appear. They enjoyed some success as credit institutions and defenders of local agricultural interests, although they were concentrated in peasant regions where the church retained considerable influence. There were other aspects to the 'Catholic revival'. In Spain and Portugal, Catholic Congresses including clergy and laity met periodically from the 1880s to discuss issues judged vital to the church. A moderately effective Catholic press emerged, although it never matched the circulation of its secular counterpart. In Spain, Catholic leagues were

34 Jiménez Duque, *La espiritualidad en el siglo XIX español*, pp. 146–60; Neto, *O Estado, a Igreja*, pp. 463, 486.
35 Cited in Neto, *O Estado, a Igreja*, p. 481.
36 Andrés Gallego, *Pensamiento y acción social de la Iglesia en España*, pp. 203–6; Neto, *O Estado, a Igreja*, pp. 444–5.

organised by several bishops after 1900 to defend the church at local level. The success of the multitude of associational initiatives launched by clergy and laity was uneven, but it represented a remarkable degree of institutional recovery compared to the church's catastrophic situation during the 1830s. But after 1900, controversy over the church's place in Portuguese and Spanish society entered a new and conflictive period. The extraordinary expansion of the religious orders revived debate over religious orders that led to the passage of legislation (1901) to limit their future growth in both countries. A recent study of Spanish anticlerical incidents between 1900 and 1910 shows that they expanded from a limited geographical base to become national in scope. In Portugal during the same period, various groups, including the Associaçao dos Livres-Pensadores and the Freemasons gathered in the Grande Oriente Lusitano Unido, as well as others, constituted 'an authentic anticlerical front' of considerable influence.[37] The growing strength of republicanism with its commitment to the separation of church and state also posed a clear danger to the consensus that had sustained the civil ecclesiastical *modus vivendi* for decades.

In Spain, the growth of radical social movements, socialism, anarchism and anarchosyndicalism, all hostile towards the church in varying degrees, introduced a new element in the old struggle over the church. In Barcelona, the emergence after 1901 of the Radical Republican Party with a demagogic programme of anticlericalism, especially towards the religious orders, contributed to the violence of the Tragic Week (1909) when eighty church buildings were put to the torch, the worst example of violence against the church since 1834–5.

The Tragic Week did not lead to the political revolution its supporters expected. But in Portugal the triumphant republican revolution of 1910 saw the clergy's worst fears realised through what Pope Pius X saw as 'an incredible series of excesses and crimes which have been enacted in Portugal for the oppression of the church'.[38] The Portuguese church survived better than this dark assessment suggests. But the new republic abolished the church's financial, educational and legal privileges, and for good measure administered a dose of the regalism that had been part of Portuguese history since the days of absolute monarchy. The civil authorities imitated an old regalist tactic by forbidding

---

37 Andrés Gallego and Pazos, *La Iglesia en la España contemporánea*, vol. 1, pp. 290–6; Catroga, 'O livre-pensamento contra a Igreja', p. 344.

38 *Iamdudum: encyclical of Pope Pius X on the Law of Separation in Portugal*, 24 May 1911 (www.thecatholiclibrary.org/Docs/Popes/257_Pius X/Encyclicals/iamdudum.html).

the publication of papal documents without the government's consent and by imposing restrictions on religious processions outside the church buildings. There was no question of implementing the nineteenth-century republican formula of 'a free church in a free state'. The Second Spanish Republic (1931–9) did not go this far, but it remained a prisoner of the regalist ghosts of the past.

24

Latin America: the church and national independence

JOHN LYNCH

The post-colonial church

The collapse of the Bourbon state and the onset of colonial rebellion in Spanish America were observed by the church not simply as secular events but as a conflict of ideologies and a struggle for power that vitally affected its own interests. Controlled as it was by the colonial state, the Bourbon church reacted to the trials of the state. And in the war of ideas the church saw allegiance to Spain, obedience to monarchy and repudiation of revolution as moral imperatives and their denial as a sin. Yet the church in America did not speak with a single voice.

The majority of the bishops rejected the revolution and remained loyal to Spain. They owed their appointments to the crown, they had sworn allegiance to the king, and they were under immediate pressure to conform and deliver to the king a docile people. Bishops were urged 'to cooperate by their example and their doctrine in preserving the rights of legitimate sovereignty which belongs to the king our lord'. During these years bishops helped to finance, arm and activate anti-insurgency forces, and they launched weapons as well as anathemas against their enemies.

The clergy were divided but many, especially among the lower clergy who were predominantly creole (American-born), supported the cause of independence. Some priests played leading roles in the struggle, many more were activists in the rebel ranks, and numerous volunteers served as chaplains in the armies of liberation. In Mexico the early insurgency was dominated by priests, two in particular: Miguel Hidalgo, a country priest of progressive views, and José María Morelos, another reformist and a natural guerrilla leader. On their defeat they were not only executed by royal authority but also condemned and excommunicated by the church.

The turning point for the church in Spanish America was the year 1820, when a liberal revolution in Spain forced the king to renounce absolutism and accept the constitution of 1812. The new regime promptly exported itself to the colonies, where it had immediate implications for the church. Spanish liberals were just as imperialist as Spanish conservatives and offered no concessions to independence. They were also aggressively anticlerical, attacking the church, its privileges and its property. The combination of radical liberalism and renewed imperialism was too much even for the royalist bishops in America, many of whom now lost confidence in the king and began to question the basis of their allegiance. While these events unfolded, the war of independence began to turn in favour of the republicans; at Boyacá in 1819 the era of the great victories opened and with it the eyes of the prelates.

During this time of crisis the church in America received little help from Rome. Ignorant of the meaning of colonial grievance and creole nationalism, the popes judged the movements of independence in Spanish America as an extension of the revolutionary upheaval they observed in Europe, and they gave their support to the Spanish crown. The encyclical *Etsi Longissimo* (30 January 1816) exhorted the bishops and clergy of Spanish America to 'destroy completely' the revolutionary seed sown in their countries and to make clear to their people the dire consequences of rebellion against legitimate authority.[1] When Ferdinand VII was restored to absolute power in Spain (1823) and revived hopes, however unrealistic, of the reconquest of America, Leo XII urged the Spanish American hierarchy (*Etsi Iam Diu*, 1824) to come to the 'defence of religion and legitimate power'. The popes thus made support for the Bourbon monarchy and Spanish rule a matter of conscience, and appeared to deny the possibility of a Latin American church. These positions were impossible to maintain and in due course the papacy had to see reason and, from 1835, to recognise the new states. In the meantime the policy of the Holy See had caused a backlash of anticlericalism, helped to demoralise the church in America, and debased the currency of papal encyclicals.

The church in accepting independence also accepted its conservative character, and so it paid little heed to the claims of Indians and blacks. The church had ceased to be a colonial institution but retained traces of a colonial mentality. Yet independence was an opportunity as well as a challenge. The American church, free from the suffocating grasp of the Bourbon state, could now look directly to Rome for leadership and authority; at first it looked in vain, but in course of time, when the papacy responded to the needs of America, the church moved from Spain to Rome, from Iberian religion to universal religion. The history of the church in nineteenth-century Latin America developed in

---

1 Leturia, *Relaciones entre la Santa Sede e Hispanoamérica*, vol. 11, pp. 90, 110–13, 365–71.

two phases. In the first, 1820–60, a post-imperial church clung to its privileges in a time of secular state-building. In the second, 1860–1910, a reformed church clashed with liberal regimes and lost much of its public power. Throughout the century the church expanded and the faithful multiplied.

Priests and prelates

The church reflected secular society. Bishops and higher clergy were of the elites, alongside landowners, businessmen and bureaucrats. Many of the lower clergy belonged to the poor. The church inherited from its colonial past great wealth in real estate and revenue from annuities. But there were inequalities of income between upper and lower clergy, between wealthy city benefices and poor parishes in the country. In rural societies priests were often younger sons who were not expected to inherit land and found an alternative career in the church. This created a reserve of recruits for the clergy and was an asset to the church, though it did not guarantee good vocations or ensure that priests kept their vows.

The church began its new life short of priests. In post-war Venezuela in 1837 there were 200 fewer priests than in 1810 and regions such as the llanos of Apure hardly saw a priest from one year to the next. It was the common people who kept the faith alive while the bishops struggled to raise clerical numbers and standards. In Bolivia, where in 1850 the clergy were 50 per cent fewer than in 1800, the church was served by priests who were as diverse in training as they were in dedication. As elsewhere in Latin America they suffered from a poor public image, and were criticised for living with women and using parish funds for their own benefit.

In Mexico, in contrast to South America, statistics tell a story of more vigorous life. After the losses at independence, the number of clergy remained fairly constant throughout the nineteenth century. There were 3,463 in 1826, 3,232 in 1851, 3,576 in 1895, 4,015 in 1900 and 4,533 in 1910. Assuming that the number of nominal Catholics was almost coterminous with the population, this meant that in 1895 (total population 12.6 million) there were fewer than three priests for every 10,000 inhabitants, and in 1910 (total population 15.1 million) just over three. The training available for priests was expanded in this period. Diocesan seminaries increased from nine in 1826 to ten in 1851, and twenty-nine in 1910, while the Conciliar Seminary of Mexico City was raised to the status of Pontifical University in 1896.

The qualitative life of the church and the standards of the clergy were also changing. During the first decades of independence many Mexican priests, like their Peruvian counterparts, were a source of scandal rather than sanctity. But a process of reform and renewed evangelisation gathered momentum in the fifty years from 1860 to 1910. The revival was strongest in rural Mexico; a typical Mexican priest was a country priest from a middle-class family. Priests were the products of the diocesan seminary, where they learnt Latin, scholastic philosophy and theology, and were imbued with strict moral values and a deep hostility to liberalism. They embarked on pastoral work inspired by their seminary ideals, urging parishioners to regular attendance at mass and the sacraments, organising catechism classes, encouraging observance of Lent, and inculcating in their people an awareness of sin and avoidance of sex outside marriage.

Argentina, unlike Mexico and Peru, did not inherit from the colonial church an infrastructure on which it could later build. The period 1830–60 was the low tide of Argentine Catholicism, a time when it collaborated with dictatorship and traded its freedom for protection. In these vast and empty lands, bishoprics remained unfilled for decades, seminaries closed from apathy, and priests were few and far between. The national constitution of 1853 established and funded the Catholic Church as the religion of the state, which was obliged to 'support' but not 'profess' the Catholic religion. The government controlled the appointment of bishops and relations with Rome, and guaranteed toleration for other faiths. A culture of compromise was born.

From the 1860s the Argentine church renewed its mission. The metropolitan diocese of Buenos Aires was created, with its own archbishop. New seminaries were established and old ones revived. Seculars were joined by religious, and native priests by immigrant clergy. The Jesuits returned and in 1868 founded the Colegio del Salvador in Buenos Aires, successful enough to be burned down in 1875 by an anticlerical mob led by an apostate Spanish priest. The last decades of the nineteenth century were a new age for religious orders in Argentina, many of them dedicated not only to the contemplative life but also to welfare and education, and they helped to fill a gap in the social provisions of the republic, providing charitable agencies of a traditional kind. Religion acquired a political edge as Catholic action took the gospel outside the church and the cloister, and a vigorous clerical movement disputed for public space, a beneficiary of the liberal state as well as its leading critic.

Between 1880 and 1914, in an age of mass immigration and economic growth, Catholicism underwent great expansion in Argentina. In Buenos Aires there were nineteen parishes in 1900 compared to seven in 1857. This was a conservative church which still attracted people of the upper and middle classes, whose religiosity was marked by individual piety, devotion to the Sacred Heart, belief in the Immaculate Conception and allegiance to Rome. But the countryside too was Christianised, and it was here that elements of popular religion survived in prayers, hymns, processions and the cries of Martín Fierro, the voice of the rural underdog: 'vengan santos milagrosos, vengan todos en mi ayuda' ('Come down all you saints with your miracles, come to my aid').[2] Rural priests were not highly regarded by the politicians and press of Buenos Aires. Yet the church did not entirely abandon peons and their families. In Fraile Muerto an English observer described the priest as 'an Italian, and not a very clerical character, but pleasant and good natured, and having been educated as a doctor, did all he could for the bodies of his parishioners, and I trust also for their souls . . . During the cholera he exerted himself nobly for the people.'[3]

Brazil and its clergy had a different religious history from the rest of Latin America in the nineteenth century. Two particular institutions, monarchy and slavery, in both of which the clergy were involved, were inimical to the development of a modern church in an ex-colonial country. The political independence of Brazil brought no independence to the church. The almost absolute power of the Portuguese crown over colonial religion was inherited intact by the independent empire. Pedro II retained full powers of patronage and rights of intervention between Rome and Brazil. He nominated bishops, collected tithes, and paid the clergy, who became in effect government servants. 'Political priests' of this kind tended to be hostile to Rome, servants of the elite, and rarely faithful to their vows. During the monarchy (1822–89) there were only about 700 secular priests, products of state-controlled seminaries, to minister to 14 million people. Eventually, the decline and fall of the monarchy gave the church the opportunity to free itself from direct political influence and look to its own renewal. Dioceses were established, seminaries were founded, and a new and more dedicated clergy emerged. Monarchy, however, had not been the only embarrassment. The stain of slavery seeped through the whole of Brazilian society, and few institutions were left unmarked. The Catholic Church was no exception.

While the faithful relied on priests for mass and sacraments, priests depended upon bishops for selection and ordination, and the church depended on them as teachers and administrators. The Latin American episcopate was not entirely homogeneous, either in ideas or in social status. A number of church leaders came from landed elites, as did Archbishop Rafael Valentín

2 José Hernández, *Martín Fierro* (Buenos Aires: EUDEBA, 1962), p. 7.
3 Richard Arthur Seymour, *Pioneering in the Pampas* (London: Longmans, Green, and Co., 1869), pp. 80–1.

Valdivieso (1804–78) in Chile, whose family of landowners went back to colonial times. But the majority of the bishops came from the same middle ranks of society that supplied the priests, from traditional Catholic families in Mexico and Peru, from immigrant families in modern Argentina. They made their way in the church through their superior qualifications, moral character and powers of Christian leadership, rather than through social or political interests. Where the state retained an element of patronage, as in Argentina, episcopal appointments tended to be the results of compromise between the government and Rome and to produce a conventional hierarchy unlikely to disturb church or state.

In general Latin American bishops took a cautious and middle way, more prone to compromise than to conflict. But during times of crisis they varied between intransigents and those seeking a consensus with society and the state. The Mexican episcopate contained men like Eulogio Gillow, archbishop of Oaxaca (1887–1922), and Ignacio Montes de Oca, bishop of San Luis Potosí (1884–1921), both from wealthy families, both educated abroad – Gillow in England, Montes de Oca in Rome – and both true princes of the Church. Eduardo Sánchez Camacho, bishop of Tamaulipas, was different. He aroused much indignation among conservative Catholics for his attempt to reconcile the laws of the church and those of liberal reform, and for his opposition to the cult of Our Lady of Guadalupe. He was censured by the Roman Inquisition, resigned from his see, and died without the sacraments.

The political thinking of Colombia's bishops was almost entirely conservative and normally alarmed their opponents. Liberal statesmen feared the church, believing that it had great influence over consciences and could divert citizens from their proper obedience to the state. In 1852 thrice-president Tomás Cipriano de Mosquera addressed Pope Pius IX directly, arguing that liberals too were Catholics and that churchmen who intervened in political issues perverted a divine institution in the interests of one political party. The hierarchy, on the other hand, maintained a right of resistance to liberal measures when they attacked the God-given rights of the church. Both sides overstepped the limits of their competence, liberals requiring priests to obtain an official permit to perform religious services (1861), churchmen scattering excommunications like gunshots. In Chile the Catholic liberal politician Federico Errázuriz Zañartu, president of Chile in 1871–5, criticised the clergy as exploiters of the poor, incurring the wrath of Archbishop Valdivieso and other members of the hierarchy; they made it clear that outside the conservative alliance there was no place for a Catholic, only association with liberals and unbelievers. In 1874 the ageing archbishop excommunicated Errázuriz and all those in parliament who approved the suppression of the *fuero eclesiástico* (clerical immunity), a privilege from another age.

Faith and the faithful

Lay membership of the church in the nineteenth century ranged over a wide spectrum of belief and practice, from those who went to mass every Sunday to those whose only contact with religion was at baptism, first communion, marriage and death, and those whose Catholicism was primarily social and political. There was, however, an ingrained Catholicism in the majority of the people which was not easily measured by external practice but was part of national and popular culture.

The religion they received from bishops and priests often tended to be prohibitive rather than encouraging. It has been said of piety and liturgy in Chile that in many ways they expressed 'a religion of Lent, of fasting and penance, rather than a religion of Easter joy and gladness'.[4] Church teaching imposed a sharp division between the sacred and the profane, and Catholics were warned to avoid the devil, the world and the flesh. These were universal Christian values but received special emphasis in the Hispanic tradition, perpetuated by preachers who urged their congregations to 'flee all familiarity with persons of the other sex, and to avoid the slightest touch of even a thread of clothing'.

The laity knew the church as a parish, and their most immediate contact with organised religion was through their parish priest. The church had a strong pastoral presence in the older cities and provincial towns of Latin America, where numerous churches, convents and schools served the faith and enriched the skyline. In the countryside the framework was more stretched, and the ministrations of religion were more dependent on individual priests. Yet peasant commitment to the church was never in doubt. The Mexican Indians, in the past neglected and sometimes exploited by the church, were more inclined to accept the legitimacy of the clergy's authority than that of civil officials and politicians. The peasants of central Mexico, like the church, were victims of liberal policy and they resented attacks on their lands and fiestas, and other menaces of modernisation. They were the natural allies of the church, though the church hardly reciprocated or gave them the priests and resources they needed in their distant communities.

Religion did not necessarily abolish class conflict. As the parish priest of San Miguel in El Salvador reported in 1878, 'there exists a deep division between

---

4 Maximiliano Salinas, 'La Iglesia chilena ante el surgimiento del orden neocolonial', in *HGIAL*, vol. IX (1994), pp. 308–9.

the top families and the common people, a division which produces hatred and resentment'.[5] Or at least incomprehension. The Catholic elite in Mexico had little contact with the popular sectors of the church, while they were marked off from other leading groups by their religion and their politics, steadfast in defence of hierarchy in church and state. Catholic conservatives were politically destroyed by their liberal enemies during the civil wars of the Reform and subsequently kept a low profile.

In Argentina immigration had mixed effects on religion. Many Spanish, Italian and French immigrants were enemies of the church, political exiles hostile to clericalism. Many others were indifferent or would say that their work gave them no time for religion, which was best left to women and children. And some had their faith tested for the first time. A Catholic from Galicia wrote home to say, 'Paco, on arriving in Buenos Aires I have learnt on good authority that God does not exist.'[6] On the other hand, practising Catholics from northern Italy, Germany and Ireland reinforced the faith and increased vocations. Demographically Argentina remained a Catholic country, and in 1910 Catholics comprised 92 per cent of the population; but numbers countered for little in the struggle to preserve religion in the schools and in the laws of marriage, a contradiction that always bewildered the hierarchy.

In Colombia, unlike Mexico, religion was an agent of social cohesion and enabled people of different social origins to interact in common endeavours, in charity hospitals and social welfare projects. The Jesuits sought a new constituency among urban workers by changing the old devotional associations into workers' mutual aid organisations. The church became a 'familiar' institution, closely involved with people in new forms of social organisation, a unifying, not a divisive, influence. In Medellín, while the church increased its presence and penetrated the lives of the people – in parishes, pious associations, religious communities and public professions of faith – this was not introverted religion but served a humanitarian purpose, and the result was the growth of numerous philanthropic societies that brought social stability to Antioquia.

In Peru the politics of Catholics, clergy and lay, were conformist. The church was scorned by the intellectual elite as an obstacle to progress, and the corrupt and debauched rural priest became a stock character in the demonology of the Peruvian left. The church added fuel to the flames in its deference to Hispanic

---

5 Cardenal, *El poder eclesiástico en El Salvador*, p. 163.
6 E. Mignone, 'La Iglesia argentina en la organización nacional', *HGIAL*, vol. IX (1994), p. 342.

traditions and devotion to state power and social order. Yet the church did not remain aloof from the issues of the time and its action on the ground sometimes carried a clearer message than its words from the pulpit. In the period 1800–54 the church was an active agent in the demise of slavery in Peru, as it began to intervene decisively in the relationship between slaves and masters. To defend the integrity of slave marriage the church opposed the break up of slave families and moved to limit the right of slave owners to prevent marriages between slaves. Moreover, masters who attempted to sell married slaves outside the city of Lima, or who sexually abused their female slaves, might find themselves attacked not only by their slaves but also by the church.

The Peruvian Indians traditionally suffered from many exploiters, including clerics, whose extortionate behaviour frequently went far beyond the just collection of fees. But the church was not responsible for liberal legislation, which abolished Indian community lands and opened them to market forces, often cheating the Indians of their land without giving them true independence. Pastorals and pronouncements, overtly indifferent to the Indians, were not the only evidence of the church's Indian policy. In Indian rebellions of the later nineteenth century in the central and southern Andes church leaders in the diocese of Puno and elsewhere defended the interests of the Indians or at least acted as mediators between the rebels and the government. The Indians responded to these initiatives and reaffirmed their attachment to religion and respect for its ministers. In pacifying the Indians, of course, priests sometimes served government interests rather than those of the rebels, and it is difficult to assess the balance of church action in the sierra. The majority of priests in the Indian areas were white or mestizo, though many spoke Quechua or Aymara. But the allegiance of the Indians to traditional Catholicism was never in doubt, even during times of revolution, and there is no evidence that religion was used as a palliative or became an inhibiting factor in the Indians' struggle against abuses.

The absence of social conscience in the nineteenth-century church was perhaps seen above all in Brazil, where the church was a slave owner and a notable absentee among abolitionists. The secular clergy, convents and religious orders owned slaves and were among the various interest groups sustaining a slave society. It is true that some set an example. In 1866 the Benedictines, owners of some 2,000 slaves, freed all children henceforth born to female slaves in their possession, an important precedent at the time. After the Rio Branco Law of 1871, the so-called law of free birth, the Benedictine and Carmelite orders freed their slaves, several thousand in all. And individual priests campaigned for abolition. But the Brazilian church did not significantly support the abolitionist cause. Joaquim Nabuco, distinguished leader of abolition, had an audience with Pope Leo XIII in 1888 but without positive results, and throughout the antislavery campaign the Brazilian church remained a spectator of events. According to Nabuco, the Catholic church never raised its voice in favour of emancipation: 'Our clergy's desertion of the role of the Gospel assigned to it was as shameful as it could possibly be.' Reformers criticised what they saw as a triple alliance of church, slavery and monarchy as the major obstacles to national progress, and believed, however unjustly, that they would sink or swim together.

The religion of the people

Large numbers of Latin Americans deserted the Catholic Church in the nineteenth century. Reason deposed faith among the professional classes, while positivism provided an intellectual alternative to Christian doctrines. The decline of religious practice, however, was a story not only of lapsed Catholics but also of missing priests. Parishes were so large that attendance at mass was impossible for many people. While average sizes in the dioceses of Bogotá (3,732 parishioners) and Caracas (4,722) were barely manageable, parishes in the dioceses of Santiago (over 12,000) and La Paz (over 18,000) were too large for the existing clergy. And priests were declining in numbers. The ideal proportion of 1/1,000 cited for contemporary Europe and the United States was never reached in Latin America in the period 1820–1900; by 1912 the average was 4,480 to a priest, and even in Mexico, where vocations were more abundant, the average was only 1/3,000. In these conditions the cure of souls was a vain hope, and many nominal Catholics, especially those on the margin of society, were left without pastoral care for most of their lives. But the faithful were not entirely forgotten.

The church never lost its links with the popular sectors or became a captive of the elites, though the pattern of religious observance was unpredictable. There were places, especially in mestizo America, where churchgoing was regular, others where it was infrequent, others where it was once a year at Easter or thereabouts. There was also a difference between countries: on the one hand those where historically the church was strongly implanted, on the other hand those where religion was endemically weak. So Mexico was more Catholic than Honduras, Paraguay than Uruguay. The common people of Paraguay, inheritors of a Jesuit past and victims of a recent war, practised religion with a fervour that inspired a Vatican observer to report in 1878 that 'they love Catholicism almost instinctively'.[7] But outward conformity does not tell the whole story or unveil the depth of commitment, either among fervent believers or among apparently nominal ones, or among those influenced by social pressures.

The faith was secure, behaviour lamentable: this was the consensus of church opinion. The records of synods, councils and visitations describe a sinful population happy in its adultery, drunkenness, gambling, corruption, superstition and hedonism. In Santiago Archbishop Mariano Casanova devoted an entire pastoral to the perils of alcohol; elsewhere sex outside marriage seemed to be the prevailing sin. 'Yet in spite of this, the faith is preserved intact and there is much religious enthusiasm.'[8] So the priests made a distinction between morality and piety: their people were pious but sinful. Moral laxity was a feature of Latin American Catholicism that impressed all the emissaries from Rome. An apostolic delegate reported from Honduras at the end of the century: 'As for morals, behaviour is so lax that it can only be attributed to an exaggerated confidence in God's mercy or to the scandalous example of their own priests. Here it is all explained in terms of human frailty. So concubinage is widespread, tolerated by parents, who allow it before their own eyes, under the same roof.'[9] These informal relationships, in fact, were treated as virtual marriages, and the church itself admitted that the principal obstacles to marriage were not immorality but the shortage of clergy, the distances separating communities, and the lack of money to defray expenses.

To what extent did religion in Latin America divide into an official church and a popular church? Was there a religious subculture independent of the institutional church, the voice of the popular classes, existing alongside the orthodox religion of priests and bishops? Latin America produced popular forms of religion but not alternative models. The favourite practices of popular Catholicism expressed orthodox teaching on saints, indulgences, the holy souls, prayers for the dead, the veneration of relics, wearing of medals, use of holy water, and recourse to Marian shrines and cults, none of which departed from traditional doctrines. Popular religiosity and lay movements were not inherently anticlerical. They had developed to some extent in response to the absence of priests, not in opposition to them. Popular religion transcended social class. It was urban as well as rural, artisan as well as peasant, clerical as well as lay. But the church in Latin America existed within the prevailing social structure, where the poor were more prone to disease, starvation and

7 Pazos, *La Iglesia en la América del IV centenario*, p. 274.
8 Cardenal, *El poder eclesiástico en El Salvador*, p. 163.
9 Pazos, *La Iglesia de la América del IV centenario*, p. 223.

shocks of nature, and more likely to invoke their special saints and throng their favourite shrines than were the rich. Most of the fiestas were organised by particular peasant, mining or artisan groups, who sought the protection of a popular saint or the Virgin. In some cases blacks and mulattos had their own fiestas, Indians their special feast days.

The Catholics of Colombia took their religion not only into the churches but also into the streets, and popular religiosity was expressed in civic as well as pious events: in Medellín in 1875 a procession marking a civil occasion included magistrates, lawyers, doctors and professional associations, and 'in front marched the *Asociación del Sagrado Corazón de Jesús*'.[10] Religious fervour took other forms than pious women in black hurrying to early-morning mass. Faith promoted works of charity and kept the richer families concerned with the needs of the poor and helpless; the faith fulfilled secular as well as spiritual expectations. Seats were full not only in churches but also in libraries, lecture rooms, and other cultural venues where people searched for a better life, and in doing so contributed further to social integration.

In Mexico and Guatemala, countries with large Indian populations, practised and prescribed religion more or less merged, and the main disquiet of the church concerned denial and superstition rather than popular or local practices. Church authorities in Peru looked with suspicion on many of the religious practices of Andean Indians. In 1912 the bishop of Puno, Valentín Ampuero, described the religion of the Indians as distorted by ignorance: 'their religious beliefs are minimal, their Christianity is adulterated and consists in having a mass said, or praying before a saint's image on occasion of illness or death in the family or loss of a llama'.[11] Yet masses and prayers were Catholic practices, legacies of past evangelisation, and signs of present faith.

The Romanisation of the Latin American church

The doctrinal inspiration of the Latin American church in the nineteenth century came from Rome, and standards were set by Pope Pius IX (1846–78), who in December 1864 published the encyclical *Quanta Cura*, with its annex the Syllabus of Errors.[12] Catholics in Latin America easily recognised the 'errors', for they lived with them daily: liberalism, secularism, freedom of thought, and toleration. The encyclical focused the attention of Latin American Catholics obsessively on liberalism, rationalism and *laicismo* (exclusion of religion from

10 Londoño-Vega, *Religion, culture, and society in Colombia*, p. 163.
11 Jeffrey Klaiber, 'La reorganización de la Iglesia', in *HGIAL*, vol. VIII (1987), p. 301.
12 See chapters 2 and 15 above.

public affairs), and led the church into absolutist positions that delayed its integration in the modern world. Catholic moderates seeking a middle way were embarrassed by its intransigence. Conservative Catholics could appeal to it against moderates. And liberals could cite it as proof of the danger from the Catholic Church.

Latin America was a new world for Rome, and in exploring it Rome discovered that in one sense there was no such thing as a Latin American church. Nationalism affected churchmen and their policies as it did secular governments, and divisions between churches were a fact of religious life. Rome regarded them all as Latins with common origins, and unity of race, language and interests, and was astonished to observe that 'they live divided and in virtual isolation from each other, with hardly any communication or exchange of ideas and doctrines'.[13] Rome was the point of unity, and republican Latin America gave Rome more access to Catholics than the Spanish monarchy had ever allowed; by the end of the nineteenth century the Holy See had diplomatic relations with most of the countries of the sub-continent.

Latin America was a source of anxiety to Rome. Clergy were too few and not of the best. Concubinage was common and was accepted by the faithful, for 'in some parishes the family of the parish priest is known and received without scandal'.[14] Latin America, especially the River Plate countries, was served by increasing numbers of European clergy. European secular clergy, as distinct from regulars, were not always well received, and were regarded even by Rome as often ill educated, unworthy and financially motivated, dispatched by bishops who were glad to be rid of them. Nevertheless Rome was convinced that the only hope for reforming the clergy and modernising the church came from Europe, especially in the case of religious orders, whose local recruits were 'religious only in name'. It was essential to increase and improve seminaries, and to provide a model of higher education in the church. This was the function of the Colegio Pio Latinoamericano, founded in Rome in 1856 by Pius IX and subsidised by an allocation from the Latin American diocesan contributions to the Holy See. The Latin American bishops were slow to send candidates, and payments, but it was from this college that the best of bishops and seminary professors eventually came, proud bearers of degrees from the Gregorian University.

Envoys, bishops, the Catholic press, seminaries, the religious orders, these were the instruments of papal influence in Latin America, fortified by the

13 Pazos, *La Iglesia en la América del IV centenario*, p. 41.
14 Pazos, *La Iglesia en la América del IV centenario*, p. 223.

respect of Catholics for the successor of St Peter. The Latin American bishops came into direct contact with Ultramontane Catholicism in the First Vatican Council (1869–70), where they comprised forty-eight of the 700 prelates who participated in that gathering. They adopted conservative positions on matters of faith and morals, and almost without exception they supported the definition of papal infallibility. Thirty years later the Latin American episcopate had a further opportunity to affirm its allegiance to the Holy See when Pope Leo XIII convoked the first Latin American Plenary Council, a unique occasion not previously known in the history of the church.

The Council was held in Rome in 1899 in the Colegio Pio Latino-americano, a site free of national pressures and the only one acceptable to the various Latin American churches. Out of a total episcopate of 104, thirteen archbishops and forty-one bishops attended; Latin American theologians and non-episcopal experts were not called upon to play a part, and essentially this was a meeting of bishops organised according to canon law and the clerical criteria of the time, and advised by experts, most of whom had not been to Latin America. The Council deliberated on problems of paganism, superstition, ignorance of religion, socialism, masonry, the press, and other perceived dangers to religion in the modern world. The church in Latin America was depicted as a church assailed by 'the monstrous errors' of liberalism, positivism, atheism and rationalism. None of these horrors was imaginary, as the Catholics of Mexico and Central America could testify; but in general a siege mentality prevailed, and the assertion of the church's rights of jurisdiction over religious education in state schools was by this time unrealistic. There were 998 articles for the defence and propagation of the Catholic faith and the organisation of the church in Latin America, most of them inspired by Roman theology and canon law and the papal teaching of the nineteenth century rather than by any Latin American traditions and local needs, and more designed to centralise than to devolve, to conserve than to initiate. The Council's list of prevailing sins was conventional: gambling, drunkenness, lust, concubinage, adultery, obscenity and murder. But sins of injustice to workers, peasants and the poor were not a priority, and references to the social encyclical *Rerum Novarum* were brief. The Council's final letter to the clergy and people of Latin America, signed on 9 July, gave thanks for 'God's special favour' in having populated 'America so generously with a Latin and Catholic race'. In spite of its limitations, the Council left one enduring legacy, which has been identified as 'the rebirth of collegial consciousness among the Latin American episcopate, which would yield fruit in the future'.[15] This took the form of a specific instruction urging the church to hold conferences of bishops every three years in the ecclesiastical provinces of Latin America.

Directed by Roman organisation and released by the secular state, the church in Argentina, Brazil and many other countries of Latin America now had to generate its own resources, strengthen its own structures, improve the material fabric of religion, its churches, chapels and shrines, establish new seminaries, monasteries and convents, and welcome reinforcements of priests, nuns and religious from Europe, some to evangelise the towns, some the countryside. And a primary instrument of evangelisation was the Catholic parish school, whose children were marked with the new practice of first communion.

The growth of Protestantism

The nineteenth century saw the growth of another religion in Latin America, one that did not accept the jurisdiction of the Catholic Church or the primacy of the pope. The first Protestants in Latin America were foreign diplomats, merchants and residents, who from the early years of independence settled in the capitals and ports of the sub-continent, protected directly or indirectly by the British trade treaties with the new nations. Congregations and churches of Anglicans, Presbyterians and Methodists made their appearance, as tolerated enclaves rather than missionary bases. But the arrival of representatives of Bible Societies heralded further expansion, for they sought to reach beyond foreigners to the Catholic population. The Catholics of Latin America were not ignorant of the Scriptures, for they encountered them in the Epistles and Gospels of the mass. But the Bible Societies met the needs of some and led to a further phase, that of evangelisation among Catholics and unconverted Indians by missionaries, especially from the United States and now including Episcopalians and Baptists. The numbers of clergy and followers increased, especially in countries like Argentina and Brazil which received large immigrant populations in the late nineteenth century and where the Catholic Church did not immediately respond to their presence. In order to survive, the new churches and sects had to rely on liberal policies of religious toleration and separation of church and state; liberals usually welcomed the new input of skill and knowledge contributed by Protestant immigrants and regarded their work ethic as

15 Dussel, *Historia de la Iglesia en América Latina*, pp. 175–6.

an example to Catholics. Their schools were consciously liberal – in Mexico the 'daughters of Juárez' were to rival the 'Daughters of Mary'.[16] This affinity between liberalism and Protestantism further alerted the Catholic Church and caused it to rely even more on protection and privilege, determined to keep control of registration of births, marriages and deaths. Catholics equated Protestantism with secularisation, living proof of the danger of religious toleration, and further argument for alliance with conservatives and insistence on state support. Early relations between Catholics and Protestants, therefore, were tense. Protestant preachers tended to brand Catholics as superstitious, while Catholics saw Protestantism as another evil of the modern age and, from the early twentieth century, as another arm of United States influence. Yet even after a century of growth, Protestantism was a rare and exotic phenomenon in Latin America.

Church and state in a liberal world

The Romanisation of the Catholic Church took place at the same time as the liberalisation of the secular state. As the church gained in spiritual authority so it lost its temporal power, in a struggle that was not always peaceful. The pace of change, and the degree, differed from country to country. Each had its own response to a host of common problems. The church wanted to keep its traditional resources, preserve its privileges, and decide education and moral issues. The state wanted to control senior appointments, recover sources of wealth, determine national policy and marginalise Rome. In some countries anticlericalism was so strong that not only was the church disestablished but limitations were even imposed on its religious functions. Military victory over their enemies enabled the Mexican liberals to secularise schools, hospitals and charitable institutions, appropriate church property, and then proceed to attack the religious orders, expel the Sisters of Charity and forbid the holding of religious activities outside churches. But in Colombia the church remained defiant of the state and Antioquia became notorious as a 'República de curas' ('priestly republic'). In other countries, such as Argentina, a compromise was reached, and the church continued to be subsidised by the state but also dependent upon it, helpless in face of the removal of religion from state schools and the introduction of a civil marriage law. In yet other countries the church remained more or less established but had to accept state control over the

16 Jean-Pierre Bastian, 'Protestantism in Latin America', in Dussel (ed.), *The church in Latin America*, p. 329.

410

appointment of bishops. In Peru a conservative church was forced protesting into a pluralist society. Ecuador, often described as a theocracy, was in fact a small clerical state, 'an entirely Catholic nation', in which the state occupied the dominant position.

Perhaps the most important factor in determining church–state relations was the relative power and wealth of the church. Where the church was large, its clergy ubiquitous and its riches obvious, it was more likely to provoke anticlericalism and envy, both political and personal; it was also in a stronger position to defend itself. The ensuing conflict would probably be bitter, and the settlement more decisive, one way or the other. In Mexico, war of this kind (1858–60) took the church from power to persecution. Where the church was poor and weak, as in Venezuela, it did not provoke overt hostility, but nor could it defend itself, and gradually, without dramatic conflict, it would find its privileges eroded. In some cases there was a balance of power. And in Colombia, where from the 1880s an educated clergy tightened its grip on levers of power in local government, education and the press, the church gave valuable support to government and earned exceptional privileges.

In the period 1870–1914 the church in most of Latin America ceased to rely on legal and political sanctions for the promotion and protection of religion. Catholics did not at first welcome their new status or respond to conditions of independence, pluralism and toleration, but continued to look backwards to a Christian state and collaborating church as the ideals against which to judge the secular trends of the age. Yet they were not fighting innocents. Power could change liberals into monsters of illiberalism, and it was difficult for Catholics to understand decrees that expelled bishops, exiled nuns, confiscated church property, and forbade wearing soutanes in the street and carrying the viaticum to the sick. But gradually adjustment was made and the church exchanged external support for inner renewal.

25

Between east and west: the Eastern Catholic ('Uniate') churches

ROBERT J. TAFT

'Uniate'[1] churches comprise Eastern Christians who either reaffirmed their never formally broken communion with Rome, or left their Orthodox mother churches to join the Catholic communion. They derive from all seven extant Eastern Christian traditions – Armenian, Byzantine, Coptic and Ethiopian and those of Syriac provenance: East-Syrian or Mesopotamian, represented today by the Chaldean and Syro-Malabar Catholic churches, West-Syrian or Syro-Antiochene by the Syrian Catholic Church (another branch of the same tradition, the Syro-Malankara Catholic Church, dates only from the 1930s); and the Maronite Church of Lebanon, which shares elements of both East- and West-Syrian provenance. The last is the only Eastern church that is entirely Catholic, and only the Chaldean and Syro-Malabar churches are larger than their Orthodox counterparts. These churches are all mono-ethnic except those of the Byzantine tradition, which includes communities of Albanian, Georgian, Greek, Hungarian, Melkite or Arab, Romanian, and Slavic 'Greek Catholics', the name Empress Maria Theresa invented in 1774 to distinguish them from their 'Latin Catholic' coreligionists.

The history of these minorities, subject to Latin meddling and paternalism within the Roman communion and shunned by their Orthodox mother churches, was largely conditioned by their turbulent relation to these much larger church bodies in whose shadow they were fated to live.

At the sunset of the empires

The turbulent century from the Congress of Vienna until the Great War witnessed the destruction of the three territorially integral multi-ethnic empires of the day: the Austro-Hungarian empire in which Eastern Catholics flourished;

---

1 The term 'Uniate', from the Slavic neologism 'Unia', is now considered derogatory, but was not so in the period covered here. It was coined to denote a method of church union some view as politically motivated. See Suttner, *Church unity*.

the Tsarist Russian empire in which they were persecuted and violently suppressed; and the Ottoman empire in which they were initially tolerated, eventually protected and allowed to flourish, and finally massacred.

In Austria-Hungary

The Ruthenians

In the partitions of 1772, 1793 and 1795, rapacious neighbours swallowed Poland piece by piece. Austria incorporated the Ruthenians[2] of Galicia, with its capital Lvov (Lviv, Lwów, Lemburg), metropolitan see (1808) of the Greek Catholic Church to which most of the population belonged. In the Hungarian half of the Dual Monarchy the Greek Catholics comprised a multi-ethnic mix of Slavic (Croatian, Rusyn, Serbian, Slovak), Hungarian and Romanian Greek Catholics originally centred around the see of Užhorod-Mukačevo in Transcarpathia. Separate bishoprics were created at Križevci for those in Croatia and Serbia in 1777, at Gherla for the Romanians in 1853, at Hajdúdorog for the Hungarians in 1912, and at Prešov for the Slovaks in 1918. The Congress of Vienna confirmed Austro-Hungarian control over these areas, and despite the pressures of assimilation, the Greek Catholics thrived under the relatively benign Austro-Hungarian regime.

The twentieth century saw stirrings of renewal, especially in Galicia under the leadership of Lvov metropolitan Andryj Sheptytskyj (1900–44),[3] who sought to steer a delicate course between opposed Polonising and Russophile tendencies among his clergy.[4] As the most important native socio-cultural institution in the area, the Greek Catholic Church played a key role in the formation of the Ukrainian and Rusyn national consciousness, preventing assimilation by the dominant Polish and Hungarian cultures. The church became a national institution and the centre of the struggle for cultural development and emancipation.[5]

From 1880, economic conditions forced large numbers of Ruthenians to emigrate to North America, where mistreatment at the hands of the Catholic Church and its hierarchy provoked mass defections to Orthodoxy, and led

---

2 Slavic 'Greek Catholics' were called 'Ruthenians' before the consolidation of Ukrainian, Belorussian, Rusyn and Slovak national consciousness.
3 Korolevsky, *Metropolitan Andrew*.
4 With the outbreak of World War I in 1914, hundreds of Galician Ukrainians were hanged without trial by the Austrian authorities for real or alleged pro-Russian allegiance: Subtelny, *Ukraine*, p. 341.
5 Hirka, *Religion and nationality*.

ultimately to the Vatican's erecting independent Greek Catholic jurisdictions for the Galicians and Transcarpathians.[6]

The Romanians

In Transylvania, part of Hungary until the end of World War I, the Romanian Greek Catholics were subject to the Latin primate of Esztergom until 1853, when Pius IX established for them a separate ecclesiastical province centred in Blaj, with a metropolitan see and three suffragan eparchies (dioceses). Synods held at Blaj in 1872, 1882 and 1900 consolidated the organisation of the church. Romanian Greek Catholic intellectuals played a leading role in the revival and promotion of Romanian culture and national unity.[7]

Under the Tsarist yoke

The annihilation of 'Uniatism'

Ruthenians, second-class Catholics subjected to certain restrictions under independent Poland, began their Calvary in earnest when the Congress of Vienna created 'Congress Poland' subject to Tsarist Russia. After the Polish uprising of 1830–1, Nicholas I (1825–55) imposed a draconian military dictatorship on the Congress Kingdom, and after the revolt of 1863, Alexander II (1855–81) reduced it to a province of the Russian Empire and inaugurated a policy of Russification.

In 1839, Nicholas I forced 1,674,478 Greek Catholics into Orthodoxy,[8] and in 1875, under Alexander II, the last remaining eparchy of Cholm was liquidated and resistance brutally repressed with the infamous slaughter of simple villagers in Drelov on 18 January 1874, and in Pratulin on 24 January of the same year, when imperial Cossack troops fired on the Greek Catholic faithful gathered in front of their church.[9] Some 250,000 Greek Catholics were forcibly incorporated into Orthodoxy, while 70,000 recusants turned to the Latin church or were ministered to secretly by incognito Jesuit circuit riders.

Civil unrest following the humiliation of the Russo-Japanese war (1904–5) forced Nicholas II (1894–1917) to proclaim his famous Edict of Tolerance on 17 April 1905, at which 300,000 Belorussian peasants, Greek Catholics forced into Orthodoxy under his predecessor, passed to the Latin church since the Edict did not extend to Eastern Catholics.

6 Simon, 'In Europe and America'.
7 Roberson, *The Eastern Christian churches*, pp. 171–7.
8 Lencyk, *The Eastern Catholic Church*.
9 Glinka, *Diocesi ucraino-cattolica*, pp. 85–6.

'Old Believers in Communion with the Holy See'

At the turn of the century a small group of Russian Orthodox clergy and laity, dissatisfied with their state church yet aware that Catholicism in its foreign, Latin (read Polish) vesture was totally antipathetic to the Russian spirit, passed to Catholicism one by one while retaining their Russian Orthodox ethos and rite.[10] This spontaneous movement emerges into the light of history with Nicholas A. Tolstoy (1867–1938), a Russian Orthodox priest who professed Catholicism in Rome in 1894. It was at his hands that in 1896 the famous Russian philosopher Vladimir Solovyov (1853–1900), whose treatise *Russie et l'Eglise universelle* (Paris, 1889) gave ideological impetus to the movement, made his profession of the Catholic faith and received Holy Communion, apparently without thereby abandoning Orthodoxy.

Though Eastern Catholicism was still banned, the authorities turned a blind eye to this tiny group. Aided by two French Assumptionists and emboldened by the new climate, in 1909 these converts, including several former Orthodox priests, opened a Russian rite house-chapel in St Petersburg. This group called itself 'Old Believers in Communion with the Holy See' because one of their clergy, Evstafij Susalev, was a converted Old Believer priest, a confession legalised by the 1905 decree.[11] In 1907 Metropolitan Sheptytskyj of Lvov organised the church life of this group under his jurisdiction, a step Pius X approved the following year. The civil authorities closed the chapel in 1913, but the community carried on in secret, grew, and even published a periodical, *Slovo Istiny (The Word of Truth)* (1913–18), until swallowed up in the Soviet Gulag.

In the Ottoman empire[12]

Religious minorities in the Ottoman empire were organised into distinct 'communities' (*millets*), enjoying a relative autonomy under the control of their religious authorities in questions of religion and personal status (marriage, inheritance, education), but without the civil or political rights of the Muslims. Rather, they were *dhimmi*, subordinate but protected peoples, as Islamic Shari'a law required. This system, while assuring Christian minorities a degree of stability and internal autonomy *vis-à-vis* other communities and the Sublime Porte, also made religious confession the badge of national identity, turning

---

10 Wenger, *Rome et Moscou*, pp. 57–96 and *passim*; Simon, *Russicum*, pp. 14–42; Mailleux, *Exarch Leonid Feodorov*.

11 The Old Believers stem from the 1667 schism of those who broke with the Russian Orthodox Church over the liturgical reforms introduced under Patriarch Nikon (1652–8).

12 Frazee, *Catholics and sultans*; Mayeur-Jacquen, 'Les chrétiens d'orient'.

'Uniatism' into a kind of treason to the ethnic confessional community whose survival depended on numbers and unity. Worse still, the *millet* system left the 'Uniates' under the authority of the Orthodox ecclesiastical hierarchy they had abandoned.

The 'Golden Age' of the Latin missions

Catholic missionary activity in the Ottoman East, exercised chiefly by French religious orders and congregations, was interrupted by the French Revolution but recovered in the next century. Rome confirmed France's protectorate over Catholics in the Ottoman empire in 1888 and 1898. The virulent anticlericalism of the period was not for export, and France's anticlerical governments were happy to foster surrogate French influence abroad via Catholic schools and missions.[13]

Contact with the West has been a mixed blessing for Eastern Christianity, but in the nineteenth century the Catholic churches of the Middle East made rapid advances, often with the help of Latin missionaries. Schools and seminaries were founded almost everywhere, religious and monastic life renewed or restored. In addition to proselytising the Orthodox, the Latin missionaries contributed enormously to the intellectual and spiritual renewal of the 'Uniate' churches, though often at the price of the erosion of their tradition through Latinisation, and many Eastern Catholics passed to the Latin rite, albeit illegally, largely for reasons of prestige and snobbery.

Armenians

Meanwhile, each church was also living out its own particular history, none more turbulent than that of the Armenians.[14] Armenian Catholics had remained under the Armenian apostolic patriarch of Constantinople until the French ambassador pressured the Porte to recognise them as a separate *millet* in 1829. Civil jurisdiction was confided to a layman, then in 1831 to a priest with the title patriarch, while an archbishop at Constantinople exercised religious jurisdiction. In 1846 the two powers were united when Mgr Hassoun, the civil chief, was elected archbishop. When the Synod of Bzommar elected him catholicos of Cilicia in 1867, the jurisdictional anomaly was resolved and Pius IX (1846–78) united the two sees into one, transferring the patriarchate to the Ottoman capital, where it remained until after the dissolution of the empire.

13 Hajjar, *Le Vatican, la France, et le catholicisme oriental.*
14 Janin, *Les églises orientales*, pp. 355–60.

Schisms and divisions continued to plague the Armenian Catholic Church until the genocide (1915). Pius IX's bull *Reversurus* of 12 July 1867, aimed at putting an end to these problems, stipulated that henceforth Rome would choose Armenian Catholic bishops from a list of three names, that laity and lower clergy could no longer participate in patriarchal elections, and that patriarchs would have to be confirmed by Rome before exercising their office.[15] This provoked a violent reaction, and several Armenian Catholic bishops and most of the Antonine monks passed to the Armenian Orthodox Church.[16]

In letter after letter, Pius IX returned to the intractable internecine divisions provoked by lay interference in the affairs of the Armenian Catholic Church (*Non Sine Gravissimo*, 24 February 1870; *Quo Impensiore*, 20 May 1870; *Ubi Prima*, 11 March 1871; *Quartus Supra*, 6 January 1873), even appealing to the sultan to restore order. The Turkish revolution of 1908 led to further disruptions. Patriarch Terzian, unanimously elected by the synod of 1910, was deposed by the government in 1912 through the machinations of influential laity opposed to his reforms. Because of this intractable mess, Pius IX's intention to apply the dispositions of *Reversurus* to other Eastern Catholic communities was prudently shelved.

In 1850 Pius IX had established the diocese of Artvin for Armenian Catholics in the Russian empire, but Tsarist antipathy for 'Uniatism' led to its abandonment, and in 1912 the Armenian Catholics there were placed under the Latin bishop of Tiraspol.[17]

Seven of the fifteen Armenian Catholic bishoprics existing in 1914 were wiped out in the genocide, when seven bishops, 130 priests, forty nuns, and up to 100,000 faithful perished.

Maronites

The Maronites,[18] a strongly monastic community with no Orthodox counterpart, flourished early in this period under the beneficent regime of Emir Bechir (1749–1840). The immediately subsequent political turmoil, however, led to their massacre in 1842 and 1845 by the Druze. The church's inner life also suffered from outside pressures: the Latinisation of Maronite usages was reinforced by the synod of 1818. But signs of resistance presaged later reforms, when Patriarch Boulos Mas'ad (1854–90) declined the proposal of the apostolic delegate in Syria to invite Latin missionaries to the Synod of Bkerke in

---

15 Hajjar, *Les chrétiens uniates*, pp. 289ff.
16 Janin, *Les églises orientales*, pp. 356–7.
17 Roberson, *Eastern Christian Churches*, p. 253.
18 Janin, *Les églises orientales*, pp. 454–7; Hajjar, *Les chrétiens uniates, passim*.

1856, one of a series of Eastern Catholic synods of the epoch at which Latin pressure sought to impose liturgical uniformity and Latinisation. Flourishing French Jesuit institutions served the Maronites in Lebanon: the College of Ghazir, established in 1847, moved to Beirut in 1875 to become the renowned Université Saint-Joseph (1881).

Chaldeans

The Chaldean Catholic Church,[19] divided anomalously under two chief hierarchs, was united in 1830 under one patriarch, John VIII Hormizd (1830–8), resident in Mosul.[20] His second successor, Joseph VI Audo (1848–78), one of the intrepid Eastern Catholic anti-infallibilists at Vatican I, had grave dissensions with Rome, chiefly because of the Mellus schism in India (see India below). Calm returned only under Audo's successor Elias Peter II Abulyonan (1878–94). Under Patriarch Emmanuel II Thomas (1900–47) numerous Assyrians passed to the Chaldean church, including two bishops and several other clergy. In the massacres attending the dissolution of the Ottoman empire, four Chaldean bishops, numerous priests and some 70,000 faithful perished.

Syrians

The nascent Syro-Antiochene Catholic Church,[21] recognised by the Porte in 1830, expanded steadily under notable leaders like patriarchs Ignatius-Peter VII Jarhweh (1828–51) and Anthony Samhairy (1851–66). Tensions were inevitable, since this growth was at the expense of the Orthodox mother church, including the passage of one patriarch, eight bishops, and most of the faithful of entire dioceses to the Catholic communion. The Synod of Sharfeh in 1888 introduced the inevitable ill-considered Latinisations like clerical celibacy. Patriarch Ignatius Ephrem II Rahmani (1898–1929), a vigorous, creative patriarch and renowned Syriac scholar, gave this church an international visibility disproportionate to its modest size. This community, too, suffered in the Turkish massacres of about 1,500,000 Christians in Upper Mesopotamia in the aftermath of World War I.

Bulgarians and Macedonians

The movement in Bulgaria for union with Rome arose in 1859–60 from the struggle among the Bulgarian Orthodox for emancipation from the

---

19 Le Coz, *l'église d'orient*; Janin, *Les églises orientales*, pp. 422–4.
20 Habbi, 'L'unification de la hiérarchie chaldéene'.
21 Janin, *Les églises orientales*, pp. 387–9.

Hellenising Phanariots of Constantinople.[22] In 1861, Pius IX ordained the elderly archimandrite Iosif Sokolski (c. 1790–1879) as Bulgarian Catholic archbishop, and the community received recognition from the Sublime Porte. At this point the Russians, self-appointed guardians of Orthodoxy in the Ottoman empire, intervened in one of the more bizarre of their ceaseless attempts to stamp out 'Uniatism' by force. On 6 June 1861, Russian agents shanghaied Sokolski aboard a Russian vessel in the Black Sea and deported him to Odessa and ultimate confinement in Kiev, where he died in 1879.[23]

The small Catholic community rapidly grew to about 60,000 members and survived with the help of the French Assumptionists and the Polish Resurrectionists Pius IX sent to their aid. Rafail Popov succeeded Sokolski as bishop, and in 1883 apostolic vicariates were created in Adrianople and Thessaloniki, with an archbishop resident in Sofia. French Lazarists promoted further successful union movements among the Macedonian Slavs in 1874–83.[24] In the Balkan wars of 1912–13, Macedonia and Thrace, where most of the Eastern rite Catholics lived, were divided between Turkey, Greece and Serbia, and most of the Bulgarian population was expelled to Bulgaria, while in Greece and Serbia there were forced conversions of the 'Uniates' to Orthodoxy.[25]

Greeks

The formation of a small 'Uniate' community in Constantinople was initiated in 1856 by John G. Marangos, a Latin Catholic priest from Syros, who proselytised the Greek Orthodox of the capital.[26] In the 1880s two additional Byzantine Catholic communities were established in Turkish Thrace, and in 1895 the Assumptionists founded a seminary and two small Byzantine Catholic parishes in Constantinople. Pius X created an episcopal jurisdiction for this community in 1911.

Melkites

The Melkite Greek Catholic Church, begun in Syria and Lebanon at the beginning of the eighteenth century, underwent a period of persecution from their Orthodox brethren in Syria, especially in Aleppo in 1817–21, with nine martyrs in 1818, and in Damascus in 1823–4.[27] Only in 1837 was civil emancipation

---

22 Elenkov, La chiesa cattolica, esp. chs. 2–3.
23 Ibid., pp. 73–5; Grulich, Die unierte Kirche, pp. 52–6.
24 Grulich, Die unierte Kirche, esp. pp. 56–75.
25 Elenkov, La chiesa cattolica, pp. 126–7.
26 Roberson, The Eastern Christian Churches, pp. 177–8; Gatti and Korolevskij, I rite e le chiese, pp. 428–30.
27 Gatti and Korolevskij, I riti e le chiese, pp. 436–55.

assured, though vexations from the Orthodox continued for another decade. The Melkites spread to Palestine and Egypt through emigration, and in 1838 the Melkite Catholic patriarch of Antioch was given the additional titles of Jerusalem and Alexandria.

Perceived as a bastion of Arabism, more so than the Orthodox patriarchate of Antioch, beholden to the Phanariot Greeks, the Melkites acquired sympathy in the Arab world at the first stirrings of the Arab awakening. The Melkites would also become the most resistant of the 'Uniates' to the inroads of Latinisation and the erosion of their age-old patriarchal rights and independence *vis-à-vis* Rome. Patriarch Maximos III Mazloum (1833–56) resisted Latin encroachments and repudiated Roman attempts to impose the Gregorian Calendar.[28] For his trouble he had to wait two years for Roman confirmation of his election as patriarch. Undismayed, Maximos exercised his patriarchal jurisdiction anyway, holding the Melkite Synod of Aïn-Traz in 1835 and publishing its decisions without awaiting Roman approval.[29] Another intrepid Melkite defender of Oriental rights, Patriarch Gregory II Yusif (1864–97), clashed famously with Pius IX at Vatican I and left Rome to avoid voting on the constitution *Pastor Aeternus* defining papal infallibility. He assented to it later only *juxta modum,* adding the conditional codicil: 'all rights and privileges and prerogatives of the patriarchs of the Eastern Churches being respected'.[30] He played a key role in the 1894 meeting Leo XIII convoked in Rome, from which resulted the encyclical *Orientalium Dignitas* (see Leo XIII below).

Copts and Ethiopians

The union of Copts with the Catholic Church was fostered by Franciscan missionaries in the nineteenth century, and Leo XIII had the Jesuits open a seminary in 1879. In 1895, the Coptic Catholic patriarchate was restored with Kyrillos Makarios (1867–1921) as patriarch, but grave conflicts erupted in the fractured community, and in 1908 Pius X forced Kyrillos's resignation. The small community survived under an episcopal vicar apostolic while the patriarchal throne remained vacant until 1947.[31] Though Catholic missionaries were at work in Ethiopia from 1839, the Ethiopian Catholic Church did not develop its structures until after our period.[32]

---

28 Hajjar, *Un lutteur infatigable.*
29 Hajjar, *Les chrétiens uniates*, pp. 269–70.
30 Roberson, *The Eastern Christian Churches*, pp. 141–2.
31 Martin, 'Les coptes catholiques'; Janin, *Les églises orientales*, pp. 490–1.
32 Janin, *Les églises orientales*, pp. 502–3.

The Ottoman collapse

After centuries of relative stability, the Ottoman empire in the nineteenth century was menaced internally by revolt on its Balkan fringes, and externally by the designs of Russia and the meddling of France, Austria and Britain. The precariously balanced *millet* system of multiple independent communities begins to collapse for a variety of reasons: the spread of Enlightenment ideals, the rise of national consciousness and the interference of the European powers, exacting from the Porte 'capitulations' in favour of their co-religionists and missionaries.[33] Protection of Christians by the Western Powers and the concession of civil equality in 1839 conflicted with the Shari'a legislation sanctioning Muslim, not foreign protection of the *dhimmi*. This weakened and humiliated the Sublime Porte, exacerbating a situation that led to the nineteenth-century massacres, all of which occurred after the 1839 'reforms'.

The revolt of the majority Christian provinces in Greece and the Balkans led to their autonomy and ultimate independence. Meanwhile, Russia annexed Eastern Armenia, leading to the Russo-Turkish war of 1877. The pressure of incessant insurrections and European demands led to the acquisition of civil and political rights and equality by Christians in Egypt and the Ottoman empire by the middle of the century (1839–56). But the gains were a mixed blessing, increasing tensions as Christians, suspected of disloyalty in favour of their foreign protectors, sought to maintain their *millet* autonomy and privileges while enjoying their new equality before the law. In addition, the rapid educational and social progress of the Christian communities, more affluent and socially advanced than their Muslim neighbours, provoked resentment, distrust and ultimately violence, as each retreat of the disintegrating empire led to the massacre of Christians caught up in its death throes. The Kurds slaughtered the Assyrians in 1843, 1846 and 1895; the Druze massacred the Maronites in 1842 and 1845; Muslim attacks against the Christians in Aleppo in 1850 culminated in the civil war of 1860 that spread from Lebanon to Syria. When the Muslims massacred over 20,000 Christians without the slightest reaction from the Ottoman authorities, France intervened with an expeditionary force leading, in 1861, to the creation in Lebanon of an autonomous *mutasarrifa,* 80 per cent Maronite in population under a Christian governor, a status that lasted until 1914.

---

33 For a contemporary view of western responsibility for the disruptions attending the fall of the Ottoman Empire, see Sonyel, *Minorities.*

'St Thomas Christians' of India

In the sixteenth century, the Portuguese Padroão had co-opted the ancient Syro-Malabar church of the St Thomas Christians in south India and imposed on it a Latin and Latinising hierarchy. Only in the nineteenth century were efforts made to form a more effective native clergy. In 1855 a native congregation of priests, the Carmelites of Mary Immaculate, was founded and flourished to became a major force for renewal. In 1858, five seminaries were established to train the native clergy previously formed by apprenticeship to a native priest or *malpan*.

This awakening only rendered the Latin captivity more intolerable, and the Syro-Malabar Catholics simultaneously petitioned the Chaldean Catholic Patriarch Joseph VI Audo (1848–78) and Rome to send them a bishop of their own tradition. In 1861, Audo began sending bishops to Malabar despite threats of excommunication from Rome. One of the bishops, Mar Elias Mellus, proceeded to ordain priests and combat the Latin hierarchy, thereby creating the 'Mellusian schism'.[34] Audo submitted to Rome in 1876, and Mellus in 1889, but the schism, from which the present Assyrian Church in India derives, endured.

Despite these contretemps, the Syro-Malabar Catholic Church flourished and grew dramatically. But the crisis had exposed the need for reform, and in 1896 Leo XIII instituted a native Syro-Malabar hierarchy independent of both the Latins and the Chaldean patriarch. With this emancipation, the way opened for the remarkable renaissance of this church in the twentieth century.

Italo-Albanians

The one remaining glory of old Byzantine Italy anterior to the Albanian immigration of 1467–70 is the Badia Greca di S. Maria in Grottaferrata south of Rome. Founded in 1034, this monastery is the only surviving Byzantine ecclesiastical institution in uninterrupted communion with Rome since before the east–west schism. But the emancipation of the Italo-Albanian Greek Catholics in Sicily and Calabria, long subject to the local Latin hierarchy, would come only with the creation of their own bishoprics between the World Wars.[35]

---

34 Tisserant, *Eastern Christianity in India*, pp. 111–20; Mayeur-Jacquen, 'Les chrétiens d'orient', p. 824.
35 Fortescue, *The Uniate Eastern churches*, pp. 146–84; Gatti and Korolevsky, *I riti e le chiese*, pp. 474–549.

From oppression to paternalism and renewal

The period under study is full of antinomies for the 'Uniate' communities. Annihilated in Russia, they flourished in Austria-Hungary, and under the Ottomans won civil autonomy from the Orthodox *millets* and made great gains in civil rights, demographic growth, and social, educational and cultural progress. With the help of Latin missionaries they developed their own schools and other cultural and charitable institutions. At the same time, the western education received in the Latin schools, the encroachments of Rome on their autonomy and the Latinisation of their traditions led to an erosion of their identity and independence.

In 1837, *Propaganda Fide* made the Catholic patriarchs seek papal confirmation of their election and receive Vatican confirmation of synodal acts before promulgating them. The erection in 1847 of the Latin patriarchate of Jerusalem furthered the encroachments of Latinisation – its Arab faithful were almost all former Eastern Christians – and was considered an intolerable affront. The Gregorian Calendar, already in use by the heavily Latinised Maronites, was imposed on the Syrian Catholics in 1836, and on the Chaldeans the following year. Its adoption by the Melkites in 1858 provoked a schism. Things began to improve in 1862, when Pius IX created a Special Commission in Propaganda for Eastern Rite affairs.

The First Vatican Council

Shortly thereafter, Vatican I (1869–70) provoked the initial stirrings of Eastern Catholic renewal.[36] Appalled at the Ultamontane council's lack of understanding of, or respect for the distinctiveness of the Catholic East, its age-old traditions and the peculiar dignity of its supreme hierarchs, Eastern Catholic bishops at Vatican I rose up in protest. On 25 January 1870, Chaldean patriarch Joseph VI Audo, who was to play a significant role among the anti-infallibilists, took the floor in an historic speech insisting that the particular discipline of the Christian East be respected. 'His long patriarchate was a constant struggle against the desire for hegemony of the authoritarian and rigid Pope Pius IX.'[37] Two days later Joseph Papp-Szilágyi, the Romanian Catholic bishop of Nagyvárad (Grosswardein), expressed his support for Audo's views. Anyone familiar with the highly charged atmosphere of Vatican I and the authoritarian papalism of Pius IX (1846–78) could guess that the reaction would not be long

---

36 Patelos, *Vatican I*; Hajjar, 'L'épiscopat catholique'; Hajjar, *Les chrétiens uniates*, pp. 301–8.
37 Le Coz, *L'église d'orient*, p. 346.

in coming.[38] On 29 January, the pope summoned Audo to his quarters and made him subscribe to the dispositions of the bull *Reversurus* severely limiting the traditional autonomy of the Eastern hierarchies. On 19 May, the Melkite patriarch Gregory II's intervention in defence of the traditional eastern patriarchal system of government created a sensation. Attacked on all sides and deeply offended by the way Pius IX had manifested his displeasure, Gregory II took the floor again on 14 June to defend himself and to reiterate his views.

Leo XIII and the 1893 Eucharistic Congress of Jerusalem

The profound divisions in the Catholic East manifested at Vatican I could no longer be ignored, and the election of Leo XIII (1878–1903), who was to become known as 'the pope of the Christian East', marked the beginnings of the emancipation of the Eastern Catholic churches.[39] A report on 11 April 1883 by Vanutelli, apostolic delegate at Constantinople, outlined the grave Latin failures in dealing with the Catholic East. Preparations for the 1893 Eucharistic Congress of Jerusalem brought things to a head. Cardinal Langénieux, archbishop of Rheims, was Pope Leo's cardinal-legate for relations with the Eastern hierarchies in view of the upcoming congress. His courageous and far-seeing report of 2 July 1893 denounced in unvarnished terms the problems caused by the Latin missionaries' assault on the East, and stressed the need for a radically new policy.

Leo XIII took swift and decisive action. The encyclical *Praeclara Gratulationis* of 20 June 1894 was followed in the autumn by frank discussions in the Vatican where the Eastern Catholic patriarchs were encouraged to express their griefs freely, without the fear of reprisals that reigned under the repressive Pius IX. Swiftly thereafter came Leo XIII's historic encyclical *Orientalium Dignitas,* dated 30 November 1894, rightly called the 'Magna Carta' of Eastern Catholicism.

Leo XIII's decisiveness stimulated a series of new initiatives: the founding at Kadiköy (Chalcedon) of a centre, seminary and journal, *Les Echos d'Orient* (1897–1942), by the Assumptionists, whose massive accomplishments in mission and scholarship were astounding; the founding of the Catholic reviews *Revue de l'Orient Chrétien* (1896–1946) in Paris, *Bessarione* (1896–1923) and *Roma e l'Oriente* (1910–21) in Italy, and in Germany the still existing *Oriens Christianus* (1901–). And the pontificate of Pius X (1903–14) witnessed the Roman celebrations surrounding the fifteenth centenary of the death of St John Chrysostom in 1907.

---

38 On Pius IX and the Eastern Catholic churches, see Patelos, *Vatican I.*
39 Soetens, *Le Congrès eucharistique*; Esposito, *Leone XIII*, pp. 367–84; Hajjar, *Les chrétiens uniates*, pp. 309–11.

Although some Latins tried sincerely to apply the norms of *Orientalium Dignitas,* they were largely ignored or circumvented, and the sanctions against non-compliance were not enforced. By 1900 the eastern fervour of Leo XIII's pontificate had waned. Benedict XV's election in 1914 brought renewed promise for Eastern Catholicism, but that is a later chapter in this saga.

PART III

*

THE EXPANSION OF CHRISTIANITY

26

African-American Christianity

JON SENSBACH

The story of African-American Christianity is intimately entwined with the larger narrative of African-American history. In the late eighteenth and early nineteenth centuries Christianity became deeply rooted among people of African descent in North America and the Caribbean, and the black church emerged as the bedrock of African-American culture. In the years between the American Revolution and the Civil War, Afro-Christianity provided spiritual sustenance to many enslaved thousands in the American South while serving as the focal point of black community life and antislavery mobilisation in the North. After emancipation in both the South and the Caribbean, African-American congregations multiplied rapidly as millions of newly free people found an anchor in the church. In the USA, the black church was a locus for domestic and overseas missions, for protest against discrimination and violence, for black nationalism, and for debate over the relationship of African Americans to a dominant white culture that considered them second-class citizens. 'The study of Negro religion', concluded W. E. B. DuBois in *The souls of black folk* in 1903, 'is not only a vital part of the history of the Negro in America, but no uninteresting part of American history.'[1]

By the early nineteenth century, Christianity was just becoming entrenched in African-American society. Fuelled by evangelical revivals, Protestantism had made strong inroads among the enslaved and free black populations of colonial British North America and the West Indies during the second half of the eighteenth century. In many denominations from Georgia to New England, black and white Christians worshipped together in interracial congregations, and a growing number of white evangelicals believed slavery to be incompatible with

---

1 DuBois, *The souls of black folk*, p. 136. Standard overviews of African-American Christianity include Woodson, *The history of the negro church*; Washington, *Black religion*; Frazier and Lincoln, *The negro church in America*; Wilmore, *Black religion and black radicalism*; Lincoln and Mamiya, *The black church in the African American experience*; Mays and Nicholson, *The Negro's church*.

the Bible. In 1773 a slave, George Liele, founded Silver Bluff Baptist Church in South Carolina, the first black congregation in North America; in 1782 he was evacuated with British troops to Jamaica, where he founded the First Baptist Church of Kingston in 1784, thus creating an African-American evangelical link between North America and the Caribbean.[2]

After the American Revolution, the promise of spiritual egalitarianism faded as southern white evangelicals suppressed antislavery sentiment in the churches and as white northerners, increasingly disdainful of black coreligionists, sought to exclude them from worship. These developments spawned an independent African-American church movement. A key moment took place in Philadelphia in 1787, when, after enduring humiliating discrimination by white congregants, Richard Allen and Absalom Jones organised the Free African Society and withdrew from the interracial St George's Methodist Episcopal Church. In 1794 the Free African Society became St Thomas African Episcopal Church with Jones as pastor, while Allen founded Bethel African Methodist Episcopal (AME) Church, which became known as Mother Bethel. Similarly, Free African societies gave rise to AME or other black Methodist churches along the Atlantic seaboard within a few years, including an offshoot denomination, the African Methodist Episcopal Zion (AMEZ) Church. The era also saw the proliferation of black Baptist churches in both North and South. Andrew Bryan, a disciple of George Liele's, formed the First African Church of Savannah in 1788, which comprised largely enslaved members, and by the end of the century black Baptist churches arose in Williamsburg, Petersburg and Richmond. In 1800, there were an estimated 25,000 African-American Baptists, and free black northerners founded the African Baptist Church in Boston in 1805, the Abyssinian Baptist Church in New York in 1808, and the First African Baptist Church in Philadelphia in 1809.[3]

At the same time, the Caribbean was a fertile mixing ground for African and Christian religious traditions. Many enslaved Africans arriving from Congo and Angola in the eighteenth century were already Christian, having been baptised in their homeland by Portuguese and Italian missionaries. In the greater French and Spanish Caribbean, including Louisiana and Florida, thousands more received Catholic baptism. In the French colony of Saint-Domingue, a blend of Catholic and African religious practices, including voodoo, gave potent spiritual inspiration to the rebels who overthrew their masters, defeated

---

2 Raboteau, *Slave religion*, pp. 128–41.
3 George, *Segregated Sabbaths*; Frey, *Water from the rock*, pp. 243–83; Sobel, *Trabelin' on*.

the French army and declared Haitian independence between 1791 and 1804. Among Protestants, the Moravian Church had started missions to enslaved Africans in Danish, British and Dutch plantation societies in the eighteenth century. With their evangelical appeal and emphasis on cultivating a class of enslaved lay preachers, the Moravians made thousands of converts, particularly in the Danish West Indies and Antigua. That success inspired British evangelicals to launch a similarly aggressive mission campaign, and the early nineteenth century saw increasing numbers of black Baptists and Methodists in the British Caribbean.[4]

During the first half of the nineteenth century, likewise, enslaved African Americans in North America embraced Christianity with vigour as the plantation system expanded dramatically in the deep South and west of the Mississippi. With the end of the British transatlantic slave trade in 1808, the African-born proportion of the black population declined, supplanted by African Americans more receptive to Christianity. And whereas planters in the eighteenth century often tried to keep the religion away from slaves, fearing it would intensify their desire for freedom, a growing number of planters in the nineteenth century believed it their obligation to instruct slaves in Christianity, or at least in a selective version of the faith more compatible with bondage. Missionaries from all major Protestant denominations in the South preached to slaves of their Christian duty to submit to earthly authority, while planters touted their own benevolence in 'civilising' African Americans. From a white slaveholding perspective, Christianity became a central ideological buttress of the plantation system.[5]

Enslaved Christians, however, forged an alternative, and largely clandestine, belief system sometimes called the 'invisible institution' that worked in the shadow of the masters' religion. Reinterpreting the Gospels through the prism of their own life experiences, the slaves embraced a radical Christian ethic that inverted the lessons taught by white preachers. They claimed a special bond with Jesus, the rock of comfort as well as the redeemer and liberator. He suffered as they suffered; he died to save them *because* of their persecution, not despite it. Thus they considered themselves a chosen people, and Christianity became a religion of human freedom, not enslavement. These themes resonated likewise in the slaves' ready identification with the exile

4 Dubois, *Avengers of the New World*; Frey and Wood, *Come shouting to Zion*, pp. 80–8; Sensbach, *A separate Canaan*, pp. 29–43; Turner, *Slaves and missionaries*. See chapter 27 below, pp. 450–1.
5 Frey, *Water from the rock*, pp. 243–83.

and redemption of the Israelites. Old Testament characters such as Abraham, Moses, Jacob and Daniel proved heroic figures in black Christian consciousness for the special covenant with God and the promise of deliverance for His people they represented. Christianity thus became above all a messianic faith for African Americans, grounded in God's saving power in the believer's heart and in fulfilment of prophecy through the emancipation of a people. Many African Americans considered themselves God's true Christians, and white planters to be impostors.[6]

In form and function, the religion of the slaves also blended Christianity with African traditional practices passed on through generations of African-American folk culture. The inflooding of the divine spirit during the conversion experience (when 'God struck me dead', as one former slave recalled) corresponded roughly to African spirit possession in which a sacred spirit would 'ride' its human host. A standard part of Afro-Christian worship was the 'ring shout', when worshippers gathered African-style in a circle to dance, clap and sing praises in call-and-response fashion, communing with the Spirit in an ecstatic trance that often lasted hours. When they buried their dead, the slaves often adapted the Congolese practice of placing broken jugs, bits of pottery, stones, glass and other objects on the grave to release the soul and accompany it to the afterlife.[7]

Aware of the subversive nature of many aspects of black Christianity, plantation owners sought to control both the flow and the interpretation of religious messages in the slave quarters. Religious meetings in plantation 'praise houses' were chaperoned by a white preacher or other authority figure, and slaves often attended church with whites, though they were generally assigned separate seating. Laws also proscribed the teaching of literacy to slaves, especially after the Nat Turner revolt of 1831. Throughout the plantation South, however, enslaved Christians secretly gathered in 'hush arbors' in woods and swamps far away from white oversight. There they were led in prayer by lay preachers from the slave community, both male and female, many of whom continued to read and interpret the Bible in defiance of the law. It was in these meetings, too, that African-American hymns and spirituals emerged as one of America's greatest musical art forms. The spirituals spoke about 'life and death, suffering and sorrow, love and judgment, justice and mercy, redemption and conciliation'. The biblical lyricism of the spirituals sometimes disguised other intentions; to sing of 'stealing away to Jesus' might have been a coded expression for running

6 Levine, *Black culture and black consciousness*, pp. 3–80; Frey and Wood, *Come shouting to Zion*, pp. 79–129.
7 Stuckey, *Slave culture*; Creel, *'A peculiar people'*, chs. 9 and 10.

away, and the 'Canaan land' of Exodus bore easy symbolic resemblance to the slaves' promised land, Canada.[8]

The relationship of Christianity to resistance movements of the enslaved has long been a subject of fascination and debate among historians. The most famous slave revolts of the nineteenth century all had strong messianic components. Among the leaders of Gabriel's Rebellion outside Richmond in 1800 and Denmark Vesey's plot in Charleston in 1822 were both African conjurors and Christian exhorters. Charleston's two African Methodist churches – several thousand members strong – provided fertile grounds for organising and recruitment, while Vesey patterned himself after the liberator-prophets of the Old Testament.[9] In Southampton County, Virginia, in 1831, Nat Turner, an enslaved, literate Baptist preacher, read signs such as blood on the corn and hieroglyphic figures on leaves and foretold African-American liberation through apocalyptic violence: 'It was plain to me that the Saviour was about to lay down the yoke he had borne for the sins of men, and the great day of judgment was at hand.' In Jamaica, also in 1831, an equally important rebellion, the so-called Baptist War, was led by Baptist class leaders whose slogan was 'No man can serve two masters.' Some of those leaders were native Baptists, members of a separatist sect originated by George Liele and other black migrants from the USA after the American Revolution. All of these uprisings were violently suppressed and their leaders executed.[10]

For all its emphasis on the possibilities of human freedom, the slaves' Christianity might just as often have served less revolutionary ends. Perhaps, as some historians have argued, the eschatological otherworldliness of their faith served as more of a compensatory promise of freedom and salvation in the afterlife than a prescription for rebellion. Perhaps, to many, the figure of Jesus as ally and protector, as invoked in the song 'A little talk with Jesus makes it right', offered more immediate spiritual sustenance than Jesus the liberator or Moses the deliverer. Whatever the case, religion helped many thousands of enslaved people negotiate their responses to a hostile world by offering emotional and moral support in their daily struggle.[11]

North and west of slavery in the United States, black churches proliferated with the rapid growth of the free black population. Missionaries departed from

---

8 Lincoln and Mamiya, *The black church in the African American experience*, p. 350. See also Raboteau, *Slave religion*, pp. 212–88; Southern, *The music of black Americans*.

9 Harding, 'Religion and resistance among antebellum negroes'; Egerton, *He shall go out free and Gabriel's rebellion*; Genovese, *From rebellion to revolution*.

10 Nat Turner, 'Confessions', in Tragle (ed.), *Southampton slave revolt of 1831*; Turner, *Slaves and missionaries*, pp. 150–4; Holt, *The problem of freedom*, pp. 13–17.

11 Genovese, *Roll, Jordan, roll*; Alho, *The religion of the slaves*.

well-established churches in Philadelphia, New York and Boston to found new branches in other north-eastern cities such as Providence, Pittsburgh, Trenton, New Bedford, Buffalo and, as the nation spread westward, Detroit, Chicago, St Louis, Cincinnati and San Francisco. In 1815 there were some 40,000 black Methodists and about the same number of black Baptists. By 1850 those numbers had grown to 87,000 Methodists and 150,000 Baptists. In many northern and western cities and towns, the black church was the centre of African-American life. Independent churches gave black worshippers more than simply the opportunity to escape harassment and discrimination by whites – they provided spiritual sanctuary in a sympathetic setting and the opportunity for black self-determination in church affairs. Congregations served as extended kinship networks, much as African 'secret societies' had done. Religious leaders held powerful clout within the black community, and churches functioned as informal 'courts' where disciplinary problems in the community could be adjudicated. Civic meetings of all kinds were often held in churches, which also sponsored mutual aid and benevolent societies and – since education was considered fundamental to racial improvement – a variety of schools. All these functions were grounded in the reality that black theology formed the ideological crucible of struggle and redemption for African Americans who considered themselves in a kind of internal exile in a hostile country.[12]

Not surprisingly, the churches were centres of abolitionism as well as the broader African-American freedom movement. In response to attacks on blacks in Cincinnati, an organisation called the American Society of Free Persons of Colour convened at Mother Bethel Church in Philadelphia in 1830, electing an aged Richard Allen president. The group met annually until 1835, passing resolutions on civil rights, black self-defence, emigration to Canada and opposition to African colonisation. In subsequent years black churches contributed countless leaders and foot soldiers in the antislavery struggle. Dozens of black ministers such as Samuel Cornish, Henry Highland Garnet and Charles Ray became powerful spokesmen in the movement. Speakers such as Frederick Douglass, Sojourner Truth, Charles Remond and William Lloyd Garrison regularly travelled the abolitionist circuit addressing audiences at hundreds of churches. Black churches voiced increasingly militant opposition to legislation such as the Fugitive Slave Act of 1850 and to the Supreme Court's decision in the Dred Scott case of 1857. They were at the heart of the informal network of 'vigilance committees' for community self-defence, and of the underground railroad aiding fugitive slaves. The most famous

12 Horton and Horton, *In hope of liberty*, pp. 129–51.

'conductor' on the railroad, Harriet Tubman, was a member of the AME Zion Church.[13]

Tubman and Sojourner Truth were perhaps the most publicly visible and vocal examples of the role of women in African-American Christianity. Women were prominent religious leaders in traditional African societies, and during the transition to evangelical Christianity in eighteenth- and early nineteenth-century America, enslaved women became class leaders and lay exhorters on southern plantations. In the North, many free women of colour exploited greater opportunities to preach. Jarena Lee, Zilpha Elaw and a former slave known only as Elizabeth were among those who wrote memoirs describing mystical conversion experiences, a call to preach, and subsequent careers as evangelists. Most met ambivalent receptions from their own denominations, such as AME, which endorsed women's spiritual gifts but refused to ordain them. One, Rebecca Cox Jackson, left her church and joined the Shakers, who recognised her as a prophet. Other women combined spiritual awakening with messianic abolitionism and advocacy of women's rights. Maria Stewart of Boston's African Baptist Church was one of the first women to speak publicly against slavery in the early 1830s. After a religious vision, a former slave, born Isabella in upper New York state in 1797, took the name Sojourner Truth in 1843, and spent her life crusading for African-American and women's rights grounded in Christian righteousness.[14]

The churches, and black Christianity in general, lay at the core of a contentious issue for black America – African colonisation. Churchmen such as John Marrant, Lemuel Haynes and, in England, African-born Olaudah Equiano, along with white antislavery evangelicals in Britain and America, were instrumental in developing the colony of Sierra Leone in West Africa in the late 1780s. Intended as a Christian refuge for blacks disgusted with their ill treatment, the colony drew settlers from the north-east United States and Nova Scotia, where many former slaves had settled after leaving America with British soldiers following the American Revolution. The founding of the American Colonization Society in 1816 represented an unlikely coalition of black church leaders, eager to take Christian civilisation to Africa, and whites, including slaveholders, who sought to deport 'inferior' black Americans to Africa. In 1820, Daniel Coker, a former pastor of Bethel AME in Baltimore, became the first black Methodist missionary to Africa with the Colonization Society. In 1821, Lott Carey, a missionary from the interracial First Baptist

13 George, 'Widening the circle'.
14 Andrews (ed.), *Sisters of the Spirit*; Humez, *Gifts of power*; Painter, *Sojourner Truth*; Lincoln and Mamiya, *The black church in the African American experience*, pp. 274–83.

Church of Richmond, established the first Baptist congregation in the new colony of former American slaves in Liberia. But many northern free blacks rejected colonisation and an identity as Africans, preferring to force the issue of antislavery and civil rights in the USA. Arguing that 'the name African is ill applied to a church composed of American citizens', in the 1830s the African Baptist Church of Boston changed its name to the 'First Independent Church of the People of Color'. Though black churches were committed to mission within the USA, African colonisation remained a controversial flashpoint of African-American identity politics.[15]

Northern missionaries, in fact, were crucial figures in African-American religious life during the transition from slavery to freedom. By 1862, as Union armies occupied sections of the South such as the South Carolina sea islands, New Orleans, and coastal areas of Virginia and the Carolinas, AME, AME Zion and Baptist missionaries, along with white Baptist, Methodist, Presbyterian and Congregational missionaries, moved into those territories to work with the newly freed population. Among the most important black evangelists were Henry Turner, James Hall and AME Bishop Daniel Payne. Many missionaries, both black and white, were surprised at the degree to which Christianity had already taken hold in the South, including an indigenous network of black churches and preachers. But they also disdained what they considered the emotional heathenism of the freed people's worship practices and set about trying to reform them, with limited success. In the fierce competition for souls, white organisations had the advantage of more missionaries and resources, but black missionaries, some of whom had been born in the South, shared a common experience of oppression with the former slaves who gravitated to them. Across the South, even as the war continued, black and white mission organisations created new black congregations. The end of the war in 1865 unleashed the spiritual hungering of 4 million emancipated people eager to worship free from white control.[16]

Thus, the dominant feature of African-American religious life after the Civil War was the rapid expansion in church membership and in the number of independent black churches. African Americans who had worshipped as slaves in biracial churches left by the thousands to join black congregations. Providing spiritual and social anchors for freed people, these churches symbolised African-American autonomy and self-reliance. The numbers reflect this dynamic growth. AME membership grew from 20,000 in 1860 to 450,000 by

---

15 Sanneh, *Abolitionists abroad*; Horton and Horton, *In hope of liberty*, pp. 177–202, quotation on p. 201.
16 Montgomery, *Under their own vine and fig tree*, pp. 38–96; Walker, *A rock in a weary land*.

1896, while AME Zion grew from 4,600 to 350,000 members during that same period. The majority of that expansion took place in the South. In addition, another black offshoot of the Methodist Episcopal Church, South, called the Colored Methodist Episcopal Church or CME (changed to Christian Methodist Episcopal in 1954), was founded in 1866 and claimed 130,000 members by 1890. Towards the end of the nineteenth century, new black Holiness and Pentecostal churches such as the Church of God in Christ drew thousands of adherents as well. Smaller numbers of black worshippers attended Catholic, Episcopalian, Presbyterian and other churches.[17]

Far and away the largest black Christian group, however, was the Baptists. In 1850 there were some 150,000 black Baptists nationwide; by 1870 that number grew to 500,000. With 3 million parishioners in 20,000 churches nationwide by 1915, black Baptists outnumbered all other black Christians in the USA combined. Separating from white Baptists after the Civil War, black Baptists formed several independent conventions – an organisation akin to a denomination – during the 1880s, and for the next several decades these groups merged, and disunited, and coalesced again. For a few years in the early twentieth century, the National Baptist Convention, USA, represented a unified front, but in 1915 another major group, the National Baptist Convention of America, broke away.[18]

At the same time, less formal versions of Christianity mixed with African-American folk traditions remained in wide use. In both the city and the countryside, people practised conjury, voodoo and fortune-telling as alternative forms of belief parallel to, or overlapping with, church religion. For many black Americans barred from formal sources of power, folk practices provided additional access to spiritual authority and a way to enhance control over their lives.[19]

The multiplicity of Christian formats among people of African descent likewise took root in the Caribbean. Following emancipation of the slaves in the British West Indies in 1838, the popularity of English dissenting missionaries, many of whom had strongly supported the abolitionist cause, remained high.[20] In Jamaica the Baptists and Methodists claimed the largest number of adherents. They were challenged, however, by the independent Native Baptists, led by black preachers who achieved mass appeal among impoverished rural workers through their syncretistic blend of Christian and African

---

17 Lincoln and Mamiya, *The black church in the African American experience*, pp. 25, 54, 60–3.
18 *Ibid*., pp. 26–8. See also Washington, *Frustrated fellowship*.
19 Chireau, *Black magic*.
20 See chapter 27 below.

beliefs and practices involving visions, ecstatic trances and prophecies. After a series of revivals in the early 1860s, religious enthusiasm combined with political protest against the planting class when the Native Baptists helped instigate a peasant uprising in Morant Bay in 1865 that left nearly 500 dead before it was suppressed. Still, prophetic blends of Afro-Christianity became increasingly popular among working-class Jamaicans towards the end of the nineteenth century, generating a proliferation of revivalist churches and cults such as Revival Zion, Pocomania, Cumina and Convince – the forerunners of the Ras Tafari movement of the twentieth century. These groups were sometimes energised by charismatic leaders, such as Alexander Bedward, leader of the Revivalist movement between the 1890s and 1920s. Similar cults arose elsewhere in the Caribbean, such as the Spiritual Baptists in Trinidad. Other West Indian nations or colonies had their Afro-Catholic equivalents, such as Vodun in Haiti, Santeria in Cuba and the Shango cult in Trinidad. All contained strong elements of African worship, such as drumming, dancing, spirit possession, animal sacrifice and worship of African divinities in a 'total magico-religious complex'.[21]

In the United States, the rapid growth in independent churches generated a strong demand for black clergy; as one meeting of Virginia Baptists declared: 'It was manifest that the churches of the Association are decidedly in favor of having *colored pastors*.' Baptists, all the black Methodist and Methodist Episcopal denominations and others launched aggressive campaigns to train black clergy, turning out hundreds of ministers, many of them former slaves, in the decades after Emancipation. The preaching profession became one of the fastest-growing occupations among African Americans, offering status and opportunities for leadership and service. Black ministers were respected and, often, charismatic and powerful figures in the community. Many were vigorous spokesmen for political rights and racial progress. In 1870, the Rev. Hiram Revels of Mississippi, an AME clergyman, became the first black senator elected to Congress, and dozens of other black preachers held national and state elective office at some point in the post-war South. AME Bishop Henry McNeil Turner helped organise a black political base in Georgia for the Republican Party while espousing a black nationalist liberation theology and reparations for slave labour.[22]

21 Simpson, *Religious cults of the Caribbean*, p. 11. See also Holt, *The problem of freedom*, pp. 289–309; Brereton, 'Society and culture in the Caribbean', pp. 104–6; Olmos (ed.), *Creole religions of the Caribbean*.

22 Lincoln and Mamiya, *The black church in the African American experience*, pp. 204–7; Montgomery, *Under their own vine and fig tree*, pp. 307–32.

Because many preachers were uneducated, on the other hand, they were also criticised as impediments to the broader African-American freedom struggle. The younger generation, declared Frederick Douglass in 1883, demanded 'an educated, chaste and upright ministry. These old-fashioned preachers minister to passion, decry the intellect, and induce contentment in ignorance and stupidity, and are hence a hindrance to progress.' Because ministers were often thrust into the uneasy position of mediating between dominant white political and economic interests and a subordinate black constituency, they were sometimes criticised as too compliant to whites.[23]

Ministers symbolised the ambiguous role of the churches in the African-American struggle for civil, political and economic justice during Reconstruction and into the early twentieth century. Black theology remained rooted in a prophetic conviction of divine deliverance, and churches were often centres of protest, of political organisation and, when and wherever African Americans held the franchise, of voter mobilisation. In retaliation, many churches were torched by white vigilantes. During the 1870s, federal protection for African-American rights receded, launching a new era of black disenfranchisement, white terrorist violence and Jim Crow segregation, culminating in the notorious 'separate but equal' *Plessy v. Ferguson* Supreme Court ruling of 1896. Many church leaders decried the racism and killings, but in local communities across the country the church often served less as an axis of overt political protest than as a psychological sanctuary or protective shell against the abuse. Preachers who saw all too often the consequences of resistance counselled patience and caution to their flocks, fuelling further criticism from progressive black leaders that churches were bastions of social conservatism.

None the less, churches anchored the black community in crucial ways. Most importantly, the church remained a place for joyous communal celebration of the Spirit. The music, the chanted sermon, the participation of the congregation, made worship in the black church a distinctive and powerful sensory experience reinforcing the conviction of a divine presence active in the devotee's life. Churches expanded their co-operative economic self-help functions in the absence of governmental aid or social welfare organisations. Pastors helped newly emancipated people make the economic transition to freedom, emphasising from the pulpit and in Sunday school the necessity for economic and moral uplift through hard work, thrift, savings and racial solidarity. Churches, mutual aid societies and fraternal organisations founded and invested in black banks and insurance companies. The church also played a

---

23 Montgomery, *Under their own vine and fig tree*, pp. 54, 307–32.

huge role in the massive African-American migrations of the late nineteenth and early twentieth centuries. Black southerners began moving from the countryside to the city in the South and migrating north and west during Reconstruction, taking their faith with them to found new congregations. As the exodus accelerated in the early twentieth century, the black church became increasingly urban, and migrants to the city often found employment through church connections. The church was usually the focal point of urban neighbourhoods and rural landscapes alike, offering a meeting place for parishioners who walked three blocks or three miles to worship, attend Sunday school, and hold social gatherings, political rallies and auxiliary meetings. Extended kin church networks helped raise children whose families were disrupted by migration or violence. Churches helped inform constituents and shape debate by publishing dozens of newspapers at the national, state and local level. And churches helped effect dramatic changes in African-American education by sponsoring many of the black colleges, academies and seminaries founded after the Civil War. The black church, in short, was a critical clearinghouse for discussion about African-American identity and the future of the race, and it offered a forum for decision-making and action.[24]

Women, the majority of black Christians, formed the backbone of this religious culture as preachers, teachers and organisers. In the 1890s, AME Zion was the first black denomination to ordain women as deacons and elders, conferring on them the rights of ministry. Most other denominations did not follow suit until the twentieth century, and some, such as the Pentecostals, prohibited women's ordination altogether. AME women were licensed to preach in 1884, but could not gain ordination until 1948. In the decentralised Baptist church structure, congregations had the right to ordain their own pastors, but few women were granted that recognition. Still, women created ample space within their churches for leadership and education as lay exhorters, class leaders, social organisers, school teachers and missionaries. They promoted a vision of racial solidarity and self-help while using the church to challenge barriers of race and gender in the larger society and restrictions against women in their own denominations.[25]

Evangelical outreach by many black denominations intensified in the late nineteenth century. Missions were yet another endeavour in which African Americans could exert influence and leadership in a call to action for moral advancement and the salvation of the race. Evangelists in 'home missions'

---

24 Lincoln and Mamiya, *The black church in the African American experience*, pp. 240–53.
25 Higginbotham, *Righteous discontent*; Collier-Thomas, *Daughters of thunder*; Dodson, 'Nineteenth-century A.M.E. preaching women', pp. 276–92.

reached out to their own communities and to regions in the USA perceived to be deficient in Christian enlightenment. Missionaries also founded new congregations in the Caribbean. Missions to Africa, however, took on a special symbolic significance by linking Christian providentialism with an emotional connection to black Americans' African ancestral heritage.[26] Supporters of missions often referred to Africa as the 'dark continent', as did white missionaries and imperialists, but insisted that racial solidarity with Africans made black evangelists uniquely qualified to take the word there. As one publication put it: 'The Special Mission of the AME Church to the Darker Races is to "Teach the Mind to Think, the Heart to Love, the Hand to Work." ' AME missionaries ventured to Liberia and, in the 1890s, to South Africa, where they acted as catalysts to the formation of the Ethiopian church movement.[27] In planting the church there, an AME bishop explained in 1902 that black Africans 'have for long centuries become the victims of customs and habits not in keeping with the better life which is the result only of Christian civilization'. Inspired by a pan-African consciousness infused with the doctrine of racial uplift, black American missionaries created an internationalist evangelical Protestant network between the USA, Africa and the Caribbean by the late nineteenth century.[28]

By the early twentieth century, the centrality of black Christianity in African-American culture was widely known, and the black church became a subject of scholarly study. Carter G. Woodson's magisterial *The history of the negro church*, published in 1921, was a landmark work of scholarship that remains influential. But it was in *The souls of black folk* of 1903, perhaps the most important book ever published about black America, that W. E. B. DuBois expressed a more prophetic vision of religion in the redemption of African Americans. The black church, he wrote, 'is the social center of Negro life in the United States, and the most characteristic expression of African character . . . The church often stands as a real conserver of morals, a strengthener of family life, and the final authority on what is Good and Right. Thus one can see in the Negro church today, reproduced in microcosm, all that great world from which the Negro is cut off by color-prejudice and social condition.' DuBois lamented a persistent 'deep religious fatalism' that he said was a legacy of slavery. But he predicted a renewal of the 'deep religious feeling of the real Negro heart' that

---

26 For a fuller exposition of this theme see chapter 35, pp. 583–4.
27 See chapter 35 below, pp. 576–92.
28 Becker, 'The black church'; Campbell, *Songs of Zion*; Martin, *Black Baptists and African missions*; Drake, *The redemption of Africa and black religion*; Moses, *The golden age of black nationalism*.

would inspire a massive protest against injustice: 'Some day the Awakening will come, when the pent-up vigor of ten million souls shall sweep irresistibly toward the Goal, out of the Valley of the Shadow of Death, where all that makes life worth living – Liberty, Justice, and Right – is marked "For White People Only"'. When DuBois died sixty years later at the age of ninety-six, his vision was on the verge of being realised.[29]

29 DuBois, *The souls of black folk*, pp. 136, 140, 145.

27

Christian missions, antislavery and the claims of humanity, c.1813–1873

BRIAN STANLEY

During the period c.1813–73 Protestant forms of Christianity were implanted in southern and western Africa and Australasia, greatly extended their limited influence in South Asia, the Caribbean and the Dutch East Indies, and gained precarious footholds in East Africa and the vast Chinese empire. In terms of geographical coverage, though not of numbers of converts, this was an age of rapid Protestant missionary expansion. At the beginning of this period, the Catholic presence in the non-western world was weak in comparison. Despite Napoleon's reconstitution of the French religious orders in 1805 and Pius VII's re-establishment of the Jesuit order in 1814, Catholic missions had not yet recovered from the catastrophes of the revolutionary era. It is estimated that in 1820 there were no more than twenty missionary priests in India, and only about 270 throughout the globe.[1] By 1873, Catholic missions were again a force to be reckoned with, and increasingly feared by their Protestant rivals. Old orders had been reconstituted, and new ones founded, among them the Marists (1817), the Missionaries of the Most Holy Heart of Mary (1841) and the Society of Missionaries of Africa or White Fathers (1868). Other missionary orders, such as the Paulist Fathers (1858), owed their origin to the vision, shared by Catholics and Protestants alike, of the evangelisation of the burgeoning European immigrant communities in North America: the United States continued to be classified by the Vatican as a mission territory until 1908.

The majority missionary tradition in this period – that of evangelical Protestantism – displayed three predominant features, all of which had implications for the ways in which missions related to indigenous peoples, colonial authorities, traders and settlers. First, the tradition was marked by an international, transatlantic and pan-evangelical or ecumenical character. In this period, to a greater degree than in the decades that followed, its missionaries were people

---

1 Delacroix, *Histoire universelle*, vol. III, pp. 169–70.

for whom national identity and the imperial designs of their respective governments were matters of secondary importance. Second, evangelical missions exhibited a paradoxical blend between evangelistic zeal, simple biblicism and the Enlightenment motifs of progress, liberty, civilisation, education and the unity of humanity. The very close association between the missionary and antislavery movements exemplifies this union of evangelistic and humanitarian impulses. However, the apparent failure of that common project to deliver the pattern of 'improvement' of the African race that was originally expected carried consequences that were played out into the high Victorian period and beyond. Third, Protestant missions were infused by a voluntaristic philosophy, in relation both to their domestic organisation and to their commitment to the planting of churches on the mission field which would enshrine the voluntary ideal of independence in terms of finance, personnel and dynamic for expansion. The movement's severest challenges were posed by the obstacles which persistently thwarted the full implementation of this ideal. At many points, though not at others, these three emphases were paralleled in the Catholic missionary tradition, and some of these similarities will be noted as the chapter proceeds.

The changing shape of international Protestant fraternity

As the offspring of the eighteenth-century evangelical awakenings, nineteenth-century Protestant missions were connected by networks of information and personnel that crossed national, denominational and indeed continental boundaries. Paradoxically, Protestant missions in this period were more internationalist than some Catholic orders, which were more strictly national in recruitment and perspective. Evangelical approaches to missionary training and accreditation sat more loosely to national and denominational affiliation than subsequently became the case. A Lusatian recruit to the London Missionary Society (LMS, 1795), Gottlob Brückner (1783–1857), reveals the intricacy of the weave of the European evangelical tapestry. In 1806 Brückner entered the Berlin mission seminary run by the pietist Johannes Jänicke, who later founded the Berlin Missionary Society (1824). On request from the (largely Dutch Reformed) Netherlands Missionary Society (NMS, 1797) Brückner was sent in 1808 to Holland, including a spell at the Moravian settlement at Zeist, to prepare for service in India. Diverted by the Napoleonic wars to England, he enrolled at the Gosport seminary run by the Scottish Congregationalist David Bogue. Ordained in London by a Dutch Reformed minister, he was sent by the LMS to Java in 1814. There Brückner became a Baptist, joining the Baptist

Missionary Society (BMS, 1792), and worked for over forty years, chiefly on translating the New Testament into Javanese. Despite his Baptist affiliation, Brückner's work prompted the NMS to expand its work in Java, and another German, J. F. C. Gerické of the Netherlands Bible Society, used his translation as a basis for his own Javanese version, published in 1848.

Throughout the evangelical world 'missionary intelligence' was circulated and devoured with scant attention to national or denominational provenance. Leading missionary publicists exerted an influence far beyond their own country. On both sides of the Atlantic, for instance, the awakening of evangelical interest in China during the 1830s was largely the result of the writing and (in Europe) public speaking of the maverick Pomeranian, Karl Gützlaff (1803–51). Like Brückner, Gützlaff was schooled in pietist spirituality at Jänicke's Berlin seminary before undergoing further training in Rotterdam. In 1826 he went to the Dutch East Indies in the employ of the NMS. His passion for China led him to sever his links with that society and operate free-lance, travelling up and down the Chinese coast, distributing tracts and preaching. In 1834 he succeeded Robert Morrison as Chinese secretary to the British East India Company in Canton, and he continued to work for the British during the Opium War of 1839–42. His dubious reputation today rests in part on his links with the opium trade and the British authorities, but it should be noted that as a Pomeranian he had no interest in furthering British ambitions in China. As so often, missionary 'imperialism' had relatively little to do with nationalism. Gützlaff's legacy was diverse: one of his pamphlets inspired David Livingstone's call to missionary service; his mission principles exerted a profound influence on the Basel and Rhenish missions in their work among the Hakka Chinese, and supremely on James Hudson Taylor's China Inland Mission (1865), pioneer of the interdenominational 'faith missions'.

Patterns of correspondence and interchange varied from one sector of evangelicalism to another, and also shifted with the passing of time. The Anglican Church Missionary Society (CMS, 1799) maintained strong links until the 1850s with Lutheran pietists, but had few transatlantic connections, as the small Protestant Episcopal Church of the USA was largely unaffected by evangelical influence. The CMS did not send its first English clergyman to the mission field until 1815; until then it relied wholly for ordained personnel on German Lutherans. For several decades thereafter, the ranks of the CMS were studded with German names, many of them trained in the Berlin or Basel mission seminaries (the latter, founded in 1815, gave rise to the Basel Mission). Some were notable scholars and linguists: Johann Krapf and Johannes Rebmann in East Africa, David Hinderer in Yorubaland, Sigismund Koelle in Sierra Leone and the Near East, Karl Rhenius in south India and Karl Pfander in north-west India, all bear witness to the deep impact of continental piety and learning on the evangelical Anglican missionary tradition. It is no accident that the second and most distinguished of the holders of the Anglo-Prussian Jerusalem bishopric was Samuel Gobat, product of the Swiss *Réveil,* student in the Basel Mission seminary, and former CMS missionary in Egypt and Abyssinia. By the 1850s, the link between the CMS and the Basel Mission was weakening, the victim of hardening national sentiments and the new suspicion of Lutheran orders instilled in Anglicans by the Oxford Movement. Henry Venn, the influential secretary of the CMS from 1841 to 1872, filled the gap to an extent by engaging in regular transatlantic correspondence with Rufus Anderson, foreign secretary of the (largely Congregationalist) American Board of Commissioners for Foreign Missions (ABCFM, 1810), but this American connection was never more than a personal one. By the 1870s, the horizons of the CMS were more narrowly, and dangerously, confined by English perspectives than at any time in its previous history.

Baptists and Methodists provide a contrasting model of missionary internationalism in that their transatlantic connections were always stronger than their inter-European ones. Although the BMS had a Dutch auxiliary and recruited a few missionaries from the Netherlands, Germany and Scandinavia, there was no natural constituency in early nineteenth-century Europe for the support of Baptist missions. Baptist work in Germany and later in Russia and eastern Europe was itself a product of the nineteenth-century *Erweckung,* associated particularly with J. G. Oncken. Oncken was engaged in 1835 as a missionary to his native Germany by the second foreign missionary agency formed by American Protestants, the Triennial Convention (1814), known from 1845 as the American Baptist Missionary Union (ABMU). The first corresponding secretary of the Convention was an Englishman, William Staughton of Philadelphia, who had been one of the founders of the BMS with William Carey at Kettering in 1792. Links between the BMS and the ABMU remained strong throughout this period. The 1845 schism over slave-owning that split the swelling ranks of American Baptists between North and South reinforced the ties between Baptists in the northern states and in England, but isolated the Southern Baptist Convention, whose Foreign Mission Board was to grow into the largest of all Protestant mission agencies.

That the Methodist pattern exhibits some similarity to the Baptist one may appear surprising in view of the indebtedness of Methodism to the Moravian tradition. The register of missionaries serving with the Wesleyan Methodist Missionary Society (WMMS) is the most uniformly Anglophone in character of all the English societies. Methodists and Moravians were first cousins, but as such had gone their separate ways, despite an overture from Thomas Coke to Benjamin La Trobe in 1785–6 which had briefly raised the prospect of a Methodist–Moravian union. Moreover, the WMMS, from its origins as a national body in 1818, was not an independent voluntary society, but rather the means whereby the Methodist Conference organised its expansion in Ireland, Europe, the British colonies and beyond. For Methodists, even more than Baptists, continental Europe was not a source of missionaries but a mission field. Wesleyan missionaries were of necessity mostly English or Irish. The most famous half-exception, Thomas Birch Freeman of the Gold Coast, was the son of an African 'freedman' father and an English mother. The fact that the WMMS saw itself as existing both for the support of colonial Methodism and for the evangelisation of the 'heathen' made it more difficult for the society to distinguish between humanitarian and national concerns in situations where indigenous interests were under pressure from British settlers. The architect of South African Methodism, William Shaw, was sent to the Cape Colony in 1820 as chaplain to a large group of British colonists. As such, Shaw disagreed with John Philip of the LMS over the politics of the eastern frontier during the Xhosa wars of the 1830s and 1840s. Yet Shaw's faithful witness to the Methodist principle of a single multi-racial church embracing settlers and Xhosa had enduring significance in South Africa.

British and American Methodists had maintained close relations from the beginning, but the connections became still stronger from the 1830s as a result of the scale of Irish Methodist emigration: over 26,000 Irish Methodists emigrated between 1830 and 1869, mainly to the United States, Canada and Australia.[2] Some of them became pioneers of Methodist missions in their adopted country and in regions beyond. William Butler (1818–99), the founder of American Methodist missions in India and Mexico, was born and converted in Ireland. James Thoburn (1836–1922), the first Methodist missionary bishop of India and Malaysia, was born in Ohio of Irish stock.

A third model of interrelationship, midway between the other two, balanced continental connections with transatlantic ones, and with a growing preponderance of the latter as the century proceeded. The LMS had contributed to the foundation both of the NMS and of Jänicke's Berlin seminary. It drew its early missionaries from the Netherlands, Germany, the Austrian empire, Switzerland, Sweden, Denmark and France, as well as England and

---

2 Taggart, *The Irish in world Methodism*, p. 38.

(notably) Scotland. Yet the society also developed increasingly close connections with American evangelicals. Six of its seventeen Foreign Directors in 1815 were from the United States. The LMS and the ABCFM shared a keen interest in the evangelisation of the Pacific islands; William Ellis, former missionary in Polynesia and LMS Foreign Secretary from 1831 to 1841, corresponded regularly with Rufus Anderson on mission strategy. The LMS and the ABCFM underwent a similar evolution from original interdenominationalism towards a predominantly Congregationalist constituency. As their denominational base narrowed, the two agencies grew closer to each other, and the transatlantic nexus gradually supplanted the older European ties.

A similar trajectory is observable in the case of Scottish Presbyterians. In the first non-denominational phase of the Scottish missionary movement, before the General Assembly of the Church of Scotland sent its first missionary, Alexander Duff, to Bengal in 1830, Scottish evangelicals were closely linked through the LMS and the associated Glasgow and Edinburgh Missionary Societies to continental pietist movements and the developing Genevan *Réveil*. Thomas Chalmers avidly read the *Periodical Accounts* of the Moravian missions, and the local missionary society over which he presided at St Andrews from 1823 to 1828 was a liberal donor to Moravian mission funds. After 1830, however, the evangelicals in the Church of Scotland threw their weight behind the church's own foreign missions, and their participation in pan-European evangelical ecumenism weakened. Although Chalmers remained president of the Edinburgh Association in aid of Moravian Missions until his death in 1847, he had also accepted honorary positions with the New York Board of Foreign Missions of the Presbyterian Church and the ABCFM. The Disruption of 1843 did not halt this growing realignment in a transatlantic direction. The Free Church Foreign Missions Committee sent Alexander Duff to the USA and Canada in 1854, where his advocacy of the missionary cause had a great impact. His first address, to a crowd of 3,000–4,000 in Philadelphia, referred to America and Britain 'shaking hands across the Atlantic as the two great props of evangelic Protestant Christianity in the world'.[3] It was a sentiment that could not have been uttered in the 1790s, or even in 1813. It presaged the tone of the missionary movement over the next sixty years, culminating in the World Missionary Conference at Edinburgh in 1910, at which the descendants of continental European pietism at times felt oppressed by the weight of the British–American evangelical axis.

3 G. Smith, *The life of Alexander Duff, D.D., LL.D.*, 2 vols. (London: Hodder and Stoughton, 1879), vol. II, p. 268.

Enlightenment, antislavery and civilisation

The evangelical missionary movement was founded on the premise of the equality before God of all human beings. All were created in the image of God; all had sinned and descended into moral and social depravity; and yet all were capable of being raised by the grace of God to the heights of civilisation. Africans or Hindus or Chinese may have looked shockingly different from Europeans, yet missions could not predicate the absolute difference of the 'heathen' without collapsing into futility. Missionary support in the nineteenth century thrived on lurid tales of 'heathen' blindness and the savage cruelties of idolatry, but these tales would have been pointless if the 'blindness' and 'savagery' were innate. Missionary advocates, whilst notoriously prone to gross and offensive caricatures of the 'heathen' whom most of them had never seen, did so precisely in order that they might magnify the capacity of the gospel to emancipate the 'heathen' from their barbarism. For evangelical Christians, in contrast to much secular opinion, the barrier separating 'civilised' from 'savage', though formidable at first sight, was in principle and practice surmountable. Missionary literature thus united extreme statements of cultural difference with strong assertions of humanitarian identity.

In insisting on the fundamental unity of humanity, missions were advancing an emphasis which was not only deeply Christian, but also peculiarly characteristic of the theistic mainstream of the Enlightenment. Although the Enlightenment's zeal for the systematic classification of human phenomena contained the seeds of later biological racism, the majority of Enlightenment thinkers subscribed to an ideal of progress towards civilisation which, no less than the missionary hope of global conversion, depended on a presumption that what all humans had in common was more significant than what divided them. If what made 'the heathen' so different from us was the result of external conditions, and if those conditions were, as much Enlightenment thought argued, amenable to human engineering, then the potential was there to transform not just individuals but ultimately also the world. The premise of this confidence was, however, the assumption that processes of religious and social change would be subject to missionary control.

Almost all participants in the Protestant missionary movement shared this optimism. It was, for example, as evident among the Württemberg pietists of the Basel Mission in the Gold Coast as among the American Congregationalist missionaries to the Sandwich Islands. This ideology of Christian improvement under missionary tutelage was not a 'political theology' in the modern sense. The societies instructed their missionaries to avoid political entanglements, and, most pointedly, in the slave societies of the Caribbean to urge slaves to be obedient to their masters, in accordance with biblical teaching. But wherever political or social structures persistently thwarted the progress of Christian improvement, the underlying discourse of individual rights and the claims of humanity was thrust to the surface, and missionaries found themselves compelled to seek subversion of those structures.

The Caribbean was a religious laboratory which revealed both the power and the limitations of evangelical improvement. The Dissenting chapels of the BMS, LMS and WMMS created an alternative society of spiritual egalitarianism in which Bible-reading, preaching and prayer dissolved the distinctions between slave and free. The alarmed slave-owners placed increasing restrictions on missionary operations, but such repression, intensified following the slave rebellions in Demerara in 1823 and Jamaica in 1831, served to turn cautious evangelicals into strident advocates of emancipation.[4] The abolition of slavery was now regarded as the only means of assuring gospel freedom and hence the raising of the degraded and enslaved African to the full dignity of humanity. Slave emancipation in 1833–4, and even more the ending of apprenticeship in 1838, were hailed as turning-points in history, markers which set 'before' and 'after' in a juxtaposition that mirrored the transformation of Christian conversion itself. The slogans that reverberated through the celebratory meetings in Jamaica on 1 August 1838 proclaimed that 'Africa is free' and 'Britons never will be slaves'.[5] The combination of liberationist and imperial motifs jars on the modern ear, but expressed an ideology of Britannia's empire as a realm of Protestant faith and civil liberties that had solidified into the dominant narrative of British imperial expansion as early as the 1730s.[6]

With slavery dispatched, the pathway to Christian transformation of the African population of the Caribbean seemed clear. The chapels were full, and in Jamaica Baptist missionaries settled former slaves in 'free villages' intended to turn them into prosperous independent producers and church members capable of sustaining their own gospel ministry. But from the 1840s such dreams evaporated as the sugar trade collapsed and Christian stewardship with it. In the Baptist churches of Jamaica, Trinidad and the Bahamas, many of which owed their origins to black preachers from the United States rather than missionaries, the indigenous traditions of African-American Christianity reasserted themselves, challenging the word-centred orthodoxy of British evangelicals

---

4 On the role of Christianity in early nineteenth-century slave rebellions see chapter 26 above.
5 Hall, *Civilising subjects*, pp. 117–20, 180.
6 Armitage, *The ideological origins of the British empire*, passim.

with a Holy Spirit religion of power and ecstatic experience, shading at its dark edges into the syncretism of myalism and *obeah* sorcery. A BMS deputation in 1859–60 responded by vainly trying to reassert missionary tutelage, looking to more pastors from England and a longer period of collegiate pastoral training for Jamaicans to stop the rot. By the 1860s evangelical hopes for the regeneration of the children of Africa had shifted from the Caribbean to West Africa.

In other parts of the globe, missionary humanitarians were by the 1830s finding the progress of Christian transformation blocked by the hardening impact of European settlers and traders on indigenous peoples within or near the frontiers of British settlement, such as the Maori, or the Xhosa of the Cape Colony. The Parliamentary Select Committee on Aborigines was set up in 1836 in response to pressure from T. F. Buxton and the missionary lobby, to consider what measures should be adopted to secure for such peoples 'the due observance of Justice and the protection of their Rights; to promote the spread of Civilization among them, and to lead them to the peaceful and voluntary reception of the Christian Religion'.[7] Witnesses to the Committee included the secretaries of the CMS, LMS and WMMS, and serving missionaries such as John Philip and William Shaw from the Cape Colony, William Yate from the CMS New Zealand mission, and John Williams of the LMS from the South Pacific. These witnesses were unanimous in their testimony that conversion to Christianity offered the only sure hope of eliminating 'savagery' and 'barbarism', a conclusion which pointed Buxton's Report firmly in the direction of seeing missions as the cement of a benevolent empire. Yet their evidence also revealed a growing sense among missionaries that pure evangelism might not be enough. Shaw, Yate and Williams all urged that the preaching of the word must be accompanied by a concurrent process of 'civilisation', challenging the social and economic structures of 'heathen' societies by the introduction of the plough, the 'useful arts' and habits of 'industry'.

Such testimony added weight to the thesis that John Philip had already advanced in his influential *Researches in South Africa*. The apparent indolence of the Khoi population, Philip argued, was not to be attributed to any intrinsic defect in the African race. Rather 'we are all born savages' and are all naturally indolent. The continuing improvidence of the Khoi was the product of their status as virtual slaves, deprived of an independent economic base and the freedom to sell their labour to the best market. Philip cited Adam Smith,

---

7 *Report from the select committee on aborigines (British settlements) together with the minutes of evidence, appendix and index*, Parliamentary Papers 1836, VII (538), p. iii.

Fergusson, Malthus and Ricardo in support of his contention that liberty was the necessary precondition for industry, but civil liberty in itself was inadequate without the aid of Christianity, whose conviction of the incalculable worth of the human soul could alone impart 'the thinking principle' that was the first step towards true civilisation.[8]

By the late 1830s the arguments of Philip and Buxton's Aborigines Report had become evangelical orthodoxy. Preaching the word remained as central as it was in the days of Wesley or Whitefield, but missionaries were now much more aware of the structural constraints that both slave and nomadic societies imposed on the process of 'improvement'. Their persuasion of the necessity of an independent economic base for indigenous people owed much to Scottish political economy but also reflected the accumulating wisdom of field experience. Voluntaryism was intrinsic to Congregational and Baptist tradition, and by now part of Methodist tradition also. But in the mission field, it was increasingly the case that all, even Anglicans or Presbyterians, were *de facto* voluntaryists: the missionary objective was, as the Select Committee's terms of reference put it, 'the voluntary reception of the Christian Religion', and voluntary reception implied voluntary support. The preoccupation of early and mid-Victorian missions with instilling the virtues of agricultural production and free commercial exchange has been blamed by John and Jean Comaroff for unleashing the spirit of capitalism in the world of the southern Tswana, and contributing to the creation in South Africa of a 'population of peasant-proletarians trapped in a promiscuous web of economic dependencies'.[9] If this was indeed the result, it was the very opposite of missionary intentions, which were remarkably congruent with the goals of modern development theory in its concern to enable rural communities to achieve the economic independence which permits human capabilities to develop and flourish.

T. F. Buxton applied the conclusions of the Aborigines Report to his African Civilisation Society (1839) and the resulting Niger expedition of 1841. Buxton's concern was to counter the African slave trade by drawing out 'the capabilities of Africa, and thence to deduce the possibility of her becoming peaceful, flourishing, and productive, by the force of legitimate commerce'. Yet true evangelical that he was, Buxton placed no confidence in commerce or civilisation without the saving grace of the gospel: 'It is the Bible and the plough that

---

8 J. Philip, *Researches in South Africa: illustrating the civil, moral, and religious condition of the native tribes . . .* , 2 vols. (London: J. Duncan, 1828), vols. I, pp. 362–78; II, pp. 315–16, 355–70.
9 Comaroff and Comaroff, *Of revelation and revolution*, vol. II, pp. 163–4.

must regenerate Africa.'[10] Although the Niger expedition ended in disaster, the theory that lay behind it lived on in the principles of Henry Venn and David Livingstone. Venn's African Native Agency Committee (1845) sought 'the social and religious improvement of Africa by means of her own sons', who were to be brought to England to train in useful arts such as brick-laying, printing, and the production and marketing of cotton.[11] Venn encouraged cotton cultivation at Abeokuta in the hope that a cash crop for export would stifle the illegitimate commerce of the slave trade and raise up an educated middle class that would prove the foundation of a self-supporting church. Livingstone similarly looked to Zambezi cotton to drive out the slave trade from East Africa and incidentally remove from Lancashire consciences the burden of dependence on American slave-grown cotton. The 'colonies' which Livingstone envisaged for the Zambezi region were not staging posts for European expansion, but an adaptation for nineteenth-century Africa of St Boniface's eighth-century monastic communities in Germany, which were centres of education and agricultural innovation.[12] For both Venn and Livingstone 'commerce and Christianity' was no blueprint for imperial exploitation but a slogan for the development of self-sustaining African communities, whose channels of free commercial exchange would also be the conduits whereby the gospel would spread from village to village.

This ideology was not a British peculiarity. The Basel Mission responded similarly to the growth of the colonial plantation economy on the Gold Coast by encouraging the creation of autonomous village communities capable of sustaining themselves by skills in craft and husbandry. The Mission set up its own trading company in 1859 to encourage such communities to engage on their own account in the palm oil and cocoa trades, rather than remaining dependent on the existing networks of colonial trade. In the 1870s both the Church of Scotland and the Free Church of Scotland pursued a parallel vision in what is now Malawi through their respective missions at Blantyre and Livingstonia (the latter with its own trading company, the African Lakes Company). Neither was the linkage of commerce and Christianity exclusively Protestant, although its most influential advocates were evangelicals. The Alsatian Catholic convert from orthodox Judaism François Libermann, who founded the Missionaries of the Most Holy Heart of Mary in 1841 and then presided over their merger with the Holy Ghost Fathers in 1848, emphasised

---

10 C. Buxton (ed.), *Memoirs of Sir Thomas Fowell Buxton, Bart.*, edited by his son, 3rd edn (London: J. Murray, 1851), pp. 443, 451.
11 Shenk, *Henry Venn*, p. 68.
12 Ross, *David Livingstone*, pp. 122–3.

the importance of making the laity 'teachers, farmers and master-craftsmen', if Africans were to be raised above subsistence level and enabled to develop their full human potential. Like Buxton, he argued both that the inculcation of industry was indispensable to civilisation and that true civilisation was impossible without Christian faith.[13]

The planting of an indigenous church

The objective of planting indigenous churches that would be capable of sustaining their own life, growing their own pastoral ministry and initiating mission on their own account was shared by almost all missions in this period. Posterity has paid most attention to the statements of 'Three-Self' principles produced by Henry Venn and Rufus Anderson, but the fact that two mission strategists on either side of the Atlantic arrived independently at similar conclusions is less surprising if one regards them as seeking to elucidate the principles which would guarantee the achievement of a generally accepted goal. The conference on missions held at Liverpool in 1860 (the second in an ecumenical series which began in New York in 1854 and culminated in Edinburgh in 1910) was unambiguous in its commitment to the planting of 'native' churches that would be self-reliant, self-supporting and self-governing, and in its opposition to the persistent tendency of missionaries to retain control as the pastors of 'native' churches.

With appropriate ecclesiological nuances, these aims were shared by missions in the Catholic tradition. W. G. Tozer and Edward Steere, pioneers of the Anglo-Catholic Universities' Mission to Central Africa (UMCA, 1858–9), were unequivocal in their insistence that the aim of the mission was to plant an independent African church, not one subject to European tutelage. Roman Catholic mission strategists echoed the refrain. François Libermann argued that missions must follow apostolic precedent, by basing 'ourselves from the very beginning on a stable organization indigenous to the soil which we want to cultivate. The formation of a native clergy . . . supplies the only means whereby the light of the Gospel can be widely diffused and the Church solidly established in the countries where we are called to work.'[14] Similarly, the Italian priest Daniel Comboni founded the Verona Fathers in 1867 as the first step towards the fulfilment of a vision for 'the regeneration of Africa by Africa' through the creation of an African apostolate.

13 Koren, *To the ends of the earth*, pp. 257–9.
14 *Ibid.*, p. 255.

The commitment to the implanting of independent churches contained multiple ambiguities both in theory and in practice. At the theoretical level, it was unclear whether 'civilisation' was a good or a bad thing. Inasmuch as civilisation implied the acquisition of the tools for economic self-sufficiency, it was to be endorsed. But if it meant the imposition of western patterns of organisation and thought, missionary opinion was divided. Both Catholic and Protestant strategists, even as they commended the necessity of socio-economic 'civilisation', could advocate a repudiation of western cultural accoutrements. Thus Libermann, who insisted that 'our mission . . . consists not only in announcing the faith but also in initiating the peoples to our European civilization', also urged his missionary priests in Africa to 'rid yourselves of Europe, its customs and mentality' and 'become Negroes with the Negroes'.[15] In similar terms, Venn could set before Samuel Crowther in 1858 the vision of filling up 'the distance between Lagos and the Niger with civilization, through missionary operations and lawful commerce', yet also admonish J. C. Taylor, Crowther's Igbo colleague in the Niger mission, when returning to West Africa after his ordination by the bishop of London in 1859, to 'let all European habits, European tastes, European ideas, be left behind you'.[16] By the 1870s, a strengthening reaction against the prominence of European habits was discernible in missions across the ecclesiastical spectrum from the UMCA to the CIM.

Was human equality itself a 'European idea'? Rufus Anderson, though confident that ultimately the gospel would raise the Hawaian or the Hindu to the same exalted level of civilisation as that reached by New Englanders, developed a profound scepticism towards all missionary talk about 'civilisation' and its embodiment in education in the English medium, believing that such policies encouraged unrealistic and expensive expectations among indigenous Christians. His scepticism extended even to the wisdom of permitting 'native' pastors to enjoy equal status with missionaries. Those who were granted equal status would expect equal pay, with the result that self-support would never be achieved. Congregational independency without missionary hierarchy was doomed to futility.[17]

Anderson's doubts about whether pure Congregationalism was suitable for impoverished and poorly educated infant Christian communities were paralleled in a variety of contexts from the 1840s onwards. Missionaries were stationed by their home committees, and were thus effectively appointed as

---

15 *Ibid.*, p. 260.
16 Shenk, *Henry Venn*, pp. 33, 75–6.
17 Harris, *Nothing but Christ*, p. 114.

pastors over local congregations. Those congregations often worshipped in buildings erected with funds remitted from Europe or North America. Yet Baptist, Congregationalist and some Free Church of Scotland missionaries professed an ecclesiology that vested the right to call or dismiss a minister, and the control of church property, in the gathered congregation. It is hardly surprising that from Spanish Town to Grahamstown disputes surfaced in which congregations asserted the democratic rights inherent in their own Dissenting missionaries' traditions, only to find themselves opposed by the very same missionaries, appealing to the supposedly higher claims of paternal responsibility and the authority of the missionary committee.[18] Racial pride, and convictions of the missionary's 'fatherly' role, pushed those of congregational principles closer to *de facto* episcopal or presbyterian polity, even as missionary strategists from established churches, such as Venn, looked increasingly towards Nonconformist churches for their models of self-support and self-propagation. The resulting ecclesiological convergence contained the seeds of twentieth-century ecumenism, especially in India.

The difficulty of deciding whether denominational polity was a 'thing indifferent' or of the essence of the faith became apparent at the 1860 Liverpool conference. Joseph Mullens of the LMS Calcutta mission insisted that indigenous churches, no less than indigenous converts themselves, should not be 'hybrids': they should be expected to conform neither to western architectural taste nor even to such 'technicalities' of western ecclesiastical principle as the Thirty-Nine Articles or the Deed of Demission which effected the Scottish Disruption in 1843. He was firmly answered by other speakers, including William Shaw and William Tweedie, Convener of the Free Church's Foreign Missions Committee, who denied that their respective denominational principles were mere technicalities to be discarded on crossing the oceans. The conference minute on 'native churches' was a diplomatic masterpiece, designed to paper over the cracks between the two positions.[19]

The sharpest ambiguities were those thrown up by experience in India, where the dynamics of a caste society tied converts into more absolute dependence on missionary protection than anywhere else. All missions shared the same ideal of planting a self-sustaining Indian church, yet all failed to a greater or lesser extent to implement the ideal. In 1854 the CMS had a Christian community in north India of over 7,000 Christians, yet not one was ordained. In

---

18 Hall, *Civilising subjects*, pp. 192–9; De Gruchy, *The London Missionary Society in southern Africa*, pp. 120–55.
19 *Conference on missions held in 1860 at Liverpool* (London: James Nisbet, 1860), pp. 283–91, 309–13.

1867, of the fifty-six churches planted by the BMS in India, only one had an Indian pastor wholly supported by the membership. In parts of the south, mission churches were stronger and more able to support their own ministry. By 1870 the LMS Travancore mission had eleven ordained ministers and 210 native preachers. In Ceylon, missions initially prospered more in the Buddhist and Sinhalese south than in the Hindu and Tamil north. The Methodist mission, initiated by Thomas Coke in 1813, had seventeen Sinhalese ministers by 1863, but only two Tamil ministers in 1859, when John Kilner was appointed chairman of the Tamil District. Kilner was one of the few missionaries in the sub-continent who had some success in disentangling the structures of church and mission and freeing promising indigenous leaders from their status as paid agents of the foreign mission. By his return to England in 1875, there were eighteen Tamil Methodist ministers. Conversely, in the Buddhist south, the outlook for the church deteriorated from the 1870s in the aftermath of a series of public debates between Buddhist and Christian champions. David de Silva, a Sinhalese Methodist minister and notable Pali scholar trained by Daniel Gogerly of the WMMS, led the Christian side in an epic confrontation at Pānadurē in 1873. Ironically, de Silva's attempts to vanquish Buddhism with the weapons of the Enlightenment proved counter-productive to the Christian cause. The future of Protestant Christianity in south Asia lay not with the handful of educated and usually high-caste products of missionary education, but with people movements among the poor and the outcastes, movements that missionaries neither initiated nor directed.

28

The Middle East: western missions and the Eastern churches, Islam and Judaism

HELEEN MURRE-VAN DEN BERG

Introduction

In the nineteenth century, the Middle East became the scene of intensive religious encounters between representatives of Christianity and Islam, and between Christianity and Judaism, as well as between those representing western forms of Christianity (Protestantism and Roman Catholicism) and the members of the Eastern churches. These encounters took place in a rapidly changing part of the world, where western influence by way of diplomatic and commercial relationships was strong and where mundane interests on both sides were thoroughly mixed with religious interests. French and British diplomatic relationships with the Ottoman empire, already strong in the seventeenth and eighteenth centuries, in the nineteenth century helped to strengthen the constitutional rights of the minority communities of Jews and Christians, whereas western support (notably from Russia) of the separatist movements in the Greek, Balkan and Caucasian provinces of the Ottoman empire helped to reduce its size considerably, at the same time increasing the percentage of Muslim inhabitants of the remaining Ottoman state. The other important Middle Eastern state of the time, Persia, also experienced growing western influence, culminating in the 'strangling of Persia' by Russia and Great Britain at the end of the nineteenth century. Under Muhammed Ali (1805–48), Egypt gained independence from the Ottoman empire, but in 1882 became the first Middle Eastern state to be occupied by a western country, Great Britain.

Religion in the Middle East displayed great variety: about 75 per cent of the population belonged to Islam, rather evenly divided among Sunni and Shi'a, but including also groups like the 'Alawi in the Syrian provinces. In addition, northern Mesopotamia had its Yezidies, Lebanon its Druze, Palestine its Samaritans, Persia its Zoroastrians; this last country also witnessed in the 1840s the birth of the Baha'i faith. Small but ancient communities of Jews were found in almost all cities of the Middle East, while Palestine started to welcome growing numbers of Jewish immigrants from the West.

The Christians of the Middle East, after the Muslims the biggest single group, consisted of many different denominations. Of these, the Coptic Church in Egypt, the Armenian Church in the Ottoman empire and Persia, and the Syrian Orthodox Church in northern Mesopotamia represented the miaphysite opposition to the Council of Chalcedon (451), whereas the (Assyrian) Church of the East, in northern Mesopotamia and north-western Persia, represented the continuation of the Church of Persia which had identified with the theologies of Nestorius and Theodore of Mopsuestia in the same period. The Chalcedonian tradition was represented by the Greek Orthodox or 'Rum' Church, mainly to be found in the western provinces of the Ottoman empire.[1] In the seventeenth and eighteenth centuries, Roman Catholic missionaries in Aleppo and other cities of the Ottoman empire had successfully laboured for the union of these churches with Rome, although only the Maronite Church (which had established strong links with the Roman Catholic Church during the crusading period) as a whole had accepted the authority of the pope. All other churches split over this issue and rival Catholic hierarchies were created.[2] In general, the level of education of the members and clergy of the churches of the East was not high, and lay religious life was maintained primarily by oral transmission of the basic texts (in church as well as in informal settings outside the church) almost everywhere in the Middle East. Exceptions were found, however, especially in places with a long-established Catholic presence such as Aleppo or an international city like Istanbul. Churches that were located far removed from the centres of the day, like the Syrian Orthodox Church in eastern Turkey and the Church of the East in Persia, remained almost untouched by western influences.

It is to this world that Protestant and Catholic missionaries of the early nineteenth century directed their attention in a series of encounters that had lasting implications for the relations of Western Christians with Eastern Christians, Jews and Muslims.

---

1 See volume v. On the christological positions, see also Brock, 'The "Nestorian" Church'. The name 'Rum' ('Roman') refers to the historical connection of this church with the Byzantine Church in the East Roman empire.
2 See chapter 25 above. On the earlier Catholic missions, see Heyberger, Les chrétiens du Proche-Orient.

Historical outline

Although Henry Martyn's translation of the New Testament into Persian (1812) stands almost unconnected to the ensuing Protestant mission work in the Middle East, his work was often seen as the beginning of it. Martyn, an East India Company chaplain sent to India in 1806, spent little more than a year in the Middle East (1811–12), but he was the first to translate the New Testament into one of Islam's important languages, an achievement which won the admiration of generations of missionaries in the same region. However, it was not in Persia and not among the Muslim population that the next steps were taken: the Church Missionary Society (CMS) took up work in the Middle East by establishing a mission post on Malta, then a British possession, in 1815, and from there started work on the isle of Syra (Syros) in 1828, in Egypt in 1825 and in Smyrna (Izmir) in 1830. Although the work was led by the Briton William Jowett, most of the CMS missionaries of the time were of German descent, such as F. Schlienz on Malta and J. R. T. Lieder in Egypt. German-speaking missionaries were also active in the Russian Caucasus, where the Basel Mission started work among German immigrants in 1821, but also established contacts with local Armenians and Muslims in Shusha and other towns of the region. Another of their missionaries was Karl Gottlieb Pfander, sent out in 1825 to the Caucasus and Persia. He became famous for his apologetic work *Mizan ul-Haqq*, 'The balance of truth', which defended Christianity against Islam and was translated into many other Middle Eastern languages, remaining popular among Protestant missionaries throughout the nineteenth century. In the years up to 1830, the American Board of Commissioners for Foreign Missions (ABCFM) also laid the foundations for its Middle Eastern missions. Between 1819 and 1825, Levi Parsons and Pliny Fisk travelled from Malta to Syria and Palestine, distributing Bibles and tracts, but were unable to establish a permanent mission post. In the late 1820s, 'missionary researches' to identify suitable mission posts were undertaken by Eli Smith and Harrison G. O. Dwight, who travelled all the way through what is now Turkey into western Persia. Itinerant work was also undertaken by the eccentric Joseph Wolff of the London Society for Promoting Christianity amongst the Jews (or London Jews' Society – LJS), who visited Jewish communities all over the Middle East, Central Asia and India, whereas John Nicolayson went back and forth in Syria and Palestine between 1826 and 1828.

Between 1830 and 1845, mission work in the Middle East became firmly consolidated, and Protestant missionaries succeeded in establishing and maintaining permanent posts, the CMS in Egypt (1825–65), the LJS in Istanbul (1826) and Jerusalem (1833), and the ABCFM in Beirut (1824), Istanbul (1831), Izmir (1834) and various other places in Lebanon and central and eastern Turkey, as well as in Iran (Urmia 1834). Except for the abortive attempt by James Lyman Merrick in Persia (1835–42) and LJS work among Jews, these mission posts directed their activities mostly to the members of the Eastern churches, among which the Armenians of Turkey and the members of the Church of the East in Persia were particularly receptive. In fact, initial successes led some of the missionaries to believe that reform from within the Eastern churches was not only possible and desirable, but also attainable in the short term.

Early Protestant successes became one of the factors that stimulated Roman Catholic orders, such as the newly re-established Jesuits and the Lazarists (established by St Vincent de Paul), to start new missions in the Middle East in the 1830s and 1840s. Long-established mission work in the Middle East, like that of the Franciscans and Carmelites in Palestine and of the Dominicans and Capuchins in Mesopotamia and Persia, was taken up again with new fervour. From the 1860s onwards, the Roman Catholic missions experienced the largest growth in their history. A new element was the entrance of female congregations, the first of which were the Filles de la Charité who started work in Beirut in the late 1840s and later worked also in Persia and Egypt. Other important congregations were those of the Sœurs de Saint-Joseph de l'Apparition (Syria, Egypt) and the Dames de Nazareth (Palestine). The Catholic orders focused primarily on the strengthening of the existing Uniate churches, but the ultimate aim of uniting all eastern churches to the Roman Catholic Church and the conversion of Muslims to Christianity was never abandoned.[3]

In the early 1840s, owing perhaps partly to Catholic influence, but also to changes within the Eastern churches themselves, opposition against Protestant interference grew, leading to the excommunications of those sympathising with the Protestants and the ensuing establishment of separate Protestant congregations in Istanbul in 1846 and Beirut in 1848. In this period, a few smaller missions also found their way into the Middle East. These included Anglican and Episcopalian missions to eastern Turkey and the beginnings of the Anglo-Prussian bishopric in Jerusalem, which was headed by Michael Solomon Alexander from 1842 to 1845 and explicitly limited its mission work to the Jewish community.

Under his successor, the former CMS missionary Samuel Gobat, work among the Jews was cut short and replaced by work among the Arabic Christians where he expected a more favourable response. For this the bishop

---

3 Verdeuil, 'Travailler à la renaissance', and Michel, 'Les mission latines en Orient'.

soon asked the help of CMS missionaries, who returned to Palestine in 1851. Mission work among the Jews meanwhile was continued by the LJS, in Palestine and Istanbul. In 1849, the first Protestant church building in the Middle East, Christ Church in Jerusalem, was consecrated, although at that time the majority of its congregation consisted of Europeans, complemented by a few Jewish converts. In Egypt and Iran, where the missionaries (CMS and ABCFM) were more reluctant to form separate Protestant churches and the circumstances for reform were more favourable, the need for separation had not yet arisen. In Egypt, this changed when in 1854 American Presbyterians started work in Cairo and from the beginning aimed at the formation of a Protestant church, which came into being not long after the beginning of the mission. In Iran, Protestant congregations did not formally disconnect themselves from the Church of the East, and for quite some time the bishops allowed 'reformed' and 'old' congregations to exist alongside each other. A fully separate Protestant church was not instituted till 1871. Although the schools of the missions were usually open to Muslims also, the fact that these schools attracted large numbers of Christians (both Protestant and others) made Muslims shun them, whereas the missionaries' involvement in the affairs of the Protestant congregations left them little time to engage in special projects aimed at Muslims.

It was only in the last decades of the nineteenth century, when fresh generations of evangelically minded missionaries entered the field, and under the impact of institutional changes such as the division of the ABCFM into the largely congregational ABCFM and the Presbyterian Board of Missions (1870), that missions among Muslims became an important priority of the mission boards. This change of policy was facilitated by growing western influence and political pressure on Middle Eastern governments (including the British occupation of Egypt in 1882), leading to limited toleration of personal religious choices on the one hand and to a growing interest of Muslims in western religion and culture on the other. New mission posts were opened that worked almost exclusively among Muslims, such as those of the ABCFM in Iran (Tehran 1872, Tabriz 1873, Kermanshah 1894), the CMS in Iran and Iraq (Ispahan 1869, Baghdad 1882) and Aden (Keith Falconer, 1886–7), and some of the new CMS work in Egypt (W. H. T. Gairdner, 1899). Missionaries of the American Dutch Reformed Church opened new fields in southern Iraq (Basra 1891, Bahrain 1892), where members of the Zwemer family played an important role. An additional factor enabling mission work among Muslims was a renewed emphasis on education and medicine. Modern institutions such as universities and hospitals were greatly appreciated and provided many opportunities for closer contacts with the Muslim population. However, publications of the early twentieth century breathe an optimism about the apparent weaknesses of Islam and the imminent 'victory' of Christianity that was not supported by any significant number of conversions of Muslims.[4]

In the latter part of the nineteenth century, the Eastern churches again attracted the attention of western missionaries. The Russian Orthodox felt a special responsibility for the Rum Orthodox, especially towards the Arabic-speaking population of Syria and Palestine that was often neglected by the Greek-speaking hierarchy. Russian Orthodox support was also welcomed by the Assyrians of north-western Persia, where thousands of members of the Church of the East were admitted to the Russian Orthodox Church in the late 1890s. Among the Assyrians, Anglicans about ten years earlier had restarted their project towards strengthening the Church of the East, while Lutherans of various countries were also working in the same direction. By that time, the work of the Anglicans in Jerusalem had again changed direction, renouncing all 'proselytism', and under the direction of George F. P. Blyth supported educational work among Jews, Muslims and the Druze, aimed at better relationships with the Eastern churches, even if this led to conflict with the CMS.[5]

By 1914, Protestant missionaries in the Middle East faced a wider range of possibilities than ever before. Missions were active in almost every part of the Middle East, Protestant churches flourished, and relationships with the Eastern churches had generally improved. At the same time, however, missions started to feel the impact of developments that were not wholly unconnected with the mission work itself: the emerging nationalistic consciousness of Armenians and Assyrians contributed to growing distrust of the Christian communities within the Ottoman empire, whereas rising levels of education made young Christian men look for opportunities abroad, not infrequently leading to permanent emigration and thus weakening the position of Christians. During the First World War many missionaries left, and although those who remained played an important role in organising relief for the suffering Armenians, Syrian Orthodox and Assyrians of the Church of the East, the war in many cases put an end to ongoing mission work.

Objectives and motivation

Although the above overview of the nineteenth-century missions might suggest otherwise, there is little doubt that converting Muslims to Christianity

---

4 Compare Zwemer, *Islam*.
5 Tibawi, *British interests in Palestine*, pp. 215–62.

formed the initial aim of the Protestant mission boards. Early publications make clear that both missionaries and administrators were convinced that Christianity alone guaranteed forgiveness of sins and eternal happiness on the one hand, and provided a sound basis for a modern and civilised society on the other. In their opinion, Islam did neither. Converting Muslims to Christianity therefore was just as important as converting 'pagans' in other parts of the world. Although some modifications in the views of Islam occurred in the course of the nineteenth century, missionaries of the early twentieth century held the same essential beliefs: that Islam did not provide eternal salvation for the individual and would not be compatible with modern society. In both periods, the importance of the mission among Muslims was underlined by detailed studies of the condition and various subdivisions of Islam, its world-wide spread, the basic tenets of the faith, and its rules and customs. From the very beginning, the missionaries realised that the governments of the Middle East, at the local level as well as at the level of the Ottoman and Persian states, were unlikely to accept missionary activities aimed at converting Muslims to Christianity. In addition, they thought Muslims to be extremely bigoted and not at all inclined to accept Christian teachings from a foreigner. As if this were not reason enough to expect no easy successes among Muslims, they thought that the degenerate state of the Christians of the Middle East would constitute another reason why Muslims would not readily be converted to Christianity. This explains why the 'reformation' or 'spiritual awakening' of Eastern Christians began to replace the conversion of Muslims as the missions' first aim and why, indeed, all of the first mission posts were established in places with considerable Christian communities.

What did Protestant missionaries have in mind when they wrote about the reformation of the Eastern churches? In their opinion, the Eastern churches displayed almost none of the characteristics of a true church. On the contrary, they worshipped images, Mary and large numbers of saints, their services were 'ritualistic in the extreme', priests were guilty of 'simony' (getting paid directly for saying mass, baptising and marrying), some of the churches prac-tised oral confession, and most of the clergy were hardly literate and unable to explain basic dogmas to their congregations. Most important of all was the fact that being baptised was generally considered as enough to be counted as a Christian. 'True conversion', in the evangelical sense of the word, was something these 'nominal' Christians had never heard of. The missionaries' favourite way of expressing the difference between their belief and that of the local Christians was that between 'spiritual' and 'material' religion: theirs was the religion of the heart, of true conviction, belief that existed independently of outward liturgical forms, and which ideally was complemented by indifference to worldly concerns such as wealth and political security. The 'material' religion of the people of the Middle East (Christians as well as Muslims) was characterised by the importance of outward appearance: the correct forms of prayer, the languages of the liturgy, the icons and church buildings, as well as by worldly concerns such as safeguarding regular income and security and well-being for the community as a whole. This negative view of the religious state of the Christians of the Middle East underlay the missionaries' conviction that reformation of these churches towards an evangelical model was of the utmost importance.

Whereas in the early days mission work among Muslims was not a priority, the reformation of the Eastern churches was worked for wholeheartedly. Especially among the Armenians and the Assyrians of the Church of the East, the missionaries' efforts seemed to bear fruit: educational initiatives were welcomed, preaching by missionaries in the Eastern churches was accepted and, in the 1840s, revivals took place in which Eastern Christians appropriated evangelical spirituality. Many of these early converts, young men and women, became missionaries among their own people and contributed to the spread of the evangelical message. These successes, however, led to reactions from the church hierarchies, who were disinclined to transfer power to foreign missionaries or their own lower clergy. Such opposition stimulated the formation of separate Protestant churches, and mission work in the second half of the nineteenth century in many respects centred on the extension and consolidation of the resulting Protestant congregations, not unlike Roman Catholic mission work, which aimed first and foremost at strengthening the Uniate churches.

Another possible motive for mission in the Middle East was what the missionaries thought of as the region's 'backwardness'. Judging from their publications (both at home and in the Middle East), the missionaries propagated a form of modernity which included good education for all, domestic hygiene, efficiency in the household as well as in the public domain, fair dealings in commerce, democratic institutions instead of authoritarian governments, a free press, equal relationships in marriage, and women's active participation in public life through education. American Protestants were the most typical proponents of such views on modernity; Europeans often tended to be somewhat more conservative. However, in line with the assumption that Islam was not easily compatible with modernity, the missionaries usually did not consider modernisation as a goal in itself, and for most of the century, in the Middle East as in other Protestant mission fields, 'civilisation' was seen more as a logical and irresistible result of the conversion process than as either a prerequisite for conversion or a separate object of mission.[6] In comparison, Roman Catholic missionaries give the impression of being less optimistic about progress in general and the possible benefits of European influence. However, their views on the education of women (for the benefit of the Christian family) and of the clergy (for the benefit of the congregations) were not very different from those of the more conservative Protestants.

The conversion of the Jews, the third religious community in the Middle East, was of less importance to Protestant missionary ideology than might have been expected. Significant numbers of the early missionaries shared a millennial world-view in which the conversion of the 'heathen' was a necessary stage in the beginning of the millennium and the return of Christ. In the first half of the nineteenth century, however, only a minority of those with more or less precise millennial expectations had definite views on the position of the Jewish people in such a scheme. This minority expected that the Jews would return to Palestine, acquire some kind of independent state, and convert to Christ. It was only the LJS that acted on such hopes, although even in this society not all members shared these explicit expectations. The LJS, alongside missions among Jews in Europe, also sponsored missions among the Jews of the Middle East, though without much success. Although missionaries of other organisations shared a certain interest in the position of the Jews in the Middle East and some were interested in identifying the 'lost tribes', it seems that most missions, once they had focused on the Eastern Christians, had little interest in pursuing missions among Jews.[7]

Although the majority of missionaries to the Middle East did not share the premillennial expectations that gained popularity in the late 1820s, there are strong indications that many of those involved in Middle Eastern missions (including the administrators at home who influenced the global distribution of funds) shared a common vision of the importance of the Middle East to the Christian faith. In 1860, the ABCFM spent about 45 per cent of its income on its missions in Turkey and Iran.[8] Although most publications did not elaborate on this special importance and during the course of the century less and less referred to millennial expectations, their authors often used terms like the 'Holy Land' when referring to Palestine, or 'Bible Lands' when referring to the whole region. Of the few authors who reflected theologically on this

---

6 See chapter 27 above.
7 Compare Kochav, '"Beginning at Jerusalem"', Perry, 'The American Board of Commissioners', pp. 251–94, and Bebbington, *Evangelicalism in modern Britain*, pp. 82–3.
8 Perry, 'The American Board of Commissioners', p. 275.

special position of the Middle East, William Thomson was perhaps the most important. His *The Land and the Book* (1868) considered the Holy Land to be an 'integral part of the Divine Revelation', of as much importance for the understanding of the story of Jesus in the New Testament as was the Old Testament.[9] Whereas Thomson's 'geopiety'[10] was inspired mainly by its relevance for understanding the biblical message, expressions that were employed by other authors indicate that some of the crusading spirit survived in Protestant circles. Rufus Anderson, the administrator and historian of the ABCFM, spoke about the 'republication' of the gospel in Bible lands.[11] Such a formulation indicates that Protestants of this period thought that Christianity had some kind of historic right in the Middle East. The fact that these countries witnessed the birth of Christianity, saw its first extension and flowering, but also saw it almost disappear in the course of the centuries, gave Christians a special responsibility for the conversion of their inhabitants.

Missions among the Muslims and Christians of the Middle East, therefore, were motivated not only by the intrinsic importance of every individual conversion or by the millennial expectation of worldwide preaching of the gospel as heralding the second coming of Christ, but also by the importance of the region in the nineteenth-century Protestant world-view. This world-view also gave rise to an additional motivating factor: the all-pervading sense of rivalry with Roman Catholic missions, who were their main competitors in winning the favour of the Christians of the Middle East.

The expansion of Roman Catholic influence among the Christians of the East was much resented by Protestants and thought to be the prime factor explaining these churches' lukewarm witness in the Middle East. In addition, they suspected Catholic missionaries of inciting opposition against their work, and they attributed not a few of their failures to Catholic interventions. More than the attraction exerted by the 'Holy Land', it was anti-Catholic rhetoric that played an important role in their publications, inducing their readers at home to fund their missions among the Eastern Christians more abundantly, and fortifying the early eastern Protestants against Catholic influence. The Catholics, in turn, used the relative success of the Protestant missions to propagate their mission in combating secularism and heresy, both seen (in the Middle East as well as in France) as intimately connected to Protestantism. In addition, the opposition of the Greek hierarchies was seen as one of the prime factors preventing larger gains from among the Eastern Christians.

9 Thomson, *The Land and the Book*, p. xv.
10 Vogel, *To see a promised land*.
11 Anderson, *History of the missions*, vol. i, p. xi.

Methods and results

The basis of Protestant mission work in the Middle East was formed by the partnership of 'public preaching' and 'conversation', in which evangelical truths were conveyed to Muslims and 'nominal' Christians. Rufus Anderson was particularly convinced of the importance of public preaching, which seems to have been one reason why missions among Muslims, where public preaching was out of the question, never gained his full support. Evangelistic goals, however, also infused the other departments of mission work – education, publishing in the local languages, and medical and social care. Primary schools, apart from basic literacy, offered knowledge of the Bible and Christian history on the one hand, and modern western knowledge (geography, secular history, arithmetic, natural sciences) on the other. 'Seminaries' offered advanced training for future Protestant leadership: 'pastor' positions for boys and 'teacher' positions for boys and girls. Both schools and evangelistic activities were in need of vernacular publications: Bibles, Christian literature, journals and schoolbooks. The missions often had their own printing presses, and while the CMS had much of the printing done in Malta, the ABCFM had mission presses in Izmir, Beirut and Urmia, where printing in a variety of local languages was executed. Many other missions also had small printing establishments. The third department that occupied much of the missionaries' time was that of medical care. From the beginning, most mission stations included a physician, for the double function of safeguarding the health of the members of the mission and of using medical help as a way to gain the hearts of the people. In the second half of the century, in pace with developments in America and Europe, the single physician was replaced by fully fledged hospitals with additional medical dispensaries at outposts.

Mission work often started with one or two male ordained missionaries, who initially were sent out single, but by the 1840s usually were married. In those cases, their wives participated as much as possible in the mission work, often by establishing girls' boarding schools. In the 1830s and 1840s the unmarried female missionary made her way to the Middle East, taking over much of the burden of the wives of the missionaries (who also had to care for their own families) in the educational projects, and participating fully in the 'conversational' aspect of the evangelistic work. Later in the century, women played a key role as physicians and nurses. From the beginning, local Christians were employed to assist the missionaries in translating and printing, as well as in teaching. Their contributions soon became indispensable and often the number of local co-workers of the missionaries far outnumbered the western missionaries. The local Christians functioned as pastors in the Protestant churches, as teachers in the schools, and as evangelists and Bible women in the more remote regions. In the latter half of the century also the medical professions became popular. Roman Catholic missions displayed the same variety of activities, including the overall emphasis on teaching. In addition, the female congregations, like the Protestant women, were very active in the medical professions. The contribution of Middle Eastern Christians to Roman Catholic work can be illustrated very clearly by the increasing number of indigenous religious who entered the orders in the Middle East. They, for example among the Filles de la Charité, accounted for up to 41 per cent of all religious in 1914.[12]

Judged by their own conversionist aims, the work of the Protestant missions to a large extent was a failure. The number of Muslim converts in the early years of the twentieth century was very small (a 1906 estimate suggests a maximum of 200 converts from Islam in the entire region, forming a tiny minority among some 30,000 communicants in the Protestant congregations of the Middle East).[13] The Eastern churches were carrying on much as before, Roman Catholicism was strengthened rather than weakened, whereas Christianity in general was not regaining the territories it had lost over the centuries to Islam.

Despite this overall failure of the initial aims, however, the missionaries could point to small successes that to them made their work worthwhile. The first of these was the existence of small but vigorous Protestant communities all over the Middle East. Although not part of the missionaries' original plans, their existence and modest growth appeared to promise the ultimate victory of evangelical spirituality in the region. These small communities suggested that 'new faith' could find a home in 'ancient lands' and exert a positive influence on the Middle East as a whole. This was also proved by the fact that the Eastern churches, sometimes supported by missions from the Russian Orthodox, High Church Anglicans/Episcopalians and Lutherans, in the second half of the nineteenth century went through a modernising process in which better education of the clergy and lay leaders formed the basis for new spiritual life in the community as a whole, among other things by establishing communal schools on a modern basis.

---

12 Verdeuil, 'Travailler à la renaissance', p. 281.
13 Cf. Zwemer, *Islam*, pp. 217–18 and Richter, *A history of Protestant missions*, p. 421, where further statistics on the state of Protestant missions of his day can be found. For geographical and statistical data on the Catholic missions, see Werner, *Katholischer Missions-Atlas*, pp. 9 and 16–20.

Another result that the missionaries highly appreciated, but which was not fully part of the initial aims, was the fact that their modernising and civilising activities met with relative success, especially towards the end of the century. As part of a broader movement of growing western influence, missionary education was appreciated by many, while the publications of the mission presses, either directly or indirectly (by stimulating responses by Islamic or secular presses) contributed to the spread of knowledge and the development of new literatures in Arabic and other languages. In this way, the missionaries felt part of the general westernising and modernising movement that can be distinguished in the late nineteenth and early twentieth centuries, and which, among other things, led to growing equality between Christians and Muslims and the first steps of a democratisation process in the Ottoman and Persian empires.

However, there was a downside to this modernising process. A connection between the missionaries' involvement with the Christian communities on the one hand, and the deterioration of intercommunal relationships on the other, cannot be denied. In a process that had started in the seventeenth century under western influence, the Christian communities rose in wealth and influence *vis-à-vis* the Muslims, a trend which was reinforced by nineteenth-century missionary activities, from which the Christian communities benefited more than the Muslims. This process resulted in growing nationalistic consciousness among the Christians, most prominently among the Armenian communities in the Ottoman empire, which was one of the factors that led to the Armenian massacres in the late nineteenth century and during the First World War.[14] The migration of Christians from the Ottoman and Persian domains (to British-ruled Egypt as well as to the Americas) that started in the late nineteenth century can be seen partly as a result of the better education and wider world-view of the Christians, but also as a sign of the limited possibilities of using these advantages within the context of the Islamic Middle East. Rather than strengthening Christian presence in the Middle East, as had been their aim, missionaries contributed to the fragmentation, dispersion and even decimation through massacre of the Christian communities.

Another unforeseen result of the missionaries' interest in the Middle East was that the 'Holy Land' became an important focus of popular piety among Protestants, as it had already among the Orthodox (from the Middle East and elsewhere) and Roman Catholics. Thomson's immensely popular *The Land and the Book*, combined with the numerous reports in domestic mission

---

14 Cf. Quataert, *The Ottoman Empire*, pp. 183–6.

publications, stimulated biblical scholarship at home and biblical archaeology in the Middle East, and also gave rise to the new phenomenon of Protestant pilgrimages to Palestine. Protestant Christians gained an enduring interest in this part of the world. In addition, missionaries were among the first to bring home to the Christian public in America and Europe the importance of Islam in the modern world. Although the majority of their publications described Islam as a religion that should be rejected as unscriptural and idolatrous and that eventually would disappear, these publications displayed genuine interest in, and sometimes outspoken admiration for, the faith of the Muslims, especially in regard to simplicity and consistency in life and prayer (which were sometimes compared favourably with the more elaborate practices of the Eastern Christians). This ambiguous assessment of Islam was often complemented by sincere attachment to individual Muslims with whom the missionaries became acquainted. A rather mixed message on Islam and the Middle East thus found its way into western Christian consciousness.

Concluding remarks

When the practical considerations that guided missionary administrators of the early nineteenth century in the choice of suitable mission fields are taken into account, the rather bleak prospects of mission work in the Middle East (also visible to nineteenth-century observers) suggest that other motivations were in play. The most important of these was the conviction that Islam constituted the archenemy of true Christianity (Mohammed was regularly portrayed as the eastern Antichrist) and that the 'Lands of the Bible' ultimately should be in Christian rather than Muslim hands. For Protestants, the strong presence of the Roman Catholic missions in the Middle East constituted an additional reason: the works of the pope, the 'western Antichrist', should be counteracted as much as possible. In response, Protestant initiatives in this region incited Catholic missions to work with all the more fervour for the union of the Eastern churches with Rome.

Neither Protestant nor Catholic missions could avoid entanglement in the colonial politics of the nineteenth century. British, Russian and French interventions in this region were not infrequently orchestrated by missionaries who wanted their beneficiaries to be protected from oppressive measures from local governments or other groups, or who wanted to have rival missions expelled or hindered in their work. Again a great deal of ambiguity is to be detected: the missionaries used the western powers as much as possible to their advantage, but at the same time many missionaries (among whom not a few Americans) earnestly believed that they could remain neutral and could abstain from making choices in the political arena.

Although the conversion of Muslims proved too difficult a task and the reawakening of the Eastern Christians only succeeded very partially, the missionaries were by 1914 confident that their work had contributed to the spiritual well-being and the necessary modernising of the Middle East as a whole. The negative effects of their activities were not yet fully visible and only after the Second World War would other interpretations of their work predominate in missionary circles.

29

Christians and religious traditions in the Indian empire

ROBERT ERIC FRYKENBERG

The story of most Christians in India begins in the south. For others, the story begins later, and elsewhere. Each Christian community has had its own separate lineage (*vamshāvali*), or tradition. By the beginning of the nineteenth century, three main streams of Christian tradition – Orthodox (Syrian/Thomas), Catholic (Roman) and Protestant (pietist/evangelical) – existed and can be followed. Hundreds of new communities, mainly Catholic and Protestant, came into being, in processes of proliferation that were increasingly complex. Scattered far and wide, to the farthest corners of the sub-continent, and beyond, these communities evolved within the dynamics of a Hindu and imperial matrix.

The Hindu Raj

During the first half of the nineteenth century, as processes of imperial integration reached completion, all principalities within the sub-continent were brought together under the shadow of a single overarching political system. Under the East India Company, a partnership of Europeans and Indians gathered enough resources to make this possible. This system, known as the 'Indian empire' or the 'Raj', coined the twin concepts 'Hindu' and 'India', signifying things that had never before happened.

This empire was, in many respects, a 'Hindu Raj'. Beneath the euphemism of 'religious neutrality' (or 'non-interference') was a clear-eyed logic of power. The entire structure – vital flows of information and revenue – depended upon collaboration with 'Hindu' or 'native' elites belonging to the highest castes. It was these elites who, working alongside European scholars and thinkers, and missionaries, collaborated in the making of what would later become known as 'Hinduism'.

It is good to remember that the terms 'Hindu' and 'Hinduism' are relatively recent. Distinctions between things religious and non-religious are modern.

In earlier times, to be 'Hindu' was to be native to 'Hindustan'. Terms like 'Hindu-Muslim' and 'Hindu-Christian' were not uncommon. The emergence of 'Hinduism' as a religious concept was also a byproduct of collaboration between Indians and Europeans. The concept was not British, 'colonial' or 'Orientalist' (in the pejorative sense now fashionable). Many high-caste, mainly Brahman pandits helped to perfect a 'rule of law' that, while British in procedure, was Hindu in substance. Scores of Indian scholars in each locality played as large a role as scholars from the west. When the Baptist missionary William Ward (1769–1823) defined 'Hindooism' as a single religious system,[1] he was merely taking the logic of collaborative orthodoxy to the next level. The process begun under Warren Hastings in the 1770s, and pursued by John Holwell, Nathaniel Halhed and Sir William Jones, culminated a century later in the works of Monier Monier-Williams and Max Müller. Müller's fifty-volume *Sacred Books of the East* is still the foundation for this 'constructed' Hinduism. Also, when the Company's governments took over religious endowments within its territories (in Bengal Presidency in 1810 and Madras in 1817), they inadvertently defined and reified a parallel array of 'Hindu' institutions – with up to 10,000 pukka temples per district – so that all seemed to be part of a seamlessly single 'Hinduism'.

India's Christians, and missionaries from abroad, faced official indifference and hostility. Officials studiously avoided interfering with established traditions, taking care to make sure the Raj was not identified as 'Christian'. Contradictions occurred – as when Christians 'on the ground' were asked to serve as chaplains, teachers or emissaries. For the sake of expedience, subventions were paid to Roman Catholic vicars apostolic for clerics to serve as chaplains for Irish contingents; and, after 1792, the evangelical lobby got 'missionary chaplains' admitted into Company service. William Carey, forbidden entry into Bengal, worked in the tiny Danish enclave of Serampore (Srirampur). While his *An enquiry into the obligations of Christians to use means for the conversion of the heathens* (1792), inspired by the deeds of Moravian and pietist missionaries such as C. F. Schwartz, stirred up a wave of voluntarism, he himself was not allowed to cross the Hugli into Calcutta until offered a position at Fort William College. Not until after voluntary missionary agencies and 'free-trade' interests opposed to the Company's commercial monopoly formed an alliance was this barrier broken. A heated 'pamphlet war', and much lobbying by 'saints' among Company's Directors (such as Charles Grant) and friends

---

1 W. Ward, *Account of the writings, religion, and manners of the Hindoos*, 4 vols. (Serampore: Mission Press, 1811).

in Parliament (Wilberforce, Thornton, *et al.*), occurred before the 1792 'Pious Clause' was finally reinserted into the Charter Renewal Act of 1813. Thereafter, missionaries or merchants denied entry to India could appeal for redress.

Even so, nineteenth-century missionaries faced resistance. Ever wary of tactlessness that might lead to disorder, authorities summarily expelled any missionary or overzealous officer whose actions provoked unrest. Europeans daring to slight Hindu and Muslim practices, as 'devilish' or 'heathen', could be deported. Sir Thomas Munro, while governor of Madras (1820–27), censured and removed mofussil (*mufassal*: interior, country or rural) officers who used their positions for personal evangelism. When Lord Bentinck, yielding to reformers and missionaries, decreed the abolition of female infanticide and widow-burning (1827), outrage among the gentry (*bhadralog*) of Calcutta was such that 30,000 signed a 'Sacred Petition', protesting against the violation of 'religious freedoms'. But when devout civil and military Christian servants of the Company signed a protest against government involvement in 'idolatrous practices' – such as the managing of 'Hindu' temple properties and functions; protecting pilgrimages; requiring Christian soldiers to attend Hindu festivals; forcing thousands, even Christians, to pull Temple Cars (*Rath Yatras*) in honour of local deities (when some were crushed); or turning a blind eye to temple 'dancing girls' (*devadasis*), thereby consigning untold thousands into lives of perpetual prostitution – they were reprimanded or sacked. Bishop George Spencer was rebuked; and General Peregrine Maitland returned to London to launch the Anti-Idolatry Connexion League. In the 1840s, Lord Tweeddale (Governor of Madras, 1842–8) was censured and recalled for using the term 'heathen' in official communications and favouring missionary schools. His actions provoked a rally of the 'Hindu Community of Madras' where 70,000 signed a petition to parliament. 'Proselytising zeal' was blamed for the Great Rebellion (Mutiny) of 1857 and lesser uprisings going back to the Vellore Mutiny of 1806. Long after 1858, missionaries sympathising with the nationalist cause, or Anglican prelates engaged in ecclesiastical imperialism, evoked displeasure. Missionaries (such as the American Congregationalist R. Allen Hume) who were among the founding members of the Indian National Congress were often viewed with suspicion.

The Thomas tradition

In November 1806, in an event of pivotal importance, Mar Dionysius I, *metrān* (metropolitan bishop) of the *Jacoba* (Syrian) Christians, received the evangelical Company chaplain Claudius Buchanan at his palace in Kandanāt. Described as an old man, with a long white beard, seated among his *kattanārs* (priests), holding a silver crozier curved at the top in the Greek style, and wearing a pontifical cope with a round mitre on his head, he represented a proud and ancient people. The provost of Fort William College had come from Lord Wellesley to make an alliance. Told that few Syriac copies of Scripture remained and that the local *kattanārs* were ill trained and poor, Buchanan offered help. He would get Scriptures translated into Malayālam and printed, so that all would have access to Holy Writ in their mother tongue. He would also help to set up a seminary for training *kattanārs*. Highly pleased, the *metrān* presented Buchanan with a copy of the Syriac Scriptures said to be a thousand years old. He was less enthusiastic about a possible union between the Syrian and Anglican communions. Buchanan soon returned to Britain, where his *Christian researches in Asia* (1811) brought him renown. Mar Dionysius soon died, and his nephew Metrān Mathan Mar Thoma VII presided in his place.

The ancient Christians of Malabar were 'Hindu' – Hindu in culture, Christian in faith, and Syrian in doctrine, polity and ritual. Tracing their origins to 52 A D, and the arrival of the Apostle Thomas at Malankara, there was no denying the canonical status of their tradition – nor of the multiple arrivals among their ranks, over centuries, of refugees from Zoroastrian and Islamic persecutions. Nor can there be any denying the ritual purity and rank of this high-caste community within the caste structure (*varnāshramadharma*). Mostly landed merchant-warriors, they possessed distinctly 'Hindu' customs: husbands tied *thālis* on the necks of their brides; they ceremonially took 'marriage cloths'; in the case of the elite Malankara Nazranis, they wore a tonsure like Nayars and Brahmans and lived in *tharavād* houses; and they strictly avoided pollution in matters of inter-dining, inter-marriage and disposing of their dead. In their hereditary priesthood, each new cleric succeeded his mother's brother; families of some *kattanārs* and *metrāns* traced lineages (*vamshāvalis*) from Brahman converts of the Apostle as far back as seventy or eighty generations. While patriarchs (catholicos) of Antioch and Babylon competed for sway over prelates in India, the Thomas Christians themselves seem to have been little bothered about doctrines, whether Diophysite (Nestorian) or Monophysite (Jacobite: *Jakoba* or *Yacoba*). Resorting to defensive, self-insulating strategies for survival, their gospel seems to have gone into a long hibernation, all but hermetically sealed for a thousand years.

The Portuguese, when they arrived, had been welcomed as allies against oppressive rulers and maritime predators; but later, when their Estado da India tried to impose total Catholic hegemony upon the ancient Thomas Christians, they were resented. After the Synod of Udayamperur (Diamper) in 1599, Syrian clerics, doctrines and rituals were cast aside and Syrian libraries burned. Nevertheless, resistance to Catholic hegemony continued, with local leaders showing great resilience in surviving cultural domination. In 1653, at a solemn assembly of notables and *kattanārs* at Koonen Cross (*Koonen Kurisu*), Thomas Christians for the first time consecrated their own Indian *metrān*. Followers of Mar Thoma I, called the 'Puthencoor' (New Group), continued to struggle against domination. After the Dutch conquered Cochin, a *Jakoba metrān* arrived in Malabar, sent by the catholicos of Antioch (from Debhikr). His efforts to take control led to further struggles for ecclesiastical ascendancy – between Antioch and Babylon, as well as with Rome.

The first two British Political Residents in Travancore and Cochin were Colin Macaulay (1800–10) and Sir John Munro (1811–19). In 1809 and 1811, after Company troops put down insurgencies and 'rescued' him, Maharajah Raja Rama Varma (d. 1814) made Munro diwan; and under Lakshmi Rani (d. 1814) and Parvati Rani (1814–29), he became virtual ruler of Travancore. Both Residents, devout evangelicals, favoured Thomas Christians, showing a partiality that would have brought reprimands elsewhere in India. Munro rescued Christians from compulsory service and temple taxes, and appointed Christians to district judgeships. When the Malayālam translation of the Syriac Scriptures was completed, he had copies printed and placed in every church. In 1813, on lands endowed by the Rani, a seminary was established in Kottayam. By 1816, training of pastors (*kattanārs*) and teachers (*malpāns*) had begun, with instruction both in Malayālam and Syriac, twenty-five enrolled students and the *metrān* himself in residence. Four CMS missionaries – Thomas Norton, Benjamin Bailey, Joseph Fenn and Henry Baker – taught in the seminary and were allowed to preach in Thomas Christian churches.

The year 1816 also saw the death of Mar Dionysus. On Munro's request, Mar Philoxenos became *metrān*. But Philoxenos, pleading bad health, soon consecrated Punnathra George *kattanār*. Metrān Mar Dionysius III convened the Synod of Māvēlikkara in 1818, with missionaries sitting on each side, as if by right. When the assembly of *kattanārs* was asked to make all ceremonies, doctrines and rites conform to the Scriptures (as interpreted by the missionaries), Konāṭṭu, a leading *malpān*, warned that changes were coming too rapidly – clergy were marrying, schools opened, Malayālam Scriptures read each Sunday, and images removed.

Munro retired in 1820, and relations soon deteriorated. Hindu resentments against Thomas Christians resurfaced and suspicions of missionaries increased. After Mar Dionysius III died in 1825, the new *metrān*, elected by a synod of clergy and laity, was Philipose *malpān*. Consecrated as Mar Dionysius IV, he did little to hinder increasing anti-Christian sentiment. Christians who lost government positions found the new Resident less than sympathetic. At the same time, another clash erupted between the new *metrān* and agents of the patriarch. The quarrel, that continues to this day, was not just between Malankara and Antioch, between Indian and Syrian authority, but between opposed parties of Thomas Christians, each claiming patriarchal support whenever this suited its purpose. As resentments against missionary interference and new ideas about conformity to biblical norms over the old ways increased, Bishop Reginald Heber, then on his last journey as the second Anglican bishop of Calcutta, tried to pour oil on the waters. Daniel Wilson, bishop from 1832, took a harder line. Irate Thomas Christians, assembling at Māvēlikkara in 1836, firmly rejected Wilson's views and reaffirmed their ancient tradition. This synod ended formal connections between Thomas Christians and Anglicans. Ongoing struggles over the Kottayam property served to make the rupture permanent.

Two evangelical groups of Thomas Christians emerged from the thirty years of Anglo-Syrian collaboration. The smaller group became Anglican (CMS). The larger, while appreciating lessons learned at Kottayam College, committed themselves to reforms within the Thomas Christian tradition. Their leader, Abraham *malpān*, resigned from the college and became a veritable 'Wycliffe' among his own people. In his large congregation at Mar Marāmanu, worship services were held in Malayālam and non-biblical elements were removed. Yet, wanting not to abandon ancient tradition but to legitimise and preserve reforms, he laid hands upon his nephew, Matthew, and sent him as his emissary to the patriarch of Antioch, then in Mardin. This young man, having studied in Kottayam and Madras, made a good impression on the patriarch. Consecrated Metrān Mar Matthew Athanasius, he returned to India with a commission to restore order. But when he arrived in Travancore, his authority was immediately challenged. Mar Dionysius refused to recognise his credentials and accused him of being a puppet of European (*Pfarangi*) missionaries and subverting ancient traditions. A perplexed patriarch sent Mar Kurilos to investigate. Mar Kurilos, on reaching India, declared himself to be the only legitimate *metrān*. The Travancore government, in 1852, decided that only the documents of Mar Matthew Athanasius were genuine and that those of Mar Kurilos had been forged.

The new *metrān*, despite his deeply divided community, felt vindicated. While some *kattanārs* continued to question his credentials, feeling that the patriarch had been duped, the ancient community was gradually led towards incorporating new doctrines within its ancient tradition. The support Matthew received revealed that sympathy for reformation within the

Synod of Māvēlikkara in 1836 had never been extinguished.[2] Numbers of new schools continued to multiply and literacy rapidly increased. The Mar Thoma Evangelistic Association, founded in 1888, devoted itself to outreach among lower-caste peoples, eventually establishing ashram-like settlements. Thomas Christians steadily moved into the modern world.[3]

The Catholic Church

Catholics in nineteenth-century India faced a precarious situation. Political upheavals, in Europe and India, had brought disruption, decline and dissension. Suppression of the Jesuit order in 1773 had left many congregations in India abandoned. Capuchins, coveting Jesuit properties, had to make way for the Société des Missions Etrangères de Paris; but that society had only six missionaries – three elderly and infirm (one a bishop) and three novices. The disruptions of the French Revolution, the Napoleonic wars and the occupation of Rome had weakened papal authority. Increasingly difficult communications and funding from Europe had left Indian priests to fill the void, many of them half-trained.

The remarkable expansion of Catholic communities that had occurred over the previous three centuries was in jeopardy. Catholic orders, enjoying considerable autonomy from Lisbon and Rome, had sent forth missionaries from their monastic and collegial citadels into the countryside outside of the Estado da India. Whole communities of fisherfolk along the coasts had turned Christian, partially in defiance of Hindu and Muslim rulers. The Jesuit 'Brahmans' Roberto de Nobili in the seventeenth century and Constanzo Giuseppe Beschi in the eighteenth had established a proud Catholic tradition of Sanskrit and Tamil scholarship, and modest numbers of 'caste' people from respectable families had become Catholic.

More serious were ongoing disputes between the *padroado real* and the *Propaganda Fide*.[4] Despite its decline in world power and its flagging zeal, the Portuguese crown was still clinging to its 'rights'. Suffragan sees in Cranganore,

---

2 A parallel saga of byzantine complexity occurred among *metrāns* of the (Nestorian) patriarch of Babylon.
3 At least six communities still claim the Apostolic tradition: (1) the Orthodox Syrian Church (in two branches); (2) the Malankara Catholic Church (Syrian Rite); (3) the Independent Syrian Church of Malabar (Kunnamkulam); (4) the Church of the East (Chaldean); (5) the Mar Thoma Church; and (6) the St Thomas Evangelical Church (in two factions). 'Anglican' Thomas Christians are in the Church of South India. The Mar Thoma Syrian Evangelistic Association (begun in 1888) has run some 180 missions and ashrams.
4 The Vatican had created the *Propaganda Fide* in 1622 for sending missionaries into areas beyond Portuguese or Spanish authority.

Cochin and Mylapore often lay vacant for decades for want of papal approval. Missionaries independent of Goa[5] moving into areas under *padroado* authority were thwarted. Answering only to vicariates apostolic, they aroused fierce resistance. As a result, Catholic institutions languished; and flocks were left without shepherds.

Attempts to remedy the situation began in the 1830s. Gregory XVI, when still Cardinal Cappellari, had been in charge of *Propaganda Fide*. Acutely aware of the plight of Catholics in India, he was determined to make changes. First, he established new vicariates apostolic: Madras (1832), Bombay (1833), Calcutta and Ceylon (1834), Coromandel Coast (1835), and Pondicherry and Madurai (1836). Coimbatore, Mangalore, Pondicherry, Vishakapatnam and others followed, until there were seventeen. By the end of the century, the map of Catholic India was complete, with twenty-eight bishoprics, of which twenty-five were located within the Madras Presidency.[6] The Jesuits were restored as an order in 1814 and came back to Madurai in 1837 (after an absence of sixty-four years). Establishment of these new dioceses within the domains of the *padroado*, but answerable to *Propaganda Fide*, was an important event in the history of Catholics in India. After decades of neglect, this assault upon the *padroado* brought turbulence – reactions from padroadists provoking counter-reactions from propagandists.

The second action by Gregory XVI was an historic brief. *Multa Praeclare* (1838) publicly asserted papal supremacy over all Catholics in India, including those under the *padroado*. Henceforth, areas within the diocese of Mylapore not assigned to a vicar apostolic would go to the vicariate of Madras; likewise, untended parishes in Cranganore and Cochin went to the vicariate of Malabar. Vicars alone would be the true prelates, regardless of all previous papal bulls. The archbishop of Goa had no authority outside of Goa.

However, it was one thing to make pronouncements and another to implement them. With centuries of experience among 'country priests', padroadists had perfected skills of delay and obfuscation. While affirming papal authority, local prelates and priests strove to undermine the actions of the propagandists. Employing devices successfully utilised in the past, padroadist forces temporised, hoping to outlast the pope and 'turn' his successor.[7] Complicating matters, diplomatic relations with Lisbon had been broken since 1834.

---

5 The oldest (1637) vicariate apostolic at Bijapur and then at the Mughal (*sic: 'Mogor'*) Durbar, was begun by a Brahman Oratian; the second (1663), run by Carmelites in Dutch areas, was the vicariate apostolic of Malabar, at Varāppalli (Verapoly), in the Serra.

6 Ballhatchet, *Caste, class and Catholicism*, p. 5.

7 Boudens, *Catholic missionaries in a British colony*.

'Archbishop-elect' Dom Carvalho circulated a pastoral letter from Goa, repudiating *Multa Praeclare*, claiming it was a forgery 'extorted' by trickery and falsehood; and Dom Antonio Texeira in Cranganore and then in Mylapore did the same. Diplomatic relations being restored in 1841, Queen Dona Maria's nomination of Dom José Maria Silva y Torres as archbishop of Goa was confirmed in 1843. But the new archbishop launched attacks upon *Multa Praeclare*. Not until after the death of Gregory XVI and the accession of Pius IX in 1846, and the recall of Archbishop Silva y Torres in 1849, did negotiations make progress. Yet, even after the concordat of 1860, disputes continued to erupt and fester. Meanwhile, during these years, prelates successfully turned to officials of the Raj for redress.

Clément Bonnand, bishop of Pondicherry and vicar apostolic of the Coromandel Coast, led efforts to revive Catholic institutions in India. Years of experience among high-caste Telugus in Pirangipuram (Guntur District) had taught him that one could deal with officials of the Raj. Bonnand understood India and recognised the need to come to terms with secular authorities. Looking beyond the *padroado* and *Multa Praeclare*, and seeing that Catholics of India needed to build a stronger consensus and discipline, he sent invitations to prelates and priests of other vicariates apostolic and brought Catholics together to discuss burning issues. Discussions focused on anomalies and controversies between rival jurisdictions, the raising of native clergy, pastoral care, schools for children, seminaries for training priests, evangelisation and dealing with secular authorities, especially the British Raj. The First Synod lasted four weeks (18 January–13 February 1844).[8] These consultations set the tone for the eventual consolidation of the Catholic hierarchy of India under Leo XIII in 1886. The significance of this event for Catholicism in India can hardly be exaggerated. It laid foundations for building a comprehensive educational system and a native Indian clergy within an English-speaking Indo-British world.

Perhaps the most constructive initiative of Bishop Bonnand was his coming to terms with the Raj. Tense relations between Rome and Lisbon had in the past driven Catholics to seek frequent redress from non-Catholic regimes. Vicariates apostolic, with sees entitled '*in partibus infidelium*' ('in a place of infidel [Muslim] rule'), had often dealt with non-Catholic rulers. Carmelites of Malabar had gained concessions from the Dutch in Cochin and from the British in Bombay. Jesuits and members of the Missions Etrangères had dealt with the rulers of Madras, Madurai and Mysore. Catholics, clergy and laypeople alike, now took their disputes over caste, property or priests to the British.

8 Anchukanandam, *The first synod of Pondicherry*.

Catholics' disputes could be settled by the courts and governments of the East India Company. The British no longer worried about malignant Portuguese, Dutch or French influences. After Catholics in Britain had convinced the British public of their loyalty, the repeal of the Test and Corporation Acts (1828) and passage of Catholic emancipation in 1829 rendered them eligible for public offices. Irish immigration was turning Roman Catholicism into simply another denomination in Britain. The Vatican appointed English-speaking Irish vicars apostolic. For encounters between padroadist and propagandist prelates or priests within its territories, the Raj accepted responsibility and devised the Protestant-style principle that a change of jurisdiction was possible if a majority of the people wanted it. Such proposals prompted official investigation, and the Company was frequently involved in the affairs of the Roman Catholic Church.[9]

The evangelical expansion

Evangelical expansion in south India – from Tranquebar to Thanjāvur, Tiruchirāpalli, Tirunelvēli, and thence to Travancore (at Tiruvanthapuram) – reached its highest point during the early nineteenth century, and then spread to the north. With pietist roots, via Halle missionaries who had arrived in 1706, Vellalar Christian disciples from Tranquebar and Thanjāvur had already spread a network of chapel-schools across south India. Each expansion, initiated by local leadership, was followed after roughly half a century of incubation by a mass movement among lower-caste peoples. Influential 'Hindu Christians' of Thanjāvur provide a lens for comprehending what later happened among lower-caste Christians.

The most renowned was Vedanayagam (Pillai) Sastri (1774–1864). Born in Palaiyamkottai (Tirunelvēli), son of Christian poet Devasahayam Pillai, 'adopted' and taken to Thanjāvur by Schwartz when he was twelve, Vedanayakam quickly became a master teacher, headmaster and writer. Schools, endowed by the rajahs of Thanjāvur, Shivaganga and Ramnad, had already become so famous that Company directors paid subsidies for them to train civil servants, and Brahman families vied for admission of their sons. The Tamil–English curriculum, mingling biblical with Enlightenment learning and reflecting Francke's Halle ideals, provided an education available nowhere else in India at that time. The Saraswati Mahal Library, with its science laboratory and 'Cabinet of Wonders', symbolised the Enlightenment in India.

---

9 Ballhatchet, *Caste, class and Catholicism*, p. 5.

Vedanayakam, like Serfoji Maharajah a disciple of C. F. Schwartz, never abandoned his sense of being a Vellālar of noble birth, nor his reverence for classical or high *Sangam* (*Cankam*) culture. An evangelical and an intellectual, he was both founder and fountainhead of modern Tamil literature and learning. There was hardly a subject on which he did not write. His students learned about events and places all over the world. In lyric Tamil verse, he described the wonders of the universe and the wonders of God's grace; the wonders of what science revealed in stars of the sky, beasts and birds of the field, cities of America, Asia and Europe, and absurdities of inhuman and sinful behaviour. His *Bethlehem Kurvanchee*, a drama presenting the gospel in *kuruvanci* genre (a tale told by a wandering woman soothsayer or fortuneteller), confronted eternal verities. Yet later, when castigated by younger missionaries for observing caste customs, such as segregated seating and eating in church services, he remained adamant: what, he asked, entitled these Europeans to make such judgements? Bishop Heber had remarked upon the hypocrisy of allowing Europeans to employ servants or own slaves while condemning caste. Vedanayakam's 'Tanjore Christians' would eventually be publicly flogged, at a missionary's request, for refusing to abandon caste strictures. His hymns and songs, using standard Tamil tunes and tempos, are still sung. As 'poet-laureate' to Serfoji, the Maharajah of Thanjāvur, the title *Sastriar* was affixed to his name.[10]

Satyanathan Pillai, Schwartz's second great disciple, witnessed the first 'mass movement' of India. This outbreak spread across Tirunelvēli in 1799, after thirty years of incubation. Savarimuthu Pillai, a Company sepoy, and Rasa Clarinda, an affluent Brahman Christian, had opened a 'prayer-school' at Palaiyamkottai before Satyanathan came as the first pastor-missionary to the area. David Sundaranandam, commissioned to bring the gospel to his own people, was a powerful and charismatic preacher. Whole villages of 'Shanars' (now known as 'Nadars') became Christian, sometimes turning temples into prayer-school halls. These events aroused the wrath of local landlords and warlords ('poligars': *palaiyakarrars*). Many new Christians suffered violence, chapel-schools were destroyed and books were burned. Thousands who lost their homes, and were stripped and sent into the jungle to die, established biblical 'villages of refuge'. In the decades that followed, Mudulur ('First Village') was

---

10 Vedanayakam was soon followed by H. A. Krishna Pillai. A Thanjāvur Vellālar convert who taught in one of the modern schools, Krishna Pillai's greatest work was his epic *Irakshaniya Vāttirikam,* a poetic rendering of *Pilgrim's Progress* set within the classical Tamil idiom.

followed by Megnanapuram, Sawyerpuram, Jerusalem, Nazareth, Dohnavur, Suviseshapuram, Anandapuram and many other settlements.

By 1806, this fledgling community had lost its leaders. But after James Hough (another of the evangelical Company chaplains) was stationed at Palaiyamkottai (1814–20) and heard Tamil hymns being sung in local prayer-halls, he determined to come their rescue, by paying for Bibles, schoolbooks and teacher-preachers out of his private means. In 1820, Hough wrote to the new CMS corresponding committee in Madras asking for a missionary. The person sent to Tirunelvēli was a brilliant if fiery Prussian named Karl Rhenius (1790–1838). Rhenius, a Prussian ex-soldier of Moravian convictions who had survived the Napoleonic wars, soon became a heroic figure among the villages of Tirunelvēli. He encouraged, instructed, trained, translated, and held public debates. His wife ran schools for girls and women, teaching basic literacy and home health – setting a pattern that would be followed throughout India. As his disciples fanned out across the countryside, the earlier mass movement of conversion was rekindled. Thousands of Shanars, again sometimes whole villages, turned Christian. Thereafter, during every decade of the century, the Tirunelvēli Christian community doubled and sometimes tripled. As village congregations proliferated, hundreds of chapel schools were established, and voluntary self-help societies to care for the homeless, widows and orphans were also formed. Teacher shortages sometimes led to the recruitment of Catholics and non-Christians, some of whom also converted. Colleges and seminaries and hospitals were built; and the entire society of Tirunelvēli was transformed. A graphic picture of this new culture, covering the years 1838 to 1873, has been left in a three-volume Tamil diary by Savariraya Pillai, a Christian village teacher-preacher.

The social revolution in Tirunelvēli, in turn, brought severe reactions, especially from landed gentry and religious notables. Persecution, riots and violent attacks upon Christian villages broke out and continued sporadically for decades. As early as 1828, a voluntary society called the Vibuthi Sangam or 'Ashes Society', modelled after Christian societies, organised efforts to thwart mass conversions. Occasionally, Company officials had to be called in to keep the peace. During the 1840s, local court decisions were appealed to the High Court in Madras. What developed in Tirunelvēli, almost unique in India, was Hindu–Christian communalism, with sporadic violence against Nadars (formerly Shanars) who no longer accepted a menial place in society.

Evangelical expansion in Travancore began with 'Vedamanickam' ['Gem of Knowledge'] (d. 1827), whose pre-Christian name was 'Maha Rasan'.

Disillusioned after a pilgrimage to Chidambaram, he and his nephew (Masillamoni) responded to the Christian message while stopping in Thanjāvur to visit his sister and her family. In 1799, Vedamanickam carried seeds of his new faith to his family village in Mylaudy. There his following soon grew to several hundred, and he returned to Thanjāvur for help in recruiting pastors and teachers. William Tobias Ringeltaube, a zealous young Prussian of the LMS who had recently begun working among the Shanars of Nagarkoil, joined him.

But, within the steeply structured agrarian system of Travancore, the existence of this small community was an offence. Caste people, including Thomas Christian, Nayar and Brahman landlords, were not prepared to let low-caste people take liberties. Such people, whether Christian or not, were 'soil slaves' and, as such, polluting. That such people dared to declare their faith was enough for them to be accused, beaten, deprived of meagre possessions and threatened with death. Sons were taken away for corvée (forced or gratuitous) labour, and daughters for worse purposes. Women were beaten for daring to cover their bosoms. Pukka houses not being allowed, chapel-schools were burned, teachers imprisoned and Sabbath days denied.[11]

Eventually, as in Tirunelvēli, after fifty years of incubation and modest growth, mass movements broke out. People in several communities, among non-slave castes (e.g. Nadars, Arrians, Izhavas and Kuravars) and slave castes (e.g. Pulaiyars and Paraiyars), sought liberation from fear of demons and emancipation from bondage and oppression. Each movement occurred when leaders within a particular caste led their people into the new faith. Supporting infrastructures – schools to bring literacy, local teacher-preachers (catechists), etc. – were provided by missionaries (LMS and CMS in particular). Protests against oppression, violent reactions against conversion, and petitions to the Maharajah or British Resident followed disturbances and deaths. Finally, in 1855, under pressure from British authorities, slavery was abolished. Again, in 1859, as news of civil disabilities aroused further public outrage, Sir Charles Trevelyan, Governor of Madras, asked for explanations from the Maharajah. The Brahman-Nayar gentry of Travancore blamed missionaries. The chain of events continued: between progressive Christian conversions, demands from lower castes and reactions from local gentry. Leaders within each Christian community, despite support from missionaries, also began to become more assertive and resentful of missionary paternalism.

---

11 Hardgrave, 'The breast-cloth controversy'.

What had happened in Tirunelvēli and Travancore is a template for understanding what later took place in other parts of Tamil and Telugu country, and, eventually, among lowest caste (*āvarna*) and aboriginal (*ādivasi*) peoples of the north and, especially, in the north-east. As new waves of conversion occurred and brought new Christian communities into existence in other parts of India, educational, medical and social infrastructures were provided by missionaries.

Mass movements in Telugu country from the 1860s onward, replicating what was happening further south, began with a Madiga Christian, Yerragunthla Periah, and his wife Nagama. After hearing the gospel message from a converted relative, they went to Ongole and were baptised by John Clough, an American Baptist missionary. A Mala Christian movement gained momentum with support from American Lutherans in Guntur and Rajahmundry; and movements among other communities were supported by various Anglican, Catholic and Brethren missionaries from many countries.

Similarly, among forest peoples in the hills, movements of conversion gradually increased in volume and frequency. Across a wide belt of interior and exterior frontiers, from Kanya Kumari up through central India, into areas of Assam surrounding the Brahmaputra Valley, and across Burma, even to the Thai border, conversions occurred among hundreds of separate peoples, such as Badigas, Chenchus, Yerrakulas, Bheels, Khonds (Gonds), Mundas, Santals, Khasis, Mizos, Nagas, Garos, Chins, Kachins and Karens (of Burma), and many more. All of these were peoples who had never been Sanskritised or Islamicised and were only too eager to escape from conditions of brutality and insecurity.

Perhaps the most dramatic changes occurred among peoples in mountains around the edges of the Assam Valley, especially among Naga and Khasi tribes. In each instance, initial efforts seemingly failed. Yet the groundwork laid in the 1830s and 1840s brought results thirty years later, when individual Assamese Christians ventured into the hills with the gospel, putting their lives at risk from headhunters. Missionaries, American Baptists and Welsh Presbyterians in particular, followed. Living in primitive houses, they mastered local languages, translated Scriptures, set up printing presses, and ran schools for both children and adults. As village congregations increased in number and size and as local youths acquired literacy and became teachers, preachers and evangelists, more and more villages asked for schools and teachers. Eventually, revolutionary transformations occurred.

'New Molung' (Molung-yimsen), the first Naga Christian community, exemplifies this pattern. Formed in 1876 as a 'village of refuge', its story began years earlier in the river town of Shibsagar where Subongmeren, an Ao Naga who had come down into the valley to barter, met the Assamese evangelist Godhula and invited him to come and live in his home village. But Godhula's conversion and training, in turn, had occurred many years earlier under the American Baptist Miles Bronson (1812–83) who, with Nathan Brown, had failed to reach the Nagas. British Baptist missionaries, even earlier, had opened the door for American Baptists in Assam. Thus, on foundations long abandoned and then resumed by Godhula, the American Baptists Edward and Mary Clark became the first missionaries to settle among the Nagas. They were followed by many others. But, throughout the ensuing decades, it was the Naga preachers and teachers who carried the gospel to new tribes: from the Ao Nagas to the Angami Nagas, the Sema Nagas and fifty others. A very similar story can be told about the Garo, Khasi, Abhor, Mishmi, Lushai and other peoples. Thus, while the Ahom-Hindu cultural heartland in the Assam Valley remained largely impervious to Christianity, the cultures of aboriginal peoples in the surrounding hills and mountains were increasingly, and profoundly, altered. This pattern, to a lesser degree, was replicated in Maharashtra, Gujarat, Orissa and other regions of the north.

Aboriginal peoples became Christian without ever becoming either 'Hindu' or 'Indian', a circumstance that would cause problems, especially for the national government. In each instance, the gospel was reinterpreted in new ways, so as to fit prevailing conditions, older traditions and local challenges. Lives of peoples inhabiting ever lower strata or ever more remote frontier areas were touched and transformed, especially among women and children. Social reforms, together with educational and health services, reached peoples in hitherto neglected sectors of society, such as aboriginals and outcastes, including impoverished and impaired and disease-stricken elements. Notions of humanity and society expanded, suggesting that all – men, women and children alike, no matter what their birth or condition – should be intrinsically equal, at least in the eyes of the law. For the first time in history, universal literacy became more than an ideal. As newly literate people went on to high schools and colleges, as these joined movements for reform and self-determination, changes so engendered had revolutionary implications. Local Christian leaders within each community, aided by missionaries, played pivotal and reciprocal roles.

The cultural impact

As already indicated, while missionaries were neither the primary vehicles of the Christian message nor the primary agents of conversion within the cultural matrix or 'mother tongue' of each people, they were the primary vehicles of modern learning, science and medicine. Such being the case, the apex of missionary efforts consisted of institutions of higher learning in every major city. Interestingly, the influence of these institutions, antedating a parallel system of government institutions, was more among Hindu and Muslim elites than Christians. Beginning with William Carey's Serampore College in 1818, Alexander Duff's Calcutta Institution in 1830, John Wilson's Bombay College in 1835, and John Anderson's Madras Christian College (1838), and perhaps culminating in Forman Christian College (1865) in Lahore, along with a parallel development of women's (or zenana) Christian colleges across the land, these institutions catered primarily for the highest classes. As the nineteenth century came to an end, theologically liberal missionaries in the post-Darwinian climate began to extol Brahmanical and Islamic civilisations and conceive of the conversion of India in more developmental terms. For upper-class, intellectually eclectic missionaries, such as William Miller of Madras Christian College, the 'downward filtration' strategy of Duff was replaced by 'upward fulfilment' as a way to bring about more conversions among the elites. The task, therefore, was to permeate Indian society with Christian values. To this end, Christians needed to influence the elites who were taking to western education in such droves. Since much in the life and conduct of Hindus and Muslims was already praiseworthy, an evolutionary strategy was articulated by J. N. Farquhar: all religions being, in some measure, divinely inspired, Hinduism would lead Indians towards Christ, with missionaries striving for dialogue and mutual understanding. This kind of thinking in the west, called 'fulfilment theory', gained wider acceptance, especially among some missionaries. Put forward at the World Parliament of Religions at Chicago in 1892 and the World Missionary Conference at Edinburgh in 1910, this view gained ground.[12]

In vast areas of north India where Christians were thinly spread, some converts of high birth became highly regarded among both Christians and non-Christians: for example, Salih Abdul Masih (1765–1827), Lal Behari Day (1824–94), Nilakantha [Nehemiah] Goreh (1825–95), Krishna Mohan Banerjea (1813–85), Imad-ud-din (1830–1900), Narayan Vaman Tilak (1862?–1919), Pandita Ramabai [Saraswati; Dongre-Medhavi] (1858–1922), Kali Charan Chatterji (1839–1916), Brahmabhāndav Upādhyāya (1861–1907), Narayan Vaman Tilak (1862?–1919) and Sadhu Sundar Singh (1889–1929?). Four of these may

---

12 See chapter 34 below.

serve to exemplify influential Christian leaders of the late nineteenth century.

Maulvi Imad-ud-din, from the time of his conversion, followed by his ordination as a clergyman and evangelist, sought to convince members of his prestigious (*ashrāf*) class within the Muslim community that his new faith rested upon truths that could bring any person closer to God. In contrast to 'Hindu convert theology', the writings in 'Muslim Christian theology' by Imad ud-din provided Christians with fresh understandings of religious traditions in India. This was especially so since 'Imad-ud-din was so prolific.

Pandita Ramabai Saraswati, despite her enormous grasp of Sanskrit lore, was outraged at the treatment of women. Disillusioned by the inconsistencies of the Brahmo Samaj while in Calcutta, she happened upon Luke's Gospel in Assam and became fascinated. Nehemiah Goreh helped to resolve some of her doubts. But, in England, she refused the confining discipline of Anglo-Catholic sisters. Fêted in America by high-society women, her work on *The high-caste Hindu woman* (1887) made her world-famous. Returning to India in 1889, she devoted the rest of her life to rescuing 'child' widows. At her famous Mukti Mission, opened at Kedgaon in 1898, her spiritual quests continued, until an Indian form of 'Holy Spirit' revival broke out in 1905. Turning from society elites and rationalist theologies, her restless search for freedom (*mukti*) drove her into evangelicalism and towards 'holiness'. Her last days were devoted to a new translation of the Marathi Bible.

Narayan Vaman Tilak, a celebrated Brahman poet and thinker, read the Bible and was converted. But he insisted on being baptised by an Indian and not by a foreigner. His life-long quest or *parampara* was to reconcile his cultural heritage with commitment to Christ. Dedicated to the emancipation of the oppressed and marginalised, especially non-Brahmans, untouchables and women, he became editor of *Dnyānodaya*, an eight-page Marathi weekly operated by the American Marathi Mission. Tilak's enormous corpus of writings included some 700 hymns, many of which are still sung. He urged Indian Christians to shed dependency upon the west and eradicate denominational divisions. During his last years, he became a mendicant *bhakta sannyāsi* – giving up all connections except his family and home.

'Sadhu' Sundar Singh was a Sikh-Christian convert whose vision of Christ in 1904 changed his life. He never accepted European modes of thought, explaining: 'Indians need the Water of Life, but not the European cup.' He became a wandering mendicant or 'Christian sadhu', devoting himself to remote hill peoples, adopting an ascetic and ecstatic or *bhakti* fervour, and shunning the stuffy preaching of 'missionary churches'.

The qualities of dual identity

Christians and Christianity, as such, have never existed solely in the abstract – except as ideals. By itself, the adjective 'Christian' is a property of something else. The term implies 'diminishment' – positional subordination.[13] Things 'Christian' are activities, entities, communities, missions, institutions and individuals that are defined in relationship to, and subject to, the person of Jesus Christ. So seen, there is no such thing as an 'Indian' Christian – or a 'World' Christian. There are only earth-bound, 'hybrid' or 'hyphenated' Christians, pinned to the earth by local cultures and languages. Within the Indian empire, all Christians were hybrid and hyphenated – unable to escape contextual identities rooted, first and foremost, in family and lineage.

The gospel message, in its humanising universality, directly challenged the fissiparous tendencies of religious traditions in India, Christian and non-Christian alike. It uncovered a basic contradiction between *varnāshramadharma,* as defined by birth and privileged by classical tradition (*sanāthanadharma*), and the Christian doctrine of a single *imago Dei* for all humankind. Missionaries from abroad being alien, no movement occurred that was not conveyed in the local agent's 'mother tongue'. No local church or congregation escaped being a hyphenated entity. What has been traced here, therefore, is the hyphenised and hybridised character, or 'dual identity', of each Christian community.

Two shadows never disappeared. The first and most ceaseless lay in conflicts among Christians, whether Indian or western, Catholic or Protestant, Anglican or Nonconformist, Mar Thoma (Syrian) or Nazrani, Jacobite or Nestorian, conservative or liberal, divisions that were often rooted in caste. In dimensions historical and theological, every single group that had existed also continued to exist. Unity and diversity, polarities and contradictions, acceptance of common humanity without repudiation of lineage persisted.

A second shadow for Indians, Christian and non-Christian alike, was the presence of foreign missionaries themselves. Missionaries were alien, agents of change and disturbers of the status quo. Clashes between alien influences and indigenous institutions were more than religious or theological. They were cultural and political. Christians opposed by political regimes, both alien and native, found common ground and mutual support. But when alien Christians (missionaries) and alien rulers found common ground, Indian Christians found themselves marginalised and relegated to colonial domination. Yet the evangelising efforts of missionaries – whether Catholic or Protestant,

---

13 I owe this insight to David Lyle Jeffrey of Baylor University.

British or non-British – rarely benefited from colonialism. Indeed, precolonial, noncolonial and anticolonial missionaries, taken together, far outnumbered those British missionaries of the Anglican establishment who strove for another fiefdom of Christendom. While many British Nonconformist missionaries identified themselves, emotionally, with colonial rule (whose minions often despised them), some were anticolonial. None was more so than the Salvation Army. Most Catholic missionaries were not British but French, Italian, Irish, etc., and many Protestant missionaries from North America or northern Europe remained ambivalent towards British rule. Ambivalence toward the Raj existed also among recruits from lower classes within non-British societies, and from 'faith' missions that operated outside traditional systems of ecclesiastical control. Even before 1914, maverick missionaries such as R. Allen Hume, C. F. Andrews or Amy Carmichael were attaining prominence for their anti-imperial and pro-nationalist sympathies, and some later became friends of Gandhi.

New forces challenged the Raj late in this period. Drawn mainly from modernising Hindu elites, the same communities that had helped to construct the Raj, the same sinews of manpower, money and methods had also helped to bring modern 'India' and 'Hinduism' into being. The new challenges came from those who, through curiosity and dexterity, gained a mastery over the English language, English channels of communication, and English technology. This aspiring and affluent 'New India' – journalists, lawyers, physicians, teachers, bureaucrats, businessmen and landed gentry – influenced imperial policy. 'Hindus' and 'nationalists' now saw themselves as 'true Indians' in distinction from the tiny European group who occupied the high seats and whose 'colonial' society became increasingly 'foreign.' Only a few Christians belonged to this 'New India'.

Conclusion

New Christian communities by the hundreds, each ethnically distinct, proliferated throughout the Indian empire between Waterloo and World War I. The process was highly complex and sometimes convoluted. Each community, moved by unique circumstances, preconditions and contexts, developed its own story, many still uncollected. New communities, high-caste Christians and low-caste (*āvarna*) Christians, as well as 'no-caste' Christians (*ādivasis*: aboriginals or tribals), came into being. Distributed unevenly, the largest regional concentrations were in the south and, later, in the north-east. Malayālam-speaking communities of high-caste ancient Christians were densely concentrated in towns and villages along the Malabar Coast from Kanya Kumari as far north as Mangalore. Converts from both respectable caste and lowest-caste communities were also concentrated most densely in southernmost Tamil-speaking districts. Communities also came into being in Telugu-speaking districts along the Coromandel Coast, as well as in interior districts of the Deccan. Tribal Christians were concentrated in hill ranges dividing one region from another, especially surrounding the Brahmaputra in Assam and the Irrawaddy in Burma. In the north and west, over the vast Indo-Gangetic plains, as well as in the wilds of central India and the Deccan, along coastal plains of the Konkan from Gujarat almost down to Goa, as well as the uplands behind them, converts also came mainly from the lowest castes and forest peoples.

Christian movements seem to have been most successful when least connected to empire. Movements of conversion occurred not because of, but despite, imperial expansion, in places removed from imperial control. Movements of Christian expansion also tend not to have been led by foreign missionaries, and least of all by missionaries from the established churches of England and Scotland,[14] whose greatest achievements lay in building institutions of higher learning benefiting the Hindu elites of Calcutta, Madras, Bombay and other modern cities. Nonconformist and non-British missionaries (from America, Europe or Australia) provided more encouragement and infrastructures for new Christian communities from lower social strata. Again, within the contexts of 'formal', as distinct from 'informal', empire, depending on how such terms are defined, movements with the most spectacular results occurred in principalities not yet directly under Indo-British rule: in Thanjāvur and Tirunelvēli before they came under direct rule, in Travancore, and in tribal areas of the north-east. Conversely, modern Hinduism and revivalist forms of Hindutva can be understood as consequences of the Raj and of British missions within territories of the Raj. Hypotheses such as these need further investigation, looking at the anomalies and contradictions of relations between Christians and the Indian empire. Thus, ironically, Christian movements sometimes fared far better in areas beyond or outside of direct imperial rule: in the domains, for example, of the Velama Nayakas of Madurai, Marava Tevars of Ramnad, Setupatis of Sivaganga, Kallar Tondaimans of Pudukottai, Maratha Rajas of Thanjāvur, or the Nayar Raja Vermas of Travancore in the south; and in the tribal domains of the Nagas, Khasis and Garos of the north-east, as well as Kachins, Shans and Karens of Burma.

---

14 Tirunelvēli diocese may appear to be an exception; but the first movements there resulted from the efforts of the very 'Tanjore Christians' whom Schwartz and other Tranquebar missionaries had trained.

30

Christianity in East Asia: China, Korea and Japan

DANIEL H. BAYS AND JAMES H. GRAYSON

The nineteenth-century history of Christianity in China, Korea and Japan has some features in common. In each case it was seen at times as a danger to the authorities and the elite, whether as potential internal rebellion or as a link to a foreign threat. At times it also appealed to alienated elites as well as to the lower classes, and was seen by yet others in all three countries as a perceived path to modernisation of the state and society. However, the Christian histories of the three also seem sufficiently distinct from one another to describe them separately, and that is what this chapter will do.

China

In the long century from the early 1800s to 1914, Christianity evolved from the status of an illegal heterodox sect to that of a religion under foreign missionary control, closely associated with the west and its privileged position in China gained through the unequal treaties. In the years after 1900, however, currents of change in Chinese society involved some urban sectors of the Christian (mainly Protestant) community, both foreign and Chinese, in reform, modernisation and nation-building projects.

Christianity 1807–1860: Catholic continuities and Protestant beginnings

As a result of the early mission efforts of the Roman Catholic Church, including those of the Jesuit pioneer Matteo Ricci (1552–1610), and owing to a generally favourable stance of the imperial authorities towards the missionaries, in the early 1700s there were about 300,000 Chinese Catholics. But the imperial decree of 1724 which proscribed Christianity and expelled all missionaries (except a handful of Jesuits who were kept on to operate the Bureau of Astronomy at the court in Peking) resulted in a steady decline in the Catholic community. Now with the legal status of a heterodox and illegal cult, deprived of European missionary leadership (with the exception of the occasional priest who was smuggled into the country from Macao), and only inadequately served by the few ordained Chinese priests, the Catholic communities operated in a quasi-underground fashion. Nevertheless, persecution was usually only sporadic, and in the 1790s there remained some 200,000 Catholics, concentrated in the provinces of Sichuan, Jiangsu and Chihli (today's Hebei). These communities operated increasingly under the direction of lay catechists and other Chinese leaders, including some women in orders of Christian virgins. Then after 1800, partly owing to increased government sensitivity to heterodoxy because of the White Lotus Rebellion of the late 1790s and other religious sectarian unrest, Catholics came under renewed and frequent persecution and suppression in the early nineteenth century.

Meanwhile, Protestant missions began in 1807 with the arrival of Robert Morrison (1782–1834) of the London Missionary Society (LMS). The first several decades of Protestant work were both geographically and functionally restricted. Missionaries, like merchants, could reside for only part of the year in a small harbour area of Canton (Guangzhou, the capital of Guangdong province), or year-round in nearby Portuguese Macao. Thus the first generation of Protestant missionaries also did extensive work among the Chinese communities in South-East Asia, especially in Malacca, Penang and other sites. By 1839 and the outbreak of the Opium War there were more than twenty Protestant missionaries in the Canton–Macao–South-East Asia orbit, mostly British. The first non-British Protestant was the flamboyant Karl Friedrich August Gützlaff (1803–51); the first Americans were Elijah Coleman Bridgman (1801–61) and David Abeel (1804–46) of the American Board of Commissioners for Foreign Missions, who arrived in Canton in 1830.

These early Protestant missionaries made few converts (fewer than a hundred by 1840), but did important work in laying the foundations of the missionary enterprise. Morrison compiled the first Chinese–English dictionary, and with the help of William Milne (1785–1822) published the first translation of the Bible into Chinese in 1819. Morrison also founded in 1818 the first missionary educational institution of note for Chinese, the Anglo-Chinese College, which operated in Malacca until 1843, when it moved to Hong Kong. Finally, the opening of a hospital at Canton in 1835 by the American Dr Peter Parker (1804–88) marked the beginnings of medical missions.

After the Opium War of 1839–42, the treaties which China signed with Britain and other western powers from 1842 to 1844 constituted much of the basic edifice of the imperialist treaty system which lasted well into the twentieth century. As part of the 1840s treaties and linked agreements, France, which proclaimed itself protector of all Catholic missions of whatever nationality, succeeded both in moderating the ban on Christianity by an imperial edict of toleration, and in gaining the concession that former church buildings should be restored to Catholic ownership. Although foreigners were supposed to be limited to the five port cities stipulated in the treaties, the existence of old-established Catholic communities in the interior caused many missionary priests to travel widely, and their newly established legal privilege of extra-territoriality (which they enjoyed with all foreigners) made them relatively immune from harsh treatment by Chinese authorities. The late 1840s and 1850s were a period of rejuvenation for Catholic missions, with many new missionaries from several orders arriving (almost sixty Jesuits alone). This was also a period of suppression and eradication by the European missionaries of some of the patterns of indigenous Chinese clergy and lay leadership that had emerged in the long decades of absence of the Europeans, especially in old Catholic strongholds like those in Jiangsu province. The coerciveness and insensitivity of the reimposition of European control in the 1840s caused a near-revolt in the Catholic communities in Jiangsu. From this period on, European hegemony in the Catholic Church would prevail until well into the twentieth century.

Before 1860 Protestant missionaries had no significant number of converts beyond the five coastal treaty port cities where they were permitted to reside under provisions of the treaties of the 1840s. The one exception to this pattern was the successful evangelisation in the 1850s of some communities of Hakka (Chinese people, but of distinct ethnicity and culture) in Guangdong province. Although linked to the Basel Mission in Hong Kong, the evangelisation was the work of Hakka Christians, some being products of Karl Gützlaff's ill-fated Chinese Christian Union of the late 1840s, which used native evangelists based in Hong Kong to penetrate and distribute Scriptures in the interior. Gützlaff's scheme, reviled as a disaster by missionary opinion because of its abuses, was in many ways a precursor of indigenisation policies of the twentieth century. With fewer than a hundred missionaries in the five port cities as late as 1860, in these years some Protestants continued the foundational literary work of previous decades. A new and erudite translation of the Bible in classical style, the 'Delegates' Version', was produced with much effort and considerable controversy over the proper term for God; it became the most popular translation for decades, until efforts later in the century to create a more usable translation resulted in the vernacular 'Union Version,' finally published in 1919. The 1840s also saw James Legge (1815–97) of the LMS, soon after arrival in Hong Kong, take up his monumental decades-long task of translating (with capable

Chinese assistants) the entire Confucian canon, eventually published as *The Chinese classics*.

In the twenty years from 1840 to 1860, the most important set of events related to Christianity was the Taiping Rebellion, which nearly overthrew the Qing dynasty, wreaked vast damage to city and countryside alike, and cost millions of lives in the lower Yangzi valley from 1850 to its bloody denouement in Nanjing in 1864. Profoundly influenced by Christianity, and perhaps best seen as a variety of folk or indigenised Christianity, the unorthodox ideas of Taiping founder Hong Xiuquan (1814–64) were dismissed by foreign missionaries. But to the dynastic government and the elite class (gentry) or literati, the iconoclastic anti-Confucian content of Taiping ideology was anathema, and they viewed the Taipings unambiguously as Christians, thus confirming their conviction that Christianity meant social disorder and sedition. This perception was a large obstacle to Christian evangelism in the decades after 1860.

1860–1900: growth, conflict and institution-building
Completion of the treaty framework

In the diplomatic settlements resulting from the second China war of the late 1850s, France expanded upon its role as protector of Catholic missions. The Sino-French Treaty of 1858 and the Sino-French Convention of 1860 included new guarantees for Chinese Christians to practise their faith without harassment, and for Catholic priests to preach and reside anywhere in the empire (eliminating the old restriction to treaty ports for foreigners). Among elaborations of the rights now given to Christians was the right of missionaries to rent or purchase land anywhere, and erect buildings. Although these provisions first appeared in the French treaties, all the western powers soon had equivalent rights extended to them through the most-favoured-nation clause that was part of all the treaties. These clauses granting unfettered missionary travel and property rights throughout the interior were instrumental in engendering local tensions and violence during the rest of the century.

Local society: adaptation, irritants and incidents

After 1860, with the entire empire thrown open to penetration by missionaries, both the Catholic and the Protestant sectors, especially the latter, increased rapidly. In 1890, there were over 700 Catholic missionaries, but more than 1,300 Protestants. Many of the Protestants at first stayed in the treaty port cities along the seacoast and major rivers, but with aggressive new 'faith missions' such as the China Inland Mission of J. Hudson Taylor (1832–1905) leading the way (the CIM was already the largest single Protestant mission in China by 1890), most missions steadily expanded inland as well. Catholic missionaries on the other hand, who were distributed around the country through vicariates apostolic assigned to different orders, tended to organise rural communities of converts as cohesive components of local society. In so doing they normally constituted a simple addition to the complex mix of local social organisations that interacted in a usually peaceful competition for resources and influence in local society. But this process of change in the local balance of social or economic power also constituted a threat to the existing social order, especially to the prerogatives of the educated local elite or gentry class, already suspicious of Christianity because of its association with the despised Taiping rebels. By using their outside resources to build schools and clinics (and for Catholics, orphanages) and by using their special treaty rights to interfere in lawsuits on behalf of converts, both Catholic and Protestant missionaries could spark gentry-inspired *jiaoan* ('missionary cases') involving attacks on church property, or even riots injuring or killing Chinese Christians or foreign missionaries. Sometimes local tensions aroused by resentment of Christians' alleged privileges or special treatment contributed to cases of popular grass-roots violence not engineered by the elite. For example, anger at perceived advantage in a lawsuit, or at Christians' exemption from paying the subscription fee for 'idolatrous' temple festivals or fairs, could stimulate acts of retaliation against Christians or missionaries. When such acts occurred, the treaty rights of the foreigners (often in their practical effect extended to the Chinese Christians) could bring the case to the attention of officials and diplomats in Peking, with resulting headaches for all and possible official recriminations, reprimands and indemnities.

Institutional growth

The decades between 1860 and 1900 saw an explosive burst of institution-building in the Christian project in China, especially among Protestants. The missionary community in China was commissioned and sent there by denominational mission boards, which were becoming more bureaucratised and professionalised by the end of the century. Even the CIM, the antithesis of a complex organisation in its early years, was forced by its very size to adopt a more bureaucratically driven style. Most Protestant missionaries remained in large or medium-sized cities, where increasing numbers of them spent most of their time not in churches or street chapels (more preaching was devolving to Chinese colleagues), but in schools, hospitals and clinics, in publishing offices (for secular as well as Christian literature), and in the management of other services such as famine relief. Moreover, the cultural confidence that characterised most Victorian missionaries led them to assume that with the Christianisation of China would naturally come its westernisation – of political, social and economic patterns – as well. Very few worried about foisting culture along with Christ upon the Chinese. In education, for example, although Catholic communities often had elementary schools, which usually did not teach English or a western curriculum, Protestants had 50,000 students in a system which went all the way up to higher middle school and even 'college' (post-middle school) level. In most of these institutions one studied a western curriculum, including English.

The achievements of these years among Protestants were facilitated by a generation of strong-willed, resilient, indefatigable personalities who lived a long time, including over a half-century in China: Hudson Taylor of the CIM, Griffith John (1831–1912) of the LMS, US Presbyterian Hunter Corbett (1835–1920), Chauncey Goodrich (1836–1925) of the American Board, Martha Crawford (1830–1909) of the Southern Baptists, and others.

The Chinese role

In most aspects of missionary endeavour in the late 1800s, and especially in the reports and publicity written for the home constituency in Europe or North America, the foreign missionary took centre stage. In the great nationwide Shanghai conferences of Protestants in 1877, 1890 and 1907, the first two had no known Chinese delegates, and the 1907 conference had fewer than ten Chinese out of 1,100 delegates. Yet Chinese collaboration and assistance was crucial for all missions, especially those of the Protestants, whose many institutions needed Chinese staff to do most of the real work. By 1900, in addition to more than 800 foreign priests there were nearly 500 Chinese priests (but no Chinese bishops until 1926). In 1905 there were 3,440 Protestant foreign missionaries, about 300 ordained Chinese pastors, but over 10,000 Chinese staff of Protestant mission stations and institutions. This growth in institutional personnel indicates that by the turn of the century a number of Chinese, especially in urban coastal areas, had found in Protestantism a channel of upward mobility; these communities of urban converts, many of them products of the mission school systems, would become important participants in modernising activities in the twentieth century.

At the same time, many Protestant and most Catholic converts were rural, finding in Christianity a community providing identity, security and a religious faith which resonated with familiar strains of Chinese popular religion. Chinese rural converts' agendas in conversion and affiliation with Christian communities varied from the utilitarian (whether advantage in a lawsuit or miraculous healing of a sickness) to empowerment in the world of the supernatural. These agendas did not necessarily follow missionary expectations. For example, Pastor Xi of Shanxi, who was active in the 1880s and 1890s in establishing Christian opium refuges, gave himself the name Shengmo, 'queller of demons', and although he often co-operated with CIM missionaries he never took orders from them, always preserving his independence of action.

Pre-1900 Chinese reformism and Christianity

Reformist currents in Chinese society before 1900 had many links with Christianity, especially with Protestant missionaries and their writings and translations. From the mid-nineteenth century, missionary efforts in education, medicine, famine relief and publishing drew the interest of some Chinese, though for several decades these were not from the elite gentry class. Despite the persistence of patriarchal attitudes among missionaries themselves, the explicit agenda of 'uplifting' Chinese women, pursued by a missionary force that was for Protestants more than half female, was a frequent topic in mission circles. Missionaries campaigned as much against footbinding as against the opium trade, and the missionary school system was, until the 1890s and for most regions of the country until well after 1900, the only place where Chinese girls could receive a systematic education, especially a western education, outside the home.

Direct Protestant missionary influence on the political structure of the nation reached a high point in the mid to late 1890s. In the aftermath of China's humiliating defeat by Japan in 1895, elite thinkers such as Kang Youwei (1858–1927) and Liang Qichao (1873–1929) derived many reformist ideas, including national economic development and even notions of constitutionalism and political reform, from a few western missionaries who targeted their efforts on the educated class of Chinese society. Through their publications and personal contacts as well, the British Baptist Timothy Richard (1845–1919) and the Americans Young J. Allen (1836–1907) and Gilbert Reid (1857–1927) played an important role in transmitting reformist ideas to key Chinese thinkers. By this time there was also a modern revolutionary movement in China, led by activists such as Sun Yat-sen (1866–1925) who were not of the elite but were nationalistic and modern in outlook. Many of these individuals, including

Sun and some of his key associates, had received a western-style missionary education and were themselves Christians.

1901–1914: Christianity in a changing China

Seldom has the turn of a century in a given country also constituted such a watershed between historical eras as the year 1900 did in China. The Boxer Uprising (formerly often called the Boxer Rebellion) was a violent antiforeign and anti-Christian popular upheaval in north China that took the lives of over 200 foreign missionaries, many thousands of Chinese Christians, and tens of thousands of Chinese who bore the brunt of the retaliation of the military forces of the eight western nations that in turn invaded and occupied north China later in 1900 and 1901. Ironically, this undoubted tragedy ushered in a period of more than two decades during which both the foreign mission enterprise in China and Chinese Christian communities seemed to flourish. One might even call this period, which continued to the early 1920s, the 'golden age' of the Sino-foreign Christian endeavour in China. These years were punctuated halfway through by the political demise of the dynasty and establishment of a republic in 1912.

Protestants

The Qing government, abandoning the resistance to change long characteristic of it, pursued an ambitious reform agenda during the decade after 1900, including abolition of the old examination system, promotion of modern education, and creation of a constitutional political system. Many reform projects were ones where Protestant missionaries and Chinese Christian leaders had an established track record of advocacy and competence, such as a modern school system including schools for girls. Until Chinese schools with a new curriculum could develop in sufficient numbers to meet the demand, that is until the second decade of the century, Protestant schools, in a system now capped by post-secondary level colleges in major cities, set the standard for modern education. Even after Chinese government schools multiplied rapidly, the mission schools continued to enjoy a high reputation and impressive growth. In 1915 there were almost 170,000 students in mission schools (as opposed to 17,000 in 1889).

Protestant growth between 1900 and 1915 was impressive by all indices. Foreign missionaries numbered about 3,500 in 1905 and 5,500 in 1915, well on the way towards their eventual high-water mark of 8,000 in the 1920s. Chinese Protestants, about 100,000 in 1900, numbered almost 270,000 communicants

(330,000 baptised) in 1915; this growth would also continue into the 1920s. The Chinese Protestant community began to come into its own as a partner with foreign missionaries in the years after 1900. Most Chinese Protestants undoubtedly were rural, and of only modest means. However, with the Christian school system having provided upward mobility for many urban converts, by the years after 1900 there had come into being fairly prosperous Chinese communities in several coastal cities. Well-educated and respected Chinese Protestants were active in social and political reform in cities such as Fuzhou in the period 1900–15, founding YMCAs, leading anti-footbinding or opium suppression societies, and holding office in provincial legislatures before and after the Revolution of 1911–12 which toppled the Qing dynasty and established a republic. Sun Yat-sen, a Protestant, was the first provisional president of the Republic in 1912.

As the resources and leadership potential grew in parts of the Chinese Protestant community, a natural desire for autonomy or even outright independence from missionary control surfaced. In Shanghai, a group of Chinese Christian businessmen and professionals formed the Chinese Christian Union in 1903. Soon after that, Shanghai Presbyterian Pastor Yu Guozhen (1852–1932) spearheaded a movement to create several fully independent churches in the Shanghai area. These developments were paralleled by a comparable formation of a federation of former mission-run churches in the Beijing area that declared their effective independence in the years before and after 1910. Foreign missionaries were largely indifferent to the desire for autonomy of some Chinese Christians, as shown by the almost total absence of Chinese colleagues at the great centenary mission conference of 1907. After the spur towards indigenisation provided by the World Missionary Conference of 1910, the creation of a Sino-foreign China continuation committee to follow up its initiatives, and a personal visit to China by John R. Mott (1865–1955, head of the worldwide Edinburgh continuation committee), the missionary community became more open to real partnership with a new generation of Chinese church leaders. By the end of the period covered here, dynamic young Protestant leaders like Cheng Jingyi (1881–1939) and Yu Rizhang (David Yui, 1882–1936) were rising rapidly in visibility. But the problem of power-sharing between missionaries and Chinese was not effectively addressed until well into the 1920s. In this regard missionaries in Korea seem to have moved faster than those in China.

We leave the Protestant community as of about 1914 in the midst of change, and just as several even more momentous changes were underway but as yet barely visible: a proliferation of new radical mission groups such as

Pentecostals; formation of some new independent Chinese Christian groups outside the Sino-foreign Protestant institutions, with no links at all to foreign missionaries; and a rising tide of nationalism in China which would soon have a devastating impact on missions and Christian communities.

Catholics

Like the Protestants, the Roman Catholic communities in China recovered quickly from the Boxer chaos, and in the ensuing years continued to expand, mainly in rural areas. In 1912 there were 1.4 million Catholics (more than a quarter of them in Hebei province), with about 1,470 foreign and 730 Chinese priests. The Catholic community was more self-contained than the Protestants. It had as yet few modern schools beyond the primary level, and also lagged behind Protestants in medical work and publishing efforts, especially on secular topics. Shortly after 1900 France renounced her protectorate of all non-French missions, even as several new Catholic orders made their initial appearance on the field in China. In the United States, the Catholic Foreign Mission Society of America and a seminary were established in 1911. This would soon become the Maryknoll Fathers and Brothers, whose first missionary priests went to China in 1918.

Some leading Chinese Catholics were impatient with the slowness of the church to participate in national reform and modernisation activities, especially in higher education. Ma Xiangbo (1840–1939) was a brilliant Jesuit priest who was instrumental in laying the groundwork for three important Catholic universities between 1903 and 1913, two in Shanghai and one in Peking. The latter, which would eventually become Furen University, was also the work of Ying Lianzhi (1867–1926), an important Catholic layman and publisher of the respected Tianjin daily *Dagongbao*. Nevertheless, the Catholic Church as a whole remained fairly indifferent to such reform initiatives, and, even more than in the Protestant case, positions of power remained firmly in the hands of foreigners. The one foreign priest who would later spearhead a movement to indigenise the power structure of the Catholic Church in China, Father Vincent Lebbe (1877–1940), a Belgian, had already come to China in 1901, and was forming his views on indigenisation, but would not begin the open advocacy of them until after 1915.

Russian Orthodoxy

From 1685 onwards, a few representatives of the Russian Orthodox Church were permitted to reside in a small ecclesiastical study mission in Peking, but did not work among the Chinese. After 1860 and establishment of a Russian legation in the capital, some evangelising activities were pursued, and an Orthodox community of a few hundred existed by 1900. After 1900, under the direction of the energetic bishop Innocent Figourovsky (1864–1931) and an increased staff of clergy, the Orthodox mission expanded to several provinces, and in 1915 claimed a Chinese baptised membership of 5,000.

Korea

The beginnings: early Roman Catholicism, 1784–1800

With the establishment of the Chosŏn dynasty (1392–1910) in the late fourteenth century by a group of radical Neo-Confucian scholars, Korea underwent a thorough process of social and political change which created the most Con-fucianised society in East Asia. Central to the vision of these radical reformers was the concept of family relationships, which was given visual expression in the performance of the ancestral rituals called *chesa*. Neo-Confucian philoso-phy, although highly ethical, was non-theistic. From the seventeenth century onward, certain Confucian scholars found the orthodox philosophy of the state to be arid and questioned its non-theistic basis. Although many of these scholars were well aware of the writings of Jesuit missionaries in China such as Matteo Ricci and of the spread of Roman Catholicism there, they expressed little interest in Catholicism until the last quarter of the eighteenth century. In 1784, Yi Sŭnghun, who had been a member of a study group set up in 1777 to study the Jesuit tracts, accompanied his father to Peking, made contact with the missionary priests, and was baptised. Upon returning to Korea, he began to proselytise amongst his circle of friends and relatives, who in turn created an ecclesiastical organisation based upon what Yi had seen in Peking. These Korean Catholics accepted the church's teaching on participation in Confucian ancestral rites as being idolatrous. In 1785, the government, horrified at the refusal of Catholics to participate in *chesa* rites, issued an edict suppressing Catholicism on the basis that it was undermining social morality and in 1786 also banned the importation of any Catholic literature. In the same year, Kim Pŏmu, a government interpreter, became the first martyr following his arrest and torture for refusing to perform *chesa*. At this stage, the majority of the early Catholics were highly educated, coming from either the aristocratic *yangban* class or the bureaucratic *chungin* class. In 1791 two cousins, Kwŏn Sangyŏn and Yun Chich'ung, were the first martyrs to be executed for their Christian beliefs because they had burned their ancestral tablets. Within the first decade of its history, two important features of Korean Catholicism had already emerged – self-propagation and persistence under conditions of severe persecution. Korean Catholicism was not initially the work of foreign missionaries, and thus had sufficient internal strength to maintain itself against great social and political forces.

The appointment of the first missionary was the result of concerns by the bishop in Peking that the fledgling community had created an ecclesiastical structure which was not apostolic in character, i.e. it had not been created by the Roman Catholic Church. The first priest was Father Chou Wên-mu, a Chinese who, owing to the threat of persecution, upon arrival in 1795 sought refuge in the home of an aristocratic lady, Kang Wansuk. In that year, there were some 4,000 believers. By 1800, the Catholic community had increased to 10,000, causing great concern amongst governmental circles who saw this development as a social and a political threat because of Catholicism's recruitment of people from the lower classes. With the sudden death of the tolerant King Chŏngjo in 1800, his young son came to the throne as a boy. King Sunjo's grandmother, who ruled as queen regent, initiated the first of a series of violent persecutions which were to last for three-quarters of a century.

Three-quarters of a century of persecution: 1800–1871

The Sinyu Persecution of 1801 marks the end of the church of scholar aristocrats and the beginning of an underground, persecuted church of the people. Part of the ferocity of this first great persecution was due to the contents of a letter written by Hwang Sayong to the bishop in Peking appealing for a western navy and army to protect the fledgling church. Reading this intercepted letter convinced many government officials that Catholicism endangered both the moral fabric of society by its objections to the performance of the *chesa* rites, and the existence of the state through its apparent connections to European powers. In the Sinyu persecution many of the key aristocratic leaders of the church were executed, while those who survived either fled to remote rural areas and hid themselves, or divested themselves of their high-class status by taking up menial jobs such as potters and itinerant pedlars. In this way, they came into contact with the poorest and most distressed members of Korean society, with the result that Catholicism spread rapidly amongst the lowest level of society.

Following the conclusion of this first national persecution, local suppressions of Catholicism continued to occur, most notably between 1811 and 1814. After that time, national persecutions broke out roughly every twelve years, the Ŭrhae Persecution of 1815, the Chŏnghae Persecution of 1827 and the

Kihae Persecution of 1839. The latter, the most severe since 1801, was sparked off by the discovery of French missionaries in the country, again raising fears of conquest by a foreign power. Although there was a smaller persecution in 1846, the next major national persecution did not occur until 1866, when Russian attempts to seize a part of Korean territory triggered the Great Persecution which lasted for five years. The appearance of a French fleet off the Korean coast in the same year, attempts by foreign traders to desecrate the tomb of the prince regent's father in 1868, and the arrival of an American fleet in Korean waters in 1871, further fanned the flames of the Great Persecution. The periodicity of these national persecutions and the continuity of more local ones, show the concerns of government officials about the extent to which the church had taken root amongst the lower classes, and the potential subversion which it posed to traditional social mores and national sovereignty.

Following the execution of Father Chou in 1801, there was no clerical oversight of the Christian community until 1831, when a vicariate apostolic over Korea was created, with responsibility for the mission being given to the Société des Missions Etrangères de Paris (SMEP). Although the first missionary bishop died before reaching Korea, a Chinese priest, Liu Fang-chi, did enter Korea in that year and was joined in 1836 by the first western priest, Father Pierre Philibert Maubant. In 1837, Father Jacques Honoré Chastan and Bishop Laurent Marie Joseph Imbert joined them. Between 1831 and 1834, church membership recovered significantly, trebling to 9,000 persons, nearly the same numbers as in the 1790s. However, the execution of all of the French clergy in the 1839 persecution smashed any hopes for a quiet period of growth. The church was again left without clerical supervision until the arrival of Bishop Jean Joseph Ferréol and Father Marie Antoine Nicolas Daveluy in 1845.

The execution of Kim Taegon in 1846 deprived the fledgling church of its first Korean priest, and Bishop Ferréol's subsequent death from exhaustion in 1853 further weakened it. Bishop Siméon François Berneux, who had arrived in 1856, reported in the following year that community membership numbered over 15,000. This is remarkable, considering both the severity of the persecution of the church and its lack of clerical supervision for nearly fifty years. However, these advances were destroyed during the Great Persecution of 1866–71, when the prince regent tried to eradicate once and for all the pernicious influences of Catholicism and its strange doctrines. With the execution of 8,000 adherents and nine French clergy, half of the community were martyred for their faith.

Cautious growth: 1871–1910

The removal of the prince regent and the accession of King Kojong to the throne in 1871 brought about the end of this final persecution. Amongst the Catholic community a ghetto mentality developed which in this period focused on the growth of the church itself, with little concern for social issues and little awareness of the historical events taking place around them. In 1876, five years after the end of the Great Persecution, two priests who had fled to China were able to return to Korea, and were joined in 1877 by Bishop Félix Clair Ridel. Although the government deported the bishop in 1878, and another priest in 1879, by 1881 it had ceased its harassment of priests as a result of Korea's attempt to establish diplomatic relations with the western powers. In these novel conditions of tolerance, the church began to flourish. By 1882 there were 12,500 believers, an increase of 5,500 persons or 44 per cent since the end of the Great Persecution. Two decades later, in 1910, the number of adherents had grown by 500 per cent to 73,000 persons who were in the care of fifteen Korean priests and fifty-six foreign clergy. The church celebrated its history of persecution by building martyrs' memorials such as Yakhyon Church (1893) near the execution ground outside the Little West Gate of Sŏul, and the Cathedral Church of St Mary (1898) on the site of the home of the first Korean martyr, Kim Pomu.

The advent of Protestantism: 1882–1910

Although there were Protestant missionary probes made by Karl Friedrich August Gützlaff in 1832, by Robert Jermain Thomas in 1866 and 1867 along the west coast of Korea, and by Alexander Williamson from Manchuria in late 1860s, none of these attempts led to the initiation of formal missionary activity. John Ross of the United Presbyterian Church of Scotland mission in Manchuria was the first missionary to have any impact on Korea. Working with a team of translators, by 1882 he had translated portions of the New Testament into Korean using the Korean alphabet rather than Chinese characters. By 1887 the entire New Testament was available. This translation introduced key theological terms which are still current, such as *Hananim* (Ruler of Heaven) for God. Moreover, Ross's converts were responsible for the establishment of the first Protestant communities in north-western Korea, in the capital, and in the Korean communities in the Jiandao (Kando in Korean) region along the northern bank of the Yalu River. The existence of Protestant communities in Korea before the arrival of foreign missionaries in 1884 is a testimonial to Ross's conviction that Christianity was spread best through the agency of local

Christians. Protestantism in Korea, like Catholicism, was self-evangelised from the beginning.

From the mid-1880s foreign missionaries began to arrive, including Horace N. Allen (1884) and Horace G. Underwood of the Northern Presbyterian Church, USA (1885), and Henry G. Appenzeller of the Northern Methodist Church, USA (1885). Almost immediately afterwards, several other missionaries, mostly Methodists and Presbyterians from the United States, arrived in Korea so that by the end of the 1880s, a foreign mission enterprise was well under way, built upon the foundations laid by the earliest converts. Because the open propagation of Christianity was still prohibited by the prince regent's anti-Christian edict of 1866, most overt missionary work until the mid-1890s was accomplished through educational and medical institutions. However, baptisms and the creation of church organisations did take place, although surreptitiously throughout the 1880s. Many of Korea's major institutions trace their origins to this period, including three medical institutions, Paejae Boys' High School, Ewha Girls' High School (which later established Ewha Woman's University), the first modern publishing house the Tri-Lingual Press, and the Religious Tract Society.

In 1890, the missionaries, who had begun to plan a formal strategy for mission and the creation of an independent church, asked John L. Nevius, a Northern Presbyterian missionary and mission strategist in Shandong, China, to explain his mission methods to them. The principles which he enunciated, now called the Nevius Method, for creating a self-propagating, self-governing and self-supporting church, became the standard mission policy for all major Protestant groups in Korea. Although not large, the numbers of converts during the 1890s increased significantly. Contrasted with missions in China or Japan at a similar stage, Protestant missionaries in Korea saw greater success in this respect. The Church of England (SPG) mission was inaugurated with the arrival of Bishop Charles J. Corfe, a High Churchman, in 1890. This decade saw increased literary and scholarly work, notably with the creation of a Korean–English dictionary and translations of devotional works such as *The pilgrim's progress*, and the creation of a Permanent Executive Bible Translation Committee in 1893, an outgrowth of an earlier body, to produce a standard Korean translation to replace the Ross translation.

In the decade leading up to Japan's annexation of Korea in 1910, Protestant adherence grew to over 10,000 persons, a result which is often attributed to the Great Revival of 1907 in P'yŏngyang which affected communities throughout the peninsula and even in Manchuria. Although the event must be seen within the context of the political uncertainties of the time, the Great Revival did release a spiritual energy amongst the Koreans which led to a nationwide movement for evangelism. In 1910, the percentage of the population who adhered to Protestant Christianity was greater than in Japan.

The rapid growth of Protestant Christianity in Korea in its first twenty-five years may be attributed to several factors. The first was the impact of the Ross translation and the efforts made by Ross's initial converts, who established Korean Protestant communities even before the arrival of foreign missionaries. The second was the emphasis on indigenous evangelism and the adoption of the Nevius Method. The third was the appeal of institutional work in education and medicine to young progressive Koreans who had rejected Confucianism and the political traditions of the nation because they were perceived to have left the state corrupt and ill-prepared to meet the changed circumstances of the nineteenth century. Nationalism, progress and Christian faith became linked in the minds of many young progressive Koreans such as Sŏ Chaep'il (Philip Jaisohn), Yi Sŭngman (Syngman Rhee) and Yun Ch'iho. Many of these young men saw that education was the way to restore national sovereignty and dignity by raising the educational level of the nation. The fact that today many Korean schools claim a Christian, but not a mission, foundation is due to the efforts of Korean Christians in the first decade of the twentieth century.

A fourth contributor to Protestant growth was the Comity Agreement of 1908. All Protestant missionaries, except for the Anglicans, agreed to a division of the peninsula into mission spheres in order to avoid competition between denominations and mission bodies, reflecting the intradenominational mission agreements of the 1890s. At the same meeting in 1908, the missionaries also agreed to establish a United Church of Christ in Korea, a proposal subsequently rejected by the home denominations. None the less, the creation of a tradition of co-operation, the use of a single translation of the Bible and a common hymnal, and pan-denominational institutional activities helped to create a sense of a common Protestant Christianity by the end of the first decade of the twentieth century, even if this was not reflected in institutional structures.

A final factor was the priority given by the missions to the training of an indigenous clergy along with the early establishment of church institutions. By 1910, the first Korean theological candidates of all denominations had been trained and ordained, Korean missionaries had been sent out to other communities, and presbyteries and other church organisations had been created.

Russian Orthodoxy: a foothold

The origins of the Orthodox Church in Korea may be traced back to the presence of a chaplain in the Russian legation in Sŏul from the 1890s. The small numbers of Koreans who joined the Orthodox faith then were augmented by Koreans who had lived in eastern Siberia and had returned to Korea before 1900. In that year, the Holy Synod in Moscow formed a mission to Korea and appointed Archimandrite Chrysanthus Shchetkovsky to take charge of the mission. In 1903, the king granted land near the Russian legation for a church, and various liturgical materials were translated. By 1912, the first Korean Orthodox priest, Kang Hant'ak, had been trained and ordained.

Japan

Roman Catholicism, the second advent: 1859–1910

Following the severe persecutions of the Roman Catholic Church in the early seventeenth century at the beginning of the Tokugawa shogunate (1600–1868), the surviving Christians went underground, forming groups known latterly as *Kakure Kirishitan* (Hidden Christians). The Treaty of Commerce and Friendship which Japan concluded with France in 1858 permitted the arrival in 1859 of the first Roman Catholic missionary priest to Japan since the beginning of the shogunate. Fr Prudence-Séraphim-Barthélemy Girard was a member of the Société des Missions Etrangères de Paris (SMEP) to which the Vatican had assigned the mission work in Japan, as it had in Korea. Fr Girard was followed soon afterwards by other French priests and nuns, as well as a number of Protestant missionaries from Europe and North America. In 1865, the construction of the first Roman Catholic church in Nagasaki, scene of some of the most severe persecutions of the church in the seventeenth century, led to the discovery of some 20,000 Hidden Christians. The overthrow of the shogunate in 1868 and establishment of a new regime under the Meiji Emperor bent on the modernisation of Japan created conditions that led in 1873 to the removal of anti-Christian edicts promulgated in the early years of the Tokugawa period. By that year, 14,000 of the Hidden Christians had rejoined the Roman Catholic Church. In 1876, the Vatican divided the Japanese mission into two vicariates apostolic, one each for northern and southern Japan. The next decade and a half, until 1890, was a period of quiet growth in circumstances of general tolerance and acceptance of the work of the church's missionaries. The continued success of the SMEP mission is indicated by the fact that within twelve years' time, by 1888, the Japan mission was divided again, with the creation of a third vicariate apostolic in central Japan, followed within three years by the creation of a local episcopal hierarchy, with the bishop of Tokyo created as the archbishop over the whole Japanese ecclesiastical structure in 1891.

In the first decades of mission, the church was strongest in the southern vicariate because of the pre-existence of the Hidden Christians there. Paradoxically, their membership in the church was also an obstacle to the further expansion of the church within broader Japanese society because they were seen to be backward, uneducated and unsophisticated at a time when Japan was trying to become 'modern' and 'advanced'. The stigma of Catholics being 'unsophisticated' and 'uneducated' was an issue which the cultivated priests of the SMEP attempted to tackle, but not until a later date. Up until 1890, the work of the Japan mission focused largely on evangelism and pastoral work, with little institutional outreach. Compared to their Protestant counterparts, the early Catholic missionaries paid less attention to institutional missionary work such as educational and medical missions.

The years 1889 and 1890 mark a watershed in Japanese missionary work, Catholic or Protestant, as it was then that the Japanese Constitution (1889) and the Imperial Rescript on Education (1890) were promulgated. These documents contained elements which promoted the concepts of state Shintō, that is of the divinity of the ruling house and the requirement of patriotic Japanese to give reverence to the emperor, his ancestors, and objects associated with the imperial House. The promulgation of these documents also coincided with a rise in Japanese nationalism which continued well into the new century. These events concerned the church authorities enough to convene a synod in 1895 to discuss the issues. Statistics show that Roman Catholic membership in this period remained largely static; as a percentage of the national population the church actually declined. In the period 1890–1910, rising public criticism of the church in the media was reflected in a decline in the number of catechumens and even in violent actions against church property. In the aftermath of the 1905 Treaty of Portsmouth concluding the Russo-Japanese War, a Catholic church in Tokyo was burned.

The period 1890–1910 also witnessed an increase in the numbers of mission bodies working in Japan, and an increase in educational, medical and literary work. From 1904 onwards, some fifteen new missionary orders entered Japan, including the Dominicans and the Society of the Divine Word. These new missionary societies represented a variety of European and North American countries bringing an ethnic mix in the missionary effort which had been absent previously. The significant increase in missionaries and mission bodies required a restructuring of ecclesiastical territory so that there would be only one mission body working in a diocese or designated region. Newspapers, magazines and journals were published as a form of missionary outreach, most notably *Tenchijin* (Man of the Universe, 1898), a journal aimed at intellectuals to debate great moral and religious issues. In spite of this literary activity, the first complete translation of the New Testament did not appear until 1910.

The advent of Protestantism: 1859–1910

The first phase of Protestant missions in Japan began with the arrival of a small cohort of missionaries from North America in 1859, including Dr James C. Hepburn of the Northern Presbyterian Church and the Rev. Guido F. Verbeck of the Dutch Reformed Church. Over the next decade, a continuing trickle of missionaries from various North American missionary societies augmented the missionary presence. Until the revocation in 1873 of the anti-Christian edicts from the Tokugawa era, these men and women worked largely in areas of educational and medical mission and not in direct evangelistic activities. Verbeck, in particular, gained such a significant reputation as an educator that in 1870 the new Meiji government asked him to establish a tertiary educational institution which eventually became Tokyo Imperial University. However, actual Christian conversion was slow until 1872. From 1859 to 1872, missionaries baptised only ten people, but following the revocation of the anti-Christian edicts this situation changed dramatically.

The Annual Week of Prayer held in January 1872 may be taken to be the starting point of the growth of Japanese Protestantism. Japanese participants evinced a religious fervour which became more pronounced throughout this decade. In September of the same year, Protestant missionaries held a convention at which two important decisions were taken, to create a New Testament Translation Committee, and to work towards creating a unified church of Christ in Japan. Both of these decisions reflected the high degree of ecumenicity amongst the early missionaries. A great increase in adherence to Protestantism took place from this decade until the 1890s, significantly amongst the dispossessed *samurai* or warrior class. Although a small percentage of the national population, by the early 1890s they constituted about 40 per cent or more of Protestant Christians. Young *samurai*, often progressive in their outlook and key in their leadership of the church, are comparable to the progressive *yangban* elite in Korea who provided the leadership for both the early Catholic and Protestant churches there. The most remarkable feature of the Japanese Protestants of the 1870s is the formation of bands of young men, students of a missionary educator, who dedicated themselves to Christ, such as the Yokohama Band (1872), the Kumamoto Band (1876), the Sapporo Band (1876) and others. From these bands came the generation of Japanese church leadership which began to make itself felt from the 1880s. The Kumamoto Band in particular was instrumental in sustaining Doshisa University and its theological school. Growth in Protestant adherence continued until, as with the Roman Catholic Church, it was stymied when the Constitution and the Imperial Rescript on Education were promulgated.

The case of Uchimura Kanzō is symbolic of the problems facing all Japanese Christians in an era of rising nationalism. His refusal to bow before the Imperial Rescript at his school became a *cause célèbre*, leading to an attack on his character by a leading nationalist scholar and the loss of his job. Although the rate of increase in the numbers of new Japanese adherents and pupils at Christian schools declined significantly after this time, Japanese Protestant Christians took a leading role in social issues and had an ethical influence beyond their actual numbers. Christians, such as Uchimura, led criticism of the Japanese government's two wars in Korea, the Sino-Japanese war of 1894–5 and the Russo-Japanese war of 1904–5, while other Christians were responsible for the creation of the Social Democratic Party in 1901 and the first trade union in 1912. Most Japanese Christians, however, were more accepting of their government's military views, and were comfortable with the social circumstances around them.

Russian Orthodoxy

The Russian Orthodox Church in Japan was shaped largely by the mission policy of its first priest Father Nicholai who stressed the absolute separation of politics and mission work. He arrived in Hakodate on Hokkaido island in 1861 and was joined by Fr Anatolius in 1871. By 1875, the first Japanese priests, Frs Paul Sawabe and John Sakai had been ordained. Like all Christian groups, the Orthodox Church experienced growth until the 1890s, when rising nationalism hindered further growth – in this case especially fierce because of the overt geopolitical rivalry and military conflict with Russia. None the less, the cathedral was consecrated in Tokyo in 1891 and many theological works in Japanese were printed.

31

Christianity in Indochina

PETER C. PHAN

By Indochina here is meant the three countries now known as Cambodia, Laos and Vietnam which, together with Burma, Thailand and Malaya, form the easternmost region of the Indochinese peninsula. Culturally and religiously, all these countries have been influenced by both India and China. In 1859, France captured the three south-eastern provinces of Vietnam, and in 1862 turned them into its colony and named it Cochinchina. In 1883, France made the northern and central parts of Vietnam (Tonkin and Annam respectively) into its protectorates. In 1887, it merged Vietnam with Cambodia to form the Union of French Indochina, to which Laos was added in 1893. In addition to politics which bound these three countries together, their Christian churches are so deeply intertwined, with Vietnam often sending missionaries into the other two countries, that a joint treatment of their Christian histories is appropriate.

Christianity in Vietnam, 1815–1915: a century of bloodshed and growth

The century of Vietnamese Christianity under consideration falls within the rule of the Nguyen dynasty (1802–1945) at whose hands it suffered the longest and bloodiest persecutions. Moreover, it was during the Nguyen dynasty that France colonised Vietnam, and its rule, which began in 1862, lasted until 1954. Hence, this period of the history of Vietnamese Christianity also partially overlaps with the history of French colonisation of Vietnam and must be considered in relation to it.

Vietnamese Christianity was born during the turbulent seventeenth century, and its fortunes in the next two centuries ebbed and flowed with the changing policies of the Trinh and the Nguyen lords. Although the Le dynasty was still the official ruler of the country in the seventeenth century, Vietnam was *de facto* divided into two parts and was ruled by two rival families, the Trinh and the Nguyen, the former in the north and the latter in the south. The Trinh and Nguyen lords permitted the missionaries to preach, or expelled them, depending on their usefulness in obtaining weapons and commercial exchange from their native countries. The Jesuits (notably Alexandre de Rhodes) were the first to begin, with the support of Portugal under the *padroado* system, a sustained mission in the south in 1615 and in the north in 1627.[1] Their work was later strengthened by the missionaries sent by the *Propaganda Fide* (founded in 1622), mostly members of the Société des Missions Etrangères de Paris (founded in 1664; henceforth, MEP). In 1659, two dioceses were established, called *Dang Ngoai* [the Exterior Part] or *Bac Ha* [the North] and *Dang Trong* [the Interior Part] or *Nam Ha* [the South]. François Pallu and Pierre Lambert de la Motte were appointed as apostolic vicars for the exterior and the interior dioceses respectively. According to de Rhodes's report to the *Propaganda Fide* in 1650, there were 300,000 Christians in Vietnam, with an average annual increase of 15,000. The converts came from a variety of religious backgrounds. Their leaders had been Confucian literati and Buddhist monks, whereas the masses had practised a mixture of Taoism and indigenous Vietnamese religion. For all of them the cult of ancestors had been central.

Since the north and the south were mutually hostile, to avoid charges of spying for the enemy, missionaries carried out their work in the two parts of the country in almost total separation from each other. In 1679, the exterior diocese was split into two, one called the Western diocese and the other the Eastern diocese. In 1757, the Eastern diocese was assigned to the Dominican province of the Most Holy Rosary of the Philippines.

In 1777, three brothers, known as the Tay Son (after the locality where they started the rebellion) succeeded in crushing the Trinh clan in the north and dismantling the Nguyen clan in the south. One of the Nguyen descendants, Nguyen Anh, then seventeen years old, survived. Later, in 1784, again defeated by the Tay Son, Nguyen Anh escaped to Thailand, where he met the French bishop Pigneau de Béhaine (1742–99), who was also taking refuge there from the war. It was a fateful meeting. Through the military help of de Béhaine, Nguyen Anh regained his political power, eventually unifying Vietnam and establishing his own dynasty. But the bishop's appeal to his native country for arms opened the door for French colonisation.

The church under Gia Long (1802–20)

The church, in both the north and the south, had suffered sporadic persecutions before the Nguyen dynasty. In the north, the first Catholic to be killed for his

---

1 On the work of the Jesuits, especially Alexandre de Rhodes, see Phan, *Mission and catechesis*.

faith was a soldier named Francis, in 1640. In the south, the first martyr was the nineteen-year-old catechist Andrew of Phu Yen in 1644. Two years later, also in the south, two more catechists, Ignatius and Vincent, were killed. From the eighteenth century, in addition to Vietnamese Catholics, numerous foreign missionaries, bishops and priests were put to death by both Trinh and Nguyen lords. In the north, the martyrs included Francisco de Federich and Mateo Liciniana (1745) and Vincent Liem and Jacinto Castañeda (1773). In the south, persecution raged from 1698 to 1725 and again from 1750 to 1765. Under the Tay Son reign, Catholics were also ferociously persecuted, accused of following a false religion and suspected of support for Tay Son's enemy, Nguyen Anh. Two Vietnamese priests were killed in 1798: Nguyen Van Trieu and John Dat.

Nguyen Anh (Gia Long) inaugurated the Nguyen dynasty in 1802, put in place a new administrative system, and built a new imperial capital in Phu Xuan (today Hue), located in the centre of the country. Under his two-decade reign, the church enjoyed freedom and peace. In gratitude to de Behaine, Gia Long revoked all decrees against Christianity, mandated religious tolerance, and forbade the forcible collection of money from Catholics to underwrite the costs of public worship. However, Gia Long remained personally opposed to Christianity, because he found the practice of monogamy burdensome, and because he rejected as blasphemous the Catholic condemnation of ancestor veneration.

Vietnam and France in the nineteenth century

Some consideration of the relations between Vietnam and France is necessary to understand the history of Vietnamese Christianity in the nineteenth century. These relations were at first mercantile. The French were not the first to seek trade with Vietnam. Other Europeans had preceded them: the Portuguese in 1535, the Dutch in 1636, the English in 1672. As mentioned above, between 1627 and 1672, the north (the Trinh clan) and the south (the Nguyen clan) were in constant warfare with each other, and the Portuguese and the Dutch could make profits from the arms trade, the former favoured the south (with Faifo as a busy seaport), while the latter favoured the north (with Pho Hien as the commercial centre). France, which had founded its own Compagnie des Indes Orientales in 1664 (the same year as the MEP), opened its first trading office in Pho Hien only in 1680. By that time, however, with peace restored between the north and the south, profits from the arms trade declined substantially.

The commercial interests of the Compagnie des Indes Orientales were assisted by French missionaries, especially by Bishop François Pallu, the first apostolic vicar to Tonkin, who made frequent reports on the political and commercial situation of Indochina to Jean-Baptiste Colbert, minister of finance and founder of the Compagnie. But attempts to gain a commercial foothold in Vietnam by adventurous individuals such as Pierre Poivre (1719–96) from the middle of the seventeenth to the middle of the nineteenth century came to naught, either because they were rebuffed by the anti-foreigner policy of the Nguyen kings, or because France under Louis XVI, Napoleon I and Louis-Philippe did not have the resources to do business with Asia.

Under Napoleon III (1852–70) French interest in Vietnam revived. Fearing that Britain would extend its political and commercial influence into South-East Asia, Napoleon III decided to move into Vietnam, by diplomacy and by force if necessary. Under the pretext of protecting French missionaries from the persecution by Nguyen Anh's successors, Minh Mang (1820–40) and Tu Duc (1847–83), and urged on by François Pellerin, bishop of Hue, who assured him that there would be an uprising of Vietnamese Catholics to welcome French soldiers as heroes and liberators, Napoleon ordered an attack on Tourane (today Da Nang). Under the command of General Rigault de Genouilly, French troops took over Tourane in 1858, though Pellerin's prediction failed to materialise. De Genouilly then moved to Saigon and in 1859 took over the three south-eastern provinces (Gia Dinh, Bien Hoa and Dinh Tuong). Tu Duc was forced in 1862 to sign the so-called Saigon treaty in which Vietnam was required to surrender to France its three south-eastern provinces, open its three ports for exclusive trade with France, pay a war indemnity of 4 million piasters, and grant freedom of action to the missionaries. Not content with these acquisitions, France annexed three more, south-western provinces (Vinh Long, An Giang and Ha Tien) in 1867.

Discovering that the route to trade with China did not lie along the Mekong River in the south, but following the Red River in the north, Admiral Dupré, governor of Cochinchina, ordered Captain Francis Garnier to lead an attack on Hanoi in 1873. This military adventure, though much opposed by Paris, was supported by Paul Puginier, bishop of Hanoi (1869–92), who advocated turning the north of Vietnam into a French protectorate. The defeat of Hanoi led to another twenty-two article treaty in 1874, Article IX of which stipulated that missionaries had the right to preach and that the Vietnamese were free to follow the Christian faith. In 1882, Le Myre de Vilers, governor of Cochinchina, ordered Captain Henri Rivière to storm Hanoi. With the fall of the city, another thirty-seven article treaty was signed, of which Article I stipulated that the whole of Vietnam be a protectorate of France. This treaty was later renewed and confirmed in 1884 in a nineteen article treaty known as Paternôtre. The south of Vietnam, known as Cochinchina, continued to be a French colony; Tonkin (the north) and Annam (the centre) became French protectorates. The independence which Vietnam had won from China in the tenth century was now lost, not to be recovered until 1954.

Vietnamese Christianity under the Nguyen dynasty and French colonial rule

The fortunes of Vietnamese Christianity were intimately linked to the varying reactions of the Nguyen kings to France's designs over Vietnam as well as to the policies of the French colonial administration. Though tolerant towards Christianity, Gia Long followed a policy of closure to western powers, including France whose military aid he had sought, as a means for national survival. For his successor he chose one of his sons, who would continue his policy of isolation from the west. Following his father, Minh Mang (1820–40) at first tolerated Christianity, but in 1825, 1826 and 1830 issued instructions forbidding the coming of new missionaries and ordering existing missionaries to gather in one place, thus effectively eliminating their ministry.

On 6 January 1833, encouraged by his mandarins, Minh Mang issued an edict proscribing throughout the country what he termed *ta dao* (the erroneous or evil religion) on the grounds that Christianity taught the existence of heaven and hell, condemned the worship of the Buddha and the ancestors, and promoted sexual immorality. The king ordered Christians to renounce their faith by stepping on the crucifix (*qua khoa*), and their leaders to be arrested and killed so as 'to destroy the roots of the *ta dao*'. Minh Mang also promulgated a list of ten 'holy instructions', of which the seventh commanded the 'learning of the true religion' (and by implication, the rejection of the false one). In all, under Minh Mang, from 1833 to 1840, over one hundred lay Catholics, fifteen catechists, twenty Vietnamese priests and nine foreign missionaries, both French and Spanish (François Isidore Gagelin, Joseph Marchand, Jean Cornay, Domingo Henáres, Ignacio Delgado, José Fernández, François Jaccard, Gilles Delamotte and Pierre Borie) were martyred.

Minh Mang's successor, Thieu Tri (1840–7), unlike his father, was not hostile to Christianity. Nevertheless, he did not revoke any of his father's edicts, so that under his rule how Christians fared depended on the zeal of local mandarins. In general, the church enjoyed relative peace. No foreign missionary was killed, and only three Vietnamese Christians were martyred. Unfortunately, on 15 April 1847, the French navy attacked Tourane and sank several Vietnamese ships. This unprovoked aggression angered Thieu Tri, who ordered the persecution of missionaries and Christians in retaliation. However, only one Vietnamese Christian was killed as a result.

Under Thieu Tri's successor, Tu Duc (1847–83), the church suffered the longest and bloodiest persecution. It was also under his thirty-six-year reign that France invaded Vietnam, ending Vietnam's long independence on 6 June 1884, less than a year after Tu Duc's death (15 July 1883). These two facts must be kept together when studying the history of Vietnamese Christianity in the nineteenth century. Tu Duc's hostility towards Christians rose and fell in response to his perceptions of the threat that Christians were alleged to pose to the survival of his dynasty and kingdom, either in collaboration with the French invaders or in support of internal rebellions.

At first, Tu Duc's reign augured well for Vietnamese Catholics. Upon ascending the throne at the age of seventeen, he pardoned and released all Christians imprisoned for their faith. But their hopes were dashed a year later when Tu Duc issued a decree forbidding the *ta dao*, in which he accused Christians of abandoning ancestor worship and practising superstition. He ordered the killing of missionaries by having stones tied to their necks and thrown into the sea. Vietnamese priests were to be arrested for investigation and, if they did not renounce their faith, banished to dangerous regions, with the words *ta dao* branded on their cheek. The simple faithful, on the other hand, because of their ignorance, were not to be killed, imprisoned or exiled, but were still severely punished if they did not renounce their faith.

On 21 March 1851, Tu Duc issued another decree with more or less the same instructions. This time, besides reiterating that the *ta dao* forbade the veneration of ancestors, the Buddha and the spirits, he added that Christian priests preached about 'heaven and the holy kingdom' and that they encouraged their followers to die rather than renounce their faith by showing 'the picture of Christ crucified on the cross'. Moreover, not only foreign missionaries but also Vietnamese priests, as well as those who harboured missionaries, were now to be killed, irrespective of their age, by being cut into two pieces and thrown into the river.

In September 1855, following a revolt led by the sympathisers of the Hau Le dynasty against the Nguyen dynasty to which Christians were accused of having lent their support, Tu Duc promulgated a decree which not only commanded that missionaries and Vietnamese priests be decapitated, their heads displayed in public for three days and then thrown into the river, but also ordered the burning of churches and community houses and forbade public gatherings of Christians. In short, the decree ended, 'every means should be used to destroy the *ta dao*'.

In 1856 de Montigny was sent by Napoleon III on a mission to South-East Asia, including Vietnam, to negotiate trade. Two ships, the *Catinat* and *La Capricieuse*, went ahead of him. When the *Catinat* was anchored outside Tourane, the court forbade food and water to be sold to the ship, and its captain ordered the bombardment of the Vietnamese defences near the harbour. The captain of *La Capricieuse* sent a letter to Tu Duc demanding trade and freedom to preach and practise the Christian faith. De Montigny himself arrived in Tourane on 23 January 1857 but was not received by the court. Before leaving, he made a show of force by firing cannon balls into the harbour and sent Tu Duc a letter threatening punishments if the king did not cease persecuting the Christians. Tu Duc was furious at these provocations and leaned harder on Vietnamese Christians who were accused of assisting the foreign enemy.

Oil was added to fire when in May of the same year François Pellerin, bishop of Hue, urged in Saigon that, to assure the rights of Vietnamese Christians, France should sign a treaty with Vietnam, a French consulate should be established, Vietnam's ports should be opened for trade, and a contingent of the French navy should be permanently posted. In short, according to the bishop, France should occupy Vietnam and make it into its protectorate. Later that year, Pellerin departed for France to urge military intervention and was received twice by Napoleon III. The emperor acceded to his proposal and assigned the task to General Rigault de Genouilly, leading to his attack on Tourane in 1858 and the fall of Saigon the following year.

In fury, Tu Duc issued another decree on 6 June 1857 reconfirming his policies of persecution, claiming this time (with wild exaggeration) that 'four-tenths' of the population had become Christian and that the 'pestilence' of the *ta dao* would be spread throughout the land if something were not done. He ordered that Christians be forced to celebrate weddings and funerals according to the traditional rituals as well as to practise the veneration of spirits and ancestors, under pain of having the words *ta dao* branded on their cheeks.

Things got worse when in 1858 a Catholic layman in the north by the name of Ta Van Phung, who had changed his name to Le Duy Minh (after the Hau Le dynasty), started an armed uprising against Tu Duc. He asked de Genouilly for military assistance (who refused for fear of creating difficulties with Tu Duc) and rallied Catholics to his cause. Two Vietnamese Dominican priests joined his army. However, in May 1858, Bishop Melchior Sampedro (who was martyred by being cut into five pieces on 28 July 1858) forbade all Catholics under pain of excommunication to join the revolt. In spite of Sampedro's condemnation of the rebellion as 'unjust, useless, and foolish',

Tu Duc put him to death and intensified his persecutions simply because the leader of the revolt was a Catholic.

After de Genouilly attacked Tourane and took over the south-eastern provinces, on 15 December 1859, Tu Duc issued another edict, this time aiming at those mandarins who were Catholic. They were to be stripped of all grades and functions, and those who refused to disown their faith were to be killed immediately if they held high positions. In 17 January 1860, Tu Duc promulgated another decree declaring that he would not grant freedom to the *ta dao*, even at the request of the 'barbarian foreigners'. In July of the same year, an edict was issued against religious sisters, especially the Lovers of the Cross, a congregation founded by Pierre Lambert de la Motte.

The most devastating edict against Vietnamese Christians was still to come. On 5 August 1861, in an attempt to destroy Christianity at its roots, Tu Duc promulgated the so-called 'dispersal' edict which included the following measures: (1) dispersal of all Christians, even those who had renounced their faith, into non-Christian villages; (2) supervision of every Christian by five non-Christians in every village; (3) destruction of all Christian villages and communities; (4) distribution of all the lands owned by Christians to non-Christians who would cultivate them and pay taxes to the court on their earnings; (5) branding of the cheeks of Christians, on the one side with the words *ta dao* and on the other with the names of their villages and counties. As a result, hundreds of thousands of Catholic families were dispossessed and their members separated from each other, and the practice of the faith made impossible.

Politically and militarily, however, Tu Duc was losing everywhere. As already mentioned, in 1862 he was forced to accept the Saigon Treaty whose provisions included the grant of religious freedom to Christians. As a result of this treaty, at the end of 1862 Tu Duc issued an amnesty, which declared that all Christian old men, old women and children would be freed from imprisonment, whether they had renounced their faith or not. All Christian officials who had sincerely renounced their faith would also be liberated, but if they lived in an all-Christian village, they had to be detained where they were, even if they had renounced their faith. Officials as well as young men who had not renounced their faith were to be detained until they sincerely abandoned their faith. All lands, houses and possessions which had been confiscated from Christians would be restored to them.

On 15 March 1876, at France's request, Tu Duc renewed his edict of toleration which included the following provisions: terminating all acts of persecution of Catholics, freedom of religion, abolition of all restrictions regarding the number of Catholics meeting in churches, equal treatment of Christians and non-Christians in employment, restitution of confiscated properties, and allowing foreign missionaries to acquire or rent land to build churches, schools or orphanages. It is estimated that under Tu Duc, between 1848 and 1860, twenty-five missionaries, 300 Vietnamese priests, and 30,000 lay faithful were martyred.

The Van Than movement and Christianity under the last Nguyen kings (1864–1915)

France's gradual occupation of Vietnam, and the humiliating treaties it subsequently imposed, provoked widespread insurrections. Among the many nationalist movements seeking to overthrow French domination, the Van Than (the literati sympathisers) was the most virulently anti-Christian. It consisted of mandarins and those schooled in Confucianism who saw their privileges ruined by the occupying powers, whose domination of Vietnam they blamed on the followers of the *ta dao*. Accusing Christians of collaborationism, this group adopted the motto *Binh Tay Sat Ta* (destroy the West, i.e. France, and kill the followers of the evil religion, i.e. Christians). Between 1873 and 1888, armed bands of Van Than roamed the country, burning thousands of Catholic villages and killing numerous priests, nuns, and more than 60,000 lay Catholics. In 1864, Tu Duc, following the ratification of the 1874 treaty with France, attempted to rein in the Van Than's atrocities but to little avail.

One of the most famous battles between the Van Than and the Catholics occurred in 1885 at Tra Kieu in the province of Quang Nam. Surrounded by the Van Than on 1 September 1885, the Catholic village, under the direction of MEP missionary Father Bruyère, decided to defend itself with an army of 350 young men and 500 women. On the twenty-first day, the siege was broken with a decisive victory over the Van Than's far more numerous army of troops, elephants and cannons. Vietnamese Catholic tradition records that the Van Than attributed their defeat to a mysterious woman whom they saw standing on the top of the church preventing their cannons from hitting their targets.

Subsequently, Tra Kieu became one of the two Marian sites of pilgrimages in Vietnam. The other is La Vang, a small Catholic village with about 150 inhabitants, about eighty miles north of Hue, the ancient imperial capital, in the Quang Tri province. The Marian tradition at La Vang originated some eighty years earlier. King Canh Thinh (1792–1802), knowing that his opponent Nguyen Anh was being assisted by Bishop Pigneau de Béhaine, and fearing that Catholics would collaborate with his enemy, ordered them to be killed. Catholics fled to La Vang where, according to the tradition, a lady of great beauty appeared to them, clad in white and surrounded by light, holding the Infant Jesus on her arms, with two charming boys each holding a torch and standing at either side. She walked back and forth several times in front of the Christians, her feet touching the ground, and promised to protect them. Ever since, La Vang has been the most important Vietnamese Marian site, and Our Lady of La Vang has been proclaimed Our Lady of Vietnam. Because of these two apparitions, devotion to Mary is one of the distinguishing characteristics of Vietnamese Catholicism's popular piety.

After Tu Duc's death (1883), a succession of nine kings were installed and swiftly removed either by the court of Hue or by the French colonial government until the Nguyen dynasty came to an end in 1945. Of these kings, the most important from the standpoint of Vietnamese Christianity was Ham Nghi (1884–5), who was put on the throne at the age of twelve by two anti-French mandarins, Nguyen Van Tuong and Ton That Thuyet. He was shortly replaced by the French government with Dong Khanh (1885–9). Ham Nghi escaped and with Ton That Thuyet began a movement called Can Vuong (save the king). On 20 October 1885, they issued a proclamation calling for the extermination of Christians. Their call was responded to by the Van Than, who went on a bloody rampage against Catholics. The burning and killing did not end until Ham Nghi was arrested by the French army on 26 September 1886 and was exiled to Algeria in 1888. The Van Than movement gradually disintegrated and its demise brought peace to the church.

In addition to persecutions by the Nguyen dynasty and the Van Than, French colonial rule also created no small troubles for Vietnamese Christianity. Beginning in 1864, the church, or more precisely the diocese, of Saigon, which was located in Cochinchina, started receiving financial support from the colonial government in the amount of 40,000 francs per year, later increased to 145,000. This money was payment for priests and religious engaged in education and health care and the construction and maintenance of churches (the most expensive of which was the cathedral of Saigon, built in 1880 at the cost of 2,500,000 francs). Protests against this subsidy brought it to an end in 1881. Later, the anticlerical policies of the Third Republic, especially those of 1901, which aimed at secularising church properties and the educational system, and which Emile Combes (1835–1921) tried to enforce in the French colonies, created severe difficulties for the church in Cochinchina.

The growth of the church in the nineteenth century

Despite persecution under the Nguyen dynasty and harassment by the colonial government, Vietnamese Christianity in the nineteenth century experienced phenomenal growth. As mentioned above, two dioceses had been established in Vietnam in 1659, the exterior (northern) and the interior (southern). In 1679, the exterior diocese was split into two: *tay* (western) and *dong* (eastern). In 1846, the western diocese was itself divided into *tay ky* (western), now Hanoi, and *nam ky* (southern), now Vinh; and in 1895, another diocese was added, called *Doai*, later known as *Hung Hoa*. In 1901, a further diocese was established, *Thanh*, later known as *Phat Diem*. In 1848, the eastern diocese was divided into two: *dong ky* (eastern), now Hai Phong, and *trung ky* (central), now Bui Chu. In 1883, a new diocese was founded called *Bac* (northern), later known as *Bac Ninh*. In 1913, another diocese was established, *Phu Doan*, later known as *Lang Son*. Thus, by 1915, in the exterior or northern part of the country, there were eight dioceses. The four in the west were entrusted to the MEP, and the four in the east to the Dominicans.

In the interior or southern part, in 1844, the diocese was divided into *Dong* (eastern), now Qui Nhon, and *Tay* (western), now Saigon (since 1975, *Ho Chi Minh City*). In 1850, a diocese was added to the western diocese, called *Bac* (northern), now Hue. In the same year, a diocese was also added into the eastern diocese, called *Cao Mien*, now Phnom Penh (Cambodia). By 1915, there were therefore four dioceses in the interior or southern part of the country. Clearly, in the nineteenth century, the centre of gravity of Vietnamese Christianity was located in the north. By 1915, there were thus twelve dioceses in Vietnam. The number of Catholics was estimated at 870,000, an increase from 400,000 in 1860, not counting the 130,000 killed during the persecution under the Nguyen dynasty and by the Van Than. The number of priests in 1900 was 385.

During the nineteenth century, several religious orders, male and female, came to Vietnam, in addition to the already present Jesuits, Dominicans, Franciscans and MEP. They were the Sisters of Saint Paul (1860) the Carmelite Sisters (1861) and the Christian Brothers of St Jean-Baptiste de la Salle (1866).

During this century several important churches were built, including the cathedrals of Hanoi (1886, Gothic style), Saigon (1880, Gothic and Roman style) and Hue (1902, Gothic style). The most famous is the church at Phat Diem, built by a priest by the name of Tran Luc (1825–99), popularly known as Cu Sau. Fourteen years in preparation and four years in construction (1891–5), the church is unique in Asia for its magnificent oriental architecture.

Christianity in Cambodia, 1815–1915

Christianity made its first appearance in Cambodia in 1553, when the Portuguese Dominican Gaspar da Cruz presented himself at the royal court of Longvek. Another Portuguese Dominican, Sylvester d'Azevedo, came in 1574 to work among the Khmer. In the early seventeenth century, a number of Japanese Catholics, a group of Portuguese Eurasians from the Moluccan Islands (Indonesia) and Vietnamese Christians arrived in the country to avoid persecution, and together with Portuguese Cambodians they made up the Christian communities of Cambodia. In 1665, Louis Chevreuil was sent by the MEP to do missionary work there, but he left in the same year, frustrated by the indifference of the population. In 1768, Gervais Levavaseur, of the MEP, began work among the Khmer. Besides translating the principal prayers and a catechism into Khmer, he composed a Khmer–Latin dictionary.

It was not until the nineteenth century that there was a significant number of Christians (predominantly Vietnamese) in Cambodia. As mentioned above, the diocese of Cao Mien (now Phnom Penh) was created in 1850. Earlier, Cambodia had been part of the western diocese of the interior part of Vietnam, later known as Saigon. Indeed, when the interior part was divided into two dioceses in 1844, i.e. eastern (Qui Nhon) and western (Saigon), the latter included not only the two central provinces (Binh Thuan and Di Linh) and the six southern provinces of Vietnam (Bien Hoa, Saigon, My Tho, Vinh Long, Chau Doc and Ha Tien) but also the whole of Cambodia and the southern part of Laos. The Catholic population of the new diocese, which was entrusted to Bishop Dominique Lefèbvre (1844–64), was estimated at 23,000, and there were three missionaries (Jean Miche, Pierre Duclos and Charles Fontaine) and sixteen Vietnamese priests.[2]

Given the vastness of the new diocese, in 1850 Bishop Lefèbvre proposed that a new diocese be carved out of his territory. It was named Cao Mien (Vietnamese for Cambodia). Jean Miche was appointed apostolic vicar of the new diocese, which covered the whole of Cambodia. Several years earlier, Miche and four other missionaries (Marie-Laurent Cordier, Louis Ausoleil, Edme Sylvestre and François Beuret) had attempted a mission to Cambodia but achieved only very meagre success. At its foundation, the diocese of Cao Mien had only 600 Catholics, most of them Vietnamese expatriates, Cambodians of Vietnamese origin or Portuguese Cambodians. Internecine war had destroyed much of the country, including the few Catholic communities established by bishops Armand Lefèbvre and Guillaume Piguel between 1759 and 1780.

To a greater extent than Vietnam, Cambodia was deeply steeped in Buddhism, and though neither government nor people was openly hostile

2 See Louvet, *La Cochinchine religieuse*, vol. ii, pp. 154–6.

to Christianity, there were few conversions. Bishop Miche established the diocesan centre at Pinhalu (near Phnom Penh). Tragedy soon struck the young diocese with the premature deaths of Father Basset in 1853 and Father Triaire in 1859. In 1867, another priest, Father Barreau, was killed by pirates. In 1865, after the death of Bishop Dominique Lefèbvre, Bishop Miche was transferred to Saigon as his successor, and at his departure there were 2,500 Christians. Given the small number of Catholics in the Cao Mien diocese, Bishop Miche proposed to the Holy See to detach the two provinces of Ha Tien and Chau Doc from the diocese of Saigon and annex them to the diocese of Cao Mien, thus adding to it some 6,000 Catholics. Louis Ausoleil was made vicar general of the diocese (1869–74). He was succeeded by Marie-Laurent Cordier (1874–82), who was made apostolic vicar (1882–95).

In 1892, the diocese had one bishop (Cordier), twenty-nine missionaries, twelve Vietnamese priests, thirty catechists, one seminary with seventy-five students, thirty-five Sisters of the Sacred Heart of Mary, eighty-six Sisters of Providence (twenty-six French, sixty Vietnamese and Cambodian), and 21,130 Christians.

Christianity in Laos, 1815–1915

In the mid-fourteenth century a powerful kingdom called Lan Xang was founded among the Laotians, the majority of whom were descendants of Thai tribes, by Fa Ngoun (1353–73), who introduced Khmer civilisation and Theravāda Buddhism. In subsequent centuries Lan Xang waged intermittent wars with its neighbours and succeeded in expanding its territory. In 1707, however, Lan Xang was split by internal dissensions into two kingdoms: Luang Prabang in the north and Vientiane in the south. During the next century the two states were overrun by the neighbouring countries. In the nineteenth century, they were dominated by Siam (Thailand) and Vietnam. When France colonised Vietnam, it forced Siam to recognise a French protectorate over Laos, and in 1893 it incorporated Laos into the Union of French Indochina.

Christian mission in Laos was first attempted in 1642 by the Jesuit missionary Giovanni Maria Leria, assisted by a number of Vietnamese catechists. After five years he was forced to leave the country without significant results since, like Cambodia, Laos was deeply influenced by Buddhism. For the next two centuries, there was no trace of any Christian community. Christian mission in Laos, especially in Luang Brabang, was not resumed until 1858 by Bishop Miche, who assigned Ausoleil and Triaire to the task. Unfortunately, Triaire died of fever in 1859, and Ausoleil had to returned to Bangkok.

In 1870, *Propaganda Fide* charged Bishop Dupond of Bangkok to undertake the evangelisation of Laos but his death in 1872 prevented him from carrying out the task. His successor, Jean-Louis Vey (1875–1909), sent Prodhomme and Perraux to begin a mission in Kengkoi, and by 1880 there were 250 Christians. In 1881, Vey charged Prodhomme and Xavier Guego to begin another mission in Ubon. In 1885, there were 485 Christians and 1,500 catechumens, and three years later, there were 648 Christians and 4,500 catechumens. In 1878, a mission was started in north-eastern Laos, but it was terminated with the killing of twelve priests in 1884 and five more in 1889. Mission was also carried out in southern Laos after the country was turned into a French protectorate in 1893. In 1896, Vey proposed that an apostolic vicariate be established in Laos, and it was erected by Pope Leo XIII on 4 May 1899.

Protestant Christianity in Indochina until 1915

Protestantism was a latecomer to Indochina. The need for Protestants to evangelise Indochina was not noted until 1887 by A. B. Simpson, the founder of the Christian and Missionary Alliance (CMA). His fellow Canadian, Robert A. Jaffray (1873–1945), was commissioned by the CMA for south China in 1896. From his headquarters in Wuchow, Jaffray carried out his ministry for China, Indochina and the neighbouring islands. In 1889, Jaffray travelled by boat down the Red River and arrived in Hanoi to explore possibilities for mission, but owing to French hostility he was not able to establish a Protestant mission.

In 1911, Jaffray led two missionaries to Tourane (Da Nang) and was received by Charles Bonnet, of the British and Foreign Bible Society. When Bonnet left for France because of ill health, Jaffray bought his house and turned it into the first Protestant centre. In 1916, Jaffray became the representative of the CMA Indochina Mission. He negotiated with the French governor-general for freedom for Protestant missionaries to work in Vietnam.

Protestants did not begin mission in Cambodia until 1922, when two Americans, D. Ellison and A. Hammon, of the CMA, started to evangelise the Khmers. Ellison founded a Bible school at Battambang in 1925, and Hammon started Bible translation.

The first Protestant missionary to Laos was the American Presbyterian Daniel McGilvray (1828–1911). Ordained in 1857, McGilvray arrived in Thailand in 1858 as a member of the Bangkok Station, Siam Mission. In 1868, he moved to Chiang Mai, the chief city in northern Thailand, and founded a new Presbyterian mission, the Laos Mission. By early 1869, there were six conversions, but a persecution in September of that year killed two and scattered the rest. From 1870 to 1890, McGilvray was the leader of the Laos Mission and succeeded in establishing several rural Christian communities. In 1878, he played a leading role in obtaining the so-called Edict of Toleration from the Thai central government which granted certain civil rights to Christian converts.

32

Christianity as church and story and the birth of the Filipino nation in the nineteenth century

JOSÉ MARIO C. FRANCISCO

Throughout the nineteenth century, Christianity in the islands named after Philip II of Spain faced profound social change initiated by economic and political forces of modernity and culminating in the emergence of the Filipino nation. As Benedict Anderson's analysis of nationalism suggests, this emergence as 'an imagined political community' involved a complex cultural process rooted in changing perceptions of community, language and lineage.[1]

Christianity's reaction to these changes and participation in the growth of nationalism have marked its place in Philippine society then as now. Implicated in politics because of its nature and stature, the colonial church reacted to different groups and concerns involved in the nationalist and revolutionary movements. But beyond those in the church's direct influence, Christianity offered a paradigm of redemption in the Christ story that a wider population appropriated and later read to envision social relations different from Spanish aims. Both as church and story, Christianity's response was based on the dynamics between Spanish Catholicism and native culture.

Beyond transplanting Spanish Catholicism

Early studies often described the encounter between the Spanish and the native as a unilateral process of transplanting the entire imperial ethos, including Catholicism, and thus spoke of 'Hispanisation'.[2] These works, which relied primarily on Spanish sources, suffer from their primary focus on events and leaders and their representation of natives as passive objects of the colonial enterprise. More recent historians include non-traditional and often vernacular sources to write social history, and draw on anthropological studies of cross-cultural contact, or theological discussions of the relations between faith and

---

1 Anderson, *Imagined communities*, pp. 1–36.
2 Phelan, *The hispanization of the Philippines*, pp. 153–61.

culture.[3] Their analyses show that evangelisation in the Philippines can be construed not as transplantation of Spanish Catholicism, but as a dynamic encounter between Spanish and native which grew from intermittent contacts into a prolonged relationship founded on religious and political considerations and punctuated by episodic collisions.[4]

While this encounter occurred within the *patronato real de la iglesia de las Indias*, the right and conduct of Spanish conquest were seriously questioned by the Dominican Bartolomé de las Casas.[5] Owing to this earlier discussion and the absence of extensive highly centralised civilisations as in the new world, colonisation of the islands was characterised by skirmishes between the Spanish and small native settlements rather than wide-scale destruction of the local population and culture. Moreover, early Augustinian missionaries disagreed with colonial authorities over the treatment of natives. This and other important church concerns, such as local slavery and polygamy, were discussed by the Synod of Manila (1582–6).[6]

Of greater impact was the synod's decision to use local languages in evangelising, a practical decision later interpreted by nationalists as denying education in Spanish to natives. With painstaking diligence, missionaries romanised the vernacular syllabary and produced grammars and sermon anthologies, catechisms and novenas. Though extremely cautious of the intrusion of 'pagan' beliefs, choosing for instance the Spanish *Dios* rather than the Tagalog *Bathala* for 'God', they nevertheless used for baptism the Tagalog word *'binyag'* which referred to the Muslim rite of purification.[7] Codified in native vocabulary laden with local connotations, Christian doctrines of the afterlife[8] or of being *'alipin ng Dios* (slaves of God)'[9] assumed new nuances. Moreover, other texts developed from official practice by church personnel were often used in aural-oral contexts, being chanted and dramatised during communal outdoor occasions such as Holy Week processions and patronal fiestas. In bringing the Christ story into native hearts and minds, they transformed the vernaculars into a language of redemption and created a Christianity easily appropriated by natives. This story's earliest major text is Gaspar Aquino de Belen's *Pasiong Mahal* (Sacred Passion) (1704).[10] Related to Spanish antecedents and published

3 See, respectively, Ileto, *Pasyon and revolution* and Schumacher (ed.), *Readings in Philippine church history*.
4 Bitterli, *Cultures in conflict*, pp. 20–51.
5 Schumacher, *Readings in Philippine church history*, pp. 5–11.
6 *Ibid.*, pp. 28–33.
7 Peralta (ed.), *Reflections on Philippine culture*, pp. 46–7.
8 Rafael, *Contracting colonialism*, pp. 167–209.
9 Francisco (ed.), *Sermones*, pp. 370–95.
10 See De Belen, *Mahal na passion*.

with church approval, this great Tagalog poem told the Christ story using biblical characters, especially Jesus, with native sensibilities and lessons related to ordinary experience.

The church also played an extensive role in the colony's social organisation and development. It reduced scattered settlements into towns patterned after Spain's, worked with local leaders and involved natives in teaching catechism and leading prayers for the dying. Established in most lowland settlements by the early seventeenth century, it provided schools for religious instruction and general education, charitable services for the sick and orphaned, and even technical know-how in agriculture. Parish priests were respected for their knowledge and their defence of natives from abusive Spanish and native authorities. In return, some natives lived their faith through exemplary service, like Ignacia del Espiritu Santo, or martyrdom, like Lorenzo Ruiz. Through these various institutions and its influential clergy, the church held a firm social presence by the end of the eighteenth century.

The dynamic encounter between Spanish Catholicism and native culture occurred within the related but distinct spheres of Christianity as story and as church, involving complex processes of negotiation that Rafael has compared to 'translation'.[11] This exchange transcended intentions and expectations on both sides. Spanish missionaries remained concerned over lapses into 'paganism' while natives transformed Christianity as their own. Moreover, the early disputes between missionaries and colonisers prefigured the eventual dissociation of the church from colonial authority, thus providing more space for native intervention.

Resistance was never absent because of the oppressive effects of the ecclesiastical and colonial infrastructure.[12] Protests against abusive friars took place. Some natives responded to forced labour and taxes through revolts with nativist or religious significations; others retreated to the mountains. But only with significant social change could an alternative to the colonial establishment emerge.

Economic and political forces of modernity

The seeds of this change were planted during the first quarter of the nineteenth century. Increased trade with other nations and the victory of Spain's liberals introduced developments that opened the colony to modernity. Thus

---

11 Rafael, *Contracting colonialism*, pp. 211–19.
12 Constantino, *The Philippines*, pp. 86–112.

while European Catholicism struggled with the Enlightenment's legacy in the modern world, the colonial church faced local developments which paved the way for social critique.

Following the official demise in 1815 of the lucrative galleon trade between Manila, Mexico and Spain, and the grant in 1822 by the Spanish Cortes of trading privileges to non-Spanish companies, other countries increased trade with the opening of ports, starting with Manila in 1834. This commercial growth stimulated domestic agricultural production of tobacco, sugar and abaca, and established an export economy.[13] Land became highly valued as a source of wealth and power, not only among the Filipino hacenderos of Pampanga, Batangas and western Visayas and the friar orders who owned the large haciendas of Bulacan, Laguna and Cavite, but also among their lessees, who became hacenderos in their own right. Though such prosperity benefited some who were already prominent, such as municipal officeholders, it brought forth Spanish or Chinese mestizo and native families who possessed great influence in their rural or urban localities and also aspired to equal Spaniards in urbanity and learning.[14] From this elite came many of the self-described *ilustrados* (the enlightened) and other prominent figures in the nationalist and revolutionary movements.

The other significant development began with the victory of anticlerical liberals in the 1830s. These political changes in Spain had direct consequences on the relations between the church and the government as well as between Spanish religious orders and native diocesan clergy. Though antichurch, the Spanish liberal government allowed friars to be sent because of their assistance in ensuring loyalty to Spain. These missionaries were loyal to Spain but wary of liberal ideas. This ambivalence fuelled related long-standing issues within the colonial church: episcopal visitation rights and the secularisation of parishes.[15]

The first concerned a bishop's right to visit parishes under religious orders, a right affirmed by the Council of Trent but contested within Spanish colonies because of the *patronato*. Its implementation aggravated tensions between religious orders and diocesan bishops. Moreover, bishops often turned over parishes under religious orders to inadequately trained native clergy. When Archbishop Basilio Sancho de Santa Justa y Rufina of Manila did so in 1768, Spanish churchmen used its disastrous consequences to claim natives were ill-suited for the priesthood.[16]

---

13 Legarda, *After the galleons*, pp. 93–144.
14 Cullinane, *Ilustrado politics*, pp. 8–48.
15 Anderson (ed.), *Studies in Philippine church history*, pp. 44–64.
16 Schumacher, *Readings in Philippine church history*, pp. 200–10.

The second issue, the secularisation of parishes, turned explosive in 1826 when a royal decree ordered that parishes held by the native clergy be returned to friars upon vacancy. This move revealed growing Spanish suspicion of the native clergy and the government's desire to displace them. Diocesan priests with higher degrees from church institutions in Manila became more militant. Led by Pedro Pelaez, vicar-capitular of the Manila archdiocese, and Fr Mariano Gomez of the Cavite clergy, they planned to ask Spain for equal treatment for the native clergy.[17]

These developments had important consequences for the church. First, the rise of the landed elite strengthened church involvement in higher education and at the same time made the church vulnerable to political attack because of the friar estates. Together with the native clergy, the wealthy studied at the Dominican-run Universidad de Santo Tomas and Colegio de San Juan de Letran, and the Jesuit-run Ateneo Municipal, and this education led some to espouse liberal ideas. Second, internal church disputes became wider political questions, generating tension in the church between Spanish and native. Thus the native clergy had greater reason to align themselves with their school contemporaries among the elite who considered the inefficient and inconsistent policies of the often-changing colonial administrators to be obstacles to economic progress.

The epic function of the Christ story

Because of the shortage of priests, the growing tension between Spanish religious and native diocesan clergy, and the uneasy alliance between church and government, few parishes received genuine pastoral care from the church. Consequently, the influence of a vibrant religiosity based on the Christ story and its symbolic world became stronger and wider throughout the nineteenth century.

The magisterial narrative of this religiosity, the *Pasyong Henesis* (the Genesis Passion narrative) (1812),[18] was an updated Aquino de Belen text framed between Creation and the Last Judgement, chanted antiphonally and dramatised during Lent. With its native imagery, it replaced epics suppressed by missionaries, inviting natives to see the world in its light and to follow Jesus's path of interiority from suffering to life, thus locating personal experience and communal identity within the Christ story as meta-narrative.

17 Schumacher, *Revolutionary clergy*, pp. 6–12.
18 Javellana (ed.), *Casaysayan*.

This epic function is illustrated by the way in which significant pasyon vocabulary and themes were echoed by Apolinario de la Cruz (known as Hermano Pule), a lay worker in a Manila hospital, and the Cofradia de San José which he established in 1832 upon being barred from any religious order as an *indio*.[19] Given its popularity in his hometown of Tayabas and its general exclusion of Spaniards and mestizos, its ascetical practices and secret rituals were judged heretical by the local priest, and the group was denied official recognition and massacred in 1841 by government forces who put Pule's severed head on a stake.

The Cofradia's world-view and resolve to resist reflected the symbolic vision and linguistic vocabulary of the pasyon tradition. Empowered to see events in the light of the Christ story, they acted with great interior resolve in solidarity with Jesus's life unto death. Moreover, their ritual meals prefigured a heavenly order free from colonial inequalities. In his poetic adaptation of the Augustinian Pedro de Herrera's work, Pule used Thomistic ideas to describe the attributes of those in heaven, and envisioned their relations as equality, the exact opposite of earthly differences in appearance, intelligence, wealth and status. Their practice and vision indicate how the epic-like pasyon shaped the Cofradia's ethos and identity as well as how their reading of the Christ story within the colonial context evoked relations of fraternity.

Similar images of alternative social relations are found in some metrical romances (*auit*) imported from Mexico and adapted by lay persons from Spanish medieval stories of Christians and Moors. Though not explicitly devotional like the pasyon, these chanted and dramatic presentations during religious feasts do not represent secularisation or discontinuity with the Christ story as Lumbera or Ileto suggests.[20] Although charting the convoluted loves of nobles and their struggles for power, their underlying quest for personal and social wellbeing remained rooted in the Christian journey from suffering to life. Like pasyon performances, they brought the Christ story out of church premises and into the lives of the people, thus opening the story to new readings.

One such *auit* is Francisco Balthazar Balagtas's *Florante at Laura* (1838?), in which Florante is helped by a Moor to save Laura and to restore order 'within and around my wretched land [where] betrayal reigns supreme'.[21] The kingdom's struggle for justice and Florante's desire for Laura reflect the Christian journey from suffering to liberation expressed in terms of a cosmic order

19 Ileto, *Pasyon and revolution*, pp. 37–91.
20 Lumbera, *Tagalog poetry*, p. 135; Ileto, *Filipinos and their revolution*, p. 2.
21 Carlos Ronquillo (ed.), *Pinagdaanang buhay ni Florante at Laura sa cahariang Albania* (Manila: Imprenta de Ramirez y Giraudier, 1921), stanza 14.

governing social and personal affairs. Characters invoke 'merciful heaven' and act according to 'reason' or 'natural law' in their quest for love and justice.[22] Both in its description of tyranny and in its vision of wellbeing, Balagtas's *auit* was an implicit critique of the colonial situation and an expression of the desire for change.

Such aspirations based on the Christ story were rehearsed in many groups and movements formed from the mid-nineteenth century up to the first decade of American occupation.[23] Like Pule's Cofradia, some were led by charismatic leaders seen as Christ figures forming nativist communes. Others became involved in the Revolution and subsequent resistance against the Americans.

This influence of the Christ story extended to many from different social strata who participated in its practices. At times suppressed by the church as doctrinally heterodox or socially dangerous,[24] these practices provided narrative logic for individual piety and social behaviour as well as social occasions for groups of natives to gather. As meta-narrative, the Christ story might be described as the subversive memory within native society, offering a language of liberation and a vehicle for alternative social relations.[25]

Ferment among native leaders and its impact on Christianity

While religiosity based on the Christ story evoked such visions across native society, similar desires grew among native leaders within and outside the church, the educated native clergy and the ilustrados, whether of wealthy origins or not. From the 1850s, more native priests contested official moves to take their parishes. They clashed with orders of friars who appeared more loyal to Spain than to the church and viewed those critical of colonial policies as freemasons. Led by the mestizo Fr José Burgos, they forged links to defend their rights with ilustrado reformist lawyers and businessmen in Manila and abroad.[26]

These activities intensified Spanish animosity against the native clergy, which exploded on 20 January 1872 when some soldiers in Cavite killed their commander and seized Fort San Felipe.[27] Based on a soldier's doubtful

---

22 Reyes (ed.), *200 Taon*, pp. 129–40.
23 Ileto, *Pasyon and revolution*, pp. 197–313.
24 Javellana (ed.), *Casaysayan*, pp. 14–15.
25 Francisco, 'The Christ story as the subversive memory'.
26 Schumacher, *José Burgos*, pp. 24–8.
27 Artigas y Cuerva, *The events of 1872*.

testimony and the governor general's arrest orders signed before the mutiny, Frs Gomez, Burgos and Jacinto Zamora, collectively known as Gomburza, were executed as conspirators. Many native priests thus doubted the possibility of significant reform within the colonial church and supported the Propaganda Movement begun by Filipinos in Spain to campaign for the general extension of Spanish peninsular law to the colony.[28]

Others groups seeking change found the friars a convenient political target despite their decreased numbers and improved training. The landed elite coveted the friars' extensive haciendas but were not generally anti-religious as they participated in local church activities or were kin to native priests. Ilustrados from the elite, such as Marcelo H. del Pilar, and from the lower classes, such as Apolinario Mabini, saw friars as personifications of antiquated notions contrary to liberal ideals of equality and enlightenment and as obstacles to the propagation of these ideals because of their influence as parish priests.[29] Those influenced by freemasonry were clearly antifriar as well as antireligious.

These perceptions of friars among the ilustrados found expression in José Rizal's celebrated novels, *Noli me tangere* (Touch me not) (1887) and *El filibusterismo* (Subversion) (1891).[30] The friars Damaso and Salvi personify greed, ambition and lust. Rizal's anticlericalism was shaped by his family's conflict with Dominican friars over land, his education in Europe and exposure to liberal thought and freemasonry. But his Catholic childhood and continuing contact with Jesuit teachers also informed his thought. His critique of Christianity sought to 'unmask the hypocrisy which, under the cloak of Religion, came among us to impoverish us, to brutalize us'.[31] This critique owed much to current rationalist notions of religion, which church personnel, including his former Jesuit mentor Pablo Pastells, could not understand because of their ideological opposition to European liberalism.[32] At the end of his second novel, the figure of Padre Florentino, said to have been based on Fr Burgos, embodies his vision of a Christianity freed from all that Padre Damaso and Padre Salvi represented.

These different strands of growing anticolonial and nationalist sentiments struck at the heart of the colonial church and widened cracks within its clergy. The native clergy shared many of these sentiments, but, bound together with

---

28 Schumacher, *The propaganda movement*, pp. 6–9.
29 Agoncillo, *The revolt of the masses*, pp. 278–83.
30 *Noli me tangere*, trans. M. Soledad Lacson-Locsin (Makati: Bookmark Inc., c. 1996) and *El filibusterismo*, trans. M. Soledad Lacson-Locsin (Makati: Bookmark Inc., c. 1996).
31 Wenceslao E. Retana, *Vida y escritos del Dr. José Rizal* (Madrid: Victoriano Suarez, n.d.), pp. 125–6.
32 Bonoan, *The Rizal–Pastells correspondence*, pp. 40–79.

foreign missionaries under the *patronato*, could not allow them to threaten the foundation of their mission. Moreover, the church had to deal with lay leaders whose education came from secular sources and whose decisions led to the tumultuous events of the Revolution.

The Revolution: church response and Christian participation

Contrary to claims made during the Marcos dictatorship of the 1970s that reform and revolution were mutually exclusive options in the late nineteenth century,[33] the nationalist movement paved the way for the 1896 outbreak by awakening many to colonial injustices. Those within the church faced the Revolution in ways consistent with the native clergy's participation in, and the colonial church's reaction to this movement. The revolutionaries' behaviour towards the church similarly reflected their earlier views. Thus attitudes within both the church and the Revolution were far from monolithic.

Andres Bonifacio's *Katipunan* (Brotherhood), founded in 1892 to unite Filipinos and obtain independence from Spain, launched the Revolution in Manila without the initial support of nationalist leaders of the educated and wealthier classes.[34] Its anticlerical and antireligious sentiments were confirmed when the Augustinian Fr Mariano Gil alerted the civil authorities, thus precipitating the premature start of the armed revolt.

Though friars suffered captivity or death throughout the military campaign, provincial revolutionary forces, especially in central and southern Luzon, treated the church differently. In Cavite, where the campaign was most successful despite factionalism, revolutionary leaders like Emilio Aguinaldo, head of the Magdalo faction and later President of the Philippine Republic, had links with the church and even ensured that friars were allowed to escape or, if captured, were treated with courtesy.[35]

The church reacted to the Revolution in partisan ways. Friars became suspicious even of those not criticised by revolutionary forces like the Jesuits. The native clergy, despite some initial hesitation, generally supported the Revolution. Many, like Fr Esteban del Rosario of Ternate, who reportedly called it 'a holy war', rallied the people;[36] some, like Fr Gregorio Crisostomo of Tanay,

33 Constantino, *The making of a Filipino*, pp. 1–22.
34 Borromeo-Buehler, *The cry of Balintawak*, pp. 24–47.
35 [Emilio] Aguinaldo, *Mga gunita ng himagsikan* (n.p., 1964), pp. 70, 85.
36 Telesforo Canseco, 'Historia de la insurreccion filipina en Cavite', original in Archivo de la Provincia del Santo Rosario, University of Sto Tomas Manila, Microfilm in Rizal Library, Ateneo de Manila University, pp. 56, 62–3.

joined the military campaign; and a few, such as Fr Pedro Dandan, participated in the Cavite revolutionary councils. Because of this involvement, Spanish officials and civilians imprisoned or executed native priests, especially in the Ilocos and Bicol regions.

However, the greater involvement of Christians came from ordinary supporters of the Revolution. According to contemporary witnesses, they participated with great devotion in traditional practices and masses offered 'for revolutionaries who had died in battle as for the Spaniards, inasmuch as . . . all were Christians'.[37] Moreover, friars were generally spared during attacks and asked to be their parish priests. Underlying these events was the influence of the Christ story on those who saw their revolutionary involvement as part of their faith.[38]

These relations changed with the ascendancy of anti-religious leaders like Mabini within the short-lived Philippine Republic, proclaimed on 12 June 1898. They sought authority over the church similar to the *patronato's* because of the importance of church support for revolutionary success. Apart from such irritants as local leaders usurping church fees and property or discouraging church marriage in favour of the newly established civil marriage, the matter of church jurisdiction proved crucial. Church life had to be re-established under ecclesiastically legal structures, but the revolutionary government refused to acknowledge the friar bishops' authority.

Moreover, church–state relations generated heated debate during the 1898 Malolos Congress.[39] Native clergy led by Fr Mariano Sevilla remained committed to nationalist ideals but also protected the integrity of the church. Catholics in the Congress like Felipe Calderon wanted Catholicism declared the state religion against anticlerical leaders who supported the constitutional separation of church and state. Though there was victory by one vote, the provision for separation was not promulgated.

Fr Gregorio Aglipay, Mabini's contemporary in Letran, rose to prominence as ecclesiastical governor of Nueva Segovia and received the post of military vicar general at this time of strained relations.[40] In agreement with revolutionary leaders, he sought to exercise jurisdiction over the native clergy independently of existing church authorities. The church's refusal to lift his excommunication pushed him to accept the leadership of the schismatic Iglesia Filipina Independiente (IFI) initiated by Isabelo de los Reyes Sr.

---

37 Canseco, 'Historia', p. 98.
38 Ileto, *Pasyon and revolution*, pp. 93–139.
39 Schumacher, *Revolutionary clergy*, pp. 81–5.
40 Anderson (ed.), *Studies in Philippine church history*, pp. 223–54.

These differences among individuals and leaders within both the Revolution and Christianity indicate the complex process attending the emergence of the Filipino nation. Arguing against the stereotype of a proletarian Revolution taken over and betrayed to the Americans by the wealthy ilustrado class, Schumacher speaks of 'the many revolutions within the one Revolution', the distinct views and interests of the liberal ilustrados, the economic elite, the native clergy and the masses which were interwoven into the fabric of an 'imagined nation' at the outbreak of the Revolution.[41] Within this complex process was born 'a new historical person: the Filipino [into whom] disappeared, for most political purposes at least, the *indio*, the mestizo, and the *criollo*'.[42]

Similarly, Christian involvement in the Revolution must be seen as including the native clergy and the ordinary supporters of the Revolution. The native clergy's general support and active engagement grew out of their nationalist advocacy of racial equality within the church and their loss of hope in the possibility of reforms under the colonial framework. Those influenced by the Christ story among supporters of the Revolution participated because of their solidarity (*pakikiramay*) with Christ and their desire for *kalayaan* (freedom) which, as Ileto points out,[43] differed from ilustrado *independencia*. Through the participation of both groups seeking alternative social relations, the Revolution finally dissociated the church from the Patronato.

More challenges to Christianity with American involvement

American involvement in the Philippines came through the Spanish-American war, when Admiral George Dewey's forces sank the Spanish fleet in Manila Bay on 1 May 1898. Six months after Aguinaldo proclaimed independence in repudiation of his earlier pact with the Spaniards, the Philippines were ceded by Spain in the Treaty of Paris on 10 December 1898, and subsequently retained, according to American President William McKinley, 'to educate the Filipinos, and uplift and civilize and Christianize them'.[44] Protestant missionary boards then sent missionaries as early as 1899 and formed an Evangelical Union, which excluded the Episcopal Church under Bishop Charles Brent that chose to preach instead to non-Christian tribes in northern Luzon and Mindanao.[45]

---

41 Schumacher, *Revolutionary clergy*, pp. 268–74.
42 Anderson, *The spectre of comparisons*, p. 257.
43 Ileto, *Pasyon and revolution*, p. 225.
44 James F. Rusling, 'Interview with President McKinley', *The Christian Advocate* 78 (20 January 1903), pp. 137–8.
45 Anderson (ed.), *Studies in Philippine church history*, pp. 279–300.

Soon after the Malolos Republic, hostilities between Americans and Filipinos started in early 1899 at different locations. The sporadic nature of resistance and conflict among leaders led to the early surrender and collaboration of many elite factions. But resistance continued until 1910 from groups the Americans called 'bandits (*tulisanes*)' and through popular literature with socialist Christ figures.

The native clergy joined this struggle because of their nationalism and suspicion of American attitudes towards religion. Many provided money and intelligence to the resistance in Luzon and the Visayas, and others, like Fr José Natera of Albay, even joined military attacks.[46] In retaliation, American forces tried to exile priest-leaders such as Fr Manuel Roxas, tortured other anti-American priests and committed atrocities in Cebu and Samar.

After the gradual establishment of American civil government, pending issues for the normalisation of church life had to be resolved among many stakeholders – the American government, native leaders, the IFI and the different Catholic voices from the native clergy, the Spanish friars, and some American church leaders and the Holy See. The most urgent and politically sensitive of these concerned the friars, most of whom returned home voluntarily. Some thirty-six priests insisted with Fr Aglipay that all church leadership be Filipino.[47] The remainder of the total 600, loyal to the Holy See and led by Fr Sevilla, blocked the reassignment of friars to parishes that were taken over by the native clergy. Early American Catholic leaders, especially Archbishop Placide Chappelle of Louisiana, the Holy See's apostolic delegate, proved unable to settle the issue because of prejudice against and suspicion of Filipinos. After an American delegation under William Howard Taft of the Second Philippine Commission visited Rome, the Holy See publicly refused to bar friars from parishes but privately agreed that they be sent only if the parishes did not object.[48]

A related issue was the question of church property in the form of estates, buildings, foundations and even cemeteries. Negotiations begun during Taft's visit to Rome led to the sale of more than 420,000 acres owned by the Augustinians, Dominicans and Recollects to the government, but only to be taken up by Filipino and American corporations later.[49] Realising that further delays in settling ownership of properties which changed hands during the fighting would work against American interests, the Philippine

46 Schumacher, *Revolutionary clergy*, pp. 164–8.
47 Anderson (ed.), *Studies in Philippine church history*, pp. 227–41.
48 Arbeiza, *Reseña histórica*, pp. 157–75.
49 Connolly, *Church lands*, pp. 1–6.

Commission passed a law giving the Supreme Court jurisdiction over such cases. In 1906, the court ordered the return of church property seized by the IFI to the Catholic Church, and in 1909, the turnover of other assets to their rightful owners.

Reorganisation of the Catholic Church proceeded with the appointment of Archbishop Giovanni Battista Guidi, a more open apostolic delegate, and the issuance of *Quae Mari Sinico* (1902), the new Apostolic Constitution replacing the *patronato*. But even with such structures in place and the 1906 appointment of the first Filipino bishop, Fr Jorge Barlin of Nueva Caceres, the Catholic Church remained disoriented from the aftermath of war and schism and the prospect of facing American state bureaucracy and church–state separation. Thus it became wary of political involvement, though some lay leaders sought election to the first Philippine Assembly in 1907 as Catholic candidates. Moreover, its influence through education diminished because of the lack of English-speaking church personnel and American Catholics in civil service. American Protestants in the public school system hindered the Catholic presence and at times fanned anti-Catholic sentiments.[50] The Catholic Church retreated from the public domain and remained Hispanic in its cultural ethos until the arrival of church personnel of other nationalities who were better equipped to deal with the new regime.

Christianity played a multifaceted role as church and story in what became the historical trajectory of nineteenth-century colonial society, the birth of the Filipino nation. It 'translated' the Christ story, thereby transforming the vernacular into a language of liberation and providing an epic paradigm for leading individual and social lives in terms of solidarity with Jesus. This story's many textual incarnations and communal performances created physical space for natives to gather as communities, as well as imaginative space for them to envision social bonds other than colonial relations.

This same concern over native status proved crucial for the dissociation of the church from the *patronato* and thus of evangelisation from colonisation. By offering higher education to the native clergy and others, the colonial church unknowingly contributed to their awakening to a common lineage as Filipinos and to a desire for what they envisioned to be equality, fraternity or progress. This 'enlightenment' infused with liberal thought and consequently rejected by Spanish church and civil authorities led to the Revolution that broke up the colonial church. This process of purification left the church unsettled, initially

---

50 Anderson (ed.), *Studies in Philippine church history*, pp. 301–24.

unable to speak in a new language under a new regime. Christianity would subsequently seek to find its voice as story and as church, both Catholic and Protestant, and face with the rest of Philippine society what has been described as the nineteenth century's legacy of an 'unfinished revolution'[51] and 'a nation aborted'.[52]

51 Ileto, *Filipinos and their revolution*, pp. 177–201.
52 Quibuyen, *A nation aborted*.

33

Christianity in Australasia and the Pacific

STUART PIGGIN AND ALLAN DAVIDSON

Christianity in Australia

Origins and foundations

Christianity came to Australia with the settlement of Sydney Cove in 1788, before the French Revolution and the formation of the major British evangelical missionary societies. In Australia, in contrast to the rest of the Pacific, it came as a chaplaincy to soldiers and convicts rather than as a mission to the indigenous people. From its origins in Australia, then, Christianity has been seen as part of the apparatus of law and order. The transformation of a convict society into a nation of the healthy and law-abiding may be understood as one of Christianity's major achievements in the nineteenth century. Australians may have had difficulty in resisting materialism and secularism, but there was no doubt in anybody's mind that, in the nineteenth century, Australia was a Christian country. The great majority of the settler population identified with a Christian denomination, either really or nominally. Christianity was a major factor in shaping the Australian colonies.

A new denominational mix

Although the Church of England had the largest percentage adherence of any denomination in Australia until 1986 when it was overtaken by the Catholics, membership of other denominations was greater as a percentage of the population than in England, in itself creating a different religious culture. Nonconformists, especially Congregationalists and Calvinistic Methodists, were revered early settlers in New South Wales to which they came *en route* to, or after displacement from, the Pacific islands to which they were sent by the London Missionary Society (LMS).

Wesleyan Methodists, by contrast, did not start well. They held their first class meetings in Sydney and nearby Parramatta in 1812, but membership was still only 126 in 1831. By the 1840s that had changed dramatically, after several revivals swept through the Sydney district. These revivals were often associated with the name of John Watsford, the first Australian-born Methodist clergyman. Revivals within Australian Methodism probably explain the growth of that denomination from 6.7 per cent of the population in 1861 to 10.2 per cent in 1901. Methodism was the great success story of nineteenth-century Australian Christianity.

Catholics represented about 25 per cent of the population in the colonies for much of the nineteenth century (South Australia and Tasmania had a lower percentage). Yet it was not until 1820 that they were allowed to have their own priests, and though most of the Catholic convicts were Irish, the first two members of the hierarchy appointed by Rome in 1833 were English Benedictines, John Bede Polding and William Ullathorne. On the establishment of a diocesan structure in 1842, the ascendancy of Irish bishops in Australian Catholicism began, and with it the consolidation of strong Irish Catholic subcultures, fertile soil for sectarianism. There were those who transcended sectarian prejudices. Caroline Chisholm, 'the immigrants' friend', a devout and philanthropic Protestant before marrying a Catholic, and then becoming one herself, gave equal support to the 11,000 people of whatever country of origin and religion whom personally she settled on the land. She thought of wives and children as God's police and believed the family to be far more the guardians of society than clergy and teachers.

John Dunmore Lang, Australia's first Presbyterian minister, arrived in Sydney in 1823. He promoted Protestant immigration to Australia, and campaigned unceasingly and unscrupulously in the pulpit, press and parliament for democratic rights in three colonies. He was also an early prophet of federation and republicanism. Presbyterians, who first started to meet in New South Wales in 1809, represented more conservative traditions and manners than their notorious clerical founder.

Baptists did not hold their first service in Sydney until 1831, and, unlike their American counterparts, then remained among the smallest of the main Christian denominations in Australia. The Churches of Christ and the Seventh Day Adventists came in the second half of the century, the Salvation Army in 1880. In 1883 Charles Strong formed the Australian Church, a liberal breakaway from the Victorian Presbyterians. It did not thrive. In contrast to American Christianity and the Christianity which developed in other parts of the South Pacific, Australia produced few genuinely indigenous Christian movements until the twentieth century when Aboriginal and charismatic indigenous churches were formed.

Other visions

The colonies of Western Australia, Victoria, South Australia and Queensland were the products of different visions from those which had led to the creation of the earlier penal settlements. They were Puritan and dissenting counters to, rather than spin-offs from, the convict colonies of New South Wales and Van Diemen's Land (renamed Tasmania in 1853). In Western Australia, the Swan River Colony was designed to be a duplication of rural England, replete with landlords and tenants. Major Frederick Chidley Irwin, in charge of the 13th Regiment, commissioned in 1828 to provide military protection to the new settlement at Swan River, conducted church services in his own home and built a church near the present site of the Anglican cathedral in Perth.

Victoria and South Australia were populated by Nonconformist and evangelical middle-class migrants displaced from Britain by the grim recession of the 1830s. Victoria was settled in 1834, and religious observance came with the settlers. Melbourne quickly became more observably 'holy' than Sydney, and Victoria the most enterprising of the colonies, a conspicuous example of the Protestant ethic.

South Australia was settled in 1838, the product of a dissenting vision. George Fife Angas, a devout Baptist and prosperous ship-owner, injected capital and pious young settlers, with a good gender balance, into the new colony. Among those Angas enticed to South Australia were German Lutherans who established the tradition of evangelical Lutheranism in Australia. The colony won self-government as early as 1856, and gave women the right to vote in council elections in 1861 and the right to vote and stand for parliament in 1894. Douglas Pike aptly described South Australia as a 'Paradise of Dissent'.[1] In the strange dialectic of religious history, the Anglicans, under Bishop Augustus Short, were dragged, kicking and often screaming, into Anglo-Catholicism, and the Catholic bishop, Patrick Geoghegan, initiated a Catholic education system which was to be emulated in all the other colonies.

Queensland had convict settlements before its creation as a separate colony in 1859, but, thanks to the efforts of John Dunmore Lang, was able to boast many staunch Protestant settlers among its pioneers, including evangelical Lutherans and Baptists. They established a robustly anti-Catholic society. That soon met with an equally stout response from the newly appointed Catholic bishop, James Quinn. In 1862 he established the Queensland Immigration Society. Many Catholic immigrants poured into Queensland, driven out of Ireland by famine and denied entry to the USA because of the Civil War.

1 Pike, *Paradise of dissent*.

Missions to the Aborigines

From the first settlement, for a generation Aboriginal people were largely ignored by the church. The great missionary societies in Britain were fully stretched financially and in their imaginations in reaching the 'higher' civilisations of India and China, and the more romantic of missionary challenges in the South Seas islands and in Africa. Catholic missionaries were few in number and even later in coming. In the first sixty years of settlement, all the missions to indigenous Australians failed dismally.

The first official missionary to Australia was the Rev. William Walker, a Wesleyan, who arrived in 1821. Aboriginal people were, he contended, the descendants of Ham, the son of Noah, on whose offspring Noah had put a curse. Walker also concluded that Aborigines could not continue to 'go walkabout' and be Christian. They were now to be settled on land reservations, where the missionaries would train them in the skills of agriculture and manufacturing. From 1825 in quick succession, 10,000 acre grants for missions were made to the Congregationalist, Anglican and Wesleyan missionaries. They all failed quickly. At the LMS mission near Lake Macquarie, Lancelot Threlkeld laboured largely on translation work until 1841, by which date none of the Awabakal survived to read his work.

There was less abject failure in the second half of the nineteenth century. Two Moravian missions in Western Victoria lasted from 1858 to 1905, when they became self-governing and financially independent communities. Then there were missions whose 'success' may be attributed to the charismatic men who ran them: the Lutheran, Carl Strehlow, at Hermannsburg in the Northern Territory; Dom Rosendo Salvado, the Spanish Benedictine bishop, at New Norcia in Western Australia; and John Gribble of the Church of England Warangesda Mission in New South Wales. Common to all the relatively successful missions were a measure of recognition of Aboriginal culture, teaching in the vernacular, recognition of indigenous leadership, and the insight, earlier denied, that Aboriginal people had their own spirituality.

In 1908 the Church of England began its Roper River Mission, the Catholics began work on Bathurst Island in 1911, and in 1916 the Methodists established a mission in Goulburn Island. They proved more successful than the earlier missions in the southern states. This was partly because Aborigines in the north were not swamped by a majority of whites, were able to retain more of their customs and culture, and were readily employable in the cattle industry. It became apparent that the Aboriginal population was increasing again, for which Christian missionaries deserve a modicum of credit.

Education and secularity

In the first settlements, it was assumed that the Church of England was responsible for all education. In 1825 Australia's first archdeacon, Thomas Hobbes
Scott, was appointed 'Visitor' to all schools, and one-seventh of the land of New
South Wales was vested in the Church and Schools Corporation, an Anglican
monopoly, to finance the education system. This arrangement failed, largely
because a much greater percentage of the population was non-Anglican than
in England.

In his Church Act of 1836, the Governor of New South Wales, Richard
Bourke, offered state aid to the major denominations to assist them in building
churches and paying the stipends of their ministers. This Act was duplicated in
other Australian colonies with far-reaching effect. They effectively bankrolled
sectarian rivalry, which was to become a major theme in Australian religious
and social history. The other side of that coin, however, is that the colonial
populations were very well supplied with religious services and pastoral care,
with typically four churches (Anglican, Catholic, Presbyterian, Methodist)
being built in even small towns, all of about the same value and therefore
prestige, and often on opposite street corners near the centre of town. Then,
when one of the four decided they should update, by replacing their Georgian
colonial building with a neo-Gothic one, the other three quickly followed suit.
Anthony Trollope, visiting Australia in 1871–2, observed, 'wherever there is a
community there arises a church, or more commonly churches ... The people
are fond of building churches.'[2]

Bourke also sought to subsidise the school systems offered by the various
denominations, supplemented, in places where there were no church schools,
by a common curriculum taught in one school. This failed owing to opposition
from the Anglicans, who wanted to retain their educational monopoly, but by
1880 'free, compulsory and secular' education was established in New South
Wales and close to that year in the other colonies and in New Zealand. These
state systems, which allowed religious instruction from visiting ministers, were
not the product of anti-Christian feeling. They were what the majority of the
Protestant laity wanted, systems which would allow the Christian religion
a positive role in developing civic-mindedness in the rising generation. Until
the 1950s the state education systems achieved that end and were, arguably,
Protestantism's finest achievement in the realm of social engineering.

Roman Catholics, influenced by Pius IX's condemnation of secular, state-
controlled education, created and funded with considerable sacrifice their own

---

2 Trollope, *Australia*, p. 240.

education system, for which they received no state aid at all until 1963. In 1866 in South Australia, the highly educated romantic Fr Julian Tenison Woods, and the practical, courageous Mary MacKillop, who was beatified in 1995, founded the Sisters of St Joseph. A teaching order, the Josephites had, at the time of MacKillop's death in 1909, almost a thousand teaching sisters and they modelled the way Catholics could build an education system without state aid. By 1901 there were 100,000 pupils in Catholic schools. This heroic campaign intensified Catholic identity, which was compounded with Irish anti-British feeling and galvanised the sectarian divide between Catholic and Protestant, a prominent feature of Australian social life until Vatican II. Nineteenth-century Australian Catholics were a minority sub-culture: alienated, defensive, introspective and clericalised; but cohesive, focused on the papacy, certain that to be Christian one had to be Roman, and, though depressed economically, better off than they had been before coming to Australia. It was a sub-culture which nurtured Australia's most notorious bush ranger, Ned Kelly, and a number of rebels in the Eureka Stockade in 1854, but it helped the poor Irish convicts and immigrants to survive more than to rebel.

Legislating for a Christian nation

The majority of the Australian population in the second half of the nineteenth century were Protestants who believed in the separation of church and state. They also believed, however, that the prosperity of the nation and the freedoms of its people depended on the morality and values of the Christian religion, and that the practice of righteousness should have the force of law behind it.

Protestant Christians argued that sabbath observance had made Britain great and free, and that Australia should follow Britain and not the Continent. In 1889, the New South Wales Council of Churches was formed, representing the six major Protestant denominations (Anglicans, Presbyterians, Wesleyans, Primitive Methodists, Baptists and Congregationalists). Similar councils were formed in the next decade in other colonies. Their chief task was to protect the Christian Sunday. Colonial legislatures did resist Protestant pressure to ban Sunday concerts, newspapers and public transport, but these concessions apart, the legislative brakes were kept on the secularisation of the sabbath until 1966.

Protestants were also eager for legislative restraints on the liquor industry. The Anglican rector Francis Bertie Boyce urged on the government the principle of 'local option', where residents could keep alcohol out of their community by a majority vote. This was actually achieved in 1882 in an act which also prohibited Sunday Trading. Temperance campaigners believed that giving women the vote would lead to strong antidrink legislation. In 1882 the Women's Christian Temperance Union, formed eight years earlier in the USA, began in Sydney. Among the Australian women associated with the Union who had worldwide renown was Bessie Harrison Lee (Cowie). Occasionally Australians and New Zealanders 'added value' to the messages of temperance, purity and women's rights which they imported from America, and not only exported them back to America, but ran ahead of Britain and the great majority of the American states in reforms such as women's suffrage.

Nowhere did the Protestants strive to defend a Christian country so much as in the matter of marriage. In 1886 the debate over the Divorce Extension Bill was at its height. The debate was over the appropriateness of making the Bible the basis of law. Sir Alfred Stephen, a devout Anglican and former chief justice of New South Wales, argued that Jesus's teaching in Matthew 5:31–2 was an ethical ideal, and that to impose it on all without consideration of specific circumstances was to lack compassion. Alfred Barry, Anglican bishop of Sydney, countered on the basis of Matthew 19:3–9 that marriage is a lifelong, indissoluble union, given to humanity at creation, and that it could be dissolved only by adultery. Many of his clergy and laity opposed Barry's stand on the indissolubility of marriage. In 1892 Stephen's Divorce Bill became law, and before the turn of the century civil divorce was legalised in every Australian colony.

Gender

Women's suffrage, divorce and temperance were all aspects of a deeper social movement, involving the domestication of the male and the feminisation of society. The churches were integral to this movement, as they were in Britain and America, but Australians responded to that involvement in a unique way. Two male types competed for ideological dominance in nineteenth-century Australia. One was the stereotypical bushman who drank copiously, gambled energetically and swore hard. In nineteenth-century Australia there was an observably high abuse of women and children by men who preferred to be with their mates on drinking binges, and the incidence of malnutrition among wives and children was also a serious social problem. The answer was 'Domestic Man'. He read the *Methodist*, and supported temperance, family and the church. The ideal of Domestic Man was consciously propagated by such organisations as the YMCA, which in the 1870s sought to extend 'home influence' to all the boys in the colonies.

Women won not only the vote. Aided by clergy and the demand of capitalism for a sober and industrious workforce, they also won the fight to domesticate their men. But it was a victory won at a price. The Christian moralisers were saddled with the label of 'wowser', by which was meant a hypocrite, a Wesleyan, a puritanical kill-joy. The term caught on like wild-fire. Catholics were never wowsers. True, they were just as puritanical as the Protestants over sex. But gambling and drinking were popular among Irish Catholics, who were as untroubled by their capacity to enjoy themselves as they were by their failure to achieve respectability in the eyes of their Protestant tormentors.

Australian Protestant males did not glory in being labelled 'wowsers'. They were keen to demonstrate that they had not been feminised. They spoke fervently of 'muscular Christianity' and were eager to endorse the popular male creed of 'mateship'. 'Mateship' was a genuinely indigenous, working-class creed championed by Henry Lawson, Australia's most famous poet. Said to be the creation of the bushman and the gold miner, it had one doctrine: that at all times and whatever the cost, a man should stick by his mate. Lawson argued that it distilled the essence of Christianity and was also the answer to the problems created in society by the bickering churches.

Nation building

In the last two decades of the nineteenth century, Australian workers sought to civilise capitalism, first by industrial power in unionism, and then by political power in the formation of the Labor Party. Christian values were foundational to both. W. G. Spence, the organiser of the enormous shearers and work-ers unions, was a Presbyterian elder as well as a preacher for the Primitive Methodists and the Bible Christians. A teetotaller and a leader in the temper-ance movement, he insisted that he was doing what Jesus would have him do for the downtrodden of society. He wrote in 1892: 'New Unionism was simply the teachings of that greatest of all social reformers, Him of Nazareth, whom all must revere.'[3]

With the spectacular failure of unionism in the Maritime Strike of 1890, the working man turned to politics, and in 1891 the New South Wales Labor Party was formed. The stereotype, that the Labor Party was formed as an ally of the Catholic Church, was fixed in the Protestant imagination and Catholic folklore very early in the Party's history. The evidence rather sug-gests that the Labor Party became strongly Catholic rather than started that way. The number of Catholics elected in the 1891 election to represent Labor is disputed: it was somewhere between three and five. In the 1894 election no Catholics were elected to represent Labor. There was no great

---

3 *The Worker*, 4 June 1892.

united Catholic vote which was just waiting to end the Protestant political ascendancy.

The truth is that the early Labor Party owed more to Protestant workers than to Catholic. In the inner suburbs of Sydney, the population did not consist mainly of the Catholic Irish working class, but of Protestants. Anglican and Primitive Methodist churches far outnumbered Catholic churches in Redfern, Darlington and Glebe. J. S. T. McGowen, who was to become New South Wales's first Labor premier, was an Anglican lay preacher and Sunday School superintendent at St Paul's Redfern, an evangelical stronghold under the Rev. Francis Bertie Boyce, the temperance campaigner. However, a disproportionate number of evangelical Protestant Labor politicians had difficulties with signing the pledge and felt compelled to leave the Labor Party by their very Protestant commitment to freedom of conscience. The ideal of the brotherhood of man, which they bequeathed to the Labor Party, was secularised.

The ambivalence which Australians felt about their experience of Christianity at the beginning of the twentieth century was nicely reflected in the debates over the constitution of the Australian Commonwealth enacted in 1901. The preamble speaks of 'humbly relying on the blessing of Almighty God', while section 116 affirms that there are to be no religious establishments and no religious tests for holding office. The majority of Australians wanted to 'recognise' the Deity, but, weary of sectarianism and allergic to establishments, they would not allow preference to any denomination. The great majority of Australians adhered to a Christian denomination, a sizeable minority attended church weekly, and most wanted their society and their children to be shaped by the teachings of Christ. But they were wary of entrusting either their souls or their civic life to the clergy.

Missionary expansion in the Pacific

The missionary impact

The explorations by Europeans, notably Captain James Cook, the Enlightenment view of the 'noble savage', and the growth of evangelical missionary interest in Britain all contributed to Protestant Christianity coming to the Pacific Islands at the end of the eighteenth century. The LMS sent its first missionaries to Tonga, Tahiti and the Marquesas, where they arrived in 1797. The Anglican evangelical Church Missionary Society (CMS) sent its first British missionaries to New Zealand in 1814. Both societies initially aimed at civilising and Christianising the indigenous populations. Samuel Marsden, Anglican chaplain in New South Wales, provided support for the LMS missionaries. He initiated, and supervised from Australia, the CMS work in New Zealand.

Early failures in Tonga and the Marquesas, opposition and apathy in Tahiti and New Zealand, questioned the missionaries' methodology and optimism. Missionary isolation and local hostility led to the withdrawal of some missionaries. While Pacific peoples at first welcomed missionaries to live among them, they saw them primarily as the bearers of European goods and as people to facilitate trade. The missionaries brought a message of sin and redemption, the need for conversion, the setting aside of Sunday as a holy day, the imposition of strict moral behaviour (which many other non-missionary Europeans by their lifestyle rejected) and an iconoclastic attitude towards indigenous culture, its symbols and rituals. For the local people, with a strong sense of community identity and belonging, the individual call to conversion which attempted to reproduce the missionaries' own religious experience was quite alien.

During the first fifteen years in Tahiti and New Zealand missionaries began to learn the local languages. Henry Nott in Tahiti and Thomas Kendall in New Zealand laid foundations for the translation of the Bible, Nott completing the Tahitian Bible in 1835. Tahitians from about 1815 and Maori after 1830 were intrigued by the process of reading and writing and attracted to the medium as well as to the Christian message. Literacy brought a new source of *mana* or power which communicated new ideas. Social, economic, political and cultural changes resulting from European and missionary influences had a profound influence on tribal societies in the Pacific. The missionary impact was caught up in the maelstrom which Pacific peoples faced. The effect of muskets on tribal warfare in New Zealand in the 1820s and the introduction of previously unknown European diseases resulting in high rates of death are examples of influences which created instability in traditional patterns of warfare, health and welfare.

The acceptability of the Christian message, after its initial rejection, was closely aligned with the internal power dynamics within Pacific societies. The Polynesian peoples living in the geographical triangle stretching from Hawaii in the north to Easter Island in the east and New Zealand in the south were chiefly societies in which birth and rank gave status. Powerful chiefs such as Pomare II in Tahiti, Kamehamaha II in Hawaii and, later, Tamati Waka Nene and Hone Heke in New Zealand, Malietoa in Samoa, Taufa'ahau in Tonga and Cakobau in Fiji were affected by Christianity and were among those who used it for their own political ends. The European principle of 'where the king, there the people' found expression in Polynesia as 'where the chief, there the people'. Evangelical missionaries were faced with tribal conversions or people movements which challenged their attempts to create Christian societies. In Tahiti and the surrounding islands the missionaries introduced law codes as one way of regulating and trying to encourage Christian behaviour. The emergence of leading chiefs who were associated with the missionaries as 'kings' in Tahiti, Hawaii and Tonga represented a Pacific missionary adaptation of monarchical government.

The relative homogeneity of culture, language and social structure in Polynesia facilitated the dispersion of Christianity. In contrast, Melanesia, with its hundreds of languages, complex geography, wide variety of social patterns and customs, and tropical diseases such as malaria, was more difficult to evangelise. Some missionaries, notably Robert Codrington and Charles Fox of the Melanesian Mission, George Brown and Lorimer Fison, both Methodists, and Maurice Leenhardt of the Paris Evangelical Missionary Society, made significant anthropological contributions to understanding the societies and people they worked among.

Indigenous agency and missionary support

The spread of Christianity throughout Polynesia was facilitated by indigenous agency and missionary support. Pacific islanders as they travelled to different islands spontaneously introduced Christianity. John Williams of the LMS, who arrived in Tahiti in 1817, moved to Raiatea where he trained native teachers. Two teachers were taken by Williams to Aitutaki in the Cook Islands in 1821, where they were very successful. In 1823 Papehia was left at Rarotonga, where he facilitated the rapid acceptance of Christianity. Williams left teachers in Samoa in 1830. Both in the Cook Islands and in Samoa, European missionaries joined these teachers in creating Christian communities. The acceptance of Christianity resulted in churches in which local ways were integrated with missionary values. Similar developments occurred in New Zealand, where Maori who had come into contact with the missionaries and their message acted, during the 1830s, as evangelists in areas hitherto unvisited by Europeans.

John Williams brought Polynesian missionaries to the New Hebrides (Vanuatu) but was killed at Erromanga in 1839. A generation later, hundreds of LMS and Methodist Polynesian islander missionaries volunteered and were brought to Melanesia, where some were killed and many died of disease. They lived with the local people, learnt their languages and were crucial in promoting the spread of Christianity. There are questions as to how far they were exploited by the European missionaries and their organisations. Some, such as Ruatoka, an LMS teacher in Papua, and Semisi Nau, a Methodist islander missionary in the Solomon Islands, were outstanding exemplars of dedication, persistence and fearlessness. Others, with only a rudimentary understanding of Christianity, could be domineering and as insensitive to local cultures as some of the European missionaries.

The contribution of missionary women, whether as wives, religious or missionaries, has received little attention in historical writing until recently. Their work, particularly among women, is increasingly recognised as a vital contribution to evangelisation in the Pacific. Indigenous women such as Kaahumanu in Hawaii, as well as the wives of indigenous missionaries, helped promote Christianity from within the Pacific women's world.

Comity and its limits

Protestant missionaries in the Pacific accepted the comity principle. The LMS expanded throughout eastern Polynesia to the Cook Islands, Samoa, Niue and Tuvalu. The American Board of Commissioners for Foreign Missions commenced work in Hawaii in 1820. Methodists worked in Tonga from 1822 and Fiji from 1835. Samoa was an exception to the comity principle, with both Methodist and LMS influences. Methodists began working in New Zealand in 1822. Presbyterians were involved in the southern islands of the New Hebrides from 1848, with support coming from Nova Scotia, Australia and New Zealand. G. A. Selwyn, Anglican bishop of New Zealand from 1841 to 1869, founded the unique Melanesian Mission in 1849. The Mission brought Melanesians, first to New Zealand, and from 1867 to Norfolk Island, for training with the hope that they would act as teachers and evangelists when they returned to their homes in the northern New Hebrides and Solomon Islands. J. C. Patteson was consecrated missionary bishop of Melanesia in 1861. The LMS began in New Caledonia in 1840 and in Papua in 1871. Methodists commenced in New Britain in 1875 under the notable leadership of George Brown, extending to Papua (1891) and the Solomon Islands (1902). Lutherans were involved in German New Guinea from 1886. Anglicans from Australia began in eastern Papua in 1891.

The comity principle did not operate between Protestants and Catholics, or among some independent missionary groups. Initial attempts by French Society of Mary (Marist) missionaries in the Solomon Islands (1845–7) and the New Hebrides (1847–50), and by French and Italians in Papua (1847–55), were aborted. With some exceptions, such as Wallis, Futuna and Bougainville, Catholics followed behind Protestant missionaries in establishing permanent work in the islands. Religious and national rivalries were caught up with colonial aspirations and conflict. French Picpus missionaries, from the Society of the Sacred Heart, made initial contact in the Gambiers (1834) and Tahiti (1836).

STUART PIGGIN AND ALLAN DAVIDSON

Marists made beginnings in Wallis and Futuna (1837), New Zealand (1838), Tonga (1842), New Caledonia (1843), Fiji (1844) and Samoa (1845). Permanent Catholic missions began in New Britain (1882), Papua (1885), the New Hebrides (1887) and the Solomon Islands (1898).

The Queensland Kanaka Mission, an independent Protestant mission founded by Florence Young, worked among Melanesian labourers in the Queensland sugar plantations. After Australia closed its doors to further labour traffic from the islands, the mission, renamed as the South Sea Evangelical Mission, began work on Malaita in the Solomon Islands in 1904. Seventh Day Adventists, who were active among descendants of the Bounty Mutineers and Tahitians on Pitcairn Island from 1886, and in Polynesia in the 1890s, commenced work in Papua (1908), the New Hebrides (1912) and the Solomon Islands (1914).

The colonial context

New Zealand became a British colony in 1840, with missionaries playing a crucial role in gaining the support of Maori chiefs for the Treaty of Waitangi which became the basis on which British government commenced. What became French Polynesia, the vast territory including the Marquesas and Tahiti, began as a French protectorate in 1842. British LMS and French Catholic missionaries were caught up in the colonial rivalry resulting in French intervention. In 1863 the Paris Evangelical Missionary Society took over from the LMS. British influence was extended throughout the nineteenth century over most of Polynesia and much of Melanesia. New Caledonia and the Loyalty Islands were French dependencies from 1853 and Wallis and Futuna were declared a protectorate in 1887. German commercial and missionary interests in New Guinea from 1884 to 1914, and the establishment of an Imperial Colony in Western Samoa between 1900 and 1914, ended with the occupation by Australians in New Guinea and New Zealand's military rule in Western Samoa at the beginning of World War I.

The ambiguous relationship between Christianity, commerce and colonisation was seen in different ways throughout the Pacific. The murder of Bishop Patteson in 1871 at Nukapu in the Solomon Islands probably resulted from the ruthless activities of labour traffickers recruiting young men for sugar plantations in Fiji. The establishment of the Western Pacific High Commission was a British response to Patteson's death and the perceived need to exercise control over the islands and British citizens operating in the area. The New Hebrides were contested by both French and British, with Protestant missionaries protesting loudly in the 1880s over French plans to send convicts there.

In 1906 the anomalous British-French Condominium was established over the New Hebrides. A British protectorate was established in the Solomon Islands in 1899.

The growth of the indigenous church

By 1914 missionary influence had spread throughout most regions of the South Pacific. The major exception was the New Guinea Highlands, which remained largely untouched by missionary effort until after World War II. In Polynesia Christianity had become part of the islanders' culture. European missionaries dominated the oversight of the church with a paternalistic approach and missionary societies still provided considerable funds to support them. The only independent church was the Free Church in Tonga, which under the leadership of the king, Taufa'ahau, and the premier and former Methodist minister Shirley Baker, broke away from the Australasian Church in 1885. This split gave rise to a remnant Wesleyan group led by J. E. Moulton which retained its Australasian links. The reunion of these two churches in 1924 gave rise to further schisms.

Large church buildings dominated villages and indigenous ministers were often given a semi-chiefly status. Local training institutions such as Takamoa, founded in Rarotonga in 1839, and Malua in Samoa in 1844, produced both indigenous ministers and missionaries. The Bible was available in most Polynesian languages by 1914. Hymns were usually translations of English favourites, although in the Cook Islands and Fiji they made use of traditional chant forms to tell biblical stories. Notable contributions were made in education ranging from Tupou College in Tonga, which reached high standards under J. E. Moulton, to village schools. Hospitals and health work, although often operating under considerable deficiencies, nevertheless filled a vacuum which colonial central hospitals could not meet.

In Melanesia the later arrival of missionaries and the complexity of the societies meant that Christianity was by 1914 still in the process of being accepted in many parts. The use of particular languages such as Mota in the Melanesian Mission, Motu by the LMS in Papua, Kuanua by Methodists in East New Britain, and Roviana by Methodists in the Western Solomon Islands, as a mission *lingua franca* alongside local languages, aided communication but meant that many people were hearing or reading about Christianity secondhand. The missionaries played an important role as agents of pacification. This was not without risks, as the rejection and murder of LMS missionaries James Chalmers and Oliver Tomkins and mission students at Goaribari in Papua in 1901 illustrates. At the beginning of the twentieth century some missionaries such as Charles Abel in Papua were involved in 'industrial missions', using boat-building, carpentry and coconut plantations as ways of providing training for local people in new skills to promote a wider form of human development than conversion. Selwyn and Patteson's hopes for the Melanesian Mission to promote an indigenous church were sidetracked as high imperialism from the 1880s and missionary paternalism reinforced European control.

Christianity in New Zealand

Settler influence and the Maori reaction

In New Zealand, more than elsewhere in the Pacific, missionary beginnings had to contend with the impact of European migration. The Maori mission-ary church from 1840 was increasingly alienated by the pressures brought by the settler society and its denominations. Selwyn attempted to provide Anglican episcopal oversight for both the Maori and colonial churches. The settler demand for land and Maori defence of their independence resulted in skirmishes in the 1840s, and in the 1860s a decade of war.

In the central North Island, in particular, the Maori rejection of missionary Christianity was seen in the emergence of indigenous movements combining traditional cultural elements and beliefs with biblical texts. Te Ua Haumene and Pai Marire or the Hauhau of the 1860s were dismissed with little understanding by many Pakeha (Europeans) as fanatical. Te Kooti was both a notable leader in guerrilla warfare at the end of the 1860s and the founder of what became the Ringatu church, which combined Maori and Christian values. Te Whiti and Tohu, based at Parihaka in Taranaki, from the 1870s used non-violent protest as a way of defending their land. Although arrested by the colonial government, they were not suppressed. Rua Kenana at the beginning of the twentieth cen-tury sought to give hope to his own people suffering from economic hardship and health problems, but he was unfairly imprisoned in 1915. Kingitanga, or the King movement, with both political and religious dimensions from 1858, united many Maori in the central North Island under the leadership of a Maori king. Much of the movement's inspiration came from the leadership of the notable Maori Christian chief Wiremu Tamihana Tarapipipi.

The Maori population reached its nadir in the 1890s. While independent Maori movements with their combined political and religious dimensions were important in providing leadership within the Maori world, Maori from the 1890s began embracing both the Pakeha and their own worlds as ways of promoting Maori cultural rejuvenation. Church schools for Maori were significant in encouraging this Maori renaissance. Te Aute College Students' Association, which became the Young Maori Party, influenced a generation of Maori leadership. Outstanding among its many leaders was Sir Apirana Ngata, a double graduate in law and arts, who became a member of parliament and an influential politician. An Anglican, Ngata was active in church affairs and worked tirelessly for his people and the renewal of Maori culture.

Denominational trajectories

The hopes of Henry Venn that the Anglican Maori church would become autonomous and independent under Maori leadership were undermined as the settler church became more dominant. Anglican settlers at first found themselves in an anomalous situation in New Zealand. Coming from an establishment context in England they had to adjust to a place in which no churches were established by law. Selwyn pioneered synodical government with his clergy in 1844 and 1847. After years of discussion Selwyn in 1857 called a constitutional convention which set up the church on the basis of a 'voluntary compact'. The constitution recognised 'fundamental provisions' which included the Book of Common Prayer. A general synod was constituted, which included all diocesan bishops, and established that representative clergy and laity from the dioceses should meet triennially. Dioceses under their own bishops held annual synods. For its time this was an innovative response to the needs of church government in a colonial society. Increasingly as the CMS missionaries aged and died out the Maori church was assimilated within the church structures. While Maori clergy were ordained from 1853 they were given little opportunity to exercise leadership within these structures, despite calls for a Maori bishop and representation.

The first Catholic missionaries and priests in New Zealand were Marists. Their important pioneering missionary work in the northern part of the country was undermined as a result of a dispute between Bishop Pompallier and the leader of their French order, Jean-Claude Colin. In 1850 Pompallier's diocese was divided and all the Marists were transferred to the new Wellington diocese under Bishop Philippe Viard. It was not until the 1880s that sustained Catholic work among Maori in the north resumed under the Mill Hill Fathers. Pompallier brought Sisters of Mercy from Ireland in 1850, the first of a number of women's religious orders. They made important contributions in the areas of education and social work. Outstanding among the women religious was Susanne Aubert, a Frenchwoman who initially worked in Auckland in the 1860s among Maori. She transferred to Hawkes Bay and then to the Wanganui River in 1883, where she set up her Daughters of our Lady of Compassion in 1892, and expanded to Wellington, undertaking notable work among children, the poor and 'incurables'. Her order gained papal recognition in 1917. Catholics, with their largely Irish origins and separate education system, cohered as a distinct minority, comprising on average 14 per cent of the population.

While Methodists began as a missionary church, from the 1850s they were increasingly absorbed by their work among the settler population. Missionary work among Maori suffered a severe setback during the wars of the 1860s and only slowly recovered in the following decades. Wesleyan, Free Church, Bible Christian and Primitive Methodists came to New Zealand, with the first three uniting in 1896 and the Primitives joining them in 1913 when the New Zealand Methodist Church gained its independence from the Australasian Conference. With some 10 per cent of the population, Methodists struggled to be an effective national church. A great deal of Methodist energy went into Sunday schools, where they attracted a larger proportion of the population than their constituency.

Presbyterians came to New Zealand as a settler church with their first resident minister, John Macfarlane from the Church of Scotland, arriving in Wellington in 1840. The settlement in Otago from 1848 was loosely connected with the Free Church created by the 1843 Disruption. Thomas Burns was the ordained leader of this group and together with William Cargill, the lay leader, sought to make a strong Scottish Presbyterian imprint on the society. The discovery of gold in the 1860s resulted in the influx of a very diverse population which finally put paid to the attempts to reproduce a Geneva of the South Seas. Presbyterian fissiparous tendencies reflected their Scottish origins. The attempt in 1862 to form a united church for the whole country foundered, with southern Presbyterians establishing a separate Synod of Otago and Southland in 1866. Divided by ethos, including conflict over the use of instrumental music in church worship, Presbyterians eventually achieved union in 1901. Presbyterian support for education was reflected in the foundation of Otago University in 1869. Presbyterians comprised up to 24 per cent of the population.

Smaller denominations such as Baptists, Brethren, Quakers and the Salvation Army added to the diverse denominationalism in colonial New Zealand. Catholic and Protestant bigotry reinforced sectarianism, particularly around the issue of universal primary education. In 1877 the government decided in favour of secular primary education, largely because of the sectarian spirit. Catholics vehemently objected to supporting state-funded education while having to support their own schools. Protestants worked unsuccessfully to introduce religious education into the state system. Voluntary efforts by churches in Sunday schools and youth work consequently absorbed increasing denominational energy.

Church, society and nation

As in Australia, evangelical churches strenuously campaigned in favour of prohibition, winning limited victories from the 1880s. The working class, alienated by the anti-alcohol attitudes, was mostly absent from active church membership. The Women's Christian Temperance Union was a formidable political force, achieving votes for women in 1893. Feminism, however, was difficult to sustain in colonial New Zealand and the country did not have its first woman member of parliament until 1933. Churches largely reflected their British and Irish origins in worship, architecture, organisation and ministry. The churches were active in benevolent and social work, but only a few individuals took prophetic leads over the dispossession of the Maori and the inequalities resulting from economic disparity. New Zealand's national identity was created out of its heterogeneous migrant origins, with British links remaining particularly significant. New Zealand's participation in the South African War and World War I were important markers of that identity, with churches reinforcing loyalty to God, Crown and Empire.

In just over one century the Pacific had moved from being without any Christian presence to being evangelised throughout Polynesia and New Zealand, with significant beginnings in Melanesia. European settlers brought with them to Australasia their various forms of Christianity. The sense of discontinuity between their northern origins and the southern hemisphere where the seasonal calendar was turned upside down found little creative response in church life or theology. The indigenous movements in New Zealand were better at adapting Christianity to their own needs and context. Both European missionaries and the emerging settler churches largely reflected the worlds from which they came.

34

Missions and empire, c.1873–1914

ANDREW PORTER

New directions in missionary strategy

'Christianity, commerce and civilisation': it was shown in chapter 27 above that no phrase encapsulated more pithily the fundamental dynamism which mid-nineteenth-century Christians believed underpinned the expansion of their faith overseas.[1] Nowhere was there a more pointed indication of the inde-terminate relationship that existed between empires and the global spread of missionary enterprise, two of the most important agencies both for transmit-ting and for shaping the Christian message. The connections between 'the three C's' highlighted for contemporaries both the essential framework of an expanding system of evangelisation and the ecclesiastical consequences of Christians' commitment to their obligation to spread the Word. The preaching of Christianity in tandem with the encouragement of a humane and liberal commerce was held to foster a genuinely Christian civilisation. Modelled on the developing capitalist economies of the western world, that civilisation, as it too prospered, would also develop its own churches. These were expected to become self-financing, then self-governing, and, after the emergence of suffi-cient local clergy and evangelists, self-propagating. At that point the missions' specific local task was complete, and missionaries could be released to work in fresh, hitherto unevangelised fields.

Although the most influential contributions to the exposition and popu-larisation of this missionary strategy were those of Henry Venn of the CMS and David Livingstone of the LMS, this, as was emphasised in chapter 27, was far from being a purely British perspective on missions.[2] It was at once widespread and long-lasting: Roman Catholic as well as North American Protestant missions spurred on by Rufus Anderson at the American Board of Commissioners for Foreign Missions in Boston also developed their thinking

---

1 See above, pp. 449–54.
2 See above, pp. 453–4.

along similar lines.[3] Conventional outlooks none the less invite challenge, especially when theory and practical reality diverge. In the 1860s Venn's and Livingstone's ideas had begun to encounter serious obstacles. With Anglican and Protestant achievements fewer than expected, and recruits and finances falling away, missionary enterprise in the 1870s began to move in new directions under pressure from new theologies and spiritualities. Venn's death in 1872 and Livingstone's the next year heralded a major reorientation of much evangelistic thought and practice. Catholic missions – whether new foundations like the White Fathers, or older ones beginning to recover their former vigour, such as the Société des Missions Etrangères – were equally anxious to explore new approaches.

Criticisms stemmed in the 1860s and increasingly in the 1880s and 1890s from the sense that mission funds were bringing a poor return. Church and chapel building, missionary housing, schools, teachers and medical missionaries, printing presses, and expanding administration required by insatiable fund-raising and geographical extension, were all attacked as wasting money. Income, it was alleged, would be far better spent on missionaries in the field, devoting themselves almost exclusively to evangelistic vernacular preaching, stripping away the western cultural wrapping that threatened to suffocate 'true' religion. Dean Stanley, addressing 'the ends and means of Christian Missions' in a sermon in 1873, reminded his congregation that 'In these days – when there is so much temptation to dwell on the scaffolding, the apparatus, the organization of religion, as though it were religion itself – it is doubly necessary to bear in mind what true Religion is.'[4]

Following the model of J. Hudson Taylor's China Inland Mission, established in 1865, there thus emerged various plans for missions with lean administrations, simply vetting candidates and receiving and transmitting donations to the field. All decisions about expenditure and strategy were delegated to a head of the mission on the spot. All missionaries were required to identify themselves as completely as possible with the ways of living characteristic of local peoples. For success, no more was required than a vivid faith, economy of means, and complete trust in divine provision. It was a vision, in part romantic, that appealed strongly to the increasing number of those touched by prophetical study and premillennial thinking, with its urgency in anticipating an imminent Second Coming.

---

3 Coulon and Brasseur, *Libermann*; Harris, *Nothing but Christ*.
4 F. Max Müller, *On missions: a lecture delivered in Westminster Abbey on December 3, 1873. With an introductory sermon by Arthur Penrhyn Stanley, Dean of Westminster* (London, 1873), pp. 7–8.

The pull of China was strong, and by the 1890s the CIM was the second largest of all British missions.[5] Not only was there the challenge presented by 'China's Millions', as the founder of the CIM called his newspaper. The limited European presence, and the remoteness especially of its inland provinces from western influences, were felt to be major attractions and advantages for the evangelist. Africa provided another arena for the proliferation of the 'faith missions' anxious to distance themselves from the corruptions of western settlement and empire. There, Livingstone, despite his identification with commerce and Christianity, had directed attention no less than the CIM to the 'regions beyond' by his constant travelling, notably in the Congo basin and central Africa. His style of exploration, his evangelism and his dislike of denominationalism reveal many parallels with the practice of the faith missions. The first such African venture – the Livingstone Inland Mission – was launched in 1878, with others such as the Sudan Interior Mission, the North African Mission and the Congo Balolo Mission following in the next two decades.

These missions were also propelled by the potent revivalism associated from 1875 onwards with the Keswick Conventions. Evangelical dissatisfaction with the conventional missionary societies' level of achievement opened the way for a fresh wave of North American revivalist activity, beginning with Dwight Moody and Ira Sankey's mission to Britain in 1874–5, and given new impetus by W. E. Boardman and Robert and Hannah Pearsall Smith. The interdenominational, annual Keswick gatherings were its fruit. Keswick's concern with 'the Promotion of Practical Holiness', the attainment of a 'Higher Life' through 'deliverance from the power of besetting sin', proved immensely powerful in awakening widespread missionary enthusiasm, notably among public school and university students.[6] Parallel movements began in the 1880s in North America. Spurred on by the white-hot evangelism of Arthur Tappan Pierson and a core of enthusiastic college helpers, displaying the same dissatisfaction with conventional missionary methods and an anticipation of the millennium, the Student Volunteer Movement, with its watchword 'the evangelisation of the world in this generation', was soon a major force, not only recruiting vigorously but extending its network of contacts and its influence within existing missionary bodies on both sides of the Atlantic.[7]

5 There were some 10,000 British missionaries by 1900; the CMS totalled 1,238, the CIM 811.

6 C. F. Harford (ed.), *The Keswick Convention: its message, its method and its men* (London: Marshall Bros, 1907), pp. 5–6; Porter, 'Cambridge, Keswick', pp. 5–34; Bebbington, *Holiness in nineteenth-century England*, ch. 4, 'The Keswick tradition'.

7 Robert, *Occupy until I come*.

Such currents of enthusiasm posed varying degrees of difficulty for older, more traditional missionary societies. Running counter to the latter's centralised, administratively disciplined organisation, they nevertheless drew on enormous reservoirs of faith and commitment. It was thought that failure to tap these new reserves would only see them drained away into less orthodox channels such as the CIM and its imitators or the Salvation Army. Thus the CMS, for example, went so far as to adopt missionary bands sharing the inspiration of the faith missions, such as the Eastern Africa Equatorial Mission (1885) and the New Interior Mission to mid-China (1891). All societies opened their doors to recruits steeped in the new spirituality, continental European Protestants no less than British. Some European initiatives in China were directly linked to the CIM, which had German and Finnish affiliates by the 1890s; others – by Swedes in 1882 or the Friedenshorst Deaconess Mission of 1912 – were independent but acknowledged CIM inspiration.[8]

Sometimes these adjustments could have disastrous results, especially when reforming zeal went together with uncompromising insistence on the new standards by which the reality of professed Christianity and the evidence of conversion were to be assessed. Methodists and Baptists at Lagos, for example, were torn apart in the 1880s, and the CMS was faced with the destructive Niger Crisis in 1890. Elsewhere, however, evidence of conversion meetings, personal experience of salvation, and a revived local missionary commitment all testified to Keswick's positive influence.[9]

Catholic missions offer few close parallels with the new Protestant radicalism, beyond advocating a general reserve towards secular western culture. Most were preoccupied with the clerical management and control of their affairs in the field, in the face of powerful competition from Rome and the *Propaganda Fide*, throughout this period in a markedly authoritarian or Ultramontanist mood, and from European governments, vigorously anticlerical in the case of the French or, like Portugal, anxious to reassert ancient patronage rights over the church. The self-contained Christian villages or '*chrétientés*', initially adopted by Catholic missions everywhere from Senegal to Saigon until the 1890s, were a source of security in more ways than one. In the Punjab by 1916 some 12,000 Roman Catholics were grouped in families in Christian villages of various sizes.

---

8 Latourette, *A history of Christian missions in China*, pp. 392–3, 596.
9 Webster, *The African churches among the Yoruba*; CMS archives, University of Birmingham, G3/A5/L3–4 Letterbooks, and G3/A5 In-Letters; Porter, 'Cambridge, Keswick', pp. 5–34.

The combination of eschatological concern with conviction that Christian missions needed to explore new directions was also instrumental in revitalising Protestant attention to Islam. A growing sense that Islam had for some time been neglected at Christianity's expense surfaced in the 1870s, just as Reginald Bosworth Smith wrote of Mohammedanism in Africa as 'spreading itself by giant strides almost year by year'.[10] European concern with North Africa, especially following the Ottoman crisis of 1875–8 and Britain's occupation of Egypt in 1882, the entrenchment of the Mahdist state in the Sudan (1885–98), and evidence of mounting Arab nationalism, provided a background to the evangelical persuasion that Islamic resurgence was to be interpreted as one amongst the major 'signs of the times'. Anglican opinion was particularly alive to the problem. CMS conferences in Allahabad (1873) and London (1875), and ensuing discussions, mapped out strategies for moving against Islam from Sierra Leone, the western Sudan, the Niger valley, the Punjab, Aden and Cairo (where the CMS re-established itself in 1882). General Charles Gordon's death at Khartoum in 1885, and analogies such as that drawn by Douglas Thornton – 'the Arabic language is read by as many people as Chinese' – only intensified a widespread concern.[11] Protestant and Catholic interests also came closest in their common concern to combat Islam. New Roman Catholic missions, for example those of Daniel Comboni and Cardinal Lavigerie, built outwards from bases in Africa itself – Cairo, Algiers and Carthage – their sights fixed on the Nile, the western and eastern Sudan, and eventually East Africa.

Ambiguous relationships with empire

Widely shared perceptions of the need for the reform and revival of mission societies and their members' activities or Christian standards in the field if Christianity was to expand, often led to an insistence on the separation of evangelisation and the essentials of the faith from empire and western culture. However, this path was neither possible nor appealing to all missions. The Anglo-Catholic Universities' Mission to Central Africa trod a very different road, combining insistence on episcopal and clerical authority with the Catholic emphasis on poverty, in the construction of an entirely new mission. Facing many problems in the mid-century, Scottish missions were no more immune than others to demands that they rethink the means of Christianity's

---

10 R. Bosworth Smith, *Mohammed and the Mohammedans* (London: Smith, Elder, 1874), pp. 31–2.
11 W. H. T. Gairdner, *Douglas Thornton: a study in missionary ideals and methods*, 3rd edn (London: Hodder and Stoughton, 1909), p. 95.

diffusion overseas. With other societies, falling receipts and deep divisions over strategy resulted in the gradual adaptation of the two great means to the propagation of Christianity established by their leading lights, Alexander and David Livingstone, rather than any radical, one-sided reform.

In India the Duff tradition of depending for Christianity's diffusion on higher education in the English language provoked mounting reservations, especially among Christians at home where vernacular preaching was far more favoured. 'I am not sure that the farther young men advance in literature and science they are led nearer to Christ', wrote the convenor of the Church of Scotland's Foreign Missions Committee.[12] However, by the 1890s, the way forward was found not in the abolition of colleges but in the leaven of compromise – in William Milner's words, 'more evangelistic work alongside our Education institutions'.[13] Other missionaries found in themselves vocations of a newer and different order: as medical missionaries, considering their 'work to be of distinct value as a means of presenting the pitifulness of the Christian religion', or in wielding 'the grand lever' for the Christian transformation of Hindu society as vernacular evangelists to the 'pariahs' (outcastes or dalits).[14] They were encouraged as far as funds would allow.

Adaptation of the Livingstone tradition was both perhaps more complete than that of Duff and certainly no less fraught, proceeding as it did in the context of Africa's late nineteenth-century partition among the European colonial powers. Both the Free Church and the established Church of Scotland only slowly and reluctantly reworked the 'commerce and Christianity' formula. The new stations of Livingstone and Blantyre, established in 1876 in what later became Nyasaland (Malawi), owed more in conception to the secure, self-supporting and independent settlement of Lovedale in the eastern Cape Colony, perhaps even to Moravian examples, than to David Livingstone's own general planning and foot-loose antislavery rhetoric. Such trade as the Scottish missions managed to encourage did not flourish and was controlled not by Africans but by the Glaswegians of the African Lakes Company. The education they provided proved of little value outside the mission stations themselves. Not until the end of the century did the situation change, with the establishment of white settler-run plantations and a measure of British administration.

---

12 J. C. Heardman to J. Wilson, 6 March 1878, National Library of Scotland, MS/7534, f. 98.
13 W. Milner to G. Smith (Secretary to the FMC, FCS), 24 April 1883, National Library of Scotland, MS/7838, f. 79.
14 A. Alexander to G. Smith, 27 Feb. 1884, National Library of Scotland, MS/7845, ff. 1–2; G. Peattie to Prof. T. Lindsay, 30 March 1893, MS/7846, f. 251.

Conditions in many parts of east and central Africa were unstable and insecure. The Scots in Nyasaland faced constant disruption from slave raiding and local warfare, as well as the activities of the Portuguese and, after 1888, Cecil Rhodes's British South Africa Company. Lacking the power to control wider events, they turned instead to the British government to secure the conditions in which Christianity could be promoted. Instructions to the Blantyre missionaries – 'You must always keep in view the fact that you are labouring to found and build up a Christian Church, and not laying the foundations of a British Colony or of a small State'[15] – sounded increasingly hollow.

This situation was widely replicated during the partition of Africa. Missions haunted the corridors of the international conferences in Berlin (1884–5) and Brussels (1890), and their respective ministries of foreign affairs. Immediate goals were often temporarily defined in starkly secular terms: 'we should have the backing of all who have sunk capital or life or labour in our part of Africa. Our object should be the limitation of Portugal . . . to the river Ruo, and a 3 per cent tariff.'[16] Alliances of convenience for a time brought many societies not only rapprochement with secular business and wary officialdom, but access on the ground and political weight – in Buganda, the Congo basin, 'Rhodesia' (Ndebeleland and Mashonaland), Asante and Yorubaland. On the one hand the Methodist Dennis Kemp declared his 'firm conviction that the British Army and Navy are today used by God for the accomplishment of His purposes'.[17] On the other, where previously he had found missionaries exceedingly tiresome, Harry Johnston (the one-time British Commissioner for Central Africa) praised missions for doing government's work for them. 'As their immediate object is not profit, they can afford to reside at places till they become profitable. They strengthen our hold over the country, they spread the use of the English language, they induct the natives into the best kind of civilization and in fact each mission station is an essay in colonization.'[18]

Neither in Africa nor in other parts of the world was this situation to last. French missions were prepared on occasion to welcome their government's backing, where it might bring them secure access and keep Protestant heretics at bay, as in the Franco-Vietnamese Treaty of 1874. However, they were normally very reluctant to call on state aid, given its persistently anticlerical

---

15 Hanna, *The beginnings of Nyasaland*, p. 41.
16 J. M. McMurtrie to A. Hetherwick, 22 Dec. 1886, and to J. Rankin, 23 Dec. 1886, National Library of Scotland, MS/7534, ff. 270, 273.
17 D. Kemp, *Nine years at the Gold Coast* (London: Macmillan, 1898), pp. 194, 232–4, 256.
18 Oliver, *Sir Harry Johnston*, p. 182.

character in response both to domestic republican needs as well as to those of colonial officials. Relations between Catholic bishops and missionaries during the French conquest of Indochina were for the most part very fraught behind a superficial and frequently ruptured façade of shared national identity.[19] As the missionary sense of self-sufficiency recovered, so in their eyes officials' stock fell. The limited expediency of empire and political involvement was recognised anew as secular empire builders settled in and missionary enterprise became everywhere once more a necessary object for official regulation. Where the priorities of evangelisation had for a while demanded imperial protection, by the early 1900s they had begun to welcome a renewed separation of missions and empire.

The Muslim world retained a dual configuration. Much of it, distanced from Christianity and western influence, continued to attract those sharing the outlook of the 'faith missions'; no less vast areas subject to British rule also created particular obligations to foster Christianity. In India, J. N. Farquhar, the YMCA National Student Secretary for India and Ceylon, saw in the political and educational dimensions of Islamic revival openings for Christian missions; on a world scale he shared the contemporary concern with 'the Mohammedan problem'.[20] However, missions' dramatic urgency, spiced as it often still was with premillennial speculation, alienated governments of all kinds. In India the traditional insistence on religious neutrality was upheld. In the Sudan, Christian teaching and preaching were severely restricted under British rule, Lord Cromer (Britain's long-serving Consul General in Cairo) admitting the excellence of missionary intentions but emphasising their defective judgement. 'They will, if under some control, probably do much good on a small scale.'[21] British representatives in Nigeria and the western Sudan thought and acted similarly.

In China too, where evangelism was equally liable to provoke hostile reactions, European official support increasingly fell short of most missionaries' expectations. Missions' insistence on their treaty rights, their political involvements in defence of church members, their property dealing, and ill-informed tangling with kinship, lineage and village conflicts, created minefields that officials were keen to skirt. The mixture of governments' unwillingness to pursue missionary questions with ill-chosen interventions notably by French

---

19 Tuck, *French Catholic missionaries*.
20 Farquhar to J. R. Mott, 15 April 1909, Mott Papers 45/29/521, Yale University Divinity School Library.
21 Lord Cromer (Evelyn Baring), *Modern Egypt*, 2 vols. (London: Macmillan, 1909), vol. 1, p. 234.

and German authorities on behalf of their own nationals contributed greatly to the Boxer Uprising in 1899–1901. The large number of missionaries killed in that upheaval – some fifty Catholics and 135 Protestants with fifty-three of their children – indicated the wisdom of official caution.

Even in territories where European imperial control was more secure, missionaries and officials distanced themselves from each other. The White Fathers in Tanganyika were only able to protect themselves against the German authorities by extending their recruitment to German Catholics. Competitive Christianity often fell foul of attempts on all sides to impose denominational spheres of influence or 'comity' agreements. Originally desired by officials anxious to preserve decorum and amity within small white communities and 'prestige' in the eyes of indigenous outsiders, they frequently proved unworkable even when Protestants alone were involved.[22] In many colonial territories, governments had long provided funds to assist missionary schools, clinics and even hospitals. These too, especially schools, were fruitful sources of dispute between missions and governments. Missionaries of all denominations intent on securing a place for Christianity in the curriculum clashed with officials concerned to preserve their religious neutrality and 'standards' in secular education, not least when the consequences involved British government support for Catholic schools at Protestant expense.

Talk of problems to be faced, the complexity of missionary adaptation and the variability of mission statistics could none the less not disguise the fact that expansion was almost everywhere the order of the day and missionary societies were multiplying. By 1914, more than 10 per cent of India's 5,465 Protestant missionaries were drawn from continental Europe, chiefly from the Basel, Gossner and Leipzig missions but also including Swedes, Danes and Norwegians. The variety of national background among India's some 4,000 Catholic missionaries was even greater. Southern Africa's Protestant missionary numbers grew with the efforts of the Hermannsburg Mission and the Missions des Eglises Libre de la Suisse Romande. In China, the Scheutveld Fathers drew on Dutch and Belgium recruits, and whether counted as adherents, baptised church members or communicants, Christian numbers increased. Baptised Catholics, for example, rose from 383,000 (1870) to 1.43 million (1912); Chinese Catholic priests grew from 371 in 1890 to 721 in 1912.[23] These international connections were further tightened by the notable tendency of European migrants to North America to add their own missionary efforts to those

22 Cooke, 'The Roman Catholic mission in Calabar', pp. 89–98.
23 Latourette, *History of the expansion of Christianity*, vol. v, pp. 364–70, vol. vi, pp. 157, 179–86, 269–75, 293, 356.

of their new home. Continental European backgrounds to missions from the United States were particularly strong in the North American Lutheran churches.

The personnel of the missionary movement

Missions not only had to decide where and how to promote knowledge of Christianity, but had to find those best able to continue building up the churches and to continue the work once Europe's missionaries had moved on. This was in part a metropolitan task, but also an international one and, above all, one that involved local indigenous people. The need for missionary volunteers and supporting finance prompted two major developments in this period. The first lay in the recruitment of women, first in fund-raising and administration, and increasingly as young single women for the mission field. Among the Protestant missions, women constituted a majority of their workforce by about 1900,[24] but their deployment was no less a Roman Catholic and continental European phenomenon. Sisterhoods and female orders proliferated, such as the Sisterhood of the Holy Heart of Mary, the Irish Congregation of St Joseph of Cluny and the Belgian Congregation of the Immaculate Heart of Mary. Anglo-Catholic communities and sisterhoods followed, such as St Hilda's in Lahore (1880s) and the Sacred Passion in Zanzibar (1910), open to local as well as European women. For the historian this raises important questions, so far insufficiently examined and male superintendence notwithstanding, as to the relation of gender to the variants of the Christian message imparted. These touch on issues such as widowhood, marriage, celibacy and the nature of Christian family life. Occupational patterns among missionaries also changed with the increase in numbers of salaried females. Women were concentrated in teaching, domestic training and health care. In countries such as India they played a crucial role in everything to do with women and children, especially in the 'zenanas' or enclosed domestic quarters of the higher castes, 'regions beyond' inaccessible to male missionaries.[25]

It is especially striking how the growth in numbers of women missionaries was closely tied after 1870 not only to the involvement of missions in healing and welfare, but to the general professionalisation of missionary vocations. There had long been a place for medicine in the mission field, but its priority reflected primarily missionaries' need for self-preservation. David

---

24 Maughan, 'Regions beyond and the national church', p. 364.
25 Robert, *American women in mission*.

Livingstone's medicine chest was not principally designed as the foundation of a new missionary strategy. Treatment of local people was an incidental expression of Christian benevolence, and along with some of his contemporaries Livingstone was equally keen to learn of efficacious African remedies. Missionaries with medical skills were welcome, but medical missionaries were only systematically recruited from the late 1870s, and even then in small numbers. The slow expansion of roles for women in medical practice at home, and the foundation of bodies such as the Delhi Female Medical Mission (1867) and the London School of Medicine for Women (1874), prompted more and more women to combine missionary roles and medical qualifications. By 1909 one tenth of the American women's missionary movement – 147 doctors and 91 trained nurses – was engaged in medical missions and training. Medical missions perhaps held a vital key above all to the Christianisation of Asia. By 1900, of 258 women on the British Medical Register, 72 were serving as medical missionaries; in India 'the total number of qualified medical missionaries, from Britain and elsewhere . . . stood at 169: 88 women and 81 men'.[26] There were many more with lesser degrees of expertise elsewhere.

Recruitment of women overlapped with that other burgeoning constituency for recruits provided by the universities, theological training colleges and seminaries. The enormous late-century increase in missionary volunteers came overwhelmingly from these institutions. Women and university students, attracted in large numbers to conferences such as Keswick and Mildmay and, in the United States, Northfield and Niagara, not only fuelled each other's enthusiasm but constituted the bedrock of the expanding international student movement. The Student Volunteer Movement and the British Student Volunteer Missionary Union, together with the World Student Christian Federation and the YMCA/YWCA, recruited internationally. While not missionary societies as such, from Sapporo to San Francisco they publicised the global need for Christian missionaries in pursuit of the SVM's own slogan, 'the evangelisation of the world in this generation'. At a time when colonial powers, especially the Germans, French and Belgians, were demonstrating strong preferences for missionaries of their own nationality, the SVM powerfully reinforced the ecumenical and international character of the missionary movement. International conferences culminating in the World Missionary Conference at Edinburgh (1910), regional gatherings such as the all-India decennial meetings, and those devoted to the Muslim world at Cairo (1906) and Lucknow (1911), strengthened both the missionary

---

26 *Ibid.*, p. 162; Fitzgerald, 'A "peculiar and exceptional measure"', p. 195.

movement's self-reliance and its self-sufficient independence of imperial structures.

Religious revival, new sources of missionary volunteers and finance, international solidarity, the more proficient practical and theological training of missionaries noticeable by 1914, the patterns of missionary–government relations and the exploitation of new geographical fields, all assisted the process of evangelisation. None, however, could reduce the centrality for both missions and church building of indigenous evangelists, active church members and local church leaders. It is rapidly becoming recognised as a truism that Africans have always heard the gospel principally from other Africans. Almost certainly the same has been true for other peoples. This gives the instruction, encouragement and promotion of successive generations of local Christians a peculiar importance.

Indigenous missionaries were, like converts, drawn from many different walks of life, but often too from among the poor, the unfortunate and the dispossessed who made up very large proportions of Christian communities outside Europe and the north Atlantic world. Hence the enormously wide range represented by figures such as the former Hindu apologist and rationalist Nehemiah Goreh (1825–85); Pandita Ramabai Sarasvati (1858–1922), scholar, Hindu social reformer, baptised by Anglo-Catholics and turning late in life to a Keswick-style Christianity; the Xhosa William Koyi (1846–88) who went as a pupil from Lovedale to Blantyre to work with the Ngoni from 1876 to 1888; the numerous African agents of the CMS Yoruba mission who sustained the church through the crises of the 1890s; and the Bugandan catechists spreading the gospel in western Kenya. Goreh and Ramabai were highly educated Brahmans, belonging to those elite groups whose members had often taken Christianity seriously, either on the route to personal conversion or as reformers of their own religious traditions. Men such as Koyi, and still more the large numbers of Punjabi Bible women, often the wives of local catechists, were at once no less remarkable and more numerous. All but illiterate and with few manual skills at the age of twenty-five when he first reached Lovedale in 1871, William Koyi none the less impressed James Stewart and made steady headway in classes, such that his offer as an evangelist in 1876 was accepted. At Blantyre he continued to impress Europeans and his African contemporaries with his steady character, organisational gifts, and ability as an interpreter to cultivate lasting Ngoni respect for the mission.[27] Similarly placed was Thomas Johnson on the Niger. A shoemaker with no formal education, he nevertheless became

---

27 On Koyi, see Thompson, *Touching the heart*.

schoolmaster first at Akassa and then at Brass, where in 1878, after nearly two decades, Bishop Crowther wrote of him 'working single-handed . . . with the assistance of his zealous wife'.[28] Modest tasks such as preliminary religious instruction, a painstaking persistence in conveying a Christian frame of reference and sense of community or purpose through visits to the sick and elderly, and a dependable pastoral presence, were all essential contributions made by ordinary Christians to the process of early church growth.

Race, religion and ecumenism

However, talent, dedication and acceptability to local peoples, even 'true religion', were not necessarily enough for agents to overcome the barriers to indigenous advancement and church leadership. In this 'high imperial age', belief in the universality of human nature and the direct relevance of Christianity's message to all mankind survived intact to a greater extent among missionaries than elsewhere. Nevertheless, operating in a world where belief in innate racial distinctions and a hierarchy of cultures determined by race was widespread, where Christianity's fundamental egalitarianism was increasingly mocked and ethnicity was commonly seen to set limits to individual capacity, subjected missions to uncomfortable compromises.[29] Where 'race' was woven into the justifications for empire and subordination, the goal of an indigenous-led Christian church was liable to be widely seen as an eccentric rejection of 'the white man's burden'. Evangelical Christianity neither necessarily nor completely immunised missionary activists against the conventional wisdom.

'Race' was nevertheless not the only calculus that was used to shape Christianity's translation, expansion and institutionalisation. Missionaries were often amazed and outraged at 'the barbarous colour madness of many of [their] fellow-countrymen', astounded and saddened by 'the unspeakable want of knowledge, injustice, rapid self contradictions, [and] ungrounded assertions' concerning Africans and other non-Europeans.[30] Notably in central and southern Africa the SPG, Scottish Presbyterians and Wesleyans showed how missionaries agonised over the choice between separate churches where indigenous leaders could most easily emerge, and colour-blind churches where whites would none the less rule the roost. In debates over indigenous

---

28 Tasie, *Christian missionary enterprise*, p. 60.
29 Stanley, 'Church, state, and the hierarchy of "civilisation"'.
30 S. T. Pruen to R. Lang, 30 June 1886, CMS Archives G3/A5, f. 220; J. Wells, *The life of James Stewart*, 4th edn (London: Hodder and Stoughton, 1909), pp. 283–4.

advancement in a world of limited resources which made hard choices unavoidable, missionaries were only too well aware that to educate and advance small numbers to the priesthood, or instead to bring on larger numbers of evangelists, might both be seen by Africans as racially discriminatory courses of action. As the consecration of V. S. Azariah, the first Indian Anglican bishop, in 1912 demonstrated, promotions within the church unavoidably raised awkward questions of Christians' status and acceptability in the eyes of other indigenous but non-Christian social or political parties.

Among the seemingly endless examples of friction in the relations between missions and local churches or individual Christians after 1880, the most far-reaching was that on the Niger in West Africa which culminated in 1891 with the enforced retirement and death of Bishop Samuel Ajayi Crowther. Many of the day-to-day details – accusations of missionary paternalism or racism, the corruption or unacceptable worldliness of 'native agents', the failure of indigenous authority to discipline the church, financial disputes and irregularities, sexual misdemeanours and insobriety – were duplicated in other fields irrespective of denomination. The chief significance of this serious crisis lay in the destruction for the time being of the CMS's central vision, implemented in West Africa in 1864, of an indigenous church and its mission under indigenous episcopal leadership. This upheaval occurred in circumstances of extreme bitterness, in which racial disputes, the new Keswick spirituality, conflicting visions of the future church and eschatological speculation combined to undermine faith in indigenous leadership far beyond the Niger and to exclude the appointment of another African bishop to an Anglican diocese until 1951. The Roman Catholic Holy Ghost Fathers in Nigeria agreed with Crowther's critics as to the mistaken policy of undue reliance on African catechists. At a time, however, when the development of an indigenous clergy was ever more necessary, events such as those on the Niger held it back, by serving everywhere to reinforce foreign missionaries' notions of hierarchy and their insistence on 'standards' in rigorous clerical training and lay instruction.

The consequences of such debates, still more of intolerance and misjudged decisions, overcautiousness and pusillanimity on the part of many missionaries, were often far-reaching. Especially in Africa they resulted in divided congregations, schisms, and, as a result of indigenous initiatives, the emergence of separate or independent churches, some of them moulding western forms of Christian belief and ritual to their own tastes, others rooting themselves firmly in traditional religious practice.[31] Crises notwithstanding, divisions both

31 See chapter 35 below.

within and between the missions and the mission churches thus failed to curb the vitality of indigenous Christianity. They also provoked fresh reflections on the future of Christianity and the direction of the missionary enterprise. Putting the Niger conflicts behind them, many were inclined on entering the new century to agree with J. N. Farquhar in reasserting for a fresh generation that priority lay with the global challenge to Christianity posed by 'two problems . . . beyond all others, the Oriental problem and the Mohammedan problem', brought to the fore by 'the explosive processes of Western thought' operating on Asia.[32] It was in part to address these problems that the World Missionary Conference of 1910 was mounted in Edinburgh.

The Edinburgh conference was one of several contemporary developments emphasising the missionary movement's shared preoccupations and interest in common solutions. This ecumenical slant, signalled in the conference's pronounced interdenominational character, was no less evident in the constitution of the Presbyterian Church in India in 1904, and the formation in 1908 of the South India United Church. At the Kikuyu Conference of 1913, East African missionaries sounded similar notes in their discussions of ecclesiastical polity, common baptismal procedures and intercommunion. However, the World Missionary Conference represented far more than the closing of Protestant ranks detected by those fearful for their ecclesiastical or denominational identity. More than any previous general conference, such as those at London in 1888 and New York in 1900, in the Report of its Commission IV Edinburgh addressed the question of what Christians could learn from other religions. To know what was 'really alive in the non-Christian religions', 'what had the power of keeping men back from Christ, or of preparing the way for faith in him', had implications for Christian theologians as well as missionaries. In particular Islam, notwithstanding its legalistic character, had grasped truths vital to all religion in its stress on the unity of God. So too Hinduism, despite its moral and social failures, had grasped certain 'profound and vital truths' concerning salvation, redemption, dissatisfaction with the world and 'the mystical element in the Christian religion'.[33] Together with animism, Buddhism and Confucianism, 'all these religions without exception disclose elemental needs of the human soul', and 'in their higher forms they plainly manifest

32 Farquhar to Mott, 15 April 1909, Mott Papers 45/29/521, Yale University Divinity School Library.
33 World Missionary Conference, 1910, *Report of Commission IV: the missionary message in relation to non-Christian religions* (Edinburgh and New York: Oliphant, Anderson and Ferrier, 1910), pp. 244–55.

the working of the Spirit of God'. To comprehend how this was so was to understand more fully the Christian revelation and how to bring it home to non-Christians. In encountering other religions, 'the merely iconoclastic attitude is . . . radically unwise and unjust'.[34]

These views reflected those of thoughtful missionaries such as Farquhar, whose influential book developing a theology of fulfilment, in which Christianity was presented as 'the Crown of Hinduism', was published in 1913.[35] In asserting the value of 'comparative religion' and calling for the incorporation of 'this science' into missionary training and theological education, the Commission was publicising a major shift taking place in missionary approaches to evangelism. To some it caused great offence, especially by its sympathetic handling of Hinduism, and in a postscript to its published report the Commission conceded that it had dealt 'almost entirely with the nobler side of the non-Christian religions'.[36] Nevertheless, publication went far to bring the non-Christian religions in from the cold, gave them a place in the Christian dispensation of providence, and encouraged an openness and open-mindedness in the discussion of both Christianity and other 'world religions' until recently hardly even the limited preserve of ethnographers and anthropologists.

---

34 *Ibid.*, p. 267. See Cracknell, *Justice, courtesy and love*, ch. 4.
35 J. N. Farquhar, *The Crown of Hinduism* (London: Oxford University Press, 1913). See Sharpe, *Not to destroy but to fulfil*.
36 World Missionary Conference, 1910, *Report of Commission IV*, pp. 278–9.

35

Ethiopianism and the roots of modern African Christianity

OGBU U. KALU

No fire without smoke: the texture of colonial Christianity as the backdrop to Ethiopianism

Certain forces from the home bases of missionaries combined with the emergent modes of African appropriation to reshape the face of African Christianity in the period from 1885 to the First World War. The Berlin Conferences of 1884–5 that initiated the partition of Africa by the European powers had an enormous effect on the relationship between the white missionaries and the Africans. The impact of colonial rule brought the gospel down to the grassroots and gave missionaries new opportunities to attempt to domesticate their values in African cultural terrains. Africans responded by weaving Christian strands of their own. Similarly, the World Missionary Conference of 1910 endeavoured to reformulate a new vision of the missionary enterprise even though it had no powers of enforcement. The dominant note of ecumenical consolidation of the vision kept the missionary spirit alive in the midst of growing institutionalisation, rivalry within the enterprise, the resilience of primal cultures, and the rising powers of the colonial state.

Partition introduced virulent forms of European nationalism into the continent. The mission churches embellished this spirit with denominational stripes. The Berlin Conference's demand for physical presence rather than mere declarations of areas of influence opened the African interior to missionary gaze. It was a moot point whether colonies were acquired in a fit of official absent-mindedness or by the machinations of the men-on-the-spot; the character of the cross-cultural process changed. European self-confidence replaced the initial respect for African chiefs as colonial weaponry was now at the behest of gospel bearers. The scale of missionary activities was enormously enlarged, making analysis complex; competition among missionaries became rife: broadly, Catholics squared off against Protestants but there were intramural competitions among the Catholic orders and Protestant denominations because they came from different nations. Sometimes rivalry determined the pace, direction and nature of the Christian presence.

Missionary policy was forged amidst the competing claims of colonial ambitions, evangelical spirituality and obligations to the indigenous peoples. The allegation that missionaries colluded with the colonial governments must take into account that these intimate enemies contested over cultural policy, educational curricula and the moral temper of governance, and also the curious fact that colonialism benefited Islam more than several jihads could ever accomplish. The texture of colonial Christianity contained four strands that would challenge the indigenous peoples and evoke responses. First, *the character of the missionary presence* was exhibited in such varied contexts as the mission centres of southern and central Africa, the protection of the settler communities in eastern Africa, and the increasing rejection of the large space that progressives such as Henry Venn advocated for African agency in West Africa. The second strand was a *cultural policy* that despised indigenous realities and embedded racism in mission practice. Third, the *institutionalisation* of mission agencies ignored the pneumatological resources of the gospel, sapped the vigour of the original evangelical spirituality and encrusted the monopoly of decision-making processes and the practice of faith. Fourth, *translation* of the Scriptures exposed the underbelly of the missionary enterprise and produced unintended consequences.

The net effect of the first three strands loaded the cross of humiliation on African shoulders. Missionaries shared the Enlightenment world-view of the age and the negative image of Africa. While they used education to create an elite that would mediate the new dispensation and carry the gospel to their people, education served as an instrument of rivalry and a means of evangelisation; therefore, the range in the curricula was limited. Some missionaries disdained the educated 'black Englishman' and stoutly resisted the belief in African capacity nurtured by Henry Venn. From the fate of the native pastorate in Sierra Leone, through the delimitation of the powers of Samuel Crowther's Niger bishopric, to his disgrace and the ousting of Africans from such high posts, the character of the Christian presence in Africa was beclouded by racism. Missionaries showed more respect for south Asian and east Asian cultures. In Africa this cultural policy created physical and psychological burdens and gave the enterprise a negative image embedded in a certain way of reading the Bible and in paternalistic principles that emphasised hierarchy, discipline and control. Race was particularly a major aspect of the Christian story in eastern and southern Africa. When Winston Churchill visited Kenya in 1906 as the Under-Secretary of State for the Colonies, he compared its racial issue to 'rhinoceros questions – awkward, thick-skinned, and horned, with a short sight, an evil temper, and a tendency to rush blindly upwind upon any alarm'. That was a swipe at the settlers who reserved a sports cup named the *Kifaru* (Rhinoceros) for themselves.[1] Settlers implicated all whites by creating social and geographical boundaries between themselves and the indigenes. Ironies pervaded as white civilisation, envisioned as the redemption of Africans, held them back, chafing for self-expression.

Control and the quest for a monopolistic interpretation of Christianity occupied the centre of much missionary ideology. This controlling attitude affected the pattern of African responses. For instance, the Africa Inland Mission among the Kikuyu from 1895 recruited only personnel who demonstrated strong piety, personal conversion and passion for evangelism, and could fund themselves. But their piety demonised local cultures and created tight-knit separate communities of believers (*athomi*). The tension between them and the rest of the community was so strong that the Kenyan novelist Ngugi wa Thiong'o has described this type of Christianity as a *River Between*. After 1914 such tensions would intensify, splintering the Kikuyu nation into competing Christianities. Nevertheless, the Kikuyu would reject, not Christianity itself, but the mode of evangelisation practised by the missionaries. Much to the contrary, their nationalism contested the liberation offered by missionaries as being less than the translated Bible promised.[2]

Why did missionaries fail to disengage from the frontier mounted by the settlers? There appeared to be a strong evangelical reticence towards practical issues of social justice: for some it was the result of premillennial eschatology; for others it was the emphasis on the individual in their theology; for most, the openness that invited all people to be converted failed to dissolve the frontier of racial exclusion. The Anglicans and Scottish Presbyterians who were a part of the establishment were most inclined to accept the hegemony and justice of colonial rule. Most whites lived under fear of the African; the dark skin, large numbers and cultures steeped in alien religiosity frightened outsiders. Control measures were adopted as a survival technique.

From this perspective, the wave of 'Ethiopianism' in Africa from 1860 to the turn of the century may be viewed as an example of African response to colonial Christianity. According to a key figure, the Sierra Leonean medical doctor Africanus Beale Horton (1835–83), it was a response to the European nationalism of the period that resulted in the partition of Africa and the change in

---

1 Lonsdale, 'Mission Christianity', p. 196.
2 Lonsdale, 'Kikuyu Christianities'.

white temperament which sought to restrain African initiative with European domination.[3] This chapter sets out to do three things: first to explore the concept, 'Ethiopianism'; second, to situate it within the context of African responses to missionary Christianity that gained momentum from the nineteenth century; and third, to examine its impact on the future of Christianity in Africa.

The lens: moral economy and agency

Certain concepts could be useful for the task. The notion of 'moral economy', employed by the social historian E. P. Thompson to describe the failure by those in authority in early modern England to meet traditional and customary obligations towards the ruled, may be helpful. Thompson characterised those expectations, embodied in values and roughly approximating to a consensus, as 'moral economy'. This concept could apply to the context of colonial Christianity in which the original motives included saving Africans from the evil caused by the nefarious slave trade, obeying the Great Commission, and bringing the resources of the kingdom of God to the continent. Within the colonial structure built on the tripod of civil administration, legitimate trade and judiciary, missionaries through their new socialising techniques constructed a civilising moral economy. To the extent that internal contradictions and discernible benefits existed within the structure, the new indigenous members were compelled to respond to the structure. By structure is meant the ways social forces constrained, shaped and/or determined human behaviour within such contexts.

Another dimension to the maintenance of the structure or moral economy is the concept of legibility. Indigenous people could be rendered 'legible' by using simple characterisations, forms of representation that essentialised, and employed stereotypes, simplifications and prejudices. Nineteenth-century missionaries constructed physical and psychological tools for 'reading' the new converts. The mission compound and its allocation of space, the regimen in boarding schools and mission compounds, ethical boundaries, character formation strategies and the dynamics of church polity were all designed to make the converts legible. Here, a variation of rational choice theory becomes helpful, arguing that individuals and communities respond to structures by choosing either to accept them with *loyalty*, or to *voice* their dissent, or even to take measures to *exit* from them. A loyalist may be an unsatisfied customer

3 Fyfe, *Africanus Horton*.

who gives voice to dissent in non-obtrusive ways or calls for reform to be achieved from within the system. Harris W. Mobley illustrates the pattern with an example from Ghana.[4] He draws a distinction between the literature of tutelage by courteous critics and the radical genre of critical literature by a second generation that avoided such deferential, tentative nuances. The new voices criticised the missionary's secluded habitation, social distance and vocational dominance. They explored the negative dimensions of missionary institutionalism or structure, harping on the imposition of ecclesiastical forms, the replacement of village community with church membership, marriage issues and the retarding effects of rivalry. They suspected the use of schools as a means of evangelisation and faulted the missionary interpretation of Christianity, especially its failure to relate to indigenous beliefs. The ambiguity in the structure did not escape notice, recognising what was dubbed as 'coast conscience' that afflicted a minority of daring European 'progressives' who cared for the welfare of Africans.

In contemporary social sciences, radicalism is profiled as 'agency'. Agency is used to refer to how individuals and groups self-consciously shape their behaviour within such structures. It is the ability to make decisions, initiate redemptive actions and counter vulnerability or the inability to take decisions for oneself or one's community. Agency is a visioning gift that sees beyond simple tasks of survival and defines the importance of activism on behalf of self and community. As applied here, it refers to the dual processes by which black people may work for as well as against social structures and institutions: a measure of self-invention that mines psychological roots to combat models for internalising negative self-images. Colonialism was not just an administrative structure but also a psychological instrument that humiliated and wounded the soul and embedded a certain dependency as the victim internalised the values of the master figure. In church historiography, agency is a tool for analysing both the patterns of insertion of the gospel and the modes of appropriation; or how agents responded in the process of culture-encounter. Those described as 'Ethiopians' were agents who 'set to work' the missionary message, responded to the larger import of its moral values and gave voice to whispers from the ranges of infra-politics – that zone where the ruled talk freely about their rulers. Since missionary racial and cultural ideologies jarred most prominently against the biblical values that their translation of the gospel betrayed, and since the cultural hardware of the enterprise was intimidating, these two issues dominated the first African response to the missionary message.

4 Mobley, *The Ghanaian's image of the missionary*.

Ethiopianism: myth and memory

Ethiopianism was a movement with many strands. It was rooted in the Bible; specifically in the passage in Psalm 68:31 that prophesied that 'Princes shall come out of Egypt; Ethiopia shall soon stretch out her hands unto God.' The prophetic reading of this passage is traced to African Americans who in the golden age of black nationalism from 1850 to 1925 crafted an empowering exegesis around this passage. It has inspired generations who refashioned it freely. The Ethiopian tradition sprang from certain shared political and religious experiences and found expression in slave narratives, the exhortations of conspiratorial slave preachers, folklore and the songs of slaves. After 1872, it moved beyond the nostalgia of prideful heritage to communal assertion. The intellectual origin may include the impact of European ideals filtered through American revolutionary rhetoric to inspire African Americans who returned to the motherland. The Christianity of the returnees, argues Sanneh, was stamped with the values of antislavery and promoted as the cause of the oppressed and stigmatised.[5] It called for freeing Africans from the religious and political tutelage of Europeans. The core concerns included a quest for a place of their own, for identity, self-respect and an opportunity to nurse Africa back to its old glory. That glory was imaged with the achievements of ancient Egypt, Nubia and Ethiopia. There was a conflation of myth and history. Ethiopia was both a place and an ideological symbol and there is little doubt about the achievements of Egypt in science, architecture and government. The contributions of ancient Egypt were injected into western civilisation through the Greeks and mistaken for Greek ingenuity. The contributions of this part of Africa to the consolidation of the theology and identity of early Christianity are equally immense. Ethiopianism, therefore, has three broad strands: in African-American diasporic experience, West African manifestations and southern African genre. In all incarnations, it fuelled black nationalism.

The first task is to explore the search for heroic roots that often fails to underscore patches in the story. It is a puzzle why the Egyptians did not refer to themselves as *Kushites* but applied the term *Kush* to the region south of the first cataract of the Nile, and to the descendants of Ham, the son of Noah who witnessed his drunken father's nakedness. The notion of a curse was introduced into the story even though it was Canaan who was cursed. Did the ancient Egyptians perceive themselves as related to the Kush? Historically, the relationship between Egypt and the Kushite region was fraught with ambiguity. Egypt was attracted to the mineral wealth, and to commercial

---

5 Sanneh, *Abolitionists abroad*.

and cultural exchanges with the region that stood between it and central Africa, as well as the trade with Arabs from the Red Sea island of Dahlak and the sea port of Adulis. Nubians patronised the cultic temples at Philae (Aswan). Archaeological evidences of Egyptian cultural presence in the interior of the Nubian region abound. Meanwhile, the Blemmyes, ancestors of the Beja of modern Sudan, constantly raided the southern Egyptian regions around Thebes and Philae. It is said that the rich Nubian kingdom of Meroe was once located around Napata; when the Nubians attacked Egyptian towns, the latter took revenge, sacked its capital and forced its relocation down the Nile. The treasurer to the Queen Mother, Candace of Meroe, made it into the pages of the Bible as Philip met him returning from a pilgrimage to Jerusalem.[6] He was reading the Septuagint.

Matters darkened as the translators of the Septuagint Bible in 300 BC mistakenly translated the Hebrew *Kush* into the Greek, *Aithiop*, a word that the Greeks used for any country south of their known world and derived from their word for black face, *aithiops*. The entire region from Egypt to Ethiopia / Abyssinia thus became known as Ethiopia. This explains how 'Ethiopianism' as a movement sought to re-create and moor itself onto the prideful, golden age of African civilisation, the splendour of the kingdoms of Meroe and Aksum that survived the Islamic onslaught of the seventh century and retained the pristine traditions of early Christianity. In European imagination, this was the kingdom of Prester John, whose myth lured many crusaders into arduous sojourns and served as a key component of Iberian voyages of the fifteenth century. Ethiopia was an enchanted place, whose monarch claimed to be the Lion of Judah, a scion of the Queen of Sheba and King Solomon; whose land is said to hold the ark of the covenant and who defeated the Italians at Adwa in March 1896 to prove that the whites were not invincible. Ethiopians maintained their independence into modern times, though Nubia collapsed into Islamic embrace in the fifteenth century. 'Ethiopian' passed into the nineteenth-century imagination as a generic term for blacks, the descendants of Ham and Cush. The Rastafarians of the West Indies equally celebrate this conflation of myth and historical memory because the movement was, like Ethiopianism, a form of cultural appreciation, a social and historical excavation, a recovery and recontextualisation of black traditions of emancipation hidden from consciousness of black peoples by colonial hegemony.

However, recent archaeological literature on the alluring Queen of Sheba, whose image rivals that of Delilah and of Cleopatra, locates her in south Arabia

---

6 Acts 8:27.

rather than in Nubia or Ethiopia. Indeed, it was the dynasty of Tewodros of Ethiopia (1855–68) that contrived the Solomonic succession into a messianic ideology of a king whose coming had long been prophesied. He would later add 'the son of David and of Solomon' to his official titles. Ethiopia was portrayed as the land from whence the Queen of Sheba journeyed to consort with Solomon and produce the heritage of the monarchy. Tewodros superseded the story of the Falasha linkage with ancient Israel and conjured a myth. The Falasha or Beta-Israel trace a genuine religious heritage to Israel. Some Victorian observers claimed that there was a Semitic physiognomic resemblance; this is debatable.[7] The Falasha maintained a Mosaic tradition with a strong asceticism that borrowed elements of the indigenous culture. They inhabited a number of communities, mostly in northern Ethiopia, and were despised. The term *falasi* meant 'stranger'. Various Christian kings of Ethiopia sought to counter the Falasha claim to a more authentic heritage and tried to Amharise them. They became generally poor, powerless artisans; some could not afford to retain the Mosaic rituals. The *zemana mesafent*, rule of princes (1769–1855), when the central authority virtually dissolved, was the worst period for the Falasha as the princes disenfranchised their lands. In the mid-nineteenth century, missionary efforts by Jewish organisations such as the London Society for Promoting Christianity Amongst the Jews, attempted to consolidate their Jewish heritage and later to promote repatriation to Israel.

Thus, Ethiopian kings constructed the Hebraic linkage by disestablishing the direct line. The myth about Ethiopia, therefore, conflated different genres: the staggering achievements of ancient Egypt, the work of the early Christian apologists in Alexandria and Carthage, the gilded kingdoms of Nubian Meroe, the exploits of Aksum, and the endeavours of various Abyssinian kings who sustained the Christian kingdom in the face of Islamic onslaught until Yohannes and Menelik modernised it. The defeat of the Italians crowned all these into a prideful past for Africans. Ethiopia became a symbol of African redemption, a political and religious ideology that continued to inspire for generations to come.

'God is a Negro': Ethiopianism in African-American imagination

Henry McNeal Turner (1834–1915), bishop in the African Methodist Episcopal Church, was perhaps the greatest protagonist of the Ethiopian cause.

7 Seeman, 'The question of kinship', pp. 101–2.

Confronted with a keen sense of the sovereignty of God and the humiliation confronting black people at home and abroad, he designed a providential theology hewn from the belief that God has the interest of Negroes so much at heart that he is a Negro. God brought them as slaves to America to acquire the resources of the gospel for redeeming the fatherland. Black Manifest Destiny conferred a responsibility. Many other African Americans, such as Alexander Crummell (1819–98), Martin Delany (1812–85) and Henry Garnet (1815–82), contributed to developing the idea. Some understood the prophecy in Psalm 68:31 to mean that Africa would be saved from heathenism; others grandly imagined it to say that Africa would one day rule the world. For all, it explained the forced dispersion, countered the prevalent Hamitic theory, and imposed a sacred duty. African Americans were the instruments for achieving God's design. Each commentator prescribed how the task could be accomplished. Some urged the exercise of black religious genius and commitment evident in Simon Cyrene's assistance to Jesus. Crummell imagined the black intellectuals as agents for redeeming the fatherland through religion. Delany, a Harvard-trained medical doctor, harped on the cultivation of self-help ('elevation'), education and skills. Such trained manpower would return to Africa to develop it. Henry Turner laboured to inspire and mobilise Africans in black churches.

All agreed on emigration and the imperative to appropriate the best of Anglo-Saxon civilisation. Garnet buttressed the dream with an organisational structure. He scripted a constitution in 1858 for the American Colonization Society based on a voluntary and cooperative mobilisation and redirection of the energy of black people. For Turner, America held no hopes for the black person. Incidentally, the period coincided with white realisation that the challenges of the climate in certain parts of Africa required black personnel. They toured institutions to recruit and founded others for training such personnel. Other blacks suspected white motives because those who did not care for the welfare of blacks in the United States could not possibly sympathise with Africans at home. The ACS suffered challenges because of funding, the robust opposition of integrationists, and the American Civil War that distracted focus, but its ideal flowed into various Pan-African movements in later years. In many ways, their activism buttressed the daring of the Nova Scotians and Maroons who had emigrated in 1792 to Sierra Leone and whose example inspired the foundation of Liberia in 1822. African Americans articulated some of the key themes that would be picked up on the continent precisely because some protagonists, such as Edward Wilmot Blyden (1832–1912), participated from both sides of the Atlantic.

'We are no longer slaves': voice and antistructure in West Africa

Beyond myth and ideology, Ethiopianism was a daring voice of new confidence that was manifested in the Native Pastorate experiment by the CMS in Sierra Leone; it breathed with the hope that Africans would bear the responsibility to evangelise Africa, build an autonomous church devoid of denominations and break European domination of the church. It dreamt of developing a Negro state with a different type of education that included a tertiary facility; one that would mobilise Christian and Muslim resources in the African interest; one that would preserve African culture, language and racial distinctives. Ironically it would do all these by absorbing the best in European culture. There was no rejection of European culture in the programme. It wanted only a share in an envisioned new dispensation rooted in a prophecy of the destiny of the black race. The emphasis was on reimagining the race in the face of white denigration. This explains the strand in Ethiopianism that urged awareness and activist protest about the fate of oppressed Africans in the Congo, the West Indies, South Africa and Fernando Po.[8]

Jehu Hanciles has rooted the West African manifestation of Ethiopianism in Henry Venn's vision of the euthanasia of missionary control that promoted a counter-imagination built on confidence in African ability and created space for the indigenes to run their churches. Venn advised missionaries to build nucleus congregations, study and respect indigenous peculiarities, and avoid mistaking black nationalism for presumption or ingratitude. He predicted that the desire to supersede denominational distinctions would grow.[9] James 'Holy' Johnson of Freetown, and later of the CMS Yoruba mission, expressed this view when he wrote in April 1873:

> The desire to have an independent church closely follows the knowledge that we are a distinct race, existing under peculiar circumstances and possessing peculiar characteristics, the desire to preserve this distinction uninjured, the conviction that it would materially contribute to give a purely native character and power to our religious profession, and that the arrangements of foreign Churches made to suit their own local circumstances can hardly be expected to suit our own in all their details.[10]

Johnson anticipated the roots of the indigenisation project of the future and can be seen as a forerunner of the moratorium debate of the 1970s. The

---

8 Ayandele, *The missionary impact on modern Nigeria*, p. 187.
9 Hanciles, *Euthanasia of mission*.
10 Ayandele, *Holy Johnson*, p. 42.

Native Pastorate caused a vigorous debate over the availability of educated personnel, funding and the marginalised role of whites. While this was going on, an ideological fire from the African-American emigration activists engulfed the West African educated elite who chafed under white control of decision-making processes in the churches and state.

Crucial to the nationalism of the period was the use of the Bible to legitimate racial ideology. It shared the diatribe by African-American protagonists such as Martin Delany who countered culture-based hermeneutics by declaring that 'we are no longer slaves, believing any interpretation that our oppressors may give the word of God, for the purpose of deluding us to the more easy subjugation; but freemen'.[11] Ethiopianism went beyond passive radicalism, that is, a coping mechanism against ideological and material disadvantage, to an active radicalism that sought to remove the source of the control system. African response would gradually move from voicing opposition to the moral economy of missionary structure to antistructural agency. Some nationalists gave voice to dissent through their writings but remained within the structure; others sought to emasculate missionary structures.

By networking through Sierra Leone, Liberia, Gold Coast and Nigeria, Ethiopians in West Africa built a formidable following among the sector of the new elite who refused to be coopted. It bonded the stars of West Africa. To name but a few: in the Gold Coast, J. E. Casely Hayford (Ekra-Agiman, 1868–1930), a brilliant lawyer and Methodist layman, wrote *Ethiopia Unbound* (1911) and initiated a critical tradition which rejected the literature of tutelage characteristic of missionary protégés. As an admirer of Wilmot Blyden, his activism centred on mobilising the entire West African colonies in educational and political matters. Unlike Casely Hayford, the educationist Mensah Sarbah (b. 1864) avoided an open attack on missionaries but offered an insightful work on Fanti customary laws that would show the moral foundations of an African community. Attoh Ahuma (1863–1921) broke away and affiliated his Gold Coast African Methodist Church to the bastion of African-American self-assertion, the American Methodist Episcopal Zion, in 1896.

In Nigeria, a leader in the Southern Baptist mission, David Brown Vincent (1860–1917), took to wearing only Yoruba clothes, founded a school with no foreign support and in 1888 seceded from the Southern Baptists to form the Native Baptist Church in Lagos, the first indigenous church in West Africa. In 1894 he reverted to his original name, Mojola Agbebi. Similarly, another Yoruba, E. M. Lijadu (1862–1926), refused to be insulted by an Anglican agent,

---

11 Wilmore, *Black religion and black radicalism*, p. 137.

funded his 'Self-Supporting Evangelist Band' (1900) through trade, and wrote two books in which he tried to articulate Christian theology with indigenous knowledge, arguing that the Yoruba deity, Orunmila, was a prefiguration of Jesus. The educationist Henry Car asserted that education was a crucial tool for building the African self-image. Car and the more famous Ghanaian J. E. K. Aggrey (1875–1927) of the African Methodist Episcopal Zion Church, inspired a generation of educationists. The ambiguity in the movement was encapsulated in the career of James 'Holy' Johnson (c. 1836–1917) who led the movement before he was transferred from Sierra Leone to Lagos. He had a reputation for unbending evangelicalism and as an agitator for African rights to education and ecclesiastical independence. He insisted on fighting the battle from inside the Anglican Church and would not be persuaded to secede. He did not even accept the platform of polygamy as the basis for Ethiopianism. The same pragmatism characterised the ideals of Julius Ojo-Cole who was not averse to borrowing the best of other civilisations to improve Africa as long as it was affirmed that each race of people possessed its genius and must unite, and cooperate to foster a spirit of national consciousness and radical pride. He was a founding member of the West African Students' Union, published the journal *West African Review* and sought to introduce a new type of education in West Africa.[12] Many of the Ethiopianists were inspired by Blyden but did not share Blyden's optimism about the spread of Islam. From Liberia, Blyden travelled widely to promote the cause in Africa and America. His lecture in Lagos in 1891, entitled 'The return of the exiles', encapsulated the heart of the movement. Acknowledging the sacrifices of white missionaries, he argued none the less that the destiny of Christianity lay in the hands of Africans or, as a weekly newspaper in Sierra Leone reported a speech by Agbebi in 1892, 'the sphinx must solve her own riddle. The genius of Africa must unravel its own enigma.' Blyden braided cultural, religious and political strands of nationalism into a coherent prophetic logic of African response to the missionary structure and message. As he told the sixty-third meeting of the American Colonization Society in 1880:

> Africa may yet prove to be the spiritual conservatory of the world. Just as in past times, Egypt proved the stronghold of Christianity after Jerusalem fell, and just as the noblest and greatest of the Fathers of the Christian Church came out of Egypt, so it may be, when the civilised nations, in consequence of their wonderful material development, have had their spiritual perceptions darkened and their spiritual susceptibilities blunted through the agency of a

12 Olusanya, 'Julius Ojo-Cole'.

capturing and absorbing materialism, it may be, that they may have to resort to Africa to recover some of the simple elements of faith; for the promise of that land is that she shall stretch forth her hands unto God.[13]

Blyden thus foresaw the coming shift in the centre of gravity of Christianity from the north to the south Atlantic and its import for Africa. Perhaps, the significance of the movement can best be gleaned from the fact that African Christians choreographed all three movements of loyalty, voice and exit; as some loyally memorised the script written by the missionaries, others voiced their dissent through publications and the media; gradually, a few, such as Mojola Agbebi, led a movement of exit to form Native African Churches which split from the mission-founded ones to experiment with interdenominational Christianity. In Nigeria, there were six main branches of the movement: three split from mainline churches and three sprouted thereafter on their own. By the 1921 census, these churches in aggregate constituted the third largest form of Christianity in southern Nigeria. The Ethiopian cultural register included the rejection of European baptismal names; the use of African clothes; praying for chiefs instead of the British monarch; and accepting polygamists into church membership. They contested missionary polity, liturgy and ethics from an honest appropriation of biblical principles.[14] Indeed, by 1914 two of the Native Baptist churches had returned into fellowship with the Southern Baptist Convention. The image of a syncretistic endeavour is fictional.

This may explain the changing pattern of white responses to Ethiopianism. The conservative ones were often regarded as useful for controlling the natives, while those influenced by African Americans, such as the African Orthodox Church in Zimbabwe, were viewed as subversive, to be hounded out of the religious space. For the most part, Ethiopianism pursued the symbols of modernity such as education, but used antistructural strategy to protest against the arrogance of power. Beyond cultural nationalism, Ethiopianism restructured the ecclesiology and theology of the missionary churches and encapsulated the dilemmas of blending missionary endeavour, colonisation and endogenous development in African societies. It confronted externality in African Christianity by asserting that all forms of Christianity are tribal and that a truly African Christianity was possible, even though its full character would emerge only with time: in the words of the Akamba proverb, 'cattle are born with ears, they grow horns later'. Ethiopians laid the foundations for modern forms of

---

13 Lynch, *Edward Wilmot Blyden*, p. 147; see the discussion of Blyden's visit to Egypt, pp. 55–7.
14 Webster, *The African churches among the Yoruba*, p. xvi.

African nationalism, whether in the political or ecclesiastical realm, and initiated the current debates on enculturation and vernacularisation in African theology. They voiced a new form of Christianity in Africa.

Agency and exit: Ethiopianism in southern and central Africa

In southern and central Africa, three interesting dimensions intrigue: first, the question of why Africans reacted with such confidence to the new face of missionary Christianity; second, the different faces of Ethiopianism in the region, where the movement occurred independently, though rooted in the same principles as in West Africa; third, the role of African-American black churches in catalysing and sustaining African radicalism. Certain regional characteristics equally emerged: race was more prominent than culture in white settler communities; exit was sometimes forced and sometimes adopted out of frustration; the political dimension was buttressed by the religious as churches provided havens from the brutality and humiliations of the structure, and served as the forum for mobilising dissent until the character of radicalism changed and the weight of frustration produced the violent genre of Ethiopianism. For instance, in 1892, Mangena M. Mokone (1851–c. 1936), an ordained Wesleyan Methodist, rejected the racial segregation of the church and withdrew to found his Ethiopian Church in Pretoria. Four years later, he contacted the African Methodist Episcopal Church (AMEC) through the agency of his niece, Charlotte Manye. She was a member of a group of singers stranded in the United States after a tour of America in 1893. The intervention of an African Methodist Episcopal minister got her into Wilberforce College in Ohio, where she graduated with honours. The two churches united. Mokone's agent, James M. Dwane (1848–1915), was made the General Superintendent of the AMEC but in 1900 broke off and took his group into the Anglican Church, maintaining its quasi-independent identity as 'the Order of Ethiopia'.

A pattern of enclavement dominated the character of the missionary presence in the region, perhaps derived from the model of treating delinquents in Europe. African responses varied from loyalty to exit in rejection of the enclavement pattern. Nehemiah Tile (d. 1891) left the Wesleyans in Tembuland in 1884; P. J. Mzimba abandoned the Presbyterians of Lovedale in 1890 just as Charles Domingo would exit from the Livingstonia Mission in Nyasaland in 1908. African-American influence was important, as the visit of Bishop Henry Turner to South Africa in 1898 did much to galvanise the Ethiopian movement of the period to the consternation of the settlers. His liaison with Dwane catalysed tremendous growth in the Cape Colony, Orange Free State and Transvaal. A cultural aside is that it was Mankayi Enoch Sontonga (c. 1873–1905), a product of the Lovedale Institution and member of Mzimba's African Presbyterian Church, who composed the famous song 'Nkosi Sikelel' i-Afrika' in 1897. This has become the theme song of African liberation, forms the national anthem of Zambia and Zimbabwe, and has been incorporated into the national anthem of South Africa.

Collectively, these men rejected the racism, insults, control, and European cultural and religious domination that frequently overshadowed the evangelical spirit in the missionary enterprise. They harped on the themes of a non-denominational African Christianity; self-expression; political and ecclesiastical freedom and interethnic mobilisation. Dwane's antiwhite rhetoric may have been strident but there was something inexplicable that galled Africans in this period. This can be well illustrated by the case of John Chilembwe's exit from white tutelage in Nyasaland (modern Malawi). Like Mzimba and Domingo, Chilembwe (c. 1871–1915) was nurtured by a loving missionary who placed much hope on his loyalty. Joseph Booth of the Zambezi Industrial Mission raised him from the position of a cook to status as a son and put him in a black college in West Virginia. Chilembwe returned in 1900 to Nyasaland a changed person and founded the Providence Industrial Mission at Chiradzu which was supervised by an African-American Baptist missionary through its first six years. His preference for ebony kinship frightened the whites, even though they had no sympathy for Booth, who was later deported. Chilembwe's resort to violence in 1915 was only one of seven cases that stoked white scares about Ethiopianism between 1906 (the last Zulu Bambata rebellion) and 1927. African-American churches were blamed as the external agitators of African unrest until the Watch Tower challenge to civil polity (led in Nyasaland by Booth's former protégé Elliot Kamwana) became the dread of white politics in southern Africa between 1909 and 1915. Indeed, white fears severely throttled the African-American missionary impulse. The underlying reasons for the tense socio-political environment in the period were the political restructuring and creation of the Union in 1910, the increased alienation of land from the indigenes, and the decline of the status of educated blacks, who responded by forming the South African Native National Council in 1912 and sent a delegation to London to protest against the South Africa Native Land Act of 1913. Though some Ethiopians were involved, a political force took over control. Even in the United States, black nationalism took a political colour as Garveyism and the United Negro Improvement Association captured the centre stage.

It could be argued that after 1915 Ethiopianism as a movement started to lose momentum, so that by 1930 it had become disengaged from the religious terrain and merged into a larger Pan-Africanist political movement that had operated since 1896 as a component of a larger ideology.[15] Various reasons can be canvassed for this trend, some of which were discernible even before 1915. First is the diverse character of missionary ideologies; this meant that no single person or group represented the whole. Within the same missionary movement some perceived the dangers of the missionary's cultural hardware and voiced African discomfort. Others went even further to wonder whether managerial mission did not overshadow the role of the Holy Spirit. The strength of the missionary enterprise lay in the capacity for internal criticism. Some aspects of missionary practices countered and chipped away the rough edges of its other manifestations, and hence weakened the appeal of the Ethiopian churches.

Second, Africans appropriated those resources in a variety of ways and differently in time perspective. The vision, sacrifice and range of social services by missionaries benefited Africans in their quest to adjust to new power realities. The effect of Bible translation, the power of the gospel working in spite of the bearers, thus appreciating and yet limiting human agency, ensured that Christianity began to answer the questions raised by the interior of the prevailing world-views and the tensions encountered with colonialism. Soon African agents carried the burden of evangelisation and grew more confident with the times. African Bible women who visited kraals in the Transvaal enthused with a hot gospel increasingly became adept. Xhosa evangelists worked in Malawi in the 1870s. South Africa was like a nodal point from which many migrant labourers, as black missionaries, fanned into the contiguous countries.

Third, by the turn of the century, the character of Christian presence and the mode of appropriating the gospel had changed; further shifts in geopolitics reshaped the character of Christianity in Africa. For instance, political parties emerged in West Africa as cultural nationalism shifted to political nationalism. The reshaped character of Christian presence can be illustrated by the immense efforts made to consolidate the enterprise through ecumenical endeavour and indigenisation. The World Missionary Conference of 1910 depicts the character of this strand. After Edinburgh, many missionary groups shifted from comity or mere friendship among whites in foreign lands to more formal co-operation. They negotiated boundaries and delimited areas of operation to avoid rivalry, and later, following Indian precedent, founded National

15 Esedebe, *Pan Africanism*, ch. 2.

Councils of Churches. Examples include Nigeria, Zambia, Madagascar, Swaziland and Angola.

Fourth, the hopes of Edinburgh did not fully materialise because the whole missionary field soon became confused, insecure and vulnerable with the outbreak of the First World War in 1914. As it dragged on longer than anticipated, missionary logistics would become endangered: posts, supplies, transportation and manpower. Nevertheless, the War would enlarge the space for African roles and initiative and thus reduce racial tensions. Moreover, mass movements of conversion to Christianity would enable a new era of consolidation for the mission churches after 1914.

Conclusion: the enduring legacy of Ethiopianism

In 1964, the Nigerian Methodist theologian E. B. Idowu gave a series of radio talks, 'Towards an indigenous church', that sounded like a close reading of earlier Ethiopian themes. The indigenisation project that followed decolonisation so mirrored the design of Ethiopianism that the movement can be said to have nurtured the roots of modern African Christianity. Ethiopianism deployed Christianity as an instrument to reconstruct the development of African cultural and political nationalism. Later African indigenous churches uncovered the Achilles heel of missionary Christianity and also revealed the limits of the Ethiopian response. The legacies of the Ethiopian movement were, however, numerous: the quests to appropriate the gospel and modernity with dignity; to be both an African and a Christian; to express faith from an indigenous world-view and spirituality so that Africans could respond to their own realities and culture in the spheres of liturgy, polity and ethics; to tap the resources of indigenous knowledge in communicating the kerygma; and to practise local initiatives in evangelism, decision-making processes, ecclesial structures and funding. Some Ethiopians even advocated dialogue with other faiths by responding to Islam without confrontation. Dialogue was an African idea long before missionaries woke up to its import.

36

The outlook for Christianity in 1914

BRIAN STANLEY

It was not uncommon for Christian observers surveying the world in the years before the First World War to give voice to what may now appear as a vainly deluded sense that they were living in days of portentous significance for the future of Christianity. Although the consciousness of standing at a turning point in Christian history was most marked among evangelical Protestants who anticipated a missionary breakthrough in the Orient, Catholics were not entirely immune from the trend. Catholic modernists, almost as much as their liberal Protestant counterparts, constructed progressive 'new theologies' that would supposedly be free of the constraints of superstition and archaic dogma and liberate the Christian spirit to confront the intellectual and social challenges of the modern age. Catholic 'Christian democrats' and leaders of workers' associations, heartened by the encouragement offered by *Rerum Novarum* (1891), sought to achieve a synthesis of historic faith with the new co-operative forms of social and economic organisation of the modern world.

Pioneering international gatherings of Christian leaders such as the Latin American Plenary Council convened by Leo XIII in Rome in May–July 1899, the Pan-Anglican Congress in London in June 1908, or the World Missionary Conference in Edinburgh in June 1910, encouraged the heady mood of expectancy: 17,000 people attended one or more sessions of the Pan-Anglican Congress, numbers which Archbishop Randall Davidson claimed to be 'without parallel in European history'.[1] Two years later, Davidson, delivering the opening address at the Edinburgh conference, appropriated the eschatological words of Christ in the gospel narratives of the Transfiguration to assert, that, provided the world church gave to foreign missions the support that they deserved, 'it may well be that "there be some standing here tonight who shall not taste of death till they see," – here on earth, in a way we know not now, – "the Kingdom

---

1 Stephenson, *Anglicanism and the Lambeth conferences*, p. 126.

of God come with power'".[2] The American Methodist bishop of Peking, James W. Bashford, addressing the same conference, gave hyperbolic reinforcement to Davidson's view that the world stood poised on the fulcrum of extraordinary religious change: 'Not since the days of the Reformation, not indeed since Pentecost, has so great an opportunity confronted the Christian Church.'[3] The excitement of a new century, the unprecedented extent of recent colonial acquisitions by European Christian nations (especially in Africa), the revolution in transport currently being effected by steamships and railways, and the multiplying signs of spiritual and intellectual ferment in the historic civilisations of Asia, all seemed to point to the hand of providence, beckoning the church forward into a new era of global Christian expansion.

Even a comparatively small regional conference, such as the first and more controversial of the Kikuyu ecumenical conferences that took place in East Africa in June 1913, was invested by some with quite exceptional historical significance. A leader in *The Times* of 4 December 1913 saw no incongruity in adding the name of Kikuyu to a uniquely Anglican and hybridised version of apostolic succession that extended from Constantinople and Nicaea, through Trent, Augsburg and Dort, to the Hampton Court and Savoy conferences of seventeenth-century England.[4] In the eyes of such ecumenical enthusiasts, the healing of the divisions of the centuries was about to begin in the newly tilled Christian soil of East Africa. For other Anglicans, of course, notably the Anglo-Catholic Bishop Frank Weston of Zanzibar, Kikuyu was very far from being an apostolic event, but even Weston, in his indignation at the 'heresy' and 'schism' supposedly involved in Kikuyu's pioneering celebration of a Protestant ecumenical eucharist, was doing his best to ensure that this apparently minor conference was written into the pages of church history.[5]

Weston's robust dismissal of pan-Protestant experiments in ecumenism from the perspective of a firmly Anglo-Catholic view of tradition was symptomatic of a range of responses by conservative Christians to the innovatory and often radical spirit that had seized sections of the churches. Catholic modernism received its come-uppance from Pius X in 1907 in the decree *Lamentabili* and the encyclical *Pascendi*, and in the systematic purge of modernist influence which followed. Pius also reasserted the control of clergy and hierarchy over

---

2 World Missionary Conference, 1910, vol. IX, The history and records of the conference (Edinburgh and London: Oliphant, Anderson and Ferrier, n.d.), p. 150.
3 *Ibid.*, p. 246.
4 Willis, *Towards a united church*, p. 18.
5 Smith, *Frank Bishop of Zanzibar*, p. 149.

the workers' movement. In the Anglican communion, doctrinal revisionism, as represented by *Foundations*, the collection of modernist essays edited by B. H. Streeter in 1912, was dealt with less severely, but none the less received its ripostes, not merely from conservatives such as Weston, but more significantly from liberal Catholic Anglicans such as Charles Gore, bishop of Oxford. In the United States, twelve slim paperback volumes by conservative scholars appeared between 1910 and 1915, under the title *The Fundamentals*, recalling American Protestants to the 'simple truths' of personal Bible religion, and anticipating the emergence after the war of the new reactionary movement of 'fundamentalism'. *The Fundamentals*, however, were markedly less 'fundamentalist' than their post-war offspring. The essays did not repudiate scientific historical criticism of the Bible *per se*, but only its illegitimate application; and the most important of the essays that dealt with evolution, by G. F. Wright of Oberlin College, did not so much attack evolution in principle as argue that 'by no stretch of legitimate reasoning can Darwinism be made to exclude design'.[6] Perhaps most revealing of all was the fact that R. J. Campbell, Congregationalist author of *The new theology* (1907), had by 1915 withdrawn his radically immanentist book from circulation and quietly returned to the Anglican fold he had left as a young man twenty years before.[7] Some expressions of Christian confidence in the new possibilities of the twentieth century had thus worn thin even before the outbreak of war.

Consciousness that present opportunities and future prospects were unprecedented depended on an awareness, however distorted, of the past: Edinburgh had been linked with Pentecost, and Kikuyu with Constantinople. But commemoration of the past could lay bare the disturbing extent to which the apparent ecumenical harmony of Edinburgh concealed continuing deep divergences even among the non-Roman Christian traditions of northern Europe. By 1914 Christians belonging to the Lutheran and Reformed churches were already looking forward to the four hundredth anniversary of the Reformation, conventionally reckoned to have begun on 31 October 1517 with the posting of Luther's Ninety-Five Theses. An invitation to the Church of England to participate officially in the celebrations was the occasion for Randall Davidson's famous letter of reply to Ernst von Dryander, chief court chaplain to the Kaiser, on 1 August 1914, in which Davidson had to explain the inability of the Church of England to participate in any commemoration

---

6 Marsden, *Fundamentalism and American culture*, pp. 118–23; G. F. Wright, 'The passing of evolution', in *The Fundamentals: a testimony to the truth*, 12 vols. (Chicago: Testimony Publishing Company [1910–15]), vol. VII, pp. 10, 19.
7 Clements, *Lovers of discord*, p. 43.

'which might, however unintentionally, take the form, or at least bear some appearance, of a declaration of a coherent and solidly united Protestantism against a coherent and solidly united Catholicism'. The archbishop went on to express a deeper anxiety, caused by the deteriorating aspect of international affairs: 'War between two great Christian nations of kindred race and sympathies is, or ought to be, unthinkable in the twentieth century of the Gospel of the Prince of Peace.'[8]

Davidson was expressing a sense of historical portentousness of a rather more ominous kind than that which he had voiced at Edinburgh in 1910. The prospect of conflict between 'the two great Christian nations' of Britain and Germany was properly unthinkable in the new century of Christian ecumenism and the supposed redundancy of war as a means of settling international disputes, yet the unthinkable now had to be contemplated. The 1910 conference had been premised on the linked assumptions that the world could be divided into Christendom and heathendom, and that the territorial extension of the former at the expense of the latter offered the only hope for peace, civilisation and progress. The ideology of Christendom, which had attained its most self-confident expression in the opening decade of the century, was about to be dealt a blow from which it was never fully to recover.

But what, after all, was a 'Christian nation'? In 1815 most of Europe would have given the answer that a Christian 'nation' (or, more likely at that date, 'kingdom') was one in which the state supplied constitutional recognition of the divine truth of the Christian revelation by its endowment of the national church and legal protection of its privileged status. By 1914 such a definition was becoming much less tenable, for established churches – though still powerful in England, Scandinavia and Germany – were rarer and weaker than they had been a century earlier, in part because churches which owed external allegiance to Rome or Canterbury had been increasingly perceived as obstacles to the construction of truly 'national' identities. Even those churches which retained their established status, such as the Church of England or the Catholic Church in most of Latin America, no longer wielded the monopolistic power that they had in 1815. In the course of the nineteenth century, as chapter 4 has made clear, voluntary and Dissenting forms of evangelical Christianity had exploded, although by 1914 the peak of Nonconformist growth in Britain had already passed. The expansion of evangelicalism eroded the hegemonic status of established churches, especially in England, Wales and Sweden. In England urbanisation further tipped the balance in favour of religious

8 Bell, *Randall Davidson*, pp. 732–3.

Dissent. Elsewhere in Europe, notably in France, Spain and Germany, as also in Latin America, secularism or anticlericalism had played a greater part in the weakening of churchgoing and the fabric of Christendom. Paradoxically, the nation that in 1914 offered the most vibrant and confident (albeit competitive) model of the permeation of national life by Christian influence – the United States – was founded on the constitutional principle of the repudiation of any formal link between church and state.

The century before 1914 had witnessed numerous examples of the weakening or dissolution of establishments. In Germany, the process of state consolidation instituted by the Congress of Vienna had necessitated some relaxation of state control of the *Landeskirchen*, though full separation of church and state remained a distant prospect in the new German empire after 1871. In Italy, secularisation of the property and privileges of the Catholic Church had begun in Piedmont as early as 1850 and had been extended to the new kingdom of Italy from the early 1860s. Colombia in 1853 was the first Latin American country to witness the separation of church and state, though Catholicism was reinstated by the 1887–8 constitution as the official religion of the state. In Argentina, Brazil and Chile, Catholicism was similarly recognised as the official religion, but the days of state subsidy for the Catholic Church had come to an end. The most famous act of separation of church and state – that in France in 1905–7 – met with total rejection by Pius X; the resulting estrangement between church and nation appears to have accelerated a marked decline in the principal indices of religious observance.[9] In Portugal, the republican revolution of 1910 which deprived the Catholic Church of its financial, educational and legal privileges provoked Pius to similar outrage (see chapter 23).

In the British empire, the process of severance was generally less painful, with the possible exception of the disestablishment of the Irish church in 1869–71, which was greeted by Irish Anglicans with dismay (see chapter 19). In this period the process was also incomplete, but no less significant in the long term, for it began to create the space for definitions of Christian and even Anglican identity that were no longer explicitly tied to Englishness. In the Australian and Canadian colonies the temporary introduction from the 1830s of concurrent endowment for all Christian denominations who wanted it terminated the status of the Church of England as the sole appointed guardian of Christian tradition. The idea of a Christian nation survived, but without the exclusive constitutional nexus that had seemed so indispensable to European Christians in the early nineteenth century. The ruling of the Judicial Committee of the

---

9 McManners, *Church and state in France*, p. 169.

Privy Council on the Colenso case in 1865 confirmed the voluntary status of the Anglican church in the self-governing Cape Colony, and hence spelt the end of Anglican establishment in the other self-governing colonies where state support of the Church of England remained a reality. The colonial legislature in Jamaica disestablished the Anglican church in 1870, though that in Barbados opted to retain Anglican establishment – the only church in the Anglican communion other than the Church of England to retain such status well into the second half of the twentieth century.[10] In Wales, that most ancient and proximate part of the British empire, legislation was passed in 1914 to disestablish the Church of England, though this could not be fully implemented until 1920.

In Britain's Asian colonies, any form of establishment appeared increasingly as a spiritual liability in an age of rising nationalism. The Anglican bishop of Ceylon, R. S. Copleston, welcomed the process of disestablishment, initiated in 1881 and completed in 1886, as an aid to the effectiveness of his tiny church.[11] In India, with its much larger English population, the dismantling of the Anglican and more modest Presbyterian establishments set up by the East India Act of 1813 would not come until 1927–30,[12] but the Episcopal Synod of 1912–13 set the 'Church of England in India' firmly on the road towards constitutional autonomy. It was already clear to far-sighted Anglicans that the Indian establishment was a *'damnosa hereditas'*, producing indefensible anomalies: in 1913 the bishop of Calcutta received an annual salary from public funds of 72,260 rupees, 'nearly twice as much as all Roman Catholic Archbishops, Bishops, Priests, together'.[13]

Nationalism, though it should be seen as much older than the nineteenth century,[14] had in the hundred years before 1914 been peculiarly fertile, giving birth to new nation-states in Italy and Germany, and latterly connecting the diverse political aspirations of emerging educated elites in Asia. Western missions, intrigued by the prospect of capturing those elites for Christ, viewed the stirrings of Indian and Chinese nationalism with benevolent but guarded approval, provided such impulses were confined to constitutional channels.

---

10 Thompson, *Into all lands*, p. 275. The Anglican church in Barbados was not completely disestablished until 1977.
11 *Ibid.*, p. 381.
12 The 1813 Act provided not simply for an Anglican bishopric in Calcutta, but also for the appointment from Company revenues of a Church of Scotland chaplain in each of the presidencies of Bengal, Madras and Bombay.
13 Grimes, *Towards an Indian church*, pp. 102, 112–17; O'Connor, *Gospel, Raj, and Swaraj*, pp. 166, 205.
14 Hastings, *The construction of nationhood*, pp. 1–34.

The 1911 Republican Revolution in China was hailed by many western Christians with unbridled enthusiasm: it unleashed a passion for education on a western model and some of its leaders displayed sympathies for Christianity – President Yuan Shih-k'ai only fleetingly, but much more permanently in Sun Yat-sen's case. The possibility that the new modernising Chinese nationalism would make common cause with the existing tradition of antiforeignism in China, which had surfaced with such violence in the Boxer Uprising of 1899–1900, seemed happily remote in 1914. Yet the expectation that Christianity and Chinese nationalism could achieve harmonious coexistence would soon prove illusory. The claim of the state under the Guomindang to be the final arbiter of morals and ideology undermined the central rationale for the heavy investment of China missions in education and resulted in the antimission reaction of 1920–8. Within a decade of 1914, western Protestant confidence that east Asian civilisations could be propelled along the road towards a European model of Christendom had largely evaporated. Only Korea, where nationalism assumed a stable pro-Christian and pro-western alignment in response to the Japanese protectorate of 1905 and annexation of 1910, and whose Protestant churches continued to grow rapidly after the First World War, would be left as a pledge that the evangelical hope of a Christian Asia might not be wholly vacuous.

The anticipation of a new era for Christendom that was so widely shared in the decade before 1914 was built on fragile foundations. Christendom was in fact about to enter an extended period of deepening crisis in its ancient European heartlands. The cultural self-confidence that was so marked a feature of the Edwardian period would not survive the Great War intact. At the same time in Asia revitalised, militant and newly systematic forms of Hinduism and Buddhism, in addition to the Chinese version of the western secular ideology of Marxism, were to prove far more doughty opponents than anyone realised in 1914. Conversely, nobody in 1914 foresaw that the most spectacular advances for both Catholic and Protestant Christianity in the remainder of the twentieth century would take place in 'primitive' Africa, a continent that in the opening years of the century appeared to be about to succumb to the southward advance of Islam. The tens of thousands of converts in the Ivory Coast and Gold Coast who in 1914 renounced their fetishes and were baptised in response to the preaching of the wandering Liberian prophet William Wadé Harris pointed towards the future shape of the Christian faith, not simply in Africa, but in other continents also. In the twentieth century, the story of Christianity would only in part be about the political vicissitudes and theological arguments that continued to beset the national churches of territorial Christendom. Movements inspired by the Spirit, impatient of traditional ecclesiastical structures, led by both male and female prophets and preachers, and often made up of the poor and marginalised, would move towards the centre of the stage, at first largely unnoticed but by the end of the century too prominent to be ignored.

Select general bibliography

Anderson, Benedict, *Imagined communities: reflections on the origin and spread of nationalism* (London: Verso, 1983).

Ayandele, E. A., *The missionary impact on modern Nigeria, 1842–1914* (London: Longmans, 1966).

Bebbington, D. W., *Evangelicalism in modern Britain: a history from the 1730s to the 1980s* (London: Unwin Hyman, 1989).

Blackbourn, David, *Marpingen: apparitions of the Virgin Mary in Bismarckian Germany* (Oxford: Clarendon Press, 1993).

Brekus, Catherine A., *Strangers and pilgrims: female preaching in America, 1740–1845* (Chapel Hill and London: University of North Carolina Press, 1998).

Breward, Ian, *A history of the churches in Australasia* (Oxford: Oxford University Press, 2001).

Butler, Cuthbert, *The Vatican Council: the story told from inside in Bishop Ullathorne's letters*, 2 vols. (London: Longmans, Green and Co., 1930).

Callahan, W. J., *Church, politics and society in Spain, 1750–1874* (Cambridge, MA: Harvard University Press, 1984).

Carlen, Claudia (ed.), *The papal encyclicals 1740–1878* (Ann Arbor, MI: The Pierian Press, 1981).

Chadwick, Owen, *The popes and European revolution* (Oxford: Clarendon Press, 1981).

A history of the popes, 1830–1914 (Oxford: Clarendon Press, 1998).

Cholvy, Gérard and Hilaire, Yves-Marie, *Histoire religieuse de la France contemporaine, 1800–1880*, 3 vols. (Toulouse: Privat, 1985–8).

Clark, Christopher and Kaiser, Wolfram (eds.), *Culture wars: secular–Catholic conflict in nineteenth-century Europe* (Cambridge: Cambridge University Press, 2003).

Clark, J. C. D., *English society 1688–1832: ideology, social structure and political practice during the ancien regime* (Cambridge: Cambridge University Press, 2000).

Connolly, Sean J., *Religion and society in nineteenth-century Ireland* (Dundalk: Dundalgan Press, 1985).

Cox, Jeffrey, *Imperial faultlines: Christianity and colonial power in India, 1818–1940* (Stanford: Stanford University Press, 2002).

Cracknell, Kenneth, *Justice, courtesy and love: theologians and missionaries encountering world religions, 1846–1914* (London: Epworth Press, 1995).

Ehler, Sidney Z. and Morrall, John B. (eds.), *Church and state through the centuries: a collection of historic documents with commentaries* (London: Burns and Oates, 1954).

Fremantle, Anne (ed.), *The papal encyclicals in their historical context* (New York: G. P. Putnam's Sons, 1956).

Gibson, Ralph, *A social history of French Catholicism 1789–1914* (London and New York: Routledge, 1989).

Gilbert, A. D., *Religion and society in industrial England: chapel and social change, 1740–1914* (London: Longman, 1976).

Harris, Paul, *Nothing but Christ: Rufus Anderson and the ideology of Protestant foreign missions* (New York: Oxford University Press, 1999).

Harris, Ruth, *Lourdes: body and spirit in the secular age* (London: Allen Lane, 1999).

Hatch, Nathan O., *The democratization of American Christianity* (New Haven: Yale University Press, 1989).

Hennesey, James, *American Catholics: a history of the Roman Catholic community in the United States* (Oxford: Oxford University Press, 1981).

Heslam, Peter S., *Creating a Christian worldview: Abraham Kuyper's lectures on Calvinism* (Grand Rapids, MI: Eerdmans, 1998).

Holmes, J. Derek, *The triumph of the Holy See: a short history of the papacy in the nineteenth century* (London and Shepherdstown: Burns and Oates and the Patmos Press, 1978).

Hope, Nicholas, *German and Scandinavian Protestantism, 1700–1918* (Oxford: Clarendon Press, 1995).

Kossmann, E. H., *The Low Countries 1780–1940* (Oxford: Clarendon Press, 1978).

Larkin, Emmet, 'The Devotional Revolution in Ireland, 1850–75', *American Historical Review* 77 (1972), 625–52.

Lausten, M. S., *A church history of Denmark* (Aldershot: Ashgate, 2002).

McLeod, Hugh, *Religion and the people of western Europe, 1789–1989* (Oxford: Oxford University Press, 1997).

McManners, John, *Church and state in France, 1870–1914* (London: SPCK, 1972).

Marsden, George M., *Fundamentalism and American culture: the shaping of twentieth-century evangelicalism: 1870–1925* (New York: Oxford University Press, 1980).

Molony, John N., *The Roman mould of the Australian Catholic Church* (Melbourne: Melbourne University Press, 1969).

Nielsen, Fredrik, *The history of the Papacy in the XIXth century*, trans. A. J. Mason, 2 vols. (London: John Murray, 1906).

Nockles, Peter B., *The Oxford Movement in context: Anglican High Churchmanship 1760–1857* (Cambridge: Cambridge University Press, 1994).

Noll, Mark A., *A history of Christianity in the United States and Canada* (Grand Rapids, MI: Eerdmans, 1992).

O'Farrell, Patrick, *The Catholic Church and community in Australia: a history* (Melbourne: Nelson, 1977, revised 1985 and 1992).

Porter, Andrew, *Missions versus empire? British Protestant missions and overseas expansion* (Manchester: Manchester University Press, 2004).

Prickett, Stephen, *Romanticism and religion: the tradition of Coleridge and Wordsworth in the Victorian Church* (Cambridge: Cambridge University Press, 1976).

Robert, Dana, *American women in mission: a social history of their thought and practice* (Macon, GA: Mercer University Press, 1996).

Rowell, Geoffrey, *The vision glorious: themes and personalities of the Catholic revival in Anglicanism* (Oxford: Oxford University Press, 1983).

Roxborogh, John, *Thomas Chalmers: enthusiast for mission. The Christian good of Scotland and the rise of the missionary movement* (Carlisle: Paternoster Press, 1999).

Samuelsson, K., *From great power to welfare state: 300 years of Swedish social development* (London: Allen and Unwin, 1968).

Sanneh, Lamin, *Abolitionists abroad: American blacks and the making of modern West Africa* (Cambridge, MA: Harvard University Press, 1999).

Sheehan, J. J., *German history 1770–1866* (Oxford: Clarendon Press, 1989).

Sperber, Jonathan, *Popular Catholicism in nineteenth-century Germany* (Princeton: Princeton University Press, 1984).

Tuck, Patrick J. N., *French Catholic missionaries and the politics of imperialism in Vietnam, 1857–1914: a documentary survey* (Liverpool: Liverpool University Press, 1987).

Vaiss, Paul (ed.), *From Oxford to the people: reconsidering Newman and the Oxford Movement* (Leominster: Gracewing, 1996).

Walker, Pamela J., *Pulling the devil's kingdom down: the Salvation Army in Victorian Britain* (Berkeley: University of California Press, 2001).

Webster, J. B., *The African churches among the Yoruba 1888–1922* (Oxford: Clarendon Press, 1964).

Wilmore, G. S., *Black religion and black radicalism: an interpretation of the religious history of Afro-American people*, revised edn (Maryknoll, NY: Orbis, 1998).

Wintle, M. J., *Pillars of piety: religion in the Netherlands in the nineteenth century* (Hull: Hull University Press, 1987).

An economic and social history of the Netherlands 1800–1920: demographic, economic and social transition (Cambridge: Cambridge University Press, 2000).

Wittberg, Patricia, *The rise and decline of Catholic religious orders: a social movement perspective* (Albany: State University of New York Press, 1994).

Wolffe, John, *The Protestant crusade in Great Britain 1829–1860* (Oxford: Clarendon Press, 1991).

Chapter bibliographies

2 The papacy

Aubert, Roger, *et al.*, *The Church between revolution and restoration* (trans. Peter Becker), Hubert Jedin and John Dolan (eds.), *History of the Church*, vol. VII (London: Burns and Oates, 1981).

The Church in the age of liberalism (trans. Peter Becker), Hubert Jedin and John Dolan (eds.), *History of the Church*, vol. VIII (London: Burns and Oates, 1981).

The Church in the industrial age (trans. Margit Resch), Hubert Jedin and John Dolan (eds.), *History of the Church*, vol. IX (London: Burns and Oates, 1981).

Barmann, Lawrence F., *Baron Friedrich von Hügel and the Modernist crisis in England* (Cambridge: Cambridge University Press, 1972).

Binchy, D. A., *Church and state in Fascist Italy* (London: Oxford University Press, 1941).

Blackbourn, David, *Marpingen: apparitions of the Virgin Mary in Bismarckian Germany* (Oxford: Clarendon Press, 1993).

Blakiston, Noel, *The Roman question: extracts from the despatches of Odo Russell from Rome 1858–1870* (London: Chapman and Hall, 1962).

Butler, Cuthbert, *The Vatican Council: the story told from inside in Bishop Ullathorne's letters*, 2 vols. (London: Longmans, Green and Co., 1930).

Chadwick, Owen, *The popes and European revolution* (Oxford: Clarendon Press, 1981).

A history of the popes 1830–1914 (Oxford: Clarendon Press, 1998).

Clark, Christopher and Kaiser, Wolfram (eds.), *Culture wars: secular–Catholic conflict in nineteenth-century Europe* (Cambridge: Cambridge University Press, 2003).

Duffy, Eamon, *Saints & sinners: a history of the popes* (New Haven: Yale University Press, 1997), at pp. 214–53.

Ehler, Sidney Z. and Morrall, John B. (eds.), *Church and state through the centuries: a collection of historic documents with commentaries* (London: Burns and Oates, 1954).

Furlong, Paul and Curtis, David (eds.), *The Church faces the modern world: Rerum Novarum and its impact* (Hull: Earlsgate Press, 1994).

Hales, E. E. Y., *Pio Nono: a study in European politics and religion in the nineteenth century* (London: Eyre and Spottiswoode, 1954).

The Catholic Church in the modern world: a survey from the French Revolution to the present (London: Eyre and Spottiswoode, 1958).

Revolution and papacy 1769–1846 (London: Eyre and Spottiswoode, 1960).

Heyer, Friedrich, *The Catholic Church from 1648 to 1870*, trans. D. W. D. Shaw (London: Adam and Charles Black, 1969).

Holmes, J. Derek, *The triumph of the Holy See: a short history of the papacy in the nineteenth century* (London and Shepherdstown: Burns and Oates and the Patmos Press, 1978).

Jemolo, A. C., *Church and state in Italy, 1850–1950*, trans. David Moore (Oxford: Basil Blackwell, 1960).

Jodock, Darrell (ed.), *Catholicism contending with modernity: Roman Catholic Modernism and anti-Modernism in historical context* (Cambridge: Cambridge University Press, 2000).

McManners, John, *Church and state in France, 1870–1914* (London: SPCK, 1972).

Manning, H. E., *The true story of the Vatican Council* (London: Burns and Oates, 1877).

Mattei, Roberto de, *Blessed Pius XI* (Leominster: Gracewing, 2004).

Misner, Paul, *Social Catholicism in Europe from the onset of industrialization to the First World War* (London: Darton Longman and Todd, 1991).

Nielsen, Fredrik, *The history of the papacy in the XIXth century*, trans. A. J. Mason, 2 vols. (London: John Murray, 1906).

Pollard, John, 'Italy', in Tom Buchanan and Martin Conway, (eds.), *Political Catholicism in Europe, 1918–1965* (Oxford: Clarendon Press, 1996), pp. 69–96.

  The Vatican and Italian Fascism, 1929–32: a study in conflict (Cambridge: Cambridge University Press, 1985).

Rerum Novarum: Ecriture, contenu et reception d'une encyclique: Actes du colloque international organisé par l'Ecole française de Rome et le Greco no. 2 du CNRS (Rome: Ecole française de Rome, 1997).

Vidler, A. R., *Prophecy and papacy: a study of Lamennais, the Church and the Revolution* (London: SCM Press, 1954).

  A century of Social Catholicism 1820–1920 (London: SPCK, 1964).

Wiseman, Nicholas, *Recollections of the last four popes and of Rome in their times* (London: Hurst and Blackett, 1858).

3 Theology and the revolt against the Enlightenment

Abrams, M. H., *The mirror and the lamp: Romantic theory and the critical tradition*, new edn (Oxford: Oxford University Press, 1979).

Barth, K., *Die protestantische Theologie im 19. Jahrhundert* (Zurich: Evangelische Verlag, 1947).

Berlin, Isaiah, 'Joseph de Maistre and the origins of Fascism', in *The crooked timber of humanity* (London: Fontana, 1990), pp. 91–174.

Brandes, George, *Friedrich Nietzsche* (London: Heinemann, 1914).

Clark, J. C. D., *English society 1688–1832: ideology, social structure and political practice during the ancien regime* (Cambridge: Cambridge University Press, 2000).

Coleridge, S. T., *Table talk*, ed. Carl Woodring, 2 vols. (London, Routledge, 1990).

  Aids to reflection, ed. J. Beer (London: Routledge, 1993).

Gore, Charles (ed.), *Lux mundi: a series of studies in the religion of the incarnation* (London: John Murray, 1889).

Hedley, R. D., *Coleridge, philosophy and religion: aids to reflection and the mirror of the spirit* (Cambridge: Cambridge University Press, 2000).

Heron, Alasdair I. C., *A century of Protestant thought* (Guildford: Lutterworth Press, 1980).

Hirsch, E., *Geschichte der neuern evangelischen Theologie im Zusammenhang mit der Theologie Überhaupt*, 5 vols. (Gütersloh: C. Bertelsmann, 1949–54).

Holmes, Richard, *Coleridge: early visions* (London: Hodder and Stoughton, 1989).

Lebrun, R. A., *Joseph de Maistre: an intellectual militant* (Kingston and Montreal: McGill-Queen's University Press, 1988).

Mill, J. S., 'Coleridge', in *Utilitarianism and other essays: J. S. Mill and Jeremy Bentham*, ed. Alan Ryan (Harmondsworth: Penguin, 1987).

Newman, J. H., *Apologia pro vita sua*, ed. M. J. Svaglic (Oxford: Clarendon Press, 1967).

Newsome, David, *Two classes of men: Platonism and English Romantic thought* (London: John Murray, 1974).

Oßwald, Bernard, *Anton Günther: theologisches Denken im Kontext einer Philosophie der Subjektivität* (Paderborn: Schöningh, 1990).

Pocock, J. G. A., *Barbarism and religion*, 3 vols. (Cambridge: Cambridge University Press, 1999–2003).

Powell, Samuel M., *The Trinity in German thought* (Cambridge: Cambridge University Press, 2001).

Prickett, Stephen, *Romanticism and religion: the tradition of Coleridge and Wordsworth in the Victorian Church* (Cambridge: Cambridge University Press, 1976).

  Words and the Word: language, poetics and biblical interpretation (Cambridge: Cambridge University Press, 1986).

Reardon, Bernard M. G., *Liberalism and tradition: aspects of Catholic thought in nineteenth-century France* (Cambridge: Cambridge University Press, 1975).

  Religion in the age of Romanticism: studies in early nineteenth-century thought (Cambridge: Cambridge University Press, 1985).

  Religious thought in the Victorian age: a survey from Coleridge to Gore, 2nd edn (London and New York: Longman, 1995).

Sanders, C. R., *Coleridge and the Broad Church movement: studies in S. T. Coleridge, Dr Arnold of Rugby, J. C. Hare, Thomas Carlyle and F. D. Maurice* (Durham, NC: Duke University Press, 1942).

Smart, Ninian, *et al.* (eds.), *Nineteenth-century religious thought in the West*, 3 vols. (Cambridge: Cambridge University Press, 1985).

Welch, Claude, *Protestant thought in the nineteenth century*, 2 vols. (New Haven: Yale University Press, 1972–85).

Willey, Basil, *Nineteenth-century studies: Coleridge to Matthew Arnold* (Cambridge: Cambridge University Press, 1949).

  More nineteenth-century studies: a group of honest doubters (Cambridge: Cambridge University Press, 1956).

Young, B. W. *Religion and enlightenment in eighteenth-century England: theological debate from Locke to Burke* (Oxford: Clarendon Press, 1998).

4 The growth of voluntary religion

United Kingdom

Bebbington, D. W., *Evangelicalism in modern Britain: a history from the 1730s to the 1980s* (London: Unwin Hyman, 1989).

  Victorian Nonconformity (Bangor: Headstart, 1992).

Binfield, Clyde, *So down to prayers: studies in English Nonconformity, 1780–1920* (London: Dent, 1977).

Brown, Callum G., *Religion and society in Scotland since 1707* (Edinburgh: Edinburgh University Press, 1997).

Cashdollar, C. D., *A spiritual home: life in British and American Reformed congregations, 1830–1915* (University Park, PA: Pennsylvania State University Press, 2000).

Cox, Jeffrey, *The English churches in a secular society: Lambeth, 1870–1930* (New York: Oxford University Press, 1982).

Davies, Rupert *et al.* (eds.), *The history of the Methodist Church in Great Britain*, 4 vols. (London: Epworth Press, 1965–88).

Field, C. D., 'The social structure of English Methodism: eighteenth–twentieth centuries', *British Journal of Sociology* 28 (1977), 199–225.

'Adam and Eve: gender in the English Free Church constituency', *Journal of Ecclesiastical History* 44 (1993), 63–79.

Gilbert, A. D., *Religion and society in industrial England: chapel and social change, 1740–1914* (London: Longman, 1976).

Hempton, David and Hill, Myrtle, *Evangelical Protestantism in Ulster society, 1740–1890* (London: Routledge, 1992).

Hillis, Peter, 'Presbyterianism and social class in mid-nineteenth-century Glasgow: a study of nine churches', *Journal of Ecclesiastical History* 32 (1981), 47–64.

Isichei, Elizabeth, *Victorian Quakers* (Oxford: Oxford University Press, 1970).

Jerrome, Peter, *John Sirgood's way: the story of the Loxwood Dependants* (Petworth: Window Press, 1998).

Jones, R. Tudor, *Congregationalism in Wales*, ed. Robert Pope (Cardiff: University of Wales Press, 2004).

Faith and the crisis of a nation: Wales, 1890–1914, ed. Robert Pope (Cardiff: University of Wales Press, 2004).

Larsen, Timothy, *Friends of religious equality: Nonconformist politics in mid-Victorian England* (Woodbridge: Boydell and Brewer, 1999).

Lovegrove, D. W., *Established church, sectarian people* (Cambridge: Cambridge University Press, 1988).

McLeod, Hugh, *Religion and society in England, 1850–1914* (Basingstoke: Macmillan, 1996).

Munson, James, *The Nonconformists: in search of a lost culture* (London: SPCK, 1991).

Oldstone-Moore, Christopher, *Hugh Price Hughes: founder of a new Methodism, conscience of a new Nonconformity* (Cardiff: University of Wales Press, 1999).

Ross, Andrew, 'Student kaleidoscope', in D. F. Wright and G. D. Badcock (eds.), *Disruption to diversity: Edinburgh divinity, 1846–1996* (Edinburgh: T. and T. Clark, 1996), pp. 203–19.

Smith, Mark, *Religion in industrial society: Oldham and Saddleworth, 1740–1865* (Oxford: Clarendon Press, 1994).

Snell, K. D. M. and Ell, P. S., *Rival Jerusalems: the geography of Victorian religion* (Cambridge: Cambridge University Press, 2000).

Walker, Pamela J., *Pulling the devil's kingdom down: the Salvation Army in Victorian Britain* (Berkeley: University of California Press, 2001).

Watts, Michael R., *The Dissenters*, vol. II: *The expansion of evangelical Nonconformity* (Oxford: Clarendon Press, 1995).

Outside the United Kingdom

Brandenburg, Hans, *The meek and the mighty: the emergence of the evangelical movement in Russia* (New York: Oxford University Press, 1967).

Breward, Ian, *A history of the churches in Australasia* (Oxford: Oxford University Press, 2001).

Hatch, N. O., *The democratization of American Christianity* (New Haven: Yale University Press, 1989).

Hope, Nicholas, *German and Scandinavian Protestantism, 1700–1918* (Oxford: Clarendon Press, 1995).

McLoughlin, W. G., *New England Dissent, 1630–1833*, 2 vols. (Cambridge, MA: Harvard University Press, 1971).

Noll, M. A., *A history of Christianity in the United States and Canada* (Grand Rapids, MI: Eerdmans, 1992).

Piggin, Stuart, *Evangelical Christianity in Australia: Spirit, word and world* (Melbourne: Oxford University Press, 1996).

Pike, Douglas, *Paradise of Dissent* (Carlton: Melbourne University Press, 1967).

Rawlyk, G. A. (ed.), *Aspects of the Canadian evangelical experience* (Montreal and Kingston: McGill-Queen's University Press, 1997).

Stunt, T. C. F., *From awakening to secession: radical evangelicals in Switzerland and Britain, 1815–35* (Edinburgh: T. and T. Clark, 2000).

Wemyss, Alice, *Histoire du réveil, 1790–1849* (Paris: Les Bergers et les Mages, 1977).

5 Catholic revivalism in worship and devotion

Altholz, J. L., *The Liberal Catholic movement in England: the 'Rambler' and its contributors 1848–1864* (London: Burns and Oates, 1962).

Bossy, John, *The English Catholic community 1570–1850* (London: Darton, Longman and Todd, 1975).

Cholvy, Gérard, and Hilaire, Yves-Marie, *Histoire religieuse de la France contemporaine, 1800–1880*, 3 vols. (Toulouse: Privat, 1985–8).

Connolly, G. P., 'Catholicism in Manchester and Salford, 1770–1850: the quest for "le chrétien quelconque"', unpublished PhD thesis, 3 vols., University of Manchester (1980).

Gibson, Ralph, *A social history of French Catholicism, 1789–1914* (London and New York: Routledge, 1989).

Gilley, S. W., 'Vulgar piety and the Brompton Oratory, 1850–1860', *Durham University Journal* 43 (1981), 15–21.

Hastings, Adrian, *African Catholicism: essays in discovery* (London: SCM Press, 1989).

Heimann, Mary, *Catholic devotion in Victorian England* (Oxford: Clarendon Press, 1995).

'St Francis and modern English sentiment', in S. Ditchfield (ed.), *Christianity and community in the West: essays for John Bossy* (Aldershot: Ashgate, 2001), pp. 278–93.

Lamberts, Emiel, 'L'Internationale noire', in Emiel Lamberts (ed.), *The Black International, 1870–1878: the Holy See and militant Catholicism in Europe* (Brussels: Institut historique belge de Rome, 2002), pp. 15–101.

Larkin, Emmet, 'The devotional revolution in Ireland, 1850–75', *American Historical Review* 77 (1972), 625–52.

McLeod, Hugh, *Religion and the people of western Europe 1789–1970* (Oxford: Oxford University Press, 1981).

McSweeney, Bill, *Roman Catholicism: the search for relevance* (Oxford: Blackwell, 1980).

Molony, John N., *The Roman mould of the Australian Catholic Church* (Melbourne: Melbourne University Press, 1969).

Morris, Charles R., *American Catholic: the saints and sinners who built America's most powerful church* (New York: Times Books, 1997).

O'Brien, Susan, 'Making Catholic spaces: women, decor, and devotion in the English Catholic Church, 1840–1900', in D. Wood (ed.), *The Church and the Arts*, Studies in Church History 28 (Oxford: Blackwell, 1992), pp. 449–64.

Sperber, Jonathan, *Popular Catholicism in nineteenth-century Germany* (Princeton, NJ: Princeton University Press, 1984).

Taves, Ann, *The household of faith: Roman Catholic devotions in mid-nineteenth-century America* (Notre Dame, IN: University of Notre Dame Press, 1986).

Wilson, A., *Blessed Dominic Barberi: supernaturalized Briton* (London and Glasgow: Sands, 1967).

Wolffe, John, *The Protestant crusade in Great Britain, 1829–1860* (Oxford: Clarendon Press, 1991).

6 Women preachers and the new Orders

A: Women preachers in the Protestant churches

Anderson, Olive, 'Women preachers in mid-Victorian Britain: some reflexions on feminism, popular religion and social change', *Historical Journal* 12 (1969), 467–84.

Billington, Louis, '"Female labourers in the church": women preachers in the northeastern United States, 1790–1840', *Journal of American Studies* 19 (1985), 369–94.

Brekus, Catherine A., *Strangers and pilgrims: female preaching in America, 1740–1845* (Chapel Hill and London: University of North Carolina Press, 1998).

Cazden, Elizabeth. *Antoinette Brown Blackwell: a biography* (Old Westbury, NY: Feminist Press, 1983).

Chilcote, Paul W., *John Wesley and the women preachers of early Methodism* (Metuchen, NJ: American Theological Association Library and Scarecrow Press, 1991).

Dayton, Lucille Sider and Dayton, Donald W., '"Your daughters shall prophesy": feminism in the holiness movement', *Methodist History* 14 (1976), 67–92.

Dodson, Jualynne, *Engendering church: women, power and the AME Church* (Lanham, MD: Rowman and Littlefield, 2001).

Gill, Sean, *Women and the Church of England: from the eighteenth century to the present* (London: SPCK, 1994).

Graham, E. Dorothy, 'Chosen by God: the female travelling preachers of early Primitive Methodism', *Proceedings of the Wesley Historical Society* 49 (1993), 77–95.

Hassey, Janette, *No time for silence: evangelical women in public ministry around the turn of the century* (Grand Rapids: Zondervan Academie, 1986).

Holmes, Janice, *Religious revivals in Britain and Ireland, 1859–1905* (Dublin: Irish Academic Press, 2000).

Hovet, Theodore, 'Phoebe Palmer's "altar phraseology" and the spiritual dimension of woman's sphere', *Journal of Religion* 63 (1983), 264–80.

Kienzle, B. Mayne and Walker, P. J. (eds.), *Women preachers and prophets through two millennia of Christianity* (Berkeley and Los Angeles: University of California Press, 1998).

Larson, Rebecca, *Daughters of light: Quaker women preaching and prophesying in the colonies and abroad, 1700–1775* (New York: Alfred A. Knopf, 1999).

Lenton, John, '"Labouring for the Lord": women preachers in Wesleyan Methodism 1802–1932: a revisionist view', in Richard Sykes (ed.), *Beyond the boundaries: preaching in the Wesleyan tradition* (Oxford: Applied Theology Press, 1998), pp. 58–86.

Muir, Elizabeth Gillan, *Petticoats in the pulpit: the story of early nineteenth-century Methodist women preachers in Upper Canada* (Toronto: United Church Publishing House, 1991).

Plant, Helen, '"Subjective testimonies": women Quaker ministers and spiritual authority in England: 1750–1825', *Gender and History* 15 (2003), 296–318.

Robert, Dana L., *American women in mission: a social history of their thought and practice* (Macon, GA: Mercer University Press, 1996).

Tucker, Cynthia Grant, *Prophetic sisterhood: liberal women ministers of the frontier, 1880–1930* (Boston: Beacon Press, 1990).

Tucker, Ruth A. and Liefeld, Walter, *Daughters of the church: women and ministry from New Testament times to the present* (Grand Rapids: Zondervan Academie, 1987).

Valenze, Deborah, *Prophetic sons and daughters: female preaching and popular religion in industrial England* (Princeton: Princeton University Press, 1985).

Walker, Pamela J., *Pulling the devil's kingdom down: the Salvation Army in Victorian Britain* (Berkeley and Los Angeles: University of California Press, 2001).

Wilson, Linda, 'An investigation into the decline of female itinerant preachers in the Bible Christian sect up to 1850' unpublished MA thesis, Cheltenham and Gloucester College of Higher Education (1992).

'"Constrained by zeal": women in mid-nineteenth century Nonconformist churches', *Journal of Religious History* 23 (1999), 185–202.

B. New religious orders for women

Bradshaw, Sue, 'Religious women in China: an understanding of indigenization', *Catholic Historical Review* 67 (1982), 28–45.

Coburn, Carol K. and Smith, Martha, *Spirited lives: how nuns shaped Catholic culture and American life, 1936–1920* (Chapel Hill and London: University of North Carolina Press, 1999).

Danyleweycz, Marta, *Taking the veil: an alternative to marriage, motherhood, and spinsterhood in Quebec, 1840–1920* (Toronto: McClelland and Stewart, 1987).

De Maeyer, J., Leplae, S. and Schmieal, J. (eds.), *Religious institutes in western Europe in the 19th and 20th centuries: historiography, research and legal position*, KADOC-International Studies on Religion, Culture and Society 1 (Louvain: University of Louvain, 2004).

Dufourcq, Elisabeth, *Une forme de l'expansion française: les congrégations religeuses féminines hors d'Europe de Richelieu à nos jours: histoire naturelle d'une diaspora*, 4 vols. (Paris: Librairie de l'Inde sarl 1993).

Eijt, José, *Religieuzen vrouwen: bruid, moeder, zuster. Geschiedenis van twee Nederlandse zuster-congregaties, 1820–1940* (Nijmegen and Hilversum: Katholiek Studiecentrum, 1995).

Gibson, Ralph, *A social history of French Catholicism 1789–1914* (London and New York: Routledge, 1989).

Gould, Virginia and Nolan, Charles, *No cross, no crown: black nuns in nineteenth-century New Orleans* (Bloomington: Indiana University Press, 2001).

Harline, Craig, 'Actives and contemplatives: the female religious of the Low Countries before and after Trent', *Catholic Historical Review* 81 (1995), 541–67.

Langlois, Claude, *Le catholicisme au féminine: les congrégations françaises à supérieure générale au XIX siècle* (Paris: Le Cerf, 1984).

MacGinley, Mary Rosa, *A dynamic of hope: institutes of women religious in Australia* (Sydney: Crossing Press, 1996).

McMillan, James F., *France and women 1789–1914: gender, society and politics* (London: Routledge, 2000).

Magray, Mary Peckham, *The transforming power of the nuns: women, religion and cultural change in Ireland, 1750–1900* (New York and Oxford: Oxford University Press, 1998).

Meiwes, Relinde, *'Arbeiterinnen des Herrn': Katholische Frauenkongregationen im 19. Jahrhundert*, Geschichte und Geschlechter 30 (Frankfurt: Campus Verlag, 2000).

Mumm, Susan, *Stolen daughters, virgin mothers: Anglican sisterhoods in Victorian Britain* (London and New York: Leicester University Press, 1999).

O'Brien, Susan, 'Religious life for women', in V. A. McClelland and M. Hodgetts (eds.), *From without the Flaminian gate: 150 years of Roman Catholicism in England and Wales 1850–2000* (London: Darton, Longman and Todd, 1999), pp. 108–41.

Rapley, Elizabeth, *Les dévôtes: women and the church in seventeenth-century France* (Montreal: McGill-Queen's University Press, 1990).

Rocca, G., 'La vita religiosa dal 1878 al 1922', in Elio Guerriero and Annibale Zambarbieri (eds.), *La chiesa e la società industriale (1878–1922)*, 2 vols. (Balsamo: Cinisello, 1990), vol. II, pp. 137–59.

Thompson, M. S., 'Women, feminism and new religious history: Catholic sisters as a case study', in P. R. Vandermeer and R. P. Swierenga (eds.), *Belief and behaviour: essays in the new religious history* (New Brunswick: Rutgers University Press, 1991).

'Cultural conundrum: sisters, ethnicity, and the adaptation of American Catholicism', *Mid-America: An Historical Review* 74 (1992), 205–30.

Tihon, A., 'Les religieuses en Belgique du XVIII au XX siècle: approche statistique', *Revue Belge d'Histoire Contemporaine* 7 (1976), 1–54.

Turin, Yvonne, *Femmes et religieuses au XIX siècle: le féminisme en religion* (Paris: Nouvelle Cité, 1989).

Walsh, Barbara, *Roman Catholic nuns in England and Wales 1800–1937: a social history* (Dublin and Portland, OR: Irish Academic Press, 2002).

Williams, Margaret, *The Society of the Sacred Heart: history of a spirit 1800–1975* (London: The Catholic Book Club, 1978).

Wittberg, Patricia, *The rise and decline of Catholic religious orders: a social movement perspective* (Albany: State University of New York Press, 1994).

Wynants, Paul, 'Les religieuses de vie active en Belgique et aux Pays-Bas 19th–20th siècles', in *Deux mille ans d'histoire de l'église: bilan et perspectives historiographiques*. Special issue of *Revue d'Histoire Ecclésiastique* 15 (Louvain, 2000), 238–56.

7 Church architecture and religious art

Architecture

General studies

Clarke, B. F. L., *Anglican cathedrals outside the British Isles* (London: SPCK, 1958).

De Maeyer, Jan and Verpoest, Luc (eds.), *Gothic Revival: religion, architecture and style in western Europe 1815–1914* (Leuven: Universitaire Pers Leuven, 2000).

Dixon, Roger and Muthesius, Stefan, *Victorian architecture* (London: Thames and Hudson, 1978).

Hitchcock, Henry-Russell, *Early Victorian architecture in Britain*, 2 vols. (New Haven: Yale University Press, 1954).

Architecture: nineteenth and twentieth centuries, 3rd edn (Harmondsworth: Penguin Books, 1968).

Lewis, Michael J., *The Gothic Revival* (London: Thames and Hudson, 2002).

Little, Bryan, *Catholic churches since 1623* (London: Robert Hale, 1963).

Middleton, Robin and Watkin, David, *Neoclassical and 19th century architecture* (New York: Harry N. Abrams, 1980).

Architects

Great Britain and Ireland

Atterbury, Paul (ed.), *A. W. N. Pugin: master of the Gothic Revival* (New Haven and London: Yale University Press, 1995).

Atterbury, Paul and Wainwright, Clive (eds.), *Pugin: a Gothic passion* (New Haven and London: Yale University Press, 1994).

Crook, J. Mordaunt, *William Burges and the High Victorian dream* (London: John Murray, 1981).

De L'Hôpital, Winifred, *Westminster Cathedral and its architect*, 2 vols. (London: Hutchinson, 1919).

McFadzean, Ronald, *The life and work of Alexander Thomson* (London: Routledge and Kegan Paul, 1979).

Quiney, Anthony, *John Loughborough Pearson* (New Haven and London: Yale University Press, 1979).

Sheehy, Jeanne J. J., *McCarthy and the Gothic Revival in Ireland* (Belfast: Ulster Architectural Heritage Society, 1977).

Stamp, Gavin and McKinstry, Sam (eds.), *'Greek' Thomson* (Edinburgh: Edinburgh University Press, 1994).

Thompson, Paul, *William Butterfield* (London: Routledge and Kegan Paul, 1971).

United States

Van Rensselaer, Mariana Grisworld, *Henry Hobson Richardson and his works* (New York: Houghton, Mifflin, 1888).

France

Auzas, Pierre-Marie, *Eugène Viollet-le-Duc, 1814–1879* (Paris: Caisse Nationale des Monuments Historiques, 1979).

Bercé, Françoise and Foucart, Bruno (eds.), *Viollet-le-Duc: architect, artist, master of historic preservation* (Washington, DC: The Trust for Museum Exhibitions, 1987).

Leniaud, Jean-Michel, *Jean-Baptiste Lassus 1807–1857: ou le temps retrouvé des cathédrales* (Geneva: Droz, 1980).

The Netherlands

Cuijpers, P. J. H., *Het Werk van Dr. P. J. H. Cuijpers* (Amsterdam: van Holkema and Warendorf, 1917).

Germany and Austria

Börsch-Supan, Helmut and Grisebach, Lucius (eds.), *Karl Friedrich Schinkel: Architektur, Malerei, Kunstgewerbe* (Berlin: Verwaltung der Staatlichen Schlösser und Gärten, Schloos Charlottenburg, 1981).

Güttler, Peter, *et al.*, *Berlin: Brandenburg: ein Architekturführer* (Berlin: Ernst und Sohn, 1993).

Milde, Kurt, *Neorenaissance in der deutschen Architektur des 19. Jahrhunderts* (Dresden: VEB, 1971).

Rave, Paul Ortwin, *Berlin: Bauten für die Kunst, Kirchen, Denkmalpflege* (Berlin: Deutscher Kunstverlag, 1942).

Painting and sculpture

Helsted, Dyveke, Henschen, Eva and Jørnæs, Bjarne, *Thorvaldsen* (Copenhagen: The Thorvaldsen Museum, 1990).

Hilton, Timothy, *The Pre-Raphaelites* (London: Thames and Hudson, 1970).

Hofmann, Werner, *Caspar David Friedrich* (London: Thames and Hudson, 2000).

Piantoni, Gianna and Susinno, Stefano, *I Nazareni a Roma* (exhibition catalogue, Rome: De Luca, 1981).

Susinno, Stefano (ed.), *The Pre-Raphaelites* (exhibition catalogue, London: The Tate Gallery and Penguin Books, 1984).

Maestà di Roma da Napoleone all'Unità d'Italia (exhibition catalogue, Rome: Electa, 2003).

Vaughan, William, *German Romantic painting*, 2nd edn (London: Thames and Hudson, 1994).

8 Musical trends and the western church

Adelmann, Dale, *The contribution of Cambridge ecclesiologists to the revival of Anglican choral worship 1839–62* (Aldershot: Ashgate, 1997).

Blume, Friedrich, *Classic and Romantic music* (London: Faber and Faber, 1972).

Bradley, Ian, *Abide with me: the world of Victorian hymns* (London: SCM Press, 1997).

Dahlhaus, Carl, *Nineteenth-century music*, trans. J. Bradford Robinson (Berkeley and Los Angeles: University of California Press, 1989).

Dibble, Jeremy, *Charles Villiers Stanford: man and musician* (Oxford: Oxford University Press, 2002).

Einstein, Alfred, *Romantic music* (London: J. M. Dent and Sons, 1947).

Gatens, William J., *Victorian cathedral music in theory and practice* (Cambridge: Cambridge University Press, 1986).

Horton, Peter, *Samuel Sebastian Wesley: a life* (Oxford: Oxford University Press, 2004).

Hutchings, Arthur, *Church music in the nineteenth century* (London: Herbert Jenkins, 1967).

Mongrédien, Jean, *French music from the Enlightenment to Romanticism 1789–1830*, trans. S. Frémaux (Portland, OR: Amadeus Press, 1996).

Orledge, Robert, *Gabriel Fauré* (London: Eulenberg Books, 1979).

Ringer, Alexander (ed.), *The early Romantic era. Between revolutions: 1789 and 1848* (London: Macmillan, 1990).

Rosselli, John, *Music and musicians in nineteenth-century Italy* (London: Batsford, 1991).

Rushton, Julian, *Classical music: a concise history from Gluck to Beethoven* (London: Thames and Hudson, 1986).

Samson, Jim (ed.), *The late Romantic era: from the mid-19th century to World War I* (London: Macmillan, 1991).

Ursprung, O., *Die katholische Kirchenmusik* (Potsdam: Akademische Verlagsgesellschaft Athenaion, 1931–3).

Thibaut, A. F. J., *Über Reinheit der Tonkunst* (Heidelberg: J. C. B. Mohr, 1825); *On purity in musical art*, trans. W. H. Gladstone (London: John Murray, 1877).

Temperley, N., 'Mozart's influence on English music', *Music and Letters* 42 (1961), 307–18.
  The music of the English parish church (Cambridge: Cambridge University Press, 1979).

Verba, Cynthia, *Music and the French Enlightenment: reconstruction of a dialogue 1750–1764* (Oxford: Clarendon Press, 1993).

Watson, J. R., *The English hymn: a critical and historical study* (Oxford: Oxford University Press, 1997).

White, Harry, *The keeper's recital: music and cultural history in Ireland, 1770–1970* (Cork: Cork University Press in association with Field Day, 1998).

Whittall, Arnold, *Romantic music: a concise history from Schubert to Sibelius* (London: Thames and Hudson, 1987).

Zaslaw, Neal (ed.), *The Classical era: from the 1740s to the end of the 18th century* (London: Macmillan, 1989).

Zon, Bennett, *The English plainchant revival* (Oxford: Oxford University Press, 1999).

9 Christianity and literature in English

Brown, Stephen J., *Novels and tales by Catholic writers: a catalogue* (Dublin: Central Catholic Library, 1940).

Chadwick, Owen, *The Victorian Church* (Parts 1 and 2) (London: Adam and Charles Black, 1966, 1970).

Cunliffe, Marcus (ed.), *American literature to 1900* (*History of literature in the English language*, vol. VIII) (London: Barrie and Jenkins, 1973).

Cunningham, Valentine, *Everywhere spoken against: Dissent in the Victorian novel* (Oxford: Clarendon Press, 1975).

Gill, Stephen, *William Wordsworth: a life* (Oxford: Oxford University Press, 1989).

Gilley, Sheridan, 'John Keble and the Victorian churching of Romanticism', in J. R. Watson (ed.), *An infinite complexity: essays in Romanticism* (Durham: University of Durham Commemoration Series, 1982).

'Father William Barry, priest and novelist', *Recusant History* 20 (1999), 523–51.

Hennell, Michael, 'Evangelicalism and worldliness 1770–1870', in G. J. Cuming and Derek Baker (eds.), *Popular belief and practice*, Studies in Church History 8 (Cambridge: Cambridge University Press, 1972), pp. 229–36.

Heuser, Herman J., *Canon Sheehan of Doneraile* (London: Longmans, Green and Co., 1918).

Jay, Elisabeth, *The religion of the heart: Anglican Evangelicalism and the nineteenth century novel* (Oxford: Clarendon Press, 1979).

Jay, Elisabeth (ed.), *The Evangelical and Oxford movements* (Cambridge: Cambridge University Press, 1983).

Maison, Margaret, *Search your soul, Eustace: a survey of the religious novel in the Victorian age* (London and New York: Sheed and Ward, 1961).

John Oliver Hobbes: her life and work (London: The Eighteen Nineties Society, 1976).

Marsh, Jan, *Christina Rossetti: a literary biography* (London: Jonathan Cape, 1994).

Martin, Robert Bernard, *Tennyson: the unquiet heart: a biography* (Oxford: Clarendon Press, 1980).

Morley, Edith J. (ed.), *Henry Crabb Robinson on books and their writers*, 3 vols. (London: J. M. Dent and Sons, 1938).

Ormond, Leonée, *Alfred Tennyson: a literary life* (London: Macmillan, 1993).

Oulton, Carolyn, *Literature and religion in mid-Victorian England: from Dickens to Eliot* (Basingstoke: Palgrave Macmillan, 2003).

Paley, Morton D., *Energy and the imagination: a study of the development of Blake's thought* (Oxford: Oxford University Press, 1970).

Prickett, Stephen, *Romanticism and religion: the tradition of Coleridge and Wordsworth in the Victorian Church* (Cambridge: Cambridge University Press, 1976).

Rosman, Doreen M., '"What has Christ to do with Apollo?": evangelicalism and the novel, 1800–30', in Derek Baker (ed.), *Renaissance and renewal in Christian history,* Studies in Church History 14 (Oxford: Blackwell, 1977), pp. 301–11.

Evangelicals and culture (London: Croom Helm, 1984).

Sanders, Andrew, *The Victorian historical novel 1840–1880* (London: Macmillan, 1978).

The short Oxford history of English literature, 3rd edn (Oxford: Oxford University Press, 2004).

Tennyson, G. B., *Victorian devotional poetry: the Tractarian mode* (Cambridge, MA: Harvard University Press, 1981).

Walder, Dennis, *Dickens and religion* (London: Allen and Unwin, 1981).

Westbrook, Perry D., *A literary history of New England* (Bethlehem, PA: Lehigh University Press, 1988).

Wheeler, Michael, *Death and the future life in Victorian literature and theology* (Cambridge: Cambridge University Press, 1990).

White, Norman, *Hopkins: a literary biography* (Oxford: Oxford University Press, 1992).

Woolf, Robert Lee, *Gains and losses: novels of faith and doubt in Victorian England* (London: John Murray, 1977).

10 **Christian social thought**

A: Catholic social teaching

Antonazzi, Giovanni (ed.), *L'enciclica Rerum Novarum: testo autentico e redazioni preparatorie dai documenti originali* (Rome: Edizioni di Storia e Letteratura, 1957).

Calvez, Jean-Yves, SJ and Perrin, Jacques, SJ, *The church and social justice: the social teachings of the popes from Leo XIII to Pius XII (1878–1958)* (London: Burns and Oates, 1961).

Carlen, Claudia (ed.), *The papal encyclicals 1740–1878* (Ann Arbor, MI: The Pierian Press, 1981).

The papal encyclicals 1878–1903 (Raleigh, NC: McGrath Publishing, 1981).

De Gasperi, Alcide, *I tempi e gli uomini che prepararano la 'Rerum Novarum'* (Milan: Vita e Pensiero, 1945).

Ehler, Sidney Z. and Morrall, John B. (trans. and ed.), *Church and state through the centuries: a collection of historical documents with commentaries* (London: Burns and Oates, 1954).

Fremantle, Anne (ed.), *The papal encyclicals in their historical context* (New York: G. P. Putnam's Sons, 1956).

Molony, John, *The emergence of political Catholicism in Italy: Partito Popolare 1919–1926* (London: Croom Helm, 1977).

The worker question: a new historical perspective on Rerum Novarum (Melbourne: Collins Dove, 1991).

'The making of Rerum Novarum, April 1890–May 1891', in Paul Furlong and David Curtis (eds.), *The Church faces the modern world: Rerum Novarum and its impact* (Hull: Earlsgate Press, 1994), pp. 27–39.

Rickard, John, *H. B. Higgins: the rebel as judge* (Sydney: Allen and Unwin, 1984).

B: The social thought of the Protestant churches

Anstey, Roger, *The Atlantic slave trade and British abolition, 1760–1810* (London: Macmillan, 1975).

Christensen, Torben, *Origin and history of Christian Socialism, 1848–54* (Aarhus: Universitetsforlaget, 1962).

Göhre, P. S., *The evangelical-social movement in Germany* (London: Ideal, 1898).

Heslam, P. S., *Creating a Christian worldview: Abraham Kuyper's lectures on Calvinism* (Grand Rapids, MI: Eerdmans, 1998).

Howse, E. M., *Saints in politics: the 'Clapham Sect' and the growth of freedom* (London: George Allen, and Unwin, 1953).

Jones, Peter d'A., *The Christian Socialist revival, 1877–1914* (Princeton: Princeton University Press, 1968).

Lausten, M. S., *A church history of Denmark* (Aldershot: Ashgate, 2002).

Samuelsson, K., *From great power to welfare state: 300 years of Swedish social development* (London: Allen and Unwin, 1968).

Scott, F. D., *Sweden: the nation's history* (Minneapolis: University of Minnesota Press, 1977).

Soloway, R. A., *Prelates and people: ecclesiastical social thought in England 1783–1852* (London and Toronto: Routledge and Kegan Paul and University of Toronto Press, 1969).

Thompson, D. M., 'John Clifford's social gospel', *Baptist Quarterly* 31 (1986), 199–217.
'The emergence of the Nonconformist social gospel in England', in K. Robbins (ed.), *Protestant evangelicalism: Britain, Ireland, Germany and America c.1750–c.1950*, Studies in Church History, Subsidia 7 (Oxford: Blackwell, 1990), pp. 255–80.
'R. W. Dale in context', in C. Binfield (ed.), *The cross and the city*, Supplement no. 2 to *Journal of the United Reformed Church History Society* 6 (1999), 16–25.

Ward, W. R., *Theology, sociology and politics: the German Protestant social conscience, 1890–1933* (Berne: Peter Lang, 1979).

Wearmouth, R. F., *Methodism and the working-class movements of England, 1800–1850* (London: Epworth Press, 1937).

Wintle, M., *Pillars of piety: religion in the Netherlands in the nineteenth century, 1813–1901* (Hull: Hull University Press, 1987).
An economic and social history of the Netherlands, 1800–1920 (Cambridge: Cambridge University Press, 2000).

Wright, T. R., *The religion of humanity: the impact of Comtean positivism on Victorian Britain* (Cambridge: Cambridge University Press, 1986).

11 Christianity and the sciences

Bowler, Peter J., *The eclipse of Darwinism: anti-Darwinian evolution theories in the decades around 1900* (Baltimore and London: Johns Hopkins University Press, 1983).
The non-Darwinian revolution: reinterpreting a historical myth (Baltimore and London: Johns Hopkins University Press, 1988).

Brooke, John Hedley, *Science and religion: some historical perspectives* (Cambridge: Cambridge University Press, 1991).

Corsi, Pietro, *Science and religion: Baden Powell and the Anglican debate, 1800–1860* (Cambridge: Cambridge University Press, 1988).

Daum, Andreas, *Wissenschaftspopularisierung im 19. Jahrhundert: Bürgerliche Kultur, naturwissenschaftliche Bildung und die deutsche Öffentlichkeit 1848–1914* (Munich: R. Oldenbourg, 1998).

Ellegård, Alvar, *Darwin and the general reader: the reception of Darwin's theory of evolution in the British periodical press, 1859–1872* (Chicago and London: University of Chicago Press, 1990, reprinted from the 1958 original).

Ferngren, Gary B. (ed.), *The history of science and religion in the western tradition: an encyclopedia* (New York and London: Garland Publishing, 2000).

Gillispie, Charles C., *Genesis and geology: a study in the relations of scientific thought, natural theology, and social opinion in Great Britain, 1790–1850*, new edn (Cambridge, MA: Harvard University Press, 1996; 1st edn 1951).

Greene, Mott T., 'Genesis and geology revisited: the order of nature and the nature of order in nineteenth-century Britain', in David C. Lindberg and Ronald L. Numbers (eds.), *When science and Christianity meet* (Chicago: University of Chicago Press, 2003), pp. 139–59.

Gregory, Frederick, *Nature lost? Natural science and the German theological traditions of the nineteenth century* (Cambridge, MA and London: Harvard University Press, 1992).

Kippenberg, Hans Gerhard, *Die Entdeckung der Religionsgeschichte: Religionswissenschaft und Moderne* (Munich: Beck, 1997).

Kraus, Hans-Joachim, *Geschichte der historisch-kritischen Erforschung des Alten Testaments* (Neukirchen: Verlag der Buchhandlung des Erziehungsvereins, 1956).

Lindberg, David C. and Numbers, Ronald L. (eds.), *God and nature: historical essays on the encounter between Christianity and science* (Berkeley: University of California Press, 1986). *When science and Christianity meet* (Chicago: University of Chicago Press, 2003).

Livingstone, David N., *Darwin's forgotten defenders: the encounter between evangelical theology and evolutionary thought* (Grand Rapids and Edinburgh: Eerdmans and Scottish Academic Press, 1987).

Putting science in its place: geographies of scientific knowledge (Chicago and London: University of Chicago Press, 2003).

Moore, James R., *The post-Darwinian controversies: a study of the Protestant struggle to come to terms with Darwin in Great Britain and America 1870–1900* (Cambridge: Cambridge University Press, 1979).

'Geologists and interpreters of Genesis in the nineteenth century', in David C. Lindberg and Ronald L. Numbers (eds.), *God and nature: historical essays on the encounter between Christianity and science* (Berkeley: University of California Press, 1986), pp. 322–50.

Mullin, Robert Bruce, 'Science, miracles, and the prayer-gauge debate', in David C. Lindberg and Ronald L. Numbers (eds.), *When science and Christianity meet* (Chicago: University of Chicago Press, 2003), pp. 203–24.

Nelson, G. Blair, '"Men before Adam!": American debates over the unity and antiquity of humanity', in David C. Lindberg and Ronald L. Numbers (eds.), *When science and Christianity meet* (Chicago: University of Chicago Press, 2003), pp. 161–81.

Numbers, Ronald L., 'Science and religion', *Osiris* 1 (2nd series) (1985), 59–80.

The creationists: the evolution of scientific creationism (New York: Alfred A. Knopf, 1992).

Darwinism comes to America (Cambridge, MA: Harvard University Press, 1998).

Riper, A. Bowdoin Van, *Men among the mammoths: Victorian science and the discovery of human prehistory* (Chicago and London: University of Chicago Press, 1993).

Roberts, Jon H., *Darwinism and the divine in America: Protestant intellectuals and organic evolution, 1859–1900* (Notre Dame, IN: University of Notre Dame Press, 2001).

Rudwick, Martin J. S., 'The shape and meaning of earth history', in David C. Lindberg and Ronald L. Numbers (eds.), *God and nature: historical essays on the encounter between Christianity and science* (Berkeley: University of California Press, 1986), pp. 296–321.

Rupke, Nicolaas A., *The great chain of history: William Buckland and the English school of geology (1814–1849)* (Oxford: Clarendon Press, 1983).

Richard Owen: Victorian naturalist (New Haven and London: Yale University Press, 1994).

Russell, Bertrand, *Religion and science*, new edn (London, Oxford and New York: Oxford University Press, 1961; 1st edn 1935).

Soulimani, Andrea Alaoui, *Naturkunde unter dem Einfluss christlicher Religion. Johann Andreas Wagner (1797–1861): Ein Leben für die Naturkunde in einer Zeit der Wandlungen in Methode, Theorie und Weltanschauung* (Aachen: Shaker Verlag, 2001).

Turner, Frank M., 'The Victorian conflict between science and religion: a professional dimension', *Isis* 69 (1978), 356–76.

Contesting cultural authority: essays in Victorian intellectual life (Cambridge: Cambridge University Press, 1993).

Young, Robert M., *Darwin's metaphor: nature's place in Victorian culture* (Cambridge: Cambridge University Press, 1985).

12 History and the Bible

Addinall, P., *Philosophy and biblical interpretation: a study in nineteenth-century conflict* (Cambridge: Cambridge University Press, 1991).

Clements, R. E., 'George Stanley Faber (1773–1854) as biblical interpreter', in P. Mommer *et al.* (eds.), *Altes Testament – Forschung und Wirkung: Festschrift für Henning Graf Reventlow* (Frankfurt-am-Main: Peter Lang, 1994) pp. 247–68.

'The intellectual background of H. H. Milman's *The History of the Jews* (1829) and its impact on English biblical scholarship', in H. Graf Reventlow *et al.* (eds.), *Biblical studies and the shifting of paradigms 1850–1914*, Journal for the Study of the Old Testament Supplement Series 192 (Sheffield: Sheffield Academic Press, 1995), pp. 246–71.

Cook, J. G., 'Loisy, Alfred Firmin (1857–1940)', in J. H. Hayes (ed.), *Dictionary of biblical interpretation* (Nashville: Abingdon Press, 1999), vol. II, pp. 87–9.

De Vaux, R., *The Bible and the Ancient Near East* (London: Darton, Longman and Todd, 1966).

Flegg, Columba G., *'Gathered under apostles': a study of the Catholic Apostolic Church* (Oxford: Clarendon Press, 1992).

Guy, Jeff, *The heretic: a study of the life of John William Colenso 1814–1833* (Pietermaritzburg: University of Natal Press; Johannesburg: Ravan Press, 1983).

Idestrom, Rebecca G. S., *From biblical theology to biblical criticism: Old Testament scholarship at Uppsala University 1866–1922*, Coniectanea Biblica, Old Testament Series 47 (Stockholm: Almqvist and Wiksell, 2000).

Klatt, W., *Hermann Gunkel: zu seiner Theologie der Religionsgeschichte und zur Entstehung der formgeschichtlichen Methode*, FRLANT 100 (Göttingen: Vandenhoeck and Ruprecht, 1969).

Kümmel, W. G., *The New Testament: the history of the investigation of its problems* (London: SCM Press, 1973).

Lagrange, M.-J., *Père Lagrange: personal reflections and memoirs* (New York: Paulist Press, 1985).

McClelland, C. E., *State, society and university in Germany, 1700–1914* (Cambridge: Cambridge University Press, 1980).

Parker, D., 'The New Testament', in J. W. Rogerson (ed.), *The Oxford illustrated history of the Bible* (Oxford: Oxford University Press, 2001), pp. 110–33.

Rogerson, John W., *Old Testament criticism in the nineteenth century: England and Germany* (London: SPCK, 1984).

W. M. L. de Wette: founder of modern biblical criticism: an intellectual biography, Journal for the Study of the Old Testament Supplement Series 126 (Sheffield: Sheffield Academic Press, 1992).

'British responses to Kuenen's pentateuchal studies', in P. B. Dirksen *et al.* (eds.), *Abraham Kuenen (1828–1891): his major contributions to the study of the Old Testament*, Oudtestamentische Studien 29 (Leiden: E. J. Brill, 1993), pp. 91–104.

Sheehan, J. J., *German history 1770–1866* (Oxford: Clarendon Press, 1989).

Treloar, G. R., *Lightfoot the historian: the nature and role of history in the life and thought of J. B. Lightfoot (1828–1889) as churchman and scholar*, Wissenschaftliche Untersuchungen zum Neuen Testament 2, Reihe 103 (Tübingen: Mohr Siebeck, 1998).

13 Popular religion and irreligion in countryside and town

Blackbourn, D., *Marpingen: apparitions of the Virgin Mary in Bismarckian Germany* (Oxford: Clarendon Press, 1993).

Bornewasser, J. A., 'Thorbecke and the churches', *Acta Historiae Neerlandicae* 7 (1974), 146–69.

Boulard, F., *Introduction to religious sociology: pioneer work in France*, English edn (London: Darton, Longman and Todd, 1960).

Callahan, W. J., *Church, politics and society in Spain, 1750–1874* (Cambridge, MA: Harvard University Press, 1984).

Chadwick, Owen, *The popes and European revolution* (Oxford: Clarendon Press, 1981).

  A history of the popes, 1830–1914 (Oxford: Clarendon Press, 1998).

Christian, W. W. Jr, *Person and God in a Spanish valley* (New York: Seminar Press, 1972).

Davies, Horton, *Worship and theology in England*, vol. III: *From Watts and Wesley to Maurice, 1690–1850* (Princeton : Princeton University Press, 1961).

Devlin, Judith, *The superstitious mind: French peasants and the supernatural in the nineteenth century* (New Haven: Yale University Press, 1987).

Everitt, Alan, *The pattern of rural dissent: the nineteenth century* (Leicester: University of Leicester Department of English Local History, 1972).

Gill, Robin, *The myth of the empty church* (London: SPCK, 1993).

Green, S. J. D., *Religion in the age of decline: organisation and experience in industrial Yorkshire, 1870–1920* (Cambridge: Cambridge University Press, 1996).

Harris, Ruth, *Lourdes: body and spirit in the secular age* (London: Allen Lane, 1999).

Hope, Nicholas, *German and Scandinavian Protestantism, 1700–1918* (Oxford: Clarendon Press, 1995).

Kiernan, V. G., *The revolution of 1854 in Spanish history* (Oxford: Clarendon Press, 1966).

Kossmann, E. H., *The Low Countries* (Oxford: Clarendon Press, 1978).

Lannon, F., *Privilege, persecution, and prophecy: the Catholic Church in Spain, 1875–1975* (Oxford: Clarendon Press, 1987).

Lausten, M. S., *A church history of Denmark* (Aldershot: Ashgate, 2002).

Le Bras, G., *Etudes de sociologie religieuse*, 2 vols. in 1 (Paris: Presses Universitaires de France, 1955).

  L'église et le village (Paris: Flammarion, 1976).

McLeod, H., *Religion and society in England, 1850–1914* (Basingstoke: Macmillan, 1996).

  Religion and the people of western Europe, 1789–1989 (Oxford: Oxford University Press, 1997).

Samuelsson, K., *From great power to welfare state* (London: Allen and Unwin, 1968).

Schmidt, Leigh Eric, *Holy fairs: Scotland and the making of American revivalism*, 2nd edn (Grand Rapids, MI: William B. Eerdmans, 1989).

Scott, F. D., *Sweden: the nation's history* (Minneapolis: University of Minnesota Press, 1977).

Sperber, J., *Popular Catholicism in nineteenth-century Germany* (Princeton : Princeton University Press, 1984).

Thompson, D. M., 'The churches and society in nineteenth-century England: a rural perspective', in G. J. Cuming and D. Baker (eds.), *Popular belief and practice*, Studies in Church History 8 (Cambridge: Cambridge University Press, 1972), pp. 267–76.

Vlekke, B. H. M., *Evolution of the Dutch nation* (London: Dobson, Roy, 1951).

Wintle, M., *An economic and social history of the Netherlands, 1800–1920* (Cambridge: Cambridge University Press, 2000).

14 Catholic Christianity in France, 1815–1905

Acomb, E. M., *The French Laic Laws* (New York: Columbia University Press, 1941).

Anderson, R. D., *Education in France 1848–1870* (Oxford: Clarendon Press, 1975).

Aston, Nigel, *Christianity and Revolutionary Europe, c.1750–1830* (Cambridge: Cambridge University Press, 2002).

Boutry, P. and Cinquin, M., *Deux pèlerinages au XIXe siècle: Ars et Paray-le-Monial* (Paris: Beauchesne, 1980).

Bowman, E. P., *Le Christ romantique* (Geneva: Droz, 1973).

Brown, Marvin L., *Louis Veuillot: French Ultramontane Catholic journalist and layman 1813–1883* (Durham, NC: Moore, 1977).

Bush, J. W., 'Education and social status: the Jesuit College in the early Third Republic', *French Historical Studies* 9 (Spring 1975), 83–104.

Capéran, L., *L'anticléricalisme et l'affaire Dreyfus, 1897–1899* (Toulouse: Imprimerie Régionale, 1948).

Caron, J., *Le Sillon et la démocratie chrétienne, 1894–1910* (Paris: Plon, 1967).

Chevallier, P., *La séparation de l'église et de l'école: Jules Ferry et Léon XIII* (Paris, 1981).

Cholvy, Gérard and Hilaire, Yves-Marie, *Histoire religieuse de la France contemporaine*, 3 vols. (Toulouse: Privat, 1985–8).

Christophe, Paul, *Les choix du clergé dans les Révolutions de 1789, 1830 et 1848*, 2 vols. (Lille: privately published, 1976).

Cubitt, Geoff, *The Jesuit myth: conspiracy theory and politics in nineteenth-century France* (Oxford: Clarendon Press, 1993).

Curtis, Sarah, *Educating the faithful: religion, schooling and society in nineteenth- century France* (Dekalb: Northern Illinois University Press, 2000).

Ford, Caroline, *Creating the nation in provincial France: religion and political identity in Brittany* (Princeton: Princeton University Press, 1993).

Gibson, Ralph, 'Missions paroissiales et réchristianisation en Dordogne au XIXe siècle', *Annales du Midi* 98 (1986), 213–36.

A social history of French Catholicism 1789–1914 (London: Routledge, 1989).

Gough, Austin, *Paris and Rome: the Gallican Church and the Ultramontane campaign 1848–1853* (Oxford: Clarendon Press, 1986).

Harris, Ruth, *Lourdes: body and spirit in the secular age* (London: Allen Lane, 1999).

Hazareesingh, S., *Intellectual founders of the Republic: five studies in nineteenth-century political thought* (Oxford: Oxford University Press, 2001).

Hazareesingh, S. and Wright, V., *Francs-maçons sous le Second Empire: les loges provinciales du Grand-Orient à la veille de la Troisième République* (Rennes: Presses Universitaires de Rennes, 2001).

Jonas, Raymond, *France and the cult of the Sacred Heart: an epic tale for modern times* (Berkeley, Los Angeles and London: University of California Press, 2000).

Kselman, T., *Miracles and prophecies in nineteenth-century France* (New Brunswick, NJ: Rutgers University Press, 1983).

'The dechristianisation of death in modern France', in Hugh McLeod and Werner Ustorf (eds.), *The decline of Christendom in Western Europe 1750–2000* (Cambridge: Cambridge University Press, 2003), pp. 145–62.

Lafon, J., *Les prêtres, les fidèles et l'état: le ménage à trois du XIXe siècle* (Paris: Beauchesne, 1970).

Lalouette, J., *La libre pensée en France 1848–1940* (Paris: Albin Michel, 1997).

Langlois, C., *Le catholicisme au féminin: les congrégations à supérieure générale au XIXe siècle* (Paris: Editions du Cerf, 1984).

Larkin, Maurice, *Church and state after the Dreyfus affair: the separation issue in France* (London: Macmillan, 1974).

Lebrun, J., *Lamennais, ou l'inquiétude de la liberté* (Paris: Fayard-Mame, 1981).

Le Guillou, L., *L'évolution de la pensée religieuse de Félicité Lamennais* (Paris: A. Colin, 1966).

McManners, John, *Church and state in France 1870–1914* (London: SPCK, 1972).

McMillan, James F., 'Religion and politics in nineteenth-century France: further reflections on why Catholics and Republicans couldn't stand each other', in Austen Ivereigh (ed.), *The politics of religion in an age of revival* (London: Institute of Latin American Studies, 2000), pp. 43–55.

'"Priest hits girl": on the front line of the war of the two Frances', in C. Clark, and W. Kaiser (eds.), *Culture wars: secular–Catholic conflict in nineteenth-century Europe* (Cambridge: Cambridge University Press, 2003), pp. 77–101.

'Rediscovering Louis Veuillot: the politics of religious identity in nineteenth-century France', in Nigel Harkness *et al.* (eds.), *Visions/revisions: essays on nineteenth-century French culture* (Oxford and Berne: Peter Lang, 2004), pp. 305–22.

Maurain, J., *La politique ecclésiastique du Second Empire de 1852 à 1869* (Paris: F. Alcan, 1930).

Mayeur, J.-M., *Un prêtre démocrate, l'abbé Lemire (1853–1928)* (Paris: Casterman, 1968).

Montclos, X. de, *Lavigerie, le Saint-Siège et l'église* (Paris: E. de Boccard, 1965).

Montuclard, M., *Conscience religieuse et démocratie chrétienne: la deuxième démocratie chrétienne en France, 1891–1902* (Paris: Editions du Seuil, 1965).

Moody, J. N., *The Church as enemy: anticlericalism in nineteenth-century French literature* (Washington, DC: Corpus Books, 1965).

Partin, Malcolm O., *Waldeck-Rousseau, Combes and the Church: the politics of anticlericalism, 1899–1905* (Durham, NC: Duke University Press, 1969).

Phayer, J. M., 'The cult of the Cross in France 1815–1840', *Journal of Social History* 11 (Spring 1978), 346–65.

Phillips, C. S., *The Church in France 1789–1848* (London: SPCK, 1936).

Pierrard, P., *Louis Veuillot* (Paris: Beauchesne, 1998).

Poulat, E., *Eglise contre bourgeoisie: introduction au devoir du catholicisme actuel* (Tournai: Casterman, 1977).

Scott, I., *The Roman question and the Powers, 1848–1965* (The Hague: Martinus Nijhoff, 1969).

Sedgwick, A., *The Ralliement in French politics 1890–8* (Cambridge, MA: Harvard University Press, 1965).

Sevrin, E., *Les missions religieuses en France sous la Restauration* (Saint-Mandé: Procure des Prêtres de la Miséricorde, 1948).

Sorlin, Pierre, *Waldeck-Rousseau* (Paris: A. Colin, 1966).

'La Croix' et les Juifs (1880–1899) (Paris: B. Grasset, 1967).

Weill, G., *Histoire de l'idée laïque en France au XIXième siècle* (Paris: F. Alcan, 1929).

15 Italy: the church and the *Risorgimento*

Brady, Joseph H., *Rome and the Neapolitan revolution of 1820–21* (New York: Octagon Books, 1976).

Butler, Cuthbert, *The Vatican Council: the story told from inside in Bishop Ullathorne's Letters* (New York: Longmans, Green and Co., 1930).

Carlen, Claudia (ed.), *The papal encyclicals 1740–1878* (Ann Arbor, MI: The Pierian Press, 1981).

    Papal pronouncements: a guide, vol. 1: *Benedict XIV to Paul VI* (Ann Arbor, MI: The Pierian Press, 1990).

Colapietra, Raffaele, 'Il diario Brunelli del conclave del 1823', *Archivio Storico Italiano* 120 (1962), 76–146.

    La Chiesa tra Lamennais e Metternich: il pontificato di Leone XII (Brescia: Morcelliana, 1963).

Coppa, Frank J., '*Realpolitik* and conviction in the conflict between Piedmont and the papacy during the *Risorgimento*', *Catholic Historical Review* 54 (1969), 579–612.

    'Cardinal Antonelli, the Papal States and the Counter-Risorgimento', *Journal of Church and State* 16 (1974), 453–71.

    'Cardinal Giacomo Antonelli: an accommodating personality in the politics of confrontation', *Biography* 2 (1979), 283–302.

    Pope Pius IX: crusader in a secular age (Boston: Twayne Publishers, 1979).

    Cardinal Giacomo Antonelli and papal politics in European affairs (Albany: State University of New York Press, 1990).

    The origins of the Italian wars of independence (London: Longman, 1992).

    The modern papacy since 1789, vol. v of the Longman History of the Papacy (London and New York: Longman, 1998).

Coppa, Frank J. (ed.), *Controversial concordats: the Vatican's relations with Napoleon, Mussolini and Hitler* (Washington, DC: The Catholic University of America Press, 1999).

Engel-Janosi, Friedrich, 'French and Austrian political advice to Pius IX, 1846–1848', *Catholic Historical Review* 38 (1952), 1–20.

Fremantle, Anne (ed.), *The papal encyclicals in their historical context* (New York: G. P. Putnam's Sons, 1956).

Gabriele, Mariano (ed.), *Il carteggio Antonelli-Sacconi (1858–1860)*, 2 vols. (Rome: Istituto per la Storia del Risorgimento Italiano, 1962).

Holmes, J. Derek, *The triumph of the holy see: a short history of the papacy in the nineteenth century* (London: Burns and Oates, 1978).

Kertesz, G. A. (ed.), *Documents in the political history of the European continent* (Oxford: Clarendon Press, 1968).

Leonetti, Alfonso and Pastore, Ottavio, *Chiesa e Risorgimento* (Milan: Edizione Avanti, 1963).

Maiolo, Giovanni (ed.), *Pio IX da Vescovo a pontifice: lettere al Card. Luigi Amat, Agosto 1839–Luglio 1848* (Modena: Società Tipografico Modenese, 1943).

Martina, Giacomo, *Pio IX*, 3 vols. (Rome: Università Gregoriana Editrice, 1974–90).

    Pio IX: chiesa e mondo moderno (Rome: Studium, 1976).

Massari, Giuseppe, *Diario delle cento voci* (Bologna: Cappelli, 1959).

Metternich-Winneburg, Prince Richard (ed.), *Memoirs of Prince Metternich, 1773–1835*, trans. Mrs Alexander Napier, 8 vols. (New York: Howard Fertig, 1970).

Momigliano, Eucardio (ed.), *Tutte le encicliche dei sommi Pontefici* (Milan: dall'Oglio, editore, 1959).

Monti, Antonio, *Pio IX nel Risorgimento Italiano con documenti inediti* (Bari: Laterza, 1928).

Nielsen, Fredrik, *History of the papacy in the XIX century*, trans. Arthur James Mason, 2 vols. (London: John Murray, 1906).

O'Dwyer, Margaret M., *The papacy in the age of Napoleon and the Restoration: Pius VII, 1800–1823* (New York: University Press of America, 1985).

Reinerman, Alan, 'Metternich and the papal condemnation of the Carbonari, 1821', *Catholic Historical Review* 54 (1968), 55–69.

Austria and the papacy in the age of Metternich: I – between conflict and cooperation, 1809–1830 (Washington, DC: Catholic University of America Press, 1979).

Serafini, Alberto, *Pio Nono: Giovanni Maria Mastai Ferretti dalla giovinezzza alla morte nei suoi scritti e discorsi editi e inediti* (Vatican City: Tipografia Poliglotta Vaticana, 1958).

16 Catholicism, Ireland and the Irish diaspora

Campion, Edmund, *Australian Catholics* (Ringwood, Victoria: Viking, 1987).

Clark, C. M. H., *A history of Australia*, vol. 1: *From the earliest times to the age of Macquarie* (Melbourne: Melbourne University Press, 1962).

Connolly, Sean J., *Priests and people in pre-Famine Ireland, 1780–1845* (London and New York: Gill and Macmillan and St Martin's Press, 1982).

Religion and society in nineteenth-century Ireland (Dundalk: Dundalgan Press, 1985).

Corish, Patrick J., *The Irish Catholic experience: a historical survey* (Dublin: Gill and Macmillan, 1985).

Maynooth College 1795–1995 (Dublin: Gill and Macmillan, 1995).

Corish, Patrick J. (ed.), *A history of Irish Catholicism* (Dublin: Gill and Macmillan (not in order by volume: 1967–72), vols. I–VI.

Dolan, Jay P., *The immigrant church: New York's Irish and German Catholics, 1815–1865* (Baltimore and London: Johns Hopkins University Press, 1975).

The American Catholic experience: a history from colonial times to the present (New York: Doubleday, 1985).

Fallows, Marjorie R., *Irish Americans: identity and assimilation* (Englewood Cliffs, NJ: Prentice Hall, 1979).

Fogarty, Gerald P., *The Vatican and the American hierarchy from 1870 to 1965* (Stuttgart: Anton Hiersemann, 1982).

Gilley, Sheridan, 'The Roman Catholic Church and the nineteenth-century Irish diaspora', *Journal of Ecclesiastical History* 35 (1984), 188–207.

Gleason, Philip (ed.), *Catholicism in America* (New York: Harper and Row, 1970).

Graham, B. J. and Proudfoot, L. J. (eds.), *An historical geography of Ireland* (London: Academic Press, 1973).

Hennesey, James, *American Catholics: a history of the Roman Catholic community in the United States* (Oxford: Oxford University Press, 1981).

Keenan, Desmond, *The Catholic Church in nineteenth-century Ireland: a sociological study* (Dublin: Gill and Macmillan, 1983).

Kelly, James and Keogh, Dáire, *History of the Catholic diocese of Dublin* (Dublin: Four Courts Press, 2000).

Kerr, Donal A., *Peel, priests and politics: Sir Robert Peel's administration and the Roman Catholic Church in Ireland, 1841–1846* (Oxford: Clarendon Press, 1982).

'Government and Roman Catholics in Ireland, 1850–1940', in Donal A. Kerr *et al.* (eds.), *Religion, state and ethnic groups*, vol. II: *Comparative studies on governments and non-dominant ethnic groups in Europe, 1850–1940* (Aldershot: Dartmouth Pub. Co. for the European Science Foundation, 1992), pp. 277–311.

'*A nation of beggars'? Priests, people, and politics in Famine Ireland, 1846–1852* (Oxford: Clarendon Press, 1994).

Larkin, Emmet, 'Economic growth, capital investment, and the Roman Catholic Church in nineteenth-century Ireland', *American Historical Review* 72 (1967), 852–84.

'The Devotional Revolution in Ireland, 1850–75', *American Historical Review* 77 (1972), 625–52.

'Church, state and nation in modern Ireland', *American Historical Review* 80 (1975), 1244–76.

The making of the Roman Catholic Church in Ireland, 1850–1860 (Chapel Hill: University of North Carolina Press, 1980).

The consolidation of the Roman Catholic Church in Ireland, 1860–1870 (Dublin: Gill and Macmillan, 1987).

Lee, Joseph, *The modernisation of Irish society: 1848–1918* (Dublin: Gill and Macmillan, 1973).

Miller, David, 'Irish Catholicism and the Great Famine', *Journal of Social History* 9 (1975), 81–98.

Molony, John N., *The Roman mould of the Australian Catholic Church* (Melbourne: Melbourne University Press, 1969).

Moran, Gerard, *A radical priest in Mayo: Fr Patrick Lavelle: the rise and fall of an Irish Nationalist 1825–86* (Dublin: Four Courts Press, 1994).

Moran, Gerard (ed.), *Radical Irish priests 1660–1970* (Dublin: Four Courts Press, 1998).

Murphy, Terrence and Byrne, Cyril J. (eds.), *Religion and identity: the experience of Irish and Scottish Catholics in Atlantic Canada: selected papers from a conference on Roman Catholicism in Anglophone Canada* (St John's, Newfoundland: Jesperson Press, 1987).

O'Farrell, Patrick, *St Mary's Cathedral, Sydney 1821–1971* (Surry Hills: Devonshire Press, 1971).

The Catholic Church and community in Australia: a history (Melbourne: Nelson, 1977).

The Irish in Australia (Kensington, New South Wales: New South Wales University Press, 1987).

O'Sullivan, Patrick (ed.), *Religion and identity*, vol. v: *The Irish world wide* (London: Leicester University Press, 1996).

Sheils, W. J. and Wood, Diana (eds.), *The churches, Ireland and the Irish*, Studies in Church History 25 (Oxford: Blackwell, 1989).

Swift, Roger and Gilley, Sheridan, *The Irish in the Victorian city* (London: Croom Helm, 1985).

The Irish in Britain 1815–1939 (London: Pinter Publishers, 1989).

The Irish in Victorian Britain: the local dimension (Dublin: Four Courts Press, 1999).

17 Catholic nationalism in Greater Hungary and Poland

A: Hungary

Adriányi, Gabriel, *Die Stellung der ungarischen Kirche zum österreichischen Konkordat von 1855* (Rome: privately published, 1963).

Fünfzig Jahre ungarischer Kirchengeschichte, 1895–1945, Studia Hungarica 6 (Mainz: Verlag von Hase and Koehler, 1974).

Ungarn und das I. Vaticanum, Bonner Beiträge zur Kirchengeschichte 5 (Cologne and Vienna: Böhlau-Verlag, 1975).

Beiträge zur Kirchengeschichte Ungarns, Studia Hungarica 30 (Munich: Trofenik-Verlag, 1986).

Kleine Kirchengeschichte Ungarns, Studien zur Geschichte Ungarns 5 (Herne: Verlag Gabriele Schäfer, 2003).

Geschichte der katholischen Kirche in Ungarn, Bonner Beiträge zur Kirchengeschichte 26 (Cologne, Weimar and Vienna: Böhlau-Verlag, 2004).

Gergely, Jenö, *Katolikus egyház, magyar társadalom 1890–1986* (Budapest: Tankönyvkiado, 1989).

Gratz, Gusztáv, *A dualizmus kora: Magyarország története 1867–1918*, 2 vols. (Budapest: Magyar Szemle Társ, 1934).

Haltmayer, Josef (ed.), *Die katholischen Donauschwaben in der Doppelmonarchie 1867–1918* (Stuttgart: Verlag Buch und Kunst Kettlerhaus, 1977).

Hanák, Péter (ed.), *Studien zur Geschichte der österreichisch-ungarischen Monarchie* (Budapest: Akadémiai Kiadó, 1961).

Hanák, Péter, *et al.*, *Magyarország története 1848–1918*, 2 vols. (Budapest: Tankönyvkiado, 1972).

Hermann, Egyed, *A katolikus egyház története Magyarországon 1914-ig*, Dissertationes Hungaricae ex Historia Ecclesiae 1 (Munich: Aurora Könyvek, 1973).

Nyisztor, Zoltán, *Ötven esztendö: Századunk katolikus megujhodása* (Vienna: Becs Opus Mystici Corporis, 1962).

Salacz, Gábor, *Egyház és állam Magyarországon a dualizmus korában 1867–1918*, Dissertationes Hungaricae ex Historia Ecclesiae 2 (Munich: Aurora Könyvek, 1974).

Steed, H. Wickham, Phillips, Walter Alison and Hannay, David, *A short history of Austria-Hungary and Poland* (London: Encyclopaedia Britannica Co., 1914).

Török, Jenö, *A katolikus autonómia mozgalom 1848–1871* (Budapest: Stephaneum, 1941).

B: Poland

Billot, C. C., *Honorat Kominski 1829–1916* (Paris: Editions Notre Dame de la Trinité, 1982).

Chlebowczyk, Józef, *On small and young nations in Europe: nation-forming processes in ethnic borderlands in east-central Europe* (Wrocław: Zaklad Narodowy im. ssolinskich Wydawnictwo Polskiej Akademii Nauk, 1980).

Davies, Norman, *God's playground: a history of Poland*, 2 vols. (Oxford: Clarendon Press, 1981).

Delsol, Chantal and Maslowski, Michel (directors), *Histoire des idées politiques de l'Europe centrale* (Paris: Presses Universitaires de France, 1998).

Delsol, Chantal, Maslowski, Michel and Nowicki, Joanna (directors), *Mythes et symboles politiques en Europe centrale* (Paris: Presses Universitaires de France, 2002).

Hrytsak, Jaroslav, *Historia Ukrainy 1772–1999: Narodziny nowoczesnego narodu (Birth of a modern nation)* (Lublin: Instytut Europy Środkowo-Wschodniej, 2000).

Kiaupa, Zigmantas, *The history of Lithuania*, trans. S. C. Rowell (Vilnius, Lithuania: Baltos Lankos, 2002).

Kieniewicz, Stefan, 'Eglises et nationalités en Europe centrale-orientale au XIXe s.', in *The common Christian roots of the European nation: an international colloquium in the Vatican*, 2 vols. (Florence: Le Monnier, 1982), vol. 1, pp. 127–36.

'Polish revolutionaries of the nineteenth century and the Catholic Church', in David Loades and Katherine Walsh (eds.), *Faith and identity: Christian political experience*, Studies in Church History Subsidia 6 (Oxford: Basil Blackwell, 1990), pp. 147–59.

Kłoczowski, Jerzy, 'The place of the Jews in the socio-religious history of Poland and the Polish-Lithuanian-Ruthenian commonwealth', in Andrzej K. Paluch (ed.), *The Jews in Poland*, 2 vols. (Cracow: Research Centre on Jewish History and Culture in Poland, Jagiellonian University, 1992), Subsidia 6, vol. 1, pp. 77–91.

'Christianisme et nationalité dans l'Europe du centre est', in Jacques Gadille and Jean-Marie Mayeur (directors), *Histoire du Christianisme des origines à nos jours* (Paris: Declée, 1995), pp. 703–29.

A history of Polish Christianity (Cambridge: Cambridge University Press, 2000).

Kłoczowski, Jerzy (ed.), *Histoire religieuse de la Pologne* (Paris: Centurion, 1987).

Belarus, Lithuania, Poland, Ukraine: the foundations of historical and cultural traditions in east-central Europe (Lublin: Institute of East-Central Europe; Rome: Foundation of John Paul II, 1994).

Kłoczowski, Jerzy and Beauvois, Daniel (eds.), *Historia Europy Środkowo-Wschodniej*, 2 vols. (Lublin: Instytut Europy Środkowo-Wschodniej, 2000).

Magocsi, Paul R., *A history of Ukraine* (Seattle: University of Washington Press, 1996).

Olszamowska-Skowrońska, Z., 'La suppression des diocèses catholiques par le gouvernement russe après l'insurrection de 1843', *Antemurale* 9 (1965), 41–130.

'Tentatives d'introduire la lange russe dans les églises latines de la Pologne orientale (1865–1903)', *Antemurale* 11 (1967), 47–169.

Olszewski, Daniel, 'Le rôle des églises dans le processus nation-formateurs en Europe-centrale et orientale au declin du XIXe s. et au début du XXe s.', in *The common Christian roots of the European nation: an international colloquium in the Vatican*, 2 vols. (Florence: Le Monnier, 1982), vols. 1, pp. 1110–14.

Parot, Joseph John, *Polish Catholics in Chicago, 1850–1920: a religious history* (DeKalb: Northern Illinois University Press, 1981).

Shibeko, Zakhar Vasil'evich, *Historia Bialorusi: 1795–2000* (Lublin: Instytut Europy Środkowo-Wschodniej, 2002).

Snyder, Timothy, *The reconstruction of nations: Poland, Ukraine, Lithuania, Belarus 1569–1999* (New Haven: Yale University Press, 2003).

Sporluk, Roman, *Russia, Ukraine and the breakup of the Soviet Union* (Stanford, CA: Hoover Institution Press, 1999).

Trzeciakowski, Lech, 'The Prussian state and the Catholic Church in Prussian Poland, 1871–1914', *Slavic Review* 26 (1967), 618–37.

Wandycz, Piotr Stefan, *The lands of partitioned Poland 1795–1918*, vol. VII: *A history of east central Europe* (Seattle: University of Washington Press, 1974).

The price of freedom: a history of east central Europe from the Middle Ages to the present (London and New York: Routledge, 2001).

Wlodarski, S. W., *The origin and growth of the Polish National Catholic Church* (Scranton, PA: Polish National Catholic Church, 1974).

Zamoyski, Adam, *The Polish way: a thousand-year history of the Poles and their culture* (New York: F. Watts, 1988).

Zaprudnik, Jan, *Belarus: at a crossroads in history* (Boulder, CO: Westview Press, 1993).

Zernack, Klaus, *Polen und Russland: zwei Wege in der europäischen Geschichte* (Berlin: Propyläen Verlag, 1994).

18 Christianity and the creation of Germany

Altgeld, Wolfgang, *Katholizismus, Protestantismus, Judentum: über religiös begründete Gegensätze und nationalreligiöse Ideen in der Geschichte des deutschen Nationalismus* (Mainz: Matthias-Grünewald Verlag, 1992).

'German Catholics', in Rainer Liedtke and Stephan Wendehorst (eds.), *The emancipation of Catholics, Jews and Protestants: minorities and the nation state in nineteenth-century Europe* (Manchester: University of Manchester Press, 1999), pp. 100–21.

Anderson, Margaret Lavinia, 'The *Kulturkampf* and the course of German history', *Central European History* 19 (1986), 82–115.

Besier, Gerhard, *Religion Nation Kultur: die Geschichte der christlichen Kirchen in den gesellschaftlichen Umbrüchen des 19. Jahrhunderts* (Neukirchen-Vlyun: Neukirchener Verlag, 1992).

Bigler, Robert M., *The politics of German Protestantism: the rise of the Protestant Church elite in Prussia, 1815–1848* (Berkeley: University of California Press, 1972).

Blackbourn, David, *The long nineteenth century: a history of Germany, 1870–1918* (Oxford: Oxford University Press, 1998).

Bowman, William David, *Priest and parish in Vienna, 1780–1880*, Studies in Central European Histories (Boston: Humanities Press, 1999).

Boyer, John W., *Political radicalism in late imperial Vienna: origins of the Christian Social movement 1848–1897* (Chicago: University of Chicago Press, 1981).

Culture and political crisis in Vienna: Christian Socialism in power, 1897–1918 (Chicago: University of Chicago Press, 1995).

Breuilly, John, *The formation of the first German nation-state 1800–1871* (London: Macmillan, 1996).

Clark, Christopher, 'German Jews', in Rainer Liedtke and Stephan Wendehorst (eds.), *The emancipation of Catholics, Jews and Protestants: minorities and the nation state in nineteenth-century Europe* (Manchester: University of Manchester Press, 1999), pp. 122–47.

Götz von Olenhusen, Irmtraud, *Klerus und abweichendes Verhalten: zur Sozialgeschichte katholischer Priester im 19. Jahrhundert: die Erzdiöcese Freiburg* (Göttingen: Vandenhoeck and Ruprecht, 1994).

Gross, Michael B., *The war against Catholicism: liberalism and the anti-Catholic imagination in nineteenth-century Germany* (Ann Arbor: The University of Michigan Press, 2004).

Huber, Ernst Rudolf and Huber, Wolfgang (eds.), *Staat und Kirche im 19. und 20. Jahrhundert: Dokumente zur Geschichte des deutschen Staatskirchenrechts*, 5 vols. (Berlin: Duncker und Humblot, 1973–95).

Hübinger, Gangolf, 'Confessionalism', in Roger Chickering (ed.), *Imperial Germany: a historiographical companion* (Westport, CT: Greenwood Press, 1996), pp. 156–84.

Lamberti, Marjorie, *State, society and the elementary school in imperial Germany* (New York: Oxford University Press, 1989).

Langewiesche, Dieter, 'Reich, Nation und Staat in der jüngeren deutschen Geschichte', *Historische Zeitschrift* 254 (1992), 341–81.

Lidtke, Vernon L., *The alternative culture: socialist labor in imperial Germany* (New York and Oxford: Oxford University Press, 1985).

Nipperdey, Thomas, *Deutsche Geschichte 1866–1918*, 2 vols. (Munich: C. H. Beck, 1990–2).

Germany from Napoleon to Bismarck: 1800–1866 (Princeton: Princeton University Press, 1996).

Nowak, Kurt, *Geschichte des Christentums in Deutschland: Religion, Politik und Gesellschaft vom Ende der Aufklärung bis zur Mitte des 20. Jahrhunderts* (Munich: C. H. Beck, 1995).

Rauscher, Anton (ed.), *Probleme des Konfessionalismus in Deutschland seit 1800* (Paderborn: Schöningh, 1984).

Ross, Ronald J., *The failure of Bismarck's Kulturkampf: Catholicism and state power in imperial Germany, 1871–1887* (Washington, DC: Catholic University Press of America, 1998).

Schnabel, Franz, *Deutsche Geschichte im neunzehnten Jahrhundert*, vol. IV: *Die religiösen Kräfte* (Munich: DTV, 1987).

Sheehan, James J., *German history 1770–1866* (Oxford: Oxford University Press, 1989).

Smith, Helmut Walser, *German nationalism and religious conflict: culture, ideology, politics, 1870–1914* (Princeton: Princeton University Press, 1995).

Smith, Helmut Walser (ed.), *Protestants, Catholics and Jews in Germany, 1890–1914* (Oxford: Berg, 2001).

Sperber, Jonathan, *Popular Catholicism in nineteenth-century Germany* (Princeton: Princeton University Press, 1984).

Tal, Uriel, *Christians and Jews in Germany: religion, politics, and ideology in the Second Reich, 1870–1914* (Ithaca, NY: Cornell University Press, 1975).

Wandruszka, Adam and Urbanitsch, Peter (eds.), *Die Habsburgermonarchie 1848–1918*, vol. IV: *Die Konfessionen* (Vienna: Verlag der Österreichischen Akademie der Wissenschaften, 1987).

19 Anglicanism, Presbyterianism and the religious identities of the United Kingdom

Akenson, D. H., *The Church of Ireland: ecclesiastical reform and revolution, 1800–1885* (New Haven: Yale University Press, 1971).

Bell, P. M. H., *Disestablishment in Ireland and Wales* (London: SPCK, 1969).

Bentley, J., *Ritualism and politics in Victorian Britain: the attempt to legislate for belief* (Oxford: Oxford University Press, 1978).

Best, G. F. A., *Temporal pillars: Queen Anne's bounty, the Ecclesiastical Commissioners, and the Church of England* (Cambridge: Cambridge University Press, 1964).

Bowen, D., *The Protestant crusade in Ireland, 1800–70: a study of Protestant Catholic relations between the Act of Union and disestablishment* (Dublin: Gill and Macmillan, 1978).

Brent, R., *Liberal Anglican politics: Whiggery, religion and reform 1830–1841* (Oxford: Clarendon Press, 1987).

Brooke, P., *Ulster Presbyterianism: the historical perspective 1610–1970* (Dublin: Gill and Macmillan, 1987).

Brown, C. G., 'The myth of the established Church of Scotland', in J. Kirk (ed.), *The Scottish churches and the Union Parliament 1707–1999* (Edinburgh: Scottish Church History Society, 2001), pp. 48–74.

Brown, R. L., 'In pursuit of a Welsh episcopate', in R. Pope (ed.), *Religion and national identity: Wales and Scotland c. 1700–2000* (Cardiff: University of Wales Press, 2001), pp. 84–102.

Brown, S. J., *Thomas Chalmers and the godly commonwealth in Scotland* (Oxford: Oxford University Press, 1982).

The national churches of England, Ireland, and Scotland 1801–1846 (Oxford: Oxford University Press, 2001).

Burns, A., *The diocesan revival in the Church of England c.1800–1870* (Oxford: Clarendon Press, 1999).

Cannadine, D., 'The context, performance and meaning of ritual: the British monarchy and the "invention of tradition", c. 1820–1977', in E. Hobsbawm and T. Ranger (eds.), *The invention of tradition* (Cambridge: Cambridge University Press, 1983), pp. 101–64.

Chadwick, O., *The Victorian church*, 2 vols. (London: A. and C. Black, 1966, 1970).

Clark, J. C. D., *English society 1688–1832* (Cambridge: Cambridge University Press, 1985).

Colley, L., *Britons: forging the nation 1707–1837* (New Haven: Yale University Press, 1992).

Connolly, S., *Religion and society in nineteenth-century Ireland* (Dundalk: Dundalgan Press, 1985).

Conybeare, W. J. (ed. Burns, A.), 'Church parties', in S. Taylor (ed.), *From Cranmer to Davidson: a miscellany* (Woodbridge: Boydell/Church of England Record Society, 1999), pp. 215–385.

Cragoe, M., *An Anglican aristocracy: the moral economy of the landed estate in Carmarthenshire 1832–1895* (Oxford: Oxford University Press, 1996).

Currie, R., Gilbert, A. and Horsley, L., *Churches and churchgoers: patterns of church growth in the British Isles since 1700* (Oxford: Clarendon Press, 1977).

Davies, E. T. *Religion in the industrial revolution of South Wales* (Cardiff: University of Wales Press, 1965).

A new history of Wales: religion and society in the nineteenth century (Llandybïe: Christopher Davies, 1981).

Drummond, A. L. and Bulloch, J., *The church in Victorian Scotland 1843–1874* (Edinburgh: St Andrew Press, 1975).

The church in late Victorian Scotland 1874–1900 (Edinburgh: St Andrew Press, 1978).

Forbes, D., *The Liberal Anglican idea of history* (Cambridge: Cambridge University Press, 1952).

Gash, N., *Reaction and reconstruction in English politics 1832–1852* (Oxford: Clarendon Press, 1965).

Gilbert, A. D., *Religion and society in industrial England: church, chapel and social change 1740–1914* (London: Longman, 1976).

Hanham, H. J., 'Mid-century Scottish nationalism: romantic and radical', in R. Robson (ed.), *Ideas and institutions of Victorian Britain: essays in honour of George Kitson Clark* (London: G. Bell and Sons, 1967), pp. 143–79.

Hempton, D., *Religion and political culture in Britain and Ireland from the Glorious Revolution to the decline of empire* (Cambridge: Cambridge University Press, 1996).

Hempton D. and Hill, M., *Evangelical Protestantism in Ulster society 1740–1890* (London: Routledge, 1992).

Holmes, F., *Henry Cooke* (Belfast: Christian Journals, 1981).

McBride, I., *The siege of Derry in Ulster Protestant mythology* (Dublin: Four Courts Press, 1997).

Machin, G. I. T., *Politics and the churches in Great Britain 1832 to 1868* (Oxford: Clarendon Press, 1977).

Marsh, P. T., *The Victorian church in decline: Archbishop Tait and the Church of England, 1868–1882* (London: Routledge and Kegan Paul, 1969).

Mathias, P., *The first industrial nation: an economic history of Britain 1700–1914* (London: Methuen, 1969).

Morgan, P., 'From a death to a view: the hunt for the Welsh past in the romantic period', in E. Hobsbawm and T. Ranger (eds.), *The invention of tradition* (Cambridge: Cambridge University Press, 1983), pp. 43–100.

Parsons, G. A., Moore, J. R. and Wolffe, J. (eds.), *Religion in Victorian Britain*, 5 vols. (Manchester: Open University / Manchester University Press, 1988, 1997).

Roxborogh, J., *Thomas Chalmers: enthusiast for mission: the Christian good of Scotland and the rise of the missionary movement* (Carlisle: Paternoster, 1999).

Stewart, A. T. Q., *The Ulster crisis: resistance to Home Rule, 1912–14* (London: Faber and Faber, 1967).

Wolffe, J., *The Protestant crusade in Great Britain 1829–1860* (Oxford: Clarendon Press, 1991).

God and greater Britain: religion and national life in Britain and Ireland 1843–1945 (London: Routledge, 1994).

Great deaths: grieving, religion and nationhood in Victorian and Edwardian Britain (Oxford: British Academy / Oxford University Press, 2000).

'National occasions at St Paul's since 1800', in A. Burns, D. Keene and A. Saint (eds.), *St Paul's: the cathedral church of London 604–2004* (New Haven: Yale University Press, 2004), pp. 381–91.

Young, G. M. and Handcock, W. D. (eds.), *English historical documents 1833–1874* (London: Eyre and Spottiswoode, 1956).

20 Protestant dominance: Switzerland and the Netherlands

A: Switzerland

Altermatt, Urs, *Der Weg der Schweizer Katholiken ins Ghetto: die Entstehungsgeschichte der nationalen Volksorganisationen im Schweizer Katholizismus 1848–1919* (Zurich and Cologne: Benziger, 1972, 2nd edn 1991; Fribourg: Universitätsverlag, 3rd edn 1995).

'Conservatism in Switzerland: a study in antimodernism', in 'A century of conservatism, part 2', *Journal of Contemporary History* 14 (1979), 581–610.

Katholizismus und Moderne: zur Sozial- und Mentalitätsgeschichte der Schweizer Katholiken im 19. und 20. Jahrhundert (Zurich: Benziger, 1989, 2nd edn 1991).

Katholizismus und Antisemitismus: Mentalitäten, Kontinuitäten, Ambivalenzen: Zur Kulturgeschichte der Schweiz 1918–1945 (Frauenfeld, Stuttgart and Vienna: Huber, 1999).

'Religion und Nation. Die Rolle der Religion bei der Nationalstaatenbildung Europas im 19. und 20. Jahrhundert', in Dieter Ruloff (ed.), *Religion und Politik* (Chur and Zurich: Rüegger, 2001), pp. 27–52.

'Ambivalence of Catholic modernisation', in Judith Frishman, Willemien Otten and Gerard Rouwhorst (eds.), *Religious identity and the problem of historical foundation: the foundational character of authoritative texts and traditions in the history of Christianity* (Leiden: Brill, 2004), pp. 49–75.

'Religion, Staat und Gesellschaft in der Schweiz', in *Jüdische Lebenswelt Schweiz: 100 Jahre Schweizerischer Israelitischer Gemeindebund (SIG)* (Zurich: Chronos, 2004), pp. 377–87.

Altermatt, Urs (ed.), *'Den Riesenkampf mit dieser Zeit zu wagen . . .': Schweizerischer Studentenverein 1841–1991* (Lucerne: Maihof, 1993).

Altermatt, Urs and Metzger, Franziska, 'Katholische Arbeiter und Milieuidentität in der Schweiz 1850–1950', in Claudia Hiepel and Mark Ruff (eds.), *Christliche Arbeiterbewegung in Europa 1850–1950* (Stuttgart: Kohlhammer, 2003), pp. 159–75.

'Milieu, Teilmilieus und Netzwerke. Das Beispiel des Schweizer Katholizismus', in Urs Altermatt, (ed.), *Katholische Denk- und Lebenswelten: Beiträge zur Kultur und Sozialgeschichte des Schweizer Katholizismus im 20. Jahrhundert* (Fribourg: Academic Press Fribourg, 2003), pp. 15–36.

Arx, Urs von, 'Christkatholische Kirche', in *Historisches Lexikon der Schweiz* (in preparation).

Conzemius, Victor, *Katholizismus ohne Rom: die Altkatholische Kirchengemeinschaft* (Zurich, Einsiedeln and Cologne: Benziger, 1969).

Philipp Anton von Segesser, 1817–1888: Demokrat zwischen den Fronten (Zurich: Benziger 1977).

Gäbler, Ulrich, 'Erweckungsbewegungen', in *Historisches Lexikon der Schweiz* (in preparation).

Mattioli, Aram (ed.), *Antisemitismus in der Schweiz 1848–1960* (Zurich: Chronos, 1998).

Metzger, Franziska, *Die 'Schildwache': eine integralistisch-rechtskatholische Zeitschrift 1912–1945* (Fribourg: Universitätsverlag, 2000).

'The legal situation of religious institutes in Switzerland in the context of conflicts about social and cultural modernisation and discourses about national hegemony', in Jan De Maeyer, Sofie Leplae and Joachim Schmiedl (eds.), *Religious institutes in western Europe in the 19th and 20th centuries: historiography, research and legal position* (Leuven: Leuven University Press, 2004), pp. 309–30.

'Die Reformation in der Schweiz zwischen 1850 und 1950: konkurrierende konfessionelle und nationale Geschichtskonstruktionen und Erinnerungsgemeinschaften', in Heinz-Gerhard Haupt and Dieter Langewiesche (eds.), *Nation und Religion in Europa: Mehrkonfessionelle Gesellschaften im 19. und 20. Jahrhundert* (Frankfurt and New York: Campus Verlag, 2004), pp. 64–98.

Pfister, Rudolf, *Kirchengeschichte der Schweiz*, 3 vols. (Zurich: Theologischer Verlag, 1964–).

Ruffieux, Roland, *Le mouvement chrétien-social en Suisse romande 1891–1949* (Fribourg: Universitätsverlag, 1969).

Ruffieux, Roland, *et al.* (eds.), *Geschichte der Universität Freiburg Schweiz: Institutionen, Lehre und Forschungsbereiche*, 3 vols. (Fribourg: Universitätsverlag, 1991).

Stadler, Peter, *Der Kulturkampf in der Schweiz: Eidgenossenschaft und katholische Kirche im europäischen Umkreis 1848–1888* (Zurich: Chronos, 2nd edn 1996).

Vischer, Lukas, Schenker, Lukas and Dellsperger, Rudolf (eds.), *Ökumenische Kirchengeschichte der Schweiz* (Fribourg: Universitätsverlag, 1994), especially: Olivier Fatio, 'Die protestantischen Kirchen' and 'Auseinandersetzungen und Aufbrüche innerhalb des Protestantismus', pp. 215–19, 236–46.

Von der katholischen Milieuorganisation zum sozialen Hilfswerk: 100 Jahre Caritas Schweiz, ed. by the Caritas Schweiz (Lucerne: Caritas Verlag, 2002).

Zeitschrift für Schweizerische Kirchengeschichte 90 (1996).

Zimmer, Oliver, *A contested nation: history, memory and nationalism in Switzerland, 1761–1891* (Cambridge: Cambridge University Press, 2003).

B: The Netherlands

Bank, J. and Buuren, M. van, *1900: hoogtij van burgelijke cultuur* (The Hague: SDU, 2000).

Bos, D. J., *In dienst van het koninkrijk: beroepsontwikkeling van hervormde predikanten in negentiende-eeuws Nederland* (Amsterdam: Bakker, 1999).

Heslam, P. S., *Creating a Christian worldview: Abraham Kuyper's lectures on Calvinism* (Grand Rapids, MI: Eerdmans, 1998).

Kok, J. A. de, *Nederland op de breuklijn Rome-Reformatie: numerieke aspecten van protestantisering en katholieke herleving in de noordelijke Nederlanden 1580–1880* (Assen: Van Gorcum, 1964).

Koppen, C. A. J. van, *De geuzen van de negentiende eeuw: Abraham Kuyper en Zuid-Afrika* (Wormer: Inmerc, 1992).

Kossmann, E. H., *The Low Countries 1780–1940* (Oxford: Clarendon Press, 1978).

'Some questions concerning Dutch national consciousness', *Dutch Crossing* 34 (April 1988), 1–14.

Lijphart, A., *The politics of accommodation: pluralism and democracy in the Netherlands* (Berkeley: University of California Press, 1st edn, 1968; and 2nd edn, 1975).

Lipschits, I., *De protestants-christelijke stroming tot 1940: ontstaansgeschiedenis van de Nederlandse politieke partijen, deel 1* (Deventer: Kluwer, 1977).

Miert, J. van, 'Confessionelen en de natie, 1870–1920', in *Om het christelijk karakter der natie: confessionelen en de modernisering van de maatschappij*, ed. Dirk Jan Wolffram (Amsterdam: Het Spinhuis, 1994), pp. 89–112.

Raedts, P., 'Katholieken op zoek naar een Nederlandse identiteit 1814–1898', *Bijdragen en Mededelingen betreffende de Geschiedenis der Nederlanden* 107 (1992), 713–25.

Rasker, A. J., *De Nederlandse Hervormde Kerk vanaf 1795: haar geschiedenis en theologie in de negentiende en twintigste eeuw* (Kampen: Kok, 1974).

Righart, H., *De katholieke zuil in Europa: een vergelijkend onderzoek naar het ontstaan van verzuiling onder katholieken in Oostenrijk, Zwitserland, België en Nederland* (Meppel: Boom, 1986).

Rooden, P. van, *Religieuze regimes: over godsdienst en maatschappij in Nederland 1570–1990* (Amsterdam: Bakker, 1996).

Sas, N. C. F. van, 'De mythe Nederland', *De Negentiende Eeuw* 16 (1992), 4–22.

Vis, J. and Janse, W. (eds.), *Staf en storm: het herstel van de bisschoppelijke hiërarchie in Nederland in 1853: actie en reactie* (Hilversum: Verloren, 2002).

Wintle, M. J., *Pillars of piety: religion in the Netherlands in the nineteenth century* (Hull: Hull University Press, 1987).

An economic and social history of the Netherlands 1800–1920: demographic, economic and social transition (Cambridge: Cambridge University Press, 2000).

21 Scandinavia: Lutheranism and national identity

Anderson, Benedict, *Imagined communities: reflections on the origin and spread of nationalism* (London: Verso, 1983).

Bloom, William, *Personal identity, national identity and international relations* (Cambridge: Cambridge University Press, 1990).

Brohed, Ingmar (ed.), *Church and people in Britain and Scandinavia* (Lund: Lund University Press; Bromley: Chartwell-Bratt, 1996).

Hope, Nicholas, *German and Scandinavian Protestantism, 1700–1918* (Oxford: Clarendon Press, 1995).

Hunter, L. S. (ed.), *Scandinavian churches* (London: Faber and Faber, 1965).

Hutchinson, John, *The dynamics of cultural nationalism: the Gaelic revival and the creation of the Irish nation state* (London: Allen and Unwin, 1987).

Lausten, M. S., *A church history of Denmark* (Aldershot: Ashgate, 2002).

Molland, E., *Church life in Norway, 1800–1950* (Minneapolis: Augsburg Publishing House, 1947).

Murtorinne, E., 'Den fennomanska rörelsen och Finlands kyrka 1850–1914', in Ingmar Brohed (ed.), *Kyrka och nationalism i Norden: nationalism och skandinavism i de nordiska folkkyrkorna under 1800-talet* (Lund: Lund University Press, 1998), pp. 381–91.

Østergård, U., 'Norden – europæisk eller nordisk?', *Den Jyske Historiker* 69/70 (Aarhus, 1994), pp. 7–37.

Østerlin, Lars, *Nordisk lutherdom över gränsarna* (Copenhagen: Gad, 1972).

Churches of northern Europe in profile: a thousand years of Anglo-Nordic relations (Norwich: The Canterbury Press, 1995).

Peturson, P., 'Väckelser på Island', in A. Gustavsson (ed.), *Religiösa väckelsesrörelser i Norden* (Lund: Centrum för Religionsetnologisk Forskning, 1984), pp. 85–95.

Rasmussen, P. M., *Den færøske sprogrejsning med henblik på kampen om færøsk som kirkesprog i national og partipolitisk betydning*, Annales Societatis Færoensis, Supplementum 13 (Hoydølum: P. M. Rasmussen, 1987).

Sørensen, Ø. and Stråth, B., *The cultural construction of Norden* (Oslo: Scandinavian University Press, 1997).

Thorkildsen, Dag, 'Fra Martin Luther til Eivind Berggrav: fortolkning og bruk av Rom. 13.1–7', *Norsk Teologisk Tidsskrift* 90 (1989), 105–23.

Skandinavismen: en historisk oversikt, KULTs Skriftserie 30 (Oslo: Norges Forskningsråd, 1994).

Nasjonalitet, identitet og moral, KULTs Skriftserie 33 (Oslo: Norges Forskningsråd, 1995).

Grundtvigianisme og nasjonalisme i Norge i det 19. århundre, KULTs Skriftserie 70 (Oslo: Norges Forskningsråd, 1996).

'Vekkelse og modernisering i Norden på 1800-tallet', *Historisk Tidsskrift* 98 (1998), 160–80.

Wåhlin, V., 'Religiøse vækkelsesbevæglser i Danmark', in A. Gustavsson (ed.), *Religiösa väckelserörelser i Norden* (Lund: Centrum för Religionsetnologisk Forskning, 1984), pp. 51–68.

Westin, Gunnar, *Den kristna friförsamlingen i Norden* (Stockholm, 1958).

22 'Christian America' and 'Christian Canada'

North American: general

Gaustad, Edwin Scott and Barlow, Philip L., *New historical atlas of religion in America* (New York: Oxford University Press, 2001).

Lippy, Charles H. and Williams, Peter W. (eds.), *Encyclopedia of the American religious experience*, 3 vols. (New York: Scribners, 1988).

Meinig, D. W., *The shaping of America: a geographical perspective on 500 years of history*, 4 vols. (New Haven: Yale University Press, 1986–2004).

Noll, Mark A., *A history of Christianity in the United States and Canada* (Grand Rapids, MI: Eerdmans, 1992).

The United States

Ahlstrom, Sydney E., *A religious history of the American people*, 2nd edn (New Haven: Yale University Press, 2004).

Andrews, Dee E., *The Methodists and revolutionary America* (Princeton: Princeton University Press, 2000).

Appleby, R. Scott, *'Church and age unite': the modernist impulse in American Catholicism* (Notre Dame, IN: University of Notre Dame Press, 1992).

Blumhofer, Edith L., *Her heart can see: the life and hymns of Fanny J. Crosby* (Grand Rapids, MI: Eerdmans, 2005).

Blumhofer, Edith L. and Noll, Mark A. (eds.), *Singing the Lord's song in a strange land: hymnody in the history of North American Protestantism* (Tuscaloosa: University of Alabama Press, 2004).

Brekus, Catherine, *Strangers and pilgrims: female preaching in America, 1740–1845* (Chapel Hill: University of North Carolina Press, 1998).

Brown, Candy Gunther, *The word in the world: evangelical writing, publishing, and reading in America, 1789–1880* (Chapel Hill: University of North Carolina Press, 2004).

Carey, Patrick W. (ed.), *American Catholic religious thought* (New York: Paulist Press, 1987).

Carwardine, Richard, *Evangelicals and politics in antebellum America* (New Haven: Yale University Press, 1993).

Genovese, Eugene D., *A consuming fire: the fall of the Confederacy in the mind of the white Christian South* (Athens: University of Georgia Press, 1999).

Gutjahr, Paul C., *An American Bible: a history of the Good Book in the United States, 1777–1880* (Stanford, CA: Stanford University Press, 1999).

Hatch, Nathan O., *The democratization of American Christianity* (New Haven: Yale University Press, 1989).

Hennessey, James, S.J., *American Catholics: a history of the Roman Catholic community in the United States* (New York: Oxford University Press, 1981).

Leighly, John, 'Biblical place-names in the United States', *Names* 27 (March 1979), 46–59.

McGreevy, John T., *Catholicism and American freedom: a history* (New York: W. W. Norton, 2003).

Marsden, George M., *Fundamentalism and American culture . . . 1870–1925* (New York: Oxford University Press, 1980).

Miller, Randall M., Stout, Harry S. and Wilson, Charles Reagan (eds.), *Religion and the American Civil War* (New York: Oxford University Press, 1998).

Noll, Mark A., *America's God, from Jonathan Edwards to Abraham Lincoln* (New York: Oxford University Press, 2002).

Nord, David Paul, *Faith in reading: religious publishing and the birth of mass media in America* (New York: Oxford University Press, 2004).

Schaff, Philip, *America: a sketch of its political, social and religious character*, ed. Perry Miller (Cambridge, MA: Harvard University Press, 1961).

Tocqueville, Alexis de, *Democracy in America*, ed. and trans. Harvey Claflin Mansfield and Delba Winthrop (Chicago: University of Chicago Press, 2000).

Wacker, Grant, *Heaven below: early Pentecostals and American culture* (Cambridge, MA: Harvard University Press, 2001).

Canada

Flanagan, Thomas, *Louis 'David' Riel: prophet of the new world*, 2nd edn (Toronto: University of Toronto Press, 1996).

Gauvreau, Michael, *The evangelical century: college and creed in English Canada from the Great Revival to the Great Depression* (Montreal and Kingston: McGill-Queen's University Press, 1991).

Grant, John Webster, *A profusion of spires: religion in nineteenth-century Ontario* (Toronto: University of Toronto Press, 1988).

Rawlyk, George A. (ed.), *Aspects of the Canadian evangelical experience* (Montreal and Kingston: McGill-Queen's University Press, 1997).

Van Die, Marguerite, *Religion, family, and community in Victorian Canada: the Colbys of Carrolcraft* (Kingston and Montreal: McGill-Queen's University Press, 2005).

Westfall, William, *Two worlds: the Protestant culture of nineteenth-century Ontario* (Montreal and Kingston: McGill-Queen's University Press, 1989).

23 Spain and Portugal: the challenge to the church

Aldea Vaquero, Quintín, Marín Martinez, Tomás and Vives Gatell, José (eds.), *Diccionario de historia eclesiática de España*, 5 vols. (Madrid: CSIC Instituto Enrique Flórez, 1972–87).

Almeida, Fortunato de, *História da Igreja em Portugal*, new edn, ed. Damião Peres, 4 vols. (Lisbon: Livraria Civilização, 1967–71).

Andrés Gallego, José, *Pensamiento y acción social de la Iglesia en España* (Madrid: Espasa Calpe, 1984).

Andrés Gallego, José and Pazos, Antón M., *La Iglesia en la España contemporánea*, 2 vols. (Madrid: Ediciones Encuentro, 1999).

Benet, Josep and Martí, Casimir, *Barcelona a mitjans segle XIX: el movement obrer durante el Bienni Progresista, 1854–1856*, 2 vols. (Barcelona: Curial, 1976).

Callahan, William J., *Church, politics and society in Spain, 1750–1874* (Cambridge, MA: Harvard University Press, 1984).

The Catholic Church in Spain, 1874–1998 (Washington, DC: Catholic University of America Press, 2000).

Cárcel Ortí, Vicente, *Política eclesial de los gobiernos liberales españoles, 1830–1840* (Pamplona: Ediciones Universidad de Navarra, 1975).

Cárcel Ortí, Vicente (ed.), *León XIII y los católicos españoles: informes vaticanos sobre la Iglesia en España* (Pamplona: Ediciones Universidad de Navarra, 1988).

Carmo Reis, Antonio do, *O liberalismo em Portugal e a Igreja católica: a época de Sua Majestade Imperial e Real D. Pedro* (Lisbon: Editorial Noticias, 1988).

Catroga, Fernando Joséde Almeida, *A militancia laica e a descristianização da morte em Portugal, 1865–1911*, 2 vols. (Coimbra: Publicações da Universidade Coimbra, 1988).

'O livre-pensamento contra a Igreja. A evolução do anticlericalismo em Portugal', *Revista de História das Ideias* 22 (2001), 255–354.

Corts I Blay, Ramón, Galtés I Pujol, Joan and Manent I Segimon, Albert (eds.), *Diccionari d'història eclesiàstica de Catalunya*, 3 vols. (Barcelona: Editorial Claret, 1998–2001).

Cuenca Toribio, José Manuel, 'La Iglesia sevillana en la primera época constitucional', *Hispania Sacra* 15 (1962), 149–62.

Socieda y clero en la España del XIX Siglo (Córdoba: Monte de Piedad y Caja de Ahorros, 1980).

Díaz de Cerio, F. and Núñez y Muñoz, M. F. (eds.), *Instrucciones secretas a los nuncios de España en el siglo XIX (1847–1907)* (Rome: Editrice Pontificia Università Gregoriana, 1989).

França, Luis de, *Comportamento religioso da população portuguesa* (Lisbon: Moraes Editores, 1980).

Franquelims Neiva Soares, A. S. (ed.), *O Concelho de Vila do Conde: e os inquéritos paróquiais de 1825 e 1845* (Póvoa de Varzim: Tip. Camões, 1974).

Halpern Pereira, Miriam, 'Del Antiguo Régimen al liberalismo (1807–1842)', in Hipólito de la Torre Gómez (ed.), *Portugal y España contemporáneos* (Madrid: Marcial Pons, 2000), pp. 39–64.

Jiménez Duque, Baldomero, *La espiritualidad en el siglo XIX español* (Madrid: Fundacion Universitaria Española, 1974).

Longares Alonso, Jesús, *Política y religión en Barcelona (1833–1843)* (Madrid: Editora Nacional, 1976).

Moreira Azevedo, Carlos A. (ed.), *Historia religiosa de Portugal*, 3 vols. (Lisbon: Circulo de Leitores, 2000–1).

Neto, Vitor, *O Estado, a Igreja e a sociedade em Portugal, 1823–1911* (Lisbon: Análise Social, 1998).

Oliveira, Miguel de, *História eclesiástica de Portugal*, ed. Arturo Roque de Almeida (Lisbon: Publicações Europa-América, 1994).

Revuelta González, Manuel, *Política religiosa de los liberales en el siglo XIX: trenio constitucional* (Madrid: CSIC Escuela de Historia Moderna, 1973).

La exclaustración, 1833–1840 (Madrid: Editorial Católica, 1976).

Robles, Cristóbal, *Insurrección o legalidad: los católicos y la Restauración* (Madrid: CSIC Centro de Estudios Históricos, 1988).

Rodrigues, N., 'Le Portugal', in S. H. Scholl (ed.), *150 ans de mouvement ouvrier chrétien en Europe de l'Ouest, 1789–1939* (Louvain and Paris: Editions Nauwelaerts, 1966).

Rueda, Germán and Siliveira, Luis A., 'Dos experiencias: España y Portugal', in Germán Rueda (ed.), *La desamortización en la Península Ibérica* (Madrid: Marcial Pons, 1993).

Sáez Marín, Juan, *Datos sobre la Iglesia Española contemporánea, 1768–1868* (Madrid: Editora Nacional, 1975).

Simón Segura, Francisco, *La desamortización española del siglo XIX* (Madrid: Instituto de Estudios Fiscales, 1973).

Tellería, Raimundo, *Un instituto misionero: la Congregación del Santíismo Redentor, 1732–1932* (Madrid: El Perpetuo Socorro, 1932).

24 Latin America: the church and national independence

The leading history of the church in Latin America is the multi-volume work edited by Enrique Dussel, *Historia general de la iglesia en América Latina (HGIAL)*, Comisión de Estudios de Historia de la Iglesia en América Latina (CEHILA) (Salamanca: Ediciones Sígueme, 1981–), of which vols. II, V, VI, VII, VIII and IX are relevant for coverage of the nineteenth century by countries and themes.

Auza, Néstor Tomás, *Católicos y liberales en la generación del ochenta* (Buenos Aires: Ediciones Culturales Argentinas, 1975).

  La Iglesia argentina (Buenos Aires: Ciudad Argentina, 1999).

Cardenal, Rodolfo, *El poder eclesiástico en El Salvador* (San Salvador: UCA Editores, 1980).

Cárdenas, Eduardo, *La Iglesia hispanoamericana en el siglo XX (1890–1990)* (Madrid: MAPFRE, 1992).

Demélas, Marie-Danielle and Saint-Geours, Yves, *Jerusalen y Babilonia: religión y política en el Ecuador 1780–1880* (Quito: Corporación Editora Nacional, 1988).

Dussel, Enrique D., *Historia de la Iglesia en América Latina: coloniaje y liberación (1492–1973)*, 3rd edn (Barcelona: Nova Terra, 1974).

Dussel, Enrique (ed.), *The church in Latin America 1492–1992* (Tunbridge Wells: Burns and Oates, 1992).

Dussel, Enrique and Esandi, M. M., *El Catolicismo popular en la Argentina* (Buenos Aires: Editorial Bonum, 1970).

González, Fernán E., *Partidos políticos y poder eclesiástico* (Bogotá: CINEP, 1977).

Ivereigh, Austen, *Catholicism and politics in Argentina, 1810–1960* (London: Macmillan, 1995).

Klaiber, Jeffrey, *Religion and revolution in Peru, 1824–1976* (Notre Dame, IN: University of Notre Dame Press, 1977).

  La Iglesia en el Perú: su historia social desde la Independencia (Lima: Pontificia Universidad Católica del Perú, Fondo Editorial, 1988).

Leturia, Pedro de, *Relaciones entre la Santa Sede e Hispanoamérica*, 3 vols., Analecta Gregoriana 101–3 (Rome and Caracas: Sociedad Bolivariana de Venezuela, 1959–60).

Londoño-Vega, Patricia, *Religion, culture, and society in Colombia: Medellín and Antioquia, 1850–1930* (Oxford: Clarendon Press, 2002).

Lynch, John, 'The Catholic Church in Latin America, 1830–1930', in Leslie Bethell (ed.), *The Cambridge history of Latin America*, vol. IV: *c.1870–1930* (Cambridge: Cambridge University Press, 1986), pp. 527–95.

'Revolution as a sin: the Church and Spanish American independence', in John Lynch, *Latin America between colony and nation* (London: Institute of Latin American Studies and Palgrave, 2001), pp. 109–33.

Pazos, Antón, *La Iglesia en la América del IV centenario* (Madrid: MAPFRE, 1992).

Pazos, Antón and Piccardo, Diego, *El Concilio Plenario de América Latina* (Rome: Vervuert, Iberoamericana, 2002).

Pontificia Commissio pro America Latina, *Actas y decretos del Concilio Plenario de la América Latina*, Edición facsímil (Vatican City: Libreria Editrice Vaticana, 1999).

Los últimos cien años de la evangelización en América Latina. Centenario del Concilio Plenario de América Latina: simposio histórico (Vatican City: Libreria Editrice Vaticana, 2000).

Prien, Hans-Jürgen, *Die Geschichte des Christentums in Lateinamerika* (Göttingen: Vandenhoeck and Ruprecht, 1978).

Salinas, Maximiliano, 'Cristianismo popular en Chile, 1880–1920', *Nueva Historia* 3, 12 (1984), 275–302.

Saranyana, Josep-Ignasi (ed.), *Teología en América Latina* (Madrid: Iberoamericana, and Frankfurt: Vervuert, 1999).

25 Between east and west: the Eastern Catholic churches

Elenkov, Ivan, *La chiesa cattolica di rito bizantino-slavo in Bulgaria dalla sua cosituzione nel 1860 fino alla metà del XX sec.*, trans. from the Bulgarian by Neli Radanova (Sofia: Montecchi Editore, 2000).

Esposito, Rosario F., *Leone XIII e l'oriente cristiano: studio storico-sistematico* (Rome: Edizioni Paoline, 1961).

Fortescue, Adrian, *The Uniate Eastern churches: the Byzantine rite in Italy, Syria and Egypt* (London: Burns, Oates and Washbourne, 1923).

Frazee, Charles A., *Catholics and sultans: the church and the Ottoman Empire (1453–1923)* (Cambridge: Cambridge University Press, 1983).

Gatti, Carlo and Cirillo Korolevskij, *I riti e le chiese oriental*, vol. 1: *Il rito bizantino e le chiese bizantine* (Genoa and Sampiedarena: Libreria Salesiana Editrice, 1942).

Glinka, Luigi, *Diocesi ucraino-cattolica di Cholm: liquidazione ed incorporazione alla Chiesa Russo-ortodossa* (Rome: Basiliani, 1975).

Grulich, Rudolf, *Die unierte Kirche in Mazedonien (1856–1919)*, Das östliche Christentum, Neue Folge, 29 (Würzburg: Augustinus-Verlag, 1977).

Habbi, Joseph, 'L'unification de la hiérarchie chaldéenne dans la première moitié du XIXe siècle', *Parole de l'Orient* 11 (1971), 121–43, 305–27.

Hajjar, Joseph, *Un lutteur infatigable: le patriarche Maximos III Mazloum* (Harissa: Imprimerie St Paul, 1957).

Les chrétiens uniates du Proche-orient, Collection les Univers 6 (Paris: Editions du Seuil, 1962).

'L'épiscopat catholique orientale et le 1er concile du Vatican d'après la correspondence diplomatique française', *Revue d'Histoire Ecclésiastique* 65 (1970), 423–55, 737–88.

Le Vatican, la France, et le catholicisme oriental (1878–1914): diplomatie et histoire de l'église, Bibliothèque Beachesne, Religion, Société, Politique 6 (Paris: Beauchesne, 1979).

Hirka, John-Paul, *Religion and nationality in western Ukraine: the Greek Catholic Church and the Ruthenian national movement in Galicia, 1867–1900* (Montreal and Kingston: McGill-Queen's University Press, 1999).

Janin, Raymond, *Les églises orientales et les rites orientaux*, 4th edn (Paris: Letouzey and Ané, 1955).

Korolevsky, Cyril, *Metropolitan Andrew (1865–1944)*, trans. and rev. Serge Keleher (Lvov: Stauropegion, 1993).

Le Coz, Raymond, *L'église d'orient: chrétiens d'Irak, d'Iran et de Turquie* (Paris: Editions du Cerf, 1995).

Lencyk, Wasyl, *The Eastern Catholic Church under Czar Nicholas I* (Rome and New York: Ukrainian Catholic University Press, 1966).

Mailleux, Paul, *Exarch Leonid Feodorov: bridgebuilder between Rome and Moscow* (New York: P. J. Kennedy and Sons, 1964).

Martin, Maurice, 'Les coptes catholiques 1880–1920', *Proche-Orient Chrétien* 40 (1990), 33–55.

Mayeur-Jacquen, Catherine, 'Les chrétiens d'orient au XIXe siècle: un renouveau lourd de menaces', in *Histoire du christianisme des origines à nos jours*, sous la direction de Jean-Marie Mayeur, Charles and Luce Pietri, André Vauchez and Marie Venard: tome XI: *Libéralisme, industrialisation, expansion européenne (1830–1914)* (Paris: Desclée, 1995), Cinquième partie: *Le christianisme oriental*, pp. 793–849.

Patelos, Constantin, *Vatican I et les évêques uniates: une étape éclairante de la politique romaine à l'égard des orientaux (1867–1870)*, Bibliothèque de la Revue d'Histoire Ecclésiastique 65 (Louvain: Nauwelaerts, 1981).

Roberson, Ronald, *The Eastern Christian churches: a brief survey*, 6th edn (Rome: Edizioni Orientalia Christiana, 1999).

Simon, Constantin, 'In Europe and America: the Ruthenians between Catholicism and Orthodoxy', *Orientalia Christiana Periodica* 59 (1993), 169–210.

Russicum: pioneers and witnesses of the struggle for Christian unity in Eastern Europe, vol. 1: *Leonid Feodorov, Vendelín Javorka, Theodore Romža: three historical sketches* (Rome: Opere Religiose Russe, 2001).

Soetens, Claude, *Le Congrès eucharistique international de Jérusalem (1893) dans le cadre de la politique orientale du pape Léon XIII*, Université de Louvain, Recueil de Travaux d'Histore et de Philologie, série 6, fasc. 12 (Louvain: Editions Nauwelaerts – Bibliothèque de l'Université, 1977).

Sonyel, Salâhi R., *Minorities and the destruction of the Ottoman Empire*, Atatürk Supreme Council for Culture, Language and History. Publications of the Turkish Historical Society, Serial VII, 129 (Ankara: Turkish Historical Society Publishing House, 1993).

Subtelny, Orest, *Ukraine: a history* (Toronto: University of Toronto Press, 1988).

Suttner, Ernst-Christoph, *Church unity: union or uniatism? Catholic-Orthodox ecumenical perspectives*, Placid Lecture Series 13 (Rome: Centre for Indian and Inter-religious Studies; Bangalore: Dharmaram Publications, 1991).

Tisserant, Eugène, *Eastern Christianity in India: a history of the Syro-Malabar Church from the earliest time to the present day* (Bombay and Calcutta: Orient Longmans, 1957).

Wenger, Antoine, *Rome et Moscou, 1900–1950* (Paris: Desclée de Brouwer, 1987).

XPYCOCTOMIKA. Studi e ricerche intorno a S. Giovanni Crisostomo, a cura del comitato per il XV° centenario della sua morte, 407–1907 (Rome: Pustet, 1908).

26 African-American Christianity

Alho, Olli, *The religion of the slaves: a study of the religious tradition and behaviour of plantation slaves in the United States, 1830–1864* (Helsinki: Academia Scientiarum Fennica, 1976).

Andrews, William L. (ed.), *Sisters of the Spirit: three black women's autobiographies of the nineteenth century* (Bloomington: University of Indiana Press, 1986).

Becker, William H., 'The black church: manhood and mission', *Journal of the American Academy of Religion* 40 (1972), 316–33.

Brereton, Bridget, 'Society and culture in the Caribbean: the British and French West Indies, 1870–1980', in Franklin W. Knight and Colin A. Palmer (eds.), *The modern Caribbean* (Chapel Hill: University of North Carolina Press, 1989), pp. 85–110.

Campbell, James T., *Songs of Zion: the African Methodist Episcopal Church in the United States and South Africa* (New York: Oxford University Press, 1995).

Chireau, Yvonne, *Black magic: religion and the African-American conjuring tradition* (Berkeley: University of California Press, 2003).

Collier-Thomas, Bettye, *Daughters of thunder: black women preachers and their sermons, 1850–1979* (San Francisco: Jossey-Bass, 1997).

Creel, Margaret Washington, *'A peculiar people': slave religion and community-culture among the Gullahs* (New York: New York University Press, 1988).

Dodson, Jualynne, 'Nineteenth-century A.M.E. preaching women: cutting edge of women's inclusion in church polity', in Hilah F. Thomas and Rosemary Skinner Keller (eds.), *Women in new worlds: perspectives on the Wesleyan tradition*, vol. 1 (Nashville: Abingdon, 1981), pp. 276–92.

Drake, St. Clair, *The redemption of Africa and black religion* (Chicago: Third World Press, 1970).

Dubois, Laurent, *Avengers of the New World: the story of the Haitian revolution* (Cambridge, MA: Harvard University Press, 2004).

DuBois, W. E. B., *The souls of black folk* (Chicago: McClurg, 1903).

Egerton, Douglas R., *Gabriel's rebellion: the Virginia slave conspiracies of 1800 and 1802* (Chapel Hill: University of North Carolina Press, 1993).

He shall go out free: the lives of Denmark Vesey (Madison, WI: Madison House, 1999).

Frazier, E. Franklin and Lincoln, C. Eric, *The negro church in America: the black church since Frazier* (New York: Schocken Books, 1974).

Frey, Sylvia R., *Water from the rock: black resistance in a revolutionary age* (Princeton: Princeton University Press, 1991).

Frey, Sylvia R. and Wood, Betty, *Come shouting to Zion: African American Protestantism in the American South and British Caribbean to 1830* (Chapel Hill: University of North Carolina Press, 1998).

Genovese, Eugene, *Roll, Jordan, roll: the world the slaves made* (New York: Pantheon, 1975).

From rebellion to revolution: Afro-American slave revolts in the making of the modern world (Baton Rouge: Louisiana State University Press, 1979).

George, Carol V. R., *Segregated Sabbaths: Richard Allen and the emergence of independent black churches, 1760–1840* (New York: Oxford University Press, 1973).

'Widening the circle: the black church and the abolitionist crusade, 1830–1860', in Lewis Perry and Michael Fellman (eds.), *Antislavery reconsidered: new perspectives on the abolitionists* (Baton Rouge: Louisiana State University Press, 1979), pp. 75–95.

Harding, Vincent, 'Religion and resistance among antebellum negroes', in August Meier and Elliot Rudwick (eds.), *The making of black America: essays in negro life and history* (New York: Athenaeum, 1969), vol. 1, pp. 179–97.

Higginbotham, Evelyn Brooks, *Righteous discontent: the women's movement in the black Baptist church, 1880–1920* (Cambridge, MA: Harvard University Press, 1993).

Holt, Thomas, *The problem of freedom: race, labor and politics in Jamaica and Britain, 1832–1938* (Baltimore: Johns Hopkins University Press, 1992).

Horton, James Oliver and Horton, Lois E., *In hope of liberty: culture, community and protest among Northern free blacks, 1700–1860* (New York: Oxford University Press, 1997).

Humez, Jean, *Gifts of power: the writings of Rebecca Jackson, black visionary, Shaker eldress* (Amherst: University of Massachusetts Press, 1981).

Jacobs, Sylvia M. (ed.), *Black Americans and the missionary movement in Africa* (Westport, CT: Greenwood Press, 1982).

Levine, Lawrence W., *Black culture and black consciousness: Afro-American folk thought from slavery to freedom* (New York: Oxford University Press, 1977).

Lincoln, C. Eric and Mamiya, Lawrence H., *The black church in the African American experience* (Durham, NC: Duke University Press, 1993).

Martin, Sandy D., *Black Baptists and African missions: the origins of a movement, 1880–1915* (Macon, GA: Mercer University Press, 1989).

Mays, Benjamin and Nicholson, Joseph, *The Negro's church* (New York: Russell and Russell, repub. 1969).

Montgomery, William E., *Under their own vine and fig tree: the African-American church in the South, 1765–1900* (Baton Rouge: Louisiana State University Press, 1993).

Moses, Wilson Jeremiah, *The golden age of black nationalism, 1850–1925* (New York: Oxford University Press, 1978).

Olmos, Margarite Fernandez (ed.), *Creole religions of the Caribbean: an introduction from Vodou and Santeria, to Obeah and Espiritismo* (New York: New York University Press, 2003).

Painter, Nell Irvin, *Sojourner Truth: a life, a symbol* (New York: Norton, 1995).

Raboteau, Albert J., *Slave religion: the 'invisible institution' in the antebellum South* (New York: Oxford University Press, 1978).

Sanneh, Lamin, *Abolitionists abroad: American blacks and the making of modern West Africa* (Cambridge, MA: Harvard University Press, 1999).

Sensbach, Jon F., *A separate Canaan: the making of an Afro-Moravian world in North Carolina, 1763–1840* (Chapel Hill: University of North Carolina Press, 1998).

Simpson, George E., *Religious cults of the Caribbean: Trinidad, Jamaica and Haiti* (Rio Piedras, Puerto Rico: Institute of Caribbean Studies, 1965).

Sobel, Mechal, *Trabelin' on: the slave journey to an Afro-Baptist faith*, 2nd edn (Princeton: Princeton University Press, 1988).

Southern, Eileen, *The music of black Americans: a history* (New York: Norton, 1971).

Stuckey, Sterling, *Slave culture: nationalist theory and the foundations of black America* (New York: Oxford University Press, 1987).

Tragle, Henry (ed.), *Southampton slave revolt of 1831* (Amherst: University of Massachusetts Press, 1971).

Turner, Mary, *Slaves and missionaries: the disintegration of Jamaican slave society, 1787–1834* (Urbana: University of Illinois Press, 1982).

Walker, Clarence E., *A rock in a weary land: the African Methodist Episcopal Church during the Civil War and reconstruction* (Baton Rouge: Louisiana State University Press, 1982).

Washington, James Melvin, *Frustrated fellowship: the black Baptist quest for social power* (Macon, GA: Mercer University Press, 1985).

Washington, Joseph R., *Black religion: the negro and Christianity in the United States* (Boston: Beacon, 1964).

Wilmore, Gayraud, *Black religion and black radicalism: an interpretation of the religious history of Afro-American people* (Maryknoll, NY: Orbis Books, 1983).

Woodson, Carter G., *The history of the negro church* (Washington, DC: Associated Publishers, 1921, 3rd edn 1972).

27 Christian missions, antislavery and the claims of humanity

Armitage, David, *The ideological origins of the British empire* (Cambridge: Cambridge University Press, 2000).

Comaroff, Jean and Comaroff, John, *Of revelation and revolution*, 2 vols. (Chicago and London: University of Chicago Press, 1991, 1997).

De Gruchy, John (ed.), *The London Missionary Society in southern Africa: historical essays in celebration of the bicentenary of the LMS in southern Africa, 1799–1999* (Cape Town: David Philip, 1999).

Delacroix, S., *Histoire universelle des missions catholiques d'après la conception originale de J. L. Françoisprimo*, 4 vols. (Paris: Grund, 1956–9).

Findlay, George G. and Holdsworth, W. W., *The history of the Wesleyan Methodist Missionary Society*, 5 vols. (London: Epworth Press, 1921–4).

Hall, Catherine, *Civilising subjects: metropole and colony in the English imagination, 1830–1867* (Cambridge: Polity Press, 2002).

Harris, Paul, *Nothing but Christ: Rufus Anderson and the ideology of Protestant foreign missions* (New York: Oxford University Press, 1999).

Hutchison, William R., *Errand to the world: American Protestant thought and foreign missions* (Chicago and London: University of Chicago Press, 1987).

Koren, Henry J., *To the ends of the earth: a general history of the Congregation of the Holy Ghost* (Pittsburgh, PA: Duquesne University Press, 1983).

Miller, Jon, *Missionary zeal and institutional control: organizational contradictions in the Basel Mission on the Gold Coast, 1828–1917*, Studies in the History of Christian Missions (Grand Rapids, MI, Cambridge and London: Eerdmans and RoutledgeCurzon, 2003).

Porter, Andrew N., *Missions versus empire? British Protestant missions and overseas expansion* (Manchester: Manchester University Press, 2004).

Ross, Andrew C., *David Livingstone: mission and empire* (London and New York: Hambledon and London, 2002).

Roxborogh, John, *Thomas Chalmers: enthusiast for mission. The Christian good of Scotland and the rise of the missionary movement* (Carlisle: Paternoster Press, 1999).

Shenk, Wilbert R., *Henry Venn – missionary statesman* (Maryknoll, NY: Orbis Books, 1983).

Stanley, Brian, *The History of the Baptist Missionary Society 1792–1992* (Edinburgh: T. and T. Clark, 1992).

Stanley, Brian (ed.), *Christian Missions and the Enlightenment*, Studies in the History of Christian Missions (Grand Rapids, MI, Cambridge, and Richmond: Eerdmans and Curzon Press, 2001.

Taggart, Norman W., *The Irish in world Methodism 1760–1900* (London: Epworth Press, 1986).

Walls, Andrew F., *The missionary movement in Christian history: studies in the transmission of faith* (Maryknoll, NY, and Edinburgh: Orbis Books and T. and T. Clark, 1996).

The cross-cultural process in Christian history: studies in the transmission and appropriation of faith (Maryknoll, NY, and Edinburgh: Orbis Books and T. and T. Clark, 2002).

Ward, Kevin and Stanley, Brian (eds.), *The Church Mission Society and world Christianity, 1799–1999*, Studies in the History of Christian Missions (Grand Rapids, MI, Cambridge, and Richmond: Eerdmans and Curzon Press, 2000).

Williams, C. Peter, *The ideal of the self-governing church: a study in Victorian missionary strategy* (Leiden: E. J. Brill, 1990).

Young, Richard Fox and Somaratna, G. P. V., *Vain debates: the Buddhist–Christian controversies of nineteenth-century Ceylon*, Publications of the De Nobili Research Library (Vienna: De Nobili Research Library, 1996).

28 The Middle East: western missions and Eastern churches, Islam and Judaism

Anderson, Rufus, *History of the missions of the American Board of Commissioners for Foreign Missions to the oriental churches*, 2 vols. (Boston: Congregational Publishing Society, 1873).

Bebbington, D. W., *Evangelicalism in modern Britain: a history from the 1730s to the 1980s* (London and New York: Routledge, 1989).

Brock, Sebastian, 'The "Nestorian" Church: a lamentable misnomer', *Bulletin of the John Rylands University Library of Manchester* 78 (1996), 23–35.

Coakley, J. F., *The Church of the East and the Church of England: a history of the Archbishop of Canterbury's Assyrian mission* (Oxford: Clarendon Press, 1992).

Cracknell, Kenneth, *Justice, courtesy and love: theologians and missionaries encountering world religions, 1846–1914* (London: Epworth Press, 1995).

Heyberger, Bernard, *Les chrétiens du Proche-Orient au temps de la réforme catholique (Syrie, Liban, Palestine, XVIIe–XVIIIe siècles)*, Bibliothèque des Ecoles Françaises d'Athènes et de Rome 224 (Rome: Ecole Française de Rome Palais Farnèse, 1994).

Hopwood, Derek, *The Russian presence in Syria and Palestine, 1843–1914: church and politics in the Near East* (Oxford: Clarendon Press, 1969).

Kawerau, Peter, *Amerika und die orientalischen Kirchen: Ursprung und Anfang der amerikanischen Mission unter den Nationalkirchen Westasiens* (Berlin: Walter de Gruyter, 1958).

Kochav, Sarah, '"Beginning at Jerusalem": The mission to the Jews and English evangelical eschatology', in Yeshoshua Ben-Arieh and Moshe Davis (eds.), *Jerusalem in the mind of the western world, 1800–1948*, With Eyes toward Zion 5 (Westport, CT and London: Praeger, 1997), pp. 91–107.

Lückhoff, Martin, *Anglikaner und Protestanten im Heiligen Lan: das gemeinsame Bistum Jerusalem (1841–1886)*, Abhandlungen des Deutschen Palästina-Vereins 24 (Wiesbaden: Harrassowitz Verlag, 1998).

Masters, Bruce, *Christians and Jews in the Ottoman Arab world: the roots of sectarianism*, Cambridge Studies in Islamic Civilisation (Cambridge: Cambridge University Press, 2001).

Michel, P., 'Les missions latines en Orient', *Revue de l'Orient Chrétien*, supplément trimestriel, 1/1 (1896), 88–123, 1/2 (1896) 91–136, 379–395, 2 (1807) 94–119, 176–218.

Murre-van den Berg, H. L., *From a spoken to a written language: the introduction and development of Literary Urmia Aramaic in the nineteenth century*, Publication of the 'De Goeje Fund' 28 (Leiden: Nederlands Instituut voor het Nabije Oosten, 1999).

Perry, A. F., 'The American Board of Commissioners for Foreign Missions and the London Missionary Society in the nineteenth century: a study of ideas', unpublished PhD thesis, Washington University (1974).

Quataert, Donald, *The Ottoman Empire, 1700–1922*, New Approaches to European History 17 (Cambridge: Cambridge University Press, 2000).

Richter, Julius, *A history of Protestant missions in the Near East* (Edinburgh: AMS Press, 1910).

Stock, E., *The history of the Church Missionary Society: its environment, its men and its work*, 4 vols. (London: Church Missionary Society, 1899, 1916).

Tamcke, Martin, 'Die Arbeit im vorderen Orient', in Ernst-August Lüdemann (ed.), *Vision: Gemeinde weltweit. 150 Jahre Hermannsburger Mission und evangelische-lutheranische Missionswerk in Niedersachsen* (Hermannsburg: ELM, 2000), pp. 511–47.

Thomson, William M., *The Land and the Book: or biblical illustrations drawn from the manners and customs, the scenes and scenery of the Holy Land*, 2 vols. (New York: Harper and Brothers, 1868).

Tibawi, A. L., *British interests in Palestine, 1800–1901: a study of religious and educational enterprise* (Oxford: Oxford University Press, 1961).

American interests in Syria, 1800–1901: a study of educational, literary and religious work (Oxford: Clarendon Press, 1966).

Verdeuil, C., 'Travailler à la renaissance de l'orient chrétien. Les missions latines en Syrie (1830–1945)', *Proche-Orient Chrétien* 51 (2001), 267–316.

Vogel, Lester I., *To see a promised land: Americans and the Holy Land in the nineteenth century* (University Park: The Pennsylvania State University Press, 1993).

Werner, O., *Katholischer Missions-Atlas* (Freiburg: Herder'sche Verlagshandlung, 1885).

Zwemer, Samuel M., *Islam, a challenge to faith: studies on the Mohammedan religion and the needs and opportunities of the Mohammedan world from the standpoint of Christian missions* (New York: Student Volunteer Movement for Foreign Missions, 1907).

29 Christians and religious traditions in the Indian empire

Agur, C. M., *History of the Protestant Church in Travancore* (Madras: Albion Press, 1903).

Anchukanandam, T., *The first synod of Pondicherry, 1844* (Bangalore: Kristu Jyoti Publications, 1994).

Appasamy, A. J. (Aiyadurai Jesudasan), *Sundar Singh: a biography* (London: Lutterworth Press, 1958).

Ballhatchet, K. A., *Caste, class and Catholicism in India: 1789–1914* (Richmond, Surrey: Curzon Press, 1998).

Bayly, Susan, *Saints, goddesses and kings: Muslims and Christians in South Indian society, 1700–1900* (Cambridge: Cambridge University Press, 1989).

Becker, Christopher, *History of the Catholic missions in northeast India (1890–1915)* trans. and ed. G. Stadler and S. Karotemprel (Calcutta: Firma KLM, 1980).

Early history of the Catholic missions in northeast India (1598–1890), trans. and ed. F. Leicht and S. Karotemprel (Calcutta: Firma KLM, 1989).

Boudens, R., *Catholic missionaries in a British colony: successes and failures in Ceylon, 1796–1893* (Immensee: Nouvelle Revue de Science Missionaire, 1979).

Cox, Jeffrey, *Imperial fault lines: Christianity and colonial power in India, 1818–1940* (Stanford: Stanford University Press, 2002).

Downs, Frederick S., *History of Christianity in India*, vol. v, part 5: *North East India in the nineteenth and twentieth centuries* (Bangalore: Church History Association of India [CHAI], 1992).

Eaton, Richard M., 'Comparative history as world history: religious conversion in modern India', in *Essays on Islam and Indian history* (New Delhi: Oxford University Press, 2000), pp. 45–75 (reprint from *Journal of World History* 8, 2 (Fall, 1997), 243–71).

Farias, Kranti K., *The Christian impact in south Kanara* (Mumbai: CHAI, West India Branch, 1999).

Frykenberg, Robert Eric, *Christians and missionaries in India: cross-cultural communication since 1500, with special reference to caste, conversion, and colonialism* (Grand Rapids, MI: Eerdmans; London: RoutledgeCurzon, 2003).

Gladstone, J. W., *Protestant Christianity and people's movements in Kerala: a study of Christian mass movements in relation to neo-Hindu socio-religious movements in Kerala, 1850–1936* (Trivandrum: Seminary Publications, 1984).

Grafe, Hugald, *History of Christianity in India*, vol. iv, Part 2: *History of Christianity in Tamilnadu from 1800 to 1975* (Bangalore: CHAI, 1990).

Hardgrave, R., 'The breast-cloth controversy: caste consciousness and social change in southern Travancore', *Indian Economic and Social History Review* 5, 2 (1968), 171–87.

Harper, Susan Billington, *In the shadow of the Mahatma: Bishop V. S. Azariah and the travails of Christianity in British India* (Grand Rapids, MI: Eerdmans; Richmond, Surrey: Curzon Press, 2000).

Hudson, D. Dennis, *Protestant origins in India: Tamil Evangelical Christians, 1706–1835* (Grand Rapids, MI: Eerdmans; Richmond, Surrey: Curzon Press, 2000).

Kawashima, Koji, *Missionaries and a Hindu state: Travancore 1858–1936* (New Delhi: Oxford University Press, 1998).

Mallampalli, Chandra, *Christians and public life in colonial India, 1863–1937* (London: RoutledgeCurzon, 2004).

Neill, Stephen, *A history of Christianity in India: 1707–1858* (Cambridge: Cambridge University Press, 1985).

Philip, Puthuvail Thomas, *The growth of Baptist churches in Nagaland*, 2nd edn (Guwahati: Christian Literature Centre, 1983).

Powell, Avril A., *Muslims and missionaries in pre-mutiny India* (Richmond, Surrey: Curzon Press, 1993).

Puthenpurakal, Joseph, *Baptist missions in Nagaland: a study in historical and ecumenical perspective* (Calcutta: Firma KLM, 1984).

Sengupta, Padmini, *Pandita Ramabai Saraswati: her life and work* (Bombay: Asia Publishing House, 1970).

Singh, Brijraj, *The first Protestant missionary to India* (New Delhi: Oxford University Press, 1999).

Tilak, Lakshmibai, *I follow after: an autobiography by Lakshmibai Tilak*, trans. E. J. Inkster (London and Madras: Oxford University Press, 1950).

Tiliander, Brör, *Christian and Hindu terminology: a study of their mutual relations with special reference to the Tamil area* (Uppsala: Almqvist and Wiksell, 1974).

Visvanathan, Susan, *The Christians of Kerala: history, belief and ritual among the Yakoba* (Madras and Oxford: Oxford University Press, 1993).

Webster, John C. B., *A history of the Dalit Christians in India* (San Francisco: Mellen Research University Press, 1992).

Young, Richard Fox, *Resistant Hinduism: Sanskrit sources on anti-Christian apologetics in early nineteenth-century India* (Vienna: Institut für Indologie der Universität Wien, 1981).

30 Christianity in East Asia: China, Korea and Japan

China

Bays, Daniel H. (ed.), *Christianity in China: from the eighteenth century to the present* (Stanford: Stanford University Press, 1996).

Cohen, Paul A., 'Christian missions and their impact to 1900', in John K. Fairbank (ed.), *The Cambridge history of China*, vol. x, *Late Ch'ing 1800–1911*, Part 1 (Cambridge: Cambridge University Press, 1978), pp. 543–90.

Dunch, Ryan, *Fuzhou Protestants and the making of a modern China 1857–1927* (New Haven: Yale University Press, 2001).

Latourette, Kenneth S., *A history of Christian missions in China* (New York: Macmillan, 1929).

Lutz, Jessie G. and Lutz, R. Ray, *Hakka Chinese confront Protestant Christianity, 1850–1900* (Armonk, NY: M. E. Sharpe, 1998).

Spence, Jonathan D., *God's Chinese son: the Taiping heavenly kingdom of Hong Xiuquan* (New York: Norton, 1996).

Sweeten, Alan R., *Christianity in rural China: conflict and accommodation in Jiangxi province 1860–1900*, Michigan Monographs in Chinese Studies 91 (Ann Arbor: University of Michigan Center for Chinese Studies, 2001).

Zetzsche, Jost Oliver, *The Bible in China: the history of the Union Version or the culmination of Protestant missionary Bible translation in China*, Monumenta Serica Monograph Series 45 (Sankt Augustin, Germany: Institut Monumenta Serica, 1999).

Korea

Clark, Donald N., *Christianity in modern Korea* (London: University Press of America, 1986).

Dallet, Charles, *Histoire de l'église de Corée* (1874; repr. Seoul: Royal Asiatic Society, Korea Branch, 1975).

Grayson, James Huntley, *Korea: a religious history*, revised edn (Richmond, Surrey: RoutledgeCurzon, 2002).

Kim, Chang-seok Thaddeus, *Lives of 103 martyr saints of Korea* (Seoul: Catholic Publishing, 1984).

Paik, L. George, *The history of Protestant missions in Korea: 1832–1910* (1929; repr. Seoul: Yonsei University Press, 1971).

Yu, Chai-shin (ed.), *The founding of the Catholic tradition in Korea* (Mississauga, Ontario: Korean and Related Studies Press, 1996).

Korea and Christianity (Seoul: Korean Scholar Press, 1996).

Japan

Cary, Otis, *A history of Christianity in Japan* (New York: F. H. Revell, 1909).

Drummond, Richard Henry, *A history of Christianity in Japan* (Grand Rapids, MI: Eerdmans, 1971).

Hecken, Joseph Leonard van. *The Catholic Church in Japan since 1859* (Tokyo: Herder, 1963).

Iglehart, Charles W., *A century of Protestant Christianity in Japan* (Tokyo: Charles E. Tuttle, 1959).

Ion, A. Hamish, *The cross and the rising sun*, 3 vols. (Waterloo, Ontario: Wilfrid Laurier University Press, 1990–9).

Kitagawa, Joseph M., *Religion in Japanese history* (New York: Columbia University Press, 1966).

Laures, Johannes, *The Catholic Church in Japan: a short history* (Tokyo: Charles E. Tuttle, 1954).

31 Christianity in Indochina

Faure, A., *Les Français en Cochinchine au XVIIIe siècle: Mgr. Pigneau de Béhaine, évêque d'Adran* (Paris: Challamel, 1891).

Launay, A., *Histoire générale de la Société des Missions Etrangères depuis sa fondation jusqu'à nos jours*, 3 vols. (Paris: MEP, 1920).

Histoire de la mission de Cochinchine, 1658–1823: documents historiques, 3 vols: I, 1658–1728; II, 1728–1771; III, 1771–1823 (Paris: Douniol et Retaux, 1923–5).

Louvet, L. E., *La Cochinchine religieuse*, 2 vols. (Paris: Leroux, 1885).

Monseigneur d'Adran, notice biographique (Saigon: Imprimerie de la Mission, 1896).

Nguyen, Khac Vien, *Vietnam: une longue histoire* (Hanoi: The Gioi, 1993).

Phan, Peter C., *Mission and catechesis: Alexandre de Rhodes and inculturation in seventeenth-century Vietnam* (Maryknoll, NY: Orbis Books, 1998).

Phan, Phat Huon, *The history of the Catholic Church in Vietnam* (Long Beach, CA: Cuu The Tung Thu, 2000).

Taboulet, G., 'La vie tourmentée de l'évêque d'Adran', *Bulletin de la Société des Etudes Indochinoises* 3/4 (1940), 9–14.

La geste française en Indochine: histoire par les textes de la France en Indochine des origines à 1914 (Paris: Adrien-Maisonneuse, 1955–6).

Tavernier, E., *Monseigneur Pigneau de Béhaine, évêque d'Adran* (Hanoi: Le-Van-Tan, 1943).

Tuck, P., *French Catholic missionaries and the politics of imperialism in Vietnam, 1857–1914: a documentary survey* (Liverpool: Liverpool University Press, 1987).

32 Christianity and the birth of the Filipino nation

Agoncillo, Teodoro A., *The revolt of the masses: the story of Bonifacio and the Katipunan* (Quezon City: University of the Philippines, 1956).

Anderson, Benedict, *The spectre of comparisons: nationalism, southeast Asia and the world* (London and New York: Verso, 1998).

  Imagined communities: reflections on the origin and spread of nationalism, rev. edn (Pasig City: Anvil Publishing, 2003).

Anderson, Gerald H. (ed.), *Studies in Philippine church history* (Ithaca and London: Cornell University Press, 1969).

Arbeiza, Bienvenido de, OFM Cap., *Reseña historica de los Capuchinos en Filipinas* (Pamplona: PP. Capuchinos, 1969).

Artigas y Cuerva, Manuel C., *The events of 1872: a historico-bio-bibliographical account*, trans. O. D. Corpuz, National Glories 3 (Quezon City: University of the Philippines Press, 1966).

Bitterli, Urs, *Cultures in conflict: encounters between Europeans and non-European cultures, 1492–1800*, trans. Ritchie Robertson (Stanford, CA: Stanford University Press, 1989).

Bonoan, Raul J., *The Rizal–Pastells correspondence: the hitherto unpublished letters of José Rizal and portions of Fr. Pablo Pastells's fourth letter and translation of the correspondence, together with a historical background and theological critique* (Quezon City: Ateneo de Manila University Press, 1994).

Borromeo-Buehler, Soledad, *The cry of Balintawak: a contrived controversy, a textual analysis with appended documents* (Quezon City: Ateneo de Manila University Press, 1998).

Connolly, Michael J., *Church lands and peasant unrest in the Philippines: agrarian conflict in twentieth-century Luzon* (Quezon City: Ateneo de Manila University Press, 1992).

Constantino, Renato, *The making of a Filipino (a story of Philippine colonial politics)* (Quezon City: Malaya Books Inc., 1969).

  The Philippines: a past revisited (Manila: By the author, 1975).

Cullinane, Michael, *Ilustrado politics: Filipino elite responses to American rule, 1898–1908* (Quezon City: Ateneo de Manila University Press, 2003).

De Belen, Gaspar Aquino, *Mahal na passion ni Jesu Christong Panginoon natin na tola*, ed. Rene B. Javellana (Quezon City: Ateneo de Manila University Press, c. 1990).

De la Costa, Horacio, *The Jesuits in the Philippines, 1581–1768* (Cambridge, MA: Harvard University Press, 1961).

Francisco, José Mario C., 'The Christ story as the subversive memory of tradition: Tagalog texts and politics around the turn of the century', in D. M. Roskies (ed.), *Text/politics in Island Southeast Asia: essays in interpretation*, Ohio University Monographs in International Studies, Southeast Asia Series, 91 (Athens, OH: Center for International Studies, 1993), pp. 82–110.

Francisco, José Mario C. (ed.), *Sermones, Francisco Blancas de San José OP*, Sources for Philippine Studies (Quezon City: Pulong, 1994).

Ileto, Reynaldo Clemeña, *Pasyon and revolution: popular movements in the Philippines, 1840–1910* (Quezon City: Ateneo de Manila University Press, 1979).

  Filipinos and their revolution: event, discourse, and historiography (Quezon City: Ateneo de Manila University Press, 1998).

Javellana, Rene B. (ed.), *Casaysayan nang pasiong mahal ni Jesucristong panginon natin na sucat ipag-alab nang puso nang sinomang babasa* (Quezon City: Ateneo de Manila University Press, 1988).

Kwantes, Anne C. (ed.), *Chapters in Philippine church history* (Manila: OMF Literature, 2001).

Legarda, Benito J. Jr., *After the galleons: foreign trade, economic change and entrepreneurship in the nineteenth-century Philippines* (Quezon City: Ateneo de Manila University Press, 1999).

Lumbera, Bienvenido L., *Tagalog poetry 1570–1898: tradition and influences in its development* (Quezon City: Ateneo de Manila University Press, 1986).

Phelan, John Leddy, *The hispanization of the Philippines: Spanish aims and Filipino responses 1565–1700* (Madison and London: University of Wisconsin Press, 1959).

Peralta, Jesus T. (ed.), *Reflections on Philippine culture and society: festschrift in honor of William Henry Scott* (Quezon City: Ateneo de Manila University Press, 2001).

Quibuyen, Floro C., *A nation aborted: Rizal, American hegemony and Philippine nationalism* (Quezon City: Ateneo de Manila University Press, 1999).

Radoa, Florentino and Rodriguez, Felice Noelle (eds.), *The Philippine Revolution of 1896: ordinary lives in extraordinary times* (Quezon City: Ateneo de Manila University Press, 2001).

Rafael, Vicente L., *Contracting colonialism: translation and Christian conversion in Tagalog society under early Spanish rule* (Quezon City: Ateneo de Manila University Press, 1988).

Reyes, Soledad (ed.), *200 Taon ni Balagtas: mga bagong pagtanaw at pagsusuri* (Quezon City: Balagtas Bicentennial Commission, c. 1989).

Salamanca, Bonifacio S., *The Filipino reaction to American rule 1901–1913* (Quezon City: New Day Publishers, 1984).

Schumacher, John N. *Father José Burgos: priest and nationalist* (Manila: Akeneo University Press, 1972).

Readings in Philippine church history (Quezon City: Loyola School of Theology, 1979).

Revolutionary clergy: the Filipino clergy and the nationalist movement, 1850–1903 (Quezon City: Ateneo de Manila University Press, 1981).

The propaganda movement 1880–1895: the creation of a Filipino consciousness, the making of the revolution, rev. edn (Quezon City: Ateneo de Manila University Press, 1997).

Scott, William Henry, *Cracks in the parchment curtain and other essays in Philippine history*, new edn (Quezon City: New Day Publishers, 1985).

33 Christianity in Australasia and the Pacific

General

Breward, Ian, *A history of the churches in Australasia*, Oxford History of the Christian Church (Oxford: Oxford University Press, 2001).

Withycombe, Robert S. M. (ed.), *Australian and New Zealand religious history, 1788–1988* (Canberra: ANZSTS and ATS, 1988).

Australia

Breward, Ian, *A history of the Australian churches* (Sydney: Allen and Unwin, 1993).

Campion, Edmund, *Australian Catholics* (Melbourne: Viking, 1987).

Carey, Hilary M., *Believing in Australia: a cultural history of religions* (Sydney: Allen and Unwin, 1996).

Ely, Richard, *Unto God and Caesar: religious issues in the emerging Commonwealth, 1891–1906* (Melbourne: Melbourne University Press, 1976).

Fogarty, Ronald, *Catholic education in Australia, 1806–1950* (Melbourne: Melbourne University Press, 1959).

Hutchinson, Mark and Campion, Edmund (eds.), *Re-visioning Australian colonial Christianity: new essays in the Australian Christian experience, 1788–1900* (Sydney: Centre for the Study of Australian Christianity, 1994).

Kaye, Bruce (ed.), *Anglicanism in Australia* (Carlton South: Melbourne University Press, 2002).

O'Farrell, Patrick James, *The Catholic church and community in Australia: a history* (Melbourne: Nelson, 1977; revised 1985 and 1992).

Piggin, Stuart, *Evangelical Christianity in Australia: spirit, word and world* (Melbourne: Oxford University Press, 1996).

Pike, Douglas, *Paradise of dissent* (Melbourne: Melbourne University Press, 1967).

Thompson, Roger C., *Religion in Australia* (Melbourne: Oxford University Press, 1994).

Trollope, Anthony, *Australia* (1873; St Lucia: University of Queensland Press, 1967 reprint).

Wright, Don and Clancy, Eric, *The Methodists: a history of Methodism in New South Wales* (Sydney: Allen and Unwin, 1993).

The Pacific Islands and Melanesia

Crocombe, Marjorie Tuainekore, *et al.*, *Polynesian missions in Melanesia from Samoa, Cook Islands and Tonga to Papua New Guinea and New Caledonia* (Suva: The Institute of Pacific Studies, University of the South Pacific, 1982).

Garrett, John, *To live among the stars: Christian origins in Oceania* (Geneva and Suva: World Council of Churches in association with the Institute of Pacific Studies, University of the South Pacific, 1982).

Gunson, Niel, *Messengers of grace: Evangelical missionaries in the South Seas, 1797–1860* (Melbourne: Oxford University Press, 1978).

Hilliard, David, *God's gentlemen: a history of the Melanesian Mission, 1849–1942* (St Lucia: University of Queensland Press, 1978).

Howe, K. R., *Where the waves fall: a new South Sea Islands history from first settlement to colonial rule*, Pacific Islands Monograph Series 2 (Honolulu: University of Hawaii Press, 1988).

Langmore, Diane, *Missionary lives: Papua, 1874–1914*, Pacific Islands Monograph Series 6 (Honolulu: University of Hawaii Press, 1989).

Laracy, Hugh, *Marists and Melanesians: a history of Catholic missions in the Solomon Islands* (Canberra: Australian National University Press, 1976).

Munro, Doug and Andrew Thornley (eds.), *The covenant makers: islander missionaries in the Pacific* (Suva: Pacific Theological College and The Institute of Pacific Studies at the University of the South Pacific, 1996).

Wiltgen, Ralph M., *The founding of the Roman Catholic Church in Oceania, 1825 to 1850* (Canberra: Australian National University Press, 1979).

New Zealand

Binney, Judith, *Redemption songs: a life of Te Kooti Arikirangi Te Turuki* (Auckland: Auckland University Press and Bridget Williams Books, 1995).

Clark, Paul, *'Hauhau': the Pai Marire search for Maori identity* (Auckland: Auckland University Press and Oxford University Press, 1975).

Davidson, Allan K., *Christianity in Aotearoa: a history of church and society in New Zealand* (Wellington: Education for Ministry, 1997).

Davidson, Allan K. and Lineham, Peter J. (eds.), *Transplanted Christianity: documents illustrating aspects of New Zealand church history* (Palmerston North: Department of History, Massey University, 1995).

Elsmore, Bronwyn, *Mana from heaven: a century of Maori prophets in New Zealand* (Auckland: Reed, 1999).

Like them that dream: the Maori and the Old Testament (Auckland: Reed, 2000).

King, Michael, *God's farthest outpost: a history of Catholics in New Zealand* (Auckland: Penguin, 1997).

Limbrick, Warren E. (ed.), *Bishop Selwyn in New Zealand, 1841–68* (Palmerston North: Dunmore Press, 1983).

McEldowney, Dennis (ed.), *Presbyterians in Aotearoa, 1840–1990* (Wellington: The Presbyterian Church of New Zealand, 1990).

Morrell, W. P., *The Anglican Church in New Zealand: a history* (Dunedin: Anglican Church of the Province of New Zealand, 1973).

34 Missions and empire, c.1873–1914

Ayandele, E. A., *The missionary impact on modern Nigeria 1842–1914* (London: Longman, 1966).

Bebbington, David, *Holiness in nineteenth-century England* (Carlisle: Paternoster Press, 2000).

Cooke, C. M., The Roman Catholic mission in Calabar, 1903–1960', unpublished PhD thesis, University of London (1985).

Coulon, Paul and Brasseur, Paule *et al.*, *Libermann, 1802–1852: une pensée et une mystique missionaires* (Paris: Editions du Cerf, 1988).

Cox, Jeffrey, *Imperial faultlines: Christianity and colonial power in India, 1818–1940* (Stanford: Stanford University Press, 2002).

Cracknell, Kenneth, *Justice, courtesy and love: theologians and missionaries encountering world religions, 1846–1914* (London: Epworth Press, 1995).

Fitzgerald, Rosemary, 'A "peculiar and exceptional measure": the call for women medical missionaries for India in the later nineteenth century', in R. A. Bickers and R. Seton (eds.), *Missionary encounters: sources and issues* (Richmond: Curzon Press, 1996), pp. 174–96.

Hanna, A. J., *The beginnings of Nyasaland and north-eastern Rhodesia, 1859–95* (Oxford: Clarendon Press, 1956).

Harris, Paul, *Nothing but Christ: Rufus Anderson and the ideology of Protestant foreign missions* (New York: Oxford University Press, 1999).

Hastings, Adrian, *The Church in Africa 1450–1950* (Oxford: Clarendon Press, 1994).

Latourette, K. S., *A history of Christian missions in China* (1929; repr. New York: Russell and Russell, 1967).

A history of the expansion of Christianity, 7 vols. (London: Eyre and Spottiswoode, 1938–47), vols. v and vi.

McCracken, John, *Politics and Christianity in Malawi: the impact of the Livingstonia Mission in the northern province* (Cambridge: Cambridge University Press, 1977).

Maughan, Steven, 'Regions beyond and the national church: domestic support for the foreign missions of the Church of England in the high imperial age, 1870–1914', unpublished PhD thesis, Harvard University (1995).

Oliver, Roland, *Sir Harry Johnston and the scramble for Africa* (London: Chatto and Windus, 1957).

The missionary factor in East Africa, 2nd edn (London: Longman, 1965).

Porter, Andrew, 'Cambridge, Keswick, and late nineteenth-century attitudes to Africa', *Journal of Imperial and Commonwealth History* 5 (1976), 5–34.

Religion versus empire? British Protestant missionaries and overseas expansion, 1700–1914 (Manchester: Manchester University Press, 2004).

Porter, Andrew (ed.), *The imperial horizons of British Protestant missions, 1880–1914* (Grand Rapids, MI: Eerdmans, 2003).

Robert, Dana, *American women in mission: a social history of their thought and practice* (Macon, GA: Mercer University Press, 1996).

Occupy until I come: A. T. Pierson and the evangelization of the world (Grand Rapids, MI: Eerdmans, 2003).

Sharpe, Eric J., *Not to destroy but to fulfil: the contribution of J. N. Farquhar ro Protestant missionary thought in India before 1914* (Uppsala: Gleerup, 1965).

Stanley, Brian, 'Church, state, and the hierarchy of "civilization": the making of the "missions and governments" report at the World Missionary Conference, Edinburgh 1910', in Andrew Porter (ed.), *The imperial horizons of British Protestant missions, 1880–1914* (Grand Rapids, MI: Eerdmans, 2003), pp. 58–84.

Tasie, G. O. M., *Christian missionary enterprise in the Niger Delta 1864–1918* (Leiden: E. J. Brill, 1978).

Thompson, T. Jack, *Touching the heart: Xhosa missionaries to Malawi 1876–1888* (Pretoria: UNISA Press, 2000).

Tuck, Patrick J. N., *French Catholic missionaries and the politics of imperialism in Vietnam, 1857–1914: a documentary survey* (Liverpool: Liverpool University Press, 1987).

Webster, J. B., *The African churches among the Yoruba 1888–1922* (Oxford: Clarendon Press, 1964).

35 Ethiopianism and the roots of modern African Christianity

Ayandele, E. A., *The missionary impact on modern Nigeria, 1842–1914* (London: Longmans, 1966).

Holy Johnson: pioneer of African nationalism, 1836–1917 (London: Frank Cass, 1970).

Blyden, E. W., *African life and customs* (1908; reprinted Baltimore: Black Classic Press, 1994).

Casely Hayford, J. E., *Ethiopia unbound: studies in race emancipation* (London: C. M. Phillips, 1911).

Chirenje, J. M., *Ethiopianism and Afro-Americans in South Africa, 1883–1916* (Baton Rouge: Louisiana State University Press, 1987).

Dwane, S., *Ethiopianism and the Order of Ethiopia* (Glosderry: Ethiopian Episcopal Church, 1999).

Esedebe, O., *Pan Africanism* (Enugu: Fourth Dimensions Publishers, 1980).

Fyfe, C., *Africanus Horton, 1835–1883: West African scientist and patriot* (London: Oxford University Press, 1972).

Gray, R. L., 'African American Ethiopianism: interpreting the divine redemptive mission of a chosen people', *Journal of African Christian Thought* 5 (2002), 37–46.

Hanciles, J., 'Ethiopianism: rough diamond of an African Christianity', *Studia Historiae Ecclesiasticae* 23 (1997), 75–104.

  Euthanasia of mission: African church autonomy in a colonial context (Westport, CT: Praeger, 2002).

Holden, E., *Blyden of Liberia: an account of the life and labors of Edward Wilmot Blyden, LL.D., as recorded in letters and print* (New York: Vantage Press, 1966).

Langley, J. A. (ed.), *Ideologies of liberation in black Africa* (New York: Oxford University Press, 1979).

Lonsdale, J., 'Kikuyu Christianities', *Journal of Religion in Africa* 29 (1999), 206–29.

  'Mission Christianity and settler colonialism in eastern Africa', in H. B. Hansen and M. Twaddle (eds.), *Christian missionaries and the state in the Third World* (Oxford: James Currey, 2002), pp. 194–211.

Lynch, H., *Edward Wilmot Blyden: pan Negro patriot, 1832–1912* (London: Oxford University Press, 1967).

Mobley, H. W., *The Ghanaian's image of the missionary* (Leiden: E. J. Brill, 1970).

Olusanya, G. O., 'Julius Ojo-Cole: a neglected Nigerian nationalist and educationist', *Journal of the Historical Society of Nigeria* 7 (1973), 91–101.

Parfitt, T. and Semi, E. T. (eds.), *The Beta Israel in Ethiopia and Israel: studies on the Ethiopian Jews* (Richmond: Curzon, 1999).

Sanneh, L., *Abolitionists abroad: American blacks and the making of modern West Africa* (Cambridge, MA: Harvard University Press, 1999).

Seeman, D., 'The question of kinship: bodies and narratives in the Beta-Israel–European encounter, 1860–1920', *Journal of Religion in Africa* 30 (2000), 86–120.

Shepperson, G. and Price, T., *Independent African: John Chilembwe and the origins, setting and significance of the Nyasaland native rising* (Edinburgh: Edinburgh University Press, 1958).

Webster, J., *The African churches among the Yoruba, 1888–1922* (Oxford: Clarendon Press, 1964).

Williams, W. L., *Black Americans and the evangelization of Africa, 1877–1900* (Madison: University of Wisconsin Press, 1982).

Wilmore, G. S., *Black religion and black radicalism: an interpretation of the religious history of Afro-American people*, revised edn (Maryknoll, NY: Orbis, 1998).

36 The outlook for Christianity in 1914

Bell, G. K. A., *Randall Davidson: Archbishop of Canterbury*, 2nd edn (London: Oxford University Press, 1938).

Clements, K. W., *Lovers of discord: twentieth-century theological controversies in England* (London: SPCK, 1988).

Grimes, C. J., *Towards an Indian church: the growth of the Church of India in constitution and life* (London: SPCK, 1946).

Hastings, A., *The construction of nationhood: ethnicity, religion and nationalism* (Cambridge: Cambridge University Press, 1997).

McManners, J., *Church and state in France, 1870–1914* (London: SPCK, 1972).

Marsden, G. M., *Fundamentalism and American culture: the shaping of twentieth-century evangelicalism: 1870–1925* (New York: Oxford University Press, 1980).

O'Connor, D., *Gospel, Raj, and Swaraj: the missionary years of C. F. Andrews 1904–14* (Frankfurt: Peter Lang, 1990).

Smith, H. M., *Frank Bishop of Zanzibar* (London: SPCK, 1926).

Stephenson, A. M. G., *Anglicanism and the Lambeth conferences* (London: SPCK, 1978).

Thompson, H. P., *Into all lands: the history of the Society for the Propagation of the Gospel in Foreign Parts 1701–1950* (London: SPCK, 1951).

Willis, J. J., et al., *Towards a united church 1913–1947* (London: Edinburgh House Press, 1947).

Index